CHRISTIAN SOCIAL TEACHINGS

CHRISTIAN SOCIAL TEACHINGS

A READER IN CHRISTIAN SOCIAL ETHICS

FROM THE BIBLE TO THE PRESENT

SECOND EDITION

GEORGE W. FORELL, EDITOR

REVISED AND UPDATED BY JAMES M. CHILDS

Fortress Press

Minneapolis

CHRISTIAN SOCIAL TEACHINGS
A Reader in Christian Social Ethics from the Bible to the Present
Second Edition

Cover image © Amy Allcock
Cover design: Laurie Ingram
Book design: Hillspring Books, Inc.

Library of Congress Cataloging-in-Publication Data is available
ISBN 978-0-8006-9860-7

The paper used in this publication meets the minimum requirements of American National Standard for Information Sciences—Permanence of Paper for Printed Library Materials, ANSI Z329.48-1984.
Manufactured in the U.S.A.

17   16   15   14   13   1   2   3   4   5   6   7   8   9   10

CONTENTS

PART 3: THE MEDIEVAL CHURCH

PART 4: THE REFORMATION

PART 5: POST-REFORMATION ENGLAND AND AMERICA

PART 6: EIGHTEENTH-CENTURY VOICES

PART 7: NINETEENTH-CENTURY VOICES

PART 8: NINETEENTH- AND TWENTIETH-CENTURY CATHOLIC SOCIAL TEACHING

PART 9: EARLY- TO MID-TWENTIETH-CENTURY VOICES

PART 10: TWENTIETH-CENTURY FEMINIST AND WOMANIST ETHICS

PART 11: CONTEMPORARY ISSUES: THE MID-TWENTIETH CENTURY TO THE PRESENT

A Thematic Organization of Sources

For those courses that are arranged by theme instead of chronology, I have prepared an alternative organization of the selection of readings. The following chart provides an organization of the material according to major themes that appear throughout the history of Christian social teaching as represented by the selections in this book. All selections in the anthology have been assigned to particular themes based on their most prominent features. Readers may well see in a given selection connections with other themes as well. The numbers of the chapters are listed for each of the themes to which they apply and the numbers of the applicable selections within those chapters are given in parentheses. So, for example, for the theme of "Divine Command," selection 1(1) refers to Chapter 1/Hebrew Bible, and the first selections from Exodus.

Biblical and Theological Foundations
Divine Command: 1(1), 2(1), 3(1,2), 13(3), 20(1), 24
Neighbor Love: 2(3&6), 7(4), 9(1&3), 12(1), 31(1)
Divine Judgments and Promise: 1(3), 2(2), 6(2), 7(1,2), 13(1)
Reason and Natural Law: 5(1), 6(1), 10(2&5), 13(2), 19(1,2), 27(2), 28(1), 31(3), 35(2)
Virtues: 2(1), 7(4), 8(1,2), 9(2,3), 10(4), 18(1), 20(2), 42(1-3)
Trinitarian Theology and Social Ethics: 42(1,2)

Church and State
The selections for this theme vary from strict separation of church and state to a desire to see the state Christianized and positions in between:
2(5), 3(3), 4(1), 5(3), 7(3), 10(5), 11(1, 2), 12(2, 3)
13(5), 14(1-3), 15(1), 16(1), 17, 22, 23, 30(1), 33, 34(1)

War and Peace
Just War: 7(6), 10(6), 15(2), 41(3)
Pacifism: 14(1), 18(2), 41(1)
General: 5(3), 17, 29(1), 41(2)

Justice Issues
Economic Justice: 1(2), 16(2), 27(1,2), 29(2)
Just Use of Money: 2(4), 5(2), 10 (7), 21(1)
For the Poor and Those in Need: 14(3), 16(2), 21(3), 37(4)
Social and Political Liberation: 2(2), 18(3), 21(2), 23, 25(1,2), 35 (1-3), 36(1-3), 37(1-4)
For the Social Order: 10(1), 16(1), 26, 28(2), 30(1,2), 31(2)
Sexuality and Marriage: 7(5), 35(2), 38(1-5)

Respect for Life and Creation
The Whole Creation: 8(3), 39(1-4)
The Challenge of Modern Medical Science: 40(1-5)

PREFACE

George Wolfgang Forell (September 19, 1919–April 29, 2011) was the Carver Distinguished Professor Emeritus in the Department of Religious Studies at the University of Iowa. The following tribute that appeared in the online *Journal of Lutheran Ethics* expresses the high regard in which Professor Forell was held by so many:

> George W. Forell has been one of the theological giants of the Lutheran churches in America for over half a century. During this time, he has been a major figure in helping to interpret Luther, and particularly a Lutheran understanding of Ethics, to generations of students and scholars alike. . . . Forell's influence on Lutheran churches is particularly remarkable given the fact that his teaching career has been primarily within the context of a secular state university, the University of Iowa. Here he has faithfully maintained his integrity as a Christian theologian, while at the same time being open to and respectful of all the points of view that comprise the pluralistic culture of a major university.

Notwithstanding Forell's clear identity as a Lutheran ethicist, the wide scope of his grasp and appreciation of the multiple traditions of Christian thought and ethics is amply illustrated by the discerning selections in the original version of this book.

I am grateful to Fortress Press for the invitation to undertake the revision and updating of Professor Forell's 1966 publication of *Christian Social Teachings*. It is an honor to be associated with Dr. Forell's name. I am also deeply grateful for the approval he gave for me to carry forward the continuance of his work in this project. I approach the task with a genuine sense of humility and with the fond hope that, had Professor Forell lived to see the finished project, he would have approved.

This new edition has a good deal of new introductory commentary, and newer translations of older works have been used where available and helpful. A large portion of this expanded edition is the material representative of Christian social teaching since the publication of the original volume. So much has happened since that time—I am well aware of the fact that, when all is said and done, one cannot do justice to the full range of Christian social witness in these last decades of our time within the confines of a printed book. Selections must be made, and that is the hardest part. However, despite these restraints, I am confident that the selection of readings provides leading and important voices on major themes as routinely covered in college and university courses.

There are, of course, many perspectives on matters of Christian ethics that have remained unchanged in the faith and practice of Christian communities. These convictions should be evident in the texts when the book is viewed as a whole. At the same time, new and influential contributions to social ethics have come about in response to changing cultural and political realities. The new selections have been chosen to reflect those developments. In making these new selections I have also attempted to choose those thinkers whose work has been well-established enough to claim a place in the emerging "history" of the discourse. Such a judgment may seem presumptuous but it also seems unavoidable. Additionally, I have sought to pay appropriate attention to ecclesial and ecumenical sources that claim to represent the voice of the larger community of faith. Finally, the new selections have been made following the principle that they represent "social" teaching; ethical concerns that speak to the ethos of a society and may also have implications for public policy even as they give expression to the churches' witness for justice and peace.

Readers should note that I have included three "tools" for navigating and locating the content of the many readings. First, the table of contents includes authors's names and titles of selections in several cases, for easy identification and later reference. Second, the thematic organization of sources provides key themes and topics and their location among the numerous readings in the anthology. Third, unlike the vast number of anthologies for any discipline, especially religious studies and theology, an index is provided to assist the reader in finding additional themes or subjects (for example, atonement, covenant, sacrifice), as well as important titles or selections (for example, The Ten Commandments, The Beatitudes), for ready reference. I am hopeful that these various compilations of the anthology's content will enhance the use of this volume.

James M. Childs Jr.
Trinity Lutheran Seminary
Columbus, Ohio

PART 1

Biblical Influences

HEBREW BIBLE

The ethical vocation of the people of Israel and the Christian community that followed is grounded in and takes its life from the intimate relationship God has chosen to establish with humankind. Genesis 1:26-27 tells us that humanity is created in the very image of God. It is a special relationship that human beings enjoy among all creatures. In the creation account of Genesis 2, we see God molding the first human being from the dust of the earth like the potter molds the clay and then breathing into that form the life-giving divine breath. As images of God, human beings are dependent beings, dependent upon God for life itself. God not only creates humankind but gives them the fruits of the creation for their flourishing (Genesis 1:29 and 2:16). Humanity's relationship to God is constitutive of its being. Thus, when Adam and Eve yield to the temptation of the serpent to eat the forbidden fruit and be "like God," (Genesis 3:5) they step outside the circle of their true being. In their lost innocence they must now live out the struggle between good and evil (Genesis 3:22). The ethical themes of the Hebrew Scriptures find expression in the history of this conflict of good and evil from Cain's murder of Abel forward into the New Testament.

God does not abandon a wayward humanity or the promise of creation for the harmony of all things. God's actions in history continue to reveal God as the One who desires that humankind flourish along with the whole of creation. The covenant with Abraham (Genesis 15), the deliverance of the Israelites from slavery in Egypt, the giving of the Law in the covenant of Sinai (Exodus 19–24), the covenant with David (2 Samuel 7), and the delivery of the promised land of Canaan to the tribes of Israelites are all actions in history by which God raises up a people set apart as a witness to the nations (42:6). God is at work in the world through this covenant people to bring reconciliation among the peoples (Isaiah 2:2-3; 60:1, 3) and peace throughout the creation (Isaiah 11:6-9). It is the ethical vocation of Israel to reflect these divine purposes in their conduct as a society with a special, intimate, relationship with God that echoes the promise of humankind's creation in the divine image sustained by God's active presence in history.

The prophets continually call the people to faithfulness to their covenant vocation through the practice of justice and works of mercy. As God acts with steadfast love, justice, and righteousness in the earth (Jer. 9:23), so Israel is to do likewise. The prophet Amos admonishes the people for their shallow piety and calls on them to "let justice roll down like waters, and righteousness like an ever-flowing stream" (5:24). As God has been merciful in delivering the people from slavery and giving them their land, so they are to reenact those divine actions in their own practice of mercy (Zechariah 7:9). The well known passage from Micah 6:8 is a succinct statement of Israel's calling: "He has told you, O mortal,

2

what is good; and what does the Lord require of you but to do justice, and to love kindness, and to walk humbly with your God?"

Selection 1: Exodus 20:1-17; 21:1-11, 22-25, 33-36; 22:21-27

These selections are from what is known as the "Book of the Covenant," beginning with the reminder that is the basis of Israel's ethical vocation, God's merciful deliverance of the people from slavery in Egypt. There follows the apodictic (unconditional) law that becomes known as the Ten Commandments. In time the tablets of the law would come to rest inside the Ark of the Covenant , the sign of God's mercy, as another reminder that God's grace precedes and sustains the call to obedience as a response to divine favor. That call to obedience also involves ordinances that set forth the sort of casuistic or case law illustrated in these selections. Casuistic law recognizes that social life is often complex and motives and circumstances must be sorted out. Some examples also display characteristics of that ancient culture having to do with slavery and the status of women that we would find disturbing and ethically unacceptable. When we juxtapose that with the ordinances expressing God's compassionate concern for aliens, widows, orphans, and the poor, we are alerted to a distinction biblical scholars often make between what is at the core of God's self-revelation and what is part of the cultural scenery.

20:1Then God spoke all these words: 2I am the LORD your God, who brought you out of the land of Egypt, out of the house of slavery; 3you shall have no other gods before me. 4You shall not make for yourself an idol, whether in the form of anything that is in heaven above, or that is on the earth beneath, or that is in the water under the earth. 5You shall not bow down to them or worship them; for I the LORD your God am a jealous God, punishing children for the iniquity of parents, to the third and the fourth generation of those who reject me, 6but showing steadfast love to the thousandth generation of those who love me and keep my commandments. 7You shall not make wrongful use of the name of the LORD your God, for the LORD will not acquit anyone who misuses his name. 8Remember the sabbath day, and keep it holy. 9Six days you shall labor and do all your work. 10But the seventh day is a sabbath to the LORD your God; you shall not do any work—you, your son or your daughter, your male or female slave, your livestock, or the alien resident in your towns. 11For in six days the LORD made heaven and earth, the sea, and all that is in them, but rested the seventh day; therefore the LORD blessed the sabbath day and consecrated it.

12Honor your father and your mother, so that your days may be long in the land that the LORD your God is giving you. 13You shall not murder. 14You shall not commit adultery. 15You shall not steal. 16You shall not bear false witness against your neighbor. 17You shall not covet your neighbor's house; you shall not covet your neighbor's wife, or male or female slave, or ox, or donkey, or anything that belongs to your neighbor.

21:1These are the ordinances that you shall set before them: 2When you buy a male Hebrew slave, he shall serve six years, but in the seventh he shall go out a free person, without debt. 3If he comes in single, he shall go out single; if he comes in married, then his wife shall go out with him. [4]If his master gives him a wife and she bears him sons or daughters, the wife and her children shall be her master's and he shall go out alone. [5]But if the slave declares, "I love my master, my wife, and my children; I will not go out a free person," [6]then his master shall bring him before God. He shall be brought to the door or the doorpost; and his master shall pierce his ear with an awl; and he shall serve him for life. [7]When a man sells his daughter as a slave, she shall not go out as the male slaves do. [8]If she does not please her master, who designated her for himself, then he shall let her be redeemed; he shall have no right to sell her to a foreign people, since he has dealt unfairly with her. [9]If he designates her for his son, he shall deal with her as with a daughter. [10]If he takes another wife to himself, he shall not diminish the food, clothing, or marital rights of the first wife. [11]And if he does not do these three things for her, she shall go out without debt, without payment of money.

[22]When people who are fighting injure a pregnant woman so that there is a miscarriage, and yet no further harm follows, the one responsible shall be fined what the woman's husband demands, paying as much as the judges determine. [23]If any harm follows, then you shall give life for life, [24]eye for eye, tooth for tooth, hand for hand, foot for foot, [25]burn for burn, wound for wound, stripe for stripe. [33]If someone leaves a pit open, or digs a pit and does not cover it, and an ox or a donkey falls into it, [34]the owner of the pit shall make restitution, giving money to its owner, but keeping the dead animal. [35]If someone's ox hurts the ox of another, so that it dies, then they shall sell the live ox and divide the price of it; and the dead animal they shall also divide. [36]But if it was known that the ox was accustomed to gore in the past, and its owner has not restrained it, the owner shall restore ox for ox, but keep the dead animal. [21]You shall not wrong or oppress a resident alien, for you were aliens in the land of Egypt. [22]You shall not abuse any widow or orphan. [23]If you do abuse them, when they cry out to me, I will surely heed their cry; [24]my wrath will burn, and I will kill you with the sword, and your wives shall become widows and your children orphans.

[25]If you lend money to my people, to the poor among you, you shall not deal with them as a creditor; you shall not exact interest from them. [26]If you take your neighbor's cloak in pawn, you shall restore it before the sun goes down; [27]for it may be your neighbor's only clothing to use as cover; in what else shall that person sleep? And if your neighbor cries out to me, I will listen, for I am compassionate.

Selection 2: Leviticus 25:8-9

In this tradition of the jubilee year, Israel was commanded to forgive debtors, set free those sold into slavery for their debt, and restore lands to families who had to sell them due to economic hardship. Families would then be reunited on their lands. Here we have an image of biblical justice in which people are set free from oppressive social and economic circumstances to begin life anew. It demonstrates that justice was viewed from the vantage point of those in need. Justice begins with the mercy of God and the merciful actions God demands of the people and for the people. There are echoes of the jubilee tradition in Isaiah 61:1, which Jesus read in the synagogue and applied to his own person and work (Luke 4:18-21). In both Isaiah 61 and Luke 4, elements of the jubilee are incorporated in the messianic hope for God's future reign.

^{25:8}You shall count off seven weeks of years, seven times seven years, so that the period of seven weeks of years gives forty-nine years. ⁹Then you shall have the trumpet sounded loud; on the tenth day of the seventh month—on the day of atonement—you shall have the trumpet sounded throughout all your land. ¹⁰And you shall hallow the fiftieth year and you shall proclaim liberty throughout the land to all its inhabitants. It shall be a jubilee for you: you shall return, every one of you, to your property and every one of you to your family.

Selection 3: Prophetic Accents

Amos 5:6-24

> *Amos prophesied the middle of the eighth century* BCE, *during the prosperous and peaceful reign of Jeroboam II. Things seemed good. However, Amos was harsh in his criticism of reliance on military might and of a self-congratulatory complacency mingled with immorality, injustice and shallow piety. Jesus is quoted in Matthew 9:13, "I desire mercy not sacrifice," though Hosea 6:6 shares in this same spirit, as does the epistle of James. Amos's passionate cry for justice and disdain of meaningless ritual has remained a constant summons throughout subsequent generations.*

^{5:6}Seek the LORD and live, or he will break out against the house of Joseph like fire, and it will devour Bethel, with no one to quench it. ⁷Ah, you that turn justice to wormwood, and bring righteousness to the ground! ⁸The one who made the Pleiades and Orion, and turns deep darkness into the morning, and darkens the day into night, who calls for the waters of the sea, and pours them out on the surface of the earth, the LORD is his name, ⁹who makes destruction flash out against the strong, so that destruction comes upon the fortress. ¹⁰They hate the one who reproves in the gate, and they abhor the one who speaks the truth. ¹¹Therefore because you trample on the poor and take from them levies of grain, you have built houses of hewn stone, but you shall not live in them; you have planted pleasant vineyards, but you shall not drink their wine. ¹²For I know how many are your transgressions, and how great are your sins—you who afflict the righteous, who take a bribe, and push aside the needy in the gate. ¹³Therefore the prudent will keep silent in such a time; for it is an evil time. ¹⁴Seek good and not evil, that you may live; and so the LORD, the God of hosts, will be with you, just as you have said. ¹⁵Hate evil and love good, and establish justice in the gate; it may be that the LORD, the God of hosts, will be gracious to the reüant of Joseph.

¹⁶Therefore thus says the LORD, the God of hosts, the LORD: In all the squares there shall be wailing; and in all the streets they shall say, "Alas! alas!" They shall call the farmers to mourning, and those skilled in lamentation, to wailing; ¹⁷in all the vineyards there shall be wailing, for I will pass through the midst of you, says the LORD. ¹⁸Alas for you who desire the day of the LORD! Why do you want the day of the LORD? It is darkness, not light; ¹⁹as if someone fled from a lion, and was met by a bear; or went into the house and rested a hand against the wall, and was bitten by a snake. ²⁰Is not the day of the LORD darkness, not light, and gloom with no brightness in it?

²¹I hate, I despise your festivals, and I take no delight in your solemn assemblies. ²²Even though you offer me your burnt offerings and grain offerings, I will not accept them; and the offerings of well-being of your fatted animals I will not look upon. ²³Take away from me the noise of your songs; I will not listen to the melody of your harps. ²⁴But let justice roll down like waters, and righteousness like an everflowing stream.

Isaiah 11:1-9

Isaiah prophesied in Judah during the latter part of the eighth century BCE, a worrisome time for Judah sitting as it did adjacent to the Northern Kingdom that had just been annexed by Assyria. If Amos seems to have offered no hope for escape from God's judgment, Isaiah by contrast engenders the hope of a coming messiah and a proleptic (or anticipatory) vision of a peaceable kingdom marked by harmony throughout creation and the end of "hurt and destruction." The early verses have been applied to Jesus as the Messiah. The text has been an inspiration to peacemakers and, of late, a way to connect concern for the health of the planet with God's plan of salvation.

¹¹:¹A shoot shall come out from the stock of Jesse,
  and a branch shall grow out of his roots.
²The spirit of the Lord shall rest on him,
  the spirit of wisdom and understanding,
  the spirit of counsel and might,
  the spirit of knowledge and the fear of the Lord.
³His delight shall be in the fear of the Lord.
He shall not judge by what his eyes see,
  or decide by what his ears hear;
⁴but with righteousness he shall judge the poor,
  and decide with equity for the meek of the earth;
he shall strike the earth with the rod his mouth,
  and with the breath of his lips he shall kill the wicked.
⁵Righteousness shall be the belt around his waist,
  and faithfulness the belt around his loins.
⁶The wolf shall live with the lamb,
  the leopard shall lie down with the kid,
the calf and the lion and the fatling together,
  and a little child shall lead them.
⁷The cow and the bear shall graze,
  their young shall lie down together;
  and the lion shall eat straw like the ox.
⁸The nursing child shall play over the hole of the asp,
  and the weaned child shall put its hand on the adder's den.
⁹They will not hurt or destroy on all my holy mountain;
for the earth will be full of the knowledge of the Lord
  as the waters cover the sea.

NEW TESTAMENT

The message of the New Testament might well be summarized by Jesus' words in Mark 1:15: "The time is fulfilled, and the kingdom of God has come near; repent and believe in the good news." The whole of New Testament ethics is implicit in this proclamation. It is the ethics born of repentance and faith in light of the realization that the kairos has come, the time is fulfilled, the fullness of God's reign is revealed and assured in the person and work of Jesus, the Christ. Here and elsewhere in the synoptic gospels we are told Jesus went about proclaiming that the kingdom of God is at hand (for example, Matthew 4:23) He identified the meaning of his person and work with prophetic hopes for God's future. It is in him that the messianic vision of Isaiah 61:1 and its promise of good news to the poor, the blind, the captives, and the oppressed is to be fulfilled (Luke 4: 18-21). John the Baptist's disciples question Jesus on John's behalf if he is the one for whom John was ordained to prepare the way. Jesus' answer is a yet another identification with prophetic hope and an implicit claim to be the one bringing in the reign of God: "Go tell John what you have seen and heard: the blind receive their sight, the lame walk, the lepers are cleansed, the deaf hear, the dead are raised, the poor have good news brought to them." (Luke 7:22; Matthew 11:4-5) God's promised future, proclaimed by Jesus, anticipated by his teaching and works, and sealed by his resurrection is marked by the triumph of life, wholeness, freedom and justice, peace, and community with God and each other. The Christian ethic of neighbor love seeks these values of God's promised future in the present, energized by the revelation of their coming as an integral part of the good news of Jesus Christ.

That love (agape)—which Jesus commands for God and for the neighbor (Matthew 22:37-39; Mark 12:30; Luke 10:27)—is the very core of the law and the prophets (Matthew 22:40), giving both motive and direction to the Christian ethic. Christians are to love as they have been loved by God in Christ (John 15 12). "God's love (agape) has been poured into our hearts" Paul says, "through the Holy Spirit that has been given to us."(Romans 5:5) Christ is the example of the self-giving love and servanthood (Philippians 2:4-11; Matthew 10:45) that he admonishes his disciples to embrace (Matthew 10:43-44).

While there is no explicit discourse on the connection between love and social justice, the two are clearly linked together. As we noted above, the values love seeks for the neighbor, revealed by Jesus as marks of the coming kingdom, are essential components of social justice. Beyond that connection we find Luke's gospel replete with concerns for the poor, Matthew's parable of judgment against those who have neglected the need (Matthew 25:31-46), Paul's declaration of the equality of Jew and Greek, slave and free, male and female (Galatians 3:28), and the

Epistle of James's condemnation of partiality against the poor as unbecoming for those called to love the neighbor (James 2:1-9).

Though Christian ethics is an ethics of self-giving love ready to "turn the other cheek" and "go the extra mile," the New Testament concern for justice and the social good is also realistic in recognizing and supporting the necessity of civil authority and law. The governing authorities are established by God for the common good and the punishment of evildoers. Support of governing authority is obedience to God's purposes and a matter of Christian conscience and Christian witness to the larger society. (Romans 13:1-7; 1 Peter 2:12-17) At the same time, Christians are not to obey government no matter what; governing authorities are established by God to carry out God's purposes. "We must obey God rather than any human authority." (Acts 5:29) Christians clearly support just law and recognize the need for law in an evil world while yet being ready to go beyond the law in love for the neighbor, even their enemies.

Selection 1: Matthew 5

This is the first chapter of what has been called the Sermon on the Mount, which extends through chapters six and seven. Chapter five is of particular interest because of its focus on Jesus' ethical teachings, including insight into the radical nature of love. Moreover, the tenor of Jesus' proclamation makes it clear that he is claiming the authority of the one who is bringing in the kingdom of God and creating a new state of affairs. His teaching is therefore about a way of life that for all its apparent impossibility is, nonetheless, by the grace of Christ and the encroaching reign of God, a new possibility. The chapter is readily divided into four sections. The beatitudes (1-12) can be understood as a presentation of the virtues of Christ like love that are the "blessings" of the disciples of Christ. The similes (13-14) make the point that Christians are salt and light and should "be what they are." A transitional section (17-20) is Jesus' claim to fulfill the law and the prophets, reminding his hearers that he is in continuity with God's revelation to Israel and its consummation. The "antitheses" present a radicalization of the law that drive beyond action to include motive.

The Beatitudes

⁵:¹When Jesus saw the crowds, he went up the mountain; and after he sat down, his disciples came to him.²Then he began to speak, and taught them, saying:
³ 'Blessed are the poor in spirit, for theirs is the kingdom of heaven.
⁴ 'Blessed are those who mourn, for they will be comforted.
⁵ 'Blessed are the meek, for they will inherit the earth.
⁶ 'Blessed are those who hunger and thirst for righteousness, for they will be filled.
⁷ 'Blessed are the merciful, for they will receive mercy.
⁸ 'Blessed are the pure in heart, for they will see God.

⁹ 'Blessed are the peacemakers, for they will be called children of God.

¹⁰ 'Blessed are those who are persecuted for righteousness' sake, for theirs is the kingdom of heaven.

¹¹ 'Blessed are you when people revile you and persecute you and utter all kinds of evil against you falsely on my account. ¹²Rejoice and be glad, for your reward is great in heaven, for in the same way they persecuted the prophets who were before you.

¹³ 'You are the salt of the earth; but if salt has lost its taste, how can its saltiness be restored? It is no longer good for anything, but is thrown out and trampled under foot.

¹⁴ 'You are the light of the world. A city built on a hill cannot be hidden. ¹⁵No one after lighting a lamp puts it under the bushel basket, but on the lampstand, and it gives light to all in the house. ¹⁶In the same way, let your light shine before others, so that they may see your good works and give glory to your Father in heaven.

¹⁷ 'Do not think that I have come to abolish the law or the prophets; I have come not to abolish but to fulfill. ¹⁸For truly I tell you, until heaven and earth pass away, not one letter, not one stroke of a letter, will pass from the law until all is accomplished. ¹⁹Therefore, whoever breaks one of the least of these commandments, and teaches others to do the same, will be called least in the kingdom of heaven; but whoever does them and teaches them will be called great in the kingdom of heaven. ²⁰For I tell you, unless your righteousness exceeds that of the scribes and Pharisees, you will never enter the kingdom of heaven.

²¹ 'You have heard that it was said to those of ancient times, "You shall not murder"; and "whoever murders shall be liable to judgment." ²²But I say to you that if you are angry with a brother or sister, you will be liable to judgment; and if you insult a brother or sister, you will be liable to the council; and if you say, "You fool," you will be liable to the hell of fire. ²³So when you are offering your gift at the altar, if you remember that your brother or sister has something against you, ²⁴leave your gift there before the altar and go; first be reconciled to your brother or sister, and then come and offer your gift. ²⁵Come to terms quickly with your accuser while you are on the way to court with him, or your accuser may hand you over to the judge, and the judge to the guard, and you will be thrown into prison. ²⁶Truly I tell you, you will never get out until you have paid the last penny.

²⁷ 'You have heard that it was said, "You shall not commit adultery." ²⁸But I say to you that everyone who looks at a woman with lust has already committed adultery with her in his heart. ²⁹If your right eye causes you to sin, tear it out and throw it away; it is better for you to lose one of your members than for your whole body to be thrown into hell. ³⁰And if your right hand causes you to sin, cut it off and throw it away; it is better for you to lose one of your members than for your whole body to go into hell.

³¹ 'It was also said, "Whoever divorces his wife, let him give her a certificate of divorce." ³²But I say to you that anyone who divorces his wife, except on the ground of unchastity, causes her to commit adultery; and whoever marries a divorced woman commits adultery.

³³ 'Again, you have heard that it was said to those of ancient times, "You shall not swear falsely, but carry out the vows you have made to the LORD." ³⁴But I say to you, Do not swear at all, either by heaven, for it is the throne of God, ³⁵or by the earth, for it is his footstool, or by Jerusalem, for it is the city of the great King. ³⁶And do not swear by your head, for you cannot make one hair white or black. ³⁷Let your word be "Yes, Yes" or "No, No"; anything more than this comes from the evil one.

[38] 'You have heard that it was said, "An eye for an eye and a tooth for a tooth." [39]But I say to you, Do not resist an evildoer. But if anyone strikes you on the right cheek, turn the other also; [40]and if anyone wants to sue you and take your coat, give your cloak as well; [41]and if anyone forces you to go one mile, go also the second mile. [42]Give to everyone who begs from you, and do not refuse anyone who wants to borrow from you.

[43] 'You have heard that it was said, "You shall love your neighbor and hate your enemy." [44]But I say to you, Love your enemies and pray for those who persecute you, [45]so that you may be children of your Father in heaven; for he makes his sun rise on the evil and on the good, and sends rain on the righteous and on the unrighteous. [46]For if you love those who love you, what reward do you have? Do not even the tax-collectors do the same? [47]And if you greet only your brothers and sisters, what more are you doing than others? Do not even the Gentiles do the same? [48]Be perfect, therefore, as your heavenly Father is perfect.

Selection 2: Luke 4:14-21 and Matthew 11:2-6

In each of these selections we find Jesus quoting from Isaiah. In Luke it is Isaiah 61:1 and in Matthew 11 he is quoting from a combination of Isaiah 29: 18-19, 35:5-6, and 61:1. In each case Jesus is pointing out that the works expected of the Messiah are being fulfilled in his person and work. Not only are these passages important for revealing Jesus' messianic claim as the fulfillment of prophetic hope and expectation, but the works of the Messiah reveal the will of God for healing, liberation, and justice. The hope that Jesus comes to proclaim is for the well-being of the whole person and the whole world. Thus, the Christian community is called to an ethic of peace and justice that imitates the works of its Lord. A clue to Jesus' social ethic may be found in the fact that Isaiah with its rich social teaching is the prophetic book most quoted by Jesus.

Luke 4:14-21

[4:14] Then Jesus, filled with the power of the Spirit, returned to Galilee, and a report about him spread through all the surrounding country. [15]He began to teach in their synagogues and was praised by everyone.

[16] When he came to Nazareth, where he had been brought up, he went to the synagogue on the sabbath day, as was his custom. He stood up to read, [17]and the scroll of the prophet Isaiah was given to him. He unrolled the scroll and found the place where it was written: [18]'The Spirit of the LORD is upon me, because he has anointed me to bring good news to the poor. He has sent me to proclaim release to the captives and recovery of sight to the blind, to let the oppressed go free, [19]to proclaim the year of the LORD's favor.' [20]And he rolled up the scroll, gave it back to the attendant, and sat down. The eyes of all in the synagogue were fixed on him. [21]Then he began to say to them, "Today this scripture has been fulfilled in your hearing."

Matthew 11:2-6

[11:2] When John heard in prison what the Messiah was doing, he sent word by his disciples [3]and said to him, 'Are you the one who is to come, or are we to wait for another?' [4]Jesus answered them, 'Go and tell John what you hear and see: [5]the blind receive their sight, the lame walk, the lepers are cleansed, the deaf hear, the dead are raised, and the poor have good news brought to them. [6]And blessed is anyone who takes no offence at me.'

Selection 3: Luke 10:25-37

This is perhaps Jesus's best-known parable. Being a "good Samaritan" has entered into popular parlance as a way to describe acts of kindness and help to a neighbor in need. The double love commandment given here to the lawyer occurs in Matthew and Mark as well. Only here in Luke is it accompanied by an example of love in action that we are commanded with the lawyer to emulate. That Samaritans were outcasts is well known. That Jesus makes a Samaritan the shining example suggests not only that Jesus reaches out to all people but also that his followers should do so as well; all are our "neighbors."

Luke 10:25-37

[10:25]Just then a lawyer stood up to test Jesus. "Teacher," he said, "what must I do to inherit eternal life?" [26]He said to him, "What is written in the law? What do you read there?" [27]He answered, "You shall love the LORD your God with all your heart, and with all your soul, and with all your strength, and with all your mind; and your neighbor as yourself." [28]And he said to him, "You have given the right answer; do this, and you will live." [29]But wanting to justify himself, he asked Jesus, "And who is my neighbor?" [30]Jesus replied, "A man was going down from Jerusalem to Jericho, and fell into the hands of robbers, who stripped him, beat him, and went away, leaving him half dead. [31]Now by chance a priest was going down that road; and when he saw him, he passed by on the other side. [32]So likewise a Levite, when he came to the place and saw him, passed by on the other side. [33]But a Samaritan while traveling came near him; and when he saw him, he was moved with pity. [34]He went to him and bandaged his wounds, having poured oil and wine on them. Then he put him on his own animal, brought him to an inn, and took care of him. [35]The next day he took out two denarii, gave them to the innkeeper, and said, 'Take care of him; and when I come back, I will repay you whatever more you spend.' [36]Which of these three, do you think, was a neighbor to the man who fell into the hands of the robbers?" [37]He said, "The one who showed him mercy." Jesus said to him, "Go and do likewise."

Selection 4: Luke 12:15-31

Jesus' parable of the rich fool is not an attack on wealth per se but a warning against greed. The rich fool is not condemned for having a good year but for his lack of readiness to share, a theme connected to the parable of the Rich Man and Lazarus (Luke 16: 19-21.) Both parables, found only in Luke, voice this theme of the need to be concerned for the wellbeing of others. The rich fool's dedication to his own security is a form of idolatry that closed him off from that concern for others. Followers of Christ, by contrast, are not to be anxious for their own security, but place their trust in God and dedicate themselves to the values and promises of the kingdom Jesus has come to usher in.

[12:15]And he said to them, 'Take care! Be on your guard against all kinds of greed; for one's life does not consist in the abundance of possessions.' [16]Then he told them a parable: 'The land of a rich man produced abundantly. [17]And he thought to himself, "What should I do, for I have no place to store my crops?" [18]Then he said, "I will do this: I will pull down my barns and build larger ones, and there I will store all my grain and my goods. [19]And I will say to my soul, Soul, you have ample goods laid up for many years; relax, eat, drink, be merry." [20]But God said to him, "You fool! This very night your life is being demanded of you. And the things you have prepared, whose will they be?" [21]So it is with those who store up treasures for themselves but are not rich toward God.'

Do Not Worry

[22]He said to his disciples, 'Therefore I tell you, do not worry about your life, what you will eat, or about your body, what you will wear. [23]For life is more than food, and the body more than clothing. [24]Consider the ravens: they neither sow nor reap, they have neither storehouse nor barn, and yet God feeds them. Of how much more value are you than the birds! [25]And can any of you by worrying add a single hour to your span of life? [26]If then you are not able to do so small a thing as that, why do you worry about the rest? [27]Consider the lilies, how they grow: they neither toil nor spin; yet I tell you, even Solomon in all his glory was not clothed like one of these. [28]But if God so clothes the grass of the field, which is alive today and tomorrow is thrown into the oven, how much more will he clothe you—you of little faith! [29]And do not keep striving for what you are to eat and what you are to drink, and do not keep worrying. [30]For it is the nations of the world that strive after all these things, and your Father knows that you need them. [31]Instead, strive for his kingdom, and these things will be given to you as well.

Selection 5: Romans 13 and 1 Peter 2:13—3:8

As noted in the general introduction to New Testament influences, these two texts contain admonitions to obey civil authorities that God has established for the common good. At the same time, as Paul says in the Romans text, love of neighbor is the fulfilling of the law. How the ethics of Christian love is both to support, critique, and be involved with civil authority and their mandate to promote and preserve justice remains an ongoing source of debate with positions ranging from avoidance of public life to vigorous activism. The diversity of views is to a great extent a function of differing circumstances in different places and different times, leading to different interpretations of how the texts apply. First Peter's admonition to slaves and wives to be obedient to masters and husbands is certainly received in a different light today than it would have been in first-century Palestine (see also Ephesians 5:22—6:9).

Romans 13:1-14

¹³:¹Let every person be subject to the governing authorities; for there is no authority except from God, and those authorities that exist have been instituted by God. ²Therefore whoever resists authority resists what God has appointed, and those who resist will incur judgment. ³For rulers are not a terror to good conduct, but to bad. Do you wish to have no fear of the authority? Then do what is good, and you will receive its approval; ⁴for it is God's servant for your good. But if you do what is wrong, you should be afraid, for the authority does not bear the sword in vain! It is the servant of God to execute wrath on the wrongdoer. ⁵Therefore one must be subject, not only because of wrath but also because of conscience. ⁶For the same reason you also pay taxes, for the authorities are God's servants, busy with this very thing.

⁷Pay to all what is due them—taxes to whom taxes are due, revenue to whom revenue is due, respect to whom respect is due, honor to whom honor is due. ⁸Owe no one anything, except to love one another; for the one who loves another has fulfilled the law. ⁹The commandments, "You shall not commit adultery; You shall not murder; You shall not steal; You shall not covet"; and any other commandment, are summed up in this word, "Love your neighbor as yourself." ¹⁰Love does no wrong to a neighbor; therefore, love is the fulfilling of the law.

¹¹Besides this, you know what time it is, how it is now the moment for you to wake from sleep. For salvation is nearer to us now than when we became believers; ¹²the night is far gone, the day is near. Let us then lay aside the works of darkness and put on the armor of light; ¹³let us live honorably as in the day, not in reveling and drunkenness, not in debauchery and licentiousness, not in quarreling and jealousy. ¹⁴Instead, put on the Lord Jesus Christ, and make no provision for the flesh, to gratify its desires.

1 Peter 2:13—3:8

²:¹³For the Lord's sake accept the authority of every human institution, whether of the emperor as supreme, ¹⁴or of governors, as sent by him to punish those who do wrong and to praise those who do right. ¹⁵For it is God's will that by doing right you should silence the ignorance of the foolish. ¹⁶As servants of God, live as free people, yet do not use your freedom as a pretext for evil. ¹⁷Honor everyone. Love the family of believers. Fear God. Honor the emperor. ¹⁸Slaves, accept the authority of your masters with all deference, not only those who are kind and gentle but also those who

are harsh. [19]For it is a credit to you if, being aware of God, you endure pain while suffering unjustly. [20]If you endure when you are beaten for doing wrong, what credit is that? But if you endure when you do right and suffer for it, you have God's approval. [21]For to this you have been called, because Christ also suffered for you, leaving you an example, so that you should follow in his steps. [22]"He committed no sin, and no deceit was found in his mouth." [23]When he was abused, he did not return abuse; when he suffered, he did not threaten; but he entrusted himself to the one who judges justly. [24]He himself bore our sins in his body on the cross, so that, free from sins, we might live for righteousness; by his wounds you have been healed. [25]For you were going astray like sheep, but now you have returned to the shepherd and guardian of your souls.

[3]Wives, in the same way, accept the authority of your husbands, so that, even if some of them do not obey the word, they may be won over without a word by their wives' conduct, [2]when they see the purity and reverence of your lives. [3]Do not adorn yourselves outwardly by braiding your hair, and by wearing gold ornaments or fine clothing; [4]rather, let your adornment be the inner self with the lasting beauty of a gentle and quiet spirit, which is very precious in God's sight. [5]It was in this way long ago that the holy women who hoped in God used to adorn themselves by accepting the authority of their husbands. [6]Thus Sarah obeyed Abraham and called him lord. You have become her daughters as long as you do what is good and never let fears alarm you. [7]Husbands, in the same way, show consideration for your wives in your life together, paying honor to the woman as the weaker sex, since they too are also heirs of the gracious gift of life—so that nothing may hinder your prayers.

[8]Finally, all of you, have unity of spirit, sympathy, love for one another, a tender heart, and a humble mind.

Selection 6: 1 John 4:7-21 and 1 Corinthians 13:1-7

Love of neighbor, as we have seen, is the cornerstone of the Christian ethic in all its expressions, social and individual. Nowhere in the New Testament is the utter necessity of agape for authentic Christian living more pronounced in these two texts. The wellspring of love for John is from the love of God who is love itself. For John as well as Paul, the absence of love, its actions, and the marks of its character render one's claims to true faith and morality empty and strident.

1 John 4:7-21

[4:7]Beloved, let us love one another, because love is from God; everyone who loves is born of God and knows God. [8]Whoever does not love does not know God, for God is love. [9]God's love was revealed among us in this way: God sent his only Son into the world so that we might live through him. [10]In this is love, not that we loved God but that he loved us and sent his Son to be the atoning sacrifice for our sins. [11]Beloved, since God loved us so much, we also ought to love one another. [12]No one has ever seen God; if we love one another, God lives in us, and his love is perfected in us. [13]By this we know that we abide in him and he in us, because he has given us of his Spirit.

[14]And we have seen and do testify that the Father has sent his Son as the Savior of the world. [15]God abides in those who confess that Jesus is the Son of God, and they abide in God. [16]So we have known and believe the love that God has for us. God is love, and those who abide in love abide in God, and God abides in them.

[17]Love has been perfected among us in this: that we may have boldness on the day of judgment, because as he is, so are we in this world. [18]There is no fear in love, but perfect love casts out fear; for fear has to do with punishment, and whoever fears has not reached perfection in love. [19]We love because he first loved us. [20]Those who say, "I love God," and hate their brothers or sisters, are liars; for those who do not love a brother or sister whom they have seen, cannot love God whom they have not seen. [21]The commandment we have from him is this: those who love God must love their brothers and sisters also.

1 Corinthians 13:1-7

[13:1]If I speak in the tongues of mortals and of angels, but do not have love, I am a noisy gong or a clanging cymbal. [2]And if I have prophetic powers, and understand all mysteries and all knowledge, and if I have all faith, so as to remove mountains, but do not have love, I am nothing. [3]If I give away all my possessions, and if I hand over my body so that I may boast, but do not have love, I gain nothing.

[4]Love is patient; love is kind; love is not envious or boastful or arrogant [5]or rude. It does not insist on its own way; it is not irritable or resentful; [6]it does not rejoice in wrongdoing, but rejoices in the truth. [7]It bears all things, believes all things, hopes all things, endures all things.

For Further Reading

The following select list of writings provides a mixture of primary and secondary sources related to the major parts of the anthology, and the full text of the works being excerpted will also provide rich additional reading.

Brueggemann, Walter. *Journey to the Common Good*. Louisville: Westminster John Knox, 2011.

Knight, Douglas A. *Law, Power, and Justice in Ancient Israel*. Louisville: Westminster John Knox, 2011.

Johnson, Luke Timothy. *Prophetic Jesus, Prophetic Church: The Challenge of Luke-Acts to Contemporary Christians*. Grand Rapids: Eerdmans, 2011.

Pilgrim, Walter. *Uneasy Neighbors: Church and State in the New Testament*. Minneapolis: Fortress Press, 1999.

PART 2

The Early Church

APOSTOLIC FATHERS 3

The ethical teachings of these early Christian Fathers receive their special character from the fact that they are written by Gentiles living in a pagan world. The Torah cannot be assumed; it is not an integral feature of the cultural context. Thus, practices such as abortion, infanticide, pederasty, magic, and witchcraft that were common in the Hellenistic Roman Empire needed to be confronted to an extent that would not be necessary in a Jewish environment. Then as now, the Christian ethic finds expression in engagement with the particular features of the context in which Christians find themselves. As such, the Christian moral witness takes on an apologetic function as a window to the Christian faith and its values.

To some degree a sense of the impending eschaton is shared by the first two of these writers. It is most pronounced in this statement from the Epistle of Barnabas, the earliest of these second-century writings: "The day is near when everything will perish together with the Evil One. The Lord and his reward are near" (21:3). Writing later in the century, Justin feels the need to explain the delay in the Parousia, "For the reason why God has delayed to do this [bring about the end of the world] is His regard for the human race; for He foreknows that some are to be saved by repentance, and perhaps some not yet born." Justin displays little concern over this apparent delay, however, though he doubtless shared the view that the days of the world are numbered. The hope for the Lord's return, then, surely influenced the ethical teachings of these early fathers. It helps to explain the uncompromising demands of their individualistic ethic. There is little need for a carefully nuanced social ethic designed to cope over time with a myriad of fluctuating claims, conflicts, and demands for compromise. Furthermore, in a setting and time when Christianity was an often-persecuted minority there was scant opportunity to exert influence in matters of justice and the civil order and a great need to be true to the faith in the most rigorous way possible. Somewhat in contrast, the selection from Irenaeus, written in the latter half of the second century voices more concern over the order of this world.

Selection 1: The *Epistle of Barnabas* XVII–XXI

This anonymous epistle, which enjoyed canonical status for a time in some circles, has been dated anywhere from the late first century to the early years of the second. Few if any scholars believe that it was written by Paul's colleague Barnabas, *who likely died before the book was written. Our selections from the second part of the epistle present a version of the "ways" or "paths," the "Way of Light" versus "Way of Darkness." This teaching is quite similar to the two ways teachings laid out in the Didache, another anonymous document from the same general time frame. Ironically, given the anti-Jewish rhetoric of the first part of the Epistle of Barnabas, it is generally believed that both this epistle and the Didache were derived from an earlier Jewish source adopted by Christian teachers.*

The Two Ways

18. But let us move on to another lesson and teaching. There are two ways of teaching and power, one of light and one of darkness, and there is a great difference between these two ways. For over the one are stationed light-giving angels of God, but over the other are angels of Satan. And the first is Lord from eternity to eternity, while the latter is ruler of the present era of lawlessness.

The Way of Light

19. This, therefore, is the way of light; if any desire to make their way to the designated place, let them be diligent with respect to their works. The knowledge, then, that is given to us that we may walk in it is as follows. You shall love the one who made you; you shall fear the one who created you; you shall glorify the one who redeemed you from death. You shall be sincere in heart and rich in spirit. You shall not associate with those who walk along the way of death; you shall hate everything that is not pleasing to God; you shall hate all hypocrisy; you must not forsake the Lord's commandments. You shall not exalt yourself, but shall be humble-minded in every respect. You shall not claim glory for yourself. You shall not hatch evil plots against your neighbor. You shall not permit your soul to become arrogant. You shall not be sexually promiscuous; you shall not commit adultery; you shall not corrupt children. The word of God shall not go forth from you among any who are unclean. You shall not show partiality when reproving someone for a transgression. Be humble; be quite; be one who reveres the words that you have heard. You shall not hold a grudge against your brother or sister. You shall not waver with regard to your decisions. You shall not take the Lord's name in vain. You shall love your neighbor more than your own life. You shall not abort a child nor, again, commit infanticide. You must not withhold your hand from your son or your daughter, but from their youth you shall teach them the fear of God. You must not covet your neighbor's possessions; you must not become greedy. Do not intimately associated with the lofty, but live with the humble and righteous. Accept as good the things that happen to you, knowing that nothing transpires apart from God. You shall not be double-minded or double-tongued. Be submissive to masters in respect and fear, as to a symbol of God. You must not give orders to your male slave or female servant (who hope in the same God as you) when angry, lest they cease to fear the God who is over you both, because he came to call those whom the Spirit has prepared, without regard to reputation. You shall share everything with your neighbor, and not claim that anything is your own. For if you are sharers in what is incorruptible, how much

more so in corruptible things! Do not be quick to speak, for the mouth is a deadly snare. Insofar as you are able, you shall be pure for the sake of your soul. Do not be someone who stretches out the hands to receive, but withdraws them when it comes to giving. You shall love as the apple of your eye everyone who speaks the word of the Lord to you. Remember the Day of Judgment night and day, and you shall seek out on a daily basis the presence of the saints, either laboring in word and going out to encourage, and endeavoring to save a soul by the word, or work with your hands for a ransom for your sins. You shall not hesitate to give, nor shall you grumble when giving, but you will know who is the good paymaster of the reward. You shall guard what you have received, neither adding nor subtracting anything. You shall utterly hate the evil one. You shall judge righteously. You shall not cause division, but shall make peace between those who quarrel by bringing them together. You shall confess your sins. You shall not come to prayer with an evil conscience. This the way of light.

The Way of Darkness

20. But the way of the black one is crooked and completely cursed. For it is a way of eternal death and punishment, in which lie things that destroy men's souls: idolatry, audacity, arrogance of power, hypocrisy, duplicity, adultery, murder, robbery, pride, transgression, deceit, malice, stubbornness, sorcery, magic art, greed, lack of fear of God. It is the way of persecutors of the good, of those who hate truth, love a lie, do not know the reward of righteousness, do not adhere to what is good or to righteous judgment, who ignore the widow and the orphan, are vigilant not because of fear of God, but for what is evil, from whom gentleness and patience are far removed and distant, who love worthless things, pursue a reward, have no mercy for the poor, do not work on behalf of the oppressed, are reckless with slander, do not know the one who made them, are murderers of children, corrupters of God's creation, who turn away from someone in need, who oppress the afflicted, are advocates of the wealthy, lawless judges of the poor, utterly sinful.

Concluding Remarks

21. It is good, therefore, to learn all the Lord's righteous requirements that are written here and to walk in them. For the one who does these things will be glorified in the kingdom of God; the one who chooses their opposites will perish together with his or her words. This is why there is a resurrection, this is why there is recompense.

I urge those in high positions, if you will accept some well-intentioned advice from me: you have among you those to whom you can do good—do not fail.

The day is near when everything will perish together with the Evil One. The Lord, and his reward, is near. Again and again I urge you: Be good lawgivers to one another; continue to be faithful counselors of one another; get rid of all hypocrisy among you. And may God, who rules over the whole world, give you wisdom, understanding, insight, knowledge of his righteous requirements, and patience. Be instructed by God, seeking out what the Lord seeks from you and then doing it, in order that you may be found in the day of judgment.

Selection 2: The *First Apology* of Justin Martyr 14–17, 27–29

Justin was a Palestinian who flourished in the middle of the second century and was later martyred for his faith. A Christian and a Platonist, Justin believed that the seeds of truth (the logos) were sown in all people. This was his famous teaching of the logos spermatikos (see the Second Apology, 8, 10, and 13). His apologetic efforts to defend the faith and convert his pagan hearers were thus an appeal to the truth of the logos (ultimately the Christ) of which they already have knowledge. Thus, despite the stark contrast between Justin's account of biblical ethics and pagan practices, it seems safe to assume that, given his doctrine of the logos, Justin would expect his listeners to be able to recognize the truth and obligation of these teachings. Therefore, one might hazard the thought that, individualistic though these ethical teachings may be, their accessibility to all people could provide the foundation for the sort of broadly shared social ethic that emerges later in Christian history.

The Moral Power of Christianity

14. For we warn you in advance to be on your guard, lest the demons whom we have previously accused should deceive you and divert you from reading and understanding what we say. For they strive to have you as their slaves and servants, and sometimes by appearances in dreams, sometimes by magical tricks, they subdue all who do not struggle to the utmost for their own salvation, as we do also who, after being persuaded by the Word, renounced them, and follow the only unbegotten God through His Son. Those who formerly delighted in fornication now embrace chastity alone; those who formerly made use of magical arts have dedicated themselves to good and unbegotten God; we who once valued above everything the gaining of wealth and possessions now bring what we have into a common stock, and share with everyone in need; we who hated and destroyed one another, and would not share the same hearth with people of a different tribe on account of their different customs, now since the coming of Christ, live familiarly with them, and pray for our enemies, and try to persuade those who unjustly hate us to live according to the good advice of Christ, to the end that they may share with us the same joyful hope of a reward from God the master of all. But lest we should seem to deceive, we consider it right, before embarking on our promised demonstration, to cite a few of the precepts given by Christ Himself. It is for you then, as powerful rulers, to find out whether we have been taught and do teach these things truly. Short and concise utterances come from Him, for He was no sophist, but His word was the power of God.

15. Concerning chastity he said this: "Whosoever looks upon a woman to lust after her has already committed adultery with her in his heart before God." And: "If your right eye offends you, cut it out; for it is better for you to enter into the Kingdom of Heaven with one eye, than with two eyes to be cast into eternal fire. And: "Whosoever shall marry her that is divorced from another husband, commits adultery. And: "There are some who have been made eunuchs by men, and some who were born eunuchs, and some who have made themselves eunuchs for the Kingdom of Heaven's sake; but not all can receive this saying. So that all who according to human law make

second marriages are sinners in the sight of our Master, as are those who look on a woman to lust after her. For not only the man who in act commits adultery is condemned by Him, but also the man who desires to commit adultery; since not only our deeds but also our thoughts are open before God. And many, both men and women, who have been Christ's disciples from childhood, have preserved their purity at the age of sixty or seventy years; and I am proud that I could produce such from every race of men and women. For what shall we say then of the countless multitude of those who have turned away from intemperance and learned these things? For Christ did not call the righteous and temperate to repentance, but the ungodly and licentious and unrighteous. So He said, "I came not to call the righteous, but sinners to repentance. For the Heavenly Father desires the repentance of a sinner, rather than his punishment. And concerning our affection for all people He taught so: "If you love those who love you, what new thing do you do? For even the fornicators do this. But I say to you, pray for your enemies, and love those who hate you, and bless those who curse you, and pray for those who despitefully use you." And that we should share with the needy, and do nothing for glory, He said these things; "Give to everyone who asks and turn not away from him who wishes to borrow. For if you lend to those from who you hope to receive, what new thing do you do? Even the publicans do this. Lay not up for yourselves treasure upon earth, where moth and rust corrupt and thieves break in; but lay up for yourselves treasure in heaven, where neither moth nor rust corrupts. For what will it profit a man if he should gain the whole world, but lose his own soul? Or what will he give in exchange for it? Lay up treasure therefore in heaven, where neither moth nor rust corrupts." And: "Be kind and merciful, as your Father also is kind and merciful, and makes His sun to rise on sinners and the righteous and the wicked. Take no thought what you will eat, or what you will put on: are you not better than the birds and the beast? And God feeds them. Take no thought, therefore, what you will eat or what you will wear; for your Heavenly Father knows that you need these things. But seek the Kingdom of Heaven, and all these things will be added to you. For where his treasure is, there is also the mind of man." And: "Do not do these things to be seen of men; otherwise you have no reward from your Father who is in heaven."

16. And concerning our being long-suffering and servants to all and free from anger, this is what He said: "To him that smites you on the one cheek, offer also the other; and to him that takes away your shirt do not forbid your cloak also. And whosoever shall be angry is in danger of the fire. And whosoever compels you to go one mile, follow him for two. And let your good works shine before men, that they, seeing them may wonder at your Father who is in heaven." For we ought not to quarrel; neither has he desired us to imitate wicked people, but He has exhorted us to lead all people, by patience and gentleness, from shame and evil desires. And this indeed we can show in the case of many who were once of your way of thinking, but have turned from the way of violence and tyranny, being conquered, either by the constancy of life which they have traced in [Christian] neighbors, or by the strange endurance which they have noticed in defrauded fellow travelers or have experienced in those with whom they had dealings. And concerning our not swearing at all, but always speaking the truth, He commanded thus: "Swear not at all, but let your yes be yes and your no, no. For what is more than these is from the evil one." And that we ought to worship God alone He showed us when He said: "The greatest commandment is, you shall worship

the Lord your God and Him only shall you serve with all your heart and all your strength, the Lord who made you." And, when a certain man came to Him and said, "Good, Master," He answered and said, "There is none good, except God only who made all things." Those who are found not living as He taught should understand that they are not really Christians, even if they profess, but those who do the works will be saved. For He said this: "Not everyone who says to me, Lord, Lord, will enter into the Kingdom of Heaven, but he who does the will of my Father who is in heaven. For whosoever hears me, and does what I say, hears Him who sent me. But many will say to me, Lord, Lord, have we not eaten and drunk in your name, and done wonders? And then I will say to them, Depart from me, you workers of iniquity. Then there will be weeping and gnashing of teeth, when the righteous will shine as the sun, but the wicked shall be sent into eternal fire. For many will come in my name, clothed outwardly in sheep's clothing, but inwardly being ravening wolves. By their works you will know them. And every tree that does not bring forth good fruit, is hewn down and thrown into the fire. And as to those who are not living in accordance with His teachings, but are Christians only in name, we demand that all such shall be punished by you.

17. And everywhere we try to pay to those appointed by you, more readily than all people, the taxed and assessments, as we have been taught by Him. For at that time some came and asked Him if it were necessary to pay tribute to Caesar. And He answered, "Tell me, whose image does this coin bear?" And they said, "Caesar's." And again He answered them, "Give therefore to Caesar the things that are Caesar's and to God the things that are God's. So we worship God only, but in other things we gladly serve you, acknowledging you as emperors and rules of men and women, and praying that with your imperial power you may also be found to possess sound judgment. But if you pay no regard to our prayers and frank statements, we shall suffer no injury, since we believe, or rather are indeed persuaded, that every person will suffer punishment in eternal fire according to the merit of his actions, and will give account according to the ability he has received from God, as Christ reminded us when He said, "To whom God has given more, from him more will be require.

27. But as for us, lest we should do any injustice or impiety, we have been taught that to expose newly born infants is the work of wicked people; firstly because we see that almost all those exposed, not only the girls but also the boys, are growing up to prostitution. And as the ancients are said to have reared herds of oxen, or goats, or sheep, or grazing horses, so now [we see you raise children] only for this shameful purpose; and with a view to this abomination a crowd of females and hermaphrodites and those who commit unspeakable iniquities are found in every nation. And you receive the hire from these, and levies and taxes from them, whom you ought to exterminate from your civilized world. And anyone who Makes use of these, in addition to the godless and infamous and impure intercourse, may by chance be consorting with his own child or relative or brother. And there are some, who prostitute even their own children and wives, and some are openly mutilated for the purposes of sodomy, and they refer these mysteries to the mother of the gods, and along with each of those whom you think of as gods there is depicted a serpent, a great symbol and mystery. Indeed the things which you do openly and with applause, as if the divine light were overturned and extinguished, these you charge against us; which in truth does no

harm to us who shrink from doing any of these things, but rather to those who do them and bear false witness [against us].

28. For among us the leader of the evil demons is called the serpent and Satan and the devil, as you can learn by examining our writings. Christ has foretold that he would be sent into the fire with his host and the people who follow him, and would be punished for endless ages. For the reason why God had delayed to do this is His regard for the human race; for He foreknows that some are to be saved by repentance, and perhaps some not yet born. In the beginning He made the human race with the power of thought and of choosing the truth and of acting rightly, so that all people are without excuse before God; for they have been born capable of exercising reason and intelligence. And if anyone denies that God cares for these things, either he will be some figure of thought deny His existence, or, while allowing His existence, he will assert that He rejoices in evil, or that He remains unmoved like a stone, and that neither virtue nor vice are anything, but only in the opinion of men and women these things are considered good or evil; and this is the greatest impiety and wickedness.

29. And again [we do not expose children] lest some of them, not being picked up, should die, and we become murderers. But whether we marry, it is only that we may bring up children, or whether we renounce marriage we live in perfect continence. And that you may understand that promiscuous intercourse is not among our myster- ies, one of our number recently presented to Felix, the Perfect in Alexandria, a peti- tion, asking that permission might be given to a doctor to make him a eunuch; for the doctors said that they were forbidden to do this without the permission of the Prefect. And when Felix would by no means agree to subscribe [to the petition] the youth remained single, and was satisfied with the testimony of his own conscience and that of his fellow believers. And it is not out of place, we think, to mention here Antinous, who was recently alive, and whom everybody, with reverence, hastened to worship as a god, though they knew both who he was and what was his origin.

Selection 3: Irenaeus, *Against Heresies*, Book V, Chapter 24

Irenaeus, Bishop of Lyon, lived in the latter half of the second century. He is one of the most important early Christian theologians, particularly because of his bib- lically oriented theology developed in conflict with Gnosticism. Some historians regard him as the first true systematic theologian. His conviction that the entire universe is God's is illustrated in this selection where the "kingdoms of the world" are claimed for God. With recourse to scripture Irenaeus defends the order of government and its coercive powers as agents appointed by God for justice.

1. As therefore the devil lied at the beginning, so did he also in the end, when he said, "All these are delivered unto me, and to whomsoever I will I give them." (2) For it is not he who has appointed the kingdoms of this world, but God; for "the heart of the king is in the hand of God."(3) And the Word also says by Solomon, "By me kings do reign, and princes administer justice. By me chiefs are raised up, and by me kings rule the earth." (4) Paul the apostle also says upon this same subject: "Be ye subject

to all the higher powers for there is no power but of God: now those which are have been ordained of God." (5) And again, in reference to them he says, "For he beareth not the sword in vain; for he is the minister of God, the avenger for wrath to him who does evil." (6) Now, that he spake these words, not in regard to angelical powers, nor of invisible rulers—as some venture to expound the passage—but of those of actual human authorities, [he shows when] he says, "For this cause pay ye tribute also: for they are God's ministers, doing service for this very thing." (7) This also the Lord confirmed, when He did not do what He was tempted to by the devil; but He gave directions that tribute should be paid to the tax-gatherers for Himself and Peter; (8) because "they are the ministers of God, serving for this very thing."

2. For since man, by departing from God, reached such a pitch of fury as even to look upon his brother as his enemy, and engaged without fear in every kind of restless conduct, and murder, and avarice; God imposed upon mankind the fear of man, as they did not acknowledge the fear of God, in order that, being subjected to the authority of men, and kept under restraint by their laws, they might attain to some degree of justice, and exercise mutual forbearance through dread of the sword suspended full in their view, as the apostle says: "For he beareth not the sword in vain; for he is the minister of God, the avenger for wrath upon him who does evil." And for this reason too, magistrates themselves, having laws as a clothing of righteousness whenever they act in a just and legitimate manner, shall not be called in question for their conduct, nor be liable to punishment. But whatsoever they do to the subversion of justice, iniquitously, and impiously, and illegally, and tyrannically, in these things shall they also perish; for the just judgment of God comes equally upon all, and in no case is defective. Earthly rule, therefore, has been appointed by God for the benefit of nations, (9) and not by the devil, who is never at rest at all, nay, who does not love to see even nations conducting themselves after a quiet manner, so that under the fear of human rule, men may not eat each other up like fishes; but that, by means of the establishment of laws, they may keep down an excess of wickedness among the nations. And considered from this point of view, those who exact tribute from us are "God's ministers, serving for this very purpose."

TERTULLIAN

4

Tertullian, born about 160 in Carthage, North Africa, the son of a pagan centurion attached to the Roman proconsul of that region, is one of the most rigidly moralistic theologians in Christian history. As an apologist for the Christian faith, he was and remains an outstanding representative of an extreme yet recurring Christian attitude toward society, that of complete and disdainful separation from the "world." As such, he became a prime illustration of the "Christ against Culture" type in H. Richard Niebuhr's modern classic, Christ and Culture.

Tertullian's antipathy toward the prevailing culture and its practices was only heightened by his embrace of Montanism later in his career. Montanism was a Christian apocalyptic movement that arose in the second century. It took its name from Montanus, who claimed to have received a revelation from the Holy Spirit to the effect that he, as representative prophet of the Spirit, would lead the Christian church into its final stage. Aided by two women, Maximilla and Priscilla (or Prisca), Montanus founded a sect of enthusiasts who preached the imminent end of the world, austere morality, and severe penitential discipline. The Montanist influence only sharpened and made harsher Tertullian's critique, underscoring themes like his rejection of Christian participation in the military and in public offices. In his Montanist period essay, The Chaplet, he argues that military and political pursuits clearly involve idolatrous behavior exemplified by the various crowns traditionally worn in pagan ceremonies, whether the soldier's laurel or the ruler's gold. However, by the time of his death (ca. 220) he had moved away from Montanism as well.

Tertullian's colorful writings with their linguistic features of his legal background have made him an influential figure in the history of Christian thought. However, his strong opposition to Christian involvement in secular culture, though a recurring perspective in one form or another, is not normative for the Christian tradition.

Selection 1: *Apology*, Chapters 39–45

This book dates from the time before Tertullian's involvement with Montanism. It is a vigorous and biting attack against the illegal treatment of Christians. Rather than be persecuted, the Christian community should be admired and valued for their charitable behavior and their generous lifestyle of sharing in common to meet each other's needs.

(1) Now I myself will explain the practices of the Christian Church, that is, after having refuted the charges that they are evil, I myself will also point out that they are good. We form one body because of our religious convictions, and because of the divine origin of our way of life and the bond of common hope. (2) We come together for a meeting and a congregation, in order to besiege God with prayers, like an army in battle formation. Such violence is pleasing to God. We pray, also, for the emperors, for their ministers and those in power, that their reign may continue, that the state may be at peace, and that the end of the world may be postponed. (3) We assemble for the consideration of the Holy Scriptures, [to see] if the circumstances of the present times demand that we look ahead or reflect. Certainly, we nourish our faith with holy conversation, we uplift our hope, we strengthen our trust, intensifying our discipline at the same time by the inculcation of moral precepts. (4) At the same occasion, there are words of encouragement, of correction, and holy censure. Then, too, judgment is passed which is very impressive, as it is before men who are certain of the presence of God, and it is a deeply affecting foretaste of the future judgment, if anyone has so sinned that he is dismissed from sharing in common prayer, assembly, and all holy intercourse. (5) Certain approved elders preside, men who have obtained this honor not by money, but by the evidence of good character. For, nothing that pertains to God is to be had for money.

Even if there is some kind of treasury, it is not accumulated from a high initiation fee as if the religion were something bought and paid for. Each man deposits a small amount on a certain day of the month or whenever he wishes, and only on condition that he is willing and able to do so. No one is forced; each makes his contribution voluntarily. (6) These are, so to speak, the deposits of piety. The money there from is spent not for banquets or drinking parties or good-for-nothing eating houses, but for the support and burial of the poor, for children who are without their parents and means of subsistence, for aged men who are confined to the house; likewise, for ship-wrecked sailors, and for any in the mines, on islands or in prisons. Provided only it be for the sake of fellowship with God, they become entitled to loving and protective care for their confession. (7) The practice of such a special love brands us in the eyes of some. 'See,' they say, 'how they love one another'; (for they hate one another), 'and how ready they are to die for each other.' (They themselves would be more ready to kill each other.)

(8) Over the fact that we call ourselves brothers, they fall into a rage—for no other reason, I suppose, than because among them every term of kinship is only a hypocritical pretense of affection. But, we are your brothers, too, according to the law of nature, our common mother, although you are hardly men since you are evil brothers. (9) But, with how much more right are they called brothers and considered such who have acknowledged one father, God, who have drunk one spirit of holiness, who in fear and wonder have come forth from the one womb of their common ignorance to the one light of truth! (10) Perhaps this is why we are considered less legitimate brothers, because no tragic drama has our brotherhood as its theme, or because we are brothers who use the same family substance which, among you, as a rule, destroys brotherhood.

(11) So, we are united in mind and soul has no hesitation about sharing what we have. Everything is in common among us—except our wives. (12) In this matter—which is the only matter in which the rest of men practice partnership—we dissolve partnership. They not only usurp the marriage rights of their friends with the

greatest equanimity. These results, I suppose, from the teaching they have learned from those who were older and wiser, the Greek Socrates and the Roman Cato, who shared with their friends the wives whom they had married, so that they could bear children in other families, too. (13) As a matter of fact, perhaps the wives were not exactly unwilling. For, why should they care about a chastity which their husbands had so readily given away? Oh, what an example of Attica wisdom and Roman dignity! The philosopher a pander, and the censor, too!

(14) Why wonder, then, if such dear friends take their meals together? You attack our modest repasts—apart from saying that they are disgraced by crimes—as being extravagant. It was, of course, to us that Diogenes' remark referred: 'The people of Megara purchase supplies as if they were to die tomorrow, but put up buildings as though they were never to die.' (15) However, anyone sees the bit of straw in another's eye more easily than a mote in his own. With so many tribes, courts, and sub-courts belching, the air becomes foul: If the Salii are going to dine, someone will have to give a loan; the city clerks will have to count up the cost of the tithes and extravagant banquets in honor of Hercules; for the festival of the Apaturia, for the Dionysiac revels, for the mysteries of Attica, they proclaim a draft of cooks; at the smoke of a feast of Serapis the firemen will become alarmed. But, only about the repast of the Christians is any objection brought forth.

(16) Our repast, by its very name, indicates its purpose. It is called by a name which to the Greeks means 'love.' Whatever it costs, it is gain to incur expense in the name of piety, since by this refreshment we confort the needy, not as among you, parasites contend for the glory of reducing their liberty to slavery for the price of filling their belly amdist insults, but as, before God, greater consideration is given to those of lower station. (17) If the motive of our repast is honorable, then on the basis of the motive appraise the entire procedure of our discipline. What concerns the duty of religion tolerates no vulgarity, no immorality. No one sits down to table without first partaking of a prayer to God. They eat as much as those who are hungry take; they drink as much as temperate people need. (18) They satisfy themselves as men who remember that they must worship God even throughout the night; they converse as men who know that the Lord is listening. After this, the hands are washed and lamps are lit, and each one, according to his ability to do so, reads, the Holy Scriptures or is invited into the center to sing a hymn to God. This is the test of how much he has drunk. Similarly, prayer puts an end to the meal. (19) From here they depart, not to unite in bands for murder, or to run around in gangs, or for stealthy attacks of lewdness, but to observe the same regard for modesty and chastity as people do who have partaken not only of a repast but of a rule of life.

(20) Such is the gathering of Christians. There is no question about it—it deserves to be called illegal, provided it is like those which are illegal; it deserves to be condemned, if any complaint is lodged against it on the same ground that complaints are made about other secret societies. (21) But, for whose destruction have we ever held a meeting? We are the same when assembled as when separate; we are collectively the same as we are individually, doing no one any injury, causing no one any harm. When men who are upright and good assemble, when the pious and virtuous gather together, the meeting should be called not a secret society but a senate.

Chapter 42

(1) But, on still another charge of misconduct are we arraigned: They say that we are worthless in business. How can they say that? Are we not men who live right with you, men who follow the same way of life, the same manner of dressing, using the same provisions and the same necessities of life? We are not Brahmans or Indian ascetics who dwell in forests, withdrawn from life. (2) We bear in mind that we owe thanks to the Lord our God who created us; we disdain no fruit of His works; obviously, we do restrain ourselves form an immoderate or excessive use of them. So, it is not without a Forum, not without a meat market, not without baths, shops, factories, inns, market days, and the rest of your business enterprises that we live with you—in this world. (3) We are sailors along with yourselves; we serve in the army; we engage in farming and trading; in addition, we share with you our arts; we place the products our labor at your service. How we can appear worthless for your business, when we live with you and depend on you, I do not know.

(4) If I do not attend your ceremonials, nevertheless, even on that day, I am a man. I do not bathe in the early dawn on the Saturnalia, lest I should waste both night and day; still, I do bathe at the hour I should, one which is conducive to health and which protects both my temperature and my life's blood. To become stiff and ashen after a bath—I can enjoy that when I'm dead! (5) At the feast of Bacchus I do not recline at table in public, a custom which belongs to gladiators eating their last meal; but wherever I do dine, I dine from your supplies. (6) I do not buy a wreath for my head; what business of yours is it how I use flowers as long as I bought them? I think they are more pleasing when free, unbound, and hanging loosely everywhere. But, even if the flowers are bound into a wreath, we know a wreath by our noses; let them look to it who smell through their hair!

(7) We do not attend the public games; yet, the things which are for sale at those gatherings I could, if I so desired puck up more freely in their own proper places. Of course we do not buy incense; if the Arabians complain; let the people of Saba know that more of their wares and dearer ones are spent on burying Christians than on fumigating the gods.

(8) 'At all events,' you say, 'the income of the temples is daily melting away. How few there are who still cast in a contribution!' Of course; for we cannot afford to help both men and those gods of yours, through both are begging, and we do not think that aid should be given to others than those who ask. So, then, let Jupiter hold out his hand and receiver! In the meanwhile, our mercy spends more from street to street than your religion does from temple to temple. (9) But the rest of the taxes will acknowledge a debt of gratitude to the Christians who pay their dues with the same good faith that keeps us from defrauding another; so that, if the records were checked as to how much the state treasury has lost through the deceitfulness and dishonesty of your declarations, the account could easily be calculated: The deficit on one side is balanced by the gain in the rest of the account.

Chapter 43

(1) I will frankly acknowledge, then, what group may, perhaps with good reason, complain about the unprofitable Christians. First of all, there are the pimps, panders, and their agents; secondly, the assassins, poisoners, and magicians; thirdly, fortune-tellers, soothsayers, and astrologers. (2) To be unprofitable to these is a tremendous profit. Yet, whatever loss your business suffers through this group of ours, it can be balanced by a certain protection. Of what worth do you consider – I do not say now, men who drive the evil sprits out of you; I do no say now, men who offer prayers for you to the true God, because, perchance, you do not believe that—men, I say, from whom you can have nothing to fear?

Chapter 44

(1) Yet there is a loss to the state, as great as it is real, and no one pays any attention to it; an injury to the state, and no one considers it—when so many upright men, such as we, are sacrificed, when so many of us, men of blameless character, are executed. (2) We now call to witness your actions, you who preside each day to pass judgment on prisoners, you who clear the criminals' records by passing sentences. So many guilty men are examined by you with various charges against them: The man arraigned there as a murderer, a pickpocket, a profaner of temples, a seducer or robber of those in the baths—which one of them is charged also as a Christian? Or, when Christians are brought forward with their own charge, which one of them is also of such a character as are so many of those guilty ones? (3) It is with men from your own midst that the jail is always bulging, with your own that the mines are always humming, with your own that the wild beasts are always fattened, with your own that the producers of gladiatorial shows feed the herds of criminals. No one there is a Christian—unless he is merely that; if he is something else, too, then he is no longer a Christian.

Chapter 45

(1) We, then, are the only ones who are innocent! What wonder if this must necessarily be the case? For it really must be. We have been taught our innocence by God; we understand it perfectly, as something revealed by a perfect Teacher; we guard it faithfully as something entrusted to us by a Judge who is not to be despised. (2) On the other hand, it is man's judgment that has handed over to you your [idea of] innocence; man's authority has enjoined it; therefore, you are not possessed of a moral system fully and sufficiently formidable to produce true innocence. Man's wisdom in pointing out good is in proportion to his power to exact it. It is as easy for the former to be mistaken as it is for the latter to be scorned. (3) And so, which is more complete, to say: 'Thou salt not kill,' or teach: 'Be not even angry'? Which is more perfect, to forbid adultery, or to guard against even a single glance of concupiscence? Which is more learned, to forbid evil-doing, or even an evil word? Which is more wise, not to permit an injury, or not even to allow one to reciprocate an injury? (4) Moreover, you

should know that those laws of yours, too, which seem to tend toward innocence, were borrowed from the divine Law, as from an older pattern. We have already spoken of the Age of Moses.

(5) But, how much authority have human laws, then it may happen that a man may evade them, time and again remaining concealed in his crimes, and that he sometimes despises them as he transgresses them of his own free will or through necessity? (6) Consider these things and also the short duration of every punishment, which at any rate is not going to last beyond the grave. Thus, even Epicurus would consider of slight account every pain and sorrow, expressing the opinion that a small pain is to be despised and a great one is something that will not last long. (7) But we alone who are examined under the eyes of an all-seeing God, we who foresee an eternal punishment from Him, deserve to attain to innocence because of the fullness of our wisdom and the difficulty of finding a hiding place, and because of the greatness of the torments which are to be not simply of long duration but eternal; we are in fear of Him whom he, too, will have to fear—I mean, the very one who sits to pass judgment on us, the fearful; in a word, we fear God, not the proconsul.

Selection 2: *Spectacles*, Chapters 8–10

Tertullian's disdain for military and civil service was matched by his rejection of the amusements that were a mainstay of his cultural context. The circus, the chariot races, the theater, and the gladiatorial and athletic contests were corrupt worldly pleasures incompatible with Christian piety and the province of false pagan gods.

Take note, O Christian, how many unclean deities have taken possession of the circus. You have nothing to do with a place which so many diabolic spirits have made their own. Speaking of places, this is the appropriate occasion for throwing more light on the subject in order to anticipate a question that some may raise. (8) What will happen, you say, if I enter the circus at some other time? Shall I be then, too, in danger of contamination? There is no law laid down with regard to places as such. For not only these places where people gather for the spectacles but also the temples may be entered by the servant of God without peril to his rule of life, provided that he do so for an urgent and honest reason which has no connection with the business and function proper of the place. (9) Moreover, there is no place whether streets or marketplace or baths or taverns or even our own homes that is completely free of idols: Satan and his angels have filled the whole world. (10) Yet, it is not by our being in the world that we fall away from God, but by taking part in some sins of the world. Therefore, if I enter the temple of Jupiter on the Capitol or that of Serapis as a sacrificer or worshiper, I shall fall away from God, just as I do if I enter the circus or theater as a spectator. It is not the places in themselves that defile us, but the things done in them, by which the places themselves, as we have contended, are defiled; it is by the defiled that we are defiled. (11) It is for this reason that we remind you who are those to whom places of this kind are dedicated to prove that what takes place in them is the work of those to whom the very places are sacred.

Chapter 9

(1) Next let us consider the arts displayed in the circus games. In times past, equestrian skill was simply a matter of riding on horseback, and certainly no guilt was involved in the ordinary use of the horse. But when this skill was pressed into the service of the games, it was changed from a gift of God into an instrument of the demons. (2) Accordingly, this kind of exhibition is regarded as sacred to Castor and Pollux, to whom horses were allotted 'by Mercury, as Stesichorus tells us.

Also, Neptune is an equestrian deity, since the Greeks all him Hippios ["Lord of Steeds"] (3) Moreover, concerning the chariot, the four-horse team was consecrated to the Sun; the two-horse team, to the Moon. But we also read: Erichthonius first dared to yoke four steeds to the car and to ride upon its wheels with victorious swiftness. This Erichthonius, a son of Minerva and Vulcan, fruit of lust, in truth, that fell to earth, is a demon-monster, or, rather, the Devil himself, not a mere snake.(4) If, however, the Argive Trochilus is the inventor of the chariot, he dedicated this work of his in the first place to Juno. And if, at Rome, Romulus was the first to display a four-horse chariot, he, too, in my view, has been enrolled among the idols himself, provided that he is identical with Quirinus.(5) The chariots having been produced by such inventors, it was only fitting that they clad their drivers in the colors of idolatry. For at first there were only two colors: white and red. White was sacred to Winter because of the whiteness of its snow; red, to Summer because of the redness of its sun. But afterwards, when both love of pleasure and superstition had grown apace, some dedicated the red to Mars, others the white to the Zephyrs, the green to Mother Earth or Spring, the blue to Sky and Sea or Autumn.(6) Since, however, every kind of idolatry is condemned by God, this condemnation certainly applies also to that kind which is impiously offered to the elements of nature.

Chapter 10

(1) Let us pass on to the exhibitions on the stage. We have already shown that they have a common origin with those in the circus, that they bear identical titles, inasmuch as they were called ludi ['games'] and were exhibited together with equestrian displays.(2) The pageantry is likewise the same, inasmuch as a procession is held to the theater from the temples and altars, with that whole wretched business of incense and blood, to the tune of flutes and trumpets, under the direction of the two most polluted masters of ceremonies at funerals and sacrifices: the undertaker and soothsayer.(3) And so, as we passed from the origins of the games to the spectacles in the circus, now we will turn to the performances on the stage. Because of the evil character of the place, the theater is, strictly speaking, a shrine of Venus. It was in that capacity, after all, that this type of structure gained influence in the world. (4) For many a time the censors would tear down theaters at the very moment they began to rise. In their solicitude for public morals, they foresaw, no doubt, the great danger arising from the theater's lasciviousness. In this occurrence already, then, the heathens have their own opinion coinciding with ours as evidence, and we have the foreboding situation of a merely human code of morality giving additional strength to our way of life.(5) So, when Pompey the Great, a man who was surpassed only by his theater in greatness, had erected that citadel of all vile practices, he was afraid that some

day the censors would condemn his memory. He therefore built on top of it a shrine of Venus, and when he summoned the people by edict to its dedication, he termed it not a theater, but a temple of Venus, 'under which,' he said, seats for viewing the shows.' (6) In this way he misrepresented the character of a building, condemned and worthy of condemnation, with a temple's name, and employed superstition to make sport of morality. Venus and Liber [Bacchus], however, are close companions. The two demons of lust and drunkenness have banded together in sworn confederacy. (7) Therefore, the temple of Venus is also the house of Liber. For they appropriately gave the name of Liberalia also to other stage performances which, besides being dedicated to Liber (and called Dionysia among the Greeks), were also instituted by him.(8) And, quite obviously, the arts of the stage are under the patronage of Liber and Venus. Those features which are peculiar to, and characteristic of, the stage, that wantonness in gesture and posture, they dedicate to Venus and Liber, deities both dissolute: the former by sex perversion, the latter by effeminate dress. (9) And all else that is performed with voice and melodies, instruments and script, belongs to the Apollos and the Muses, the Minervas and Mercuries. You will hate, O Christian, the things whose authors you cannot help but hate.(10) At this point we intend to make a few remarks concerning the arts and things whose authors we utterly detest in their very names. We know that the names of dead men are nothing, even as their images are nothing. But we are not unaware of the identity of those who are at work behind those displayed names and images, who exult in the homage paid to them and pretend to be divine, namely, the evil spirits, the demons. (11) We see then, also, that the arts are consecrated to the honor of those who appropriate the names of the inventors of those arts, and that they are not free from the taint of idolatry when their inventors for that very reason are considered gods. (12) Even more, as far as the arts are concerned, we ought to have gone further back and taken exception to all further arguments, on the ground that the demons, from the very beginning looking out for themselves, contrived, along with the other foul practices of idolatry, also those of the shows in order to turn man from the Lord and bind him to their glorification, and gave inspiration to men of genius in these particular arts. (13) For no one else but the demons would have contrived what was going to redound to their advantage, nor would they have produced the arts at that time through the agency of anyone except those very mining whose names and images and fables they accomplished that fraud of consecration which would work out to their advantage.

❧ *The two outstanding exponents of the theology of the Alexandrian catechetical school were Clement of Alexandria (ca. 150–ca. 215) and Origen (185–254). Clement is often considered the founder of this school, historically notable for its defense of Christ's divinity against various adoptionist Christologies that stressed Christ's humanity at the expense of his co-eternal divinity, one with the Father and the Spirit. Following Clement, Origen, who was theologically more significant, gave the school its greatest influence.*

    Clement was the author of the first book that could possibly be described as an exposition of Christian ethics, The Instructor (Paidagogos). *In his biblically grounded approach to Christian faith and life, Clement employs selected portions of the Greek philosophical tradition as a foil for his argument for the superiority of the Christian way of life. In this pursuit Clement exemplifies the perennial temptation facing ethicists, a legalistic concern for formal observance of the law instead of its spirit and intention. For Clement this extends even into manners as well as morals. Elsewhere in* The Instructor *he writes in detail about proper eating habits; "from all slavish habits and excess we must abstain and touch what is set before us in a decorous way; keeping the hand and couch and chin free from stains. . . . We must guard against speaking anything while eating: for the voice becomes disagreeable and inarticulate when it is confined by full jaws . . ." (Book II, 1, 13) Clement's discourse on eating is more than manners, however. The context is the vice of gluttony and the concern is part of a long tradition of avoiding offensive and intemperate behavior that can damage the witness to the faith. Similarly he comments on proper clothing and shoes, cosmetic jewelry and hairstyles. "Let the head of men be shaven, unless it has curly hair. But let the chin have hair. But let not twisted locks hang far down from the head, gliding into womanish ringlets. For an ample beard suffices for men" (Book III, 3). Here the concern is over the offense of homosexual and/or bisexual behavior. In addition to his concern with issues of offense, Clement, in this same treatise, also gives practical moral counsel for true and just participation in daily commerce.*

    Despite his greater prominence in the history of Christian thought, Origen did not produce a single work principally devoted to ethics. Nonetheless his reply to Celsus includes social-ethical notions that provide significant insight into the attitude of the Christian church toward political life in the time before Constantine.

Selection 1: *The Instructor*, Book I, Chapter XIII

*For Clement reason and Christian piety, lived in expectation of life everlasting
and in conformity with God's commandments, are not incompatible. One hears
echoes of Justin Martyr and an anticipation of a long tradition still to come of
revelation and reason combining in engagement with cultural context to form a
perduring ethical methodology.*

Everything that is contrary to right reason is sin. Accordingly, therefore, the philosophers think fit to define the most generic passions thus: lust, as desire disobedient to reason; fear, as weakness disobedient to reason; pleasure, as an elation of the spirit disobedient to reason. If, then, disobedience in reference to reason is the generating cause of sin, how shall we escape the conclusion, that obedience to reason—the Word—which we call faith, will of necessity be the efficacious cause of duty? For virtue itself is a state of the soul rendered harmonious by reason in respect to the whole life. Nay, to crown all, philosophy itself is pronounced to be the cultivation of right reason; so that, necessarily, whatever is done through error of reason is transgression, and is rightly called, (*amartbma*) sin. Since, then, the first man sinned and disobeyed God, it is said, "And man became like to the beasts:" being rightly regarded as irrational, he is likened to the beasts. Whence Wisdom says: "The horse for covering; the libidinous and the adulterer is become like to an irrational beast." Wherefore also it is added: "He neighs, whoever may be sitting on him." The man, it is meant, no longer speaks; for he who transgresses against reason is no longer rational, but an irrational animal, given up to lusts by which he is ridden (as a horse by his rider).

But that which is done right, in obedience to reason, the followers of the Stoics call *proshkon* and *kaqbkon*, that is, incumbent and fitting. What is fitting is incumbent. And obedience is founded on commands. And these being, as they are, the same as counsels—having truth for their aim, train up to the ultimate goal of aspiration, which is conceived of as the end (*telos*). And the end of piety is eternal rest in God. And the beginning of eternity is our end. The right operation of piety perfects duty by works; whence, according to just reasoning, duties consist in actions, not in sayings. And Christian conduct is the Operation of the rational soul in accordance with a correct judgment and aspiration after the truth, which attains its destined end through the body, the soul's consort and ally. Virtue is a will in conformity to God and Christ in life, rightly adjusted to life everlasting. For the life of Christians, in which we are now trained, is a system of reasonable actions—that is, of those things taught by the Word—an unfailing energy which we have called faith. The system is the commandments of the Lord, which, being divine statues and spiritual counsels, have been written for ourselves, being adapted for ourselves and our neighbors. Moreover, they turn back on us, as the ball rebounds on him that throws it by the repercussion. Whence also duties are essential for divine discipline, as being enjoined by God, and furnished for our salvation. And since, of those things which are necessary, some relate only to life here, and others, which relate to the blessed life yonder, wing us for flight hence; so, in an analogous manner, of duties, some are ordained with reference to life, others for the blessed life. The commandments issued with respect to natural life are published to the multitude; but those that are suited for living well, and from which eternal life springs, we have to consider, as in a sketch, as we read them out of the Scriptures.

Selection 2: The Rich Man's Salvation

> *Clement's allegorical development of Jesus' encounter with the rich young man leads to a rather carefully nuanced interpretation of how the Christian is to deal with wealth. Somewhat in contrast to the legalistic leanings we saw in the selection from* The Instructor, *Clement expounds on the spirit of Jesus' command, not its literal requirement. Riches are not to be spurned as a general rule. Rather, what wealth we have is to be used in just and compassionate concern for the needs of others. This is a theme that is also prominent in* The Instructor. *It is in keeping with the audience of cultured and often wealthy Christians he was addressing.*

. . . This is written in the gospel according to Mark, and in all the other accepted gospels the passage as a whole shows the same general sense, though perhaps here and there a little of the wording changes. And as we are clearly aware that the Saviour teaches His people nothing in a merely human way, but everything be a divine and mystical wisdom, we must not understand His words literally, but with due inquiry and intelligence we must search out and master their hidden meaning. (Mark 10:17-31)

*   *   *

What then was it that impelled him to flight, and made him desert his teacher, his supplication, his hope, his life, his previous labors? "Sell what belongs to thee." And what is this? It is not what some hastily take it to be, a command to fling away the substance that belongs to him and to part with his riches, but to banish from the soul its opinions about riches, its attachment to them, its excessive desire, its morbid excitement over them, its anxious cares, the thorns of our earthly existence which choke the seed of the true life. For it is no great or enviable thing to be simply without riches, apart from the purpose of obtaining life. Why, if this were so, those men who have nothing at all, but are destitute and beg for their daily bread, who lie along the roads in abject poverty, would, though "ignorant" of God and "God's righteousness," be most blessed and beloved of God and the only possessors of eternal life, by the sole fact of their being utterly without ways and means of livelihood and in want of the smallest necessities. Nor again is it a new thing to renounce wealth and give it freely to the poor, or to one's fatherland, which many have done before the Savior's coming, some to obtain leisure for letters and for dead wisdom, others for empty fame and vainglory—such men as Anaxagoras, Democritus and Crates.

What then is it that He enjoins as new and peculiar to God and alone life-giving, which did not save men of former days? If the "new creation," the Son of God, reveals and teaches something unique, then His command does not refer to the visible act, the very thing that others have done but to something else greater, more divine and more perfect, which is signified through this; namely, to strip the soul itself and the will of their lurking passions and utterly to root out and cast away all alien thoughts from the mind. For this is a lesson peculiar to the believer and a doctrine worthy of the Savior. The men of former days, indeed, in their contempt for outward things, parted with and sacrificed their possessions, but as for the passions of the soul, I think they even intensified them. For they became supercilious, boastful, conceited and dis-dainful of the rest of mankind, as if they themselves had wrought something superhu-man. How then could the Savior have recommended to those who were to live forever things that would be harmful and injurious for the life he promises? And there is this other point. It is possible for a man, after having unburdened himself of his property, to be none the less continually absorbed and occupied in the desire and longing for it. He has given up the use of wealth, but now being in difficulties and at the same time yearning after what he threw away, he endures a double annoyance, the absence of means of support and the presence of regret. For when a man lacks the necessities of life he cannot possibly fail to be broken in spirit and to neglect the higher things, as he strives to procure these necessities by any means and from any source.

And how much more useful is the opposite condition, when by possessing a suf-ficiency a man is himself in no distress about money-making and also helps those he ought? For what sharing would be left among men, if nobody had anything? And how could this doctrine be found other than plainly contradictory to and at war with many other noble doctrines of the Lord? "Make to yourselves friends from the mammon of unrighteousness, that when it shall fail they may receive you into the eternal habita-tions." "Acquire treasures in heaven, where neither moth nor rust doth consume, nor thieves break through." How could we feed the hungry and give drink to the thirsty, cover the naked and entertain the homeless, with regard to which deeds He threatens fire and the outer darkness to those who have not done them, if each of us were him-self already in want of all these things? But further, the Lord Himself is a guest with Zacchaeus and Levi and Matthew, wealthy men and tax-gatherers, and He does not bid the give up their riches. On the contrary, having enjoined the just and set aside the unjust employment of them, He proclaims, "Today is salvation come to this house." It is on this stipulation, —that He commands them to be shared, to give drink to the thirsty and bread to the hungry, to receive the homeless, to clothe the naked. And if it is not possible to satisfy these needs except with riches, and He were bidding us stand aloof from riches, what else would the Lord be doing than exhorting us to give and also not to give the same things, to feed and not to feed, to receive and to shut out, to share and not to share? But this would be the height of unreason.

We must not then fling away the riches that are of benefit to our neighbors as well as ourselves. For they are called possessions because they are things possessed, and wealth because they are to be welcomed and because they have been prepared by God for the welfare of men. Indeed, they lie at hand and are put at our disposal as a sort of material and as instruments to be well used by those who know. An instru-ment, if you use it with artistic skill, is a thing of art; but if you are lacking in skill, it reaps the benefit of your unmusical nature, though not itself responsible. Wealth too is an instrument of the same kind. You can use it rightly; it ministers to righteousness. But if one uses it wrongly, it is found to be a minister of wrong. For its nature is to minister, not to rule. We must not therefore put the responsibility on that which, hav-ing in itself neither good nor evil, is not responsible, but on that which has the power of using things either well or badly, as a result of choice; for this is responsible just for that reason. And this is the mind of man, which has in itself both free judgment and full liberty to deal with what is given to it. So let a man do away, not with is posses-sions, but rather with the passions of his soul, which do not consent to the better use of what he has; in order that, by becoming noble and good, he may be able to use these possessions also in a noble manner. "Saying good-bye to all we have," and "selling all we have," must therefore be understood in this way, as spoken with reference to the soul's passions.

Selection 3: Origen: *Against Celsus*, Book VIII, 73–75

In his impressive defense of the Christian faith against an intelligent and knowledgeable pagan, Origen describes here the basis for the Christian approach to political and social responsibility. Particularly noteworthy is his strong defense of Christian pacifism. Later apologists for Christian participation in military engagements would have to deal with this and other arguments against Christians participating in war that were part of the early church witness.

Chapter 73

In the next place, Celsus urges us "to help the king with all our might, and to labour with him in the maintenance of justice, to fight for him; and if he requires it, to fight under him, or lead an army along with him." To this our answer is, that we do, when occasion requires, give help to kings, and that, so to say, a divine help, "putting on the whole armour of God." And this we do in obedience to the injunction of the apostle, "I exhort, therefore, that first of all, supplications, prayers, intercessions, and giving of thanks, be made for all men; for kings, and for all that are in authority;" and the more any one excels in piety, the more effective help does he render to kings, even more than is given by soldiers, who go forth to fight and slay as many of the enemy as they can. And to those enemies of our faith who require us to bear arms for the commonwealth, and to slay men, we can reply: "Do not those who are priests at certain shrines, and those who attend on certain gods, as you account them, keep their hands free from blood, that they may with hands unstained and free from human blood offer the appointed sacrifices to your gods; and even when war is upon you, you never enlist the priests in the army. If that, then, is a laudable custom, how much more so, that while others are engaged in battle, these too should engage as the priests and ministers of God, keeping their hands pure, and wrestling in prayers to God on behalf of those who are fighting in a righteous cause, and for the king who reigns righteously, that whatever is opposed to those who act righteously may be destroyed!" And as we by our prayers vanquish all demons who stir up war, and lead to the violation of oaths, and disturb the peace, we in this way are much more helpful to the kings than those who go into the field to fight for them. And we do take our part in public affairs, when along with righteous prayers we join self-denying exercises and meditations, which teach us to despise pleasures, and not to be led away by them. And none fight better for the king than we do. We do not indeed fight under him, although he require it; but we fight on his behalf, forming a special army—an army of piety—by offering our prayers to God.

Chapter 74

And if Celsus would have us to lead armies in defence of our country, let him know that we do this too, and that not for the purpose of being seen by men, or of vainglory. For "in secret," and in our own hearts, there are prayers which ascend as from priests in behalf of our fellow-citizens. And Christians are benefactors of their country more than others. For they train up citizens, and inculcate piety to the Supreme Being; and they promote those whose lives in the smallest cities have been good and worthy, to a divine and heavenly city, to whom it may be said, "Thou hast been faithful in the smallest city, come into a great one," where "God standeth in the assembly of the gods, and judgeth the gods in the midst;" and He reckons thee among them, if thou no more "die as a man, or fall as one of the princes."

Chapter 75

Celsus also urges us to "take office in the government of the country, if that is required for the maintenance of the laws and the support of religion." But we recognise in each state the existence of another national organization founded by the Word of God, and we exhort those who are mighty in word and of blameless life to rule over Churches. Those who are ambitious of ruling we reject; but we constrain those who, through excess of modesty, are not easily induced to take a public charge in the Church of God. And those who rule over us well are under the constraining influence of the great King, whom we believe to be the Son of God, God the Word. And if those who govern in the Church, and are called rulers of the divine nation—that is, the Church—rule well, they rule in accordance with the divine commands, and never suffer themselves to be led astray by worldly policy. And it is not for the purpose of escaping public duties that Christians decline public offices, but that they may reserve themselves for a diviner and more necessary service in the Church of God—for the salvation of men. And this service is at once necessary and right. They take charge of all—of those that are within, that they may day by day lead better lives, and of those that are without, that they may come to abound in holy words and in deeds of piety; and that, while thus worshipping God truly, and training up as many as they can in the same way, they may be filled with the word of God and the law of God, and thus be united with the Supreme God through His Son the Word, Wisdom, Truth, and Righteousness, who unites to God all who are resolved to conform their lives in all things to the law of God.

CHRYSOSTOM

6

John of Constantinople (354–407) was called since the sixth century Chrysostom (gold-mouth) because of his eloquent use of the Greek language in his preaching. Indeed, his homilies are the vehicle for many of his principal theological and ethical contributions. He lived at a time after Christianity had become the ruling religion of the Roman Empire. A priest in Antioch and after 398 bishop of Constantinople, he became deeply involved in the political controversies of his time. Because of his efforts to assert the independence of the church from the emperor and his open criticism of the moral laxity of the court, he was eventually deposed and expelled. He died in exile.

Chrysostom illustrates the ethical teaching of the Christian church shortly after it had come to power and the new problems that its close association with the empire produced. In the first selection he develops the idea of natural law. Working off Paul's discussion of the law as written on the hearts of all people (Romans 2:14-15), Clement lays the foundation for ethical appeal to all people, Christian or otherwise. The historical development of natural law would become the basis for much Christian social teaching up to the present.

Selection 1: *Concerning the Statutes*, Homily XII, 9, 12–15

9. When God formed man, he implanted within him from the beginning a natural law. And what then was this natural law? He gave utterance to conscience within us; and made the knowledge of good things, and of those that are the contrary, to be self-taught. For we have no need to learn that fornication is an evil thing, and that chastity is a good thing, but we know this from the first. And that you may learn that we know this from the first, the Lawgiver, when He afterwards gave laws, and said, "Thou shalt not kill," did not add, "since murder is an evil thing," but simply said, "Thou shall not kill;" for He merely prohibited the sin, without teaching. How was it then when He said, "Thou shalt not kill," that He did not add, "because murder is a wicked thing." The reason was, that conscience had taught this beforehand; and He speaks thus, as to those who know and understand the point. Wherefore when He speaks to us of another commandment, not known to us by the dictate of consciences He not only prohibits, but adds the reason. When, for instance, He gave commandment respecting the Sabbath; "On the seventh day thou shalt do no work;" He subjoined also the reason for this cessation. What was this? "Because on the seventh day God rested from all His works which He had begun to make." And again; "Because thou

40

wert a servant in the land of Egypt." For what purpose then I ask did He add a reason respecting the Sabbath, but did no such thing in regard to murder? Because this commandment was not one of the leading ones. It was not one of those which were accurately defined of our conscience, but a kind of partial and temporary one; and for this reason it was abolished afterwards. But those which are necessary and uphold our life, are the following; "Thou shalt not kill; Thou shalt not commit adultery; Thou shalt not steal." On this account then He adds no reason in this case, nor enters into any instruction on the matter, but is content with the bare prohibition.

*　　*　　*

12. But it may be objected, that the Gentile allows nothing of this sort. Come then, let us discuss this point, and as we have done with respect to the creation, having carried on the warfare against these objectors not only by the help of the Scriptures, but of reason, so also let us now do with respect to conscience. For Paul too, when he was engaged in controversy with such persons, entered upon this head. What then is it that they urge? They say, that there is no self-evident law seated in our consciences; and that God hath not implanted this in our nature. But if so, whence is it, I ask, that legislators have written those laws which are among them concerning marriages, concerning murders, concerning wills, concerning trusts, concerning abstinence from encroachments on one another, and a thousand other things. For the men now living may perchance have learned them from their elders; and they from those who were before them, and these again from those beyond? But from whom did those learn who were the originators and first enactors of laws among them? Is it not evident that it was from conscience? For they cannot say, that they held communication with Moses; or that they heard the prophets. How could it be so when they were Gentiles? But it is evident that from the very law which God placed in man when He formed him from the beginning, laws were laid down, and arts discovered, and all other things. For the arts too were thus established, their originators having come to the knowledge of them in a self-taught manner.

13. So also came there to be courts of justice, and so were penalties defined, as Paul accordingly observes. For since many of the Gentiles were ready to controvert this, and to say, "How will God judge mankind who lived before Moses? He did not send a lawgiver; He did not introduce a law; He commissioned no prophet, nor apostle, nor evangelist; how then can He call these to account?" Since Paul therefore wished to prove that they possessed a self taught law; and that they knew clearly what they ought to do; hear how he speaks; "For when the Gentiles who have not the law, do by nature the things contained in the law, these having not the law, are a law unto themselves; which shew the work of the law written in their hearts." But how without letters? "Their conscience also bearing witness, and their thoughts the meanwhile accusing, or else excusing one another. In the day when God shall judge the secrets of men by Jesus Christ according to my gospel." And again; "As many as have sinned without law, shall perish without law; and as many as have sinned in the law, shall be judged by the law." What means, "They shall perish without law?" The law not accusing them, but their thoughts, and their conscience; for if they had not a law of conscience, it were not necessary that they should perish through having done amiss. For how

should it be so if they sinned without a law? but when he says, "without a law," he does not assert that they had no law, but that they had no written law, though they had the law of nature. And again; "But glory, honour, and peace, to every man that worketh good, to the Jew first, and also to the Gentile."

14. But these things he spake in reference to the early times, before the coming of Christ; and the Gentile he names here is not an idolater, but one who worshipped God only; unfettered by the necessity of Judaical observances, (I mean Sabbaths, and circumcision, and divers purifications,) yet exhibiting all manner of wisdom and piety. again, discoursing of such a worshipper, he observes, "Wrath and indignation, tribulation and anguish, upon every soul of man that doeth evil, of the Jew first, and also of the Gentile." Again he here calls by the name of Greek one who was free from the observance of Judaic customs. If, then, he had not heard the law, nor conversed with the Jews, how could there be wrath, indignation and tribulation against him for working evil? The reason is, that he possessed a conscience inwardly admonishing him, and teaching him, and instructing him in all things. Whence is this manifest? From the way in which he punished others when they did amiss; from the way in which he laid down laws; from the way in which he set up the tribunals of justice. With the view of making this more plain, Paul spoke of those who were living in wickedness. "Who, knowing the ordinance of God, that they which commit such things are worthy of death, not only do the same, but also consent with them that practise them." But from whence," says some one, "did they know, that it is the will of God, that those who live in iniquity should be punished with death?" From whence? Why, from the way in which they judged others who sinned. For if thou deemest not murder to be a wicked thing, when thou hast gotten a murderer at thy bar, thou shouldest not punish him. So if thou deemest it not an evil thing to commit adultery, when the adulterer has fallen into thy hands, release him from punishment! But if thou recordest laws, and prescribest punishments, and art a severe judge of the sins of others; what defence canst thou make, in matters wherein thou thyself doest amiss, by saying that thou art ignorant what things ought to be done? For suppose that thou and another person have alike been guilty of adultery. On what account dost thou punish him, and deem thyself worthy of forgiveness? Since if thou didst not know adultery to be wickedness, it were not right to punish it in another. But if thou punishest, and thinkest to escape the punishment thyself, how is it agreeable to reason that the same offences should not pay the same penalty?

15. This indeed is the very thing which Paul rebukes, when he says, "And thinkest thou this, O man, that judgest them which do such things, and doest the same, that thou shalt escape the judgment of God?" It is not, it cannot be possible; for from the very sentence, he means, which thou pronouncest upon another, from this sentence God will then judge thee. For surely thou art not just, and God unjust! But if thou overlookest not another suffering wrong, how shall God overlook? And if thou correctest the sins of others, how will not God correct thee? And though He may not bring the punishment upon thee instantly, be not confident on that account, but fear the more. So also Paul bade thee, saying, "Despisest thou the riches of His goodness, and forbearance, and longsuffering, not knowing that the goodness of God leadeth thee to repentance?" For therefore, saith he, doth he bear with thee, not that thou mayest become worse, but that thou mayest repent. But if thou wilt not, this

longsuffering becomes a cause of thy greater punishment; continuing, as thou dost, impenitent. This, however, is the very thing he means, when he says, "But after thy hardness and impenitent heart treasurest up to thyself wrath against the day of wrath, and revelation of the righteous judgment of God. Who will render to every man according to his deeds." Since, therefore, He rendereth to every man according to his works; for this reason He both implanted within us a natural law, and afterwards gave us a written one, in order that He might demand an account of sins, and that He might crown those who act rightly. Let us then order our conduct with the utmost care, and as those who have soon to encounter a fearful tribunal; knowing that we shall enjoy no pardon, if after a natural as well as written law, and so much teaching and continual admonition, we neglect our own salvation.

Selection 2: *Homilies on Matthew*, XIX, 6.1

Chrysostom interprets the petition of the Lord's Prayer "Thy will be done on earth as it is in heaven," as a call to the transformation of the world, namely, "make earth a heaven." The changing socio-political situation of the Christian church and the dissipation of imminent apocalyptic expectations pave the way for a meaningful witness in the church's social teaching. Concern for this world and a readiness to engage the culture stand in sharp contrast to the sort of attitude we saw in Tertullian.

"Thy will be done in earth, as it is in Heaven."

Behold a most excellent train of thought! in that He bade us indeed long for the things to come, and hasten towards that sojourn; and, till that may be, even while we abide here, so long to be earnest in showing forth the same conversation as those above. For ye must long, saith He, for heaven, and the things in heaven; however, even before heaven, He hath bidden us make the earth a heaven and do and say all things, even while we are continuing in it, as having our conversation there; insomuch that these too should be objects of our prayer to the Lord. For there is nothing to hinder our reaching the perfection of the powers above, because we inhabit the earth; but it is possible even while abiding here, to do all, as though already placed on high. What He saith therefore is this: "As there all things are done without hindrance, and the angels are not partly obedient and partly disobedient, but in all things yield and obey (for He saith, 'Mighty in strength, performing His word'); so vouchsafe that we men may not do Thy will by halves, but perform all things as Thou willest."

Seest thou how He hath taught us also to be modest, by making it clear that virtue is not of our endeavors only, but also of the grace from above? And again, He hath enjoined each one of us, who pray, to take upon himself the care of the whole world. For He did not at all say, "Thy will be done" in me, or in us, but everywhere on the earth; so that error may be destroyed, and truth implanted, and all wickedness cast out, and virtue return, and no difference in this respect be henceforth between heaven and earth.

AUGUSTINE

❧ *Aurelius Augustinus, born November 13, 354, in Thagaste, North Africa, became eventually the most influential theologian in Western Christendom. His thought is seminal for Roman Catholics as well as the descendants of the Lutheran and Calvinist reformation. He wrote so broadly in response to the myriad of events, social, political, theological, and ecclesial that shaped his historical context that it is a staggering task to map the many contributions he has made to the history of Christian thought. The focus for our purposes is the impact of his social thought, expressed classically in his monumental* City of God *as well as other writings that add further to our understanding of his social teaching. The power of his social teaching stands on its own, but the spiritual and intellectual power of his work on a variety of urgent theological concerns that shaped his career has given additional credence to his ethical thought. He lived seventy-six years in an age of vast social and political upheaval, reflected and addressed in all his writings, and died August 28, 430, as Bishop of Hippo while the Vandals were besieging the city. Major themes of Augustine's heritage for social teaching are reflected in the selections that follow. One will notice the dialectal pattern of his reasoning and some dualistic impulses of his platonic heritage.*

Selection 1: *Enchiridion,* Chapters 9–11

Undergirding all of Augustine's thought is the essential goodness of creation. Evil is privatio boni, *the absence of good, a deficiency, and therefore has no independent existence. Augustine's biblical materialism offers an affirmation of the created order that runs contrary to his own Manichean background that saw the existence of an evil principle at war with the divine good. Despite a certain strain of otherworldliness that has run through the Christian tradition and can be taken as an implication of the two contending cities in* City of God, *each city with its desparate beginnings and endings, this major theme in Augustine's thought commits Christians to the valuing and care for the world in which we live. It is an expression of the Creator's love that calls forth our love for the creation in response.*

Chapter 9.—What We are to Believe. In Regard to Nature It Is Not Necessary for the Christian to Know More Than that the Goodness of the Creator Is the Cause of All Things.

When, then, the question is asked what we are to believe in regard to religion, it is not necessary to probe into the nature of things, as was done by those whom the Greeks call physici; nor need we be in alarm lest the Christian should be ignorant of the force and number of the elements,—the motion, and order, and eclipses of the heavenly bodies; the form of the heavens; the species and the natures of animals, plants, stones, fountains, rivers, mountains; about chronology and distances; the signs of coming storms; and a thousand other things which those philosophers either have found out, or think they have found out. For even these men themselves, endowed though they are with so much genius, burning with zeal, abounding in leisure, tracking some things by the aid of human conjecture, searching into others with the aids of history and experience, have not found out all things; and even their boasted discoveries are oftener mere guesses than certain knowledge. It is enough for the Christian to believe that the only cause of all created things, whether heavenly or earthly, whether visible or invisible, is the goodness of the Creator the one true God; and that nothing exists but Himself that does not derive its existence from Him; and that He is the Trinity—to wit, the Father, and the Son begotten of the Father, and the Holy Spirit proceeding from the same Father, but one and the same Spirit of Father and Son.

Chapter 10.—The Supremely Good Creator Made All Things Good.

By the Trinity, thus supremely and equally and unchangeably good, all things were created; and these are not supremely and equally and unchangeably good, but yet they are good, even taken separately. Taken as a whole, however, they are very good, because their ensemble constitutes the universe in all its wonderful order and beauty.

Chapter 11.—What is Called Evil in the Universe Is but the Absence of Good.

And in the universe, even that which is called evil, when it is regulated and put in its own place, only enhances our admiration of the good; for we enjoy and value the good more when we compare it with the evil. For the Almighty God, who, as even the heathen acknowledge, has supreme power over all things, being Himself supremely good, would never permit the existence of anything evil among His works, if He were not so omnipotent and good that He can bring good even out of evil. For what is that which we call evil but the absence of good? In the bodies of animals, disease and wounds mean nothing but the absence of health; for when a cure is effected, that does not mean that the evils which were present—namely, the diseases and wounds—go away from the body and dwell elsewhere: they altogether cease to exist; for the wound or disease is not a substance, but a defect in the fleshly substance,—the flesh itself being a substance, and therefore something good, of which those evils—that is, privations of the good which we call health—are accidents. Just in the same way, what are called vices in the soul are nothing but privations of natural good. And when they are cured, they are not transferred elsewhere: when they cease to exist in the healthy soul, they cannot exist anywhere else.

Selection 2: *Enchiridion*, Chapters 9–11; 23–26

> *While God is the cause of all good, all evil—personal and social—is the revolt against God by angels and human beings. This contention reflects a belief in original sin as a matter of doctrinal concern vis à vis the Pelagians' optimistic view of human moral capacity. With regard to social ethics, it is foundational for Christian realism in the pursuit of justice, peace, and the common good, a realism that is certainly at work in the selections to follow.*

The Cause of Created Things Is the Goodness of the Creator

9. Since, therefore, we are considering what ought to be believed in the sphere of religion, we do not need to inquire into the nature of things as did those whom the Greeks call physikoi, nor need we fear that the Christian is ignorant of something they have discovered or think they have discovered concerning the properties and number of the elements, the movement and order and phases of the stars, the shape of the heavens, the kinds of animals, fruits, stones, springs, rivers, and mountains and their natures, the measurement of time and space, the indications of imminent storms and hundreds of other such things. This is because they themselves have not discovered everything, powerful as they are of intellect, eager in study, and abundantly gifted with leisure: Some matters they investigate with the power of human speculation, others on the basis of facts and experience, and, in those matters which they boast of having discovered, much is a matter of opinion rather than of knowledge. For a Christian it is enough to believe that the cause of created things, whether in heaven or on earth, visible or invisible, is nothing other than the goodness of the creator who is the one true God, and that there is nothing that is not either himself or from him, and that he is a Trinity, that is, a Father, the Son begotten from the Father, and a Holy Spirit who proceeds from the same Father and is one and the same Spirit of Father and Son.

10. By this Trinity, supremely, equally, and unchangeably good, all things have been created: They are not supremely, equally, or unchangeably good, but even when they are considered individually, each one of them is good; and at the same time all things are very good, since in all these things consists the wonderful beauty of the universe.

Evil Is the Removal of Good

11. In this universe even that which is called evil, well ordered and kept in its place, sets the good in higher relief, so that good things are more pleasing and praiseworthy than evil ones. Nor would Almighty God, "to whom," as even the pagans confess, "belongs supreme power," For what else is that which is called evil; but a removal of good? In the bodies of animals, to be afflicted with diseases and wounds is nothing other than to be deprived of health: The aim of treatment is not to make the evils which were in the body, such as diseases and wounds, move from where they were to somewhere else, but rather that they should cease to exist, since a wound or a disease is not in itself a substance, but a defect in the substance of flesh. The flesh itself is the substance, a good thing to which those evil things, those removals of the good, know as health, occur. In the same way all evils that affect the mind are removals of natural

goods: When they are cured they are not moved to somewhere else, but when they are no longer in the mind once it has been restored to health, they will be nowhere.

Causes of Good and Evil

23. Having treated these matters with the brevity that a book like this demands, since we must know the causes of good and evil insofar as is necessary to enable us to travel along the road that leads us to the kingdom where there will be life without death, truth without error, happiness with anxiety, we must in no way doubt that the only cause of the good things that come our way is the goodness of God, while the cause of our evils is the will of a changeable good falling away from the unchangeable good, first the will of an angel, then the will of a human being.

Ignorance and Desire

24. This is the first evil that affected the rational creation, the first privation of good. Then there came even upon those who did not wish it ignorance of what should be done and desire for harmful things, together with their companions' error and suffering: When these two evils are felt to be near at hand, the movement of the mind fleeing them is called fear. Further, when the mind gains the things it desires, however harmful and empty they may be, since it does not realize their true nature because of its error, it is either overcome with a sick pleasure or inflated with an empty joy. These are, as it were, the sources of sickness sources not of abundance but of deprivations from which all the unhappiness of rational nature flows.

Death of the Body

25. However, this nature, in the midst of all its evils, has not been able to lose the appetite for happiness. Rather, these evils are common to both human beings and angels who have been condemned for their malice by the Lord's justice. But man has also his own special penalty, since he has been punished with the death of the body as well. God had threatened him with the punishment of death if he sinned, bestowing free will on him while still ruling him by his authority and terrifying him with the thought of death, and placing him in the bliss of paradise as if in the shadow of life, from which he was to rise to better things if he preserved his state of justice.

Adam's Sin

26. After his sin he became an exile from this place and bound also his progeny, which by his sin he had damaged within himself as though at its root, by the penalty of death and condemnation. As a result, any offspring born of him and the wife through whom he had sinned, who had been condemned together with him, born through the concupiscence of the flesh which was their punishment, carrying within it a disobedience similar to that which they had showed, would contract original sin, which would drag

it through various errors and pains to that final punishment with the deserter angels, his corruptors, masters, and accomplices. Therefore, sin came into the world through one man, and death came through sin, and so it spread to all: in him all have sinned. When he used the word world in that text, the apostle was of course referring to the whole human race.

Selection 3: *City of God* XIV, 28; XIX, 17

> *Augustine describes the two cities and the reason for the discord between them. The distinction between the two cities—heavenly versus earthly—certainly contributed to an otherworldly bias and a resultant quietism in relation to social concerns in some strands of church tradition. However, Augustine makes clear that the heavenly city in its earthly pilgrimage works in history toward the common good. Thus, the cities, though distinguished, are not separated in their concern for the peace of the earth and the common good. Augustine's perspective in this matter expresses a view that has been and remains a major outlook on the church's relation to the world.*

Book XIV, Chapter 28

Of the quality of the two cities, the earthly and the heavenly

Two cities, then, have been created by two loves: that is, the earthly by love of self extending even to contempt of God, and the heavenly by love of God extending to contempt of self. The one, therefore, glories in itself, the other in the Lord; the one seeks glory from men, the other finds its highest glory in God, the Witness of our conscience. The one lifts up its head in its own glory; the other says to its God, 'Thou art my glory, and the lifter up of mine head.' In the Earthly City, princes are as much mastered by the lust for mastery as the nations which they subdue are by them; in the Heavenly, all serve one another in charity, rulers by their counsel and subjects by their obedience. The one city loves its own strength as displayed in its mighty men; the other says to its God, 'I will love Thee, O Lord, my strength.'

Thus, in the Earthly City, its wise men, who live according to man, have pursued the goods of the body or of their own mind, or both. Some of them who were able to know God 'glorified Him not as God, neither were thankful; but became vain in their imagination and their foolish heart was darkened. Professing themselves to be wise' (that is, exalting themselves in their wisdom, under the dominion of pride), 'they became fools, and changed the glory of the incorruptible God into an image made like to corruptible man, and to birds, and four-foooted beasts, and creeping things' (for in adoring images of this kind they were either the leaders of the people or their followers); 'and they worshipped and served the creature more than the Creator, Who is blessed forever'. In the Heavenly City, however, man has no wisdom beyond the piety which rightly worships the true God, and which looks for its reward in the fellowship not only of holy men, but of angels also, 'that God may be all in all'.

Book XIX, Chapter 17

What produces peace, and what discord, between the Heavenly City and the earthly
But a household of men who do not live by faith strives to find an earthly peace in the goods and advantages that belong to this temporal life. By contrast, a household of men who live by faith looks forward to the blessings which are promised as eternal in the life to come; and such men make use of earthly and temporal things like pilgrims: they are not captivated by them, nor are they deflected by them from their progress towards God. They are, of course, sustained by them, so that they may more easily bear the burdens of the corruptible body that presses down the soul; but they do not in the least allow these things to increase such burdens.

Thus both kinds of men and both kinds of household make common use of those things that are necessary to this mortal life; but each has its own very different end in using them. So also, the earthly city, which does not live by faith, desires an earthly peace, and it establishes an ordered concord of civic obedience and rule in order to secure a kind of co-operation of men's wills for the sake of attaining the things which belong to this mortal life. But the Heavenly City—or, rather, that part of it which is a pilgrim in this condition of mortality, and which lives by faith—must of necessity make use of this peace also, until this mortal state, for which such peace is necessary, shall have passed away. Thus, it lives like a captive and a pilgrim, even though it has already received the promised of redemption, and the gift of the Spirit as a kind of pledge of it. But, for as long as it does so, it does not hesitate to obey the laws of the earthly city, whereby the things necessary for the support of this mortal life are administered. In this way, then since this mortal condition is common to both cities, a harmony is preserved between them with respect to the things that belong to this condition.

But the earthly city has had among its members certain wise men whose doctrines are rejected by the divine teaching. Deceived either by their own speculations or by demons, these philosophers believed that there are many gods who must be induced to take an interest in human affairs. They believed also that these gods have, as it were, different spheres of influence with different offices attached to them. Thus the body is the responsibility of one god, the mind that of another; and, within the body, one god has charge of the head, another of the neck, and so on with each of the parts in turn. Similarly, within the mind, one god is responsible for intelligence, another for learning, another for anger, another for desire. And so too with all the things which touch our lives: There is a god who has charge of cattle, of corn, of wine, of oil, or woodlands, of money, of navigation, of war and victory, of marriage, of birth, of fertility, and so on. But the Heavenly City knows only one God Who is to be worshipped, and it decrees, with faithful piety, that to Him alone is to be given that service which the Greeks call latreia, and which is due only to God. Because of this difference, it has not been possible for the Heavenly City to have laws of religion in common with the earthly city. It has been necessary for her to dissent from the earthly city in this regard, and to become a burden to those who think differently. Thus, she has had to bear the brunt of the anger and hatred and persecutions of her adversaries, except insofar as their minds have sometimes been struck by the multitude of the Christians and by the divine aid always extended to them.

Therefore, for as long as this Heavenly City is a pilgrim in earth, she summons citizens of all nations and every tongue, and brings together a society of pilgrims in which no attention is paid to any differences in the customs, laws, and institutions by which earthly peace is achieved or maintained. She does not rescind or destroy these things, however. For whatever differenced there are among the various nations, these all tend towards the same end of earthly peace. Thus, she preserves and follows them provided only that they do not impede the religion by which we are taught that the one supreme and true God is to be worshipped. And so even the Heavenly City makes use of earthly peace during her pilgrimage, and desires and maintains the co-operation of men's wills in attaining those things which belong to the mortal nature of man, in so far as this may be allowed without prejudice to true godliness and religion. Indeed, she directs that earthly peace towards heavenly peace: towards the peace which is so truly such that—at least so far as rational creatures are concerned—only it can really be held to be peace and called such. For this peace is a perfectly ordered and perfectly harmonious fellowship in the enjoyment of God, and of one another in God. When we have reached that peace, our life will no longer be a mortal one; rather, we shall then be fully and certainly alive. There will be no animal body to press down the soul by its corruption, but a spiritual body standing in need of nothing: a body subject in every part to the will. This peace the Heavenly City possesses in faith while on its pilgrimage, and by this faith it lives righteously, directing towards the attainment of that peace every good act which it performs either for God, or—since the city's life is inevitably a social one—for neighbor.

Selection 4: *Of the Morals of the Catholic Church*, Chapter XV, XXIV, 434, XXVI, and XXVII

Virtue is the perfect love of God, and, for Augustine, the basis of the Christian life and ethic. All other virtues, such as the classical virtues he enumerates, are dependent and derivative. The proper love of self and of neighbor is derived from it. So, we may observe that justice in relation to our neighbors is not different from love but an expression of love.

As to virtue leading us to a happy life, I hold virtue to be nothing else than perfect love of God. For the fourfold division of virtue I regard as taken from four forms of love. For these four virtues (would that all felt their influence in their minds as they have their names in their mouths!), I should have no hesitation in defining them: that temperance is love giving itself entirely to that which is loved; fortitude is love readily bearing all things for the sake of the loved object; justice is love serving only the loved object, and therefore ruling rightly; prudence is love distinguishing with sagacity between what hinders it and what helps it. The object of this love is not anything, but only God, the chief good, the highest wisdom, the perfect harmony. So we may express the definition thus: that temperance is love keeping itself entire and incorrupt for God; fortitude is love bearing everything readily for the sake of God; justice is love serving God only, and therefore ruling well all else, as subject to man; prudence is love making a right distinction between what helps it towards God and what might hinder it.

*   *   *

What of justice that pertains to God? As the Lord says, "Ye cannot serve two masters," and the apostle denounces those who serve the creature rather than the Creator, was it not said before in the Old Testament, "Thou shalt worship the Lord thy God, and Him only shalt thou serve"? I need say no more on this, for these books are full of such passages. The lover, then, whom we are describing, will get from justice this rule of life, that he must with perfect readiness serve the God whom he loves, the highest good, the highest wisdom, the highest peace; and as regards all other things, must either rule them as subject to himself, or treat them with a view to their subjection. This rule of life, is, as we have shown, confirmed by the authority of both Testaments.

*   *   *

To proceed to what remains. It may be thought that there is nothing here about man himself, the lover. But to think this, shows a want of clear perception. For it is impossible for one who loves God not to love himself. For he alone has a proper love for himself who aims diligently at the attainment of the chief and true good; and if this is nothing else but God, as has been shown. what is to prevent one who loves God from loving himself? And then, among men should there be no bond of mutual love? Yea, verily; so that we can think of no surer step towards the love of God than the love of man to man.

Let the Lord then supply us with the other precept in answer to the question about the precepts of life; for He was not satisfied with one as knowing that God is one thing and man another, and that the difference is nothing less than that between the Creator and the thing created in the likeness of its Creator. He says then that the second precept is, "Thou shalt love thy neighbor as thyself." Now you love yourself suitably when you love God better than yourself. What, then, you aim at in yourself you must aim at in your neighbor, namely, that he may love God with a perfect affection. For you do not love him as yourself, unless you try to draw him to that good which you are yourself pursuing. For this is the one good which has room for all to pursue it along with thee. From this precept proceed the duties of human society, in which it is hard to keep from error. But the first thing to aim at is, that we should be benevolent, that is, that we cherish no malice and no evil design against another. For man is the nearest neighbor of man.

Hear also what Paul says: "The love of our neighbor," he says, "worketh no ill." The testimonies here made use of are very short, but, if I mistake not, they are to the point, and sufficient for the purpose. And every one knows how many and how weighty are the words to be found everywhere in these books on the love of our neighbor. But as a man may sin against another in two ways, either by injuring him or by not helping him when it is in his power, and as it is for these things which no loving man would do that men are called wicked, all that is required is, I think, proved by these words, "The love of our neighbor worketh no ill." And if we cannot attain to good unless we first desist from working evil, our love of our neighbor is a sort of cradle of our love to God, so that, as it is said, "the love of our neighbor worketh no ill," we may rise from this to these other words, "We know that all things issue in good to them that love God."

But there is a sense in which these either rise together to fullness and perfection, or, while the love of God is first in beginning, the love of our neighbor is first in coming to perfection. For perhaps divine love takes hold on us more rapidly at the outset, but we reach perfection more easily in lower things. However that may be, the main point is this, that no one should think that while he despises his neighbor he will come to happiness and to the God whom he loves. And would that it were as easy to seek the good of our neighbor, or to avoid hurting him, as it is for one well trained and kind-hearted to love his neighbor! These things require more than mere good-will, and can be done only by a high degree of thoughtfulness and prudence, which belongs only to those to whom it is given by God, the source of all good. On this topic—which is one, I think, of great difficulty—I will try to say a few words such as my plan admits of, resting all my hope in Him whose gifts these are.

Man, then, as viewed by his fellow-man, is a rational soul with a mortal and earthly body in its service. Therefore he who loves his neighbor does good partly to the man's body, and partly to his soul. What benefits the body is called medicine; what benefits the soul, discipline. Medicine here includes everything that either preserves or restores bodily health. It includes, therefore, not only what belongs to the art of medical men, properly so called, but also food and drink, clothing and shelter, and every means of covering and protection to guard our bodies against injuries and mishaps from without as well as from within. For hunger and thirst, and cold and heat, and all violence from without, produce loss of that health which is the point to be considered.

Hence those who seasonably and wisely supply all the things required for warding off these evils and distresses are called compassionate, although they may have been so wise that no painful feeling disturbed their mind in the exercise of compassion. No doubt the word compassionate implies suffering in the heart of the man who feels for the sorrow of another. And it is equally true that a wise man ought to be free from all painful emotion when he assists the needy, when he gives food to the hungry and water to the thirsty, when he clothes the naked, when he takes the stranger into his house, when he sets free the oppressed, when, lastly, he extends his charity to the dead in giving them burial. Still the epithet compassionate is a proper one, although he acts with tranquility of mind, not from the stimulus of painful feeling, but from motives of benevolence. There is no harm in the word compassionate when there is no passion in the case.

Fools, again, who avoid the exercise of compassion as a vice, because they are not sufficiently moved by a sense of duty without feeling also distressful emotion, are frozen into hard insensibility, which is very different from the calm of a rational serenity. God, on the other hand, is properly called compassionate; and the sense in which He is so will be understood by those whom piety and diligence have made fit to understand. There is a danger lest, in using the words of the learned, we harden the souls of the unlearned by leading them away from compassion instead of softening them with the desire of a charitable disposition. As compassion, then, requires us to ward off these distresses from others, so harmlessness forbids the infliction of them.

Selection 5: *A Good Marriage*, Chapters 3, 6, 7, 10

> *Sexual intercourse for Augustine and many of the other ancients was ambigu-*
> *ous. The only moral justification for it was procreation within the marriage*
> *bond. Although companionship was also a purpose of marriage, sex within*
> *marriage without the aim of procreation was nonetheless a venial sin and ulti-*
> *mately refraining from sex within marriage when having children was not*
> *an issue he considered laudable. Refraining from sex altogether in the celi-*
> *bate life was even better. Nonetheless, sex in marriage is provided as a hedge*
> *against fornication and sexual fidelity within marriage a hedge against adul-*
> *tery. In the end Augustine judges that marriage carried on in the right spirit*
> *and without lust is a good gift of God. In this judgment he stood against the*
> *Manichean belief that creation and procreation, being of the material world,*
> *was inherently evil. Augustine's views had a profound influence on Christian*
> *sexual ethics for generations to come.*

Chapter 3

This does not seem to me to be a good solely because of the procreation of children, but also because of the natural companionship between the two sexes. Otherwise, we could not speak of marriage in the case of old people, especially if they had either lost their children or had begotten none at all. But, in a good marriage, although one of many years, even if the ardor of youths has cooled between man and woman, the order of charity still flourishes between husband and wife. They are better in proportion as they begin the earlier to refrain by mutual consent from sexual intercourse, not that it would afterwards happen of necessity that they would not be able to do what they wished, but that it would be a matter of praise that they had refused beforehand what they were able to do. If, then, there is observed that promise Therefore, married people owe each other not only the fidelity of sexual intercourse for the purpose of procreating children and this is the first association of the human race in this mortal life but also the mutual service, in a certain measure, of sustaining each other's weakness, for the avoidance of illicit intercourse, so that, even if perpetual continence is pleasing to one of them, he may not follow this urge except with the consent of the other. In this case, 'The wife has not authority over her body, but the husband; the husband likewise has not authority over his body, but the wife/ So, let them not deny either to each other, what the man seeks from matrimony and the woman from her husband, not for the sake of having children but because of weakness and incontinence, lest in this way they fall into damnable seductions through the temptations of Satan because of the incontinence of both or of one of them.

Chapter 6

In marriage, intercourse for the purpose of generation has no fault attached to it, but for the purpose of satisfying concupiscence, provided with a spouse, because of the marriage fidelity, it is a venial sin; adultery or fornication, however, is a mortal sin.

And so, continence from all intercourse is certainly better than marital intercourse itself which takes place for the sake of begetting children.

Chapter 7

While continence is of greater merit, it is no sin to render the conjugal debt, but to exact it beyond the need for generation is a venial sin; furthermore, to commit fornication or adultery is a crime that must be punished.

Chapter 10

But I know what they murmur. 'What if,' they say, 'all men should be willing to restrain themselves from all intercourse, how would the human race survive?' Would that all men had this wish, if only in 'charity, from a pure heart and a good conscience and faith unfeigned.' Much more quickly would the City of God be filled and the end of time be hastened. What else does it appear that the Apostle is encouraging when he says, in speaking of this: 1. I would that you all were as I am myself 2. or, in another place: 'But this I say, brethren, the time is short; it remains that those who have wives be as if they had none; and those who weep, as though not weeping; and those who rejoice, as though not rejoicing; and those who buy, as though not buying; and those who use this world, as though not using it, for this world as we see it is passing away. I would have you free from care.' Then he adds: 'He who is unmarried thinks about the things of the Lord, how he may please the Lord. Whereas he who is married thinks about the things of the world, how he may please his wife, and he is divided. And the unmarried woman and the virgin, who is unmarried, is concerned about the things of the Lord, that she may be holy in body and in spirit. Whereas she who is married is concerned about the things of the world, how she may please her husband. And so it seems to me that at this time only those who do not restrain themselves ought to be married in accord with this saying of the same Apostle: 'But if they do not have self-control, let them marry, for it is better to marry than to burn.

Selection 6: Peace and Just War—*City of God*, Book XV, 4; XIX, 7

Just war thinking has been associated in Christian tradition with such towering figures as Ambrose, Bishop of Milan at the time of Augustine's conversion and mentioned in Augustine's Confessions, Augustine himself, Thomas Aquinas, and Martin Luther. It has been the predominant outlook on the problem of war in the history of Christian thought. Augustine allows for the possibility that good rulers may wage just war. However, it is important to note that, in Augustine's view, while war is waged for the purpose peace, sustainable peace is an unlikely prospect. More importantly, while a war may be judged to be just, it is always tragic.

Book XV, Chapter 4

Of strife and peace in the earthly city
But the earthly city will not be everlasting; for when it is condemned to that punishment that is its end, it will no longer be a city. But it has its good in this world, and it
rejoices to partake of it with such joy as things of this kind can confer. And because
this is not the kind of good that brings no distress to those who love it, the earthly city
is often divided against itself by lawsuits, wars and strife, and by victories that either
bring death or are themselves short-lived. For if any part of that city has risen up in
war against another part, it seeks to be victorious over other nations even though it is
itself held captive by vices; and if, when it triumphs, it is lifted up in its pride, such triumph itself brings only death. If on the other hand, it considers the vicissitudes which
are the common lot of mankind, and is more distressed by the possibility of future
calamity than buoyed up by the present prosperous state of things, then its triumph is
again, only short-lived. For it will not be able to rule forever over those whom, in its
triumph, it was able to subdue.

But it is not rightly said that the goods that this city desires are not goods; for, in
its own human fashion, even that city is better when it possesses them than when it
does not. Thus, it desires earthly peace, albeit only for the sake of the lowest kind of
goods; and it is that peace which it desires to achieve by waging war. For, peace, which
the opposing parties did not have while they strove in their unhappy poverty for the
things they could not both possess at once. It is for the sake of this peace that weari-
some wars are fought, and it is by victories that are deemed glorious that it is achieved.

Indeed, when victory goes to those who fought for the juster cause, who will
doubt that such victory is a matter for rejoicing and that the ensuing peace is something to be desired? These things are goods, and they are without doubt gifts of God.
But if the higher goods are neglected, which belong to the City on high, where victory
will be secure in the enjoyment of eternal and supreme peace: if these are neglected,
and those other goods desired so much that they are thought to be the only goods, or
loved more than the goods which are believed to be higher, then misery will of necessity follow, and present misery be increased by it.

Book XIX, Chapter 7

*Of the diversity of tongues, by which communication between men is prevented; and of the
misery of wars, even those that are called just*
After the city or town comes the world, which the philosophers identify as the third
level of human society. They begin with the household, progress to the city, and come
finally to the world. And the world, like a gathering of waters, is all the more full of
perils by reason of its greater size. First of all, the diversity of tongues now divides
man from man. For if two men, each ignorant of the other's language, meet, and are
compelled by some necessity not to pass on but to remain with one another, it is easier
for dumb animals, even of different kinds, to associate together than these men, even
though both are human beings. For when men cannot communicate their thoughts
to each other, they are completely unable to associate with one another despite the
similarity of their natures; and this is because of the diversity of tongues. So true
is this that a man would more readily hold a conversation with his dog than with

another man who is a foreigner. It is true that the Imperial City has imposed on subject nations not only her yoke but also her language, as a bond of peace and society, so that there should be no lack of interpreters but a great abundance of them. But how many great wars, what slaughter of men, what outpourings of human blood have been necessary to bring this about!

Those wars are not over; but the misery of these evils has not yet come to an end. For though there has been, and is now, no lack of enemies among foreign nations, against whom wars have always been waged, and still are being waged, yet the very breadth of the Empire has produced wars of a worse kind: that is, social and civil wars. By these, the human race is made even more miserable, either by warfare itself, waged for the sake of eventual peace, or by the constant fear that conflict will begin again. I could not possibly give a suitably eloquent description of these many evils, these manifold disasters, these harsh and dire necessities. How lengthy this discourse would be, if I were to try to do so!

But the wise man, they say, will wage just wars. Surely, however if he remembers that he is a human being, he will be much readier to deplore the fact that he is under the necessity of waging even just wars. For if they were not just, he would not have to wage them, and so there would then be no wars at all for a wise man to engage in. For it is the iniquity of the opposing side that imposes upon the wise man the duty of waging wars; and every man certainly ought to deplore this iniquity since, even if no necessity for war should arise from it, it is still the iniquity of men. Let everyone, therefore, who reflects with pain upon such great evils, upon such horror and cruelty, acknowledge that this is misery. And if anyone either endures them or thinks of them without anguish of soul, his condition is still more miserable: for he thinks himself happy only because he has lost all human feeling.

For Further Reading

The following select list of writings provides a mixture of primary and secondary sources related to the major parts of the anthology, and the full text of the works being excerpted will also provide rich additional reading.

Babcock, William S., editor. *The Ethics of St. Augustine.* Atlanta: Scholars, 1991.

Benedict XVI, Pope. *The Fathers of the Church from Clement of Rome to Augustine of Hippo.* Edited by Joseph T. Lienhard, SJ. Grand Rapids: Eerdmans, 2009.

Elshtain, Jean Bethke. *Augustine and the Limits of Politics.* Notre Dame: Notre Dame University Press, 1995.

Meilaender, Gilbert. *The Way That Leads: Augustinian Reflections on the Christian Life.* Grand Rapids: Eerdmans, 2006.

Wingren, Gustaf. *Man and the Incarnation: A Study in the Biblical Theology of Irenaeus.* Translated by Ross Mackenzie. Philadelphia: Muhlenberg, 1947.

PART 3

The Medieval Church

MONASTICISM 8

As the numbers of Christians grew in the first few centuries of Christianity, so did the concern to maintain true Christian piety. This led to the development of a double standard of morality and spiritual practice. The ascetic tradition of poverty and chastity present in surrounding religious cultures and exemplified by leading figures such as Origen became the higher and holier way in contrast to the ordinary workaday life of the average Christian. The embrace of this asceticism and its formalization in the development of monastic communities expanded with the end of persecutions and Emperor Constantine's decision to make Christianity the religion of the state. It seemed clear to many Christians that this melding of church and culture was a corrupting influence. With the end of martyrdom, asceticism was for them the highest form of Christian devotion attainable.

The involvement of monasticism is, indeed, ambiguous. On the one hand, it represents denial and withdrawal. On the other hand, it became the main force for the preservation of Christian culture through the ages following the collapse of the Roman Empire. The monks preserved Western culture by transmitting it to the barbarians. They were the teachers of the West at least until the Reformation. Because of the key position of the monks and friars as the teachers of the church who kept its moral and theological traditions alive, they were of crucial importance to sustaining values foundational to Christian social thought.

Selection 1: *The Rule of Saint Benedict*

Benedict was born in Nursia, a city some one hundred kilometers northeast of Rome, about 480 CE and lived until 545 CE. While in Rome for studies he became disillusioned with the decadence he experienced there. He withdrew and turned to the ascetic life of a monk and in time founded a monastery at Monte Cassino between Rome and Naples. His Rule, composed in 543 CE, became very influential and by the ninth century superseded all others, providing the foundation for newer orders such as the Cluniacs and the Cistercians. The selections from the Rule that follow give us a good introduction to the discipline of monasticism in general and to the virtues and practices which, notwithstanding the peculiarities of monastic life, are in many ways foundational for all expressions of the Christian life of service.

Chapter IV: The Instruments of Good Works

(1) In the first place to love the Lord God with the whole heart, the whole soul, the whole strength . . . (2) Then, one's neighbor as one's self (cf. Mt 22:37-39; Mk 12:30-31; Lk 10:27). (3) Then, not to kill . . . (4) Not to commit adultery . . . (5) Not to steal . . . (6) Not to covet (cf. Rom 13:9). (7) Not to bear false witness (cf. Mt 19:18; Mk 10:19; Lk 18:20). (8) To honor all men (cf. 1 Pt 2:17). (9) And what one would not have done to himself, not to do to another (cf. Tob 4:16; Mt 7:12; Lk 6:31). (10) To deny one's self in order to follow Christ (cf. Mt 16:24; Lk 9:23). (11) To chastise the body (cf. 1 Cor 9:27). (12) Not to seek after pleasures. (13) To love fasting. (14) To relieve the poor. (15) To clothe the naked. . . (16) To visit the sick (cf. Mt 25:36). (17) To bury the dead. (18) To help in trouble. (19) To console the sorrowing. (20) To hold one's self aloof from worldly ways. (21) To prefer nothing to the love of Christ. (22) Not to give way to anger. (23) Not to foster a desire for revenge. (24) Not to entertain deceit in the heart. (25) Not to make a false peace. (26) Not to forsake charity. (27) Not to swear, lest perchance one swear falsely. (28) To speak the truth with heart and tongue. (29) Not to return evil for evil (cf. 1 Thess 5:15; 1 Pt 3:9). (30) To do no injury, yea, even patiently to bear the injury done us. (31) To love one's enemies (cf. Mt 5:44; Lk 6:27). (32) Not to curse them that curse us, but rather to bless them. (33) To bear persecution for justice sake (cf. Mt 5:10). (34) Not to be proud . . . (35) Not to be given to wine (cf. Ti 1:7; 1 Tm 3:3). (36) Not to be a great eater. (37) Not to be drowsy. (38) Not to be slothful (cf. Rom 12:11). (39) Not to be a murmurer. (40) Not to be a detractor. (41) To put one's trust in God. (42) To refer what good one sees in himself, not to self, but to God. (43) But as to any evil in himself, let him be convinced that it is his own and charge it to himself. (44) To fear the day of judgment. (45) To be in dread of hell. (46) To desire eternal life with all spiritual longing. (47) To keep death before one's eyes daily. (48) To keep a constant watch over the actions of our life. (49) To hold as certain that God sees us everywhere. (50) To dash at once against Christ the evil thoughts which rise in one's heart. (51) And to disclose them to our spiritual father. (52) To guard one's tongue against bad and wicked speech. (53) Not to love much speaking. (54) Not to speak useless words and such as provoke laughter. (55) Not to love much or boisterous laughter. (56) To listen willingly to holy reading. (57) To apply one's self often to prayer. (58) To confess one's past sins to God daily in prayer with sighs and tears, and to amend them for the future. (59) Not to fulfill the desires of the flesh (cf. Gal 5:16). (60) To hate one's own will. (61) To obey the commands of the Abbot in all things, even though he himself (which Heaven forbid) act otherwise, mindful of that precept of the Lord: "What they say, do ye; what they do, do ye not" (Mt 23:3). (62) Not to desire to be called holy before one is; but to be holy first, that one may be truly so called. (63) To fulfill daily the commandments of God by works. (64) To love chastity. (65) To hate no one. (66) Not to be jealous; not to entertain envy. (67) Not to love strife. (68) Not to love pride. (69) To honor the aged. (70) To love the younger. (71) To pray for one's enemies in the love of Christ. (72) To make peace with an adversary before the setting of the sun. (73) And never to despair of God's mercy.

Behold, these are the instruments of the spiritual art, which, if they have been applied without ceasing day and night and approved on judgment day, will merit for us from the Lord that reward which He hath promised: "The eye hath not seen, nor the ear heard, neither hath it entered into the heart of man, what things God hath prepared for them that love Him" (1 Cor 2:9). But the workshop in which we perform all these works with diligence is the enclosure of the monastery, and stability in the community.

Chapter VII: Of Humility

Brethren, the Holy Scripture crieth to us saying: "Every one that exalteth himself shall be humbled; and he that humbleth himself shall be exalted" (Lk 14:11; 18:14). Since, therefore, it saith this, it showeth us that every exaltation is a kind of pride. The Prophet declareth that he guardeth himself against this, saying: "Lord, my heart is not puffed up; nor are my eyes haughty. Neither have I walked in great matters nor in wonderful things above me" (Ps 130[131]:1). What then? "If I was not humbly minded, but exalted my soul; as a child that is weaned is toward his mother so shalt Thou reward my soul" (Ps 130[131]:2).

Hence, brethren, if we wish to reach the greatest height of humility, and speedily to arrive at that heavenly exaltation to which ascent is made in the present life by humility, then, mounting by our actions, we must erect the ladder which appeared to Jacob in his dream, by means of which angels were shown to him ascending and descending (cf. Gen 28:12). Without a doubt, we understand this ascending and descending to be nothing else but that we descend by pride and ascend by humility. The erected ladder, however, is our life in the present world, which, if the heart is humble, is by the Lord lifted up to heaven. For we say that our body and our soul are the two sides of this ladder; and into these sides the divine calling hath inserted various degrees of humility or discipline which we must mount.

The first degree of humility, then, is that a man always have the fear of God before his eyes (cf. Ps 35[36]:2), shunning all forgetfulness and that he be ever mindful of all that God hath commanded, that he always considereth in his mind how those who despise God will burn in hell for their sins, and that life everlasting is prepared for those who fear God. And whilst he guardeth himself evermore against sin and vices of thought, word, deed, and self-will, let him also hasten to cut off the desires of the flesh.

Let a man consider that God always seeth him from Heaven, that the eye of God beholdeth his works everywhere, and that the angels report them to Him every hour. The Prophet telleth us this when he showeth God thus ever present in our thoughts, saying: "The searcher of hearts and reins is God" (Ps 7:10). And again: "The Lord knoweth the thoughts of men" (Ps 93[94]:11) And he saith: "Thou hast understood my thoughts afar off" (Ps 138[139]:3). And: "The thoughts of man shall give praise to Thee" (Ps 75[76]:11). Therefore, in order that he may always be on his guard against evil thoughts, let the humble brother always say in his heart: "Then I shall be spotless before Him, if I shall keep myself from iniquity" (Ps 17[18]:24).

We are thus forbidden to do our own will, since the Scripture saith to us: "And turn away from thy evil will" (Sir 18:30). And thus, too, we ask God in prayer that His will may be done in us (cf. Mt 6:10). We are, therefore, rightly taught not to do our own will, when we guard against what Scripture saith: "There are ways that to men seem right, the end whereof plungeth into the depths of hell" (Prov 16:25). And also when we are filled with dread at what is said of the negligent: "They are corrupted and become abominable in their pleasure" (Ps 13[14]:1). But as regards desires of the flesh, let us believe that God is thus ever present to us, since the Prophet saith to the Lord: "Before Thee is all my desire" (Ps 37[38]:10).

We must, therefore, guard thus against evil desires, because death hath his station near the entrance of pleasure. Whence the Scripture commandeth, saying: "Go no after thy lusts" (Sir 18:30). If, therefore, the eyes of the Lord observe the good and the bad (cf. Prov 15:3) and the Lord always looketh down from heaven on the children of men, to see whether there be anyone that understandeth or seeketh God (cf. Ps 13[14]:2); and if our actions are reported to the Lord day and night by the angels who are appointed to watch over us daily, we must ever be on our guard, brethren, as the Prophet saith in the psalm, that God may at no time see us "gone aside to evil and become unprofitable" (Ps 13[14]:3), and having spared us in the present time, because He is kind and waiteth for us to be changed for the better, say to us in the future: "These things thou hast done and I was silent" (Ps 49[50]:21).

The second degree of humility is, when a man loveth not his own will, nor is pleased to fulfill his own desires but by his deeds carrieth out that word of the Lord which saith: "I came not to do My own will but the will of Him that sent Me" (Jn 6:38). It is likewise said: "Self-will hath its punishment, but necessity winneth the crown."

The third degree of humility is, that for the love of God a man subject himself to a Superior in all obedience, imitating the Lord, of whom the Apostle saith: "He became obedient unto death" (Phil 2:8).

The fourth degree of humility is, that, if hard and distasteful things are commanded, nay, even though injuries are inflicted, he accept them with patience and even temper, and not grow weary or give up, but hold out, as the Scripture saith: "He that shall persevere unto the end shall be saved" (Mt 10:22). And again: "Let thy heart take courage, and wait thou for the Lord" (Ps 26[27]:14). And showing that a faithful man ought even to bear every disagreeable thing for the Lord, it saith in the person of the suffering: "For Thy sake we suffer death all the day long; we are counted as sheep for the slaughter" (Rom 8:36; Ps 43[44]:22). And secure in the hope of the divine reward, they go on joyfully, saying: "But in all these things we overcome because of Him that hath loved us" (Rom 8:37). And likewise in another place the Scripture saith: "Thou, O God, hast proved us; Thou hast tried us by fire as silver is tried; Thou hast brought us into a net, Thou hast laid afflictions on our back" (Ps 65[66]:10-11). And to show us that we ought to be under a Superior, it continueth, saying: "Thou hast set men over our heads" (Ps 65[66]:12). And fulfilling the command of the Lord by patience also in adversities and injuries, when struck on the one cheek they turn also the other; the despoiler of their coat they give their cloak also; and when forced to go one mile they go two (cf. Mt 5:39-41); with the Apostle Paul they bear with false brethren and "bless those who curse them" (2 Cor 11:26; 1 Cor 4:12).

The fifth degree of humility is, when one hideth from his Abbot none of the evil thoughts which rise in his heart or the evils committed by him in secret, but humbly confesseth them. Concerning this the Scripture exhorts us, saying: "Reveal thy way to the Lord and trust in Him" (Ps 36[37]:5). And it saith further: "Confess to the Lord, for He is good, for His mercy endureth forever" (Ps 105[106]:1; Ps 117[118]:1). And the Prophet likewise saith: "I have acknowledged my sin to Thee and my injustice I have not concealed. I said I will confess against myself my injustice to the Lord; and Thou hast forgiven the wickedness of my sins" (Ps 31[32]:5).

The sixth degree of humility is, when a monk is content with the meanest and worst of everything, and in all that is enjoined him holdeth himself as a bad and worthless workman, saying with the Prophet: "I am brought to nothing and I knew it not; I am become as a beast before Thee, and I am always with Thee" (Ps 72[73]:22-23).

The seventh degree of humility is, when, not only with his tongue he declareth, but also in his inmost soul believeth, that he is the lowest and vilest of men, humbling himself and saying with the Prophet: "But I am a worm and no man, the reproach of men and the outcast of the people" (Ps 21[22]:7). "I have been exalted and humbled and confounded" (Ps 87[88]:16). And also: "It is good for me that Thou hast humbled me, that I may learn Thy commandments" (Ps 118 [119]:71,73).

The eighth degree of humility is, when a monk doeth nothing but what is sanctioned by the common rule of the monastery and the example of his elders.

The ninth degree of humility is, when a monk withholdeth his tongue from speaking, and keeping silence doth not speak until he is asked; for the Scripture showeth that "in a multitude of words there shall not want sin" (Prov 10:19); and that "a man full of tongue is not established in the earth" (Ps 139[140]:12).

The tenth degree of humility is, when a monk is not easily moved and quick for laughter, for it is written: "The fool exalteth his voice in laughter" (Sir 21:23).

The eleventh degree of humility is, that, when a monk speaketh, he speak gently and without laughter, humbly and with gravity, with few and sensible words, and that he be not loud of voice, as it is written: "The wise man is known by the fewness of his words."

The twelfth degree of humility is, when a monk is not only humble of heart, but always letteth it appear also in his whole exterior to all that see him; namely, at the Work of God, in the garden, on a journey, in the field, or wherever he may be, sitting, walking, or standing, let him always have his head bowed down, his eyes fixed on the ground, ever holding himself guilty of his sins, thinking that he is already standing before the dread judgment seat of God, and always saying to himself in his heart what the publican in the Gospel said, with his eyes fixed on the ground: "Lord, I am a sinner and not worthy to lift up mine eyes to heaven" (Lk 18:13); and again with the Prophet: "I am bowed down and humbled exceedingly" (Ps 37[38]:7-9; Ps 118[119]:107).

Having, therefore, ascended all these degrees of humility, the monk will presently arrive at that love of God, which being perfect, casteth out fear (1 Jn 4:18). In virtue of this love all things which at first he observed not without fear, he will now begin to keep without any effort, and as it were, naturally by force of habit, no longer from the fear of hell, but from the love of Christ, from the very habit of good and the pleasure in virtue. May the Lord be pleased to manifest all this by His Holy Spirit in His laborer now cleansed from vice and sin.

Selection 2: *The Rule of Saint Francis*

St. Francis of Assisi is one of the popular and even beloved figures in all of Christian history. Saint Francis's original directions for his order were simple biblical exhortations. As the order grew more specific regulations were required. The selection that follows, then, is from the third Rule sanctioned in 1223 by Pope Honorius III. It is named for Saint Francis, but he did not prepare it. The commitment of the brothers to vows of chastity, poverty, and obedience are clearly laid out as a witness in the church and too the world of the true devotion of the Christian life.

1. This is the Rule and way of life of the brothers minor; to observe the holy Gospel of our Lord Jesus Christ, living in obedience, without personal possessions, and in chastity. Brother Francis promises obedience and reverence to our Lord Pope Honorius, and to his canonical successors, and to the Roman Church. And the other brothers shall be bound to obey Brother Francis and his successors. . . .

3. The Clerical brothers shall perform the divine service according to the order of the holy Roman Church; excepting the psalter, of which they may have extracts. But the lay brothers shall say twenty-four Paternosters at Mains, five at Lauds, seven each at Prime, Terce, Sext and None, twelve at Vespers, seven at the Completorium; and they shall pray for the dead. And they shall fast from the feast of All Saints to the Nativity of the Lord; but as to the holy season of Lent, which begins after the Epiphany of the Lord and continues forty days, a season the Lord consecrated by his holy fast—those who fast during this time shall be blessed of the Lord, and those who do not wish to fast shall not be bound to do so; but otherwise they shall fast until the Resurrection of the Lord. At other times the brothers shall not be bound to fast save on the sixth day (Friday); but when there is a compelling reason the brothers shall not be bound to observe a physical fast. But I advise, warn and exhort my brothers in the Lord Jesus Christ, that, when they go into the world, they shall not quarrel, nor contend with words, nor judge others. But let them be gentle, peaceable, modest, merciful and humble, with honorable conversation towards all, as is fitting. They ought not to ride, save when necessity or infirmity clearly compels them to do so. Into whatsoever house they enter let them first say, 'Peace be to this house.' And according to the holy Gospel it is lawful for them to partake of all dishes placed before them.

4. I strictly command all the brothers never to receive coin or money either directly or through an intermediary. The ministers and guardians alone shall make provision, through spiritual friends, for the needs of the inform and for other brothers who need clothing, according to the locality, season or cold climate, at their discretion. . . .

5. Those brothers, to whom God has given the ability to work, shall work faithfully and devotedly and in such a ways that, avoiding idleness, the enemy of the soul, they do not quench the spirit of holy prayer and devotion, to which other and temporal activities should be subordinate. As the wages of their labor they may receive corporal necessities for themselves and their brothers but not coin nor money, and this will humility, as I fitting for servant of God, and followers of holy poverty.

6. The brothers shall possess nothing, neither a house, nor a place, nor anything. But, as pilgrims and strangers in this world, serving God in poverty and humility, they shall confidently seek alms, and not be ashamed, for the Lord made Himself poor in this world for us. This the highest degree of that sublime poverty, which has made you, my dearly beloved brethren, heirs and kings of the Kingdom of Heaven;

which has made you poor in goods but exalted in virtues. Let this be 'your portion,' which leads you to 'the land of the living' (Ps. cxlii. 5). If you cleave wholly to this, beloved, you will wish to have forever in Heaven nothing save the name of Our Lord Jesus Christ. Wherever the brethren are, and shall meet together, they shall show themselves as members of one family; each shall with confidence unfold his needs to his brother. A mother loves and cherishes her son in the flesh; how much more eagerly should a man love and cherish his brother in the Spirit? And if any of them fall sick and other brothers are bound to minister to him as they themselves would wish to be ministered to.

7. But if any of the brethren shall commit mortal sin at the prompting of the adversary; in the case of those sins concerning which it has been laid down that recourse must be had to the provincial ministers, the aforesaid brethren must have recourse to them without delay. Those ministers, if they are priests, shall with mercy enjoin penance: If they are not priests they shall cause it to be enjoined through others, who are priests of the order, as it seems to them most expedient in the sight of God. They must beware lest they become angry and disturbed on account of the sin of any brother; for anger and indignation hinder love in ourselves and others.

Selection 3: St. Francis's *Canticle of the Sun*

Saint Francis is probably best known for this beautiful canticle and for being so remarkably attuned to other creatures. The spirituality of his theological naturalism has marked him a kind of patron saint of our contemporary concern for the health of the environment and the ethics of loving nature.

Most high, omnipotent, good Lord,
Praise, glory and honor
and benediction all, are Thine.
To Thee alone do they belong, most High,
And there is no man fit to mention Thee.
Praise be to Thee, my Lord, with all Thy creatures,
Especially to my worshipful brother sun,
The which lights up the day, and through him dost Thou brightness give;
And beautiful is he and radiant with splendor great;
Of Thee, most High, signification gives.
Praised be my Lord, for sister moon and for the stars,
In heaven Thou has formed them clear and precious and fair.
Praised be my Lord for brother wind
And for the air and clouds and fair and every kind of weather,
By the which Thou givest to Thy creatures nourishment.
Praised be my Lord for sister water,
The which is greatly helpful and humble and precious and pure.
Praised be my Lord for brother fire,
By the which Thou lightest up the dark.
And fair is he and gay and mighty and strong.

Praised be my Lord for our sister, mother earth,
The which sustains and keeps us
And brings forth diverse fruits with grass and flowers bright.
Praised be my Lord for those who for Thy love forgive
And weakness bear tribulation.
Blessed those who shall in peace endure,
For by Thee, most High, shall they be crowned.
Praised be my Lord for our sister, the bodily death,
From the which no living man can flee.
Woe to them who die in mortal sin;
Blessed those who shall find themselves in Thy most holy will,
For the second death shall do them no ill.
Praise ye and bless ye my Lord, and give Him thanks,
And be subject unto Him with great humility.

THE MYSTICS 9

The contemplative life of the medieval mystics was a quest for the height of spiritual experience. The mystic followed a path of purgation, illumination, and, finally, the soul's communion and union with the divine. The path to that apogee of union was one marked along the way by dark nights of the soul and episodes of rapture, and ecstasy. On the face of it, the religious way of mysticism, which antedates its practice in Christianity, would seem to entail withdrawal from the concerns of this world, if not a disdain for that which is worldly. However, while this may be true of some, it is not true of all. The Christian mystics in the selections that follow clearly had concerns beyond their own spiritual journeys. Their writings and reflections have contributed to the foundations of the Christian ethic that Christian social teaching is built upon.

Selection 1: Bernard of Clairvaux, *On Love of God*

Bernard was born in 1090 at Fontaines near Dijon, the descendant of a noble family. In 1112 he entered the monastery of Citeaux and in 1115 became the first abbot of Clairvaux. From the monastery at Clairvaux, Bernard exerted considerable influence on the life of his age. With his sermons he promoted the Second Crusade the failure of which was a severe blow to him. He corresponded with popes, prelates, and kings offering his forthright instruction and admonition on concerns affecting church and state. It was his conviction that leaders in the church exist for the benefit of the people. This idea of servant leadership is surely consistent with the emphasis on love that was the overarching theme of Bernard's work. He wrote no specific treatise on mysticism itself but in the treatise, "On Loving God," the highest degree of love is virtually the equivalent of mystical union. The selections that follow from this treatise give us a glimpse of Bernard's spirituality and the manner in which he contributed to the understanding that God's love is the wellspring of the Christian life of love and the ethic that flows from it.

Chapter Six—A Brief Summary

Admit that God deserves to be loved very much, yea, boundlessly, because He loved us first, He infinite and we nothing, loved us, miserable sinners, with a love so great and so free. This is why I said at the beginning that the measure of our love to God is to love immeasurably. For since our love is toward God, who is infinite and immeasurable, how can we bound or limit the love we owe Him? Besides, our love is not a gift but a debt. And since it is the Godhead who loves us, Himself boundless, eternal, supreme love, of whose greatness there is no end, yea, and His wisdom is infinite, whose peace passeth all understanding; since it is He who loves us, I say, can we think of repaying Him grudgingly? 'I will love Thee, O Lord, my strength. The Lord is my rock and my fortress and my deliverer, my God, my strength, in whom I will trust' (Ps. 18.1f). He is all that I need, all that I long for. My God and my help, I will love Thee for Thy great goodness; not so much as I might, surely, but as much as I can. I cannot love Thee as Thou deservest to be loved, for I cannot love Thee more than my own feebleness permits. I will love Thee more when Thou deemest me worthy to receive greater capacity for loving; yet never so perfectly as Thou hast deserved of me. 'Thine eyes did see my substance, yet being unperfect; and in Thy book all my members were written' (PS. 139.16). Yet Thou recordest in that book all who do what they can, even though they cannot do what they ought. Surely I have said enough to show how God should be loved and why. But who has felt, who can know, who express, how much we should love him.

Chapter Eight—Of the First Degree of Love: Wherein Man Loves God for Self's Sake

Love is one of the four natural affections, which it is needless to name since everyone knows them. And because love is natural, it is only right to love the Author of nature first of all. Hence comes the first and great commandment, 'Thou shalt love the Lord thy God.' But nature is so frail and weak that necessity compels her to love herself first; and this is carnal love, wherewith man loves himself first and selfishly, as it is written, 'That was not first which is spiritual but that which is natural; and afterward that which is spiritual' (1 Cor. 15.46). This is not as the precept ordains but as nature directs: 'No man ever yet hated his own flesh' (Eph. 5.29). But if, as is likely, this same love should grow excessive and, refusing to be contained within the restraining banks of necessity, should overflow into the fields of voluptuousness, then a command checks the flood, as if by a dike: 'Thou shalt love thy neighbor as thyself.' And this is right: for he who shares our nature should share our love, itself the fruit of nature. Wherefore if a man find it a burden, I will not say only to relieve his brother's needs, but to minister to his brother's pleasures, let him mortify those same affections in himself, lest he become a transgressor. He may cherish himself as tenderly as he chooses, if only he remembers to show the same indulgence to his neighbor. This is the curb of temperance imposed on thee, O man, by the law of life and conscience, lest thou shouldest follow thine own lusts to destruction, or become enslaved by those passions which are the enemies of thy true welfare. Far better divide thine enjoyments with thy neighbor than with these enemies. And if, after the counsel of the son of Sirach, thou goest not after thy desires but refrainest thyself from thine appetites

(Ecclus. 18.30); if according to the apostolic precept having food and raiment thou art therewith content (I Tim. 6.8), then thou wilt find it easy to abstain from fleshly lusts which war against the soul, and to divide with thy neighbors what thou hast refused to thine own desires. That is a temperate and righteous love which practices self-denial in order to minister to a brother's necessity. So our selfish love grows truly social, when it includes our neighbors in its circle.

But if thou art reduced to want by such benevolence, what then? What indeed, except to pray with all confidence unto Him who giveth to all men liberally and upbraideth not (James 1.5), who openeth His hand and filleth all things living with plenteousness (Ps. 145.16). For doubtless He that giveth to most men more than they need will not fail thee as to the necessaries of life, even as He hath promised: 'Seek ye the Kingdom of God, and all those things shall be added unto you' (Luke 12.31). God freely promises all things needful to those who deny themselves for love of their neighbors; and to bear the yoke of modesty and sobriety, rather than to let sin reign in our mortal body (Rom. 6.12), that is indeed to seek the Kingdom of God and to implore His aid against the tyranny of sin. It is surely justice to share our natural gifts with those who share our nature.

But if we are to love our neighbors as we ought, we must have regard to God also: for it is only in God that we can pay that debt of love aright. Now a man cannot love his neighbor in God, except he love God Himself; wherefore we must love God first, in order to love our neighbors in Him. This too, like all good things, is the Lord's doing, that we should love Him, for He hath endowed us with the possibility of love. He who created nature sustains it; nature is so constituted that its Maker is its protector forever. Without Him nature could not have begun to be; without Him it could not subsist at all. That we might not be ignorant of this, or vainly attribute to ourselves the beneficence of our Creator, God has determined in the depths of His wise counsel that we should be subject to tribulations. So when man's strength fails and God comes to his aid, it is meet and right that man, rescued by God's hand, should glorify Him, as it is written, 'Call upon Me in the time of trouble; so will I hear thee, and thou shalt praise Me' (Ps. 50.15). In such wise man, animal and carnal by nature, and loving only himself, begins to love God by reason of that very self-love; since he learns that in God he can accomplish all things that are good, and that without God he can do nothing.

Chapter Nine—Of the Second and Third Degrees of Love

So then in the beginning man loves God, not for God's sake, but for his own. It is something for him to know how little he can do by himself and how much by God's help, and in that knowledge to order himself rightly towards God, his sure support. But when tribulations, recurring again and again, constrain him to turn to God for unfailing help, would not even a heart as hard as iron, as cold as marble, be softened by the goodness of such a Savior, so that he would love God not altogether selfishly, but because He is God? Let frequent troubles drive us to frequent supplications; and surely, tasting, we must see how gracious the Lord is (Ps. 34.8). Thereupon His goodness once realized draws us to love Him unselfishly, yet more than our own needs impel us to love Him selfishly: even as the Samaritans told the woman who announced that it was Christ who was at the well: 'Now we believe, not because of thy saying: for we have heard Him ourselves, and know that this is indeed the Christ, the savior of the world' (John 4.42). We likewise bear the same witness to our own fleshly nature, saying, 'No longer do we love God because of our necessity, but because we have tasted and seen how gracious the Lord is.' Our temporal wants have a speech of their own, proclaiming the benefits they have received from God's favor. Once this is recognized it will not be hard to fulfill the commandment touching love to our neighbors; for whosoever loves God aright loves all God's creatures. Such love is pure, and finds no burden in the precept bidding us purify our souls, in obeying the truth through the Spirit unto unfeigned love of the brethren (I Peter 1.22). Loving as he ought, he counts that command only just. Such love is thankworthy, since it is spontaneous; pure, since it is shown not in word nor tongue, but in deed and truth (I John 3.18); just, since it repays what it has received. Whoso loves in this fashion, loves even as he is loved, and seeks no more his own but the things which are Christ's, even as Jesus sought not His own welfare, but ours, or rather ourselves. Such was the psalmist's love when he sang: 'O give thanks unto the Lord, for He is gracious' (Ps. 118.1). Whosoever praises God for His essential goodness, and not merely because of the benefits He has bestowed, does really love God for God's sake, and not selfishly. The psalmist was not speaking of such love when he said: 'So long as thou doest well unto thyself, men will speak good of thee' (Ps. 49.18). The third degree of love, we have now seen, is to love God on His own account, solely because He is God.

Chapter Ten—Of the Fourth Degree of Love: Wherein Man Does Not Even Love Self, Save for God's Sake

How blessed is he who reaches the fourth degree of love, wherein one loves himself only in God! Thy righteousness standeth like the strong mountains, O God. Such love as this is God's hill, in the which it pleaseth Him to dwell. 'Who shall ascend into the hill of the Lord?' 'O that I had wings like a dove; for then would I flee away and be at rest.' 'At Salem is His tabernacle; and His dwelling in Sion.' 'Woe is me, that I am constrained to dwell with Mesech! '(Ps. 24.3; 55.6; 76.2; 120.5). When shall this flesh and blood, this earthen vessel that is my soul's tabernacle, attain thereto? When shall my soul, rapt with divine love and altogether self-forgetting, yea, become like a broken vessel, yearn wholly for God, and, joined unto the Lord, be one spirit with Him? When shall she exclaim, 'My flesh and my heart faileth; but God is the strength of my heart and my portion for ever' (Ps. 73.26). I would count him blessed and holy to whom such rapture has been vouchsafed in this mortal life, for even an instant to lose thyself, as if thou wert emptied and lost and swallowed up in God, is no human love; it is celestial. But if sometimes a poor mortal feels that heavenly joy for a rapturous moment, then this wretched life envies his happiness, the malice of daily trifles disturbs him, this body of death weighs him down, the needs of the flesh are imperative, the weakness of corruption fails him, and above all brotherly love calls him back to duty. Alas! that voice summons him to re-enter his own round of existence; and he must ever cry out lamentably, 'O Lord, I am oppressed: undertake for me' (Isa. 38.14); and again, 'O wretched man that I am! who shall deliver me from the body of this death?' (Rom. 7.24).

Seeing that the Scripture saith, God has made all for His own glory (Isa. 43.7), surely His creatures ought to conform themselves, as much as they can, to His will.

In Him should all our affections center, so that in all things we should seek only to do His will, not to please ourselves. And real happiness will come, not in gratifying our desires or in gaining transient pleasures, but in accomplishing God's will for us: even as we pray every day: 'Thy will be done in earth as it is in heaven' (Matt. 6.10). O chaste and holy love! O sweet and gracious affection! O pure and cleansed purpose, thoroughly washed and purged from any admixture of selfishness, and sweetened by contact with the divine will! To reach this state is to become godlike. As a drop of water poured into wine loses itself, and takes the color and savor of wine; or as a bar of iron, heated red-hot, becomes like fire itself, forgetting its own nature; or as the air, radiant with sun-beams, seems not so much to be illuminated as to be light itself; so in the saints all human affections melt away by some unspeakable transmutation into the will of God. For how could God be all in all, if anything merely human remained in man? The substance will endure, but in another beauty, a higher power, a greater glory. When will that be? Who will see, who possess it? 'When shall I come to appear before the presence of God?' (Ps. 42.2). 'My heart hath talked of Thee, Seek ye My face: Thy face, Lord, will I seek' (Ps. 27.8). Lord, thinkest Thou that I, even I shall see Thy holy temple?

In this life, I think, we cannot fully and perfectly obey that precept, 'Thou shalt love the Lord thy God with all thy heart, and with all thy soul, and with all thy strength, and with all thy mind' (Luke 10.27). For here the heart must take thought for the body; and the soul must energize the flesh; and the strength must guard itself from impairment. And by God's favor, must seek to increase. It is therefore impossible to offer up all our being to God, to yearn altogether for His face, so long as we must accommodate our purposes and aspirations to these fragile, sickly bodies of ours. Wherefore the soul may hope to possess the fourth degree of love, or rather to be possessed by it, only when it has been clothed upon with that spiritual and immortal body, which will be perfect, peaceful, lovely, and in everything wholly subjected to the spirit. And to this degree no human effort can attain: it is in God's power to give it to whom He wills. Then the soul will easily reach that highest stage, because no lusts of the flesh will retard its eager entrance into the joy of its Lord, and no troubles will disturb its peace. May we not think that the holy martyrs enjoyed this grace, in some degree at least, before they laid down their victorious bodies? Surely that was immeasurable strength of love which enraptured their souls, enabling them to laugh at fleshly torments and to yield their lives gladly. But even though the frightful pain could not destroy their peace of mind, it must have impaired somewhat its perfection.

Selection 2: Meister Eckhart, *The Talks of Instruction*, Nos. 2, 4, 5, 7, 18

Meister Eckhart was born in Hochheim, Thuringia, Germany, in 1260 of a noble family. He joined the Dominicans at Erfurt at age 15. He studied in Paris and in 1302 received the degree of Magister, which explains his name "Meister" Eckhart. As the popularity and impact of his teachings grew, he was eventually accused of heresy, which he denied with the strong support of his followers. He appealed the charges to the pope but died (sometime between 1327 and 1329)

before the matter was brought to resolution. However, some of his more eso-
teric mystical teachings were condemned in the Bull In Agro Dominico *(1329)*
by Pope John XXII. As one of the great medieval Christian mystics, Eckhart
influenced other mystics who were to follow, beginning with his student, John
Tauler, who in turn made his impress on the German Theology, *an anony-*
mous mystical treatise highly prized by Luther. In the excerpts that follow, we see
in Eckhart's approach to ethics what we might today refer to as "virtue ethics,"
in which the emphasis is upon the character of the person and the virtues that
give it expression. Eckhart is concerned with the "being" from which flows the
"doing." This correlates nicely with his view that contemplation and good works
go together; the love born of contemplation comes to fruition in action.

The strongest prayer, one well-nigh almighty in what it can effect, and the most exalted work a man can do proceed from a pure heart. The more pure it is, the more powerful, and the more exalted, useful, laudable and perfect is its prayer and work. A pure heart is capable of anything.

What is a pure heart?

A pure heart is one that is unencumbered, unworried, uncommitted, and which does not want its own way about anything but which, rather, is submerged in the loving will of God, having denied self. Let a job be ever so inconsiderable, it will be raised in effectiveness and dimension by a pure heart.

We ought so to pray that every member and faculty, eyes, ears, mouth, heart, and the senses shall be directed to this end and never to cease prayer until we attain unity with him to whom our prayers and attention are directed, namely, God.

*   *   *

Know that no man in this life ever gave up so much that he could not find something else to let go. Few people, knowing what this means, can stand it long, [and yet] it is an honest requital, a just exchange. To the extent that you eliminate self from your activities, God comes into them—but not more and no less. Begin with that, and let it cost you your uttermost. In this way, and no other, is true peace to be found.

People ought not to consider so much what they are to do as what they are; let them but be good and their ways and deeds will shine brightly. If you are just, your actions will be just too. Do not think that saintliness comes from occupation; it depends rather on what one is. The kind of work we do does not make us holy but we may make it holy. However "sacred" a calling may be, as it is a calling, it has no power to sanctify; but rather as we are and have the divine being within, we bless each task we do, be it eating, or sleeping, or watching, or any other. Whatever they do, who have not much of [God's] nature, they work in vain.

This take care that your emphasis is laid on being good and not on the number of kind of thing to be done. Emphasize rather the fundamentals on which your work depends.

*   *   *

This is the basis on which human nature and spirit are wholly good, and from which our human actions receive their worth; a mind completely devoted to God. Direct your study to this end, that God shall be great in you, so that in all your comings and goings your zeal and fervor are toward him. In fact, the more you do so, the better your behavior will be, whatever your work. Hold fast to God and he will add every good thing. Seek God and you shall find him and all good with him. Indeed, with such an attitude, you might step on a stone and it would be a more pious act than to receive the body of our Lord, thinking of yourself, and it would distract your soul far less. To the man who cleaves to God, God cleaves and adds virtue. Thus, what you have sought before, now seeks you; what once you pursued, now pursues you; what once you fled, now flees you. Everything come to him who truly comes to God, bringing all divinity with it, while all that is strange and alien flies away.

*   *   *

There are many people who are not hindered by the things they handle, since those things leave no lasting impression on their minds. It is a stage easily reached if one desires to reach it, for no creature may find a place in a heart full of God. Still we should not be satisfied, for we shall profit by assuming that things are as we are, that they are what we see and hear, however strange and unfamiliar. Then and not until then shall we be on the right road—a road to which there is no end—on which one may grow without stopping, profiting more and more by making true progress.

In all his work, and on every occasion, a man should make clear use of his reason and have a conscious insight into himself and his spirituality and distinguish God to the highest possible degree in everything. One should be, as our Lord said, "Like people always on the watch, expecting their Lord." Expectant people are watchful, always looking for him they expect, always ready to find him in whatever comes along; however strange it may be, they always think he might be in it. This is what awareness of the Lord is to be like and it requires diligence that taxes a man's senses and powers to the utmost, if he is to achieve it and to take God evenly in all things—if he is to find God as much in one thing as in another.

In this regard, one kind of work does indeed differ from another but if one takes the same attitude toward each of his various occupations, then they will be all alike to him. Thus being on the right track and God meaning this to him, he will shine, as clear in worldly things as heavenly. To be sure, one must not of himself behave intemperately or as being worldly, but whatever happens to him from without, whatever he sees or hears, let him refer it to God. The man to whom God is ever present, and who controls and uses his mind to the highest degree—that man alone knows what peace is and he has the Kingdom of Heaven within him.

To be right, a person must do one of two things: either he must learn to have God in his work and hold fast to him there, or he must give up his work altogether. Since, however, man cannot live without activities that are both human and various, we must learn to keep God in everything we do, and whatever the job or place, keep on with him, letting nothing stand in our way. Therefore, when the beginner has to do with other people, let him first commit himself strongly to God and establish God firmly in his own heart, uniting his senses and thought, his will and powers with God, so that nothing else can enter his mind.

*　　*　　*

You shall not be concerned about the style of your food and clothing, thus laying too much stress on them, but rather accustom your heart and mind to be exalted above such things, so that nothing may move you to pleasure or to love except God alone. Let your thought be above all else.

Why?

Because only a feeble spirit could be moved by the garments of appearance; the inner man should govern the outer, and only this will do for you. But if it happens that you are well off, in your heart be tranquil about it—if you can be just as glad and willing for the opposite condition. So let it be with food, friends, kindred, or anything else that God gives or takes away.

So I hold this to be best, that a man should give himself over to God and let God throw on him what he will, offenses, work, or suffering, and that then he takes them gladly and thankfully, allowing God to put such things upon him even if he does not choose them for himself. To learn from God gladly in all things, and to follow after him only, is to be on the right track. In this frame of mind, a man may enjoy his honor or comfort—if he is just as glad to take hardship and disgrace when they come along. Thus, they may eat with perfect right and good conscience who are as ready and glad to fast.

Probably this is the reason why God spares his friends so many and such great wounds—which his incomparable honor would not otherwise permit: many and great are the blessings to be found in suffering. And while it would not suit God, nor would he wish to withhold any good thing, yet sometimes he does withhold these things, being content with his just good will; and again, he skips no degree of suffering because of the benefits inherent in it. Therefore, you should be content as long as God is, and inwardly so responsive to his will as not to be concerned with ways and works. Avoid especially any singularity in clothes, food, or speech, such as the use of high-flown language, for example, or eccentric mannerisms, which help not at all.

Still, you should know that not all singularity is forbidden. On many occasions, among many people, you will have to be singular. There are times when distinctive people cannot avoid standing out in many ways, for spiritually a man must conform to out Lord Jesus Christ in all things so that men may see his divine form, the reflection of him at work. In all you do, keep in yourself as perfect a likeness of him as possible. You are to sow and he is to reap. Work devotedly, with whole-hearted conviction, and thus train your mind and heart so that you may represent him at all time.

Selection 3: Catherine of Siena, *The Dialogue* or *A Treatise of Divine Providence*

Catherine of Siena was born in 3147 and died in Rome in 1380. A renowned mystic, a member of a Dominican order who experienced a spiritual marriage to Christ was at the same time very much involved in the concerns of the world. Traveling about the country with a group of followers, she was deeply involved in service to the poor and the sick. She was active in peacemaking among the

republics and principalities of Italy and in reforms of the church. She was instru-
mental in getting the pope to return to Rome from Avignon. In this excerpt
from The Dialogue *God speaks to the human soul (Catherine herself). Love*
we learn is the foundation of all virtues and the love of God is completed in the
love of neighbor whereas self-love is destructive of charity. Once again, as in the
previous selection from Meister Eckhart, we have an emphasis on the ethics of
love's character and virtues, which was certainly foundational for Catherine's
own active life of service in the world.

How virtues are accomplished by means of our neighbor, and how it is that virtues differ to such an extent in creatures.

"I have told you how all sins are accomplished by means of your neighbor, through the principles which I exposed to you, that is, because men are deprived of the affection of love, which gives light to every virtue. In the same way self-love, which destroys charity and affection towards the neighbor, is the principle and foundation of every evil. All scandals, hatred, cruelty, and every sort of trouble proceed from this perverse root of self-love, which has poisoned the entire world, and weakened the mystical body of the Holy Church, and the universal body of the believers in the Christian religion; and, therefore, I said to you, that it was in the neighbor, that is to say in the love of him, that all virtues were founded; and, truly indeed did I say to you, that charity gives life to all the virtues, because no virtue can be obtained without charity, which is the pure love of Me.

"Wherefore, when the soul knows herself, as we have said above, she finds humility and hatred of her own sensual passion, for she learns the perverse law, which is bound up in her members, and which ever fights against the spirit. And, therefore, arising with hatred of her own sensuality, crushing it under the heel of reason, with great earnestness, she discovers in herself the bounty of My goodness, through the many benefits which she has received from Me, all of which she considers again in herself. She attributes to Me, through humility, the knowledge which she has obtained of herself, knowing that, by My grace, I have drawn her out of darkness and lifted her up into the light of true knowledge. When she has recognized My goodness, she loves it without any medium, and yet at the same time with a medium, that is to say, without the medium of herself or of any advantage accruing to herself, and with the medium of virtue, which she has conceived through love of Me, because she sees that, in no other way, can she become grateful and acceptable to Me, but by conceiving, hatred of sin and love of virtue; and, when she has thus conceived by the affection of love, she immediately is delivered of fruit for her neighbor, because, in no other way, can she act out the truth she has conceived in herself, but, loving Me in truth, in the same truth she serves her neighbor.

"And it cannot be otherwise, because love of Me and of her neighbor are one and the same thing, and, so far as the soul loves Me, she loves her neighbor, because love towards him issues from Me. This is the means which I have given you, that you may exercise and prove your virtue therewith; because, inasmuch as you can do Me no profit, you should do it to your neighbor. This proves that you possess Me by grace in your soul, producing much fruit for your neighbor and making prayers to Me, seeking with sweet and amorous desire My honor and the salvation of souls. The soul, enamored of My truth, never ceases to serve the whole world in general, and more or less in a particular case according to the disposition of the recipient and the ardent desire of the donor, as I have shown above, when I declared to you that the endurance of suffering alone, without desire, was not sufficient to punish a fault.

"When she has discovered the advantage of this unitive love in Me, by means of which, she truly loves herself, extending her desire for the salvation of the whole world, thus coming to the aid of its neediness, she strives, inasmuch as she has done good to herself by the conception of virtue, from which she has drawn the life of grace, to fix her eye on the needs of her neighbor in particular. Wherefore, when she has discovered, through the affection of love, the state of all rational creatures in general, she helps those who are at hand, according to the various graces which I have entrusted to her to administer; one she helps with doctrine, that is, with words, giving sincere counsel without any respect of persons, another with the example of a good life, and this indeed all give to their neighbor, the edification of a holy and honorable life. These are the virtues, and many others, too many to enumerate, which are brought forth in the love of the neighbor; but, although I have given them in such a different way, that is to say not all to one, but to one, one virtue, and to another, another, it so happens that it is impossible to have one, without having them all, because all the virtues are bound together. Wherefore, learn, that, in many cases I give one virtue, to be as it were the chief of the others, that is to say, to one I will give principally love, to another justice, to another humility, to one a lively faith, to another prudence or temperance, or patience, to another fortitude. These, and many other virtues, I place, indifferently, in the souls of many creatures; it happens, therefore, that the particular one so placed in the soul becomes the principal object of its virtue; the soul disposing herself, for her chief conversation, to this rather than to other virtues, and, by the effect of this virtue, the soul draws to herself all the other virtues, which, as has been said, are all bound together in the affection of love; and so with many gifts and graces of virtue, and not only in the case of spiritual things but also of temporal. I use the word temporal for the things necessary to the physical life of man; all these I have given indifferently, and I have not placed them all in one soul, in order that man should, perforce, have material for love of his fellow. I could easily have created men possessed of all that they should need both for body and soul, but I wish that one should have need of the other, and that they should be My ministers to administer the graces and the gifts that they have received from Me. Whether man will or no, he cannot help making an act of love. It is true, however, that that act, unless made through love of Me, profits him nothing so far as grace is concerned. See then, that I have made men My ministers, and placed them in diverse stations and various ranks, in order that they may make use of the virtue of love.

"Wherefore, I show you that in My house are many mansions, and that I wish for no other thing than love, for in the love of Me is fulfilled and completed the love of the neighbor, and the law observed. For he, only, can be of use in his state of life, who is bound to Me with this love."

Thomas Aquinas is the most outstanding example of medieval scholastic theology. His thought has been a dominant force in Roman Catholicism to this day. As late as 1879 he was declared by Pope Leo XIII in his encyclical **Aeterni Patris** the standard theologian of that Christian communion. Indeed, Aquinas's theology and ethics have been formative for Catholic social teaching on economic and political matters as well as sexual ethics.

Born in 1225 in the castle of Roccasecca in Italy, the son of Count Landolf (of Aquin), Thomas spent his life in monasteries and universities studying and teaching. From 1259 to 1268 he was lecturer at the papal curia in Italy. He later taught in Paris and Naples. He died in 1274 on his way to the council of Lyon. Thomas's major contribution is the utilization of the philosophy of Aristotle for a systematic and comprehensive articulation of the Christian faith. In this effort he also dealt creatively with social ethics not only as a theologian but also as a commentator on Aristotle's Nicomachean Ethics. At the heart of his grand synthesis between Aristotelian philosophy and Christian theology is the continuity of nature and grace and grace as the transformer of nature. In an era when the teachings of the Christian faith provided the foundations of the culture, Thomas had no need to defend the faith against competing philosophies. Therefore, he could confidently appropriate the thought of Aristotle and just as confidently provide an ethical system that would be taken as normative for his society.

Selection 1: *Summa Theologica*, II/1, Question 90, Article 2

The strong role of reason, humanity's loftiest gift, in Aquinas's discussions of law and ethics and the emphasis on the common good as the end of law are signature features of his ethics. Commitment to the common good and the need for individual aspirations to find their validity in that context has perdured through the long history of Catholic Social teaching.

Article 2: Whether the law is always something directed to the common good?

Objection 1: It would seem that the law is not always directed to the common good as to its end. For it belongs to law to command and to forbid. But commands are directed to certain individual goods. Therefore the end of the law is not always the common good.

Objection 2: Further, the law directs man in his actions. But human actions are concerned with particular matters. Therefore the law is directed to some particular good.

Objection 3: Further, Isidore says (Etym. v, 3): "If the law is based on reason, whatever is based on reason will be a law." But reason is the foundation not only of what is ordained to the common good, but also of that which is directed private good. Therefore the law is not only directed to the good of all, but also to the private good of an individual.

On the contrary, Isidore says (Etym. v, 21) that "laws are enacted for no private profit, but for the common benefit of the citizens."

I answer that, As stated above (A[1]), the law belongs to that which is a principle of human acts, because it is their rule and measure. Now as reason is a principle of human acts, so in reason itself there is something which is the principle in respect of all the rest: wherefore to this principle chiefly and mainly law must needs be referred. Now the first principle in practical matters, which are the object of the practical reason, is the last end: and the last end of human life is bliss or happiness, as stated above (Q[2], A[7]; Q[3], A[1]). Consequently the law must needs regard principally the relationship to happiness. Moreover, since every part is ordained to the whole, as imperfect to perfect; and since one man is a part of the perfect community, the law must needs regard properly the relationship to universal happiness. Wherefore the Philosopher, in the above definition of legal matters mentions both happiness and the body politic: for he says (Ethic. v, 1) that we call those legal matters "just, which are adapted to produce and preserve happiness and its parts for the body politic": since the state is a perfect community, as he says in Polit. i, 1.

Now in every genus, that which belongs to it chiefly is the principle of the others, and the others belong to that genus in subordination to that thing: thus fire, which is chief among hot things, is the cause of heat in mixed bodies, and these are said to be hot in so far as they have a share of fire. Consequently, since the law is chiefly ordained to the common good, any other precept in regard to some individual work, must needs be devoid of the nature of a law, save in so far as it regards the common good. Therefore every law is ordained to the common good.

Reply to Objection 1: A command denotes an application of a law to matters regulated by the law. Now the order to the common good, at which the law aims, is applicable to particular ends. And in this way commands are given even concerning particular matters.

Reply to Objection 2: Actions are indeed concerned with particular matters: but those particular matters are referable to the common good, not as to a common genus or species, but as to a common final cause, according as the common good is said to be the common end.

Reply to Objection 3: Just as nothing stands firm with regard to the speculative reason except that which is traced back to the first indemonstrable principles, so nothing stands firm with regard to the practical reason, unless it be directed to the last end which is the common good: and whatever stands to reason in this sense, has the nature of a law.

Selection 2: *Summa Theologica*, II/1, Question 91, Articles 1–4

In the articles that follow, Aquinas discusses the different forms of law. Of special interest is the natural law since this construct has been foundational for the ethics of the Catholic tradition including matters of social justice, sexuality, and medical practice. Here in the second article and in the selection from Question 94, we see clearly the notion that the natural law is the imprint of eternal law upon human reason. In consequence, there is a human inclination toward the good. This idea of natural law provides the justification for a broad ethical appeal beyond the precincts of the church, including the enactment of human laws consistent with natural law, grounded as it is in eternal law. It is the rather optimistic appraisal of human reason and its moral inclinations that has historically drawn the criticism of the theologians and ethicists of the churches of the Reformation who are not as sanguine about the capacities of sinful humanity. Yet, as we see in Aquinas's argument for the necessity of divine law optimism—if we can call it that—is tempered somewhat.

Article 1: Whether there is an eternal law?

Objection 1: It would seem that there is no eternal law. Because every law is imposed on someone. But there was not someone from eternity on whom a law could be imposed: since God alone was from eternity. Therefore no law is eternal.

Objection 2: Further, promulgation is essential to law. But promulgation could not be from eternity: because there was no one to whom it could be promulgated from eternity. Therefore no law can be eternal.

Objection 3: Further, a law implies order to an end. But nothing ordained to an end is eternal: for the last end alone is eternal. Therefore no law is eternal.

On the contrary, Augustine says (De Lib. Arb. i, 6): "That Law which is the Supreme Reason cannot be understood to be otherwise than unchangeable and eternal."

I answer that, As stated above (Q[90], A[1], ad 2; AA[3],4), a law is nothing else but a dictate of practical reason emanating from the ruler who governs a perfect community. Now it is evident, granted that the world is ruled by Divine Providence, as was stated in the FP, Q[22], AA[1],2, that the whole community of the universe is governed by Divine Reason. Wherefore the very Idea of the government of things in God the Ruler of the universe, has the nature of a law. And since the Divine Reason's conception of things is not subject to time but is eternal, according to Prov. 8:23, therefore it is that this kind of law must be called eternal.

Article 2: Whether there is in us a natural law?

Objection 1: It would seem that there is no natural law in us. Because man is governed sufficiently by the eternal law: for Augustine says (De Lib. Arb. i) that "the eternal law is that by which it is right that all things should be most orderly." But nature does not abound in superfluities as neither does she fail in necessaries. Therefore no law is natural to man.

Objection 2: Further, by the law man is directed, in his acts, to the end, as stated above (Q[90], A[2]). But the directing of human acts to their end is not a function of nature, as is the case in irrational creatures, which act for an end solely by their natural appetite; whereas man acts for an end by his reason and will. Therefore no law is natural to man.

Objection 3: Further, the more a man is free, the less is he under the law. But man is freer than all the animals, on account of his free-will, with which he is endowed above all other animals. Since therefore other animals are not subject to a natural law, neither is man subject to a natural law.

On the contrary, A gloss on Rom. 2:14: "When the Gentiles, who have not the law, do by nature those things that are of the law," comments as follows: "Although they have no written law, yet they have the natural law, whereby each one knows, and is conscious of, what is good and what is evil."

I answer that, As stated above (Q[90], A[1], ad 1), law, being a rule and measure, can be in a person in two ways: in one way, as in him that rules and measures; in another way, as in that which is ruled and measured, since a thing is ruled and measured, in so far as it partakes of the rule or measure. Wherefore, since all things subject to Divine providence are ruled and measured by the eternal law, as was stated above (A[1]); it is evident that all things partake somewhat of the eternal law, in so far as, namely, from its being imprinted on them, they derive their respective inclinations to their proper acts and ends. Now among all others, the rational creature is subject to Divine providence in the most excellent way, in so far as it partakes of a share of providence, by being provident both for itself and for others. Wherefore it has a share of the Eternal Reason, whereby it has a natural inclination to its proper act and end: and this participation of the eternal law in the rational creature is called the natural law. Hence the Psalmist after saying (Ps. 4:6): "Offer up the sacrifice of justice," as though someone asked what the works of justice are, adds: "Many say, Who showeth us good things?" in answer to which question he says: "The light of Thy countenance, O Lord, is signed upon us": thus implying that the light of natural reason, whereby we discern what is good and what is evil, which is the function of the natural law, is nothing else than an imprint on us of the Divine light. It is therefore evident that the natural law is nothing else than the rational creature's participation of the eternal law.

Reply to Objection 1: This argument would hold, if the natural law were something different from the eternal law: whereas it is nothing but a participation thereof, as stated above.

Reply to Objection 2: Every act of reason and will in us is based on that which is according to nature, as stated above (Q[10], A[1]): for every act of reasoning is based on principles that are known naturally, and every act of appetite in respect of the means is derived from the natural appetite in respect of the last end. Accordingly the first direction of our acts to their end must needs be in virtue of the natural law.

Reply to Objection 3: Even irrational animals partake in their own way of the Eternal Reason, just as the rational creature does. But because the rational creature partakes thereof in an intellectual and rational manner, therefore the participation of the eternal law in the rational creature is properly called a law, since a law is something pertaining to reason, as stated above (Q[90], A[1]). Irrational creatures, however, do not partake thereof in a rational manner, wherefore there is no participation of the eternal law in them, except by way of similitude.

Article 3: Whether there is a human law?

Objection 1: It would seem that there is not a human law. For the natural law is a participation of the eternal law, as stated above (A[2]). Now through the eternal law "all things are most orderly," as Augustine states (De Lib. Arb. i, 6). Therefore the natural law suffices for the ordering of all human affairs. Consequently there is no need for a human law.

Objection 2: Further, a law bears the character of a measure, as stated above (Q[90], A[1]). But human reason is not a measure of things, but vice versa, as stated in Metaph. x, text. 5. Therefore no law can emanate from human reason.

Objection 3: Further, a measure should be most certain, as stated in Metaph. x, text. 3. But the dictates of human reason in matters of conduct are uncertain, according to Wis. 9:14: "The thoughts of mortal men are fearful, and our counsels uncertain." Therefore no law can emanate from human reason.

On the contrary, Augustine (De Lib. Arb. i, 6) distinguishes two kinds of law, the one eternal, the other temporal, which he calls human.

I answer that, As stated above (Q[90], A[1], ad 2), a law is a dictate of the practical reason. Now it is to be observed that the same procedure takes place in the practical and in the speculative reason: for each proceeds from principles to conclusions, as stated above (De Lib. Arb. i, 6). Accordingly we conclude that just as, in the speculative reason, from naturally known indemonstrable principles, we draw the conclusions of the various sciences, the knowledge of which is not imparted to us by nature, but acquired by the efforts of reason, so too it is from the precepts of the natural law, as from general and indemonstrable principles, that the human reason needs to proceed to the more particular determination of certain matters. These particular determinations, devised by human reason, are called human laws, provided the other essential conditions of law be observed, as stated above (Q[90], AA[2],3,4). Wherefore Tully says in his Rhetoric (De Invent. Rhet. ii) that "justice has its source in nature; thence certain things came into custom by reason of their utility; afterwards these things which emanated from nature and were approved by custom, were sanctioned by fear and reverence for the law."

Reply to Objection 1: The human reason cannot have a full participation of the dictate of the Divine Reason, but according to its own mode, and imperfectly. Consequently, as on the part of the speculative reason, by a natural participation of Divine Wisdom, there is in us the knowledge of certain general principles, but not proper knowledge of each single truth, such as that contained in the Divine Wisdom; so too, on the part of the practical reason, man has a natural participation of the eternal law, according to certain general principles, but not as regards the particular determinations of individual cases, which are, however, contained in the eternal law. Hence the need for human reason to proceed further to sanction them by law.

Reply to Objection 2: Human reason is not, of itself, the rule of things: but the principles impressed on it by nature, are general rules and measures of all things relating to human conduct, whereof the natural reason is the rule and measure, although it is not the measure of things that are from nature.

Reply to Objection 3: The practical reason is concerned with practical matters, which are singular and contingent: but not with necessary things, with which the speculative reason is concerned. Wherefore human laws cannot have that inerrancy that belongs to the demonstrated conclusions of sciences. Nor is it necessary for every measure to be altogether unerring and certain, but according as it is possible in its own particular genus.

Whether there was any need for a Divine law?

Objection 1: It would seem that there was no need for a Divine law. Because, as stated above (A[2]), the natural law is a participation in us of the eternal law. But the eternal law is a Divine law, as stated above (A[1]). Therefore there was no need for a Divine law in addition to the natural law, and human laws derived therefrom.

Objection 2: Further, it is written (Ecclus. 15:14) that "God left man in the hand of his own counsel." Now counsel is an act of reason, as stated above (Q[14], A[1]).

Therefore man was left to the direction of his reason. But a dictate of human reason is a human law as stated above (A[3]). Therefore there is no need for man to be governed also by a Divine law.

Objection 3: Further, human nature is more self-sufficing than irrational creatures. But irrational creatures have no Divine law besides the natural inclination impressed on them. Much less, therefore, should the rational creature have a Divine law in addition to the natural law.

On the contrary, David prayed God to set His law before him, saying (Ps. 118:33): "Set before me for a law the way of Thy justifications, O Lord."

I answer that, Besides the natural and the human law it was necessary for the directing of human conduct to have a Divine law. And this for four reasons. First, because it is by law that man is directed how to perform his proper acts in view of his last end. And indeed if man were ordained to no other end than that which is proportionate to his natural faculty, there would be no need for man to have any further direction of the part of his reason, besides the natural law and human law which is derived from it. But since man is ordained to an end of eternal happiness which is inproportionate to man's natural faculty, as stated above (Q[5], A[5]), therefore it was necessary that, besides the natural and the human law, man should be directed to his end by a law given by God.

Secondly, because, on account of the uncertainty of human judgment, especially on contingent and particular matters, different people form different judgments on human acts; whence also different and contrary laws result. In order, therefore, that man may know without any doubt what he ought to do and what he ought to avoid, it was necessary for man to be directed in his proper acts by a law given by God, for it is certain that such a law cannot err.

Thirdly, because man can make laws in those matters of which he is competent to judge. But man is not competent to judge of interior movements, that are hidden, but only of exterior acts which appear: and yet for the perfection of virtue it is necessary for man to conduct himself aright in both kinds of acts. Consequently human law could not sufficiently curb and direct interior acts; and it was necessary for this purpose that a Divine law should supervene.

Fourthly, because, as Augustine says (De Lib. Arb. i, 5,6), human law cannot punish or forbid all evil deeds: since while aiming at doing away with all evils, it would do away with many good things, and would hinder the advance of the common good, which is necessary for human intercourse. In order, therefore, that no evil might remain unforbidden and unpunished, it was necessary for the Divine law to supervene, whereby all sins are forbidden.

And these four causes are touched upon in Ps. 118:8, where it is said: "The law of the Lord is unspotted," i.e. allowing no foulness of sin; "converting souls," because it directs not only exterior, but also interior acts; "the testimony of the Lord is faithful," because of the certainty of what is true and right; "giving wisdom to little ones," by directing man to an end supernatural and Divine.

Reply to Objection 1: By the natural law the eternal law is participated proportionately to the capacity of human nature. But to his supernatural end man needs to be directed in a yet higher way. Hence the additional law given by God, whereby man shares more perfectly in the eternal law.

Reply to Objection 2: Counsel is a kind of inquiry: hence it must proceed from some principles. Nor is it enough for it to proceed from principles imparted by nature, which are the precepts of the natural law, for the reasons given above: but there is need for certain additional principles, namely, the precepts of the Divine law.

Reply to Objection 3: Irrational creatures are not ordained to an end higher than that which is proportionate to their natural powers: consequently the comparison fails.

Article 4: Whether there is but one Divine law?

Objection 1: It would seem that there is but one Divine law. Because, where there is one king in one kingdom there is but one law. Now the whole of mankind is compared to God as to one king, according to Ps. 46:8: "God is the King of all the earth." Therefore there is but one Divine law.

Objection 2: Further, every law is directed to the end which the lawgiver intends for those for whom he makes the law. But God intends one and the same thing for all men; since according to 1 Tim. 2:4: "He will have all men to be saved, and to come to the knowledge of the truth." Therefore there is but one Divine *Objection 3:* Further, the Divine law seems to be more akin to the eternal law, which is one, than the natural law, according as the revelation of grace is of a higher order than natural knowledge. Therefore much more is the Divine law but one.

On the contrary, The Apostle says (Heb. 7:12): "The priesthood being translated, it is necessary that a translation also be made of the law." But the priesthood is twofold, as stated in the same passage, viz. the levitical priesthood, and the priesthood of Christ. Therefore the Divine law is twofold, namely the Old Law and the New Law.

I answer that, As stated in the FP, Q[30], A[3], distinction is the cause of number. Now things may be distinguished in two ways. First, as those things that are altogether specifically different, e.g. a horse and an ox. Secondly, as perfect and imperfect in the same species, e.g. a boy and a man: and in this way the Divine law is divided into Old and New. Hence the Apostle (Gal. 3:24,25) compares the state of man under the Old Law to that of a child "under a pedagogue"; but the state under the New Law, to that of a full grown man, who is "no longer under a pedagogue."

Now the perfection and imperfection of these two laws is to be taken in connection with the three conditions pertaining to law, as stated above. For, in the first place, it belongs to law to be directed to the common good as to its end, as stated above (Q[90], A[2]). This good may be twofold. It may be a sensible and earthly good; and to this, man was directly ordained by the Old Law: wherefore, at the very outset of the law, the people were invited to the earthly kingdom of the Chananaeans (Ex. 3:8, 17). Again it may be an intelligible and heavenly good: and to this, man is ordained by the New Law. Wherefore, at the very beginning of His preaching, Christ invited men to the kingdom of heaven, saying (Mat. 4:17): "Do penance, for the kingdom of heaven is at hand." Hence Augustine says (Contra Faust. iv) that "promises of temporal goods are contained in the Old Testament, for which reason it is called old; but the promise of eternal life belongs to the New Testament."

Secondly, it belongs to the law to direct human acts according to the order of righteousness (A[4]): wherein also the New Law surpasses the Old Law, since it directs our internal acts, according to Mat. 5:20: "Unless your justice abound more than that of the Scribes and Pharisees, you shall not enter into the kingdom of heaven." Hence the saying that "the Old Law restrains the hand, but the New Law controls the mind" (Sentent. iii, D, xl).

Thirdly, it belongs to the law to induce men to observe its commandments. This the Old Law did by the fear of punishment: but the New Law, by love, which is poured into our hearts by the grace of Christ, bestowed in the New Law, but foreshadowed in the Old. Hence Augustine says (Contra Adimant. Manich. discip. xvii) that "there is little difference [*The 'little difference' refers to the Latin words 'timor' and 'amor'—'fear' and 'love.'] between the Law and the Gospel—fear and love."

Reply to Objection 1: As the father of a family issues different commands to the children and to the adults, so also the one King, God, in His one kingdom, gave one law to men, while they were yet imperfect, and another more perfect law, when, by the preceding law, they had been led to a greater capacity for Divine things.

Reply to Objection 2: The salvation of man could not be achieved otherwise than through Christ, according to Acts 4:12: "There is no other name . . . given to men, whereby we must be saved." Consequently the law that brings all to salvation could not be given until after the coming of Christ. But before His coming it was necessary to give to the people, of whom Christ was to be born, a law containing certain rudiments of righteousness unto salvation, in order to prepare them to receive Him.

Reply to Objection 3: The natural law directs man by way of certain general precepts, common to both the perfect and the imperfect: wherefore it is one and the same for all. But the Divine law directs man also in certain particular matters, to which the perfect and imperfect do not stand in the same relation. Hence the necessity for the Divine law to be twofold, as already explained.

Selection 3: *Summa Theologica*, II/1, Question 94, Article 2

Whether the natural law contains several precepts, or only one?

Objection 1: It would seem that the natural law contains, not several precepts, but one only. For law is a kind of precept, as stated above (Q[92], A[2]). If therefore there were many precepts of the natural law, it would follow that there are also many natural laws.

Objection 2: Further, the natural law is consequent to human nature. But human nature, as a whole, is one; though, as to its parts, it is manifold. Therefore, either there is but one precept of the law of nature, on account of the unity of nature as a whole; or there are many, by reason of the number of parts of human nature. The result would be that even things relating to the inclination of the concupiscible faculty belong to the natural law.

Objection 3: Further, law is something pertaining to reason, as stated above (Q[90], A[1]). Now reason is but one in man. Therefore there is only one precept of the natural law.

On the contrary, The precepts of the natural law in man stand in relation to practical matters, as the first principles to matters of demonstration. But there are several first indemonstrable principles. Therefore there are also several precepts of the natural law.

I answer that, As stated above (Q[91], A[3]), the precepts of the natural law are to the practical reason, what the first principles of demonstrations are to the speculative reason; because both are self-evident principles. Now a thing is said to be self-evident in two ways: first, in itself; secondly, in relation to us. Any proposition is said to be self-evident in itself, if its predicate is contained in the notion of the subject: although, to one who knows not the definition of the subject, it happens that such a proposition is not self-evident. For instance, this proposition, "Man is a rational being," is, in its very nature, self-evident, since who says "man," says "a rational being": and yet to one who knows not what a man is, this proposition is not self-evident. Hence it is that, as Boethius says (De Hebdom.), certain axioms or propositions are universally self-evident to all; and such are those propositions whose terms are known to all, as, "Every whole is greater than its part," and, "Things equal to one and the same are equal to one another." But some propositions are self-evident only to the wise, who understand the meaning of the terms of such propositions: thus to one who understands that an angel is not a body, it is self-evident that an angel is not circumscriptively in a place: but this is not evident to the unlearned, for they cannot grasp it.

Now a certain order is to be found in those things that are apprehended universally. For that which, before aught else, falls under apprehension, is "being," the notion of which is included in all things whatsoever a man apprehends. Wherefore the first indemonstrable principle is that "the same thing cannot be affirmed and denied at the same time," which is based on the notion of "being" and "not-being": and on this principle all others are based, as is stated in Metaph. iv, text. 9. Now as "being" is the first thing that falls under the apprehension simply, so "good" is the first thing that falls under the apprehension of the practical reason, which is directed to action: since every agent acts for an end under the aspect of good. Consequently the first principle of practical reason is one founded on the notion of good, viz. that "good is that which all things seek after." Hence this is the first precept of law, that "good is to be done and pursued, and evil is to be avoided." All other precepts of the natural law are based upon this: so that whatever the practical reason naturally apprehends as man's good (or evil) belongs to the precepts of the natural law as something to be done or avoided.

Since, however, good has the nature of an end, and evil, the nature of a contrary, hence it is that all those things to which man has a natural inclination, are naturally apprehended by reason as being good, and consequently as objects of pursuit, and their contraries as evil, and objects of avoidance. Wherefore according to the order of natural inclinations, is the order of the precepts of the natural law. Because in man there is first of all an inclination to good in accordance with the nature which he has in common with all substances: inasmuch as every substance seeks the preservation of its own being, according to its nature: and by reason of this inclination, whatever is a means of preserving human life, and of warding off its obstacles, belongs to the natural law. Secondly, there is in man an inclination to things that pertain to him more specially, according to that nature which he has in common with other animals: and in virtue of this inclination, those things are said to belong to the natural law, "which nature has taught to all animals" [*Pandect. Just. I, tit. i], such as sexual intercourse, education of offspring and so forth. Thirdly, there is in man an inclination to good, according to the nature of his reason, which nature is proper to him: thus man has a natural inclination to know the truth about God, and to live in society: and in this respect, whatever pertains to this inclination belongs to the natural law; for instance, to shun ignorance, to avoid offending those among whom one has to live, and other such things regarding the above inclination.

Selection 4: *Summa Theologica*, II/2, Question 58, Articles 1, 11, 12

Aquinas identifies the four cardinal virtues (the preeminent moral virtues) as prudence, justice, temperance, and fortitude. In true Aristotelian fashion, these classical virtues characterize the good person. They are dispositions toward the good that work in cooperation with the demands of natural law. As without grace human beings can do some good in response to natural law, so to some degree the cardinal virtues may be approximated without grace (I/2, Q. 65, art.2). However, grace is necessary for a greater perfection of the virtues and a more perfect response to the natural law. Grace perfects nature in Thomas's system. Moreover, the theological virtues of faith, hope, and charity are the superadded gifts of grace that lead one to supernatural happiness (I/2, Q. 62, art. 1). The selections that follow concern justice since justice is given preeminence among the cardinal virtues because of its social reach and, for our purposes, because of its abiding relevance for Christian social teaching. Examined in sixty-five questions, it receives the most comment of all the virtues. Here too we have a brief case study of how Aquinas works in correlation with Aristotle's ethics.

Article 1: Whether justice is fittingly defined as being the perpetual and constant will to render to each one his right?

Objection 1: It would seem that lawyers have unfittingly defined justice as being "the perpetual and constant will to render to each one his right" [Digest. i, 1; De Just.

et Jure 10. For, according to the Philosopher (Ethic. v, 1), justice is a habit which makes a man "capable of doing what is just, and of being just in action and in intention." Now "will" denotes a power, or also an act. Therefore justice is unfittingly defined as being a will.

Objection 2: Further, rectitude of the will is not the will; else if the will were its own rectitude, it would follow that no will is unrighteous. Yet, according to Anselm (De Veritate xii), justice is rectitude. Therefore justice is not the will.

Objection 3: Further, no will is perpetual save God's. If therefore justice is a perpetual will, in God alone will there be justice.

Objection 4: Further, whatever is perpetual is constant, since it is unchangeable. Therefore it is needless in defining justice, to say that it is both "perpetual" and "constant."

Objection 5. Further, it belongs to the sovereign to give each one his right. Therefore, if justice gives each one his right, it follows that it is in none but the sovereign: which is absurd.

Objection 6. Further, Augustine says (De Moribus Eccl. xv) that "justice is love serving God alone." Therefore it does not render to each one his right.

I answer that, The aforesaid definition of justice is fitting if understood aright. For since every virtue is a habit that is the principle of a good act, a virtue must needs be defined by means of the good act bearing on the matter proper to that virtue. Now the proper matter of justice consists of those things that belong to our intercourse with other men, as shall be shown further on (2). Hence the act of justice in relation to its proper matter and object is indicated in the words, "Rendering to each one his right," since, as Isidore says (Etym. x), "a man is said to be just because he respects the rights [jus] of others."

Now in order that an act bearing upon any matter whatever be virtuous, it requires to be voluntary, stable, and firm, because the Philosopher says (Ethic. ii, 4) that in order for an act to be virtuous it needs first of all to be done "knowingly," secondly to be done "by choice," and "for a due end," thirdly to be done "immovably." Now the first of these is included in the second, since "what is done through ignorance is involuntary" (Ethic. iii, 1). Hence the definition of justice mentions first the "will," in order to show that the act of justice must be voluntary; and mention is made afterwards of its "constancy" and "perpetuity" in order to indicate the firmness of the act.

Accordingly, this is a complete definition of justice; save that the act is mentioned instead of the habit, which takes its species from that act, because habit implies relation to act. And if anyone would reduce it to the proper form of a definition, he might say that "justice is a habit whereby a man renders to each one his due by a constant and perpetual will": and this is about the same definition as that given by the Philosopher (Ethic. v, 5) who says that "justice is a habit whereby a man is said to be capable of doing just actions in accordance with his choice."

Article 11: Whether the act of justice is to render to each one his own?

Objection 1: It would seem that the act of justice is not to render to each one his own. For Augustine (De Trin. xiv, 9) ascribes to justice the act of succoring the needy. Now in succoring the needy we give them what is not theirs but ours. Therefore the act of justice does not consist in rendering to each one his own.

Objection 2: Further, Tully says (De Offic. i, 7) that "beneficence which we may call kindness or liberality, belongs to justice." Now it pertains to liberality to give to another of one's own, not of what is his. Therefore the act of justice does not consist in rendering to each one his own.

Objection 3: Further, it belongs to justice not only to distribute things duly, but also to repress injurious actions, such as murder, adultery and so forth. But the rendering to each one of what is his seems to belong solely to the distribution of things. Therefore the act of justice is not sufficiently described by saying that it consists in rendering to each one his own. *On the contrary,* Ambrose says (De Offic. i, 24): "It is justice that renders to each one what is his, and claims not another's property; it disregards its own profit in order to preserve the common equity."

I answer that, As stated above (A8,10), the matter of justice is an external operation in so far as either it or the thing we use by it is made proportionate to some other person to whom we are related by justice. Now each man's own is that which is due to him according to equality of proportion. Therefore the proper act of justice is nothing else than to render to each one his own.

Article 12: Whether justice stands foremost among all moral virtues?

Objection 1: It would seem that justice does not stand foremost among all the moral virtues. Because it belongs to justice to render to each one what is his, whereas it belongs to liberality to give of one's own, and this is more virtuous. Therefore liberality is a greater virtue than justice.

Objection 2: Further, nothing is adorned by a less excellent thing than itself. Now magnanimity is the ornament both of justice and of all the virtues, according to Ethic. iv, 3. Therefore magnanimity is more excellent than justice.

Objection 3: Further, virtue is about that which is "difficult" and "good," as stated in Ethic. ii, 3. But fortitude is about more difficult things than justice is, since it is about dangers of death, according to Ethic. iii, 6. Therefore fortitude is more excellent than justice.

On the contrary, Tully says (De Offic. i, 7): "Justice is the most resplendent of the virtues, and gives its name to a good man."

I answer that, If we speak of legal justice, it is evident that it stands foremost among all the moral virtues, for as much as the common good transcends the individual good of one person. On this sense the Philosopher declares (Ethic. v, 1) that "the most excellent of the virtues would seem to be justice, and more glorious than either the evening or the morning star." But, even if we speak of particular justice, it excels the other moral virtues for two reasons. The first reason may be taken from the subject, because justice is in the more excellent part of the soul, viz. the rational appetite or will, whereas the other moral virtues are in the sensitive appetite, whereunto appertain the passions which are the matter of the other moral virtues. The second reason is taken from the object, because the other virtues are commendable in respect of the sole good of the virtuous person himself, whereas justice is praiseworthy in respect of the virtuous person being well disposed towards another, so that justice is somewhat the good of another person, as stated in Ethic. v, 1. Hence the Philosopher says (Rhet. i, 9): "The greatest virtues must needs be those which are most profitable to other persons, because virtue is a faculty of doing good to others. For this reason the greatest honors are accorded the brave and the just, since bravery is useful to others in warfare, and justice is useful to others both in warfare and in time of peace."

Selection 5: *Summa Theologica*, II/2, Question 60, Articles 5-6

> *Aquinas advocates judgment according to written law, which, in addition to being grounded in the public will, is normed by natural right and natural law. Included here are the responses to the objections in each article because they include the historically important principles that a law that does not conform to natural law is unjust and not binding and that the spiritual authority can intervene in secular judgments for the secular is subject to the spiritual. The former principle has been important for Christian conscience in general and the latter particularly for Catholic tradition, enduring in theory even in the midst of modernity's separation of church and state.*

Article 5: Whether we should always judge according to the written law?

Objection 1: It would seem that we ought not always to judge according to the written law. For we ought always to avoid judging unjustly. But written laws sometimes contain injustice, according to Isaiah 10:1, "Woe to them that make wicked laws, and when they write, write injustice." Therefore we ought not always to judge according to the written law.

Objection 2: Further, judgment has to be formed about individual happenings.
But no written law can cover each and every individual happening, as the Philosopher declares (Ethic. v, 10). Therefore it seems that we are not always bound to judge according to the written law.

Objection 3: Further, a law is written in order that the lawgiver's intention may be made clear. But it happens sometimes that even if the lawgiver himself were present he would judge otherwise. Therefore we ought not always to judge according to the written law.

On the contrary, Augustine says (De Vera Relig. xxxi): "In these earthly laws, though men judge about them when they are making them, when once they are established and passed, the judges may judge no longer of them, but according to them."

I answer that, As stated above (Article 1), judgment is nothing else but a decision or determination of what is just. Now a thing becomes just in two ways: first by the very nature of the case, and this is called "natural right," secondly by some agreement between men, and this is called "positive right," as stated above (Question 57, Article 2). Now laws are written for the purpose of manifesting both these rights, but in different ways. For the written law does indeed contain natural right, but it does not establish it, for the latter derives its force, not from the law but from nature: whereas the written law both contains positive right, and establishes it by giving it force of authority.

Hence it is necessary to judge according to the written law, else judgment would fall short either of the natural or of the positive right.

Reply to *Objection 1:* Just as the written law does not give force to the natural right, so neither can it diminish or annul its force, because neither can man's will change nature. Hence if the written law contains anything contrary to the natural right, it is unjust and has no binding force. For positive right has no place except where "it matters not," according to the natural right, "whether a thing be done in one way or in another"; as stated above (57, 2, ad 2). Wherefore such documents are to be called, not laws, but rather corruptions of law, as stated above (I-II, 95, 2): and consequently judgment should not be delivered according to them.

Reply to Objection 2: Even as unjust laws by their very nature are, either always or for the most part, contrary to the natural right, so too laws that are rightly established, fail in some cases, when if they were observed they would be contrary to the natural right. Wherefore in such cases judgment should be delivered, not according to the letter of the law, but according to equity which the lawgiver has in view. Hence the jurist says [Digest. i, 3; De leg. senatusque consult. 25]: "By no reason of law, or favor of equity, is it allowable for us to interpret harshly, and render burdensome, those useful measures which have been enacted for the welfare of man." On such cases even the lawgiver himself would decide otherwise; and if he had foreseen the case, he might have provided for it by law.

This suffices for the Reply to the Third Objection.

Article 6: Whether judgment is rendered perverse by being usurped?

Objection 1: It would seem that judgment is not rendered perverse by being usurped. For justice is rectitude in matters of action. Now truth is not impaired, no matter who tells it, but it may suffer from the person who ought to accept it. Therefore again justice loses nothing, no matter who declares what is just, and this is what is meant by judgment.

Objection 2: Further, it belongs to judgment to punish sins. Now it is related to the praise of some that they punished sins without having authority over those whom they punished; such as Moses in slaying the Egyptian (Exodus 2:12), and Phinees the son of Eleazar in slaying Zambri the son of Salu (Numbers 25:7-14), and "it was reputed to him unto justice" (Psalm 105:31). Therefore usurpation of judgment pertains not to injustice.

Objection 3: Further, spiritual power is distinct from temporal. Now prelates having spiritual power sometimes interfere in matters concerning the secular power. Therefore usurped judgment is not unlawful.

Objection 4: Further, even as the judge requires authority in order to judge aright, so also does he need justice and knowledge, as shown above (1, ad 1,3; 2). But a judgment is not described as unjust, if he who judges lacks the habit of justice or the knowledge of the law. Neither therefore is it always unjust to judge by usurpation, i.e. without authority.

On the contrary, It is written (Romans 14:4): "Who art thou that judgest another man's servant?"

I answer that, Since judgment should be pronounced according to the written law, as stated above (Article 5), he that pronounces judgment, interprets, in a way, the letter of the law, by applying it to some particular case. Now since it belongs to the same authority to interpret and to make a law, just as a law cannot be made save by public authority, so neither can a judgment be pronounced except by public authority, which extends over those who are subject to the community. Wherefore even as it would be unjust for one man to force another to observe a law that was not approved by public authority, so too it is unjust, if a man compels another to submit to a judgment that is pronounced by other than the public authority.

Reply to Objection 1: When the truth is declared there is no obligation to accept it, and each one is free to receive it or not, as he wishes. On the other hand judgment implies an obligation, wherefore it is unjust for anyone to be judged by one who has no public authority.

Reply to Objection 2: Moses seems to have slain the Egyptian by authority received as it were, by divine inspiration; this seems to follow from Acts 7:24-25, where it is said that "striking the Egyptian . . . he thought that his brethren understood that God by his hand would save Israel [Vulgate: 'them']." Or it may be replied that Moses slew the Egyptian in order to defend the man who was unjustly attacked, without himself exceeding the limits of a blameless defence. Wherefore Ambrose says (De Offic. i, 36) that "whoever does not ward off a blow from a fellow man when he can, is as much in fault as the striker"; and he quotes the example of Moses. Again we may reply with Augustine (QQ. Exod. qu. 2) [Cf. Contra Faust. xxii, 70 that just as "the soil gives proof of its fertility by producing useless herbs before the useful seeds have grown, so this deed of Moses was sinful although it gave a sign of great fertility," in so far, to wit, as it was a sign of the power whereby he was to deliver his people.

With regard to Phinees the reply is that he did this out of zeal for God by Divine inspiration; or because though not as yet high-priest, he was nevertheless the high-priest's son, and this judgment was his concern as of the other judges, to whom this was commanded [Exodus 22:20; Leviticus 20; Deuteronomy 13 and 17.

Reply to Objection 3: The secular power is subject to the spiritual, even as the body is subject to the soul. Consequently the judgment is not usurped if the spiritual authority interferes in those temporal matters that are subject to the spiritual authority or which have been committed to the spiritual by the temporal authority.

Reply to Objection 4: The habits of knowledge and justice are perfections of the individual, and consequently their absence does not make a judgment to be usurped, as in the absence of public authority which gives a judgment its coercive force.

Selection 6: *Summa Theologica*, II/2, Question 64, Articles 2–3 and Question 40, Article 1

Thomas's teaching on capital punishment and his classic version of just-war thinking share a common conviction that killing in each case must be enacted by public authority and for the sake of justice in society. Private killing and private war is therefore precluded as are any acts of killing that are carried out for reasons other than the preservation of justice for the common good. Both teachings have proven determinative for much of subsequent Christian teaching. Of additional interest is Thomas's use in Question 64, Articles 2 and 3, of the analogy from medicine's "principle of totality" in which the parts of the body exist for the sake of the whole and cannot be mutilated or removed unless they have become a threat to the whole. This too has become a well-established feature of medical ethics in the natural law tradition.

Q64, Article 2: *Whether it is lawful to kill sinners?*

Objection 1: It would seem unlawful to kill men who have sinned. For our Lord in the parable (Matthew 13) forbade the uprooting of the cockle which denotes wicked men according to a gloss. Now whatever is forbidden by God is a sin. Therefore it is a sin to kill a sinner.

Objection 2: Further, human justice is conformed to Divine justice. Now according to Divine justice sinners are kept back for repentance, according to Ezekiel 33:11, "I desire not the death of the wicked, but that the wicked turn from his way and live." Therefore it seems altogether unjust to kill sinners.

Objection 3: Further, it is not lawful, for any good end whatever, to do that which is evil in itself, according to Augustine (Contra Mendac. vii) and the Philosopher (Ethic. ii, 6). Now to kill a man is evil in itself, since we are bound to have charity towards all men, and "we wish our friends to live and to exist," according to Ethic. ix, 4. Therefore it is nowise lawful to kill a man who has sinned.

On the contrary, It is written (Exodus 22:18): "Wizards thou shalt not suffer to live"; and (Psalm 100:8): "In the morning I put to death all the wicked of the land."

I answer that, As stated above (Article 1), it is lawful to kill dumb animals, in so far as they are naturally directed to man's use, as the imperfect is directed to the perfect. Now every part is directed to the whole, as imperfect to perfect, wherefore every part is naturally for the sake of the whole. For this reason we observe that if the health of the whole body demands the excision of a member, through its being decayed or infectious to the other members, it will be both praiseworthy and advantageous to have it cut away. Now every individual person is compared to the whole community, as part to whole. Therefore if a man be dangerous and infectious to the community, on account of some sin, it is praiseworthy and advantageous that he be killed in order to safeguard the common good, since "a little leaven corrupteth the whole lump" (1 Corinthians 5:6).

Reply to Objection 1: Our Lord commanded them to forbear from uprooting the cockle in order to spare the wheat, i.e. the good. This occurs when the wicked cannot be slain without the good being killed with them, either because the wicked lie hidden among the good, or because they have many followers, so that they cannot be killed without danger to the good, as Augustine says (Contra Parmen. iii, 2). Wherefore our Lord teaches that we should rather allow the wicked to live, and that vengeance is to be delayed until the last judgment, rather than that the good be put to death together with the wicked. When, however, the good incur no danger, but rather are protected and saved by the slaying of the wicked, then the latter may be lawfully put to death.

Reply to Objection 2: According to the order of His wisdom, God sometimes slays sinners forthwith in order to deliver the good, whereas sometimes He allows them time to repent, according as He knows what is expedient for His elect. This also does human justice imitate according to its powers; for it puts to death those who are dangerous to others, while it allows time for repentance to those who sin without grievously harming others.

Reply to Objection 3: By sinning man departs from the order of reason, and consequently falls away from the dignity of his manhood, in so far as he is naturally free, and exists for himself, and he falls into the slavish state of the beasts, by being disposed of according as he is useful to others. This is expressed in Psalm 48:21: "Man, when he was in honor, did not understand; he hath been compared to senseless beasts, and made like to them," and Proverbs 11:29: "The fool shall serve the wise." Hence, although it be evil in itself to kill a man so long as he preserve his dignity, yet it may be good to kill a man who has sinned, even as it is to kill a beast. For a bad man is worse than a beast, and is more harmful, as the Philosopher states (Polit. i, 1 and Ethic. vii, 6).

Q64, Article 3: Whether it is lawful for a private individual to kill a man who has sinned?

Objection 1: It would seem lawful for a private individual to kill a man who has sinned. For nothing unlawful is commanded in the Divine law. Yet, on account of the sin of the molten calf, Moses commanded (Exodus 32:27): "Let every man kill his brother, and friend, and neighbor." Therefore it is lawful for private individuals to kill a sinner.

Objection 2: Further, as stated above (2, ad 3), man, on account of sin, is compared to the beasts. Now it is lawful for any private individual to kill a wild beast, especially if it be harmful. Therefore for the same reason, it is lawful for any private individual to kill a man who has sinned.

Objection 3: Further, a man, though a private individual, deserves praise for doing what is useful for the common good. Now the slaying of evildoers is useful for the common good, as stated above (Article 2). Therefore it is deserving of praise if even private individuals kill evil-doers.

On the contrary, Augustine says (De Civ. Dei i) [Can. Quicumque percutit, caus. xxiii, qu. 8: "A man who, without exercising public authority, kills an evil-doer, shall be judged guilty of murder, and all the more, since he has dared to usurp a power which God has not given him."

I answer that, As stated above (Article 2), it is lawful to kill an evildoer in so far as it is directed to the welfare of the whole community, so that it belongs to him alone who has charge of the community's welfare. Thus it belongs to a physician to cut off a decayed limb, when he has been entrusted with the care of the health of the whole body. Now the care of the common good is entrusted to persons of rank having public authority: wherefore they alone, and not private individuals, can lawfully put evildoers to death.

Q40, Article 1: Whether it is always sinful to wage war?

Objection 1: It would seem that it is always sinful to wage war. Because punishment is not inflicted except for sin. Now those who wage war are threatened by Our Lord with punishment, according to Matthew 26:52: "All that take the sword shall perish with the sword." Therefore all wars are unlawful.

Objection 2: Further, whatever is contrary to a Divine precept is a sin. But war is contrary to a Divine precept, for it is written (Matthew 5:39): "But I say to you not to resist evil"; and (Romans 12:19): "Not revenging yourselves, my dearly beloved, but give place unto wrath." Therefore war is always sinful.

Objection 3: Further, nothing, except sin, is contrary to an act of virtue.
But war is contrary to peace. Therefore war is always a sin.

Objection 4: Further, the exercise of a lawful thing is itself lawful, as is evident in scientific exercises. But warlike exercises which take place in tournaments are forbidden by the Church, since those who are slain in these trials are deprived of ecclesiastical burial. Therefore it seems that war is a sin in itself.

On the contrary, Augustine says in a sermon on the son of the centurion [Ep. ad Marcel. cxxxviii]: "If the Christian Religion forbade war altogether, those who sought salutary advice in the Gospel would rather have been counselled to cast aside their arms, and to give up soldiering altogether. *On the contrary,* they were told: 'Do violence to no man . . . and be content with your pay' [Luke 3:14. If he commanded them to be content with their pay, he did not forbid soldiering."

I answer that, In order for a war to be just, three things are necessary. First, the authority of the sovereign by whose command the war is to be waged. For it is not the business of a private individual to declare war, because he can seek for redress of his rights from the tribunal of his superior. Moreover it is not the business of a private individual to summon together the people, which has to be done in wartime. And as the care of the common weal is committed to those who are in authority, it is their business to watch over the common weal of the city, kingdom or province subject to them. And just as it is lawful for them to have recourse to the sword in defending that common weal against internal disturbances, when they punish evil-doers, according to the words of the Apostle (Romans 13:4): "He beareth not the sword in vain: for he is God's minister, an avenger to execute wrath upon him that doth evil"; so too, it is their business to have recourse to the sword of war in defending the common weal against external enemies. Hence it is said to those who are in authority (Psalm 81:4): "Rescue the poor: and deliver the needy out of the hand of the sinner"; and for this reason Augustine says (Contra Faust. xxii, 75): "The natural order conducive to peace among mortals demands that the power to declare and counsel war should be in the hands of those who hold the supreme authority."

Secondly, a just cause is required, namely that those who are attacked, should be attacked because they deserve it on account of some fault. Wherefore Augustine says (QQ. in Hept., qu. x, super Jos.): "A just war is wont to be described as one that avenges wrongs, when a nation or state has to be punished, for refusing to make amends for the wrongs inflicted by its subjects, or to restore what it has seized unjustly."

Thirdly, it is necessary that the belligerents should have a rightful intention, so that they intend the advancement of good, or the avoidance of evil. Hence Augustine says (De Verb. Dom. [The words quoted are to be found not in St. Augustine's works, but Can. Apud. Caus. xxiii, qu. 1): "True religion looks upon as peaceful those wars that are waged not for motives of aggrandizement, or cruelty, but with the object of securing peace, of punishing evil-doers, and of uplifting the good." For it may happen that the war is declared by the legitimate authority, and for a just cause, and yet be rendered unlawful through a wicked intention. Hence Augustine says (Contra Faust. xxii, 74): "The passion for inflicting harm, the cruel thirst for vengeance, an unpacific and relentless spirit, the fever of revolt, the lust of power, and such like things, all these are rightly condemned in war."

Selection 7: *Summa Theologica*, II/2, Question 66, Articles 1–2

Article 1 provides an important premise for Aquinas's belief that humans have a natural right to private property. This is a function of humanity's dominion over things of the earth, graciously given for humanity's use as an endowment of creation in the image of God. Unfortunately, this view has been distorted over time when taken by some to be a license for exploitation of resources or a rationale for acquisitiveness. Here and in the article that follows, however, there is the mitigating argument that all things come from God and are to be shared with others where there is need.

Article 1: Whether it is natural for man to possess external things?

Objection 1: It would seem that it is not natural for man to possess external things. For no man should ascribe to himself that which is God's. Now the dominion over all creatures is proper to God, according to Psalm 23:1, "The earth is the Lord's," etc. Therefore it is not natural for man to possess external things.

Objection 2: Further, Basil in expounding the words of the rich man (Luke 12:18), "I will gather all things that are grown to me, and my goods," says [Hom. in Luc. xii, 18]: "Tell me: which are thine? where did you take them from and bring them into being?" Now whatever man possesses naturally, he can fittingly call his own. Therefore man does not naturally possess external things.

Objection 3: Further, according to Ambrose (De Trin. i [De Fide, ad Gratianum, i, 1) "dominion denotes power." But man has no power over external things, since he can work no change in their nature. Therefore the possession of external things is not natural to man.

On the contrary, It is written (Psalm 8:8): "Thou hast subjected all things under his feet."

I answer that, External things can be considered in two ways. First, as regards their nature, and this is not subject to the power of man, but only to the power of God Whose mere will all things obey. Secondly, as regards their use, and in this way, man has a natural dominion over external things, because, by his reason and will, he is able to use them for his own profit, as they were made on his account: for the imperfect is always for the sake of the perfect, as stated above (Question 64, Article 1). It is by this argument that the Philosopher proves (Polit. i, 3) that the possession of external things is natural to man. Moreover, this natural dominion of man over other creatures, which is competent to man in respect of his reason wherein God's image resides, is shown forth in man's creation (Genesis 1:26) by the words: "Let us make man to our image and likeness: and let him have dominion over the fishes of the sea," etc.

Reply to Objection 1: God has sovereign dominion over all things: and He, according to His providence, directed certain things to the sustenance of man's body. For this reason man has a natural dominion over things, as regards the power to make use of them.

Reply to Objection 2: The rich man is reproved for deeming external things to belong to him principally, as though he had not received them from another, namely from God.

Reply to Objection 3: This argument considers the dominion over external things as regards their nature. Such a dominion belongs to God alone, as stated above.

Article 2: Whether it is lawful for a man to possess a thing as his own?

Objection 1: It would seem unlawful for a man to possess a thing as his own. For whatever is contrary to the natural law is unlawful. Now according to the natural law all things are common property: and the possession of property is contrary to this community of goods. Therefore it is unlawful for any man to appropriate any external thing to himself.

Objection 2: Further, Basil in expounding the words of the rich man quoted above (1, Objection 2), says: "The rich who deem as their own property the common goods they have seized upon, are like to those who by going beforehand to the play prevent others from coming, and appropriate to themselves what is intended for common use." Now it would be unlawful to prevent others from obtaining possession of common goods. Therefore it is unlawful to appropriate to oneself what belongs to the community.

Objection 3: Further, Ambrose says [Serm. lxiv, de temp.], and his words are quoted in the Decretals [Dist. xlvii., Can. Sicut hi.]: "Let no man call his own that which is common property": and by "common" he means external things, as is clear from the context. Therefore it seems unlawful for a man to appropriate an external thing to himself.

On the contrary, Augustine says (De Haeres., haer. 40): "The 'Apostolici' are those who with extreme arrogance have given themselves that name, because they do not admit into their communion persons who are married or possess anything of their own, such as both monks and clerics who in considerable number are to be found in the Catholic Church." Now the reason why these people are heretics was because severing themselves from the Church, they think that those who enjoy the use of the above things, which they themselves lack, have no hope of salvation. Therefore it is erroneous to maintain that it is unlawful for a man to possess property.

I answer that, Two things are competent to man in respect of exterior things. One is the power to procure and dispense them, and in this regard it is lawful for man to possess property. Moreover this is necessary to human life for three reasons. First because every man is more careful to procure what is for himself alone than that which is common to many or to all: since each one would shirk the labor and leave to another that which concerns the community, as happens where there is a great number of servants. Secondly, because human affairs conducted in more orderly fashion if each man is charged with taking care of some particular thing himself, whereas there would be confusion if everyone had to look after any one thing indeterminately. Thirdly, because a more peaceful state is ensured to man if each one is contented with his own. Hence it is to be observed that quarrels arise more frequently where there is no division of the things possessed.

The second thing that is competent to man with regard to external things is their use. On this respect man ought to possess external things, not as his own, but as common, so that, to wit, he is ready to communicate them to others in their need. Hence the Apostle says (1 Timothy 6:17-18): "Charge the rich of this world . . . to give easily, to communicate to others," etc.

Reply to Objection 1: Community of goods is ascribed to the natural law, not that the natural law dictates that all things should be possessed in common and that nothing should be possessed as one's own: but because the division of possessions is not according to the natural law, but rather arose from human agreement which belongs to positive law, as stated above (57, 2,3). Hence the ownership of possessions is not contrary to the natural law, but an addition thereto devised by human reason.

Reply to Objection 2: A man would not act unlawfully if by going beforehand to the play he prepared the way for others: but he acts unlawfully if by so doing he hinders others from going. On like manner a rich man does not act unlawfully if he anticipates someone in taking possession of something which at first was common property, and gives others a share: but he sins if he excludes others indiscriminately from using it. Hence Basil says (Hom. in Luc. xii, 18): "Why are you rich while another is poor, unless it be that you may have the merit of a good stewardship, and he the reward of patience?"

Reply to Objection 3: When Ambrose says: "Let no man call his own that which is common," he is speaking of ownership as regards use, wherefore he adds: "He who spends too much is a robber."

The Medieval Papacy 11

❧ *During the medieval period political and religious authorities were closely intertwined, sometimes supporting one another, often in competition with one another for power in both the ecclesial and secular realms. Issues of power arose for the most part in relation to the claims of the medieval papacy, which for centuries after the downfall of the Roman Empire came to prominence as the most stable center of leadership in Europe. Few of the most successful popes were professional theologians. Many were canon lawyers who succeeded due to their administrative skills and personal dynamism. In the selections that follow, we have two examples of high water marks in papal claims of authority. They represent a perspective in which the church has a divine right to intervene in the affairs of secular authorities, a position that would be challenged by the Reformation, but that has perdured in some form even under the changed circumstances of modernity.*

Selection 1: Pope Gregory VII excommunication decree 1076

Pope Gregory VII (1073–1085), Hildebrand, was one of most intellectually gifted popes of that era. His view of the papacy was based on an extreme interpretation of Augustine's City of God, *which involved the conviction, stated in the* Dictatus, *that the Roman church was founded by God alone, that the pontiff alone has the right to be called universal, and he alone can depose or reinstate bishops and even depose emperors. Having become embroiled with Emperor Henry IV (1056–1106) in a struggle for supremacy over the temporal and spiritual realms, he issued this decree excommunicating Henry IV on February 22, 1076.*

O St. Peter, chief of the apostles, incline to us, I beg, thy holy ears, and hear me thy servant whom thou has nourished from infancy, and whom, until this day, thou hast freed from the hand of the wicked, who have hated and do hate me for my faithfulness to thee. Thou, and my mistress the mother of God, and thy brother St. Paul are witnesses for me among all the saints that thy holy Roman church drew me to its helm against my will; that I had no thought of ascending thy chair through force, and that I would rather have ended my life as a pilgrim than, by secular means, to have seized thy throne for the sake of earthly glory. And therefore I believe it to be through thy grace and not through my own deeds that it has pleased and does please thee that the Christian people, who have been especially committed to thee, should obey me. And especially to me, as thy representative and by thy favour, has the power been granted by God of binding and loosing in Heaven and on earth. On the strength of this belief therefore, for the honour and security of thy church, in the name of Almighty God, Father, Son and Holy Ghost, I withdraw, through thy power and authority, from Henry the king, son of Henry the emperor, who has risen against thy church with unheard of insolence, the rule over the whole kingdom of the Germans and over Italy. And I absolve all Christians from the bonds of the oath which they have made or shall make to him; and I forbid any one to serve him as king. For it is fitting that he who strives to lessen the honour of thy church should himself lose the honour which belongs to him. And since he has scorned to obey as a Christian, and has not returned to God whom he had deserted-holding intercourse with the excommunicated; practising manifold iniquities; spurning my commands which, as thou dost bear witness, I issued to him for his own salvation; separating himself from thy church and striving to rend it-I bind him in thy stead with the chain of the anathema. And, leaning on thee, I so bind him that the people may know and have proof that thou art Peter, and above thy rock the Son of the living God hath built His church, and the gates of Hell shall not prevail against it.

Selection 2: *Unam Sanctam* 1302

> *As a result of a lengthy conflict between Pope Boniface VIII (1294–1303) and King Philip IV of France (1285–1314) Boniface expressed the legal claims of the papacy in his famous Bull,* Unam Sanctam, *of November 18, 1302. After Boniface's successor died, the pope that followed, Clement V, fell under the sway of King Philip IV and subsequently modified the Bull. So, as so often happened, the power shifted once again.*

Urged by faith, we are obliged to believe and to hold that there is One Holy Catholic and truly Apostolic Church. And this we firmly believe and simply confess: outside of Her, there is neither salvation, nor the remission of sins, just as the Bridegroom in the Canticles proclaims: "One is my dove, my perfect one. One is her mother; elect is she who bore her." [Canticles 6:8]. And this represents the one mystical body, whose head is Christ, and truly God [is the head] of Christ. [1 Corinthians 11:3] In Her, there is one Lord, one faith, one baptism. [Ephesians 4:5] For certainly, in the time of the Flood, the ark of Noah was one, prefiguring the one Church. And She, having been completed by [the measure of] one cubit, [Genesis 6:16] had one pilot and helmsman, that is, Noah. And outside of Her, everything standing upon the land, as we read, had been destroyed.

2. Thus, we venerate Her as the only one, just as the Lord said by the prophet: "O God, rescue my soul from the spear, and my only one from the hand of the dog." [Psalm 21:21] But he prayed for the soul, that is, for his very self, head and body together. And this body, which he named as the only one, is certainly the Church, because of the Bridegroom, the Faith, the Sacraments, and the love of the Church, united. She is that seamless tunic of the Lord which was not torn, [John 19:23-24] but was distributed by lot.

3. And so, the one and only Church is one body, one head, (not two heads like a monster), Christ certainly, and the vicar of Christ, [who is] Peter and the successor of Peter. For the Lord said to Peter himself, "Feed my sheep." [John 21:17] He said "my" generally, not solely of these or of those. By this, it is understood that all [universas] were committed to him. Therefore, if either the Greeks or others declare themselves not to be committed to Peter and his successors, they necessarily admit themselves not to be among the sheep of Christ, just as the Lord says in John, "there is one sheepfold, and only one shepherd." [John 10:16]

4. We are instructed in the Gospel sayings that in Her and within Her power, there are two swords, specifically, the spiritual and the temporal. For the Apostles say, "Behold, there are two swords here," that is, in the Church. But when the Apostles were speaking, the Lord did not respond, "it is too much," but "it is sufficient." [Luke 22:38] Certainly, whoever denies that the temporal sword is in the power of Peter, misunderstands the word of the Lord, saying: "Put your sword into its sheath." [Matthew 26:52] Therefore, both are in the power of the Church, namely, the spiritual sword and the material. But indeed, the latter is to be exercised on behalf of the Church; and truly, the former is to be exercised by the Church. The former is of the priest; the latter is by the hand of kings and soldiers, but at the will and sufferance of the priest.

5. Now one sword ought to be under the other sword, and so the temporal authority is to be subject to the spiritual authority. For though the Apostle said: "there is no authority except from God and those who have been ordained by God," [Romans 13:1] still they would not have been ordained unless one sword were under the other sword. And so what is inferior should be led forward by another, to what is highest. For, according to blessed Dionysius, it is a law of divine power that what is lowest is to be led forward by what is intermediate, to what is highest.

6. Therefore, it is not in accord with the order of the universe that all things should be absolutely equal, but rather the lowest through the intermediate, and the lower through the higher, in order. And so, to whatever extent the spiritual power excels beyond the worldly, in both dignity and rank, we must, to the same extent, clearly admit that the spiritual surpasses the temporal. And this, nevertheless, we distinguish with clear eyes from the gift of tithes, and from benediction and sanctification, by the reception of the authority itself, and by the government of the things themselves. For truth is the witness that the spiritual authority holds [the ability] to establish the earthly authority, and to judge if it might not have been good. And this, concerning the Church and the authority of the Church, the prophecy of Jeremiah verifies: "Behold, today I have appointed you over nations and kingdoms" [Jeremiah 1:10] and the rest that follows.

7. Therefore, if the earthly power goes astray, it will be judged by the spiritual power; but if a lesser spiritual power goes astray, [it will be judged] by its superior; and truly, if the highest [power] goes astray, it will not be able to be judged by man, but by God alone. And so the Apostle testifies, "The spiritual man judges all things, but he himself is judged by no one." [1 Corinthians 2:15]

8. But this authority, even though it may be given to a man, and may be exercised by a man, is not human, but rather divine [power], having been given by the divine mouth [of Christ] to Peter, and to him as well as to his successors, by [Christ] Himself, [that is, to him] whom He had disclosed to be the firm rock, just as the Lord said to Peter himself: "Whatever you shall bind," [Matthew 16:19] etc. Therefore, whoever resists this authority, such as it has been ordain by God, resists the ordination of God. [Romans 13:2] Otherwise, he would be proposing two principles to exist, as did Manichaeus, and this we judge to be false and heretical. For Moses testified that God created heaven and earth, not in the beginnings, but "in the beginning." [Genesis 1:1]

9. Moreover, that every human creature is to be subject to the Roman pontiff, we declare, we state, we define, and we pronounce to be entirely from the necessity of salvation.

For Further Reading

The following select list of writings provides a mixture of primary and secondary sources related to the major parts of the anthology, and the full text of the works being excerpted will also provide rich additional reading.

Aquinas, Thomas. *Political Writings*. Cambridge Texts in the History of Political Thought. Edited and translated by R. W. Dyson. Cambridge: Cambridge University Press, 2002.

Boff, Leonardo. *Francis of Assisi: A Model for Human Liberation*. Translated by John W. Diercksmeier. Maryknoll: Orbis, 2006.

Edwards, Steven Anthony. *Interior Acts: Teleology, Justice, and Friendship in the Religious Ethics of Thomas Aquinas*. New York and London: University Press of America, 1986.

Evans, Gillian Rosemary. *Bernard of Clairvaux*. New York: Oxford University Press, 2000.

Fatula, Mary Ann, O.P. *Catherine of Siena's Way*. Wilmington: Michael Glazier, 1987.

Koritansky, Peter Karl. *Thomas Aquinas and the Philosophy of Punishment*. Washington, DC: Catholic University of America Press, 2012.

Sorrell, Roger. *St. Francis of Assisi and Nature: Tradition and Innovation in Western Christian Attitudes toward the Environment*. New York: Oxford University Press, 1988.

Tobin, Frank. *Meister Eckhart: Thought and Language*. Philadelphia: University of Pennsylvania Press, 1986.

Wood, Charles T., ed. *Philip the Fair and Boniface VIII: State vs. Papacy*. New York: Holt, Rinehart and Winston, 1967.

PART 4

The Reformation

MARTIN LUTHER

12

A German Augustinian monk and later university professor at Wittenberg, Luther was the most important of the early leaders of the Reformation. Born in Eisleben in 1483, he died in 1546 in the very same town while on a journey.

Though he rarely left Saxony and had been outside Germany only once as a young monk, he influenced the entire Christian world of his day with his enormous literary activity. The significance of his theology continues to exert itself, but his importance for Christian social teaching has sometimes been overlooked. In the Christendom of Luther's day, the tight interweaving of church and society meant that reform of the church often meant reforms in the social fabric as well. Even the famous Ninety-Five Theses of 1517 against the sale of indulgences is not just a theological concern; it was a concern for the use of indulgences as an exploitation of the faith and fear of the people in order to fill the coffers of Rome and thereby divert them from giving instead to the needs of the poor.

Selection 1: *Treatise on Christian Liberty*, 1520

This is a truly foundational treatise for understanding Luther's approach to the Christian ethic. By God's saving grace the Christian is set free from the judgment of the law. The life of neighbor love after the pattern of the Christ is a fruit of faith in this promise. We love as we have first been loved. The life of faith active in love is also at the core of Luther's important concept of vocation; in the freedom of the gospel all are "kings and priests" called to be Christ to others in all of life, including support of civil authorities and their mandate to serve the common good. The vocation shared by all the baptized gave ordinary Christians outside the ranks of the clergy and monastics a sense of call to be God's person in the world and made all activities of life a channel for that service and witness.

Many people have considered Christian faith an easy thing, and not a few have given it a place among the virtues. They do this because they have not experienced it and have never tasted the great strength there is in faith. It is impossible to write well about it or to understand what has been written about it unless one has at one time or another experienced the courage which faith gives a man when trials oppress him. But he who has had even a faint taste of it can never write, speak, meditate, or hear enough concerning it. It is a living "spring of water welling up to eternal life," as Christ calls it in John 4[:14].

As for me, although I have no wealth of faith to boast of and know how scant my supply is, I nevertheless hope that I have attained to a little faith, even though I have been assailed by great and various temptations; and I hope that I can discuss it, if not more elegantly, certainly more to the point, than those literalists and subtle disputants have previously done, who have not even understood what they have written.

To make the way smoother for the unlearned—for only them do I serve—I shall set down the following two propositions concerning the freedom and the bondage of the spirit:

A Christian is a perfectly free lord of all, subject to none.

A Christian is a perfectly dutiful servant of all, subject to all.

These two theses seem to contradict each other. If, however, they should be found to fit together they would serve our purpose beautifully. Both are Paul's own statements, who says in I Cor. 9[:19], "For though I am free item all men, I have made myself a slave to all," and in Rom. 13[:8], "Owe no one anything, except to love one another." Love by its very nature is ready to serve and be subject to him who is loved. So Christ, although he was Lord of all, was "born of woman, born under the law" [Gal. 4:4], and therefore was at the same time a free man and a servant, "in the form of God" and "of a servant" [Phil. 2:6-7].

*   *   *

Furthermore, to put aside all kinds of works, even contemplation, meditation, and all that the soul can do, does not help. One thing, and only one thing, is necessary for Christian life, righteousness, and freedom. That one thing is the most holy Word of God, the gospel of Christ, as Christ says, John 11[:25], "I am the resurrection and the life; he who believes in me, though he die, yet shall he live"; and John 8[:36], "So if the Son makes you free, you will be free indeed";

*   *   *

You may ask, "What then is the Word of God, and how shall it be used, since there are so many words of God?" I answer: The Apostle explains this in Romans 1. The Word is the gospel of God concerning his Son, who was made flesh, suffered, rose from the dead, and was glorified through the Spirit who sanctifies. To preach Christ means to feed the soul, make it righteous, set it free, and save it, provided it believes the preaching. Faith alone is the saving and efficacious use of the Word of God, according to Rom. 10[:9]: "If you confess with your lips that Jesus is Lord and believe in your heart that God raised him from the dead, you will be saved." Furthermore, "Christ is the end of the law, that every one who has faith may be justified" [Rom. 10:4]. Again, in Rom. 1[:17], "He who through faith is righteous shall live." The Word of God cannot be received and cherished by any works whatever but only by faith. Therefore it is clear that, as the soul needs only the Word of God for its life and righteousness, so it is justified by faith alone and not any works; for if it could be justified by anything else, it would not need the Word, and consequently it would not need faith.

Wherefore it ought to be the first concern of every Christian to lay aside all confidence in works and increasingly to strengthen faith alone and through faith to grow in the knowledge, not of works, but of Christ Jesus, who suffered and rose for him, as Peter teaches in the last chapter of his first Epistle (1 Pet. 5:10). No other work makes a Christian.

*   *   *

This is that Christian liberty, our faith, which does not induce us to live in idleness or wickedness but makes the law and works unnecessary for any man's righteousness and salvation.

From this you once more see that much is ascribed to faith, namely, that it alone can fulfill the law and justify without works. You see that the First Commandment, which says, "You shall worship one God," is fulfilled by faith alone. Though you were nothing but good works from the soles of your feet to the crown of your head, you would still not be righteous or worship God or fulfill the First Commandment, since God cannot be worshiped unless you ascribe to him the glory of truthfulness and all goodness which is due him. This cannot be clone by works but only by the faith of the heart. Not by the doing of works but by believing do we glorify God and acknowledge that he is truthful. Therefore faith alone is the righteousness of a Christian and the fulfilling of all the commandments, for he who fulfills the First Commandment has no difficulty in fulfilling all the rest.

*   *   *

All of us who believe in Christ are priests and kings in Christ, as 1 Pet. 2[:9] says; "You are a chosen race, God's own people, a royal priesthood, a priestly kingdom, that you may declare the wonderful deeds of him who called you out of darkness into his marvelous light."

The nature of this priesthood and kingship is something like this: First, with respect to the kingship, every Christian is by faith so exalted above all things that, by virtue of a spiritual power, he is lord of all things without exception, so that nothing can do him any harm. . . . Not only are we the freest of kings, we are also priests forever, which is far more excellent than being kings, for as priests we are worthy to appear before God to pray for others and to teach one another divine things. These are the functions of priests, and they cannot be granted to any unbeliever. Thus Christ has made it possible for us, provided we believe in him, to be not only his brethren, co-heirs, and fellow-kings, but also his fellow-priests. Therefore we may boldly come into the presence of God in the spirit of faith [Heb. 10:19, 22] and cry "Abba, Father!" pray for one another, and do all things which we see done and fore-shadowed in the outer and visible works of priests.

*   *   *

Let this suffice concerning the inner man, his liberty, and the source of his liberty, the righteousness of faith. He needs neither laws nor good works but, on the contrary, is injured by them if he believes that he is justified by them.

Now let us turn to the second part, the outer man. Here we shall answer all those who, offended by the word "faith" and by all that has been said, now ask, "If faith does all things and is alone sufficient unto righteousness, why then are good works commanded? We will take our ease and do no works and be content with faith." I answer: not so, you wicked men, not so. That would indeed be proper if we were wholly inner and perfectly spiritual men. But such we shall be only at the last day, the day of the resurrection of the dead. As long as we live in the flesh we only begin to make some progress in that which shall be perfected in the future life. For this reason the Apostle in Rom. 8[:23] calls all that we attain in this life "the first fruits of the Spirit" because we shall indeed receive the greater portion, even the fullness of the Spirit, in the future. This is the place to assert that which was said above, namely, that a Christian is the servant of all and made subject to all. Insofar as he is free he does no works, but insofar as he is a servant he does all kinds of works.

*   *   *

The following statements are therefore true: "Good works do not make a good man, but a good man does good works; evil works do not make a wicked man, but a wicked man does evil works." Consequently it is always necessary that the substance or person himself be good before there can be any good works, and that good works follow and proceed from the good person, as Christ also says, "A good tree cannot bear evil fruit, nor can a bad tree bear good fruit" [Matt. 7:18]. It is clear that the fruits do not bear the tree and that the tree does not grow on the fruits, also that, on the contrary, the trees bear the fruits and the fruits grow on the trees. As it is necessary, therefore, that the trees exist before their fruits and the fruits do not make trees either good or bad, but rather as the trees are, so are the fruits they bear; so a man must first be good or wicked before he does a good or wicked work, and his works do not make him good or wicked, but he himself makes his works either good or wicked.

*   *   *

As an example of such life the Apostle cites Christ, saying, "Have this mind among yourselves, which you have in Christ Jesus, who, though he was in the form of God, did not count equality with God a thing to be grasped, but emptied himself, taking the form of a servant, being born in the likeness of men. And being found in human form he humbled himself and became obedient unto death" [Phil. 2:5-8]. This salutary word of the Apostle has been obscured for us by those who have not at all understood his words, "form of God," "form of a servant," "human form," "likeness of men," and have applied them to the divine and the human nature. Paul means this: Although Christ was filled with the form of God and rich in all good things, so that he needed no work and no suffering to make him righteous and saved (for he had all this eternally), yet he was not puffed up by them and did not exalt himself above us and assume power over us, although he could rightly have done so; but, on the contrary, he so lived, labored, worked, suffered, and died that he might be like other men and in fashion and in actions be nothing else than a man, just as if he had need of all these things and had nothing of the form of God. But he did all this for our sake, that he might serve us and that all things which he accomplished in this form of a servant might become ours. . . . Hence, as our heavenly Father has in Christ freely come to our aid, we also ought freely to help our neighbor through our body and its works, and each one should become as it were a Christ to the other that we may be Christs to one another and Christ may be the same in all, that is, that we may be truly Christians.

*　*　*

Of the same nature are the precepts which Paul gives in Rom. 13[:1-7], namely, that Christians should be subject to the governing authorities and be ready to do every good work, not that they shall in this way be justified, since they already are righteous through faith, but that in the liberty of the Spirit they shall by so doing serve others and the authorities themselves and obey their will freely and out of love. The works of all colleges, monasteries, and priests should be of this nature. Each one should do the works of his profession and station, not that by them he may strive after righteousness, but that through them he may keep his body under control, be an example to others who also need to keep their bodies under control, and finally that by such works he may submit his will to that of others in the freedom of love.

We conclude, therefore, that a Christian lives not in himself, but in Christ and in his neighbor. Otherwise he is not a Christian. He lives in Christ through faith, in his neighbor through love. By faith he is caught up beyond himself into God. By love he descends beneath himself into his neighbor. Yet he always remains in God and in his love, as Christ says in John 1[:51], "Truly, truly, I say to you, you will see heaven opened, and the angels of God ascending and descending upon the Son of man."

Selection 2: *Temporal Authority: To What Extent It Should Be Obeyed*, 1522

This is one of the most important treatises for understanding Luther's view of the relationship between church and state. Although the term "doctrine of the two kingdoms" was not coined until the 1930s, Luther's teaching of God's two modes of governance has been a prominent feature of the Lutheran heritage of social teaching since the publication of this treatise. In this and in subsequent writings, such as "The Commentary on the Sermon on the Mount," Luther set forth his well-known distinction between God's two governments, the spiritual and the temporal, and with that the twofold ethical responses demanded of Christians. In advancing this distinction Luther sought to address the intrusion of civil authority into the spiritual domain of the church and, at the same time, to oppose both the Roman Catholic view of the temporal power of the church and sectarian teachings of withdrawal from civil affairs. However, in the nineteenth century the distinction Luther drew became for many Lutherans a dualistic doctrine of separation; the church should stick to purely spiritual matters and not concern itself with matters of public policy. The quietism that resulted in some quarters of Lutheranism was a setback for Lutheran social ethics. When one reads in this

*treatise Luther's critique and admonition to the temporal authorities, a quietistic
outlook could hardly be discerned.*

First, we must provide a sound basis for the civil law and sword so no one will doubt
that it is in the world by God's will and ordinance. The passages which do this are the
following: Romans 12, "Let every soul [seele] be subject to the governing authority,
for there is no authority except from God; the authority which everywhere [allenthal-
ben] exists has been ordained by God. He then who resists the governing authority
resists the ordinance of God, and he who resists God's ordinance will incur judgment." Again, in 1 Peter 2[:13-14], "Be subject to every kind of human ordinance,
whether it be to the king as supreme, or to governors, as those who have been sent by
him to punish the wicked and to praise the righteous."

*   *   *

Second. There appear to be powerful arguments to the contrary. Christ says in Matthew 5[:38-41], "You have heard that it was said to them of old: An eye for an eye,
a tooth for a tooth. But I say to you, do not resist evil; but if anyone strikes you on
the right cheek, turn to him the other also. And if anyone would sue you and take
your coat, let him have your cloak as well. And if anyone forces you to go one mile,
go with him two miles," etc. Likewise Paul in Romans 12[:19], "Beloved, defend not
yourselves, but leave it to the wrath of God; for it is written, 'Vengeance is mine; I will
repay, says the Lord.' " And in Matthew 5[:44], "Love your enemies, do good to them
that hate you." And again, in I Peter 2 [3:9], "Do not return evil for evil, or reviling for
reviling," etc. These and similar passages would certainly make it appear as though in
the New Testament Christians were to have no temporal sword.

Hence, the sophists also say that Christ has thereby abolished the law of Moses.
Of such commandments they make "counsels" for the perfect they divide Christian
teaching and Christians into two classes. One part they call the perfect, and assign
to it such counsels. The other they call the imperfect, and assign to it the commandments. This they do out of sheer wantonness and caprice, without any scriptural basis.
They fail to see that in the same passage Christ lays such stress on his teaching that
he is unwilling to have the least word of it set aside, and condemns to hell those who
do not love their enemies. Therefore, we must interpret these passages differently,
so that Christ's words may apply to everyone alike, be he perfect or imperfect. For
perfection and imperfection do not consist in works, and do not establish any distinct
external order among Christians. They exist in the heart, in faith and love, so that
those who believe and love the most are the perfect ones, whether they be outwardly
male or female, prince or peasant, monk or layman. For love and faith produce no
sects or outward differences.

Third. Here we must divide the children of Adam and all mankind into two
classes, the first belonging to the kingdom of God, the second to the kingdom of the
world. Those who belong to the kingdom of God are all the true believers who are
in Christ and under Christ, for Christ is King and Lord in the kingdom of God, as
Psalm 2[:6] and all of Scripture says. . . . If all the world were composed of real Christians, that is, true believers, there would be no need for or benefits from prince, king,
lord, sword, or law. . . . Why is this? It is because the righteous man of his own accord

does all and more than the law demands. But the unrighteous do nothing that the law demands; therefore, they need the law to instruct, constrain, and compel them to do good. A good tree needs no instruction or law to bear good fruit; its nature causes it to bear according to its kind without any law or instruction.

Fourth. All who are not Christians belong to the kingdom of the world and are under the law. There are few true believers, and still fewer who live a Christian life, who do not resist evil and indeed themselves do no evil. For this reason God has provided for them a different government beyond the Christian estate and kingdom of God. He has subjected them to the sword so that, even though they would like to, they are unable to practice their wickedness, and if they do practice it they cannot do so without fear or with success and impunity. . . . If this were not so, men would devour one another, seeing that the whole world is evil and that among thousands there is scarcely a single true Christian. No one could support wife and child, feed himself, and serve God. The world would be reduced to chaos. For this reason God has ordained two governments: the spiritual, by which the Holy Spirit produces Christians and righteous people under Christ; and the temporal, which restrains the un-Christian and wicked so that—no thanks to them—they are obliged to keep still and to maintain an outward peace. Thus does St. Paul interpret the temporal sword in Romans 13[:3], when he says it is not a terror to good conduct but to bad. And Peter says it is for the punishment of the wicked [1 Pet. 2:14].

If anyone attempted to rule the world by the gospel and to abolish all temporal law and sword on the plea that all are baptized and Christian, and that, according to the gospel, there shall be among them no law or sword—or need for either—pray tell me, friend, what would he be doing? He would be loosing the ropes and chains of the savage wild beasts and letting them bite and mangle everyone, meanwhile insisting that they were harmless, tame, and gentle creatures; but I would have the proof in my wounds. Just so would the wicked under the name of Christian abuse evangelical freedom, carry on their rascality, and insist that they were Christians subject neither to law nor sword, as some are already raving and ranting.

To such a one we must say: Certainly it is true that Christians, so far as they themselves are concerned, are subject neither to law nor sword, and have need of neither. But take heed and first fill the world with real Christians before you attempt to rule it in a Christian and evangelical manner. This you will never accomplish; for the world and the masses are and always will be un-Christian, even if they are all baptized and Christian in name. Christians are few and far between (as the saying is). Therefore, it is out of the question that there should be a common Christian government over the whole world, or indeed over a single country or any considerable body of people, for the wicked always outnumber the good.

*　　*　　*

For this reason one must carefully distinguish between these two governments. Both must be permitted to remain; the one to produce righteousness, the other to bring about external peace and prevent evil deeds. Neither one is sufficient in the world without the other.

Fifth. But you say: if Christians then do not need the temporal sword or law, why does Paul say to all Christians in Romans 13[:1], "Let all souls be subject to the governing authority," and St. Peter, "Be subject to every human ordinance" [1 Pet. 2:13], etc., as quoted above? Answer: I have just said that Christians, among themselves and by and for themselves, need no law or sword, since it is neither necessary nor useful for them. Since a true Christian lives and labors on earth not for himself alone but for his neighbor, he does by the very nature of his spirit even what he himself has no need of, but is needful and useful to his neighbor. Because the sword is most beneficial and necessary for the whole world in order to preserve peace, punish sin, and restrain the wicked, the Christian submits most willingly to the rule of the sword, pays his taxes, honors those in authority, serves, helps, and does all he can to assist the governing authority, that it may continue to function and be held in honor and fear. Although he has no need of these things for himself—to him they are not essential—nevertheless, he concerns himself about what is serviceable and of benefit to others, as Paul teaches in Ephesians 5[:21—6:9].

Just as he performs all other works of love which he himself does not need—he does not visit the sick in order that he himself may be made well, or feed others because he himself needs food—so he serves the governing authority not because he needs it but for the sake of others, that they may be protected and that the wicked may not become worse. He loses nothing by this; such service in no way harms him, yet it is of great benefit to the world. If he did not so serve he would be acting not as a Christian but even contrary to love; he would also be setting a bad example to others who in like manner would not submit to authority, even though they were not Christians. In this way the gospel would be brought into disrepute, as though it taught insurrection and produced self-willed people unwilling to benefit or serve others, when in fact it makes a Christian the servant of all. Thus in Matthew 17[:27] Christ paid the half-shekel tax that he might not offend them, although he had no need to do so.

Sixth. You ask whether a Christian too may bear the temporal sword and pun-ish the wicked, since Christ's words, "Do not resist evil," are so clear and definite that the sophists have had to make of them a "counsel." Answer: You have now heard two propositions. One is that the sword can have no place among Christians; therefore, you cannot bear it among Christians or hold it over them, for they do not need it. The question, therefore, must be referred to the other group, the non-Christians, whether you may bear it there in a Christian manner. Here the other proposition applies, that you are under obligation to serve and assist the sword by whatever means you can, with body, goods, honor, and soul. For it is something which you do not need, but which is very beneficial and essential for the whole world and for your neighbor.

In this way the two propositions are brought into harmony with one another: at one and the same time you satisfy God's kingdom inwardly and the kingdom of the world outwardly. You suffer evil and injustice, and yet at the same time you punish evil and injustice; you do not resist evil, and yet at the same time, you do resist it. In the one case, you consider yourself and what is yours; in the other, you consider your neighbor and what is his. In what concerns you and yours, you govern yourself by the gospel and suffer injustice toward yourself as a true Christian; in what con-cerns the person or property of others, you govern yourself according to love and tolerate no injustice toward your neighbor. The gospel does not forbid this; in fact, in other places it actually commands it.

Part Two: How Far Temporal Authority Extends

We come now to the main part of this treatise. Having learned that there must be temporal authority on earth, and how it is to be exercised in a Christian and salutary manner, we must now learn how far its arm extends and how widely its hand stretches, lest it extend too far and encroach upon God's kingdom and government. The temporal government has laws which extend no further than to life and property and external affairs on earth, for God cannot and will not permit anyone but himself to rule over the soul. Therefore, where the temporal authority presumes to prescribe laws for the soul, it encroaches upon God's government and only misleads souls and destroys them. We want to make this so clear that everyone will grasp it, and that our fine gentlemen, the princes and bishops, will see what fools they are when they seek to coerce the people with their laws and commandments into believing this or that.

*   *   *

For my ungracious lords, the pope and the bishops, are supposed to be bishops and preach God's word. This they leave undone, and have become temporal princes who govern with laws which concern only life and property. How completely they have turned things topsy-turvy! They are supposed to be ruling souls inwardly by God's word; so they rule castles, cities, lands, and people outwardly, torturing souls with unspeakable outrages.

Similarly, the temporal lords are supposed to govern lands and people outwardly. This they leave undone. They can do no more than strip and fleece, heap tax upon tax and tribute upon tribute, letting loose here a bear and there a wolf. Besides this, there is no justice, integrity, or truth to be found among them. They behave worse than any thief or scoundrel, and their temporal rule has sunk quite as low as that of the spiritual tyrants. For this reason God so perverts their minds also, that they rush on into the absurdity of trying to exercise a spiritual rule over souls, just as their counterparts try to establish a temporal rule. . . . But, you say: Paul said in Romans 13[:1] that every soul [seele] should be subject to the governing authority; and Peter says that we should be subject to every human ordinance [1 Pet. 2:13]. Answer: Now you are on the right track, for these passages are in my favor. St. Paul is speaking of the governing authority. Now you have just heard that no one but God can have authority over souls. Hence, St. Paul cannot possibly be speaking of any obedience except where there can be corresponding authority. From this it follows that he is not speaking of faith, to the effect that temporal authority should have the right to command faith. He is speaking rather of external things, that they should be ordered and governed on earth. His words too make this perfectly clear, where he prescribes limits for both authority and obedience, saying, "Pay all of them their dues, taxes to whom taxes are due, revenue to whom revenue is due, honor to whom honor is due, respect to whom respect is due" [Rom. 13:7]. Temporal obedience and authority, you see, apply only externally to taxes, revenue, honor, and respect. Again, where he says, "The governing authority is not a terror to good conduct, but to bad" [Rom. 13:3], he again so limits the governing authority that it is not to have the mastery over faith or the word of God, but over evil works.

Part Three

Now that we know the limits of temporal authority, it is time to inquire also how a prince should use it. . . . He must depend neither upon dead books nor living heads, but cling solely to God, and be at him constantly, praying for a right understanding, beyond that of all books and teachers, to rule his subjects wisely. For this reason I know of no law to prescribe for a prince; instead, I will simply instruct his heart and mind on what his attitude should be toward all laws, counsels, judgments, and actions. If he governs himself accordingly, God will surely grant him the ability to carry out all laws, counsels, and actions in a proper and godly way.

First. He must give consideration and attention to his subjects, and really devote himself to it. This he does when he directs his every thought to making himself useful and beneficial to them; when instead of thinking, "The land and people belong to me, I will do what best pleases me," he thinks rather, "I belong to the land and the people, I shall do what is useful and good for them. My concern will be not how to lord it over them and dominate them, but how to protect and maintain them in peace and plenty." He should picture Christ to himself, and say, "Behold, Christ, the supreme ruler, came to serve me; he did not seek to gain power, estate, and honor from me, but considered only my need, and directed all things to the end that I should gain power, estate, and honor from him and through him. I will do likewise, seeking from my subjects not my own advantage but theirs. I will use my office to serve and protect them, listen to their problems and defend them, and govern to the sole end that they, not I, may benefit and profit from my rule." In such manner should a prince in his heart empty himself of his power and authority, and take unto himself the needs of his subjects, dealing with them as though they were his own needs. For this is what Christ did to us [Phil. 2:7]; and these are the proper works of Christian love.

*   *   *

He must take care to deal justly with evildoers. Here he must be very wise and prudent, so he can inflict punishment without injury to others. Again, I know of no better example of this than David. He had a commander, Joab by name, who committed two underhanded crimes when he treacherously, during his own lifetime, did not have him put to death but commanded his son Solomon to do so without fail [1 Kings 2:5-6], doubtless because he himself could not do it without causing even greater damage and tumult. A prince must punish the wicked in such a way that he does not step on the dish while picking up the spoon, and for the sake of one man's head plunge country and people into want and fill the land with widows and orphans. Therefore, he must not follow the advice of those counselors and fire-eaters who would stir and incite him to start a war, saying, "What, must we suffer such insult and injustice?" He is a mighty poor Christian who for the sake of a single castle would put the whole land in jeopardy.

In short, here one must go by the proverb, "He cannot govern who cannot wink at faults." Let this be his rule: Where wrong cannot be punished without greater wrong, there let him waive his rights, however just they may be. He should not have regard to his own injury, but to the wrong others must suffer in consequence of the penalty he imposes. What have the many women and children done to deserve being made widows and orphans in order that you may avenge yourself on a worthless tongue or an evil hand which has injured you?

Here you will ask: "Is a prince then not to go to war, and are his subjects not to follow him into battle?" Answer: This is a far-reaching question, but let me answer it very briefly. To act here as a Christian, I say, a prince should not go to war against his overlord—king, emperor, or other liege lord—but let him who takes, take. For the governing authority must not be resisted by force, but only by confession of the truth. If it is influenced by this, well and good; if not, you are excused, you suffer wrong for God's sake. If, however, the antagonist is your equal, your inferior, or of a foreign government, you should first offer him justice and peace, as Moses taught the children of Israel. If he refuses, then—mindful of what is best for you—defend yourself against force by force, as Moses so well describes it in Deuteronomy 20[:10112]. But in doing this you must not consider your personal interests and how you may remain lord, but those of your subjects to whom you owe help and protection, that such action may proceed in love. Since your entire land is in peril you must make the venture, so that with God's help all may not be lost. If you cannot prevent some from becoming widows and orphans as a consequence, you must at least see that not everything goes to ruin until there is nothing left except widows and orphans.

In this matter subjects are in duty bound to follow, and to devote their life and property, for in such a case one must risk his goods and himself for the sake of others. In a war of this sort it is both Christian and an act of love to kill the enemy without hesitation, to plunder and burn and injure him by every method of warfare until he is conquered (except that one must beware of sin, and not violate wives and virgins). And when victory has been achieved, one should offer mercy and peace to those who surrender and humble themselves. In such a case let the proverb apply, "God helps the strongest." This is what Abraham did when he smote the four kings, Genesis 14; he certainly slaughtered many, and showed little mercy until he conquered them. Such a case must be regarded as sent by God as a means to cleanse the land for once and drive out the rascals.

What if a prince is in the wrong? Are his people bound to follow him then too? Answer: No, for it is no one's duty to do wrong; we must obey God (who desires the right) rather than men [Acts 5:29]. What if the subjects do not know whether their prince is in the right or not? Answer: So long as they do not know, and cannot with all possible diligence find out, they may obey him without peril to their souls.

Selection 3: *Against the Robbing and Murdering Horde of Peasants*, ca. 1525

Luther was much distressed by the peasants' revolt against their rulers. The earlier book he mentions, a response to the peasants' Twelve Articles spelling out their grievances, was an admonition that brought little result. This harsher word spells out Luther's distress at the misrepresentation of his teaching as a justification of the revolt and his concern for the devastation that will result. Luther's defense of the nobility against the oppressed peasantry helped give credence to later interpretations of Luther's two realms doctrine that construed the primary role of the church in society to be obedient to the divinely ordained civil authority in matters of civil order. At the same time, it is clear that the revolt exerted its own brand of brutality.

In my earlier book on this matter, I did not venture to judge the peasants, since they had offered to be corrected and to be instructed; and Christ in Matthew 7[:1] commands us not to judge. But before I could even inspect the situation, they forgot their promise and violently took matters into their own hands and are robbing and raging like mad dogs. All this now makes it clear that they were trying to deceive us and that the assertions they made in their Twelve Articles were nothing but lies presented under the name of the gospel. To put it briefly, they are doing the devil's work. This is particularly the work of that archdevil who rules at Mühlhausen [Thomas Münzer], and does nothing except stir up robbery, murder, and bloodshed; as Christ describes him in John 8 [:44], "He was a murderer from the beginning." Since these peasants and wretched people have now let themselves be misled and are acting differently than they promised, I, too, must write differently of them than I have written, and begin by setting their sin before them, as God commands Isaiah [58:1] and Ezekiel [2:7], on the chance that some of them may see themselves for what they are. Then I must instruct the rulers how they are to conduct themselves in these circumstances.

The peasants have taken upon themselves the burden of three terrible sins against God and man; by this they have abundantly merited death in body and soul. In the first place, they have sworn to be true and faithful, submissive and obedient, to their rulers, as Christ commands when he says, "Render to Caesar the things that are Caesar's" [Luke 20:25]. And Romans 13 [:1] says, "Let every person be subject to the governing authorities." Since they are now deliberately and violently breaking this oath of obedience and setting themselves in opposition to their masters, they have forfeited body and soul, as faithless, perjured, lying, disobedient rascals and scoundrels usually do. St. Paul passed this judgment on them in Romans 13 [:2] when he said that those who resist the authorities will bring a judgment upon themselves. This saying will smite the peasants sooner or later, for God wants people to be loyal and to do their duty.

In the second place, they are starting a rebellion, and are violently robbing and plundering monasteries and castes that are not theirs; by this they have doubly deserved death in body and soul as highwaymen and murderers. Furthermore, anyone who can be proved to be a seditious person is an outlaw before God and the emperor; and whoever is the first to put him to death does right and well. For if a man is in open rebellion, everyone is both his judge and his executioner; just as when a fire starts, the first man who can put it out is the best man to do the job. For rebellion is not just simple murder; it is like a great fire, which attacks and devastates a whole land. Thus rebellion brings with it a land filled with murder and bloodshed; it makes widows and orphans, and turns everything upside down, like the worst disaster. Therefore let everyone who can, smite, slay, and stab, secretly or openly, remembering that nothing can be more poisonous, hurtful, or devilish than a rebel. It is just as when one must kill a mad dog; if you do not strike him, he will strike you, and a whole land with you.

In the third place, they cloak this terrible and horrible sin with the gospel, call themselves "Christian brethren," take oaths and submit to them, and compel people to go along with them in these abominations. Thus they become the worst blasphemers of God and slanderers of his holy name. Under the outward appearance of the gospel, they honor and serve the devil, thus deserving death in body and soul ten times over. I have never heard of a more hideous sin. I suspect that the devil feels that the Last Day is coming and therefore he undertakes such an unheard-of act, as though saying to himself, "This is the end, therefore it shall be the worst; I will stir up the dregs and knock out the bottom." God will guard us against him! See what a mighty prince the devil is, how he has the world in his hands and can throw everything into confusion, when he can so quickly catch so many thousands of peasants, deceive them, blind them, harden them, and throw them into revolt, and do with them whatever his raging fury undertakes.

It does not help the peasants when they pretend that according to Genesis 1 and 2 all things were created free and common, and that all of us alike have been baptized. For under the New Testament, Moses does not count; for there stands our Master, Christ, and subjects us, along with our bodies and our property, to the emperor and the law of this world, when he says, "Render to Caesar the things that are Caesar's" [Luke 20:25]. Paul, too, speaking in Romans 12 [13:1] to all baptized Christians, says, "Let every person be subject to the governing authorities." And Peter says, "Be subject to every ordinance of man" [I Pet. 2:13]. We are bound to live according to this teaching of Christ, as the Father commands from heaven, saying, "This is my beloved Son, listen to him" [Matt. 17:5].

For baptism does not make men free in body and property, but in soul; and the gospel does not make goods common, except in the case of those who, of their own free will, do what the apostles and disciples did in Acts 4 [:32-37]. They did not demand, as do our insane peasants in their raging, that the goods of others—of Pilate and Herod—should be common, but only their own goods. Our peasants, however, want to make the goods of other men common, and keep their own for themselves. Fine Christians they are! I think there is not a devil left in hell; they have all gone into the peasants. Their raving has gone beyond all measure.

Now since the peasants have brought [the wrath of] both God and man down upon themselves and are already many times guilty of death in body and soul, and since they submit to no court and wait for no verdict, but only rage on, I must instruct the temporal authorities on how they may act with a clear conscience in this matter.

First, I will not oppose a ruler who, even though he does not tolerate the gospel, will smite and punish these peasants without first offering to submit the case to judgment. He is within his rights, since the peasants are not contending any longer for the gospel, but have become faithless, perjured, disobedient, rebellious murderers, robbers, and blasphemers, whom even a heathen ruler has the right and authority to punish. Indeed, it is his duty to punish such scoundrels, for this is why he bears the sword and is "the servant of God to execute his wrath on the wrongdoer," Romans 13 [:4].

But if the ruler is a Christian and tolerates the gospel, so that the peasants have no appearance of a case against him, he should proceed with fear. First he must take the matter to God, confessing that we have deserved these things, and remembering that God may, perhaps, have thus aroused the devil as a punishment upon all Germany. Then he should humbly pray for help against the devil, for we are contending not only "against flesh and blood," but "against the spiritual hosts of wickedness in the air" [Eph. 6:12; 2:2], which must be attacked with prayer. Then, when our hearts are so turned to God that we are ready to let his divine will be done, whether he will or will not have us to be princes and lords, we must go beyond our duty, and offer the mad peasants an opportunity to come to terms, even though they are not worthy of it. Finally, if that does not help, then swiftly take to the sword.

For in this case a prince and lord must remember that according to Romans 13 [:4] he is God's minister and the servant of his wrath and that the sword has been given him to use against such people. If he does not fulfill the duties of his office by punishing some and protecting others, he commits as great a sin before God as when someone who has not been given the sword commits murder. If he is able to punish and does not do it—even though he would have had to kill someone or shed blood—he becomes guilty of all the murder and evil that these people commit. For by deliberately disregarding God's command he permits such rascals to go about their wicked business, even though he was able to prevent it and it was his duty to do so. This is not a time to sleep. And there is no place for patience or mercy. This is the time of the sword, not the day of grace.

The rulers, then, should press on and take action in this matter with a good conscience as long as their hearts still beat. It is to the rulers' advantage that the peasants have a bad conscience and an unjust cause, and that any peasant who is killed is lost in body and soul and is eternally the devil's. But the rulers have a good conscience and a just cause; they can, therefore, say to God with all confidence of heart, "Behold, my God, you have appointed me prince or lord, of this I can have no doubt; and you have given me the sword to use against evildoers (Romans 13 [:4]). It is your word, and it cannot lie, so I must fulfill the duties of my office, or forfeit your grace. It is also plain that these peasants have deserved death many times over, in your eyes and in the eyes of the world, and have been committed to me for punishment. If you will me to be slain by them, and let my authority be taken from me and destroyed, so be it: let your will be done. I shall be defeated and die because of your divine command and word and shall die while obeying your command and fulfilling the duties of my office. Therefore I will punish and smite as long as my heart beats. You will be the judge and make things right."

Thus, anyone who is killed fighting on the side of the rulers may be a true martyr in the eyes of God, if he fights with the kind of conscience I have just described, for he acts in obedience to God's word. On the other hand, anyone who perishes on the peasants' side is an eternal firebrand of hell, for he bears the sword against God's word and is disobedient to him, and is a member of the devil. And even if the peasants happen to gain the upper hand (God forbid!)—for to God all things are possible, and we do not know whether it may be his will, through the devil, to destroy all rule and order and cast the world upon a desolate heap, as a prelude to the Last Day, which cannot be far off nevertheless, those who are found exercising the duties of their office can die without worry and go to the scaffold with a good conscience, and leave the kingdom of this world to the devil and take in exchange the everlasting kingdom. These are strange times, when a prince can win heaven with bloodshed better than other men with prayer!

Finally, there is another thing that ought to motivate the rulers. The peasants are not content with belonging to the devil themselves; they force and compel many good people to join their devilish league against their wills, and so make them partakers of all of their own wickedness and damnation. Anyone who consorts with them goes to the devil with them and is guilty of all the evil deeds that they commit, even though he has to do this because he is so weak in faith that he could not resist them. A pious Christian ought to suffer a hundred deaths rather than give a hairsbreadth of consent to the peasants' cause. O how many martyrs could now be made by the bloodthirsty peasants and the prophets of murder! Now the rulers ought to have mercy on these prisoners of the peasants, and if they had no other reason to use the sword with a good conscience against the peasants, and to risk their own lives and property in fighting them, this would be reason enough, and more than enough: they would be rescuing and helping these souls whom the peasants have forced into their devilish league and who, without willing it, are sinning so horribly and must be damned. For truly these souls are in purgatory; indeed, they are in the bonds of hell and the devil.

Therefore, dear lords, here is a place where you can release, rescue, help. Have mercy on these poor people! Let whoever can stab, smite, slay. If you die in doing it, good for you! A more blessed death can never be yours, for you die while obeying the divine word and commandment in Romans 13 [:1, 2], and in loving service of your neighbor, whom you are rescuing from the bonds of hell and of the devil. And so I beg everyone who can to flee from the peasants as from the devil himself; those who do not flee, I pray that God will enlighten and convert. As for those who are not to be converted, God grant that they may have neither fortune nor success. To this let every pious Christian say, "Amen!" For this prayer is right and good, and pleases God; this I know. If anyone thinks this too harsh, let him remember that rebellion is intolerable and that the destruction of the world is to be expected every hour.

JOHN CALVIN

Calvin was the most important of the second-generation reformers. Born in 1509 at Noyon, France, he first studied law and later came under the influence of humanism and pursued linguistic studies. Soon he joined the cause of the Reformation and became its leader in the French-speaking world by virtue of his authoritative position in Geneva. From here he influenced the Reformation all over the world and made the city the headquarters of Reformed Christendom. He died in 1564.

Calvin's most influential work was his massive Institutes of the Christian Religion, the most widely disseminated systematic presentation of classical Protestantism. It went through many editions during his lifetime and contains significant aspects of his social ethics. Calvin has been blamed or praised for his supposed influence on the shape of the modern world, especially the rise of capitalism and popular democracy. In both instances there is no evidence of any direct or conscious influence. The indirect influence of certain Calvinist ideas as modified in the course of time is considerable.

Selection 1: *Institutes*, Book II, Chapter II, No. 1

Basic to Calvin's ethical teaching is his view of humanity as totally corrupt, often referred to as his doctrine of total depravity. Any ethics that ignores this situation would, according to Calvin, of necessity suggest the wrong remedy.

Man Has Now Been Deprived of Freedom of Choice and Bound Over to Miserable Servitude

(Perils of this topic: point of view established, I)

1. We have not seen that the dominion of sin, from the time it held the first man bound to itself, not only ranges among all mankind, but also completely occupies individual souls. It remains for us to investigate more closely whether we have been deprived of all freedom since we have been reduced to this servitude; and, if any particle of it still survives, how far its power extends. But in order that the truth of this question may be more readily apparent to us, I shall presently set a goal to which the whole argument should be directed. The best way to avoid error will be to consider

the perils that threaten man on both sides. (1) When man is denied all uprightness, he immediately takes occasion for complacency from that fact; and, because he is said to have no ability to pursue righteousness on his own, he holds all such pursuit to be of no consequence, as if it did not pertain to him at all. (2) Nothing, however slight, can be credited to man without depriving God of his honor, and without man himself falling into ruin through brazen confidence. Augustine points out both these precipices.

Here, then, is the course that we must follow if we are to avoid crashing upon these rocks: when man has been taught that no good thing remains in his power, and that he is hedged about on all sides by most miserable necessity, in spite of this he should nevertheless be instructed to aspire to a good of which he is empty, to a freedom of which he has been deprived. In fact, he may thus be more sharply aroused from inactivity than if it were supposed that he was endowed with the highest virtues. Everyone sees how necessary this second point is. I observe that too many persons have doubts about the first point. For since this is an undoubted fact, that nothing of his own ought to be taken away from an, it ought to be clearly evident how important it is for him to be barred from false boasting. At the time when man was distinguished with the noblest marks of honor through God's beneficence, not even then was he permitted to boast about himself. How much more ought he now to humble himself, cast down glory into extreme disgrace! At that time, I say, when he had been advanced to the highest degree of honor, Scripture attributed nothing else to him than that he had been created in the image of God [Gen. 1:27], thus suggesting that man was blessed, not because of this own good actions, but by participation in God. What, therefore, now remains for man, bare and destitute of all glory, but to recognize God for whose beneficence he could not be grateful when he abounded with the riches of his grace; and at least, but confessing his own poverty to glorify him in whom he did not previously glory in recognition of his own blessings?

Also, it is no less to our advantage than pertinent to God's glory that we be deprived of all credit for our wisdom and virtue. Thus those who bestow upon us anything beyond the truth add sacrilege to our ruin. When we are taught to wage our own war, we are but borne aloft on a reed stick, only to fall as soon as it breaks! Yet we flatter our strength unduly when we compare it even to a reed stick! For whatever vain men devise and babble concerning these matters is but smoke. Therefore Augustine with good reason often repeats the famous statement that free will is by its defenders more trampled down than strengthened. It has been necessary to say this by way of preface because some, while they hear that man's power is rooted out from its very foundations that God's power may be built up in man, bitterly loathe this whole disputation as dangerous, not to say superfluous, Nonetheless, it appears both fundamental in religion and most profitable for us.

Selection 2: *Institutes*, Book II, Chapter II, No. 13

While humanity is corrupt, people have not lost the capacity of reason for the purposes of this world, where it proves to be most useful.

Yet its efforts do not always become so worthless as to have no effect, especially when it turns its attention to things below. On the contrary, it is intelligent enough to taste something of things above, although it is more careless about investigating these. Nor does it carry on this latter activity with equal skill. For when the mind is borne above the level of the present life, it is especially convinced of its own frailty. Therefore, to perceive more clearly how far the mind can proceed in any matter according to the degree of its ability, we must here set forth a distinction. This, then, is the distinction: that there is one kind of understanding of earthly things; another of heavenly. I call "earthly things" those which do not pertain to God or his Kingdom, to true justice, or to the blessedness of the future life; but which have their significance and relationship with regard to the present life and are, in a sense, confined within its bounds. I call "heavenly things" the pure knowledge of God, the nature of true righteousness, and the mysteries of the Heavenly Kingdom. The first class includes government, household management, all mechanical skills, and the liberal arts. In the second are the knowledge of God and of his will, and the rule by which we conform our lives to it.

Of the first class the following ought to be said: since man is by nature a social animal, he tends through natural instinct to foster and preserve society. Consequently, we observe that there exist in all men's minds universal impressions of a certain civic fair dealing and order. Hence no man is to be found who does not understand that every sort of human organization must be regulated by laws, and who does not comprehend the principles of those laws. Hence arises that unvarying consent of all nations and of individual mortals with regard to laws. For their seeds have, without teacher or lawgiver, been implanted in all men.

I do not dwell upon the dissension and conflicts that immediately spring up. Some, like thieves and robbers, desire to overturn all law and right, to break all legal restraints, to let their lust alone masquerade as law. Others think unjust what some have sanctioned as just (an even commoner fault), and contend that what some have forbidden is praiseworthy. Such persons hate laws not because they do not know them to be good and holy; but raging with headlong lust, they fight against manifest reason. What they approve of in their understanding they hate on account of their lust. Quarrels of this latter sort do not nullify the original conception of equity. For, while men dispute among themselves about individual sections of the law, they agree on the general conception of equity. In this respect the frailty of the human mind is surely proved: even when it seems to follow the way, it limps and staggers. Yet the fact remains that some seed of political order has been implanted in all men. And this is ample proof that in the arrangement of this life no man is without the light of reason.

Selection 3: *Institutes*, Book II, Chapter VIII, Nos. 39, 41, 45–46

> *Calvin inserts a detailed discussion of the Ten Commandments into his Institutes, which illustrates his ethical approach. This selection reproduces a portion of his commentary on the "second table," which deals with out duties to our fellow human beings.*

Sixth Commandment

"You shall not kill." [Ex. 20:13, Vg.]

The purpose of this commandment is: the Lord has bound mankind together by a certain unity; hence each man ought to concern himself with the safety of all. To sum up, then, all violence, injury, and any harmful thing as all that may injure our neighbor's body are forbidden to us. We are accordingly commanded, if we find anything of use to us in saving our neighbors' lives, faithfully to employ it; if there is anything that makes for their peace, to see to it; if anything harmful, to ward it off; if they are in any danger, to lend a helping hand. If you recall that God is so speaking as Lawgiver, ponder at the same time that by this rule he wills to guide your soul. For it would be ridiculous that he who looks upon the thoughts of the heart and dwells especially upon them, should instruct only the body in true righteousness. Therefore this law also forbids murder of the heart, and enjoins the inner intent to save a brother's life. The hand, indeed, gives birth to murder, but the mind when infected with anger and hatred conceives it. See whether you can be angry against your brother without burning with desire to hurt him. If you cannot be angry with him, then you cannot hate him, for hatred is nothing but sustained anger. Although you dissimulated and try to escape by vain shifts—where there is either anger or hatred, there is the intent to do harm. If you keep trying to evade the issue, the Spirit has already declared that "he who hates a brother in his heart is a murderer;" the Lord brother in his heart is a murderer;" the Lord Christ has declared that "whoever is angry with his brother is liable to judgment; whoever says 'Raca' is liable to the council; whoever says 'You fool!' is liable to the hell of fire."

Seventh Commandment

"You shall not commit adultery." [Ex. 20:14, Vg.]

The purpose of this commandment is: because God loves modesty and purity, all uncleanness must be far from us. To sum up, then: we should not become defiled with any filth or lustful intemperance of the flesh. To this corresponds the affirmative commandment that we chastely and continently regulate all parts of our life. But he expressly forbids fornication, to which all lust tends, in order through the foulness of fornication, which is grosser and more palpable, in so far as it brands the body also with its mark, to lead us to abominate all lust.

Man had been created in this condition that he may not lead a solitary life, but may enjoy a helper joined to himself; then by the curse of sin he has been still more subjected to this necessity. Therefore, the Lord sufficiently provided for us in this matter when he established marriage, the fellowship of which, begun on this authority, he also sanctified by his blessing. From this it is clear that any other union apart from marriage is accursed in his sight; and that the companionship of marriage has been ordained as a necessary remedy to keep us from plunging into unbridled lust. Let us not delude ourselves, then, when we hear that outside marriage man cannot cohabit with a woman without God's curse.

Eighth Commandment

"You shall not steal." [Ex. 20:15, Vg.]

The purpose of this commandment is: since injustice is an abomination to God, we should render to each man what belongs to him. To sum up: we are forbidden to pant after the possessions of others, and consequently are commanded to strive faithfully to help every man to keep his own possessions.

We must consider that what every man possesses has not come to him by mere chance but by the distribution of the supreme Lord of all. For this reason, we cannot by evil devices deprive anyone of his possessions without fraudulently setting aside God's dispensation. Now there are many kinds of thefts. One consists in violence, when another's goods are stolen by force and unrestrained brigandage. A second kind consists in malicious deceit, then they are carried off through fraud. Another lies in a more concealed craftiness, when a man's goods are snatched from him by seemingly legal means. Still another lies in flatteries, when one is cheated of his goods under the pretense of a gift.

Let us not stop too long to recount the kinds of theft. Let us remember that all those arts whereby we acquire the possessions and money of our neighbors—when such devices depart from sincere affection to a desire to cheat or in some manner to harm—are to be considered as thefts. Although such possessions may be acquired in a court action, yet God does not judge otherwise. For he sees the intricate deceptions with which a crafty man sets out to snare one of simpler mind, until he as last draws him into his nets. He sees the hard and inhuman laws with which the more powerful oppresses and crushes the weaker person. He sees the lures with which the wilier man baits, so to speak, his hooks to catch the unwary. All these things elude human judgment and are not recognized. And such injustice occurs not only in matters of money or in merchandise of land, but in the right of each one; for we defraud our neighbors of their property if we repudiate the duties by which we obligated to them. If a shiftless steward or overseer devours his master's substance, and fails to attend to household business; if he either unjustly spends or wantonly wastes the properties entrusted to him; if the servant mocks his master; if he divulges his secrets; if in any way he betrays his life or goods; if the master, on the other hand, savagely harasses his household—all these are deemed theft in God's sight. For he who does not carry out what he owes to others according to the responsibility of his own calling both withholds and appropriated what is another's.

We will duly obey this commandment, then, if, content with our lot, we are zealous to make only honest and lawful gain; if we do not seek to become wealthy through injustice, nor attempt to deprive our neighbor of his goods to increase our own; if we do not strive to heap up riches cruelly wrung from the blood of others; if we do not madly scrape together from everywhere, by fair means or foul, whatever well feed our avarice of satisfy our prodigality. On the other hand, let this be our constant aim: faithfully to help all men by our counsel and aid to keep what is theirs, in so far as we can; but if we have to deal with faithless and deceitful men, let us be prepared to give up something of our own rather than to contend with them. And not this alone: but let us share the necessity of those whom we see pressed by the difficulty of affairs, assisting them in their need with our abundance.

Finally, let each one see to what extent he is in duty bound to others, and let him pay his debt faithfully. For this reason let a people hold all its rulers in honor, patiently bearing their government, obeying their laws and commands, refusing nothing that can be borne without losing God's favor. Again let the rulers take care of their own common people, keep the public peace, protect the good, punish the evil. So let them manage all things as if they are about to render account of their services to God, the supreme Judge. Let the ministers of churches faithfully attend to the ministry of the Word, not adulterating the teaching of salvation, but delivering it pure and undefiled to God's people. And let them instruct the people not only through teaching, but also through example of life. In short, let them exercise authority as good shepherds over their sheep. Let the people in their turn receive them as messengers and apostles of God, render to them that honor of which the highest Master of God, render to them that honor of which the highest Master has deemed them worthy, and give them those things necessary for their livelihood. Let parents undertake to nourish, govern, and teach, their children committed to them by God, not provoking their minds with cruelty or turning them against their parents; but cherishing and embracing their children with such gentleness and kindness as becomes their character as parents. As we have already said, children owe obedience to their parents. Let youth reverence old age, as the Lord has willed that age to be worthy of honor. Also, let the aged guide the insufficiency of youth with their own wisdom and experience wherein they excel the younger, not railing harshly and loudly against them but tempering their severity with mildness and gentleness. Let servants show themselves diligent and eager to obey their masters—not for the eye, but from the heart, as if they were serving God. Also, let masters not conduct themselves peevishly and intractably toward their servants, oppressing them with undue rigor, or treating them abusively. Rather, let them recognize them as their brothers, their coservants under the Lord of heaven, whom they ought to love mutually and treat humanely.

In this manner, I say, let each man consider what, in his rank and station, he owes to his neighbors, and pay what he owes. Moreover, our mind must always have regard for the Lawgiver that we may know that this rule was established for our hearts as well as for our hands, in order that men may strive to protect and promote the well-being and interest of others.

Selection 4: *Institutes*, Book III, Chapter XXI, No. 7

> *This is Calvin's brief summary of his controversial doctrine of "double predestination." Election, Calvin maintains, is not based on God's foreknowledge of those who would merit salvation but simply a decision of God's sovereign freedom prior to any other consideration.*

As Scripture, then, clearly shows, we say that God once established by his eternal and unchangeable plan those whom he long before determined once for all to receive into salvation, and those whom, on the other hand, he would devote to destruction. We assert that, with respect to the elect, this plan was founded upon his freely given mercy, without regard to human worth; but by his just and irreprehensible but incomprehensible judgment he has barred the door of life to those whom he has given over to damnation. Now among the elect we regard the call as a testimony of election. Then we hold justification another sign of its manifestation, until they come into the glory in which the fulfillment of that election lies. But as the Lord seals his elect by call and justification, so, by shutting off the reprobate from knowledge of his name or from the sanctification of his Spirit, he, as it were, reveals by these marks what sort of judgment awaits them. Here I shall pass over many fictions that stupid men have invented to overthrow predestination. They need no refutation, for as soon as they are brought forth they abundantly prove their own falsity. I shall pause only over those which either are being argued by the learned or may raise difficulty for the simple, or which impiety speciously sets forth in order to assail God's righteousness.

Selection 5: *Institutes*, Book IV, Chapter XX, Nos. 1–3, 24, 31–32

The distinction between spiritual and civil government is central to Calvin's social ethics. He seems to favor a form of government incorporating checks and balances. And while opposed to any kind of revolution, he seems to advocate the overthrow of tyrants by means of lower magistrates.

1. Differences between spiritual and civil government

Now, since we have established above that man is under a twofold government, and since we have elsewhere discussed at sufficient length the kind that resides in the soul or inner man and pertains to eternal life, this is the place to say something also about the other kind, which pertains only to the establishment of civil justice and outward morality.

For although this topic seems by nature alien to the spiritual doctrine of faith which I have undertaken to discuss, what follows will show that I am right in joining them, in fact, that necessity compels me to do so. This is especially true since, from one side, insane and barbarous men furiously strive to overturn this divinely established order; while, on the other side, the flatterers of princes, immoderately praising their power, do not hesitate to set them against the rule of God himself. Unless both these evils are checked, purity of faith will perish. Besides, it is of no slight importance to us to know how lovingly God has provided in this respect for mankind, that greater zeal for piety may flourish in us to attest our gratefulness.

First, before we enter into the matter itself, we must keep in mind that distinction which we previously laid down so that we do not (as commonly happens) unwisely mingle these two, which have a completely different nature. For certain men, when they hear that the gospel promises a freedom that acknowledges no king and no magistrate among men, but looks to Christ alone, think that they cannot benefit by their freedom so long as they see any power set up over them. They therefore think that nothing will be safe unless the whole world is reshaped to a new form, where there are neither courts, nor laws, nor magistrates, nor anything which in their opinion restricts their freedom. But whoever knows how to distinguish between body and soul, between this present fleeting life and that future eternal life, will without difficulty know that Christ's spiritual Kingdom and the civil jurisdiction are things completely distinct. Since, then, it is a Jewish vanity to seek and enclose Christ's Kingdom within the elements of this world, let us rather ponder that what Scripture clearly teaches is a spiritual fruit, which we gather from Christ's grace; and let us remember to keep within its own limits all that freedom which is promised and offered to us in him. For why is it that the same apostle who bids us stand and not submit to the "yoke of bondage" elsewhere forbids slaves to be anxious about their state, unless it be that spiritual freedom can perfectly well exist along with civil bondage? These statements of his must also be taken in the same sense: In the Kingdom of God "there is neither Jew nor Greek, neither male nor female, neither slave nor free." And again, "there is not Jew nor Greek, uncircumcised and circumcised, barbarian, Scythian, slave, freeman; but Christ is all in all." By these statements he means that it makes no difference what your condition among men may be or under what nation's laws you live, since the Kingdom of Christ does not all consist in these things.

2. The "two governments" are not antithetical

Yet this distinction does not lead us to consider the whole nature of government a thing polluted, which has nothing to do with Christian men. That is what indeed, certain fanatics who delight in unbridled license shout and boast: after we have died through Christ to the elements of this world, are transported to God's Kingdom, and sit among heavenly beings, it is a thing unworthy of us and set far beneath our excellence to be occupied with those vile and worldly cares which have to do with business foreign to a Christian man. To what purpose, they ask, are there laws without trials and tribunals? But what has a Christian man to do with trials themselves? Indeed, if it is not lawful to kill, why do we have laws and trials? But as we have just now pointed out that this kind of government is distinct from that

Spiritual and inward Kingdom of Christ, so we must know that they are not at variance. For spiritual government, indeed, is already initiating in us upon earth certain beginnings of the Heavenly Kingdom, and in this mortal and fleeting life affords a certain forecast of an immortal and incorruptible blessedness. Yet civil government has as its appointed end, so long as we live among men, to cherish and protect the outward worship of God, to defend sound doctrine of piety and the position of the church, to adjust our life to the society of men, to form our social behavior to civil righteousness, to reconcile us with one another, and to promote general peace and tranquility. All of this I admit to be superfluous, if God's Kingdom, such as it is now among us, wipes out the present life. But if it is God's will that we go as pilgrims upon the earth while we aspire to the true fatherland, and if the pilgrimage requires such helps, those who take these from man deprive him of his very humanity. Our adversaries claim that there ought to be such great perfection in the church of God that its government should suffice for law. But they stupidly imagine such perfection as can never be found in a community of men. For since the insolence of evil men is so great, their wickedness so stubborn, that it can scarcely be restrained by extremely severe laws, what do we expect them to do if they see that their depravity can go scotfree—when no power can force them to cease from doing evil?

3. The chief tasks and burdens of civil government

But there will be a more appropriate place to speak of the practice of civil government. Now we only wish it to be understood that to think of doing away with it is outrageous barbarity. Its function among men is no less than that of bread, water, sun, and air; indeed, its place of honor is far more excellent. For it does not merely see to it, as all these serve to do, that men breathe, eat, drink, and are kept warm, even though it surely embraces all these activities when it provides for their living together. It does not, I repeat, look to this only, but also prevents idolatry, sacrilege against God's name, blasphemies against his idolatry, sacrilege against God's name, blasphemies against his truth, and other public offenses against religion from arising and spreading among the people; it prevents the public peace form being disturbed; it provides that each man may keep his property safe and sound; that men may carry on blameless intercourse among themselves; that honesty and modesty may be preserved among men. In short, it provides that a public manifestation of religion may exist among Christians, and that humanity be maintained among men.

Let no man be disturbed that I now commit to civil government the duty of rightly establishing religion, which I seem above to have put outside of human decision. For, when I approve of a civil administration that aims to prevent the true religion which is contained in God's law from being openly and with public sacrilege violated and defiled with impunity, I do not here, any more than before, allow men to make laws according to their own decision concerning religion and the worship of God.

24. *Obedience is also due the unjust magistrate*
But since we have so far been describing a magistrate who truly is what he is called, that is, a father of his country, and, as the poet expresses it, shepherd of his people, guardian of peace, protector of righteousness, and avenger of innocence—he who does not approve of such government must rightly be regarded as insane.

But it is the example of nearly all ages that some princes are careless about all those things to which they ought to have given heed, and, far from all care, lazily take their pleasure. Others, intent upon their own business, put up for sale laws, privileges, judgments, and letters of favor. Others drain the common people of their money, and afterward lavish it on insane largesse. Still others exercise sheer robbery, plundering houses, raping virgins and matrons, and slaughtering the innocent.

Consequently, many cannot be persuaded that they ought to recognize these as princes and to obey their authority as far as possible. For in such great disgrace, and among such crimes, so they discern no appearance of the image of God which ought to have shone in the magistrate; while they see no trace of that minister of God, who had been appointed to praise the good, and to punish the evil. Thus, they also do not recognize as ruler him whose dignity and authority Scripture commands to us. Indeed, this inborn feeling has always been in the minds of men to hate and curse tyrants as much as to love and venerate lawful kings.

31. *Constitutional defenders of the people's freedom*
But however these deeds of men are judged in themselves, still the Lord accomplished his work through them alike when he broke the bloody scepters of arrogant kings and when he overturned intolerable governments. Let the princes hear and be afraid.

But we must, in the meantime, be very careful not to despise or violate that authority of magistrates, full of venerable majesty, which God has established by the weightiest decrees, even though it may reside with the most unworthy men, who defile it as much as they can with their own wickedness. For, if the correction of unbridled despotism is the lord's to avenge, let us not at once think that it is entrusted to us, to whom no command has been given except to obey and suffer.

I am speaking all the while of private individuals. For it there are now any magistrates of the people, appointed to restrain the willfulness of kings (as in ancient times the ephors were set against the Spartan kings, or the tribunes of the people against the Roman consuls, or the demarchs against the senate of the Athenians; and perhaps, as things now are, such power as the three estates exercise in every realm when they hold their chief assemblies), I am so far from forbidding them to withstand, in accordance with their duty, the fierce licentiousness of kings, that, if they wink at kings who violently fall upon and assault the lowly common fold, I declare that their dissimulation involves nefarious perfidy, because they dishonestly betray the freedom of the people, of which they know that they have been appointed protectors by God's ordinance.

32. Obedience to man must not become disobedience to God

But in that obedience which we have shown to be due the authority of rulers, we are always to make this exception, indeed to observe it as primary, that such obedience is never to lead us away from obedience to him, to whose will the desires of all kings ought to be subject, to whose decrees all their commands ought to yield, to whose majesty their scepters ought to be submitted. And how absurd would it be that in satisfying men you should incur the displeasure of him for whose sake you obey men themselves! The Lord, therefore, is the King of Kings, who, when he has opened his sacred mouth, must alone be heard, before all and above all men; next to him we are subject to those men who are in authority over us, but only in him. If they command anything against him, let it go unesteemed. And here let us not be concerned about all that dignity which the magistrates possess; for no harm is done to it when it is humbled before that singular and truly supreme power of God. On this consideration, Daniel denies that he has committed any offense against the king, when he has not obeyed his impious edict. For the king had exceeded his limits, and had not only been a wrongdoer against men, but in lifting up his horns against God, had himself abrogated his power. Conversely, the Israelites are condemned because they were obedient to the wicked proclamation of the king. For when Jeroboam molded the golden calves, they, to please him, forsook God's Temple and turned to new superstitions. With the same readiness, their descendants complied with the decrees of their kings. The prophet sharply reproaches them for embracing the king's edicts. Far, indeed, is the pretense of modesty from deserving praise, a false modesty with which the court flatterers cloak themselves and deceive the simple, while they deny that it is lawful for them to refuse anything imposed by their kings. As if God had made over his right to mortal men, giving them the rule over mankind! Or as if earthly power were diminished when it is subjected to its Author, in whose presence even the heavenly powers tremble as suppliants! I know with what great and present peril this constancy is menaced, because kings bear deviance with the greatest displeasure, whose "wrath is a messenger of death," says Solomon. But since this edict has been proclaimed by the heavenly herald, Peter—"We must obey God rather than men"—let us comfort ourselves with the thought that we are rendering that obedience which the Lord requires when we suffer anything rather than turn aside from piety. And that our courage may not grow faint, Paul pricks us with another goad: That we have been redeemed by Christ at so great a price as our redemption cost to him, so that we could not enslave ourselves to the wicked desires of men—much less by subject to their impiety.

THE ANABAPTISTS 14

In the sixteenth century the name "Anabaptist" was applied to a widely divergent group of reform-minded people who disassociated themselves from Luther and Zwingli and their followers as well as from the Roman Catholic Church. Often identified as constituting the "Left Wing of the Reformation" or the "Radical Reformation," their social teachings varied greatly, from the advocacy of violence and the extermination of the "godless" by Thomas Müntzer to the consistent pacifism of the Swiss groups and the followers of Menno Simons. It was the pacifist tradition that survived and whose teachings have continued to influence the social thought of Western Christianity even though strict pacifism did not become the prevailing doctrine. At the same time, the Anabaptist's strong position on the separation of church and state seems more compatible with the views held by most Americans on this matter than the more complicated interactive relationship of church and state entailed in the teachings of Luther, Calvin, or the Jesuits.

Selection 1: *The Schleitheim Confession of Faith*

The Schleitheim Confession of Faith *was prepared at a conference of Swiss Brethren in 1527. The section here reproduced deals with the separation of the true Christians from the wicked. It is a principle example of the Anabaptist conviction that Christians are bound to withdraw from the cultural and civil life of the world as being irreconcilably in conflict with the teachings of Christ. In effect they sought to create a parallel society, which recognized certain claims of the civil government only if they did not countermand Christ's teachings as they understood them. There are echoes here of Tertullian and others in the tradition of Christian thought.*

We have been united concerning the separation that shall take place from the evil and the wickedness which the devil has planted in the world, simply in this; that we have no fellowship with them, and do not run with them in the confusion of their abominations. So it is; since all who have not entered into the obedience of faith and have not united themselves with God so that they will to do His will, are a great abomination before God, therefore nothing else can or really will grow or spring forth from them than abominable things. Now there is nothing else in the world and all creation than good or evil, believing and unbelieving, darkness and light, the world and those who are [come] out of the world, God's temple and idols. Christ and Belial, and none will have part with the other.

To us, then, the commandment of the Lord is also obvious, whereby He orders us to be and to become separated from the evil one, and thus He will be our God and we shall be His sons and daughters.

Further, He admonishes us therefore to go out from Babylon and from the earthly Egypt, that we may not be partakers in their torment and suffering, which the Lord will bring upon them.

From all this we should learn that everything which has not been united with our God in Christ is nothing but an abomination which we should shun. By this are meant all popish and repopish works and idolatry, gatherings, church attendance, winehouses, guarantees and commitments of unbelief, and other things of the kind, which the world regards highly, and yet which are carnal or flatly counter to the command of God, after the pattern of all the iniquity which is in the world. From all this we shall be separated and have no part with such, for they are nothing but abominations, which cause us to be hated before our Christ Jesus, who has freed us from the servitude of the flesh and fitted us for the service of God and the Spirit whom He has given us.

Thereby shall also fall away from us the diabolical weapons of violence—such as sword, armor, and the like, and all of their use to protect friends or against enemies—by virtue of the word of Christ: "you shall not resist evil.

*　　*　　*

We have been united as follows concerning the sword. The sword is an ordering of God outside the perfection of Christ. It punishes and kills the wicked and guards and protects the good. In the law the sword is established over the wicked for punishment and for death and the secular rulers are established to wield the same.

But within the perfection of Christ only the ban is used for the admonition and exclusion of the one who has sinned, without the death of the flesh, simply the warning and the command to sin no more.

Now many, who do not understand Christ's will for us, will ask; whether a Christian may or should use the sword against the wicked for the protection and defense of the good, or for the sake of love.

The answer is unanimously revealed: Christ teaches and commands us to learn from Him, for He is meek and lowly of heart and thus we shall find rest for our souls. Now Christ says to the woman who was taken in adultery, not that she should be stoned according to the law of His Father (and yet He says, "What the Father commanded me, that I do") but with mercy and forgiveness and the warning to sin no more, says: "Go, sin no more." Exactly thus should we also proceed, according to the rule of the ban.

Second, is asked concerning the sword: whether a Christian shall pass sentence in disputes and strife about worldly matters, such as the unbelievers have with one another. The answer: Christ did not wish to decide or pass judgment between brother and brother concerning inheritance, but refused to do so. So should we also do.

Third, is asked concerning the sword: whether the Christian should be a magistrate if he is chosen thereto. This is answered thus: Christ was to be made king, but He fled and did not discern the ordinance of His Father. Thus we should also do as He did and follow after Him, and we shall not walk in darkness. For He Himself says: "Whoever would come after me, let him deny himself and take up his cross and follow me." He Himself further forbids the violence of the sword when He says: "The princes of this world lord it over them etc., but among you it shall not be so." Further Paul says, "Whom God has foreknown, the same he has also predestined to be conformed to the image of his Son," etc. Peter also says: "Christ has suffered (not ruled) and has left us an example, that you should follow after in his steps." Lastly, one can see in the following points that it does not befit a Christian to be a magistrate: the rule of the government is according to the flesh, that of the Christians according to the Spirit. Their houses and dwelling remain in this world, that of the Christians is in heaven. Their citizenship is in this world, that of the Christians is in heaven. The weapons of their battle and warfare are carnal and only against the flesh, but the weapons of Christians are spiritual, against the fortification of the devil. The worldly are armed with steel and iron, but Christians are armed with the armor of God, with truth, righteousness, peace, faith, salvation, and with the Word of God. In sum: as Christ our Head is minded, so also must be minded the members of the body of Christ through Him, so that there be no division in the body, through which it would be destroyed. Since then Christ is as is written of Him, so must His members also be the same, so that His body may remain whole and unified for its own advancement and upbuilding. For any kingdom which is divided within itself will be destroyed.

VII. We have been united as follows concerning the oath. The oath is a confirmation among those who are quarreling or making promises. In the law it is commanded that it should be done only in the name of God, truthfully and not falsely. Christ, who teaches the perfection of the law, forbids His [followers] all swearing, whether true or false; neither by heaven nor by earth, neither by Jerusalem nor by our head; and that for the reason which He goes on to give: "For you cannot make one hair white or black." You see, thereby all swearing is forbidden. We cannot perform what is promised in the swearing, for we are not able to change the smallest part of ourselves.

Now there are some who do not believe the simple commandment of God and who say, "But God swore by Himself to Abraham, because He was God (as He promised him that He would do good to him and would be his God if he kept His commandments). Why then should I not swear if I promise something to someone?" The answer: hear what the Scripture says: "God, since he wished to prove overabundantly to the heirs of His promise that His will did not change, inserted an oath so that by two immutable things we might have a stronger consolation (for it is impossible that God should lie)." Notice the meaning of the passage: God has the power to do what He forbids you, for everything is possible to Him. God swore an oath to Abraham, Scripture says, in order to prove that His counsel is immutable. That means: no one can withstand and thwart His will; thus He can keep His oath. But we cannot, as Christ said above, hold or perform our oath, therefore we should not swear.

Others say that swearing cannot be forbidden by God in the New Testament when it was commanded in the Old, but that it is forbidden only to swear by heaven, earth, Jerusalem, and our head. Answer: hear the Scripture. He who swears by heaven, swears by God's throne and by Him who sits thereon. Observe: swearing by heaven is forbidden, which is only God's throne; how much more is it forbidden to swear by God Himself. You blind fools, what is greater, the throne or He who sits upon it?

Others say, if it is then wrong to use God for truth, then the apostles Peter and Paul also swore. Answer: Peter and Paul only testify to that which God promised Abraham, whom we long after have received. But when one testifies, one testifies concerning that which is present, whether it be good or evil. Thus Simeon spoke of Christ to Mary and testified: "Behold: this one is ordained for the falling and rising of many in Israel and to be a sign which will be spoken against."

Christ taught us similarly when He says: Your speech shall be yea, yea; and nay, nay; for what is more than that comes of evil. He says, your speech or your word shall be yes and no, so that no one might understand that He had permitted it. Christ is simply yea and nay, and all those who seek Him simply will understand His Word. Amen.

Selection 2: Thomas Müntzer, *Sermon to the Princes*

> *Thomas Müntzer is grouped with the Anabaptists even though their theological concerns, particularly regarding baptism, were not central to his mission. A principle instigator and leader of the Peasant's Revolt in Saxony (See Luther's reaction above in* Against the Robbing Murderous Hordes of Peasants) *Müntzer could hardly be representative of the pacifist strain. In the selection from his sermon of July 13, 1524, here reproduced, he attempted to win the rulers of electoral Saxony for his kind of extremism.*

Interpretation of the second chapter of the prophet Daniel, preached by Thomas Müntzer, servant of the word of God, in the castle at Allstedt before the great and revered dukes and rulers of Saxony. Allstedt, 1524.

First of all the text of the above chapter from the prophet Daniel's predictions was read out and translated in its straight forward meaning, and then the whole sermon was delivered in accordance with the text as follows:

In view of the wretched, ruinous condition of the poor Christian Church it should be realised that no advice or help can be given until we have industrious, unflagging servants of God who are ready, day in, day out, to promote the knowledge of the Biblical books through singing, reading, and preaching. This will mean, however, that either the heads of our delicate priests get used to taking some hard knocks, or else they will have to abandon their trade. What alternative is there, while ravaging wolves are so grievously devastating the Christian people, like God's vineyard described in Isaiah 5, Psalm 79? St. Paul, after all, teaches us to school ourselves in songs of divine praise, Ephesians 5. For our situation today is the same as that of the good prophets Isaiah, Jeremiah, Ezekiel, and the others, when the whole congregation of God's elect had become completely caught up in idolatrous ways. As a result, not even God could help them, but had to let them be captured and transported and tormented under the heathen until they learned to recognize his holy name again, as Isaiah 29, Jeremiah 15 Ezekiel 36 and Psalm 88 testify.

Nonetheless in our own time and that of our fathers, our poor Christian people has shown even greater obstinacy while going to incredible lengths to claim the divine name for itself, Luke 21, 2 Timothy 3. The devil, of course and his servants, love to deck themselves out like this, 2 Cor. 1, and do it so alluringly that the true friends of God are seduced, and—despite the most determined efforts—are almost incapable of seeing their mistake, as Matthew 24 points out so clearly . . .

Alas! Christ, the gentle son of God, is a mere scarecrow or a painted puppet in our eyes compared with the great titles and names of this world, although he is the true stone, hurled from the great mountain into the sea, into the pomp and affluence of this world, Psalm 45. He is the stone torn from the great mountain without human hands, who is called Jesus Christ. . . . The shame of it! Of this lamentable abomination (of which Christ himself speaks in Matthew 24) that he should be ridiculed so pitiably by these devilish Masses, by such superstitious sermons, rituals and behaviour; for they worship after all, nothing but an idol carved of wood. Truly a superstitious, wooden priest and a coarse, clumsy and gnarled people, unable to comprehend the simplest pronouncement of God. Isn't that a sin, a shame, a cause for grief. . . . He has become a doormat for the whole world. Hence all the unbelieving Turks, pagans, and Jews have had an easy time ridiculing us regarding us as fools; one is, after all, bound to regard as mad those who refuse to hear any mention of the spirit of their faith. Hence the suffering of Christ is nothing but a fairground spectacle in the eyes of these abandoned scoundrels . . .

We will need, that is, the very clearest wisdom of God, Wisdom 9, which can only spring from the pure unfeigned fear of God. This alone can equip us with its mighty arm to exercise vengeance on the enemies of God with burning zeal to God . . .

However, if we are to see him as he really is then we have to become conscious every day of the revelation of God. How rare and scarce that has become in this scoundrelly world! For the sly proposals of our crafty scholars will rain down on us the whole time, and hinder us still more from progressing in the pure knowledge of God, Wisdom 4, Psalm 36. This sort of thing has to be averted by the fear of God. If we preserved this, and this alone, in our hearts-in its purity and entirety-then the holy people of Christ would easily come to the spirit of wisdom and the revelation of the divine will . . .

This seems to be the way of all but a few of the biblical scholars today. With very few exceptions they teach that God no longer reveals his divine mysteries to his dear friends through genuine visions or direct words etc. So they adhere to their bookish ways, Ecclesiasticus 34 and make a laughing-stock of those who have experience of the revelation of God. . . .

Now comes the text: "King Nebuchadnezzar had a dream, but it eluded him, etc." [Daniel 2]. . . .

> [At last Müntzer begins to exegete the key passage of scripture for his sermon. The context is as follows: Nebuchadnezzar, King of the neo-Babylonian empire, has had a strange dream. He first consulted his court advisors, demanding that they describe the king's dream before interpreting it (no easy task). Daniel, one of the Jewish leaders transported from Jerusalem to Babylonia, informs the great and troubled king that he can relate to him the images of the dream and their hidden meanings through the gift of God's wisdom. At this point in Müntzer's sermon, he compares contemporary so-called 'biblical scholars' to the astrologers and councilors attending Nebuchadnezzar.]

Such biblical scholars are like the soothsayers, who publicly deny that there is any revelation from God, but in fact obstruct the Holy Spirit's work. They set themselves up as instructors to the whole world, and anything which does not suit their academic approach is branded at once as devilish, although they themselves are not assured of their own salvation, essential as that is, Rom. 8. They can chatter away beautifully about faith and brew up a drunken faith for poor, confused consciences. The reason for all this is their uninformed judgment, based on their abhorrence of the poisonous, accursed dreams of the monks, through whose odious deceptions the devil realised all his plans. Indeed, he was able to deceive many pious but uninformed members of the elect, who gave immediate and total credence to these visions and dreams, with all their mad beliefs. Add to this their monastic rules and the wild, hypocritical idolatry prescribed to them by the devil, against which the Colossians were strongly warned by St. Paul in the second chapter. But the accursed monkish dreamers did not know how to become aware of the power of God, and adhered stubbornly to their perverse views. Nowadays they are being exposed to the whole world for the idle good-for nothings that they are, their sin and shame emerging more clearly every day. They are still too crazed to recognize their blindness.

It is true—I know it for a fact—that the spirit of God is revealing to many elect and pious men at this time the great need for a full and final reformation in the near future. This must be carried out. For despite all attempts to oppose it the prophecy of Daniel retains its full force—whether anyone believes it or not, as Paul says in Romans 3. This text of Daniel then is as clear as the bright sun, and the work of ending the fifth Empire of the world is now in full swing. The first Empire is explained by the golden knob—that was the Babylonian—the second by the silver breastplate and arm-piece—that was the Empire of the Medes and Persians. The third was the Greek Empire, resonant with human cleverness, indicated by the bronze; the fourth the Roman Empire, an Empire won by the sword, an Empire ruled by force. But the fifth is the one we see before us, which is also of iron and would like to use force, but it is patched with dung (as anyone can see if they want to) that is, with the vain schemings of hypocrisy, which swarms and slithers over the face of the whole earth. For any one who does not practice deception is regarded as a real idiot. What a pretty spectacle we have before us now—all the eels and snakes coupling together immorally in one great heap! The priests and all the evil clerics are the snakes, as John, who baptised Jesus, called them, Matthew 3, and the secular lords and rulers are the eels, symbolised by the fishes in Leviticus 11.

Thus the kingdoms of the devil have smeared themselves with clay. Oh, my dear lords, what a fine sight it will be when the Lord whirls his rod of iron among the old pots, Psalms 2. Therefore, my dearest, most revered rulers, learn true judgment from the mouth of God himself. Do not let yourself by seduced by your hypocritical priests into a restraint based on counterfeit clemency and kindness. For the stone dislodged from the mountain by no human hand, is a large one now; the poor laity and the peasants have a much sharper eye for it than you. Yes, God be praised, it has grown so large that if other lords or neighbors of yours thought to persecute you for the sake of the gospel, they would now be driven out by their own subjects. I know this of a certainty . . .

For the condition of the holy people of Christ has become so pitiable, that up to now not even the most eloquent tongue could do it justice. Therefore a new Daniel must arise and expound your dreams to you and, as Moses teaches in Deuteronomy 20, he must be in the vanguard, leading the way. He must bring about a reconciliation between the wrath of the princes and the rage of the people. For once you really grasp the plight of the Christian people as a result of the treachery of the false clergy and the abandoned criminals your rage against them will be boundless beyond all imagining. There is no doubt that you will be embittered and deeply regret all your benevolence to them in the past. Since they have used most sweet-sounding words to urge calamitously wrong judgments on you, Wisdom 6, quite contrary to the honest truth. For they have made such a fool of you that everyone swears by the saints that in their official capacity princes are just pagans, that all they have to do is to maintain civic order. Alas, my fine fellow, the great stone will come crashing down soon and smash such rational considerations to the ground, as Christ says in Matthew 10: 'I am not come to send peace, but the sword.' But what is one to do with the sword? Exactly this: sweep aside those evil men who obstruct the gospel! Take them out of circulation! . . . They [the 'biblical scribes'] deny that faith must be tested like gold in the fire, 1 Peter 1; Psalm 139. This, however, makes Christian faith worse than a dog's when it hopes for a piece of bread when the table is set. This is the sort of faith which the false biblical scholars display to the poor, blind world. They do not see the absurdity of this, because they preach solely to feed their stomachs, Phil. 3. As Matthew 12 says, with hearts like theirs they cannot say anything else. Now if you are to be true rulers, you must seize the very roots of government, following the command of Christ. Drive his enemies away from the elect; you are the instruments to do this . . .

Our scholars come and—in their godless, fraudulent way—understand Daniel to say that the Antichrist should be destroyed without human hands when it really means that he is intimidated already, like the inhabitants of the promised land when the chosen people entered it. Yet, as Joshua tells us, he did not spare them the sharp edge of the sword. Consult Psalm 43 and I Chronicles 13 and you will find it explained thus: they did not win the land by the sword, but by the power of God, but the sword was the means used, just as eating and drinking is a means for us to stay alive. Hence the sword, too, is necessary to eliminate the godless, Rom. 13. To ensure, however, that this now proceeds in a fair and orderly manner, our revered fathers, the princes, who with us confess Christ, should carry it out. But if they do not carry it out the sword will be taken from them Daniel 7, for then they would confess him in words but deny him in deeds, Titus 1. The sort of peace they should offer enemies is seen in Deuteronomy 2. If they want to be spiritual, and yet refuse to give an account of their knowledge of God, I Peter 3, then they should be done away with, 1 Cor. 5. But, like pious Daniel, I intercede on their behalf where they are not opposed to God's revelation. But where they do the opposite let them be strangled without mercy . . .

There is no doubt that many who have never been put to the test will be similarly offended by this little book, because I say with Christ, Luke 19, Mt. 18 and with Paul, 1 Cor. 5, and with the guidance of the whole divine law, that one should kill the godless rulers, and especially the monks and the priests who denounce the holy gospel as heresy and yet count themselves the best Christians. Then their hypocritical, counterfeit clemency will turn to incredible fury and bitterness. It will leap to the defense of the godless and say: Christ never killed anyone etc.' And because the friends of God waste their breath so lamentably on the wind the prophecy of Paul is fulfilled, 2 Tim. 3: "In the last days the pleasure-lovers will certainly give the impression of clemency but they will deny it any power." Nothing on earth has a fairer form or appearance than counterfeit clemency. Hence every nook and cranny is full of vain hypocrites, none of whom is courageous enough to speak the real truth. In order, then, that the truth may really begin to dawn you rulers must (God willing—whether you do it gladly or not) be guided by the conclusion of this chapter, where Nebuchadnezzar installed the holy Daniel in office to judge fairly and well, as the holy spirit says, Psalm 57. For the godless have no right to live, unless by the sufferance of the elect, as is written in the book of Exodus, chapter 23. Rejoice, you true friends of God, that the hearts of the enemies of the cross have fallen into their boots, for they have no choice but to do right, though they never dreamt of doing so. If we fear God, why should we be alarmed by rootless, feckless men, Numbers 14, Joshua 11. So be bold! He to whom all power is given in heaven and on earth wants to lead the government, Matthew 28. To you most beloved, may God grant eternal protection. Amen.

Selection 3: Menno Simons, *Reply to False Accusations*

Menno Simons (1496–1561) became the most influential leader of the pacifist Anabaptists. The Anabaptists suffered widespread persecution often on the basis of false accusations. Simons made a number of attempts to bring persecution to an end. This selection is perhaps his final effort, dated by some at 1552. He attempts first of all to persuade the rulers that he and his followers are not to be associated with the radical Anabaptists called Münsterites who took over the city of Münster in an attempt to establish a theocracy. Then in this excerpt he rebuts the charge that Anabaptists do not obey civil authority. From this defense we learn not only about the Anabaptist attitude toward government but also about Simons's views on how rulers should govern justly according to Christ and the Bible.

In the second place, they say that we will not obey the magistracy.

Answer. The writings that we have published during several years past prove clearly that this accusation against us is untrue and false. We publicly and unequivocally confess that the office of a magistrate is ordained of God, even as we have always confessed, since according to our small talent we have served the Word of the Lord. And moreover, in the meantime, we have obeyed them when not contrary to the Word of God. We intend to do so all our lives. For we are not so stupid as not to know what the Lord's Word commands in this respect. Taxes and tolls we pay as Christ has taught and Himself practiced. We pray for the imperial majesty, kings, lords, princes, and all in authority. We honor and obey them. 1 Tim. 2:2; Rom. 13:1. And yet they cry that we will not obey the magistrates, in order that they may disturb the hearts of those that have authority and excite them to all unmercifulness, wrath, and bitterness against us, and that by their continual agitation the bloody sword may be used against us without mercy and never be sheathed, as may be seen They ceaselessly excite the magistracy by such gross falsehood, and moreover say Yea and Amen to everything the magistracy commands or does, whether it is agreeable to the Scriptures or not. Thus they by their pleasant doctrine lead these souls into destruction and loss. They seek not their salvation but their own enjoyment and gain. Therefore before God, it is the truth; love compels us respectfully and humbly to show all high officials (some of whom would do right if they knew it and had some Hanani to point it out to them, since it is concealed by the preachers) what the Word of the Lord commands them, how they should be minded, and how they should rightfully execute their office to the praise and glory of the Lord. And it shall be, said Moses, when the king sitteth upon the throne of his kingdom, that he shall take this second law from the priests and Levites and copy it into a book. And it shall be with him and he shall read therein all the days of his life, that he may learn to fear the Lord his God, to keep all the words of this law and these statutes, to do them (Dear sirs, mark, it reads, To do them). His heart shall not be lifted up above his brethren and he shall not turn aside from the commandments to the right hand or the left. He shall not multiply horses to himself; neither shall he multiply wives to himself, nor silver and gold. Deut. 17:16-20. Concerning rulers, Jethro speaks to Moses, Provide out of all the people able men, such as fear God, men of truth, hating covetousness, and place them over them to be rulers. Ex. 18:21. Moses says, And I charged your judges at that time saying, Hear the causes between your brethren, and judge righteously between every man and his brother, and the stranger that is with him. Ye shall not respect persons in judgment; but ye shall hear the small as well as the great; ye shall not be afraid of the face of man; for the judgment is God's. Deut. 1:16, 17. Jehoshaphat, the king of Judah, said to the judges, Take heed what ye (Io; for ye judge not for man, but for the Lord, who is with you in judgment. Oh, an important and heroic word! Wherefore now let the fear of the Lord be upon you; take heed and do it; for there is no iniquity with the Lord our God, nor respect of person, nor taking of gifts. 2 Chron. 19:6, 7.

Paul says, Rulers are not a terror to good works, but to evil. (Mark ye, rulers to whom this office pertains.) Wilt thou then not be afraid of the power? Do that which is good, and thou shalt have praise of the same; for he is the minister of God to thee for good. But if thou do that which is evil, be afraid; for he beareth not the sword in vain; for he is the minister of God, a revenger to execute wrath upon him that doeth evil. Rom. 13:3, 4.Behold, beloved rulers and judges, if you take to heart these Scriptures and diligently ponder them, then you will observe, first, that your office is not your own but God's, so that you may bend your knees before His majesty; fear His great and adorable name, and rightly and reasonably execute your ordained office. Then you will not so freely with your perishable earthly power invade and transgress against Christ, the Lord of lords in His kingdom, power, and jurisdiction, and with your iron sword adjudicate in that which belongs exclusively to the eternal judgment of the Most High God, such as in faith and matters pertaining to faith. In the same vein Luther and others wrote in the beginning, but after they came to greater and higher estate they forgot it all. Dear sirs, observe how very much Moses, Joshua, David, Ezekiel, Josiah, Zerubbabel, and others are praised in the Scriptures because they feared the Lord, and faithfully and diligently kept His commandments, counsel, and word. If you will lift up your hearts above the mountains and will not hear what the mouth of the Lord commands you, but listen only to the inventions of your flesh; if you will not acknowledge that you are the officers and servants of the Lord, and that of Him you have received country and people, then you cannot possibly avoid the judgment of Him who has made you to be such exalted potentates, commanders, heads, and rulers. (By all means get this.) Before God, Croesus and Irus are worth equally much. Therefore sincerely fear and love your God with all your hearts. Examine the Scriptures, and ponder how the great Lord in His wrath on account of their tyranny, cruelty, pride, blasphemy, disobedience, and idolatry, has without mercy overturned and destroyed the thrones of great and mighty kings and lords, such as Pharaoh, Nebuchadnezzar, Sennacherib, Antiochus, Saul, Jeroboam, Ahab, and others, as may be clearly and plainly read in the Scriptures. Secondly, you may understand from these Scriptures that you are called of God and ordained to your offices to punish the transgressors and protect the good; to judge rightly between a man and his fellows; to do justice to the widows and orphans, to the poor, despised stranger and pilgrim; to protect them against violence and tyranny; to rule cities and countries justly by a good policy and administration not contrary to God's Word, in peace and quiet, unto the benefit and profit of the common people, to rule well. You should eagerly seek and love the holy Word (by which the soul must live), the name and the glory of God, and in Scriptural fairness promote and maintain the same as much as possible. You see, dear sirs and rulers, this is really the office to which you are called. Whether you fulfill these requirements piously and faithfully, I will leave to your own consideration. I think with holy Jeremiah that you have all broken the yoke and rent the bands. For you reject and detest as an abomination and a venomous serpent the dear Word which you should introduce, in the pure fear of God. The false teachers and prophets who deceive the whole world, and whom according to the Word of God we should shun, are kept in high esteem by you. The poor miserable sheep who in their weakness would sincerely fear and obey the Lord, and who would not speak an evil word to anyone because they dare not do aught against His Word; who lead a pious, penitent life and make the right use of His holy sacraments according to the Scriptures, abhor with mortal fear all false doctrines, sects, and wickedness, these are exiled from city and country and are often sentenced to fire, water, or the sword. Their goods are confiscated; their children, who according to the words of the prophet are not responsible for the transgressions of their fathers (assuming that the fathers were guilty as they assert), these are thrust forth, divested and naked, and the labor and sweat of their parents they must leave in the hands of these avaricious, greedy, unmerciful, and blood-thirsty bandits. Oh, no, ye beloved lords and judges, we will leave it to your own judgment whether this is to protect the good and punish the evil, to judge justly between man and man; to do justice to the widow, orphan, and stranger, as the Scriptures teach and your office implies. No, dear sirs, the thing is now in reverse gear. The policy is to punish the good and to protect the evil. We see daily that of which the prophets complained. Perjurers, usurers, blasphemers, liars, deceivers, harlots, and adulterers are in no danger of death, but those that fear and love the Lord are every man's prey. The prophet says, Behold, the princes of Israel, every one in thee is mighty to shed blood In thee have they set light by father and mother; in the midst of thee have they dealt by oppression with the stranger: in thee have they vexed the fatherless and the widow. Ezek. 22. Read the prophetic Scriptures and you will find what terrible threats the holy and faithful men of God have ever prophesied of such evils and abuses.

And if you now despise these our admonitions, they nevertheless are the firm truth; this you must acknowledge in your hearts, it would seem. For it is manifest and undeniable that in our Netherlands the lascivious, bad, and good-for-nothing men whom they call pastors, ministers, masters, and teachers, some of whom wrong one woman or girl after the other, men who live in all manner of willfulness, ungodliness, idolatry, are dead drunk day and night, and do not know a single word of the Lord correctly, these men rob by their shameful trickery many God-fearing people, who before God and His angels seek nothing but to lead a righteous and unblamable life according to the direction of the Word of God. They rob them of their country, honor, possessions, and even life, while they the deceivers live at liberty and ease. Inasmuch as the scale of justice is so badly out of balance, and since you are nevertheless chosen and ordained of God to judge without respect of persons and to deliver from the hands of the oppressor all the afflicted and oppressed strangers; therefore we pray you humbly, most beloved rulers and judges, for the sake of Him who has called and chosen you to your office, 'not to believe these cruel and envious men who according to Peter are born to naught but corruption and torture and who are always publicly and privately making us so obnoxious by their shouting that men do not want to hear or see us. We pray you not to believe them so long as they in our presence do not prove (which we are sure they cannot do) against us that which they every day from their throne of pestilence and mockery so shamelessly proclaim to the world, to the shame and injury of great numbers of pious and God-fearing people. Dear sirs, we beseech you for Christ's sake to fear and love God sincerely, believe His true Word and act justly.

THE JESUIT LEGACY AND
FRANCISCO DE SUÁREZ 15

The reformation of the Roman Catholic Church by the Council of Trent and the character of post-Tridentine Roman Catholicism were profoundly influenced by the Spanish knight Ignatius of Loyola (1491–1556), the founder of the Jesuit Order (Societas Jesu). After his own conversion in 1521, the care of men's souls and the defense of the papacy became Loyola's main interests. The Order founded by him and approved by Pope Paul III in 1540 was dedicated to absolute obedience to the pope. A mighty educational force in Roman Catholic countries and all over the world, it determined the character of the so-called "Counter-Reformation."

Selection 1: Francisco de Suárez:
A Treatise on Laws and God the Lawgiver, Book III, Chapter II

The Jesuits were outstanding moral theologians and produced in Suárez (1548–1619), a leading theologian of Spanish scholasticism, one of the great social philosophers of the Roman Catholic Church. In this selection, Suárez rejects the absolute power of the prince and asserts that since men are born free, the power to make human laws resides in the whole body of mankind.

In What Men Does This Power to Make Human Laws Reside Directly, by the Very Nature of Things?

1. The reason for doubt on this point is the fact that the power in question dwells either in individual men; or in all men, that is to say, in the whole body of mankind collectively regarded.

The first alternative cannot be upheld. For it is not true that every individual man is the superior of the rest; nor do certain persons, [simply] by the nature of things, possess the said power in a greater degree than other persons [on some ground apart from general superiority], since there is no reason for thus favoring some persons as compared with others.

The second alternative would also seem to be untenable. For in the first place, if it were correct, all the laws derived from such power would be common to all men.

And secondly, [so the argument runs] no source can be found, from which the whole multitude of mankind could have derived this power; since men themselves cannot be that source—inasmuch as they are unable to give that which they do not possess—and since the power cannot be derived from God, because if it were so derived, it could not change but would necessarily remain in the whole community in a process of perpetual succession, like the spiritual power which God conferred upon Peter and which for that reason necessarily endures in him or in his successors, and cannot be altered by men.

2. It is customary to refer, in connection with this question, to the opinion of certain canonists who assert that by the very nature of the case this [legislative] power resides in some supreme prince upon whom it has been divinely conferred, and that it must always, through a process of succession, continue to reside in a specific individual. The Gloss (on *Decretum*, Pt. II, causa VII, qu. I, can. ix) is cited [by way of confirmation]; but the passage cited contains simply a statement that the son of a king is lawfully king, which is a very different matter, nor does it assert that this mode of succession was perpetual among men. Another Gloss (on Decretum, Pt. I, dist. x, can. viii) is also cited, because it declares that the Emperor receives his power from God alone. But that Gloss, in its use of the exclusive word "alone," is intended to indicate simply that the Emperor does not receive his power from the Pope; it is not intended to deny that he receives it from men. For, in this very passage, it is said that the Emperor is set up by the army in accordance with the ancient custom mentioned in the Decretum (Pt. I, dist. xciii, can. xxiv). The said opinion, then, is supported neither by authority nor by a rational basis, as will become more evident from what follows.

3. Therefore, we must say that this power, viewed solely according to the nature of things, resides not in any individual man but rather in the whole body of mankind. This conclusion is commonly accepted and certainly true. It is to be deduced from the words of St. Thomas ([I.-II,] qu. 90, art. 3, ad 2 and qu. 97, art. 3, ad 3) in so far as he holds that the prince has the power to make laws, and that this power was transferred to him by the community. The civil laws (Digest, I. iv. 1 and I. ii. 2, § II) set forth and accept the same conclusion. . . .

The basic reason in support of the first part of the conclusion is evident, and was touched upon at the beginning of our discussion, namely, the fact that in the nature of things al men are born free; so that, consequently, no person has political jurisdiction over another person, even as no person has dominion over another; nor is there any reason why such power should, [simply] in the nature of things, be attributed to certain persons over certain other persons, rather than vice versa. One might make this assertion only: that at the beginning of creation Adam possessed, in the very nature of things, a primacy and consequently a sovereignty over all men, so that [the power in question] might have been derived from him, whether through the natural origin of primogeniture, or in accordance with the will of Adam himself. For it is so that Chrysostom (on First Corinthians, Homily XXXIV [no. 5]) has declared all men to be formed and pro-created from Adam alone, a subordination to one sole prince being thus indicated. However, by virtue of his creation only and his natural origin, one may infer simply that Adam possessed domestic—not political—power. For he had power over his wife, and later he possessed the patria potestas over his children until they were emancipated. In the course of time, he may also have had servants and a complete household with full power over the same, the power called "domestic." But after families began to multiply, and the individual heads of individual families began to separate, those heads possessed the same power over their respective households. Political power, however, did not make its appearance until many families began to congregate into one perfect community. Accordingly, since this community had its beginning, not in the creation of Adam nor solely by his will, but rather by the will of all who were assembled therein, we are unable to make any well-founded statement to the effect that Adam, in the [very] nature of things, held a political primacy in the said community. For such an inference cannot be drawn from natural principles, since it is not the progenitor's due, by the sole force of natural law, that he shall also be king over his posterity.

But, granted that this inference does not follow upon natural principles, neither have we sufficient foundation for the assertion that God has bestowed such power upon that [progenitor], through a special donation or act of providence, since we have had no revelation to this effect, nor does Holy Scripture so testify to us. To this argument may be added the point made by Augustine and noted in our preceding Chapter [Ch. I, sect. 1], namely, that God did not say: "Let us make man that he may have dominion over men," but rather did He say: [Let us make man that he may have dominion] over other living creatures.

Therefore, the power of political dominion or rule over men has not been granted, directly by God, to any particular human individual.

4. From the foregoing, it is easy to deduce the second part of the assertion [at beginning of Section 3], namely, that the power in question resides, by the sole force of natural law, in the whole body of mankind [collectively regarded].

The proof is as follows: this power does exist in men, and it does not exist in each individual, nor in any specific individual, as has also been shown; therefore, it exists in mankind viewed collectively, for our foregoing division [into two alternatives] sufficiently covers the case.

Selection 2: Suárez, *Disputation* XIII: On Charity, Chapter 1

Suárez's discussion of war illustrates the reasoning that has undergirded non pacifist Western thought.

On War

An external contest at arms that is incompatible with external peace is properly called war, when carried on between two sovereign princes or between two states. When, however, it is a contest between a prince and his own state, or between citizens and their state, it is termed sedition. When it is between private individuals it is called a quarrel or a duel. The difference between these various kinds of contest appears to be material rather than formal, and we shall discuss them all, as did St. Thomas (II.-II, qq. 40, 41, 42) and others who will be mentioned below.

Is War Intrinsically Evil?

1. The first heresy [in connection with this subject] consists in the assertion that it is intrinsically evil and contrary to charity to wage war. . . . The second error is the assertion that war is specifically forbidden to Christians, and especially, war against Christians. So Eck maintains (*Enchiridion Locorum Communium*, Ch. xxii); and other persons of our own time, who are heretics, advance the same contention. They distinguish, however, two kinds of war, the defensive and the aggressive, which we shall discuss in Subsection 6 of this Section. The conclusions that follow will elucidate the matter.

2. Our first conclusion is that war, absolutely speaking, is not intrinsically evil, nor is it forbidden to Christians. This conclusion is a matter of faith and is laid down in the Scriptures, for in the Old Testament, wars waged by most holy men are praised (Genesis, Ch. xiv [, vv. 19-20]): "Blessed be Abram [. . .] And blessed be God by whose protection the enemies are in thy hands." We find similar passages concerning Moses, Josue, Samson, Gedeon, David, the Machabees, and others, whom God often ordered to wage war upon the enemies of the Hebrews. Moreover, the apostle Paul (Hebrews, Ch. xi [, v. 33]) said that by faith the saints conquered kingdoms. The same principle is confirmed by further testimony, that of the Fathers quoted by Gratian (*Decretum*, Pt. II, causa xxiii, qq. 1 and 2), and also that of Ambrose (*On Duties*, various chapters).

　However, one may object, in the first place, that the Lord said to David [I *Paralipomenon*, Ch. xxviii, v. 3]: "Thou shalt not build my temple because thou art a man who has shed blood."

　Secondly, it will be objected that Christ said to Peter (John, Ch. xviii [, v. 11]): "Put up thy sword into the scabbard," etc.; and that Isaias also said (*Isaias*, Ch. ii [, v. 4]): "They shall turn their swords into ploughshares [. . .] neither shall they be exercised any more to war"; and in another Chapter (Ch. xi [, v. 9]): "They shall not hurt nor shall they kill in all my holy mountain." The Prophet is speaking, indeed of the time of the coming of the Messiah, at which time, especially, it will be made clear, what is permissible and what is not permissible.

　Thirdly, at the Council of Nicaea (Ch. xi [, can. xii]), a penalty was imposed upon Christians who, after having received the faith, enrolled themselves for military service. Furthermore, Pope Leo (*Letters*, xcii [Letter clxvii, inquis. xii]) wrote that war was forbidden to Christians, after a solemn penance.

　Fourthly, war morally brings with it innumerable sins; and a given course of action is considered in itself evil and forbidden, given course of action if it is practically always accompanied by unseemly circumstances and harm to one's neighbours. [Furthermore,] one may add that war is opposed to peace, to the love of one's enemies, and to the forgiveness of injuries.

3. We reply to the first objection that [the Scriptural passage in question] is based upon the unjust slaying of Uriah; and, also, upon the particularly great reverence owed to the Temple.

　[As for the second objection, we may answer, first, that] Christ our Lord is speaking of one who on his own initiative wishes to use the sword, and in particular, of one who so desires, against the will of his prince. Moreover, the words of Isaias, especially in Ch. xi, are usually understood as referring to the state of glory. Secondly, it is said that future peace was symbolized in the coming of the Messiah, as is explained by Jerome on this point [on Isaias, Ch. xi], Eusebius (Demonstrations, Bk. I, Ch. i), and other Fathers [of the Church]; or, at least, that Isaias is referring to the spiritual warfare of the Apostles and of the preachers of the Gospel, who have conquered the world not by a material but by a spiritual sword. This is the interpretation found in Justin Martyr, in his *Second Apology* for the Christians, and in other writers.

The Council of Nicaea, indeed, dealt especially with those Christians who, for a second time, were assuming the uniform of pagan soldiers which they had once cast off. And Pope Leo, as the Gloss (on *Decretum*, Pt. II, causa xxxiii, qu. iii (*De Paenitentia*), dist. v, cans. iv and iii) explains, was speaking of those Christians who, after a public penance had been imposed upon them, were returning to war, before the penance had been completed. Furthermore, it may have been expedient for the early Church to forbid those who had recently been converted to the faith, to engage in military service immediately, in company with unbelievers, and under pagan officers.

To the argument drawn from reason, Augustine replies (*On the City of God*, Bk. XIX, last chapter [Ch. vii]) that he deems it advisable to avoid war in so far as is possible, and to undertake it only in cases of extreme necessity, when no alternative remains; but he also holds that war is not entirely evil, since the fact that evils follow upon war is incidental, and since greater evils would result if war were never allowed.

Wherefore, in reply to the confirmation of the argument in question one may deny that war is opposed to an honourable peace; rather, it is opposed to an unjust peace, for it is more truly a means of attaining peace that is real and secure. Similarly, war is not opposed to the love of one's enemies; for whoever wages war honourably hates, not individuals, but the actions which he justly punishes. And the same reasoning is true of the forgiveness of injuries, especially since this forgiveness is not enjoined under every circumstance, for punishment may sometimes be exacted, by legitimate means, without injustice.

4. Secondly, I hold that defensive war not only is permitted, but sometimes is even commanded. The first part of this proposition follows from the first conclusion, which even the Doctors cited above accept; and it holds true not only for public officials, but also for private individuals, since all laws allow the repelling of force with force (*Decretals*, Bk V, tit. xxxix, Ch. iii). The reason supporting it is that the right of self-defence is natural and necessary. Whence the second part of our second proposition is easily proved. For self-defence may sometimes be prescribed, at least in accordance with the order of charity; a fact which I have elsewhere pointed out. . . . The same is true of the defence of the state, especially if such defence is an official duty. . . . If anyone objects that in the *Epistle to the Romans* (Ch. xii [, v. 19]) these words are found: "Revenge not yourselves, my dearly beloved," and that this saying is in harmony with the passage (Matthew, Ch. v [, v. 39]): "If one strike thee on the right cheek, turn to him also the other", we shall reply with respect to the first passage, that the reference is to vengeance. . . .

5. My third conclusion is, that even when war is aggressive, it is not an evil in itself, but may be right and necessary. This is clear from the passages of Scripture cited above, which make no distinction [between aggressive and defensive wars]. The same

fact is evidenced by the custom of the Church, one that has quite frequently been approved by the Gathers and the Popes. . . .

The reason supporting our third conclusion is that such a war is often neccssary to a state, in order to ward off acts of injustice and to hold enemies in check. Nor would it be possible, without these wars, for states to be maintained in peace. Hence, this kind of warfare is allowed by natural law; and even by the law of the Gospel, which derogates in no way from natural law, and contains no new divine commands save those regarding faith and the Sacraments. The statement of Luther that it is not lawful to resist the punishment of God is indeed ridiculous; for God does not will the evils [against which war is waged,] but merely permits them; and therefore He does not forbid that they should be justly repelled.

6. It remains for us to explain what constitutes an aggressive war, and what, on the other hand, constitutes a defensive war; for sometimes that which is merely an act of defence may present the appearance of an aggressive act. Thus, for example, if enemies seize the houses or the property of others, but have themselves suffered invasion from the latter, that is no aggression but defense. To this extent, civil laws (*Code*, VIII. iv. 1 and *Digest*, XLIII. xvi. 1 and 3) are justified in conscience also, when they provide that if any one tries to dispossess me of my property, it is lawful for me to repel force with force. For such an act is not aggression, but defence, and may be lawfully undertaken even on one's own authority. The laws in question are extended to apply to him who, while absent, has been ejected from a tenure which they call a natural one, and who, upon his return, is prevented from recovering that tenure. For [the same laws decree] that any one who has been despoiled may, even on his own authority, have recourse to arms, because such an act is not really aggression, but a defence of one's legal possession. This rule is laid down in *Decretals*, Bk. II, tit. xiii, Ch. xii.

Consequently, we have to consider whether the injustice is, practically speaking, simply about to take place; or whether it has already done so, and redress is sought through war. In this second case, the war is aggressive. In the former case, war has the character of self-defense, provided that it is waged with a moderation of defence which is blameless. Now the injury is considered as beginning, when the unjust act itself, even physically regarded, is beginning; as when a man has not been entirely deprived of his rightful possession; or even when he has been so deprived, but immediately— that is, without noteworthy delay—attempts to defend himself and to reinstate himself in possession. The reason for this is as follows: When any one is, to all intents and purposes, in the very act of resisting, and attempts—in so far as is possible—to protect his right, he is not considered as having, in an absolute sense, suffered wrong, nor as having been deprived of his possession. . . .

7. Our fourth proposition is this: in order that a war may be justly waged, a number of conditions must be observed, which may be grouped under three heads. First, the war must be waged by a legitimate power; secondly, the cause itself and the reason must be just; thirdly, the method of its conduct must be proper, and due proportion must be observed at its beginning, during its prosecution and after victory. All of this will be made clear in the following sections. The underlying principle of this general conclusion, indeed, is that, while a war is not in itself evil, nevertheless, on account of the many misfortunes which it brings in its train, it is one of those undertakings that

are often carried on in evil fashion; and that therefore, it requires many justifying circumstances to make it righteous.

For Further Reading

The following select list of writings provides a mixture of primary and secondary sources related to the major parts of the anthology, and the full text of the works being excerpted will also provide rich additional reading.

Baylor, Michael G. Editor and Translator. *Revelation and Revolution: Basic Writings of Thomas Müntzer.* London and Toronto: Associated University Presses, 1993.

Biéler, André. *Calvin's Economic and Social Thought.* Edited by Edward Dommer. Translated by James Greig. Geneva: World Council of Churches, 2005.

Calvin, John. *On God and Political Duty.* Edited by John T. McNeill. Library of the Liberal Arts. New York: Bobbs-Merrill, 1956.

Höpfl, Harro, Editor and Translator. *Luther and Calvin on Secular Authority.* Cambridge: Cambridge University Press, 1993.

Forell, George. *Faith Active in Love: An Investigation of the Principles Underlying Luther's Social Ethics.* Minneapolis: Augsburg, 1959.

Lazareth, William H. *Christians in Society: Luther, the Bible, and Social Ethics.* Minneapolis: Fortress Press, 2001.

Luther, Martin. *The Christian in Society: Luther's Works,* Volumes 44–47. Philadelphia: Fortress Press, 1962–1971.

PART 5

Post-Reformation England
and America

THE PURITANS 16

❧ Puritanism *is a most complex term that has acquired connotations of rigid moralism in the popular parlance of today's world that is only vaguely related to its original meaning. While it is certainly true that Puritan divines were concerned with holiness of living, the term* puritan *originated with the efforts of this Calvinist oriented movement to reform or "purify" the Church of England of its Catholic tendencies. The puritans came to power with the victories of Oliver Cromwell, a strict Puritan, who fought against the excesses of the monarchy on behalf of parliamentary government and a simpler life of holy living. At the same time that Cromwell consolidated political power and the puritan way, more radical voices for social and political change arose from within Puritanism as represented by the two selections that follow.*

Selection 1: *An Agreement of the People*

The Levellers were theological radicals in the Puritan movement who opposed both the bishops and the state-church ambitions of the Presbyterians. The following selection from the so-called First Agreement of the People *(1647) provides a glimpse of their democratic and egalitarian agenda, a vision of the social order, which proved to be influential beyond its brief moment in history.*

Having by our late labors and hazards made it appear to the world at how high a rate we value our just freedom, and God having so far owned our cause as to deliver the enemies thereof into our hands, we do now hold ourselves bound in mutual duty to each other to take the best care we can for the future to avoid both the danger of returning into a slavish condition and the chargeable remedy of another war; for, as it cannot be imagined that so many of our countrymen would have opposed us in this quarrel if they had understood their own good, so may we safely promise to ourselves that, when our common rights and liberties shall be cleared, their endeavors will be disappointed that seek to make themselves our masters. Since, therefore, our former oppressions and scarce-yet-ended troubles have been occasioned, either by want of frequent national meetings in Council, or by rendering those meetings ineffectual, we are fully agreed and resolved to provide that hereafter our representatives be neither left to an uncertainty for the time nor made useless to the ends for which they are intended. In order whereunto we declare: —

That the people of England, being at this day very unequally distributed by Counties, Cities, and Boroughs for the election of their deputies in Parliament, ought to be more indifferently proportioned according to the number of the inhabitants; the circumstances whereof for number, place, and manner are to be set down before the end of this present Parliament.

II.

That, to prevent the many inconveniences apparently arising from the long continuance of the same persons in authority, this present Parliament be dissolved upon the last day of September which shall be in the year of our Lord 1648

III.

That the people do, of course, choose themselves a Parliament once in two years, viz. upon the first Thursday in every 2d March, after the manner as shall be prescribed before the end of this Parliament, to begin to sit upon the first Thursday in April following, at Westminster or such other place as shall be appointed from time to time by the preceding Representatives, and to continue till the last day of September then next ensuing, and no longer.

IV.

That the power of this, and all future Representatives of this Nation, is inferior only to theirs who choose them, and doth extend, without the consent or concurrence of any other person or persons, to the enacting, altering, and repealing of laws, to the erecting and abolishing of offices and courts, to the appointing, removing, and calling to account magistrates and officers of all degrees, to the making war and peace, to the treating with foreign States, and, generally, to whatsoever is not expressly or impliedly reserved by the represented to themselves: Which are as followeth.

1. That matters of religion and the ways of God's worship are not at all entrusted by us to any human power, because therein we cannot remit or exceed a tittle of what our consciences dictate to be the mind of God without wilful sin: nevertheless the public way of instructing the nation (so it be not compulsive) is referred to their discretion.

2. That the matter of impresting and constraining any of us to serve in the wars is against our freedom; and therefore we do not allow it in our Representatives; the rather, because money (the sinews of war), being always at their disposal, they can never want numbers of men apt enough to engage in any just cause.

3. That after the dissolution of this present Parliament, no person be at any time questioned for anything said or done in reference to the late public differences, otherwise than in execution of the judgments of the present Representatives or House of Commons.

4. That in all laws made or to be made every person may be bound alike, and that no tenure, estate, charter, degree, birth, or place do confer any exemption from the ordinary course of legal proceedings whereunto others are subjected.

5. That as the laws ought to be equal, so they must be good, and not evidently destructive to the safety and well-being of the people.

These things we declare to be our native rights, and therefore are agreed and resolved to maintain them with our utmost possibilities against all opposition whatsoever; being compelled thereunto not only by the examples of our ancestors, whose blood was often spent in vain for the recovery of their freedoms, Buffering themselves through fraudulent accommodations to be still deluded of the fruit of their victories, but also by our own woeful experience, who, having long expected and dearly earned the establishment of these certain rules of government, are yet made to depend for the settlement of our peace and freedom upon him that intended our bondage and brought a cruel war upon us.

Selection 2: Gerrard Winstanley, *The Law of Freedom in a Platform* or *True Magistracy Restored* (1652)

The Diggers were the most radical movement connected with the Revolution in England. Under the leadership of Gerrard Winstanley (1609–after 1660) they espoused an agrarian communism that included giving land to the very poor. The dramatic reforms the Diggers advocated seemed to them to be the logical response to the opportunity provided by the fall of the monarchy and the execution of Charles I. The effort was short-lived. Nonetheless, it highlighted the injustices of life under the monarchy and, notwithstanding the harsh penalties for law-breaking typical of its time, left behind an important affirmation of freedom and equality at a time when both were in short supply.

There shall be no buying and selling of the Earth, nor of the fruits thereof
For by the Government under Kings, the cheaters hereby have cozened the plain hearted of their creation birth-rights, and have possessed themselves in the earth and calls it theirs and not the others, and so have brought in that poverty and misery which lies upon many men.

And whereas the wise should help the foolish, and the strong help the weak; the wise and the strong destroys the weak and the simple.

And are not all children generally simple and weak and know not the things that belong to their peace till they come to ripe age, but before they come to that understanding, the cunning ones who have more strength and policy, have by this hypocritical lying, unrighteous and cheating Art of buying and selling, wrung the freedoms of the earth out of their hands, and cozened them of their birth-rights.

So that when they come to understanding, they see themselves beggars in the midst of a fruit full Land, and so the Proverb is true, plain dealing is a jewel, but he who uses it shall dye a beggar. And why?

Because this buying and selling is the nursery of cheaters, it is the Law of the Conqueror, and the Righteousness of the Scribes and Pharisees, which both killed Christ and hindered his Resurrection, as much as darkness can to put out light.

And these cunning cheaters commonly become the Rulers of the earth, and then the City Man-kind mourns, for not the wise poor man, the cunning rich man, was always made an Officer and Ruler, such a one as by his stolen interest in the earth would be sure to hold others in bondage of poverty and servitude to him and his party.

And hence arise oppression and tyranny in the earth upon the backs of the weak younger brethren, who are made younger brothers indeed, as the Proverb is, by their cunning elder brother; and as Daniel said, the basest of men under Kingly government were set to rule, who can but not obey, who can take other men's labors to live at ease, not work themselves.

Therefore there shall be no buying and selling in a Free Commonwealth, neither shall anyone hire his brother to work for him.

If the Commonwealth might be governed without buying and selling here is a Platform of Government for it, which is the ancientest Law of Righteousness to Mankind in the use of the Earth, and which is the very height of earthly Freedoms. But if the minds of the people, through covetousness and proud ignorance, will have the Earth governed by buying and selling still, this same Platform, with a few things subtracted, declares an easie way of Government of the Earth for the quiet of peoples minds, and preserving of Peace in the Land.

How must the Earth be planted?
The Earth is to be planted, and the fruits reaped, and carried into Barns and Storehouses by the assistance of every family: And if any man or family want Corn, or other provision, they may go to the Storehouses, and fetch without money: If they want a Horse to ride, go into the fields in Summer, or to the Common Stables in Winter, and receive one from the Keepers, and when your Journey is performed, bring him where [73] you had him, without money. If any want food or victuals, they may either go to the Butchers shops, and receive what they want without money; or else go to the flocks of sheep, or herds of cattel, and take and kill what meat is needful for their families, without buying and selling. And the reason why all the riches of the earth are a common stock is this, Because the earth, and the labours thereupon, are managed by common assistance of every family, without buying and selling; as is shewn how more largely, in the Office of Overseers for Trades, and the Law for Storehouses. The Laws for the right ordering thereof, and the Officers to see the Laws executed; to preserve the peace of every family, and the peace of every man, and to improve and promote every Trade, is shewed in the work of Officers, and by the Laws following. None will be an enemy to this freedom, which indeed is to do to another as a man would have another do to him, but Covetousness and Pride, the spirit of the old grudging snapping Pharisees, who gives God abundance of good words, in their Sermons, in their Prayers, in their Fasts, and in their Thanksgivings, as though none should be more faithful servants to him then they: nay, they will shun the company, imprison, and kill everyone that will not worship God, they are so zealous.

Well now, God and Christ hath enacted an everlasting Law, which is Love; not onely one another of your own minde, but love your enemies too, such as are not of your minde: and, having food and raiment, therewith be content.

Now here is a trial for you, whether you will be faithful to God and Christ, in obeying his Laws; or whether you will destroy the man-childe of true Freedom, righteousness and peace, in his resurrection.

And now thou wilt give us either the tricks of a Souldier, Face about, and return to Egypt, and so declare thy self to be part of the Serpents seed, that must bruise the heel of Christ; or else to be one of the plain hearted sons of promise, or members of Christ, who shall help to bruise the Serpents head, which is Kingly oppression; and so bring in everlasting righteousness and peace into the earth. Well, the eye is now open.

Store-houses shall be built and appointed in all places, and be the common Stock.
There shall be Store-houses in all places, both in the Country and in Cities, to which all the fruits of the earth, and other works made by Tradesmen, shall be brought, and from thence delivered out again particular Families, and to every one as they want for their use; or else to be transported by Ship to other Lands, to exchange for those things which our Land will not or does not afford.

Laws for Marriage.
Every man and woman shall have the free liberty to marry whom they love, if they can obtain the love and liking of that party whom they would marry, and neither birth nor portion shall hinder the match, for we are all of one blood, Mankind; and for portion, the Common Store-houses are every man and maids portion, as free to one as to another.

If any man lie with a maid, and beget a child, he shall marry her.
If a man lie with a woman forcibly, and she cry out, and give no consent; if this be proved by two Witnesses, or the mans confession, he shall be put to death, and the woman let go free; it is rubbery of a woman's bodily Freedom.

If any man by violence endeavor to take away another mans wife, the first time of such violent offer he shall be reproved before the Congregation by the Peace-maker, the second time he shall be made a servant under the Task-master for twelve Moneths; and if he forcibly lie with another mans wife, and she cry out, as in the case when a maid is forced, the man shall be put to death.

When any man or woman are consented to live together in marriage, they shall acquaint all the Overseers in their Circuit there-with, and some other neighbors; and being all met together, the man shall declare by his own mouth before them all, that he takes that woman to be his wife, and the woman shall say the same, and desire the Overseers to be Witnesses.

No Master of a family shall suffer more meat to be dressed at a dinner or supper, then what will be spent and eaten by his houshold, Or company present, or within such a time after, before it be spoyled. If there be any spoyl constantly made in a family of the food of Man, the Overseer shall reprove the Master for it privately; if that abuse be continued in his family, through his neglect of family government, he shall be openly reproved by the Peace-maker before all the people, and ashamed for his folly; the third time he shall be made a servant for twelve Moneths under the Task-master, that he may know what it is to get food, and another shall have the oversight of his house for the time.

ROGER WILLIAMS

17

The Bloody Tenent of Persecution (July 15, 1644)

❧ *The founder of the colony of Rhode Island and its capital of Providence Plan-
tations, now Providence, Roger Williams (1603–1683) is famed for his advocacy
of the separation of church and state over against the theocratic tendencies of
the Puritans in the Massachusetts Bay colony and for his insistence on religious
freedom. As a consequence, the Rhode Island colony became a refuge for those who
suffered religious persecution. The Bloody Tenent of Persecution is generally
regarded as his most important publication. The following excerpt provides a
good outline of Williams's concerns.*

First, that the blood of so many hundred thousand souls of Protestants and Papists,
spilt in the wars of present and former ages, for their respective consciences, is not
required nor accepted by Jesus Christ the Prince of Peace.

Secondly, pregnant scriptures and arguments are throughout the work proposed
against the doctrine of persecution for cause of conscience.

Thirdly, satisfactory answers are given to scriptures, and objections produced
by Mr. Calvin, Beza, Mr. Cotton, and the ministers of the New English churches
and others former and later, tending to prove the doctrine of persecution for cause of
conscience.

Fourthly, the doctrine of persecution for cause of conscience is proved guilty of
all the blood of the souls crying for vengeance under the altar.

Fifthly, all civil states with their officers of justice in their respective constitutions and administrations are proved essentially civil, and therefore not judges, governors, or defenders of the spiritual or Christian state and worship.

Sixthly, it is the will and command of God that (since the coming of his Son
the Lord Jesus) a permission of the most paganish, Jewish, Turkish, or antichristian
consciences and worships, be granted to all men in all nations and countries; and they
are only to be fought against with that sword which is only (in soul matters) able to
conquer, to wit, the sword of God's Spirit, the Word of God.

Seventhly, the state of the Land of Israel, the kings and people thereof in peace
and war, is proved figurative and ceremonial, and no pattern nor president for any
kingdom or civil state in the world to follow.

Eighthly, God requireth not a uniformity of religion to be enacted and enforced
in any civil state; which enforced uniformity (sooner or later) is the greatest occasion

of civil war, ravishing of conscience, persecution of Christ Jesus in his servants, and of the hypocrisy and destruction of millions of souls.

Ninthly, in holding an enforced uniformity of religion in a civil state, we must necessarily disclaim our desires and hopes of the Jew's conversion to Christ.

Tenthly, an enforced uniformity of religion throughout a nation or civil state, confounds the civil and religious, denies the principles of Christianity and civility, and that Jesus Christ is come in the flesh.

Eleventhly, the permission of other consciences and worships than a state professeth only can (according to God) procure a firm and lasting peace (good assurance being taken according to the wisdom of the civil state for uniformity of civil obedience from all forts).

Twelfthly, lastly, true civility and Christianity may both flourish in a state or kingdom, notwithstanding the permission of divers and contrary consciences, either of Jew or Gentile. . . .

TRUTH. I acknowledge that to molest any person, Jew or Gentile, for either professing doctrine, or practicing worship merely religious or spiritual, it is to persecute him, and such a person (whatever his doctrine or practice be, true or false) suffereth persecution for conscience.

But withal I desire it may be well observed that this distinction is not full and complete: for beside this that a man may be persecuted because he holds or practices what he believes in conscience to be a truth (as Daniel did, for which he was cast into the lions' den, Dan. 6), and many thousands of Christians, because they durst not cease to preach and practice what they believed was by God commanded, as the Apostles answered (Acts 4 & 5), I say besides this a man may also be persecuted, because he dares not be constrained to yield obedience to such doctrines and worships as are by men invented and appointed. . . .

Dear TRUTH, I have two sad complaints:

First, the most sober of the witnesses, that dare to plead thy cause, how are they charged to be mine enemies, contentious, turbulent, seditious?

Secondly, shine enemies, though they speak and rail against thee, though they outrageously pursue, imprison, banish, kill thy faithful witnesses, yet how is all vermilion'd o'er for justice against the heretics? Yea, if they kindle coals, and blow the flames of devouring wars, that leave neither spiritual nor civil state, but burn up branch and root, yet how do all pretend an holy war? He that kills, and he that's killed, they both cry out: "It is for God, and for their conscience."

'Tis true, nor one nor other seldom dare to plead the mighty Prince Christ Jesus for their author, yet (both Protestant and Papist) pretend they have spoke with Moses and the Prophets who all, say they (before Christ came), allowed such holy persecutions, holy wars against the enemies of holy church.

TRUTH. Dear PEACE (to ease thy first complaint), 'tis true, thy dearest sons, most like their mother, peacekeeping, peacemaking sons of God, have borne and still must bear the blurs of troublers of Israel, and turners of the world upside down. And 'tis true again, what Solomon once spake: "The beginning of strife is as when one letteth out water, therefore (saith he) leave off contention before it be meddled with. This caveat should keep the banks and sluices firm and strong, that strife, like a breach of waters, break not in upon the sons of men."

Yet strife must be distinguished: It is necessary or unnecessary, godly or Ungodly, Christian or unchristian, etc.

It is unnecessary, unlawful, dishonorable, ungodly, unchristian, in most cases in the world, for there is a possibility of keeping sweet peace in most cases, and, if it be possible, it is the express command of God that peace be kept (Rom. 13).

Again, it is necessary, honorable, godly, etc., with civil and earthly weapons to defend the innocent and to rescue the oppressed from the violent paws and jaws of oppressing persecuting Nimrods (Psal. 73; Job 29).

It is as necessary, yea more honorable, godly, and Christian, to fight the fight of faith, with religious and spiritual artillery, and to contend earnestly for the faith of Jesus, once delivered to the saints against all opposers, and the gates of earth and hell, men or devils, yea against Paul himself, or an angel from heaven, if he bring any other faith or doctrine. . . .

PEACE. I add that a civil sword (as woeful experience in all ages has proved) is so far from bringing or helping forward an opposite in religion to repentance that magistrates sin grievously against the work of God and blood of souls by such proceedings. Because as (commonly) the sufferings of false and antichristian teachers harden their followers, who being blind, by this means are occasioned to tumble into the ditch of hell after their blind leaders, with more inflamed zeal of lying confidence. So, secondly, violence and a sword of steel begets such an impression in the sufferers that certainly they conclude (as indeed that religion cannot be true which needs such instruments of violence to uphold it so) that persecutors are far from soft and gentle commiseration of the blindness of others. . . .

For (to keep to the similitude which the Spirit useth, for instance) to batter down a stronghold, high wall, fort, tower, or castle, men bring not a first and second admonition, and after obstinacy, excommunication, which are spiritual weapons concerning them that be in the church: nor exhortation to repent and be baptized, to believe in the Lord Jesus, etc., which are proper weapons to them that be without, etc. But to take a stronghold, men bring cannons, culverins, saker, bullets, powder, muskets, swords, pikes, etc., and these to this end are weapons effectual and proportionable.

On the other side, to batter down idolatry, false worship, heresy, schism, blindness, hardness, out of the soul and spirit, it is vain, improper, and unsuitable to bring those weapons which are used by persecutors, stocks, whips, prisons, swords, gibbets, stakes, etc. (where these seem to prevail with some cities or kingdoms, a stronger force sets up again, what a weaker pull'd down), but against these spiritual strongholds in the souls of men, spiritual artillery and weapons are proper, which are mighty through God to subdue and bring under the very thought to obedience, or else to bind fast the soul with chains of darkness, and lock it up in the prison of unbelief and hardness to eternity. . . .

PEACE. I pray descend now to the second evil which you observe in the answerer's position, viz., that it would be evil to tolerate notorious evildoers, seducing teachers, etc.

TRUTH. I say the evil is that he most improperly and confusedly joins and couples seducing teachers with scandalous livers.

PEACE. But is it not true that the world is full of seducing teachers, and is it not true that seducing teachers are notorious evildoers?

TRUTH. I answer, far be it from me to deny either, and yet in two things I shall discover the great evil of this joining and coupling seducing teachers, and scandalous livers as one adequate or proper object of the magistrate's care and work to suppress and punish.

First, it is not an homogeneal (as we speak) but an hetergeneal commixture or joining together of things most different in kinds and natures, as if they were both of one consideration. . . .

TRUTH. I answer, in granting with Brentius that man hath not power to make laws to bind conscience, he overthrows such his tenent and practice as restrain men from their worship, according to their conscience and belief, and constrain them to such worships (though it be out of a pretense that they are convinced) which their own souls tell them they have no satisfaction nor faith in.

Secondly, whereas he affirms that men may make laws to see the laws of God observed.

I answer, God needeth not the help of a material sword of steel to assist the sword of the Spirit in the affairs of conscience, to those men, those magistrates, yea that commonwealth which makes such magistrates, must needs have power and authority from Christ Jesus to fit judge and to determine in all the great controversies concerning doctrine, discipline, government, etc.

And then I ask whether upon this ground it must not evidently follow that:

Either there is no lawful common earth nor civil state of men in the world, which is not qualified with this spiritual discerning (and then also that the very commonweal hath more light concerning the church of Christ than the church itself).

Or, that the commonweal and magistrates thereof must judge and punish as they are persuaded in their own belief and conscience (be their conscience paganish, Turkish, or antichristian) what is this but to confound heaven and earth together, and not only to take away the being of Christianity out of the world, but to take away all civility, and the world out of the world, and to lay all upon heaps of confusion? . . .

PEACE. The fourth head is the proper means of both these powers to attain their ends.

First, the proper means whereby the civil power may and should attain its end are only political, and principally these five.

First, the erecting and establishing what form of civil government may seem in wisdom most meet, according to general rules of the world, and state of the people.

Secondly, the making, publishing, and establishing of wholesome civil laws, not only such as concern civil justice, but also the free passage of true religion; for outward civil peace ariseth and is maintained from them both, from the latter as well as from the former.

Civil peace cannot stand entire, where religion is corrupted (2 Chron. 15:3, 5, 6; and Judges 8). And yet such laws, though conversant about religion, may still be counted civil laws, as, on the contrary, an oath cloth still remain religious though conversant about civil matters.

Thirdly, election and appointment of civil officers to see execution to those laws.

Fourthly, civil punishments and rewards of transgressors and observers of these laws.

Fifthly, taking up arms against the enemies of civil peace.

Secondly, the means whereby the church may and should attain her ends are only ecclesiastical, which are chiefly five.

First, setting up that form of church government only of which Christ hath given them a pattern in his Word.

Secondly, acknowledging and admitting of no lawgiver in the church but Christ and the publishing of His laws.

Thirdly, electing and ordaining of such officers only, as Christ hath appointed in his Word.

Fourthly, to receive into their fellowship them that are approved and inflicting spiritual censures against them that o end.

Fifthly, prayer and patience in suffering any evil from them that be without, who disturb their peace.

So that magistrates, as magistrates, have no power of setting up the form of church government, electing church officers, punishing with church censures, but to see that the church does her duty herein. And on the other side, the churches as churches, have no power (though as members of the commonweal they may have power) of erecting or altering forms of civil government, electing of civil officers, inflicting civil punishments (no not on persons excommunicate) as by deposing magistrates from their civil authority, or withdrawing the hearts of the people against them, to their laws, no more than to discharge wives, or children, or servants, from due obedience to their husbands, parents, or masters; or by taking up arms against their magistrates, though he persecute them for conscience: for though members of churches who are public officers also of the civil state may suppress by force the violence of usurpers, as Iehoiada did Athaliah, yet this they do not as members of the church but as officers of the civil state.

TRUTH. Here are divers considerable passages which I shall briefly examine, so far as concerns our controversy.

First, whereas they say that the civil power may erect and establish what form of civil government may seem in wisdom most meet, I acknowledge the proposition to be most true, both in itself and also considered with the end of it, that a civil government is an ordinance of God, to conserve the civil peace of people, so far as concerns their bodies and goods, as formerly hath been said.

But from this grant I infer (as before hath been touched) that the sovereign, original, and foundation of civil power lies in the people (whom they must needs mean by the civil power distinct from the government set up). And, if so, that a people may erect and establish what form of government seems to them most meet for their civil condition; it is evident that such governments as are by them erected and established have no more power, nor for no longer time, than the civil power or people consenting and agreeing shall betrust them with. This is clear not only in reason but in the experience of all commonweals, where the people are not deprived of their natural freedom by the power of tyrants.

And, if so, that the magistrates receive their power of governing the church from the people, undeniably it follows that a people, as a people, naturally consider (of what nature or nation soever in Europe, Asia, Africa, or America), have fundamentally and originally, as men, a power to govern the church, to see her do her duty, to correct her, to redress, reform, establish, etc. And if this be not to pull God and Christ and Spirit out of heaven, and subject them unto natural, sinful, inconstant men, and so consequently to Satan himself, by whom all peoples naturally are guided, let heaven and earth judge. . . .

PEACE. Some will here ask: What may the magistrate then lawfully do with his civil horn or power in matters of religion?

TRUTH. His horn not being the horn of that unicorn or rhinoceros, the power of the Lord Jesus in spiritual cases, his sword not the two-edged sword of the spirit, the word of God (hanging not about the loins or side, but at the lips. and proceeding out of the mouth of his ministers) but of an humane and civil nature and constitution, it must consequently be of a humane and civil operation, for who knows not that operation follows constitution; And therefore I shall end this passage with this consideration:

The civil magistrate either respecteth that religion and worship which his conscience is persuaded is true, and upon which he ventures his soul; or else that and those which he is persuaded are false.

Concerning the first, if that which the magistrate believeth to be true, be true, I say he owes a threefold duty unto it:

First, approbation and countenance, a reverent esteem and honorable testimony, according to Isa. 49, and Revel. 21, with a tender respect of truth, and the professors of it.

Secondly, personal submission of his own soul to the power of the Lord Jesus in that spiritual government and kingdom, according to Matt. 18 and 1 Cor. 5.

Thirdly, protection of such true professors of Christ, whether apart, or met together, as also of their estates from violence and injury, according to Rom. 13.

Now, secondly, if it be a false religion (unto which the civil magistrate dare not adjoin, yet) he owes:

First, permission (for approbation he owes not what is evil) and this according to Matthew 13. 30 for public peace and quiet's sake.

Secondly, he owes protection to the persons of his subjects (though of a false worship), that no injury be offered either to the persons or goods of any. . . .

The God of Peace, the God of Truth will shortly seal this truth, and confirm this witness, and make it evident to the whole world, that the doctrine of persecution for cause of conscience, is most evidently and lamentably contrary to the doctrine of Christ Jesus the Prince of Peace. Amen.

THE QUAKERS

18

❧ *The Society of Friends, popularly called Quakers, is a relatively small religious movement that has its roots in the religious excitement of Cromwell's revolution. The original leaders started as Puritans and moved through various transformations (Independents, Baptists) to their final religious vision. The social teachings of the Society of Friends—their pacifism, rejection of slavery and openness to the needs of enemies—have influenced Christendom quite out of proportion to their small numbers.*

Selection 1: *Rules of Discipline* [Society of Friends]

These Advices, which were to be read at least once a year in the meetings of the Society, give an impression of the spirit of the moment.

Take heed, dear friends, we intreat you, to the convictions of the Holy Spirit, who leads, through unfeigned repentance and living faith in the Son of God, to reconciliation with our Heavenly Father, and to the blessed hope of eternal life, purchased for us by the one offering of our Lord and Saviour Jesus Christ.

Be earnestly concerned in religious meetings reverently to present yourselves before the Lord, and seek, by the help of the Holy Spirit, to worship God through Jesus Christ.

Be in the frequent practice of waiting upon God in private retirement, with prayer and supplication, honestly examining yourselves as to your growth in grace, and your preparation for the life to come.

Be careful to make a profitable and religious use of those portions of time on the first day of the week, which are not occupied by our meetings for worship.

Live in love as Christian brethren, ready to be helpful one to another, and to sympathize with each other in the trials and afflictions of life.

Follow peace with all men, desiring the true happiness of all; and be liberal to the poor, endeavouring to promote their temporal, moral, and religious well-being.

With a tender conscience, and in accordance with the precepts of the Gospel, take heed to the limitations of the Spirit of Truth, in the pursuit of the things of this life.

Maintain strict integrity in all your transactions in trade, and in your other outward concerns, remembering that you will have to account for the mode of acquiring, and the manner of using, your possessions.

Watch, with Christian tenderness, over the opening minds of your offspring; enure them to habits of self-restraint and filial obedience; carefully instruct them in the knowledge of the Holy Scriptures, and seek for ability to imbue their minds with the love of their Heavenly Father, their Redeemer, and their Sanctifier.

Observe simplicity and moderation in the furniture of your houses, and in the supply of your tables, as well as in your personal attire, and that of your families.

Be diligent in the private and daily family reading of the Holy Scriptures; and guard carefully against the introduction of improper books into your families.

Be careful to place out children, or all degrees, with those friends whose care and example will be most likely to conduce to their preservation from evil; prefer such assistants, servants, and apprentices, as are members of our religious society; not demanding exorbitant apprentice fees, lest you frustrate the care of friends in these respects.

Encourage your apprentices and servants of all descriptions to attend public worship, making way for them herein: and exercise a watchful care for their moral and religious improvement.

Be careful to make your wills and settle your outward affairs in time of health; and, when you accept the office of guardian, executor, or trustee, be faithful and diligent in the fulfillment of your trust.

Finally, dear friends, let your conversation be such as becometh the Gospel. Exercise yourselves to have always a conscience void of offence towards God and towards man. Watch over one another for good; and when occasions of uneasiness first appear in any, let them be treated with in privacy and tenderness, before the matter be communicated to another: and friends, every where, are advised to maintain "the unity of the spirit in the bond of peace."

Selection 2: *Rules of Discipline* [Opposition to War]

The Quaker opposition to war is well known. It was repeatedly expressed in the Rules of Discipline.

It has been a weighty concern on this meeting, that our ancient and honourable testimony against being concerned in bearing arms, or fighting, may be maintained; it being a doctrine and testimony agreeable to the nature and design of the Christian religion, and to the universal love and grace of God. This testimony, we desire may be strictly and carefully maintained, by a godly care and concern in all to stand clear therein; so shall we strengthen and comfort one another.

And as it has pleased the Lord, by the breaking forth of the glorious light of his Gospel, and the shedding abroad of his Holy Spirit, to gather us to be a people to his praise, and to unite us in love, not only one unto another, but to the whole creation of God, by subjecting us to the government of his Son our Lord and Saviour Jesus Christ, the Prince of Peace; it behoveth us to hold forth the ensign of the Lamb of God, and by our patience and peaceable behaviour to show, that we walk in obedience to the example and precepts of our Lord and Master, who hath commanded us to love our enemies, and to do good even to them that hate us. Wherefore we intreat all who profess themselves members of our society, to be faithful to that ancient testimony, borne by us ever since we were a people, against bearing arms and fighting; that by a conduct agreeable to our profession, we may demonstrate ourselves to be real followers of the Messiah, the peaceable Saviour, of the increase of whose government and peace, there shall be no end.

* * *

Our general scruple to bear arms is well known; and truly we are satisfied that our testimony in this respect is a testimony for Messiah, of whose reign it is the glory, that "the wolf and the lamb shall feed together." Most, if not all, people admit the transcendent excellency of peace. All who adopt the petition, "Thy kingdom come," pray for its universal establishment. Some people then must begin to fulfil the evangelical promise, and cease to learn war any more. Now, friends, seeing these things cannot be controverted, how do we long that your whole conversation be as becometh the Gospel; and that while any of us are professing to scruple war, they may not in some parts of their conduct be inconsistent with that profession! It is an awful thing to stand forth to the nation as the advocates of inviolable peace; and our testimony loses its efficacy in proportion to the want of consistency in any. And we think we are at this time peculiarly called to let our light shine with clearness, on account of the lenity shown us by government, and the readiness of magistrates to afford us all legal relief under suffering. And we can serve our country in no way more availingly, nor more acceptably to Him who holds its prosperity at his disposal, than by contributing, all that in us lies, to increase the number of meek, humble, and self-denying Christians.

Selection 3: *Rules of Discipline* [Abolition of Slavery]

Quakers led the way in the abolition of slavery.
It is the sense of this meeting, that the importing of Negroes from their native country and relations by friends, is not a commendable nor allowed practice, and is therefore censured by this meeting.

We fervently warn all in profession with us, that they be careful to avoid being any way concerned in reaping the unrighteous profits arising from the iniquitous practice of dealing in Negroes, and other slaves; whereby, in the original purchase, one man selleth another, as he doth the beast that perisheth, without any better pretension to a property in him, than that of superior force; in direct violation of the Gospel rule, which teacheth all to do as they would be done by, and to do good to all; being the reverse of that covetous disposition, which furnisheth encouragement to those poor ignorant people to perpetuate their savage wars, in order to supply the demands of this most unnatural traffic, whereby great numbers of mankind, free by nature, are subjected to inextricable bondage; and which hath often been observed to fill their possessors with haughtiness, tyranny, luxury, and barbarity, corrupting the minds and debasing the morals of their children, to the unspeakable prejudice of religion and virtue, and the charity, which is the unchangeable nature, and the glory, of true Christianity.

We therefore can do no less, than, with the greatest earnestness, impress it upon friends everywhere, that they endeavour to keep their hands clear of this unrighteous gain of oppression.

This meeting having reason to apprehend, that divers under our name are concerned in the unchristian traffic in Negroes, doth recommend it earnestly to the care of friends every where, to discourage, as much as in them lies, a practice so repugnant to our Christian profession; and to deal with all such as shall persevere in a conduct so reproachful to Christianity, and to disown them, if they desist not therefrom.

We think it seasonable at this time to renew our exhortation, that friends everywhere be especially careful to keep their hands clear of giving encouragement in any shape to the slave-trade, it being evidently destructive of the natural rights of mankind; who are all ransomed by one Saviour, and visited by one divine light, in order to salvation; a traffic calculated to enrich and aggrandize some upon the misery of others, in its nature abhorrent to every just and tender sentiment, and contrary to the whole tenour of the Gospel.

It appears that the practice of holding Negroes in oppressive and unnatural bondage, hath been so successfully discouraged by friends in some of the colonies, as to be considerably lessened. We cannot but approve of these salutary endeavours, and earnestly intreat they may be continued, that, through the favour of Divine Providence, a traffic so unmerciful, and unjust in its nature, to a part of our own species made equally with ourselves for immortality, may come to be considered by all in its proper light, and be utterly abolished, as a reproach to the Christian profession.

Our testimony against the inhuman practice of slave-keeping gains ground amongst our brethren in the American colonies, and hath had some happy influence on the minds of considerate people of other denominations, in opposition to that flagrant injustice to our fellow-creatures; for whom our Saviour shed his precious blood, as well as for others, and to whom he dispenseth a measure of his grace in common with the rest of mankind.

The Christian religion being designed to regulate and refine the natural affections of man, and to exalt benevolence into that charity which promotes peace on earth, and good-will towards all ranks and classes of mankind the world over; under the influence thereof, our minds have been renewedly affected in sympathy with the poor enslaved Africans; whom avarice hath taught some men, laying claim to the character of Christians, to consider as the refuse of the human race, and not entitled to the common privileges of mankind. The contempt in which they are held, and the remoteness of their sufferings from the notice of disinterested observers, have occasioned few advocates to plead their cause. The consideration of their case being brought weightily before the last yearly meeting, friends were engaged to recommend endeavours for putting a stop to a traffic so disgraceful to humanity, and so repugnant to the precepts of the Gospel.

For Further Reading

The following select list of writings provides a mixture of primary and secondary sources related to the major parts of the anthology, and the full text of the works being excerpted will also provide rich additional reading.

Barry, John M. *Roger Williams and the Creation of the American Soul: Church, State, and the Birth of Liberty*. New York: Viking, 2012.

Calvin, James. *The Moral theology of Roger Williams: Christian Conviction and Political Ethics*. Louisville: Westminster John Knox, 2004.

McGregor, J. F., and B. Reay. *Radical Religion in the English Revolution*. Oxford: Oxford University Press, 1986.

The Spirit of the Quakers. Selected and Introduced by Geoffrey Durham. New Haven: Yale University Press an Association with the International Sacred Scripture Trust, 2010.

PART 6

Eighteenth-Century Voices

RATIONALISM

19

❧ *The so-called "Age of Reason" had a profound effect on Christian ethics. In England it found an early and eloquent spokesman sympathetic to the Christian Faith in John Locke (1632–1704). His insistence that one must make the distinction between propositions which are (1) according to reason, (2) above reason, and (3) contrary to reason, and that the teachings of the Christian faith may be "according to reason" or "above reason" but never "contrary to reason" was at the heart of Christian rationalism. It influenced the social teaching of the Christian churches by insisting that ethics be grounded in reason rather than revelation. While this approach developed first in England and found in the Anglican Bishop Joseph Butler (1692–1752) one of its most eloquent spokespersons, it profoundly influenced both continental Europe and America. Christian rationalism led Thomas Paine (1737–1809) to reject in the name of reason all claims to revelation. That the appeal to the absolute authority of human reason would eventually have this result had always been the opinion of the orthodox whose worst fears were thus confirmed.*

Selection 1: John Locke, *The Reasonableness of Christianity*

Because of the weakness of human beings in their sin, lust, carelessness and fear, they fail to find God in nature and by reason. Revelation thus provides a surer way to reasonable morality in view of the frailty and weakness of people's constitutions.

Next to the knowledge of one God; maker of all things; "a clear knowledge of their duty was wanting to mankind." This part of knowledge, though cultivated with some care by some of the heathen philosophers, yet got little footing among the people. All men, indeed, under pain of displeasing the gods, were to frequent the temples: everyone went to their sacrifices and services: but the priests made it not their business to teach them virtue. If they were diligent in their observations and ceremonies; punctual in their feasts and solemnities, and the tricks of religion; the holy tribe assured them the gods were pleased, and they looked no farther. Few went to the schools of the philosophers to be instructed in their duties, and to know what was good and evil in their actions. The priests sold the better pennyworths, and therefore had all the custom. Lustrations and processions were much easier than a clean conscience, and a steady course of virtue; and an expiatory sacrifice that atoned for the want of it, was much more convenient than a strict and holy life. No wonder then, that religion was everywhere distinguished from, and preferred to virtue; and that it was dangerous heresy and profaneness to think the contrary. So much virtue as was necessary to hold societies together, and to contribute to the quiet of governments, the civil laws of commonwealths taught, and forced upon men that lived under magistrates. But these laws being for the most part made by such, who had no other aims but their own power, reached no farther than those things that would serve to tie men together in subjection; or at most were directly to conduce to the prosperity and temporal happiness of any people. But natural religion, in its full extent, was no-where, that I know, taken care of, by the force of natural reason. It should seem, by the little that has hitherto been done in it, that it is too hard a task for unassisted reason to establish morality in all its parts, upon its true foundation, with a clear and convincing light. And it is at least a surer and shorter way, to the apprehensions of the vulgar, and mass of mankind, that one manifestly sent from God, and coming with visible authority from him, should, as a king and law-maker, tell them their duties; and require their obedience; than leave it to the long and sometimes intricate deductions of reason, to be made out to them. Such trains of reasoning the greatest part of mankind have neither leisure to weigh; nor, for want of education and use, skill to judge of. We see how unsuccessful in this the attempts of philosophers were before our Saviour's time. How short their several systems came of the perfection of a true and complete morality, is very visible. And if, since that, the christian philosophers have much outdone them: yet we may observe, that the first knowledge of the truths they have added, is owing to revelation: though as soon as they are heard and considered, they are found to be agreeable to reason; and such as can by no means be contradicted. Every one may observe a great many truths, which he receives at first from others, and readily assents to, as consonant to reason, which he would have found it hard, and perhaps beyond his strength, to have discovered himself. Native and original truth is not so easily wrought out of the mine, as we, who have it delivered already dug and fashioned into our hands, are apt to imagine. And how often at fifty or threescore years old are thinking men told what they wonder how they could miss thinking of? Which yet their own contemplations did not, and possibly never would have helped them to. Experience shows, that the knowledge of morality, by mere natural light, (how agreeable soever it be to it,) makes but a slow progress, and little advance in the world. And the reason of it is not hard to be found in men's necessities, passions, vices, and mistaken interests; which turn their thoughts another way: and the designing leaders, as well as following herd, find it not to their purpose to employ much of their meditations this way. Or whatever else was the cause, it is plain, in fact, that human reason unassisted failed men in its great and proper business of morality. It never from unquestionable principles, by clear deductions, made out an entire body of the "law of nature." And he that shall collect all the moral rules of the philosophers, and compare them with those contained in the New Testament, will find them to come short of the morality delivered by our Saviour, and taught by his apostles; a college made up, for the most part, of ignorant, but inspired fishermen.

Though yet, if any one should think, that out of the sayings of the wise heathens before our Saviour's time, there might be a collection made of all those rules of morality, which are to be found in the Christian religion; yet this would not at all hinder, but that the world, nevertheless, stood as much in need of our Saviour, and the morality delivered by him. Let it be granted (though not true) that all the moral precepts of the gospel were known by somebody or other, amongst mankind before. But where, or how, or of what use, is not considered. Suppose they may be picked up here and there; some from Solon and Bias in Greece, others from Tully in Italy: and to complete the work, let Confucius, as far as China, be consulted; and Anacharsis, the Scythian, contribute his share. What will all this do, to give the world a complete morality, that may be to mankind the unquestionable rule of life and manners? I will not here urge the impossibility of collecting from men, so far distant from one another, in time and place, and languages. I will suppose there was a Stobeus in those times, who had gathered the moral sayings from all the sages of the world. What would this amount to, towards being a steady rule; a certain transcript of a law that we are under? Did the saying of Aristippus, or Confucius, give it an authority? Was Zeno a law-giver to mankind? If not, what he or any other philosopher delivered, was but a saying of his. Mankind might hearken to it, or reject it, as they pleased; or as it suited their interest, passions, principles or humours. They were under no obligation; the opinion of this or that philosopher was of no authority. And if it were, you must take all he said under the same character. All his dictates must go for law, certain and true; or none of them. And then, if you will take any of the moral sayings of Epicurus (many whereof Seneca quotes with esteem and approbation) for precepts of the law of nature, you must take all the rest of his doctrine for such too; or else his authority ceases: and so no more is to be received from him, or any of the sages of old, for parts of the law of nature, as carrying with it an obligation to be obeyed, but what they prove to be so. But such a body of ethics, proved to be the law of nature, from principles of reason, and teaching all the duties of life; I think nobody will say the world had before our Saviour's time. It is not enough that there were up and down scattered sayings of wise men, conformable to right reason. The law of nature, is the law of convenience too: and it is no wonder that those men of parts, and studious of virtue, (who had occasion to think on any particular part of it,) should, by meditation, light on the right even from the observable convenience and beauty of it; without making out its obligation from the true principles of the law of nature, and foundations of morality. But these incoherent apophthegms of philosophers, and wise men, however excellent in themselves, and well intended by them; could never make a morality, whereof the world could be convinced; could never rise to the force of a law, that mankind could with certainty depend on. Whatsoever should thus be universally useful, as a standard to which men should conform their manners, must have its authority, either from reason or revelation. It is not every writer of morality, or compiler of it from others, that can thereby be erected into a law-giver to mankind; and a dictator of rules, which are therefore valid, because they are to be found in his books; under the authority of this or that philosopher. He, that any one will pretend to set up in this kind, and have his rules pass for authentic directions, must show, that either he builds his doctrine upon principles of reason, self-evident in themselves; and that he deduces all the parts of it from thence, by clear and evident demonstration: or must show his commission from heaven, that he comes with authority from God, to deliver his will and commands to the world. In the former way, no-body that I know, before our Saviour's time, ever did, or went about to give us a morality. It is true, there is a law of nature: but who is there that ever did, or undertook to give it us all entire, as a law; no more, nor no less, than what was contained in, and had the obligation of that law? Who ever made out all the parts of it, put them together, and showed the world their obligation? Where was there any such code, that mankind might have recourse to, as their unerring rule, before our Saviour's time? If there was not, it is plain there was need of one to give us such a morality; such a law, which might be the sure guide of those who had a desire to go right; and, if they had a mind, need not mistake their duty, but might be certain when they had performed, when failed in it. Such a law of morality Jesus Christ hath given us in the New Testament; but by the latter of these ways, by revelation. We have from him a full and sufficient rule for our direction, and conformable to that of reason. But the truth and obligation of its precepts have their force, and are put past doubt to us, by the evidence of his mission. He was sent by God: his miracles show it; and the authority of God in his precepts cannot be questioned. Here morality has a sure standard, that revelation vouches, and reason cannot gainsay, nor question; but both together witness to come from God the great law-maker. And such an one as this, out of the New Testament, I think the world never had, nor can any one say, is any-where else to be found. Let me ask any one, who is forward to think that the doctrine of morality was full and clear in the world, at our Saviour's birth; whither would he have directed Brutus and Cassius, (both men of parts and virtue, the one whereof believed, and the other disbelieved a future being,) to be satisfied in the rules and obligations of all the parts of their duties; if they should have asked him, Where they might find the law they were to live by, and by which they should be charged, or acquitted, as guilty, or innocent? If to the sayings of the wise, and the declarations of philosophers, he sends them into a wild wood of uncertainty, to an endless maze, from which they should never get out: if to the religions of the world, yet worse: and if to their own reason, he refers them to that which had some light and certainty; but yet had hitherto failed all mankind in a perfect rule; and we see, resolved not the doubts that had arisen amongst the studious and thinking philosophers; nor had yet been able to convince the civilized parts of the world, that they had not given, nor could, without a crime, take away the lives of their children, by exposing them.

⋆   ⋆   ⋆

A great many things which we have been bred up in the belief of, from our cradles, (and are notions grown familiar, and, as it were, natural to us, under the gospel,) we take for unquestionable obvious truths, and easily demonstrable; without considering how long we might have been in doubt or ignorance of them, had revelation been silent. And many are beholden to revelation, who do not acknowledge it. It is no diminishing to revelation, that reason gives its suffrage too, to the truths revelation has discovered. But it is our mistake to think, that because reason confirms them to us, we had the first certain knowledge of them from thence; and in that clear evidence we now possess them.

Selection 2: Joseph Butler, *Upon the Love of Our Neighbor*

Butler developed his social ethics in a famous series of sermons, "Fifteen Sermons Preached in Rolls Chapel." Our excerpt is from one of these, "Upon the Love of our Neighbor." One gets a sense here of his reasoned approach and a few hints of his well-known critique of Thomas Hobbes's ethical egoism, which posits that society is best served when people pursue their own self-interest and allow others to do the same.

First, It is manifest that nothing can be of consequence to mankind or any creature, but happiness. This then is all which any person can, in strictness of speaking, be said to have a right to. We can, therefore, owe no man any thing, but only to further and promote his happiness, according to our abilities. And, therefore, a disposition and endeavor to do good to all with whom we have to do, in the degree and manner which the different relations we stand in to them require, is a discharge of all the obligations we are under to them.

As human nature is not one simple uniform thing, but a composition of various parts, body, spirit, appetites, particular passions, and affections; for each of which reasonable self-love would lead men to have due regard, and make suitable provision: so society consists of various parts, to which we stand in different respects and relations; and just benevolence would as surely lead us to have due regard to each of these, and behave as the respective relations require. Reasonable good will, and right behaviour towards our fellow creatures, are in a manner the same: only that the former expresseth the principle as it is in the mind; the latter, the principle as it were, become external, i.e., exerted in actions.

And so far as temperance, sobriety, and moderation in sensual pleasures, and the contrary vices, have any respect to our fellow creatures, any influences upon their quiet, welfare, and happiness; as they always have a real, and often a near, influence upon it; so far it is manifest those virtues may be produced by the love of our neighbor, and that the contrary vices would be prevented by it. Indeed, if men's regard to themselves will not restrain them from excess, it may be thought little probable, that their love to others will he sufficient: but the reason is, that their love to other's is not, any more than their regard to themselves, just, and in its due degree. There are, however, manifest instances of persons kept sober and temperate from regard to their affairs, and the welfare of those who depend upon them. And it is obvious to every one that habitual excess, a dissolute course of life, implies a general neglect of the duties we owe towards our friends, our families, and our country.

From hence it is manifest, that the common virtues; and the common vices of mankind, may be traced up to benevolence, or the want of it. And this entitles the precept, "Thou shalt love thy neighbor as thyself," to the pre-eminence given to it; and is a justification of the apostle's assertion, that all other commandments are comprehended in it: whatever cautions and restrictions there are, which might require to be considered, if we were to state particularly and at length, what is virtue and right behaviour in mankind. [For instance: as we are not competent judges what is, upon the whole, for the good of the world, there may be other immediate ends appointed us to pursue, besides that one of doing good, or producing happiness. Though the good of the creation be the only end of the Author of it, yet he may have laid us under particular obligations, which we may discern and feel ourselves under, quite distinct from a perception, that the observance or violation of them is for the happiness or misery of our fellow creatures. And this is, in fact, the case. For there are certain dispositions of mind and certain actions, which are in themselves approved or disapproved by mankind, abstracted from the consideration of their tendency to the happiness or misery of the world; approved or disapproved by reflection, by that principle within, which is the guide of life, the judge of right and wrong. Numberless instances of this kind might be mentioned. There are pieces of treachery, which in themselves appear base and detestable to every one. There are actions, which perhaps can scarce have any other general name given them than indecencies, which yet are odious and shocking to human nature. There is such a thing as meanness, a little mind, which, as it is quite distinct from incapacity, so it raises a dislike and disapprobation quite different from that contempt, which men are too apt to have of mere folly. On the other hand, what we call greatness of mind, is the object of another sort of approbation, than superior understanding. Fidelity, honor, strict justice, are themselves approved in the highest degree, abstracted from the consideration of their tendency. Now, whether it be thought that each of these are connected with benevolence in our nature, and so may be considered as the same thing with it; or whether some of them be thought an inferior kind of virtues and vices, somewhat like natural beauties and deformities; or, lastly, plain exceptions to the general rule; thus much, however, is certain, that the things now instanced in, and numberless others, are approved or disapproved by mankind in general, in quite another view than as conducive to the happiness or misery of the world.

Secondly, It might be added, that, in a higher and more general way of consideration, leaving out the particular nature of creatures, and the particular circumstances in which they are placed, benevolence seems in the strictest sense to include in it all that is good and worthy; all that is good, which we have any distinct particular notion of. We have no clear conception of any positive moral attribute in the supreme Being, but what may be resolved up into goodness. And, if we consider a reasonable creature or moral agent, without regard to the particular relations and circumstances in which he is placed, we cannot conceive any thing else to come in towards determining whether he is to be ranked in a higher or lower class of virtuous beings, but the higher or lower degree in which that principle, and what is manifestly connected with it, prevail in him.

That which we more strictly call piety, or the love of God, and which is an essential part of a right temper, some may perhaps imagine no way connected with benevolence: yet, surely, they must be connected, if there be indeed in being an object infinitely good. Human nature is so constituted, that every good affection implies the love of itself; i.e. becomes the object of a new affection in the same person. Thus, to be righteous, implies in it the love of righteousness; to be benevolent, the love of benevolence; to be good, the love of goodness; whether this righteousness, benevolence, or goodness, be viewed as in our own mind, or in another's: and the love of God as a Being perfectly good, is the love of perfect goodness contemplated in a being or person. Thus morality and religion, virtue and piety, will at last necessarily coincide, run up into one and the same point, and love will be in all senses the end of the commandment.

PIETISM

20

❧ *The definition of "Pietism" is controversial, but its significance for the development of Christian social thought is massive. Associated with the names of Philip Jacob Spener (1635–1705), August Hermann Francke (1663–1727), and Nicolaus Ludwig Count Zinzendorf (1700–1760), the movement had precursors like Johann Arndt (1555–1621), who, however, considered himself an orthodox Lutheran and was the pastor and teacher of the most impressive dogmatician of Lutheran Orthodoxy, Johann Gerhard (1586–1637). Spener emphasized the importance of the new birth of the Christian, an emphasis that became typical for Pietists who often felt that the date of this new birth should and could be established by the individual believer. It was this individual believer who played an increasingly important part in Pietism and who was gathered in small Bible study groups, the so-called Collegia Pietatis.*

In its relation to society, Pietism was characterized by an apparently contradictory attitude: Pietists rejected the "world" and "worldliness" as a realm of evil. At the same time they made valiant and sometimes effective efforts to change this "evil world." Thus Pietism became the movement that carried Protestantism to the ends of the earth through its missionary efforts and simultaneously tried to change the situation at home through a multitude of schools, hospitals, and other institutions of Christian service. The method was to change the world by changing individuals, especially also those in positions of power. Thus August Hermann Francke established a school specifically designed to educate the sons of the nobility and other leading citizens, and the Moravians became famous for their excellent private schools.

This Pietistic approach of changing the world by changing individuals and especially the leaders of society became widely adopted and quite typical for the Protestant Christian approach to social change. It presents both its greatest strength and weakness and has its roots in the thought of the men here presented.

Selection 1: Philip Jacob Spener, *Pia Desideria*

The man who is commonly regarded as the founder of Pietism was born in Alsace and studied at the University of Strasbourg. He read both Johann Arndt's True Christianity *and many of the Puritan tracts (for example, Lewis Bayly's* Practice of Piety, *Dyke's* Mystery of Selfedeceit, *Baxter's* Call to the Unconverted*) as well as the writings of Martin Luther. In 1666 he became senior* *pastor of Frankfurt/Main, where he served for twenty years and attracted a vast number of disciples. Later he served in Dresden and Berlin, where he died in 1705. One of his most influential works is* Pia Desideria, *published during his stay at Frankfurt. Our selection is taken from this booklet and deals with the emphasis upon the spiritual priesthood of all Christians.*

Proposals to Correct Conditions in the Church

1. Thought should be given to a more extensive use of the Word of God among us. We know that by nature we have no good in us. If there is to be any good in us, it must be brought about by God. To this end the Word of God is the powerful means, since faith must be enkindled through the gospel, and the law provides the rules for good works and many wonderful impulses to attain them. The more at home the Word of God is among us, the more we shall bring about faith and its fruits.

It may appear that the Word of God has sufficiently free course among us inasmuch as at various places (as in this city) there is daily or frequent preaching from the pulpit. When we reflect further on the matter, however, we shall find that with respect to this first proposal, more is needed. I do not at all disapprove of the preaching of sermons in which a Christian congregation is instructed by the reading and exposition of a certain text, for I myself do this. But I find that this is not enough. In the first place, we know that "all scripture is inspired by God and profitable for teaching, for reproof, for correction, and for training in righteousness" (2 Tim. 3:16). Accordingly all scripture, without exception, should be known by the congregation if we are all to receive the necessary benefit. If we put together all the passages of the Bible which in the course of many years are read to a congregation in one place, they will comprise only a very small part of the Scriptures which have been given to us. The remainder is not heard by the congregation at all, or is heard only insofar as one or another verse is quoted or alluded to in sermons, without, however, offering any understanding of the entire context, which is nevertheless of the greatest importance. In the second place, the people have little opportunity to grasp the meaning of the scriptures except on the basis of those passages which may have been expounded to them, and even less do they have the opportunity to become as practiced in them as edification requires. Meanwhile, although solitary reading of the Bible at home is in itself a splendid and praiseworthy thing, it does not accomplish enough for most people.

It should therefore be considered whether the church would not be well advised to introduce the people to Scripture in still other ways than through the customary sermons on the appointed lessons.

This might be done, first of all, by diligent reading of Holy Scriptures, especially of the New Testament. It would not be difficult for every housefather to keep a Bible or at least a New Testament, handy and read from it every day or, if he cannot read, to have somebody else read. How necessary and beneficial this would be for all Christians in every station of life was splendidly and effectively demonstrated a century ago by Andrew Hyperius, whose two books on this matter were quickly translated in German by George Nigrinus and, after the little work had become quite unknown, were recently brought to the attention of people again in a new edition put out by Dr.

Elias Veyel, my esteemed former fellow student in Strasbourg and my beloved brother in Christ.

Then a second thing would be desirable in order to encourage people to read privately, namely, that where the practice can be introduced the books of the Bible be read one after another, unless one wished to add brief summaries. This would be intended for the edification of all, but especially of those who cannot read at all, or cannot read easily or well, or of those who do not own a copy of the Bible.

For a third thing it would perhaps not be inexpedient (and I set this down for further and more mature reflection) to reintroduce the ancient and apostolic kind of church meetings. In addition to our customary services with preaching, other assemblies would also be held in the manner in which Paul describes them in 1 Corinthians 14:26-40. One person would not rise to preach (although this practice would be continued at other times), but others who have been blessed with gifts and knowledge would also speak and present their pious opinions on the proposed subject to the judgment of the rest, doing all this in such a way as to avoid disorder and strife. This might conveniently be done by having several ministers (in places where a number of them live in a town) meet together or by having several members of a congregation who have a fair knowledge of God or desire to increase their knowledge meet under the leadership of a minister, take up the Holy Scriptures, read aloud from them, and fraternally discuss each verse in order to discover its simple meaning and whatever may be useful for the edification of all. Anybody who is not satisfied with his understanding of a matter should be permitted to express his doubts and seek further explanation. On the other hand, those (including the ministers) who have made more progress should be allowed the freedom to state how they understand each passage. Then all that has been contributed, insofar as it accords with the sense of the Holy Spirit in the Scriptures, should be carefully considered by the rest, especially by the ordained ministers, and applied to the edification of the whole meeting. Everything should be arranged with an eye to the glory of God, to the spiritual growth of the participants, and therefore also to their limitations. Any threat of meddlesomeness, quarrelsomeness, self-seeking, or something else of this sort should be guarded against and tactfully cut off especially by the preachers who retain leadership in these meetings.

Not a little benefit is to be hoped for from such an arrangement. Preachers would learn to know the members of their own congregations and their weakness or growth in doctrine and piety, and a bond of confidence would be established between preachers and people which would serve the best interests of both. At the same time the people would have a splendid opportunity to exercise their diligence with respect to the Word of God and modestly to ask their questions (which they do not always have the courage to discuss with their minister in private) and get answers to them. In a short time they would experience personal growth and would also become capable of giving better religious instruction to their children and servants at home. In the absence of such exercises, sermons which are delivered in continually flowing speech are not always fully and adequately comprehended because there is no time for reflection in between or because, when one does not stop to reflect, much of what follows is missed (which does not happen in a discussion). On the other hand, private reading of the Bible or reading in the household, where nobody is present who may from time to time help point out the meaning and purpose of each verse, cannot provide the reader with a sufficient explanation of all that he would like to know. What is lacking in both of these instances (in public preaching and private reading) would be supplied by the proposed exercises. It would not be a great burden either to the preachers or to the people, and much would be done to fulfill the admonition of Paul in Colossians 3:16, "Let the word of Christ dwell in you richly as you teach and admonish one another in all wisdom, and as you sing psalms and hymns and spiritual songs." In fact, such songs may be used in the proposed meetings for the praise of God and the inspiration of the participants.

This much is certain: the diligent use of the Word of God, which consists not only of listening to sermons but also of reading, meditating, and discussing (Ps. 1:2), must be the chief means for reforming something, whether this occurs in the proposed fashion or in some other appropriate way. The Word of God remains the seed from which all that is good in us must grow. If we succeed in getting the people to seek eagerly and diligently in the book of life for their joy, their spiritual life will be wonderfully strengthened and they will become altogether different people.

What did our sainted Luther seek more ardently than to induce the people to a diligent reading of the Scriptures? He even had some misgivings abut allowing his books to be published, lest the people be made more slothful thereby in the reading of the scriptures. His words in Volume 1 of the Altenburg edition of his works read:

I should gladly have seen all my books forgotten and destroyed, if only for the reason that I am afraid of the example I may give. For I see what benefit it has brought to the church that men have begun to collect many books and great libraries outside and alongside of the Holy Scriptures, and especially have begun to scramble together, without any distinction, all sorts of "fathers," "councils," and "doctors." Not only has good time been wasted and the study of Scriptures neglected, but the pure understanding of God's Word is lost…It was our intention and our hope when we began to put the Bible into German that there would be less writing and more studying and reading of the Scriptures. For all other writings should point to the Scriptures. . . . Neither fathers nor councils nor we ourselves will do so well, even when our very best is done, as the Holy Scriptures have done—that is to say, that the man who at this time wishes to have my books will by no means let them be a hindrance to his own study of the Scriptures, etc.

Luther also wrote similar things elsewhere.

One of the principal wrongs by which papal politics became entrenched, the people were kept in ignorance, and hence complete control of their consciences was maintained was that the papacy prohibited, and insofar as possible continues to prohibit, the reading of the Holy Scriptures. On the other hand, it was one of the major purposes of the Reformation to restore to the people the Word of God which had lain hidden under the bench (and this Word was the most powerful means by which God blessed his work). So this will be the principal means, now that the church must be put in better condition, whereby the aversion to Scripture which many have may be overcome, neglect of its study be counteracted, and ardent seal for it awakened.

*   *   *

3. Connected with these two proposals is a third: the people must have impressed upon them and must accustom themselves to believing that it is by no means enough to have knowledge of the Christian faith, for Christianity consists rather of practice.

Our dear Savior repeatedly enjoined love as the real mark of his disciples (John 13:34-45; 15:12; 1 John 3:10, 18, 4:7-8, 11-13, 21). In his old age dear John (according to the testimony of Jerome in his letter to the Galatians) was accustomed to say hardly anything more to his disciples than "Children, love one another!" His disciples and auditors finally became so annoyed at this endless repetition that they asked him why he was always saying the same thing to them. He replied, "Because it is the Lord's command, and it suffices if this be done." Indeed, love is the whole life of the man who has faith and who through his faith is saved, and his fulfillment, of the laws of God consists of love.

If we can therefore awaken a fervent love among our Christians, first toward one another and then toward all men (for these two, brotherly affection and general love, must supplement each other according to 2 Peter 1:7), and put this love into practice practically all that we desire will be accomplished. For all the commandments are summed up in love (Rom. 13:9). Accordingly the people are not only to be told this incessantly, and they are not only to have the excellence of neighborly love and, on the other hand, the great danger and harm in the opposing self-love pictured impressively before their eyes (which is done well in the spiritually minded John Arndt's True Christianity, IV, ii, 22 et seq.), but they must also practice such love. They must become accustomed not to lose sight of any opportunity in which they can render their neighbor a service of love, and yet while performing it they must diligently search their hearts to discover whether they are acting in true love or out of other motives. If they are offended, they should especially be on their guard, not only that they refrain from all vengefulness but also that they give up some of their rights and insistence on them for fear that their hearts may betray them and feelings of hostility may become involved. In fact, they should diligently seek opportunities to do good to their enemies in order that such self-control may hurt the old Adam, who is otherwise inclined to vengeance, and at the same time in order that love may be more deeply implanted in their hearts.

For this purpose, as well as for the sake of Christian growth in general, it may be useful if those who have earnestly resolved to walk in the way of the Lord would enter into a confidential relationship with their confessor or some other judicious and enlightened Christian and would regularly report to him how they live, what opportunities they have had to practice Christian love, and how they have employed or neglected them. This should be done with the intention of discovering what is amiss and securing such an individual's counsel and instruction as to what ought now to be done. There should be firm resolution to follow such advice at all times unless something is expected that is quite clearly contrary to God's will. If there appears to be doubt whether or not one in obligated to do this or that out of love for one's neighbor, it is always better to incline toward doing it rather than leaving it undone.

Selection 2: August Hermann Francke, *Scriptural Rules*

August Hermann Francke (1663–1727) was the organizational genius of German Pietism. In Halle, where he served as professor of theology, he founded a number of institutions (orphanage, school for children of parents unable to pay tuition, Latin school, school for the education of children of the nobility, publishing house, Bible society), which helped him to extend the Pietist influence all over the world. The following selection illustrates one aspect of Pietism, its methodical attempts at self-improvement.

Rules for the Preservation of Conscience and Good Order in Social Intercourse or Society (Scriptural Rules)

(1) Society offers many occasions for sinning. If you want to preserve your conscience, remember always that the great and majestic God by His omnipresence is always the most eminent member of any society. One should show awe in the presence of such a great Lord.

(2) Whatever you do, see to it that nobody (especially not you yourself) disturbs your inner peace and your rest in God.

(3) Never speak of your enemies except in love and to the honor of God and their best interest.

(4) Do not insist on talking much. But if God gives you the opportunity to speak, speak with respect, prudence, gentleness whenever you are certain. Use a loving seriousness and distinct and clear words, in an orderly fashion and without slurring your words, and do not repeat yourself unnecessarily.

(5) Do not presumptuously speak of the things of this world unless God is honored thereby and your neighbor improved and your pressing needs met. It is a word of the Lord: "Whatever you are doing, whether you speak or act, do everything in the name of the Lord Jesus, giving thanks to God the Father through him." (Col. 3:17)

(6) Beware of barbed or sarcastic speech. Avoid all offensive foolish or merely injudicious proverbs and sayings which might give offense. Ask others to tell you whether you tend to use such, for habit results in lack of awareness. Cursing is among the serious sins. He who curses, curses himself and all that is his.

(7) When speaking of God and your Savior speak with deep humility and reverence as if in His very presence. Be ashamed to use the name of Jesus as a mere expression.

(8) When telling stories be very careful, for the spirit of lies rules here. One tends to fill in the details from one's own imagination if memory has not retained everything. One should examine when telling a story if one does not here and there speak without certainty. Ridiculous and supercilious stories are not appropriate for the Christian. For they are either not true or at least uncertain or they are opposed to love to the neighbor or result in an abuse of spiritual things or cause the suspicion in the other person that he may be meant by the story. They also tend to encourage others to tell similar and even worse stories. Good and true examples of the virtues and those who bear witness to divine Providence, Power, Mercy, and Justice one should never forget, for one can edify greatly with such illustration. But tell them if you are certain of the facts and clearly and in an orderly fashion without adding anything. If you have forgotten some detail do not be ashamed to admit it.

(9) When speaking of yourself watch that you do not speak out of self-love.

(10) Do not change sound subjects incessantly. This is the undoing of most people who cannot talk fully about anything but start talking about one thing and then about another. Stick by your subject as long as it is not burdensome to others and by

doing so you will avoid many a misunderstanding. Edify yourself and others and collect a treasure of important subjects and sound arguments which you can discuss in detail when the need arises.

(11) Remember that certain words are of themselves evil, as for example cursing, useless swearing, rude and obscene talk. This is true also of useless words which serve no purpose and have no goal. And even those words are good who are said to honor him who already knows the word that you are about to speak. You should avoid evil and useless words for you will have to give account of every single one. Good words use eagerly.

(12) Select your company either because there is need or hope for improvement but in any case select them carefully. Some formal contact with godless people cannot be avoided but do not seek their company without compelling reason. It is more likely that they will lead you astray that than you will win them. If you have to have dealing with them be on guard.

(13) Many speeches are sound but not presented in the right company or place. In church even the best speech may become a stumbling block for the weak.

(14) In the presence of others do not speak secretively or into somebody's ear or in a foreign language. For this causes suspicion and the person excluded assumes that you do not trust him.

(15) When others speak who want to be heard by everybody present do not start an individual conversation with one member of the group, for this causes disorder and annoyance.

(16) If you tell something which you know or have heard through someone else, think first if the source of your remarks would be content to have you repeat it. If you have doubts, be quiet.

(17) If somebody interrupts you be quiet. The other person will be pleased that he is heard also and even if you were to continue he would not really hear you since he is so intent of what he is about to say.

(18) Never interrupt anybody else. For everybody is annoyed if you don't let him finish. Sometimes you may think you have gotten the point and still fail to understand what he wants to say. The other person feels secretly despised if one does not let him finish. You would not interrupt an important man whom you would like to honor. Consider when you interrupt others and you will note that you let your mouth blurt out without real forethought. You will gain the love of everybody much more easily if you listen patiently to everyone.

(19) If someone contradicts you be especially on guard. For this is the occasion for sin in society. If the honor of God and the welfare of your neighbor does not suffer don't argue. There is much argument and when it is finished both sides have less certainty of the matter than they had before. Even if somebody opposes the truth beware of all violent emotion. This is only the eagerness of the flesh. If you have presented the truth clearly and with sound reasons be content. Further quarrelling will gain little. Your opponent will give the matter more thought if he sees that you are sure of your cause and do not want to quarrel. If he learns nothing else from you he learns meekness and modesty from your example.

(20) If games or other entertainment like dancing, etc., begin take thought. You know that much indecent and rough behaviour is connected with such activities and that they are commonly followed by obscene gestures and talk and other even greater sins. It may be more advisable for you to leave quietly rather than remain

since the opportunity may lead you astray to give in to such disorderly behaviour or at least make it difficult for you to preserve the peace of God in your soul.

(21) If it is up to you to punish others because of their sins, do not make excuses that the time is inconvenient if it is really fear and timidity that keep you back. Fear and timidity must be overcome like other evil emotions. But always punish yourself first before punishing others so that your punishment will flow from compassion. Punish with love and great care and modesty in order that the other person may somehow be convinced in his conscience that he had done ill. Christ punished with one look when he looked at Peter who had denied him. Yet Peter wept bitterly. Christ would also punish with explicit and plain words. Love must here be your teacher. But do not participate in the sins of others.

(22) When it comes to eating be moderate in the use of food and drink. If you are urged to overindulge remember that these are temptations to sin against your God. Do not let yourself be led to follow the pleasantness of taste and fill your belly to the brim. It would be better for you if you were to eat more frequently but less on each occasion to preserve your soberness of mind and the aptitude to do good rather than stuffing your stomach and lose the lovely and joyful manner of a sober soul. Much eating and drinking overburdens body and soul. Consistent moderation is an important test of your spiritual intelligence. If your mouth waters to select the best food for yourself to fill yourself with dainty morsels because of their taste and to eat and drink inordinately without real hunger or thirst you still are not a moderate person.

(23) Always and in every company beware of indecent facial expressions, movements of the hands and positions of the body. They reveal disorder in the mind and betray your most secret emotions. Your dear Jesus would not have done such, why would you not follow him in outward behaviour which is of all things the least important? Let a good friend call these things to your attention since you may not be able to recognize them in yourself.

(24) Beware of unnecessary laughter. Not all laughter is forbidden. For it does happen that the most pious person rejoices so deeply because of godly, not worldly, things that his mouth bears witness with a modest laugh of the delight in his mind. But it is easy to sin here and the road is opened for a distraction of the senses (Wisdom 9:15) which soon leads to the awareness that the heart has become too frivolous when it tries to approach in deep humility the omnipresent God. Especially if others laugh at jokes and foolishness beware that you do not laugh with them. It does not please God, why does it please you. If it does not please you, then why are you laughing? If you laugh you share in the sin. If you remain serious you have punished the sin in the conscience of the useless babbler.

(25) If others have gotten off the subject or sidetracked in their discussion, see to it that you correct this with an intelligent remark as soon as possible. Thus you can avoid much diffuseness. Few use this gift yet it is most necessary.

(26) Never place yourself ahead of anyone and do not avoid the place in society which you have to take because of your status in life and to preserve good order. You are dust, the other ashes. Before God you are both equal. Therefore, as far as you are concerned ignore your status. Love is humble and awakens by its humility love in others. A conceited man is a burden to everyone.

(27) Honor all men in society but be afraid of no one. God is greater than you or he. Fear Him!

(28) Do not be sad and irritable when you are with people but rather joyful and delightful for that refreshes everyone.

(29) If you note that a certain social occasion is not necessary for you, or that God's honor could be furthered better somewhere else, or that love does not constrain you to serve your neighbor by your continued presence do not stay just for the love of company. You must not remain another instant if the only reason for your staying is to waste time. It is unbecoming for a Christian to be bored in the presence of his God. Even pious people fail here occasionally and spend time in useless words and deeds which later trouble their souls.

(30) Watch whether your heart is the same, be it in solitude or in society. If this is not the case you have much reason to seek solitude rather than society so that you may put your heart first into right order. But if solitude or society are the same to you watch that you who stand do not fall.

John Wesley   21

✤ *The founder of the Methodist movement was born in Epworth, England, on June 17, 1703, and died in London on March 2, 1791. After studies at Oxford he was ordained in 1728 as a priest of the Church of England. Even at Oxford he had participated in study groups concerned not only with personal piety but social improvement, which he expressed by visiting jails, caring for the poor and instructing underprivileged children. Contact with German Pietists (Salzburger Lutherans and Moravians) modified his theological heritage and influenced him in the development of his own theological position after his conversion experience at Aldersgate (May 24, 1738).*

Wesley's ethics is characterized by an activistic emphasis on sanctification and Christian perfection. This impressed itself upon the Methodist movement and to some extent all Anglo-Saxon Christianity. Wesley's social teachings are a peculiar combination of political conservatism and social activism. He shares with other Pietists a tendency to seek individualistic solutions to social evils and to deal with the symptoms of prevailing evils rather than their causes. Nevertheless, his influence for change was great. Though Wesley was conservative to the core, his humanitarian interests made Methodism a far more radical force for social change than its founder anticipated.

Selection 1: *The Use of Money*

Wesley's life spanned the eighteenth century, a time of great change and social dislocation the ills of which were in part depicted in the satirical and moralistic works of the painter William Hogarth, Wesley's contemporary. In his sermon on the use of money, Wesley advocates personal responsibility, honest industry, care for one's dependents, and a readiness to share one's wealth. Some contemporary activists may fear that Wesley's admonition, "gain all you can, save all you can and give all you can" is insufficiently sensitive to systemic reforms required for economic justice in a capitalist society. However, it remains an important and memorable call to a generous concern for the needs of others in Christian love.

"I say unto you, Make unto yourselves friends of the mammon of unrighteousness; that, when ye fail, they may receive you into the everlasting habitations." Luke 16:9.

*   *   *

An excellent branch of Christian wisdom is here inculcated by our Lord on all his followers, namely, the right use of money—a subject largely spoken of, after their manner, by men of the world; but not sufficiently considered by those whom God hath chosen out of the world. These, generally, do not consider, as the importance of the subject requires, the use of this excellent talent. Neither do they understand how to employ it to the greatest advantage; the introduction of which into the world is one admirable instance of the wise and gracious providence of God. It has, indeed, been the manner of poets, orators, and philosophers, in almost all ages and nations, to rail at this, as the grand corrupter of the world, the bane of virtue, the pest of human society.

But is not all this mere empty rant? Is there any solid reason therein? By no means. For, let the world be as corrupt as it will, is gold or silver to blame? "The love of money," we know, "is the root of all evil"; but not the thing itself. The fault does not lie in the money, but in them that use it. It may be used ill: and what may not? But it may likewise be used well: It is full as applicable to the best, as to the worst uses. It is of unspeakable service to all civilized nations, in all the common affairs of life: It is a most compendious instrument of transacting all manner of business, and (if we use it according to Christian wisdom) of doing all manner of good. It is true, were man in a state of innocence, or were all men "filled with the Holy Ghost," so that, like the infant Church at Jerusalem, "no man counted anything he had his own," but "distribution was made to everyone as he had need," the use of it would be superseded; as we cannot conceive there is anything of the kind among the inhabitants of heaven. But, in the present state of mankind, it is an excellent gift of God, answering the noblest ends. In the hands of his children, it is food for the hungry, drink for the thirsty, raiment for the naked: It gives to the traveller and the stranger where to lay his head. By it we may supply the place of an husband to the widow, and of a father to the fatherless. We maybe a defence for the oppressed, a means of health to the sick, of ease to them that are in pain; it may be as eyes to the blind, as feet to the lame; yea, a lifter up from the gates of death!

It is therefore of the highest concern that all who fear God know how to employ this valuable talent; that they be instructed how it may answer these glorious ends, and in the highest degree. And, perhaps, all the instructions which are necessary for this may be reduced to three plain rules, by the exact observance whereof we may approve ourselves faithful stewards of "the mammon of unrighteousness."

The first of these is (he that heareth, let him understand!) "Gain all you can." Here we may speak like the children of the world: We meet them on their own ground. And it is our bounden duty to do this: We ought to gain all we can gain, without buying gold too dear, without paying more for it than it is worth. But this it is certain we ought not to do; we ought not to gain money at the expense of life, nor (which is in effect the same thing) at the expense of our health. Therefore, no gain whatever should induce us to enter into, or to continue in, any employ, which is of such a kind, or is attended with so hard or so long labor, as to impair our constitution. Neither should we begin or continue in any business which necessarily deprives us of proper seasons for food and sleep, in such a proportion as our nature requires. Indeed, there is a great difference here. Some employments are absolutely and totally unhealthy; as those which imply the dealing much with arsenic, or other equally hurtful minerals, or the breathing an air tainted with steams of melting lead, which must at length destroy the firmest constitution. Others may not be absolutely unhealthy, but only to persons of a weak constitution. Such are those which require many hours to be spent in writing; especially if a person write sitting, and lean upon his stomach, or remain long in an uneasy posture. But whatever it is which reason or experience shows to be destructive of health or strength, that we may not submit to; seeing "the life is more" valuable "than meat, and the body than raiment." And if we are already engaged in such an employ, we should exchange it as soon as possible for some which, if it lessen our gain, will, however not lessen our health.

We are, Secondly, to gain all we can without hurting our mind any more than our body. For neither may we hurt this. We must preserve, at all events, the spirit of an healthful mind. Therefore we may not engage or continue in any sinful trade, any that is contrary to the law of God, or of our country. Such are all that necessarily imply our robbing or defrauding the king of his lawful customs. For it is at least as sinful to defraud the king of his right, as to rob our fellow subjects. And the king has full as much right, to his customs as we have to our houses and apparel. Other businesses there are, which however innocent in themselves, cannot be followed with innocence now at least, not in England; such, for instance, as will not afford a competent maintenance without cheating or lying, or conformity to some custom which not consistent with a good conscience: These, likewise, are sacredly to be avoided, whatever gain they may be attended with provided we follow the custom of the trade; for to gain money we must not lose our souls. There are yet others which many pursue with perfect innocence, without hurting either their body or mind; And yet perhaps you cannot: Either they may entangle you in that company which would destroy your soul; and by repeated experiments it may appear that you cannot separate the one from the other; or there may be an idiosyncrasy,—a peculiarity in your constitution of soul, (as there is in the bodily constitution of many,) by reason whereof that employment is deadly to you, which another may safely follow. So I am convinced, from many experiments, I could not study, to any degree of perfection, either mathematics, arithmetic, or algebra, without being a Deist, if not an Atheist: And yet others may study them all their lives without sustaining any inconvenience. None therefore can here determine for another; but every man must judge for himself, and abstain from whatever he in particular finds to be hurtful to his soul.

We are. Thirdly, to gain all we can without hurting our neighbor. But this we may not, cannot do, if we love our neighbor as ourselves. We cannot, if we love everyone as ourselves, hurt anyone in his substance. We cannot devour the increase of his lands, and perhaps the lands and houses themselves, by gaming, by overgrown bills (whether on account of physic, or law, or anything else,) or by requiring or taking such interest as even the laws of our country forbid. Hereby all pawn-broking is excluded: Seeing, whatever good we might do thereby, all unprejudiced men see with grief to be abundantly overbalanced by the evil. And if it were otherwise, yet we are not allowed to "do evil that good may come." We cannot, consistent with brotherly love, sell our goods below the market price; we cannot study to ruin our neighbor's trade, in order to advance our own; much less can we entice away or receive any of his servants or workmen whom he has need of. None can gain by swallowing up his neighbor's substance, without gaining the damnation of hell!

Neither may we gain by hurting our neighbor in his body. Therefore we may not sell anything which tends to impair health. Such is, eminently, all that liquid fire, commonly called drams or spirituous liquors. It is true, these may have a place in medicine; they may be of use in some bodily disorders; although there would rarely be occasion for them were it not for the unskillfulness of the practitioner. Therefore, such as prepare and sell them only for this end may keep their conscience clear. But who are they? Who prepare and sell them only for this end? Do you know ten such distillers in England? Then excuse these. But all who sell them in the common way, to any that will buy, are poisoners general. They murder His Majesty's subjects by wholesale, neither does their eye pity or spare. They drive them to hell like sheep. And what is their gain? Is it not the blood of these men?

*　　*　　*

And are not they partakers of the same guilt, though in a lower degree, whether Surgeons, Apothecaries, or Physicians, who play with the lives or health of men, to enlarge their own gain? Who purposely lengthen the pain or disease which they are able to remove speedily? who prolong the cure of their patient's body in order to plunder his substance? Can any man be clear before God who does not shorten every disorder "as much as he can," and remove all sickness and pain "as soon as he can?" He cannot: For nothing can be more clear than that he does not "love his neighbor as himself;" than that he does not "do unto others as he would they should do unto himself."

This is dear-bought gain. And so is whatever is procured by hurting our neighbor in his soul; by ministering, suppose, either directly or indirectly, to his unchastity, or intemperance, which certainly none can do, who has any fear of God, or any real desire of pleasing Him. It nearly concerns all those to consider this, who have any-thing to do with taverns, victualling-houses, opera-houses, play-houses, or any other places of public, fashionable diversion. If these profit the souls of men, you are clear; your employment is good, and your gain innocent; but if they are either sinful in themselves, or natural inlets to sin of various kinds, then, it is to be feared, you have a sad account to make. O beware, lest God say in that day, "These have perished in their iniquity, but their blood do I require at thy hands!"

These cautions and restrictions being observed, it is the bounden duty of all who are engaged in worldly business to observe that first and great rule of Christian wis-dom with respect to money, "Gain all you can." Gain all you can by honest industry. Use all possible diligence in your calling. Lose no time. If you understand yourself and your relation to God and man, you know you have none to spare. If you under-stand your particular calling as you ought, you will have no time that hangs upon your hands. Every business will afford some employment sufficient for every day and every hour. That wherein you are placed, if you follow it in earnest, will leave you no leisure for silly, unprofitable diversions. You have always something better to do, something that will profit you, more or less. And "whatever thy hand findeth to do, do it with thy might."

*　　*　　*

Gain all you can, by common sense, by using in your business all the understanding which God has given you. It is amazing to observe, how few do this; how men run on in the same dull track with their forefathers.

*   *   *

Having gained all you can, by honest wisdom and unwearied diligence, the second rule of Christian prudence is," Save all you can." Do not throw the precious talent into the sea: Leave that folly to heathen philosophers. Do not throw it away in idle expenses, which is just the same as throwing it into the sea. Expend no part of it merely to gratify the desire of the flesh, the desire of the eye, or the pride of life.

Do not waste any part of so precious a talent merely in gratifying the desires of the flesh; in procuring the pleasures of sense of whatever kind; particularly, in enlarging the pleasure of tasting. I do not mean, avoid gluttony and drunkenness only: An honest heathen would condemn these. But there is a regular, reputable kind of sensuality, an elegant epicurism, which does not immediately disorder the stomach, nor (sensibly, at least) impair the understanding. And yet (to mention no other effects of it now) it cannot be maintained without considerable expense. Cut off all this expense! Despise delicacy and variety, and be content with what plain nature requires.

Do not waste any part of so precious a talent merely in gratifying the desire of the eye by superfluous or expensive apparel, or by needless ornaments. Waste no part of it in curiously adorning your houses; in superfluous or expensive furniture; in costly pictures, painting, gilding, books; in elegant rather than useful gardens. Let your neighbors, who know nothing better, do this: "Let the dead bury their dead." But "what is that to thee?" says our Lord: "Follow thou me." Are you willing? Then you are able so to do.

Lay out nothing to gratify the pride of life, to gain the admiration or praise of men. This motive of expense is frequently interwoven with one or both of the former. Men are expensive in diet, or apparel, or furniture, not barely to please their appetite, or to gratify their eye, their imagination, but their vanity too. "So long as thou dost well unto thyself, men will speak good of thee." So long as thou art "clothed in purple and fine linen, and farest sumptuously" every day," no doubt many will applaud thy elegance of taste, thy generosity and hospitality. But do not buy their applause so dear. Rather be content with the honor that cometh from God.

Who would expend anything in gratifying these desires if he considered that to gratify them is to increase them? Nothing can be more certain than this: Daily experience shows, the more they are indulged, they increase the more. Whenever, therefore, you expend anything to please your taste or other senses, you pay so much for sensuality. When you lay out money to please your eye, you give so much for an increase of curiosity,—for a stronger attachment to these pleasures which perish in the using. While you are purchasing anything which men use to applaud, you are purchasing more vanity. Had you not then enough of vanity, sensuality, curiosity before? Was there need of any addition? And would you pay for it, too? What manner of wisdom is this? Would not the literally throwing your money into the sea be a less mischievous folly?

And why should you throw away money upon your children, any more than upon yourself, in delicate food, in gay or costly apparel, in superfluities of any kind? Why should you purchase for them more pride or lust, more vanity, or foolish and hurt-ful desires? They do not want any more; they have enough already; nature has made ample provision for them: Why should you be at farther expense to increase their temptations and snares, and to pierce them through with more sorrows?

Do not leave it to them to throw away. If you have good reason to believe that they would waste what is now in your possession in gratifying and thereby increasing the desire of the flesh, the desire of the eye, or the pride of life at the peril of theirs and your own soul, do not set these traps in their way. Do not offer your sons or your daughters unto Belial, any more than unto Moloch. Have pity upon them, and remove out of their way what you may easily foresee would increase their sins, and consequently plunge them deeper into everlasting perdition! How amazing then is the infatuation of those parents who think they can never leave their children enough! What! cannot you leave them enough of arrows, firebrands, and death? Not enough of foolish and hurtful desires? Not enough of pride, lust, ambition vanity? not enough of everlasting burnings? Poor wretch! thou fearest where no fear is. Surely both thou and they, when ye are lifting up your eyes in hell, will have enough both of the "worm that never dieth," and of "the fire that never shall be quenched!"

"What then would you do, if you was in my case? If you had a considerable for-tune to leave?" Whether I would do it or no, I know what I ought to do: This will admit of no reasonable question. If I had one child, elder or younger, who knew the value of money; one who I believed, would put it to the true use, I should think it my absolute, indispensable duty to leave that child the bulk of my fortune; and to the rest just so much as would enable them to live in the manner they had been accustomed to do. "But what, if all your children were equally ignorant of the true use of money?" I ought then (hard saying! who can hear it?) to give each what would keep him above want, and to bestow all the rest in such a manner as I judged would be most for the glory of God.

But let not any man imagine that he has done anything, barely by going thus far, by "gaining and saving all he can," if he were to stop here. All this is nothing, if a man go not forward, if he does not point all this at a farther end. Nor, indeed, can a man properly be said to save anything, if he only lays it up. You may as well throw your money into the sea, as bury it in the earth. And you may as well bury it in the earth, as in your chest, or in the Bank of England. Not to use, is effectually to throw it away. If, therefore, you would indeed "make yourselves friends of the mammon of unrighteousness," add the Third rule to the two preceding. Having, First, gained all you can, and, Secondly saved all you can, Then "give all you can."

In order to see the ground and reason of this, consider, when the Possessor of heaven and earth brought you into being, and placed you in this world, he placed you here not as a proprietor, but a steward: As such he entrusted you, for a season, with goods of various kinds; but the sole property of these still rests in him, nor can be alienated from him. As you yourself are not your own, but his, such is, likewise, all that you enjoy. Such is your soul and your body, not your own, but God's. And so is your substance in particular. And he has told you, in the most clear and express terms, how you are to employ it for him, in such a manner, that it may be all an holy sacri-fice, acceptable through Christ Jesus. And this light, easy service, he has promised to reward with an eternal weight of glory.

The directions that God has given us, touching the use of our worldly substance, may be comprised in the following particulars. If you desire to be a faithful and a wise steward, out of that portion of your Lord's goods which he has for the present lodged in your hands, but with the right of resuming whenever it pleases him, First, provide things needful for yourself; food to eat, raiment to put on, whatever nature moderately requires for preserving the body in health and strength. Secondly, provide these for your wife, your children, your servants, or any others who pertain to your household. If when this is done there be an overplus left, then "do good to them that are of the household of faith." If there be an overplus still, "as you have opportunity, do good unto all men." In so doing, you give all you can; nay, in a sound sense, all you have: For all that is laid out in this manner is really given to God. You "render unto God the things that are God's," not only by what you give to the poor, but also by that which you expend in providing things needful for yourself and your household.

If, then, a doubt should at any time arise in your mind concerning what you are going to expend, either on yourself or any part of your family, you have an easy way to remove it. Calmly and seriously inquire, "(1.) In expending this, am I acting according to my character? Am I acting herein, not as a proprietor, but as a steward of my Lord's goods? (2.) Am I doing this in obedience to his Word? In what Scripture does he require me so to do? (3.) Can I offer up this action, this expense, as a sacrifice to God through Jesus Christ? (4.) Have I reason to believe that for this very work I shall have a reward at the resurrection of the just?" You will seldom need anything more to remove any doubt which arises on this head; but by this four-fold consideration you will receive clear light as to the way wherein you should go.

If any doubt still remain, you may farther examine yourself by prayer according to those heads of inquiry. Try whether you can say to the Searcher of hearts, your conscience not condemning you, "Lord, thou seest I am going to expend this sum on that food, apparel, furniture. And thou knowest, I act herein with a single eye as a steward of thy goods, expending this portion of them thus in pursuance of the design thou hadst in entrusting me with them. Thou knowest I do this in obedience to the Lord, as thou commandest, and because thou commandest it. Let this, I beseech thee, be an holy sacrifice, acceptable through Jesus Christ! And give me a witness in myself that for this labor of love I shall have a recompense when thou rewardest every man according to his works." Now if your conscience bear you witness in the Holy Ghost that this prayer is well-pleasing to God, then have you no reason to doubt but that expense is right and good, and such as will never make you ashamed.

Selection 2: *Thoughts upon Slavery*

> *In this eloquent pamphlet against slavery, Wesley first describes the conditions and life of the Africans, denying the claim that they are better off as slaves. They come from fertile lands, which they administer justly. He then discusses the brutal manner of their capture and the demoralizing effect of the slave trade on Africans and Europeans alike. Against the claim that all this is done legally, he responds as follow.*

The grand plea is, "They are authorized by law." But can law, human law, change the nature of things? Can it turn darkness into light, or evil into good? By no means. Notwithstanding ten thousand laws, right is right, and wrong is wrong still. There must still remain an essential difference between justice and injustice, cruelty and mercy. So that I still ask, Who can reconcile this treatment of the Negroes, first and last, with either mercy or justice?

Where is the justice of inflicting the severest evils on those that have done us no wrong? of depriving those that never injured us in word or deed, of every comfort of life? of tearing them from their native country, and depriving them of liberty itself, to which an Angolan has the same natural right as an Englishman, and on which he sets as high a value? Yea, where is the justice of taking away the lives of innocent, inoffensive men; murdering thousands of them in their own land, by the hands of their own countrymen; many thousands, year after year, on shipboard, and then casting them like dung into the sea; and tens of thousands in that cruel slavery to which they are so unjustly reduced?

But waving, for the present, all other considerations, I strike at the root of this complicated villany; I absolutely deny all slave-holding to be consistent with any degree of natural justice.

I cannot place this in a clearer light than that great ornament of his profession, Judge Blackstone, has already done. Part of his words are as follows:—

"The three origins of the right of slavery assigned by Justinian, are all built upon false foundations: (1.) Slavery is said to arise from captivity in war. The conqueror having a right to the life of his captives, if he spares that, has then a right to deal with them as he pleases. But this is untrue, if taken generally—that, by the laws of nations, a man has a right to kill his enemy. He has only a right to kill him in particular cases, in cases of absolute necessity for self-defence. And it is plain, this absolute necessity did not subsist, since he did not kill him, but made him prisoner. War itself is justifiable only on principles of self-preservation: Therefore it gives us no right over prisoners, but to hinder their hurting us by confining them. Much less can it give a right to torture, or kill, or even to enslave an enemy when the war is over. Since therefore the right of making our prisoners slaves, depends on a supposed right of slaughter, that foundation failing, the consequence which is drawn from it must fail likewise.

"It is said, Secondly, slavery may begin by one man's selling himself to another. And it is true, a man may sell himself to work for another; but he cannot sell himself to be a slave, as above defined. Every sale implies an equivalent given to the seller, in lieu of what he transfers to the buyer. But what equivalent can be given for life or liberty? His property likewise, with the very price which he seems to receive, devolves ipso facto to his master, the instant he becomes his slave: In this case, therefore, the buyer gives nothing, and the seller receives nothing. Of what validity then can a sale be, which destroys the very principle upon which all sales are founded?

"We are told, Thirdly, that men may be born slaves, by being the children of slaves. But this, being built upon the two former rights, must fall together with them. If neither captivity nor contract can, by the plain law of nature and reason, reduce the parent to a state of slavery, much less can they reduce the offspring." It clearly follows, that all slavery is as irreconcilable to justice as to mercy.

That slave-holding is utterly inconsistent with mercy, is almost too plain to need a proof. Indeed, it is said, "that these Negroes being prisoners of war, our captains and factors buy them, merely to save them from being put to death. And is not this mercy?" I answer, (1.) Did Sir John Hawkins, and many others, seize upon men, women, and children, who were at peace in their own fields or houses, merely to save them from death? (2.) Was it to save them from death that they knocked out the brains of those they could not bring away? (3.) Who occasioned and fomented those wars, wherein these poor creatures were taken prisoners? Who excited them by money, by drink, by every possible means, to fall upon one another? Was it not themselves?

They know in their own conscience it was, if they have any conscience left. But, to bring the matter to a short issue, can they say before God, that they ever took a single voyage, or bought a single Negro, from this motive? They cannot; they well know, to get money, not to save lives, was the whole and sole spring of their motions.

But if this manner of procuring and treating Negroes is not consistent either with mercy or justice, yet there is a plea for it which every man of business will acknowledge to be quite sufficient. Fifty years ago, one meeting an eminent Statesman in the lobby of the House of Commons, said, "You have been long talking about justice and equity. Pray which is this bill; equity or justice?" He answered very short and plain, "D--n justice; it is necessity." Here also the slave-holder fixes his foot; here he rests the strength of his cause. "If it is not quite right, yet it must be so; there is an absolute necessity for it. It is necessary we should procure slaves; and when we have procured them, it is necessary to use them with severity, considering their stupidity, stubbornness, and wickedness."

I answer, You stumble at the threshold; I deny that villainy is ever necessary. It is impossible that it should ever be necessary for any reasonable creature to violate all the laws of justice, mercy, and truth. No circumstances can make it necessary for a man to burst in sunder all the ties of humanity. It can never be necessary for a rational being to sink himself below a brute. A man can be under no necessity of degrading himself into a wolf. The absurdity of the supposition is so glaring, that one would wonder any one can help seeing it.

Selection 3: *Thoughts on the Present Scarcity of Provisions*

This letter written to the editor of Lloyd's Evening Post in 1772 demonstrates Wesley's profound social concern. Though the analysis he offers of the source of these economic ills appears a bit superficial and turns to a great degree on his opposition to alcohol, he nonetheless models the need for social ethics to seek an understanding of the proximate causes of unmet needs.

Many excellent things have been lately published concerning the present scarcity of provisions; and many causes have been assigned for it, by men of experience and reflection. But may it not be observed, there is something wanting still, in most of those publications? One writer assigns and insists on one cause, another on one or two more. But who assigns all the causes that manifestly concur to produce this melancholy effect? At the same time pointing out, how each particular cause affects the price of each particular sort of provision?

I would willingly offer to candid and benevolent men a few hints on this important subject; proposing a few questions, and subjoining to each what seems to be the plain and direct answer.

I ask, First, Why are thousands of people starving, perishing for want, in every part of the nation? The fact I know; I have seen it with my eyes, in every corner of the land. I have known those who could only afford to eat a little coarse food once every other day. I have known one in London (and one that a few years before had all the conveniences of life) picking up from a dunghill stinking sprats, and carrying them home for herself and her children. I have known another gathering the bones which the dogs had left in the streets, and making broth of them, to prolong a wretched life! I have heard a third artlessly declare, "Indeed I was very faint, and so weak I could hardly walk, until my dog, finding nothing at home, went out, and brought in a good sort of bone, which I took out of his mouth, and made a pure dinner!" Such is the case at this day of multitudes of people, in a land flowing as it were, with milk and honey! Abounding with all the necessaries, the conveniences, and superfluities of Life!

Now, why is this? Why have all these nothing to eat? Because they have nothing to do. The plain reason why they have no meat is because they have no work.

But why have they no work? Why are so many thousand people, in London, in Bristol, in Norwich, in every county, from one end of England to the other, utterly destitute of employment?

Because the persons that used to employ them cannot afford to do it any longer. Many that employed fifty men, now scarce employ ten; those that employed twenty now employ one or none at all. They cannot, as they have no vent for their goods; food being so dear, that the generality of people are hardly able to buy anything else.

But why is food so dear? To come to particulars: Why does bread corn bear so high a price? To set aside partial causes, (which indeed, all put together, are little more than the fly upon the chariot wheel,) the grand cause is, because such immense quantities of care are continually consumed by distilling. Indeed, an eminent distiller near London, hearing this, warmly replied, "Nay, my partner and I generally distil but a thousand quarters a week." Perhaps so. And suppose five-and-twenty distillers, in and near the town consume each only the same quantity: Here are five-and-twenty thousand quarters a week, that is, above twelve hundred and fifty thousand a year, consumed in and about London! Add the distillers throughout England, and have we not reason to believe, that (not a thirtieth or a twentieth part only, but) little less than half the wheat produced in the kingdom is every year consumed, not by so harmless a away as throwing it into the sea, but by converting it into deadly poison; poison that naturally destroys not only the strength and life, but also the morals of our countrymen?

It may be objected, "This cannot be. We know how much corn is distilled by the duty that is paid. And hereby it appears that scarce three hundred thousand quarters a year are distilled throughout the kingdom." Do we know certainly, how much corn is distilled by the duty that is paid? Is it indisputable, that the full duty is paid for all the corn that is distilled? Not to insist upon the multitude of private stills, which pay no duty at all. I have myself heard the servant of an eminent distiller occasionally aver, that for every gallon he distilled which paid duty, he distilled six which paid none. Yea, I have heard distillers themselves affirm, "We must do this, or we cannot live." It plainly follows, we cannot judge, from the duty that is paid, of the quantity of corn that is distilled.

"However, what is paid brings in a large revenue to the king." Is this an equivalent for the lives of his subjects? Would his majesty sell a hundred thousand of his subjects yearly to Algiers for four hundred thousand pounds? Surely no. Will he then sell them for that sum, to be butchered by their own countrymen? "But otherwise the swine for the navy cannot be fed." Not unless they are fed with human flesh! Not unless they are fatted with human blood! O, tell it not in Constantinople, that the English raise the royal revenue by selling the flesh and blood of their countrymen!

But why are oats so dear? Because there are four times as many horses kept (to speak within compass) for coaches and chaises in particular, as were a few years ago. Unless, therefore, four times the oats grew now that grew then, they cannot be at the same price. If only twice as much is produced, (which, perhaps, is near the truth,) the price will naturally be double to what it was.

And as the dearness of grain of one kind will always raise the price of another, so whatever causes the dearness of wheat and oats must raise the price of barley too. To account, therefore, for the dearness of this, we need only remember what has been observed above; although some particular causes may concur in producing the same effect.

Why are beef and mutton so dear? Because many considerable farmers, particularly in the northern countries, who used to breed large number of sheep, or horned cattle, and very frequently both, now breed none at all: They no longer trouble themselves with either sheep, or cows, or oxen; as they can turn their land to far better account by breeding horses alone. Such is the demand, not only for coach and chaise horses, which are bought and destroyed in incredible numbers, but much more for bred horses, which are yearly exported by hundreds, yea, thousands, to France.

But why are pork, poultry, and eggs so dear? Because of the monopolizing of farms; perhaps as mischievous a monopoly as was ever introduced into these kingdoms. The land which was some years ago divided between ten or twenty little farmers, and enable them comfortably to provide for their families, is now generally engrossed by one great farmer. One farms an estate of a thousand a year, which formerly maintained ten or twenty. Every one of these little farmers kept a few swine, with some quantity of poultry; and, having little money, was glad to send his bacon, or pork, or fowls and eggs to market continually. Hence the markets were plentifully served; and plenty created cheapness. But at present the great, the gentlemen farmers are above attending to these little things. They breed no poultry or swine, unless for their own use; consequently they send none to market. Hence it is not strange if two or three of these, living near a market town, occasion such a scarcity of these things, by preventing the former supply, that the price of them is double or treble to what it was before. Hence, (to instance in a small article,) in the same town wherein, within my memory, eggs were sold six or eight a penny, they are not sold six or eight a groat.

Another cause (the most terrible one of all, and the most destructive both of personal and social happiness) why not only beef, mutton, and pork, but all kinds of victuals, are so dear, is luxury. What can stand against this? Will it not waste and destroy all that nature and art can produce? If a person of quality will boil down three dozen of neats' tongues, to make two or three quarts of soup, (and so proportionably in other things,) what wonder that provisions fail? Only look into the kitchens of the great, the nobility and gentry, almost without exception; (considering withal, that "the toe of the peasant treads upon the heel of the courtier;") and when you have observed the amazing waste which is made there, you will no longer wonder at the scarcity, and consequently dearness, of the things which they use so much art to destroy.

But why is land so dear? Because on all these accounts, gentlemen cannot live as they have been accustomed to do without increasing their income; which most of them cannot do, but by raising their rents. And then the farmer, paying a higher rent for the land, must have a higher price for the produce of it. This again lends to raise the price of land; and so the wheel runs round.

But why is it, that not only provisions and land, but well night every thing else, is so dear? Because of the enormous taxes which are laid on almost every thing that can be named. Not only abundant taxes are raised from earth, and fire, and water; but in England, the ingenious statesmen have found a way to lay a tax upon the very light! Yet one element remains: And surely some man of honour will find a way to tax this also. For how long shall the saucy air strike a gentleman on the face, nay, a lord, without paying for it?

But why are the taxes so high? Because of the national debt. They must be so while this continues. I have heard that the national expense, seventy years ago, was, in time of peace, three millions a year. And now the bare interest of the public debt amounts yearly to above four millions! To raise which, with the other stated expenses of government, those taxes are absolutely necessary.

To sum up the whole: Thousands of people throughout the land are perishing for want of food. This is owing to various causes; but above all, to distilling, taxes, and luxury.

Here is the evil, and the undeniable causes of it. But where is the remedy?

Perhaps it exceeds all the wisdom of man to tell: But it may not be amiss to offer a few hints on the subject.

What remedy is there for this sore evil—many thousand poor people are starving? Find them work, and you will find them meat. They will then earn and eat their own bread.

But how can the masters give them work without ruining themselves? Procure vent for what is wrought, and the masters will give them as much work as they can do. And this would be done by sinking the price of provisions; for then people would have money to buy other things too.

But how can the price of wheat and barley be reduced? By prohibiting forever, by making a full end of that bane of health, that destroyer of strength, of life, and of virtue,—distilling. Perhaps this alone might go a great way toward answering the whole design. It is not improbable, it would speedily sink the price of corn, at least one part in three. If anything more were required, might not all starch be made of rice, and the importation of this, as well as of corn, be encouraged?

How can the price of oats be reduced? By reducing the number of horses. And may not this be effectually done, (without affecting the ploughman, the waggoner, or any of those who keep horses for common work,) (1.) By laying a tax on ten pounds on every horse exported to France, for which (notwithstanding an artful paragraph in a late public paper) there is as great a demand as ever? (2.) By laying an additional tax on gentlemen's carriages? Not so much on every wheel, (barefaced, shameless partiality!) but five pounds yearly upon every horse. And would not these two taxes alone supply near as much as is now paid for leave to poison his majesty's liege subjects?

How can the price of beef and mutton be reduced? By increasing the breed of sheep and horned cattle. And this would soon be increased seven-fold, if the price of horses was reduced; which it surely would be, half in half, by the method above mentioned.

How may the price of land be reduced? By all the methods above named, as each tends to lessen the expense of housekeeping: But especially the last; by restraining luxury, which is the grand and general source of want.

How may the taxes be reduced: (1.) By discharging half the national debt, and so saving, by this single means, above two millions a year. (2.) By abolishing all useless pensions, as fast as those who now enjoy them die: Especially those ridiculous ones given to some hundreds of idle men, as governors of forts or castles; which forts have answered no end for above these hundred years, unless to shelter jackdaws and crows. Might not good part of a million more be saved in this very article?

But will this ever be done? I fear not: At least, we have no reason to hope for it shortly; for what good can we expect (suppose the Scriptures are true) for such a nation as this, where there is no fear of God, where there is such a deep, avowed, thorough contempt of all religion, as I never saw, never heard or read of, in any other nation, whether Christian, Mohammedan, or Pagan? It seems as if God must shortly arise and maintain his own cause. But, if so, let us fall into the hands of God, and not into the hands of men.

For Further Reading

The following select list of writings provides a mixture of primary and secondary sources related to the major parts of the anthology, and the full text of the works being excerpted will also provide rich additional reading.

Brendlinger, Irv A. *Social Justice through the Eyes of John Wesley: John Wesley's Theological Challenge to Slavery*. Guelph: Joshua, 2006.

Locke, John. *Writings on Religion*. Edited by Victor Nuovo. New York: Oxford University Press, 2002.

Sell, Allan P. F. *John Locke and the Eighteenth Century Divines*. Cardiff: University of Wales Press, 1997.

Stoeffler, Ernest, Editor. *Continental Pietism and Early American Christianity*. Eugene: Wipf & Stock, 2007.

Wesley, John. *Political Writings of John Wesley*. Edited and Introduced by Graham Maddox. Durham: University of Durham and Bristol: Thoemmes, 1998.

PART 7

Nineteenth-Century Voices

On Christian Social Ethics

Friedrich Schleiermacher (1769–1834) is often regarded as the theologian whose thought led the way to modern liberal theology. His apologetic effort to give an intelligible account of the Christian faith in the face of its Enlightenment critics has had a lasting impact on theology up to the present day. Ironically, in contrast to some of his liberal heirs in the nineteenth century, Schleiermacher's views on Christian social ethics are quite conservative in maintaining a strict distinction between church and state in a manner that he believed was consistent with Luther's thought. At the same time, Christians engaged in their daily vocations, including participation in the civil order, bring with them a temperament born of their relation to Christ.

2. The difficulty in regard to this part of the work of Christ consists especially in defining aright the kingly power of Christ in relation to the general divine government (a difficulty which cannot be overlooked once the subject is somewhat more closely scrutinized from a theoretical point of view), and further in defining it aright relatively to secular government (a difficulty which at once emerges in the practical treatment of the question).

The customary division of the Kingdom of Christ into the kingdom of power, the kingdom of grace, and the kingdom of glory helps us little. We have first to break it up so as to comprehend under the two latter the proper object of Christ's kingly activity, namely, the world which has become participant in redemption, while under the kingdom of power we understand the world as such, and in itself. But in taking this position, we seem to lend ourselves to the extravagant notion that there belonged to Christ a kingdom of power, as it were, before the kingdom of grace, and independent of it. Now, to say the least, such a kingdom could not possibly belong to his redemptive activity; and if the Apostles knew of such a kingdom belonging to the Word, it must have been a knowledge which, because unconnected with redemption, could not belong to Christian piety either. Anyone who thinks it necessary to interpret the expressions which they use with reference to Christ as the Word made flesh, the God man and the Redeemer, or which Christ uses of himself, as if they attributed to him the governance of the whole world, involves himself in a contradiction, not only with all the passages in which Christ himself offers petitions to the Father and refers to what the Father has retained in his own power, but also with all passages which express his intention to establish an immediate relationship, both of petition and response, between believers and the Father.

* * *

Thus there remains only the one kingdom of grace as Christ's true kingdom, as indeed it is the only one a consciousness of which really emerges in our moods of devotion, the only one of which we require knowledge for our guidance, because our active faith must be directed towards it. The two other terms in the customary division we can use only to determine the scope of this very kingdom of grace. In calling it a kingdom of power we are asserting, not only that the extension of the influence of Christ over the human race knows no limits, and that no people is able to offer it a permanently effective opposition, but also that there is no stage of purity and perfection which does not belong to Christ's Kingdom. And in calling it a kingdom of glory we are confessing our belief—of course in connection with that highest purity and perfection, only approximately given in experience—in an unlimited approximation to the absolute blessedness to be found in Christ alone. So far as the distinction between the kingly power of Christ and civil government is concerned, it would seem, after what has been said, that nothing is easier than to distinguish exactly between the two in conception. For civil government is unquestionably an institution which belongs to the general divine government of the world, and even by his own declaration is accordingly as such alien to Christ's Kingdom. On the other hand, civil government is a legal thing, and exists everywhere, even where there is no Christian religion. Hence, since it springs out of the corporate life of sinfulness, and everywhere presupposes this (for of course for the sanction of its laws it reckons upon the force of sensuous motives), it cannot as such have the slightest authority in the Kingdom of Christ. On this view the two powers seem to be held entirely apart from each other, so that the sole lordship of Christ in his Kingdom remains secure although his followers conduct themselves in worldly affairs in accordance with the regulations of the secular government, and regard everything that comes to them from it as coming from the divine government of the world. But how greatly the situation is altered as soon as we think of the secular government as exercised by Christians over Christians, is clearly to be seen in the fact that, on the one side, the Church has attempted to control the secular government in the name of Christ, while on the other, the Christian magistracy as such has claimed for itself the right to regulate the affairs of the society of believers. In order not to introduce at this point anything which belongs to Christian Ethics from which even the theological principles of Church Law must be derived—the only question we shall here have to propound is whether the Kingdom of Christ is changed in extent through the entrance of this new material relationship. Now it is certainly true that Christ must completely control the society of believers, and consequently that every member of the society must show himself, wholly and in every part of his life, to be governed by Christ. But since this depends entirely upon the inner vital relationship in which each individual stands to Christ, and since there can be no representative who exercises the kingly office of Christ in his name, this simply means that everyone, whether magistrate or private citizen, has to seek in the directions given by Christ, not indeed right directions for his conduct under civil government (for this is always a matter of the art of politics), but certainly the right temper of mind even in this relationship. On the other hand, it also remains true that no one can exert influence upon the society of believers except in the measure in which he is a pre-eminent instrument of Christ's kingly power, since otherwise the sole lordship of Christ would be imperiled. And this does not at all depend on his outward vocation; one who is called as a bondservant is not therefore a bond-servant in the society, but a freedman of the Lord, and similarly he who is called as a lord does not therefore become a lord in the society, but only a bond-servant of Christ like everyone else. So that the civil contrast between magistrate and private citizen loses all significance in the Church; it makes no difference to a man's relationship to the kingly power of Christ.

3. In this way, then, we have separated the kingly power of Christ, on the one hand, from the power which the Father has retained for himself, while on the other we have set it beyond all the resources of the civil power. The latter is undoubtedly the way in which what Luther called 'the two swords' should be kept separate from each other.

*   *   *

That is why Christianity is neither a political religion nor a religious state or a theocracy. The former are those religious fellowships which are regarded as the institutions of a particular civil society, and which rest upon the assumption that the religion is derived from civil legislation, or is related as a subordinate movement to the same higher impulse which first called the civil organization into being, so that for the sake of the civil society its members also unite in a religious fellowship, which therefore is animated by the common spirit of the society and by patriotism—these being 'fleshly motives' in the Scriptural sense. Theocracies, on the other hand, are religious fellowships which as such have subordinated the civil society to themselves; in which consequently political ambition aims at pre-eminence within the religious fellowship, and there is the underlying assumption that the religious society, or the divine revelation upon which it rests, was able to call into being the civil society—which in this sense is possible only for religious fellowships which are nationally limited. To both, then, political religions as well as theocracies, Christ puts an end through the purely spiritual lordship of his God-consciousness; and the stronger and more extensive his Kingdom becomes, the more definite becomes the severance between Church and State, so that in the proper outward separation—which, of course, may take very different forms—their agreement is ever more perfectly worked out.

Horace Bushnell 23

Politics under the Law of God

❧ *Horace Bushnell (1802–1876) was a Calvinist of Puritan background. A pastor in Hartford, Connecticut, he was both highly influential and highly controversial. In his speech,* Politics under the Law of God, *delivered in the North Congregational Church in Hartford in 1844, he argues that the ministry should provide moral guidance to government, a view that met with considerable opposition. His reference to the sin of slavery, however, became an important resource to the abolitionist movement, though Bushnell himself was disinclined to support the more aggressive steps toward change.*

We have taken up, in this country, almost universally, theories of government which totally forbid the entrance of moral considerations. Government, we think, is a social compact or agreement—a mere human creation, having as little connection with God, as little of a moral quality, as a ship of war or a public road. We do not say that government, when exerted and fashioned by man, in whatever manner, is forthwith taken by God to be his instrument and ordinance—that it is molded below and authorized or clothed with authority from above—giving thus to law a moral force, and to the civil constitution the prerogatives of a settled or established order. Rejecting such views of government, or never learning to conceive them, it results that law expresses nothing but human will, and that no one is morally bound by it. If he chooses to break it and take the penalty, or if he can shun the penalty by concealment, he is guilty of no moral wrong. It also results that a majority may at any time, and in any way, rise up to change the fundamental compact; for there is no such thing as an established order of the past, endued with a moral authority to bind their actions and determine their legitimate functions. . . . Holding such views of government, it would be wonderful if we did not separate its functions practically from God, as far as we separate them in theory. If our nature were not wiser than our philosophy, we could never feel one sentiment of moral obligation in regard to our duties as citizens. There would be no crevice left through which a sense of public virtue could leak into our minds. That the views of which I complain are atheistical in their origin, is a well know fact of history, and they show that fact in their face. That they have operated powerfully to effect the disastrous separation of politics from the constraints of duty and responsibility to God, is too evident.

    The neglect of the pulpit to assert the dominion of moral principles over what we do as citizens, has hastened and aggravated the evil I complain of. The false notion has taken possession extensively of the public mind, and received the practical assent, too generally, of the ministers of religion themselves, that they must not meddle with politics. Nothing is made of the obvious distinction between the moral principles of politics and those questions of election and of State policy which are to be decided by no moral tests. It is the solemn duty of the ministers of religion to make their people feel the presence of God's law everywhere—and especially here, where so many of the dearest interests of life—nay, the interests of virtue and religion are themselves at stake. This is the manner of the Bible. There is no one subject on which it is more full and abundant than it is in reference to the moral duty of rulers and citizens. Command, reproof, warning, denunciation—every instrument is applied to keep them under a sense of obligation to God. Some of the ministers of religion, I am afraid, want the courage to discharge their whole duty in this matter. Their position between two fiery and impetuous torrents of party feeling, is often one, I know, of great weakness, and they need to consider, when they put on their armor, whether they can meet one that cometh against them with twenty thousand. But it cannot be necessary that the duties of the ministry in the field, should be totally neglected, as they have been in many places hitherto, or if it be, we may well despair of our country.

What then shall be done?—This is the great practical question to which we are brought—a question which every good citizen, every lover of his country, every Christian, should ponder with earnestness and trembling of spirit—What shall be done?

Three things, I answer, must be done, and we cannot begin too soon. First of all, we must open our eyes to what we have done. We must see our sin, as a people, and repent of it with shame and fasting. As citizens and Christians, we must be willing to go before God, confess that we as a people have done wickedly, and ask Him to deliver us from the mischiefs we have already worked by casting off His law, and desecrating the principles of His throne. Gather the people, sanctify the congregation, assemble the elders—let the ministers of the Lord weep between the porch and the altar, and let them say, as the common prayer of all—Spare they people, O Lord, and give not their heritage to reproach! Then—

Let every man take back his personality and set up his conscience. To do in all public matters what is right and well pleasing to God. Require it of your rulers to cease from the prostitution of their office to effect the reign of their party. Require them to say what is true and do what is right, and the moment they falter, forsake them. At the same time, in the choice of your rulers, be determined to choose no man who is without character and virtue. If you have an eye that will look on a partisan, without principle, pluck it out and cast it from you. If you have a hand that will vote for wickedness, cut it off. Hear the law of God, and swear that it shall be faithfully observed and kept. *Thou shalt provide out of all the people able men, such as fear God, men of truth, hating covetousness, and place such to be rulers.*

First, let them be able men—men equal to the cares of government and policy. Think it not enough, with some who demand your vote, that a man, a man of principle, is offered to your choice—there are many such whom God never made to rule the nation. Wicked rulers are not the only curse. Woe unto thee, O land! when the king is a child; and God himself threatens it as one of his severest judgments against his people, that children shall rule over them. Besides it is nothing but an insult to principle to set it up beggared of all capacity, in the candidate, and ask your vote because it is principle. There is no readier way to make principle itself contemptible. Choose able men.

When you come to the question of moral character, the answer is more difficult, or it has, at least, become so. I do not say with some, that we are to vote for none but Christians. There are many who do not pass by that name, who are governed by the fear of God, as truly as many who do. If we proceeded by this rule, we should make religion itself a partisan, setting it in public area as a wrangler for office and power, and thus make it odious to all who are not its disciples. The fundamental law which ought to govern us, I consider to be this: That we have no right to set up, in the government below, a man who is against the government above. If we do, we put our trust in wickedness, look to wickedness to defend our rights and constitutions, and expect that wickedness will do as well for us below, as God above—all which is moral offence to God. We need not go into the heart—we cannot. But we must look for an outwardly right man, one who, in his manners and conduct, acknowledges what is right and good—a man of truth, integrity, principle; who fears God in his walk, who is just, pure, humane—in one word, *righteous*. We have no right in any case whatever to vote for another. Principle forbids it, and principle can bend to nothing.

We have a way of saying—I begin to hear it on all sides, and it seems to be taking the force of a moral maxim—that we must not require the men for whom we vote to conform to any moral standard—we must choose between evils, and take the least of the two. Whether this is maxim is propounded in reference to an existing case or alternative, it is not for me to say. I leave you to judge. If it be, I will only say that I most deeply pity such an alternative. Merciful God! Has it come to this, that in choosing rulers, we are simply to choose whether the nation shall be governed by seven devils or ten! Is this the alternative offered to our consciences and our liberties! Have we simply to choose between Sodom and Gomorrah? Hear the word of the Lord, ye rulers of Sodom, give ear unto the law of our God, ye people of Gomorrah. There is your standard—the Word of the Lord the law of your God. And whether we be of Sodom or of Gomorrah, let us go forth and hear and obey this law.

But you will say, if we do not choose the least evil, we endanger the success of the greatest—we do, in effect, vote for the greatest. That is not your fault, but the fault of those who offer you the alternative. You may choose between physical evils, and take the least. Half the wisdom of life consists in doing it. But in the case of moral evils, as between adultery and incest, blasphemy and perjury, murder and treason, you have no right to choose either, or the person guilty of either; and if you do, you implicated, before God, in the choice you make. There was never a maxim more corrupt, more totally bereft of principle, than this—that, between bad men, you are to choose the least wicked of the two. The word of God in the rule just cited, expressly excludes it. It does not say that we are to choose for rulers the least impious and wicked of two—but such as fear God—men of truth, hating covetousness. And who is it that fears God? The man who is second in wickedness to the most wicked? Who is a man of truth? One who only is not as notoriously false as another? Who is clear of covetousness? The man who is only not as greedy of the spoils as another? Besides, if you wish to have this choice of evils offered you at every election, as long as the nation exists, you have only to bow your soul to it and do what is bid you. Grant that by withholding your vote in the case supposed, you allow the worse to triumph. You have not of course done evil to your country. Look to the remoter consequences and future effects. A vote is by no means thrown away because it does not go into the balance of the main question. Give it in as a visible token of innocence and incorruptible principle—*a piece of clean white paper*. Let it be known that bad candidates must lose so many votes—that they are not available—that there are so many righteous men who fear God and will not, therefore, support them. It is too much to ask that the good citizens only shall comply, and take the lead of the wicked. If a candidate is unavailable because he is a righteous man, let it be seen that he may also be unavailable because he is wicked and ungodly man. This is wisdom—this is the true part of dignity—this is due to principle itself—this only will ever suffice to save our nation from the abyss of moral anarchy and the curse of God's judgments.

Once more, you have a duty as citizens in respect to that dismal institution which is corrupting and blighting all that is fair and sound in the public virtue. Slavery is the curse of this nation—I blush to think how tamely we have suffered its encroachments. The time has come to renounce our pusillanimity, and take counsel of God and our own dignity. We have made a farce of American liberty long enough. God's frown is upon us, and the scorn of the world is settling on our name in the earth. No politician, no citizen who loves his country, can be blind to our shame and dishonor longer. We have let that thin, which our fathers would not name in their constitution, rule and overrule us, and be the characteristic of our country. It is poisoning all the element of law, and dissolving the constraints of public virtue. And the question is now coming upon us, whether we shall not, by one more act of submission, ordain the perpetuity of this hideous power in our country, and give it a final and fixed predominance! I will not trust myself to speak on this subject. I have no words to speak what I feel. I will only say that if, by this treaty with Egypt, a new territory large enough for an empire is to be added to the domain of slavery, without some qualifications or restrictions that will neutralize the evil, our doom as a nation is, to human appearance, sealed. God, I know, is gracious, and how much he will bear I cannot tell. He is also just, and how long his justice can suffer, is past human foresight. We may never absolutely despair of the nation, till we see its pillars prostrate. But if we will obstinately hope, we must not be obstinately blind. And if we dare to look on the moral debauchery of this institution as an element of the political fabric, we cannot think it possible to make our country safe and happy in its liberties as a perpetual slavedom. I intended to speak, in closing, of the disastrous effects of our party politics, in their divorce from moral law and principle, on the general interests of religion and the church. This you will see at a glance. Our politics are now our greatest immorality, and, what is most of all fearful, the immorality, sweeps through the church of God, and taints the very disciples of the Redeemer. Let us go to God this day, and ask him with our earnest tears and supplications, in public and in private, to save our beloved country from its perils and avert the doom its sin provoke!

FREDERICK DENISON MAURICE 24

The Kingdom of Christ

❧ *F. D. Maurice (1805–1872) was widely regarded as a Christian socialist, though at the same time a critic of secular versions of socialism. He held deeply felt convictions on matters of social concern rooted in his theology of the kingdom of Christ under whose present and ongoing rule all are drawn together in community with God and each other. In our excerpt from* The Kingdom of Christ *we get a glimpse of his biblically grounded vision and mandate for the church to live out the practices of the kingdom in the present.*

To a person who has contemplated the Gospel merely as the case of certain great doctrines or fine moralities, the Acts of the Apostles must be an utterly unintelligible book. For in the specimens of the Apostles' preaching which it gives us, there are comparatively few references to the discourses or the parables of our Lord. They dwell mainly upon the great acts of death and resurrection as evidences that Jesus was the king, as expounding and consummating the previous history of the Jewish people, as justifying and realizing the truth which worked in the minds of the heathen, 'that we are his offspring'. On the other hand, a person who really looks upon the Bible as the history of the establishment of a universal and spiritual kingdom, of that kingdom which God had ever intended for men, and of which the universal kingdom then existing in the world was the formal opposite, will find in this book exactly that without which all the former records would be un-meaning.

The narrator of such transcendent events as the ascension of the Son of man into the invisible glory, or the descent of the Spirit to take possession of the feelings, thoughts, utterances of mortal men, might have been expected to stand still and wonder at that which with so entire a belief he was recording. But no, he looks upon these events as the necessary consummation of all that went before, the necessary foundations of the existence of the Church. And therefore he can quietly relate any other circumstances, however apparently disproportionate, which were demanded for the outward manifestation and development of that Church, such as the meeting of the Apostles in the upper room, and the completion of their number. If the foundation of this kingdom were the end all of all the purposes of God, if it were the kingdom of God among men, the human conditions of it could be no more passed over than the divine; it was as needful to prove that the ladder had its foot upon earth, as that it had comedown out of heaven. As we proceed, we find every new step of the story leading us to notice the Church as the child which the Jewish polity had for so many ages been carrying in its womb. Its filial relation is first demonstrated, it is shown to be an. Israelitic not a mundane commonwealth; then it is shown. that, though not mundane, it is essentially human, containing a principle of expansion greater than that which dwelt in the Roman empire.

And here lies the apparent contradiction, the real harmony, of those two aspects in which this kingdom was contemplated by the Apostles of the circumcision and by St Paul. The one witnessed for the continuity of it, the other for its freedom from all national exclusions. These, we may believe, were their respective offices. Yet, as each fulfilled the one, he was in fact teaching the other truth most effectually. St Peter and St James were maintaining the universality of the Church, while they were contending for its Jewish character and derivation. St. Paul was maintaining the national covenant, while he was telling the Gentiles that if they were circumcised Christ would profit them nothing. Take away the first testimony and the Church becomes an earthly not a spiritual commonwealth, and therefore subject to earthly limitations; take away the second, and the promise to Abraham is unfulfilled. In another sense, as the canon of Scripture shows, St Paul was more directly carrying out the spirit of the Jewish distinction, by upholding the distinctness of ecclesiastical communities according to tribes and countries, than the Apostles of Jerusalem; and they were carrying out the idea of the universality of the Church more than he did by addressing the members of it as of an entire community dispersed through different parts of the world. . . .

But we must not forget that while this universal society, according to the historical conception of it, grew out of the Jewish family and nation, it is, according to the theological conception of it, the root of both. 'That,' says Aristotle, 1 'which is first as cause is last in discovery.' And this beautiful formula is translated into life and reality in the letter to the Ephesians, when St Paul tells them that they were created in Christ before all worlds, and when he speaks of the transcendent economy as being gradually revealed to the apostles and prophets by the Spirit. In this passage it seems to me lies the key to the whole character of the dispensation, as well as of the books in which it is set forth. If the Gospel be the revelation or unveiling of a mystery hidden from ages and generations; if this mystery be the true constitution of humanity in Christ, so that a man believes and acts a lie who does not claim for himself union with Christ, we can understand why the deepest writings of the New Testament, instead of being digests of doctrine, are epistles, explaining to those who had been admitted into the Church of Christ their own position, bringing out that side of it which had reference to the circumstances in which they were placed or to their most besetting sins, and showing what life was in consistency, what life at variance, with it. We can understand why the opening of the first of these epistles, of the one which has been supposed to be most like a systematic treatise, announces that the Gospel is concerning Jesus Christ, who was made of the seed of David according to the flesh, and marked out as the Son of God with power, according to the Spirit of holiness, by the resurrection of the dead. The fact of a union between the Godhead and humanity is thus set forth as the one which the Apostle felt himself appointed to proclaim, which was the ground of the message to the Gentiles, and in which all ideas of reconciliation, of a divine life, justification by faith, sanctification by the Spirit, were implicitly contained. We can understand why the great fight of the Apostle with the Corinthians should be because they exalted certain notions, and certain men as the representatives of these notions, into the place of him who was the Lord of their fellowship, and why pride, sensuality, contempt of others, abuse of ordinances, should be necessarily consequent upon that sin. We can understand why St Paul curses with such vehemence those false teachers who had denied the Galatians the right to call themselves children of God in Christ in virtue of the new covenant, and had sent them back to the old. We may perceive that those wonderful words in which he addresses the Ephesians, when he tells them that they were sitting in heavenly places in Christ Jesus, are just as real and practical as the exhortations at the end of the same letter, respecting the duties of husbands and wives, fathers and children, and that the second are involved in the first. We may see what connexion there is between the entreaty to the Colossians not to stoop to will-worship and the service of angels, and the assertion of the fact that Christ was in them the hope of glory, and that he is the head in whom dwell all the riches of wisdom and knowledge. We may see how possible it was for some of the Philippian Church to be enemies to the cross of Christ, their god their belly, their glory their shame, not because they had not been admitted to the privileges of being members of Christ, but because they had not pressed forward to realize their claim. We may enter a little into the idea of the letters to the Thessalonians, however we may differ about the particular time or times of its accomplishment, that there must be a coeval manifestation of the mystery of iniquity and of the mystery of godliness; that the two kingdoms, being always in conflict, at certain great crises of the world are brought into direct and open collision. We shall not need any evidence of the apostolical derivation of the epistle to the Hebrews, to convince us that it unfolds the relations between the national and the universal dispensation, between that which was the shadow and that which was the substance of a divine humanity; between that which enabled the worshipper to expect a perfect admission into the divine presence, and that which admitted him to it; between that which revealed God to him as the enemy of evil, and that which revealed him as the conqueror of it. Nor is it inconsistent with any previous intimation which has been given us, that the writer of this epistle should in every part of it represent the sin of men as consisting in their unbelief of the blessings into which they are received at each stage of the divine manifestation, and that he should with solemn earnestness, mixed with warnings of a fearful and hopeless apostasy, urge those whom he is addressing to believe that the position into which they had been brought was that after which all former ages had been aspiring, and as such, to claim it. From these exhortations and admonitions the transition is easy to those Catholic epistles which some have found it so hard to reconcile with the doctrine of St Paul. And doubtless, if the faith which the epistle to the Romans and the epistle to the Hebrews adjured men, by such grand promises and dire threats, to exercise, were not faith in a living Being, who had adopted men into fellowship with himself on purpose that being righteous by virtue of that union they might do righteous acts, that having claimed their place as members of a body the Spirit might work in them to will and to do of his good pleasure, the assertions that faith without works saves, and that faith without works cannot save, are hopelessly irreconcilable. But if the idea of St Paul, as much as of St James, be that all worth may be attributed to faith in so far forth as it unites us to an object and raises us out of our-selves, no worth at all so far as it is contemplated simply as a property in ourselves; if this be the very principle which the whole Bible is developing, one does not well see what either position would be good for, if the other were wanting. If our Lord came among men that he might bring them into a kingdom of righteousness, peace, and joy, because a kingdom grounded upon fellowship with a righteous and perfect Being, the notion that that righteousness can ever belong to any man in himself, and the notion that everyone is not to exhibit the fruits of it in himself, would seem to be equally contradictions. And therefore I believe that without this consideration we shall be as much puzzled by the sketch of a Christian man's life, discipline, and conflicts, in the epistle of St Peter, and by the doctrine of St John, that love is the consummation of all God's revelations and all man's strivings, as by any former part of the book. For that men are not to gain a kingdom hereafter, but are put in possession of it now, and that through their chastisements and the oppositions of their evil nature they are to learn its character and enter into its privileges, is surely taught in every verse of the one; and that love has been manifested unto men, that they have been brought into fellowship with it, that by that fellowship they may rise to the fruition of it, and that this fellowship is for us as members of a family, so that he who loveth God must love his brother also, is affirmed again and again in express words of the other. With such thoughts in our mind, I believe we may venture, with hope of the deepest instruction, upon the study of the last book in the Bible. For though we may not be able to determine which of all the chronological speculations respecting it is the least untenable, though we may not decide confidently whether it speaks to us of the future or of the past, whether it describes a conflict of principles or of persons, of this we shall have no doubt, that it does exhibit at one period or through all periods a real kingdom of heaven upon earth, a kingdom of which the principle must be ever the same, a kingdom to which all kingdoms are meant to be in subjection; a kingdom which is maintaining itself against an opposing tyranny, whereof the ultimate law is brute force or unalloyed selfishness; a kingdom which must prevail because it rests upon a name which expresses the perfect Love, the ineffable Unity, the name of the Father, and of the Son, and of the Holy Ghost.

ABOLITIONISTS 25

❧ *Though it is a sad truth of American history that many Christians claimed biblical support for the institution of slavery and others believed it was a social issue not pertinent to the proclamation of the gospel. However, there were Christian voices raised against slavery that actively sought its abolition. Our two selections are well known speeches given by former slaves. Sojourner Truth (1797–1883), born Isabella Baumfree, after escaping slavery became inspired to be a preacher. She was a spokesperson for the anti-slavery movement and worked with Frederick Douglas, William Lloyd Garrison, and other abolitionists. In her brief speech, delivered in 1851 at the Women's Convention in Akron, Ohio, she not only raises the issue of racial discrimination in the blatant inequalities between white and black women but also the case for women's rights. Frederick Douglas's "Fourth of July" speech, delivered in Rochester, New York, at a commemoration of the Declaration of Independence on July 5, 1852, is regarded by many as one of the high water marks in eloquent and powerful anti-slavery rhetoric.*

Selection 1: Sojourner Truth, "Ain't I a Woman?"

Well, children, where there is so much racket there must be something out of kilter. I think that 'twixt the negroes of the South and the women at the North, all talking about rights, the white men will be in a fix pretty soon. But what's all this here talking about?

That man over there says that women need to be helped into carriages, and lifted over ditches, and to have the best place everywhere. Nobody ever helps me into carriages, or over mud-puddles, or gives me any best place! And ain't I a woman? Look at me! Look at my arm! I have ploughed and planted, and gathered into barns, and no man could head me! And ain't I a woman? I could work as much and eat as much as a man—when I could get it—and bear the lash as well! And ain't I a woman? I have borne thirteen children, and seen most all sold off to slavery, and when I cried out with my mother's grief, none but Jesus heard me! And ain't I a woman?

Then they talk about this thing in the head; what's this they call it? [member of audience whispers, "intellect"] That's it, honey. What's that got to do with women's rights or Negroes' rights? If my cup won't hold but a pint, and yours holds a quart, wouldn't you be mean not to let me have my little half measure full?

Then that little man in black there, he says women can't have as much rights as men, 'cause Christ wasn't a woman! Where did your Christ come from? Where did your Christ come from? From God and a woman! Man had nothing to do with Him.

If the first woman God ever made was strong enough to turn the world upside down all alone, these women together ought to be able to turn it back, and get it right side up again! And now they is asking to do it, the men better let them.

Obliged to you for hearing me, and now old Sojourner ain't got nothing more to say.

Selection 2: Frederick Douglas, "The Meaning of July Fourth for the Negro"

Fellow Citizens, I am not wanting in respect for the fathers of this republic. The signers of the Declaration of Independence were brave men. They were great men, too, great enough to give frame to a great age. It does not often happen to a nation to raise, at one time, such a number of truly great men. The point from which I am compelled to view them is not, certainly, the most favorable; and yet I cannot con-template their great deeds with less than admiration. They were statesmen, patriots and heroes, and for the good they did, and the principles they contended for, I will unite with you to honor their memory. . . .

. . . Fellow-citizens, pardon me, allow me to ask, why am I called upon to speak here to-day? What have I, or those I represent, to do with your national independence? Are the great principles of political freedom and of natural justice, embodied in that Declaration of Independence, extended to us? and am I, therefore, called upon to bring our humble offering to the national altar, and to confess the benefits and express devout gratitude for the blessings resulting from your independence to us?

Would to God, both for your sakes and ours that an affirmative answer could be truthfully returned to these questions! Then would my task be light, and my burden easy and delightful. For who is there so cold, that a nation's sympathy could not warm him? Who so obdurate and dead to the claims of gratitude that would not thankfully acknowledge such priceless benefits? Who so stolid and selfish, that would not give his voice to swell the hallelujahs of a nation's jubilee, when the chains of servitude had been torn from his limbs? I am not that man. In a case like that, the dumb might eloquently speak, and the "lame man leap as an hart."

But such is not the state of the case. I say it with a sad sense of the disparity between us. I am not included within the pale of glorious anniversary! Your high independence only reveals the immeasurable distance between us. The blessings in which you, this day, rejoice, are not enjoyed in common. The rich inheritance of jus-tice, liberty, prosperity and independence, bequeathed by your fathers, is shared by you, not by me. The sunlight that brought light and healing to you has brought stripes and death to me. This Fourth July is yours, not mine. You may rejoice, I must mourn. To drag a man in fetters into the grand illuminated temple of liberty, and call upon him to join you in joyous anthems, were inhuman mockery and sacrilegious irony. Do you mean, citizens, to mock me, by asking me to speak to-day? If so, there is a parallel to your conduct. And let me warn you that it is dangerous to copy the example of a nation whose crimes, towering up to heaven, were thrown down by the breath of the

Almighty, burying that nation in irrevocable ruin! I can to-day take up the plaintive lament of a peeled and woe-smitten people!

"By the rivers of Babylon, there we sat down. Yea! we wept when we remembered Zion. We hanged our harps upon the willows in the midst thereof. For there, they that carried us away captive, required of us a song; and they who wasted us required of us mirth, saying, Sing us one of the songs of Zion. How can we sing the Lord's song in a strange land? If I forget thee, 0 Jerusalem, let my right hand forget her cunning. If I do not remember thee, let my tongue cleave to the roof of my mouth."

Fellow-citizens, above your national, tumultuous joy, I hear the mournful wail of millions! whose chains, heavy and grievous yesterday, are, to-day, rendered more intolerable by the jubilee shouts that reach them. If I do forget, if I do not faithfully remember those bleeding children of sorrow this day, "may my right hand forget her cunning, and may my tongue cleave to the roof of my mouth!" To forget them, to pass lightly over their wrongs, and to chime in with the popular theme, would be treason most scandalous and shocking, and would make me a reproach before God and the world. My subject, then, fellow-citizens, is American slavery. I shall see this day and its popular characteristics from the slave's point of view. Standing there identified with the American bondman, making his wrongs mine, I do not hesitate to declare, with all my soul, that the character and conduct of this nation never looked blacker to me than on this 4th of July! Whether we turn to the declarations of the past, or to the professions of the present, the conduct of the nation seems equally hideous and revolting. America is false to the past, false to the present, and solemnly binds herself to be false to the future. Standing with God and the crushed and bleeding slave on this occasion, I will, in the name of humanity which is outraged, in the name of liberty which is fettered, in the name of the constitution and the Bible which are disregarded and trampled upon, dare to call in question and to denounce, with all the emphasis I can command, everything that serves to perpetuate slavery Ñ the great sin and shame of America! "I will not equivocate; I will not excuse"; I will use the severest language I can command; and yet not one word shall escape me that any man, whose judgment is not blinded by prejudice, or who is not at heart a slaveholder, shall not confess to be right and just.

But I fancy I hear some one of my audience say, "It is just in this circumstance that you and your brother abolitionists fail to make a favorable impression on the public mind. Would you argue more, an denounce less; would you persuade more, and rebuke less; your cause would be much more likely to succeed." But, I submit, where all is plain there is nothing to be argued. What point in the anti-slavery creed would you have me argue? On what branch of the subject do the people of this country need light? Must I undertake to prove that the slave is a man? That point is conceded already. Nobody doubts it. The slaveholders themselves acknowledge it in the enactment of laws for their government. They acknowledge it when they punish disobedience on the part of the slave. There are seventy-two crimes in the State of Virginia which, if committed by a black man (no matter how ignorant he be), subject him to the punishment of death; while only two of the same crimes will subject a white man to the like punishment. What is this but the acknowledgment that the slave is a moral, intellectual, and responsible being? The manhood of the slave is conceded. It is admitted in the fact that Southern statute books are covered with enactments forbidding, under severe fines and penalties, the teaching of the slave to read or to write. When you can point to any such laws in reference to the beasts of the field, then I may consent to argue the manhood of the slave. When the dogs in your streets, when the fowls of the air, when the cattle on your hills, when the fish of the sea, and the reptiles that crawl, shall be unable to distinguish the slave from a brute, then will I argue with you that the slave is a man!

For the present, it is enough to affirm the equal manhood of the Negro race. Is it not astonishing that, while we are ploughing, planting, and reaping, using all kinds of mechanical tools, erecting houses, constructing bridges, building ships, working in metals of brass, iron, copper, silver and gold; that, while we are reading, writing and ciphering, acting as clerks, merchants and secretaries, having among us lawyers, doctors, ministers, poets, authors, editors, orators and teachers; that, while we are engaged in all manner of enterprises common to other men, digging gold in California, capturing the whale in the Pacific, feeding sheep and cattle on the hill-side, living, moving, acting, thinking, planning, living in families as husbands, wives and children, and, above all, confessing and worshipping the Christian's God, and looking hopefully for life and immortality beyond the grave, we are called upon to prove that we are men!

Would you have me argue that man is entitled to liberty? that he is the rightful owner of his own body? You have already declared it. Must I argue the wrongfulness of slavery? Is that a question for Republicans? Is it to be settled by the rules of logic and argumentation, as a matter beset with great difficulty, involving a doubtful application of the principle of justice, hard to be understood? How should I look to-day, in the presence of Americans, dividing, and subdividing a discourse, to show that men have a natural right to freedom? speaking of it relatively and positively, negatively and affirmatively. To do so, would be to make myself ridiculous, and to offer an insult to your understanding. There is not a man beneath the canopy of heaven that does not know that slavery is wrong for him.

What, am I to argue that it is wrong to make men brutes, to rob them of their liberty, to work them without wages, to keep them ignorant of their relations to their fellow men, to beat them with sticks, to flay their flesh with the lash, to load their limbs with irons, to hunt them with dogs, to sell them at auction, to sunder their families, to knock out their teeth, to burn their flesh, to starve them into obedience and submission to their masters? Must I argue that a system thus marked with blood, and stained with pollution, is wrong? No! I will not. I have better employment for my time and strength than such arguments would imply.

What, then, remains to be argued? Is it that slavery is not divine; that God did not establish it; that our doctors of divinity are mistaken? There is blasphemy in the thought. That which is inhuman, cannot be divine! Who can reason on such a proposition? They that can, may; I cannot. The time for such argument is passed.

At a time like this, scorching irony, not convincing argument, is needed. O! had I the ability, and could reach the nation's ear, I would, to-day, pour out a fiery stream of biting ridicule, blasting reproach, withering sarcasm, and stern rebuke. For it is not light that is needed, but fire; it is not the gentle shower, but thunder. We need the storm, the whirlwind, and the earthquake. The feeling of the nation must be quickened; the conscience of the nation must be roused; the propriety of the nation must be startled; the hypocrisy of the nation must be exposed; and its crimes against God and man must be proclaimed and denounced.

What, to the American slave, is your 4th of July? I answer; a day that reveals to him, more than all other days in the year, the gross injustice and cruelty to which he is the constant victim. To him, your celebration is a sham; your boasted liberty, an unholy license; your national greatness, swelling vanity; your sounds of rejoicing are empty and heartless; your denunciation of tyrants, brass fronted impudence; your shouts of liberty and equality, hollow mockery; your prayers and hymns, your sermons and thanksgivings, with all your religious parade and solemnity, are, to Him, mere bombast, fraud, deception, impiety, and hypocrisy—a thin veil to cover up crimes which would disgrace a nation of savages. There is not a nation on the earth guilty of practices more shocking and bloody than are the people of the United States, at this very hour.

Go where you may, search where you will, roam through all the monarchies and despotisms of the Old World, travel through South America, search out every abuse, and when you have found the last, lay your facts by the side of the everyday practices of this nation, and you will say with me, that, for revolting barbarity and shameless hypocrisy, America reigns without a rival. . . . Allow me to say, in conclusion, notwithstanding the dark picture I have this day presented, of the state of the nation, I do not despair of this country. There are forces in operation which must inevitably work the downfall of slavery. "The arm of the Lord is not shortened," and the doom of slavery is certain. I, therefore, leave off where I began, with hope. While drawing encouragement from "the Declaration of Independence," the great principles it contains, and the genius of American Institutions, my spirit is also cheered by the obvious tendencies of the age. Nations do not now stand in the same relation to each other that they did ages ago. No nation can now shut itself up from the surrounding world and trot round in the same old path of its fathers without interference. The time was when such could be done. Long established customs of hurtful character could formerly fence themselves in, and do their evil work with social impunity. Knowledge was then confined and enjoyed by the privileged few, and the multitude walked on in mental darkness. But a change has now come over the affairs of mankind. Walled cities and empires have become unfashionable. The arm of commerce has borne away the gates of the strong city. Intelligence is penetrating the darkest corners of the globe. It makes its pathway over and under the sea, as well as on the earth. Wind, steam, and lightning are its chartered agents. Oceans no longer divide, but link nations together. From Boston to London is now a holiday excursion. Space is comparatively annihilated.—Thoughts expressed on one side of the Atlantic are distinctly heard on the other.

The far off and almost fabulous Pacific rolls in grandeur at our feet. The Celestial Empire, the mystery of ages, is being solved. The fiat of the Almighty, "Let there be Light," has not yet spent its force. No abuse, no outrage whether in taste, sport or avarice, can now hide itself from the all-pervading light. The iron shoe, and crippled foot of China must be seen in contrast with nature. Africa must rise and put on her yet unwoven garment. 'Ethiopia, shall, stretch. out her hand unto God." In the fervent aspirations of William Lloyd Garrison, I say, and let every heart join in saying it:

> God speed the year of jubilee
> The wide world o'er!
> When from their galling chains set free,
> Th' oppress'd shall vilely bend the knee,
> And wear the yoke of tyranny
> Like brutes no more.

That year will come, and freedom's reign,
To man his plundered rights again
Restore.
God speed the day when human blood
Shall cease to flow!
In every clime be understood,
The claims of human brotherhood,
And each return for evil, good,
Not blow for blow;
That day will come all feuds to end,
And change into a faithful friend
Each foe.
God speed the hour, the glorious hour,
When none on earth
Shall exercise a lordly power,
Nor in a tyrant's presence cower;
But to all manhood's stature tower,
By equal birth!
That hour will come, to each, to all,
And from his Prison-house, to thrall
Go forth.
Until that year, day, hour, arrive,
With head, and heart, and hand I'll strive,
To break the rod, and rend the gyve,
The spoiler of his prey deprive—
So witness Heaven!
And never from my chosen post,
Whate'er the peril or the cost,
Be driven.

ALBRECHT RITSCHL 26

Liberal Theology

❧ *Albrecht Ritschl was a paramount figure of the liberal theology of nineteenth-century Germany and the European continent. His embrace of historical criticism led him to abandon much of the dogma of Protestant orthodoxy and instead to a theology resonant with the ethical dimensions of Kant's critique of practical reason. Consequently, he saw Christ's kingship as one of leading, shaping, and redeeming the moral community of the church for its role in seeking and leading the community of humankind toward the kingdom of God on earth, a community of mutuality in love.*

Christianity, so to speak, resembles not a circle described from a single centre, but an ellipse which is determined by two foci. Western Catholicism has recognized this fact in its own way. For it sets itself up not merely as an institution possessed of the sacraments by which the power of Christ's redemption is propagated, but also as the Kingdom of God in the present, as the community in which, through the obedience of men and States to the Pope, Divine righteousness is professedly realized. Now it has been a misfortune for Protestantism that the Reformers did not purify the idea of the moral Kingdom of God or Christ from sacerdotal corruptions, but embodied it in a conception which is not practical but merely dogmatical. Apart from Zwingli, whose views on this point are peculiar to himself, Luther, Melanchthon, and Calvin define the Kingdom of Christ as the inward union between Christ and believers through grace and its operations. The dogmatic theologians of both Confessions unanimously propagate this view by deriving an argument for religious consolation from the protection against powers hostile to redemption enjoyed by believers in the Kingdom of Christ. Kant (vol. i. 412 fl:) was the first to perceive the supreme importance for ethics of the "Kingdom of God" as an association of men bound together by laws of virtue. But it remained for Schleiermacher first to employ the true conception of the teleological nature of the Kingdom of God to determine the idea of Christianity. This service of his ought not to be forgotten, even if he failed to grasp the discovery with a firm hand. For none of the theologians who found in him their master, with the exception of Theremin, has taken account of the importance of this idea for systematic theology as a whole. Modern pietists are accustomed to describe their favorite undertakings, especially foreign missions, directly as the Kingdom of God; but in doing so, while they touch upon the ethical meaning of the idea, they narrow its reference improperly. This circle, too, have brought the word into use, e.g. to describe the public affairs of the Church as discussed in periodicals. This use of the name, however, involves that interchange of "Church " and " Kingdom of God " which we find dominating Roman Catholicism.

Since Jesus Himself, however, saw in the Kingdom of God the moral end of the religious fellowship He had to found (vol. ii. p. 28); since He understood by it not the common exercise of worship, but the organization of humanity through action inspired by love, any conception of Christianity would be imperfect and therefore incorrect which did not include this specifically teleological aspect. We must further remember that Christ did not describe this moral task, to be carried out by the human race, in the form of a philosophical doctrine, and propagate it in a school: He entrusted it to His disciples. At the same time He constituted them a religious community through training of another kind. For when good action towards our fellow-men is subsumed under the conception of the Kingdom of God, this whole province is placed under the rule and standard of religion. And so, were we to determine the unique quality of Christianity merely by its teleological element, namely, its relation to the moral Kingdom of God, we should do injustice to its character as a religion. This aspect of Christianity, clearly, is meant to be provided for in Schleiermacher's phrase—"in which everything is referred to the redemption wrought by Jesus." For redemption is a presupposition of the Christian's peculiar dependence on God; but dependence on God is, for Schleiermacher, the general form of religious experience as distinct from a moral relationship. Now it is true that in Christianity everything is "related" to the moral organization of humanity through love-prompted action; but at the same time everything is also "related" to redemption through Jesus, to spiritual redemption, i.e. to that freedom from guilt and over the world which is to be won through the realized Fatherhood of God. Freedom in God, the freedom of the children of God, is the private end of each individual Christian, as the Kingdom of God is the final end of all. And this double character of the Christian life—perfectly religious and perfectly ethical—continues, because its realization in the life of the individual advances through the perpetual interaction of the two elements. For the life and activity of the Founder of Christianity issued at once in the redemption and the setting up of the Kingdom of God. The same fidelity in His Divine vocation enabled Him to preserve and secure both His own fellowship with the Father, and the power to lead sinners back into the same fellowship with God; and the same effect has two aspects—His disciples acknowledge Him as the Head of the Kingdom of God, and God as their Father.

Christianity, then, is the monotheistic, completely spiritual, and ethical religion, which, based on the life of its Author as Redeemer and as Founder of the Kingdom of God, consists in the freedom of the children of God, involves the impulse to conduct from the motive of love, aims at the moral organization of mankind, and grounds blessedness on the relation of sonship to God, as well as on the Kingdom of God.

This conception is indispensable for systematic theology.

For Further Reading

The following select list of writings provides a mixture of primary and secondary sources related to the major parts of the anthology, and the full text of the works being excerpted will also provide rich additional reading.

Bushnell, Horace. *Women's Suffrage: The Reform against Nature.* New York: Scribner, 1870.

Jodock, Darrell, ed. *Ritschl in Retrospect: History, Community, and Science.* Minneapolis: Fortress Press, 1995.

Maurice, Frederick Denison. *Reconstructing Christian Ethics: Selected Writings.* Edited by Ellen K. Wondra. Louisville: Westminster John Knox, 1995.

Schleiermacher, Friedrich. *Introduction to Christian Ethics.* Translated by John C. Shelley. Nashville: Abingdon, 1989.

Sungmin, John. *Theological Ethics of Friedrich Schleiermacher.* Lewiston: Edwin Mellen, 2001.

Tackach, James, ed. *The Abolitionist Movement.* Farmington Hills: Greenhaven, 2005.

PART 8

Nineteenth- and Twentieth-Century
Catholic Social Teaching

On Behalf of Workers: Industrial Revolution and the Great Depression 27

❦ *These early encyclicals voice a strong concern for the well-being of workers and justice in the face of exploitation and great disparities in the distribution of wealth. These themes are prominent in the tradition of Catholic social teaching.*

Selection 1: Leo III, *Rerum Novarum*, May 15, 1891

> Rerum Novarum *comes at the time of the Industrial Revolution and the problems of inequity workers faced in the extremes of the capitalist enterprise under the name "liberalism." Though rejecting the socialist alternative and upholding the right to private property, the encyclical calls for solidarity among the classes rather than class warfare and emphasizes the duty of Christian charity to provide for the poor and to protect the rights of all.*

That the spirit of revolutionary change, which has long been disturbing the nations of the world, should have passed beyond the sphere of politics and made its influence felt in the cognate sphere of practical economics is not surprising. The elements of the conflict now raging are unmistakable, in the vast expansion of industrial pursuits and the marvelous discoveries of science; in the changed relations between masters and workmen; in the enormous fortunes of some few individuals, and the utter poverty of the masses; the increased self reliance and closer mutual combination of the working classes; as also, finally, in the prevailing moral degeneracy. The momentous gravity of the state of things now obtaining fills every mind with painful apprehension; wise men are discussing it; practical men are proposing schemes; popular meetings, legislatures, and rulers of nations are all busied with it—actually there is no question which has taken deeper hold on the public mind.

22. Therefore, those whom fortune favors are warned that riches do not bring freedom from sorrow and are of no avail for eternal happiness, but rather are obstacles; that the rich should tremble at the threatenings of Jesus Christ—threatenings so unwonted in the mouth of our Lord—and that a most strict account must be given to the Supreme Judge for all we possess. The chief and most excellent rule for the right use of money is one the heathen philosophers hinted at, but which the Church has

traced out clearly, and has not only made known to men's minds, but has impressed upon their lives. It rests on the principle that it is one thing to have a right to the possession of money and another to have a right to use money as one wills. Private ownership, as we have seen, is the natural right of man, and to exercise that right, especially as members of society, is not only lawful, but absolutely necessary. "It is lawful," says St. Thomas Aquinas, "for a man to hold private property; and it is also necessary for the carrying on of human existence."" But if the question be asked: How must one's possessions be used?—the Church replies without hesitation in the words of the same holy Doctor: "Man should not consider his material possessions as his own, but as common to all, so as to share them without hesitation when others are in need. Whence the Apostle with, 'Command the rich of this world . . . to offer with no stint, to apportion largely.'" True, no one is commanded to distribute to others that which is required for his own needs and those of his household; nor even to give away what is reasonably required to keep up becomingly his condition in life, "for no one ought to live other than becomingly." But, when what necessity demands has been supplied, and one's standing fairly taken thought for, it becomes a duty to give to the indigent out of what remains over. "Of that which remaineth, give alms." It is a duty, not of justice (save in extreme cases), but of Christian charity—a duty not enforced by human law. But the laws and judgments of men must yield place to the laws and judgments of Christ the true God, who in many ways urges on His followers the practice of almsgiving—'It is more blessed to give than to receive"; and who will count a kindness done or refused to the poor as done or refused to Himself—"As long as you did it to one of My least brethren you did it to Me." To sum up, then, what has been said: Whoever has received from the divine bounty a large share of temporal blessings, whether they be external and material, or gifts of the mind, has received them for the purpose of using them for the perfecting of his own nature, and, at the same time, that he may employ them, as the steward of God's providence, for the benefit of others. "He that hath a talent," said St. Gregory the Great, "let him see that he hide it not; he that hath abundance, let him quicken himself to mercy and generosity; he that hath art and skill, let him do his best to share the use and the utility hereof with his neighbor."

23. As for those who possess not the gifts of fortune, they are taught by the Church that in God's sight poverty is no disgrace, and that there is nothing to be ashamed of in earning their bread by labor. This is enforced by what we see in Christ Himself, who, "whereas He was rich, for our sakes became poor"; and who, being the Son of God, and God Himself, chose to seem and to be considered the son of a carpenter—nay, did not disdain to spend a great part of His life as a carpenter Himself. "Is not this the carpenter, the son of Mary?"

24. From contemplation of this divine Model, it is more easy to understand that the true worth and nobility of man lie in his moral qualities, that is, in virtue; that virtue is, moreover, the common inheritance of men, equally within the reach of high and low, rich and poor; and that virtue, and virtue alone, wherever found, will be followed by the rewards of everlasting happiness. Nay, God Himself seems to incline rather to those who suffer misfortune; for Jesus Christ calls the poor "blessed"; He lovingly invites those in labor and grief to come to Him for solace; and He displays the tenderest charity toward the lowly and the oppressed. These reflections cannot fail to keep down the pride of the well-to-do, and to give heart to the unfortunate; to move the former to be generous and the latter to be moderate in their desires. Thus,

the separation which pride would set up tends to disappear, nor will it be difficult to make rich and poor join hands in friendly concord.

36. Whenever the general interest or any particular class suffers, or is threatened with harm, which can in no other way be met or prevented, the public authority must step in to deal with it. Now, it is to the interest of the community, as well as of the individual, that peace and good order should be maintained; that all things should be carried on in accordance with God's laws and those of nature; that the discipline of family life should be observed and that religion should be obeyed; that a high standard of morality should prevail, both in public and private life; that justice should be held sacred and that no one should injure another with impunity; that the members of the commonwealth should grow up to man's estate strong and robust, and capable, if need be, of guarding and defending their country. If by a strike of workers or concerted interruption of work there should be imminent danger of disturbance to the public peace; or if circumstances were such as that among the working class the ties of family life were relaxed; if religion were found to suffer through the workers not having time and opportunity afforded them to practice its duties; if in workshops and factories there were danger to morals through the mixing of the sexes or from other harmful occasions of evil; or if employers laid burdens upon their workmen which were unjust, or degraded them with conditions repugnant to their dignity as human beings; finally, if health were endangered by excessive labor, or by work unsuited to sex or age—in such cases, there can be no question but that, within certain limits, it would be right to invoke the aid and authority of the law. The limits must be determined by the nature of the occasion which calls for the law's interference—the principle being that the law must not undertake more, nor proceed further, than is required for the remedy of the evil or the removal of the mischief.

37. Rights must be religiously respected wherever they exist, and it is the duty of the public authority to prevent and to punish injury, and to protect everyone in the possession of his own. Still, when there is question of defending the rights of individuals, the poor and badly off have a claim to especial consideration. The richer class have many ways of shielding themselves, and stand less in need of help from the State; whereas the mass of the poor have no resources of their own to fall back upon, and must chiefly depend upon the assistance of the State. And it is for this reason that wage-earners, since they mostly belong in the mass of the needy, should be specially cared for and protected by the government.

Selection 2: Pope Pius XI, *Quadragesimo anno*, 1931

> *Pius XI wrote this encyclical on the fortieth anniversary of* Rerum novarum. *In it he celebrates and reaffirms the positions taken by Leo XII on behalf of workers, now further disadvantaged by the Great Depression. He affirms the natural law, discernable by reason, as foundational for the social nature of humankind. However, the moral law is essential if God's purposes are to be achieved. He also introduces a discussion of both distributive justice.*

42. Even though economics and moral science employs each its own principles in its own sphere, it is, nevertheless, an error to say that the economic and moral orders

arc so distinct from and alien to each other that the former depends in no way on the latter. Certainly the laws of economics, as they are termed, being based on the very nature of material things and on the capacities of the human body and mind, determine the limits of what productive human effort cannot, and of what it can attain in the economic field and by what means. Yet it is reason itself that clearly shows, on the basis of the individual and social nature of things and of men, the purpose which God ordained for all economic life.

43. But it is only the moral law which, just as it commands us to seek our supreme and last end in the whole scheme of our activity, so likewise commands us to seek directly in each kind of activity those purposes which we know that nature, or rather God the Author of nature, established for that kind of action, and in orderly relationship to subordinate such immediate purposes to our supreme and last end. If we faithfully observe this law, then it will follow that the particular purposes, both individual and social, that are sought in the economic field will fall in their proper place in the universal order of purposes, and We, in ascending through them, as it were by steps, shall attain the final end of all things, that is God, to Himself and to us, the supreme and inexhaustible Good.

56. Unquestionably, so as not to close against themselves the road to justice and peace through these false tenets, both parties ought to have been forewarned by the wise words of Our Predecessor: "However the earth may be apportioned among private owners, it does not cease to serve the common interests of all." This same doctrine We ourselves also taught above in declaring that the division of goods which results from private ownership was established by nature itself in order that created things may serve the needs of mankind in fixed and stable order. Lest one wander from the straight path of truth, this is something that must be continually kept in mind.

57. But not every distribution among human beings of property and wealth is of a character to attain either completely or to a satisfactory degree of perfection the end which God intends. Therefore, the riches that economic-social developments constantly increase ought to be so distributed among individual persons and classes that the common advantage of all, which Leo XIII had praised, will be safeguarded; in other words, that the common good of all society will be kept inviolate. By this law of social justice, one class is forbidden to exclude the other from sharing in the benefits. Hence the class of the wealthy violates this law no less, when, as if free from care on account of its wealth, it thinks it the right order of things for it to get everything and the worker nothing, than does the non-owning working class when, angered deeply at outraged justice and too ready to assert wrongly the one right it is conscious of, it demands for itself everything as if produced by its own hands, and attacks and seeks to abolish, therefore, all property and returns or incomes, of whatever kind they are or whatever the function they perform in human society, that have not been obtained by labor, and for no other reason save that they are of such a nature. And in this connection We must not pass over the unwarranted and unmerited appeal made by some to the Apostle when he said: "If any man will not work neither let him eat." For the Apostle is passing judgment on those who are unwilling to work, although they can and ought to, and he admonishes us that we ought diligently to use our time and energies of body, and mind and not be a burden to others when we can provide for ourselves. But the Apostle in no wise teaches that labor is the sole title to a living or an income.

58. To each, therefore, must be given his own share of goods, and the distribution of created goods, which, as every discerning person knows, is laboring today under the gravest evils due to the huge disparity between the few exceedingly rich and the unnumbered propertyless, must be effectively called back to and brought into conformity with the norms of the common good, that is, social justice.

59. The redemption of the non-owning workers—this is the goal that Our Predecessor declared must necessarily be sought. And the point is the more emphatically to be asserted and more insistently repeated because the commands of the Pontiff, salutary as they are, have not infrequently been consigned to oblivion either because they were deliberately suppressed by silence or thought impracticable although they both can and ought to be put into effect. And these commands have not lost their force and wisdom for our time because that "pauperism" which Leo XIII beheld in all its horror is less widespread. Certainly the condition of the workers has been improved and made more equitable especially in the more civilized and wealthy countries where the workers can no longer be considered universally overwhelmed with misery and lacking the necessities of life. But since manufacturing and industry have so rapidly pervaded and occupied countless regions, not only in the countries called new, but also in the realms of the Far East that have been civilized from antiquity, the number of the non-owning working poor has increased enormously and their groans cry to God from the earth. Added to them is the huge army of rural wage workers, pushed to the lowest level of existence and deprived of all hope of ever acquiring "some property in land," and, therefore, permanently bound to the status of non-owning worker unless suitable and effective remedies are applied.

60. Yet while it is true that the status of non owning worker is to be carefully distinguished from pauperism, nevertheless the immense multitude of the non-owning workers on the one hand and the enormous riches of certain very wealthy men on the other establish an unanswerable argument that the riches which are so abundantly produced in our age of "industrialism," as it is called, are not rightly distributed and equitably made available to the various classes of the people.

61. Therefore, with all our strength and effort we must strive that at least in the future the abundant fruits of production will accrue equitably to those who are rich and will be distributed in ample sufficiency among the workers—not that these may become remiss in work, for man is born to labor as the bird to fly—but that they may increase their property by thrift, that they may bear, by wise management of this increase in property, the burdens of family life with greater ease and security, and that, emerging from the insecure lot in life in whose uncertainties non-owning workers are cast, they may be able not only to endure the vicissitudes of earthly existence but have also assurance that when their lives are ended they will provide in some measure for those they leave after them.

62. All these things which Our Predecessor has not only suggested but clearly and openly proclaimed, We emphasize with renewed insistence in our present Encyclical; and unless utmost efforts are made without delay to put them into effect, let no one persuade himself that public order, peace, and the tranquility of human society can be effectively defended against agitators of revolution.

71. In the first place, the worker must be paid a wage sufficient to support him and his family. That the rest of the family should also contribute to the common support, according to the capacity of each, is certainly right, as can be observed especially in the families of farmers, but also in the families of many craftsmen and small

shopkeepers. But to abuse the years of childhood and the limited strength of women is grossly wrong. Mothers, concentrating on household duties, should work primarily in the home or in its immediate vicinity. It is an intolerable abuse, and to be abolished at all cost, for mothers on account of the father's low wage to be forced to engage in gainful occupations outside the home to the neglect of their proper cares and duties, especially the training of children. Every effort must therefore be made that fathers of families receive a wage large enough to meet ordinary family needs adequately. But if this cannot always be done under existing circumstances, social justice demands that changes be introduced as soon as possible whereby such a wage will be assured to every adult workingman. It will not be out of place here to render merited praise to all, who with a wise and useful purpose, have tried and tested various ways of adjusting the pay for work to family burdens in such a way that, as these increase, the former may be raised and indeed, if the contingency arises, there may be enough to meet extraordinary needs.

74. Lastly, the amount of the pay must be adjusted to the public economic good. We have shown above how much it helps the common good for workers and other employees, by setting aside some part of their income that remains after necessary expenditures, to attain gradually to the possession of a moderate amount of wealth. But another point, scarcely less important, and especially vital in our times, must not be overlooked: namely, that the opportunity to work be provided to those who are able and willing to work. This opportunity depends largely on the wage and salary rate, which can help as long as it is kept within proper limits, but which on the other hand can be an obstacle if it exceeds these limits. For everyone knows that an excessive lowering of wages, or their increase beyond due measure, causes unemployment. This evil, indeed, especially as we see it prolonged and injuring so many during the years of Our Pontificate, has plunged workers into misery and temptations, ruined the prosperity of nations, and put in jeopardy the public order, peace, and tranquility of the whole world. Hence it is contrary to social justice when, for the sake of personal gain and without regard for the common good, wages and salaries are excessively lowered or raised; and this same social justice demands that wages and salaries be so managed, through agreement of plans and wills, in so far as can be done, as to offer to the greatest possible number the opportunity of getting work and obtaining suitable means of livelihood.

Pope John XXIII
and Vatican II

28

❧ *John XXIII (1881–1963) is perhaps best remembered by the world at large as the pope who called Vatican II into session. This was a surprise if not a shock to many church leaders since it had been only ninety years since Vatican I (1869–1870), which was not convened until three hundred years after the Council of Trent. Pope John XXIII however expressed the need for* aggiornamento *(literally, "up to date") for the church. Aggiornamento then became a paramount theme of the Vatican Council, which enacted far-reaching changes in liturgy, ecumenism, and the church's relation to the world.*

Selection 1: John XXIII, *Pacem in terris* (1963)

The arms race and the cold war were in full swing at the time of this encyclical. Toward its end John XXIII does speak of the way this proliferation of deadly weapons has kept people and nations in the grip of fear and of his deep concern that this build up may yet continue. However, our excerpt presents the encyclical's more prominent theme of human rights. Here we see clearly how John XXII grounds human right in natural law.

3. God created man "in His own image and likeness," endowed him with intelligence and freedom, and made him lord of creation. All this the psalmist proclaims when he says: "Thou hast made him a little less than the angels: thou hast crowned him with glory and honor, and hast set him over the works of thy hands. Thou hast subjected all things under his feet."

Order in Human Beings
4. And yet there is a disunity among individuals and among nations which is in striking contrast to this perfect order in the universe. One would think that the relationships that bind men together could only be governed by force.

5. But the world's Creator has stamped man's inmost being with an order revealed to man by his conscience; and his conscience insists on his preserving it. Men "show the work of the law written in their hearts. Their conscience bears witness to them." And

how could it be otherwise? All created being reflects the infinite wisdom of God. It reflects it all the more clearly, the higher it stands in the scale of perfection.

6. But the mischief is often caused by erroneous opinions. Many people think that the laws that govern man's relations with the State are the same as those which regulate the blind, elemental forces of the universe. But it is not so; the laws which govern men are quite different. The Father of the universe has inscribed them in man's nature, and that is where we must look for them; there and nowhere else.

7. These laws clearly indicate how a man must behave toward his fellows in society, and how the mutual relationships between the members of a State and its officials are to be conducted. They show too what principles must govern the relations between States; and finally, what should be the relations between individuals or States on the one hand, and the world-wide community of nations on the other. Men's common interests make it imperative that at long last a worldwide community of nations

Rights

11. But first We must speak of man's rights. Man has the right to live. He has the right to bodily integrity and to the means necessary for the proper development of life, particularly food, clothing, shelter, medical care, rest, and, finally, the necessary social services. In consequence, he has the right to be looked after in the event of ill health; disability stemming from his work; widowhood; old age; enforced unemployment; or whenever through no fault of his own he is deprived of the means of livelihood.

Rights Pertaining to Moral and Cultural Values

12. Moreover, man has a natural right to be respected. He has a right to his good name. He has a right to freedom in investigating the truth, and—within the limits of the moral order and the common good—to freedom of speech and publication, and to freedom to pursue whatever profession he may choose. He has the right, also, to be accurately informed about public events.

13. He has the natural right to share in the benefits of culture, and hence to receive a good general education, and a technical or professional training consistent with the degree of educational development in his own country. Furthermore, a system must be devised for affording gifted members of society the opportunity of engaging in more advanced studies, with a view to their occupying, as far as possible, positions of responsibility in society in keeping with their natural talent and acquired skill.

The Right to Worship God According to One's Conscience

14. Also among man's rights is that of being able to worship God in accordance with the right dictates of his own conscience, and to profess his religion both in private and in public. According to the clear teaching of Lactantius, "this is the very condition of our birth that we render to the God who made us that just homage which is His due; that we acknowledge Him alone as God, and follow Him. It is from this ligature of piety, which binds us and joins us to God, that religion derives its name."

Hence, too, Pope Leo XIII declared that "true freedom, freedom worthy of the sons of God, is that freedom which most truly safeguards the dignity of the human person. It is stronger than any violence or injustice. Such is the freedom which has always been desired by the Church, and which she holds most dear. It is the sort of freedom which the Apostles resolutely claimed for themselves. The apologists defended it in their writings; thousands of martyrs consecrated it with their blood."

The Right to Choose Freely One's State in Life
15. Human beings have also the right to choose for themselves the kind of life which appeals to them: whether it is to found a family—in the founding of which both the man and the woman enjoy equal rights and duties—or to embrace the priesthood or the religious life.

16. The family, founded upon marriage freely contracted, one and indissoluble, must be regarded as the natural, primary cell of human society. The interests of the family, therefore, must be taken very specially into consideration in social and economic affairs, as well as in the spheres of faith and morals. For all of these have to do with strengthening the family and assisting it in the fulfillment of its mission.

17. Of course, the support and education of children is a right which belongs primarily to the parents.

Economic Rights
18. In the economic sphere, it is evident that a man has the inherent right not only to be given the opportunity to work, but also to be allowed the exercise of personal initiative in the work he does.

19. The conditions in which a man works form a necessary corollary to these rights. They must not be such as to weaken his physical or moral fibre, or militate against the proper development of adolescents to manhood. Women must be accorded such conditions of work as are consistent with their needs and responsibilities as wives and mothers.

20. A further consequence of man's personal dignity is his right to engage in economic activities suited to his degree of responsibility. The worker is likewise entitled to a wage that is determined in accordance with the precepts of justice. This needs stressing. The amount a worker receives must be sufficient, in proportion to available funds, to allow him and his family a standard of living consistent with human dignity. Pope Pius XII expressed it in these terms:

> Nature imposes work upon man as a duty, and man has the corresponding natural right to demand that the work he does shall provide him with the means of livelihood for himself and his children. Such is nature's categorical imperative for the preservation of man.

21. As a further consequence of man's nature, he has the right to the private ownership of property, including that of productive goods. This, as We have said elsewhere, is "a right which constitutes so efficacious a means of asserting one's personality and exercising responsibility in every field, and an element of solidity and security for family life, and of greater peace and prosperity in the State."

22. Finally, it is opportune to point out that the right to own private property entails a social obligation as well.

The Right of Meeting and Association

23. Men are by nature social, and consequently they have the right to meet together and to form associations with their fellows. They have the right to confer on such associations the type of organization which they consider best calculated to achieve their objectives. They have also the right to exercise their own initiative and act on their own responsibility within these associations for the attainment of the desired results.

24. As We insisted in Our encyclical *Mater et Magistra*, the founding of a great many such intermediate groups or societies for the pursuit of aims which it is not within the competence of the individual to achieve efficiently, is a matter of great urgency. Such groups and societies must be considered absolutely essential for the safeguarding of man's personal freedom and dignity, while leaving intact a sense of responsibility.

The Right to Emigrate and Immigrate

25. Again, every human being has the right to freedom of movement and of residence within the confines of his own State. When there are just reasons in favor of it, he must be permitted to emigrate to other countries and take up residence there. The fact that he is a citizen of a particular State does not deprive him of membership in the human family, nor of citizenship in that universal society, the common, worldwide fellowship of men.

Political Rights

26. Finally, man's personal dignity involves his right to take an active part in public life, and to make his own contribution to the common welfare of his fellow citizens. As Pope Pius XII said, "man as such, far from being an object or, as it were, an inert element in society, is rather its subject, its basis and its purpose; and so must he be esteemed."

27. As a human person he is entitled to the legal protection of his rights, and such protection must be effective, unbiased, and strictly just. To quote again Pope Pius XII: "In consequence of that juridical order willed by God, man has his own inalienable right to juridical security. To him is assigned a certain, well-defined sphere of law, immune from arbitrary attack."

Duties

28. The natural rights of which We have so far been speaking are inextricably bound up with as many duties, all applying to one and the same person. These rights and duties derive their origin, their sustenance, and their indestructibility from the natural law, which in conferring the one imposes the other.

29. Thus, for example, the right to live involves the duty to preserve one's life; the right to a decent standard of living, the duty to live in a becoming fashion; the right to be free to seek out the truth, the duty to devote oneself to an ever deeper and wider search for it.

Reciprocity of Rights and Duties Between Persons

30. Once this is admitted, it follows that in human society one man's natural right gives rise to a corresponding duty in other men; the duty, that is, of recognizing and respecting that right. Every basic human right draws its authoritative force from the natural law, which confers it and attaches to it its respective duty. Hence, to claim one's rights and ignore one's duties, or only half fulfill them, is like building a house with one hand and tearing it down with the other.

Selection 2: Vatican Council II, *Gaudium et spes* (1965)

> *This Pastoral Constitution on the Church in the Modern World emphasizes the dignity of all humanity and the need to address the rapid and often threatening changes that characterize the modern world. The excerpts below give an idea of the scope of concerns in an increasingly international and interrelated world.*

In our times a special obligation binds us to make ourselves the neighbor of every person without exception and of actively helping him when he comes across our path, whether he be an old person abandoned by all, a foreign laborer unjustly looked down upon, a refugee, a child born of an unlawful union and wrongly suffering for a sin he did not commit, or a hungry person who disturbs our conscience by recalling the voice of the Lord, "As long as you did it for one of these the least of my brethren, you did it for me" (Matt. 25:40).

Furthermore, whatever is opposed to life itself, such as any type of murder, genocide, abortion, euthanasia or willful self-destruction, whatever violates the integrity of the human person, such as mutilation, torments inflicted on body or mind, attempts to coerce the will itself; whatever insults human dignity, such as subhuman living conditions, arbitrary imprisonment, deportation, slavery, prostitution, the selling of women and children; as well as disgraceful working conditions, where men are treated as mere tools for profit, rather than as free and responsible persons; all these things and others of their like are infamies indeed. They poison human society, but they do more harm to those who practice them than those who suffer from the injury. Moreover, they are supreme dishonor to the Creator.

28. Respect and love ought to be extended also to those who think or act differently than we do in social, political and even religious matters. In fact, the more deeply we come to understand their ways of thinking through such courtesy and love, the more easily will we be able to enter into dialogue with them.

This love and good will, to be sure, must in no way render us indifferent to truth and goodness. Indeed love itself impels the disciples of Christ to speak the saving truth to all men. But it is necessary to distinguish between error, which always merits repudiation, and the person in error, who never loses the dignity of being a person even when he is flawed by false or inadequate religious notions. God alone is the judge and searcher of hearts, for that reason He forbids us to make judgments about the internal guilt of anyone.

The teaching of Christ even requires that we forgive injuries, and extends the law of love to include every enemy, according to the command of the New Law: "You have heard that it was said: Thou shalt love thy neighbor and hate thy enemy. But I say to you: love your enemies, do good to those who hate you, and pray for those who persecute and calumniate you" (Matt. 5:43-44).

29. Since all men possess a rational soul and are created in God's likeness, since they have the same nature and origin, have been redeemed by Christ and enjoy the same divine calling and destiny, the basic equality of all must receive increasingly greater recognition.

True, all men are not alike from the point of view of varying physical power and the diversity of intellectual and moral resources. Nevertheless, with respect to the fundamental rights of the person, every type of discrimination, whether social or cultural, whether based on sex, race, color, social condition, language or religion, is to be overcome and eradicated as contrary to God's intent. For in truth it must still be regretted that fundamental personal rights are still not being universally honored. Such is the case of a woman who is denied the right to choose a husband freely, to embrace a state of life or to acquire an education or cultural benefits equal to those recognized for men.

Therefore, although rightful differences exist between men, the equal dignity of persons demands that a more humane and just condition of life be brought about. For excessive economic and social differences between the members of the one human family or population groups cause scandal, and militate against social justice, equity, the dignity of the human person, as well as social and international peace.

Human institutions, both private and public, must labor to minister to the dignity and purpose of man. At the same time let them put up a stubborn fight against any kind of slavery, whether social or political, and safeguard the basic rights of man under every political system. Indeed human institutions themselves must be accommodated by degrees to the highest of all realities, spiritual ones, even though meanwhile, a long enough time will be required before they arrive at the desired goal.

58. There are many ties between the message of salvation and human culture. For God, revealing Himself to His people to the extent of a full manifestation of Himself in His Incarnate Son, has spoken according to the culture proper to each epoch.

Likewise the Church, living in various circumstances in the course of time, has used the discoveries of different cultures so that in her preaching she might spread and explain the message of Christ to all nations, that she might examine it and more deeply understand it, that she might give it better expression in liturgical celebration and in the varied life of the community of the faithful.

But at the same time, the Church, sent to all peoples of every time and place, is not bound exclusively and indissolubly to any race or nation, any particular way of life or any customary way of life recent or ancient. Faithful to her own tradition and at the same time conscious of her universal mission, she can enter into communion with the various civilizations, to their enrichment and the enrichment of the Church herself.

The Gospel of Christ constantly renews the life and culture of fallen man, it combats and removes the errors and evils resulting from the permanent allurement of sin. It never eases to purify and elevate the morality of peoples. By riches coming from above, it makes fruitful, as it were from within, the spiritual qualities and traditions of every people of every age. It strengthens, perfects and restores them in Christ. Thus the Church, in the very fulfillment of her own function, stimulates and advances human and civic culture; by her action, also by her liturgy, she leads them toward interior liberty.

59. For the above reasons, the Church recalls to the mind of all that culture is to be subordinated to the integral perfection of the human person, to the good of the community and of the whole society. Therefore it is necessary to develop the human faculties in such a way that there results a growth of the faculty of admiration, of intuition, of contemplation, of making personal judgment, of developing a religious, moral and social sense.

Culture, because it flows immediately from the spiritual and social character of man, has constant need of a just liberty in order to develop; it needs also the legitimate possibility of exercising its autonomy according to its own principles. It therefore rightly demands respect and enjoys a certain inviolability within the limits of the common good, as long, of course, as it preserves the rights of the individual and the community, whether particular or universal.

This Sacred Synod, therefore, recalling the teaching of the first Vatican Council, declares that there are "two orders of knowledge" which are distinct, namely faith and reason; and that the Church does not forbid that "the human arts and disciplines use their own principles and their proper method, each in its own domain"; therefore "acknowledging this just liberty," this Sacred Synod affirms the legitimate autonomy of human culture and especially of the sciences.

All this supposes that, within the limits of morality and the common utility, man can freely search for the truth, express his opinion and publish it; that he can practice any art he chooses; that finally, he can avail himself of true information concerning events of a public nature.

71. Since property and other forms of private ownership of external goods contribute to the expression of the personality, and since, moreover, they furnish one an occasion to exercise his function in society and in the economy, it is very important that the access of both individuals and communities to some ownership of external goods be fostered.

*　　*　　*

By its very nature private property has a social quality which is based on the law of the common destination of earthly goods. If this social quality is overlooked, property often becomes an occasion of passionate desires for wealth and serious disturbances, so that a pretext is given to the attackers for calling the right itself into question.

In many underdeveloped regions there are large or even extensive rural estates which are only slightly cultivated or lie completely idle for the sake of profit, while the majority of the people either are without land or have only very small fields, and, on the other hand, it is evidently urgent to increase the productivity of the fields. Not infrequently those who are hired to work for the landowners or who till a portion of the land as tenants receive a wage or income unworthy of a human being, lack decent housing and are exploited by middlemen. Deprived of all security, they live under such personal servitude that almost every opportunity of acting on their own initiative and responsibility is denied to them and all advancement in human culture and all sharing in social and political life is forbidden to them. According to the different cases, therefore, reforms are necessary: that income may grow, working conditions should be improved, security in employment increased, and an incentive to working on one's own initiative given. Indeed, insufficiently cultivated estates should be distributed to those who can make these lands fruitful; in this case, the necessary things and means, especially educational aids and the right facilities for cooperative organization, must be supplied. Whenever, nevertheless, the common good requires expropriation, compensation must be reckoned in equity after all the circumstances have been weighed.

72. Christians who take an active part in present-day socio-economic development and fight for justice and charity should be convinced that they can make a great contribution to the prosperity of mankind and to the peace of the world. In these activities let them, either as individuals or as members of groups, give a shining example. Having acquired the absolutely necessary skill and experience, they should observe the right order in their earthly activities in faithfulness to Christ and His Gospel. Thus their whole life, both individual and social, will be permeated with the spirit of the beatitudes, notably with a spirit of poverty.

80. The horror and perversity of war is immensely magnified by the addition of scientific weapons. For acts of war involving these weapons can inflict massive and indiscriminate destruction, thus going far beyond the bounds of legitimate defense. Indeed, if the kind of instruments which can now be found in the armories of the great nations were to be employed to their fullest, an almost total and altogether reciprocal slaughter of each side by the other would follow, not to mention the widespread devastation that would take place in the world and the deadly after effects that would be spawned by the use of weapons of this kind.

All these considerations compel us to undertake an evaluation of war with an entirely new attitude. The men of our time must realize that they will have to give a somber reckoning of their deeds of war for the course of the future will depend greatly on the decisions they make today.

With these truths in mind, this most holy synod makes its own the condemnations of total war already pronounced by recent popes, and issues the following declaration.

Any act of war aimed indiscriminately at the destruction of entire cities of extensive areas along with their population is a crime against God and man himself. It merits unequivocal and unhesitating condemnation.

The unique hazard of modern warfare consists in this: it provides those who possess modern scientific weapons with a kind of occasion for perpetrating just such abominations; moreover, through a certain inexorable chain of events, it can catapult men into the most atrocious decisions. That such may never truly happen in the future, the bishops of the whole world gathered together, beg all men, especially government officials and military leaders, to give unremitting thought to their gigantic responsibility before God and the entire human race.

85. The present solidarity of mankind also calls for a revival of greater international cooperation in the economic field. Although nearly all peoples have become autonomous, they are far from being free of every form of undue dependence, and far from escaping all danger of serious internal difficulties.

* * *

If an authentic economic order is to be established on a worldwide basis, an end will have to be put to profiteering, to national ambitions, to the appetite for political supremacy, to militaristic calculations, and to machinations for the sake of spreading and imposing ideologies.

86. The following norms seem useful for such cooperation:

(a) Developing nations should take great pains to seek as the object for progress to express and secure the total human fulfillment of their citizens. They should bear in mind that progress arises and grows above all out of the labor and genius of the nations themselves because it has to be based, not only on foreign aid, but especially on the full utilization of their own resources, and on the development of their own culture and traditions. Those who exert the greatest influence on others should be outstanding in this respect.

(b) On the other hand, it is a very important duty of the advanced nations to help the developing nations in discharging their above-mentioned responsibilities. They should therefore gladly carry out on their own home front those spiritual and material readjustments that are required for the realization of this universal cooperation.

Consequently, in business dealings with weaker and poorer nations, they should be careful to respect their profit, for these countries need the income they receive on the sale of their homemade products to support themselves.

(c) It is the role of the international community to coordinate and promote development, but in such a way that the resources earmarked for this purpose will be allocated as effectively as possible, and with complete equity. It is likewise this community's duty, with due regard for the principle of subsidiarity, so to regulate economic relations throughout the world that these will be carried out in accordance with the norms of justice.

Suitable organizations should be set up to foster and regulate international business affairs, particularly with the underdeveloped countries, and to compensate for losses resulting from an excessive inequality of power among the various nations. This type of organization, in unison with technical cultural and financial aid, should provide the help which developing nations need so that they can advantageously pursue their own economic advancement.

(d) In many cases there is an urgent need to revamp economic and social structures. But one must guard against proposals of technical solutions that are untimely. This is particularly true of those solutions providing man with material conveniences, but nevertheless contrary to man's spiritual nature and advancement. For "not by bread alone does man live, but by every word which proceeds from the mouth of God" (Matt. 4:4). Every sector of the family of man carries within itself and in its best traditions some portion of the spiritual treasure entrusted by God to humanity, even though many may not be aware of the source from which it comes.

United States
Catholic Bishops 29

Selection 1: *The Challenge of Peace: God's Promise and Our Response* (1983)

This lengthy pastoral letter from the United States Catholic bishops is strong in its concern for the prevention of nuclear war and specific in its proposals to wage peace. This is still the era of the Cold War, the fear of nuclear holocaust is real and debate about the arms race in general and theories of deterrence through nuclear arms buildup in particular were much on the minds of the public and of the bishops. This portion of the letter illustrates some of the basic premises of Catholic teaching as it applies to the matter of peace and war.

234. Preventing nuclear war is a moral imperative; but the avoidance of war, nuclear or conventional, is not a sufficient conception of international relations today. Nor does it exhaust the content of Catholic teaching. Both the political needs and the moral challenge of our time require a positive conception of peace, based on a vision of a just world order. Pope Paul VI summarized classical Catholic teaching in his encyclical, The Development of peoples: "Peace cannot be limited to a mere absence of war, the result of an ever precarious balance of forces. No, peace is something built up day after day, in the pursuit of an order intended by God, which implies a more perfect form of justice among men and women."

1. World Order in Catholic Teaching

235. This positive conception of peace sees it as the fruit of order; order, in turn, is shaped by the values of justice, truth, freedom and love. The basis of this teaching is found in sacred scripture, St. Augustine and St. Thomas. It has found contemporary expression and development in papal teaching of this century. The popes of the nuclear age, from Pius XII through John Paul II have affirmed pursuit of international order as the way to banish the scourge of war from human affairs.

236. The fundamental premise of world order in Catholic teaching is a theological truth: the unity of the human family-rooted in common creation, destined for the kingdom, and united by moral bonds of rights and duties. This basic truth about the unity of the human family pervades the entire teaching on war and peace: for the pacifist position it is one of the reasons why life cannot be taken, while for the just-war position, even in a justified conflict bonds of responsibility remain in spite of the conflict.

237. Catholic teaching recognizes that in modern history, at least since the Peace of Westphalia (1648), the international community has been governed by nation-states. Catholic moral theology, as expressed for example in chapters 2 and 3 of Peace on Earth, accords a real but relative moral value to sovereign states. The value is real because of the functions states fulfill as sources of order and authority in the political community; it is relative because boundaries of the sovereign state do not dissolve the deeper relationships of responsibility existing in the human community. Just as within nations the moral fabric of society is described in Catholic teaching in terms of reciprocal rights and duties-between individuals, and then between the individual and the state—so in the international community Peace on Earth defines the rights and duties which exist among states.

238. In the past twenty years Catholic teaching has become increasingly specific about the content of these international rights and duties. In 1963, Peace on Earth sketched the political and legal order among states. In 1966, The Development of Peoples elaborated an order of economic rights and duties. In 1979, Pope John Paul II articulated the human rights basis of international relations in his "Address to the United Nations General Assembly."

239. These documents and others which build upon them, outlined a moral order of international relations, i.e., how the international community should be organized. At the same time this teaching has been sensitive to the actual pattern of relations prevailing among states. While not ignoring present geopolitical realities, one of the primary functions of Catholic teaching on world order has been to point the way toward a more integrated international system.

240. In analyzing this path toward world order, the category increasingly used in Catholic moral teaching (and, more recently, in the social sciences also) is the interdependence of the world today, The theological principle of unity has always affirmed a human interdependence; but today this bond is complemented by the growing political and economic interdependence of the world, manifested in a whole range of international issues.

241. An important element missing from world order today is a properly constituted political authority with the capacity to shape our material interdependence in the direction of moral interdependence. Pope John XXIII stated the case in the following way:

Today the universal common good poses problems of world-wide dimensions, which cannot be adequately tackled or solved except by the efforts of public authority endowed with a wideness of powers, structure and means of the same proportions: that is, of public authority which is in a position to operate in an effective manner on a world-wide basis. The moral order itself, therefore, demands that such a form of public authority be established.

242. Just as the nation-state was a step in the evolution of government at a time when expanding trade and new weapons technologies made the feudal system inadequate to manage conflicts and provide security, so we are now entering an era of new, global interdependencies requiring global systems of governance to manage the resulting conflicts and ensure our common security. Major global problems such as worldwide inflation, trade and payments deficits, competition over scarce resources, hunger, widespread unemployment, global environmental dangers, the growing power of transnational corporations, and the threat of international financial collapse, as well as the danger of world war resulting from these growing tensions—cannot be

remedied by a single nation-state approach. They shall require the concerted effort of the whole world community. As we shall indicate below, the United Nations should be particularly considered in this effort.

243. In the nuclear age, it is in the regulation of interstate conflicts and ultimately the replacement of military by negotiated solutions that the supreme importance and necessity of a moral as well as a political concept of the international common good can be grasped. The absence of adequate structures for addressing these issues places even greater responsibility on the policies of individual states. By a mix of political vision and moral wisdom, states are called to interpret the national interest in light of the larger global interest.

244. We are living in a global age with problems and conflicts on a global scale. Either we shall learn to resolve these problems together, or we shall destroy one another. Mutual security and survival require a new vision of the world as one inter-dependent planet. We have rights and duties not only within our diverse national communities but within the larger world community.

Selection 2: *Economic Justice for All* (1986)

This pastoral letter begins with recognition of both the greatness and promise of the United States economy and the reality and threat of poverty for vast numbers of people who live within it. One finds familiar language concerning Christian social responsibility and human rights that echoes the spirit and text of Vatican II. Notwithstanding the bishops insistence that they espouse no particular political or economic philosophy the degree of specificity they are willing to offer on socio-economic issues of urgency is noteworthy. This excerpt concerning employment and poverty is illustrative.

136. Full employment is the foundation of a just economy. The most urgent priority for domestic economic policy is the creation of new jobs with adequate pay and decent working conditions. We must make it possible as a nation for every one who is seeking a job to find employment within a reasonable amount of time. Our emphasis on this goal is based on the conviction that human work has a special dignity and is a key to achieving justice in society.

137. Employment is a basic right, a right which protects the freedom of all to participate in the economic life of society. It is a right which flows from the principles of justice which we have outlined above. Corresponding to this right is the duty on the part of society to ensure that the right is the duty on the part of society to ensure that the right is protected. The importance of this right is evident in the fact that for most people employment is crucial to self-realization and essential to the fulfillment of material needs. Since so few in our economy own productive property, employment also forms the first line of defense against poverty. Jobs benefit society as well as workers, for they enable more people to contribute to the common good and to the productivity required for a healthy economy..

151. We recommend that the nation make a major new commitment to achieve full employment. At present there is nominal endorsement of the full employment ideal, but no firm commitment to bringing it about. If every effort were now being made to create the jobs reburied, one might argue that the situation today is the best

we can do. But such is not the case. The country is doing far less than it might to generate employment.

152. Over the last decade, economists, policy makers, and the general public have shown greater willingness to tolerate unemployment levels of 6 to 7 percent or even more. Although we recognize the complexities and trade-offs involved in reducing unemployment, we believe that 6 to 7 percent unemployment is neither inevitable nor acceptable. While a zero unemployment rate is clearly impossible in and economy where people are constantly entering the job market and others are changing jobs, appropriate policies and concerted private and public action can improve the situation considerably, if we have the will to do so. No economy can be considered truly healthy when so many millions of people are denied jobs by forces outside their control. The acceptance of present unemployment rates would have been unthinkable twenty years ago. It should be regarded as intolerable today.

153. We must first establish a consensus that everyone has a right to employment. Then the burden of securing full employment falls on all of us—policy makers, business, labor, and the general public—to create and implement the mechanisms to protect that right. We must work for the formation of a new national consensus and mobilize the necessary political will at all levels to make the goal of full employment a reality.

154. Expanding employment in our nation will require significant steps in both the private and public sectors, as well as joint action between them. Private initiative and entrepreneurship are essential to this task, for the private sector accounts for 80 percent of the jobs in the United States, and most new jobs are being created there. Thus, a viable strategy for employment generation must assume that a large part of the solution will be with private firms and small businesses. At the same time, it must be recognized that government has a prominent and indispensable role to play in addressing the problem of unemployment. The market alone will not automatically produce full employment. Therefore, the government must act to ensure that this goal is achieved by coordinating general economic policies, by job creation programs and by other appropriate policy measures.

200. c. *Self-help efforts among the poor should be fostered by programs and policies in both the private and public sectors.* We believe that an effective way to attack poverty is through programs that are small in scale, locally based, and oriented toward empowering the poor to become self-sufficient. Corporation, private organizations, and the public sector can provide seed money, training and technical assistance, and organizational support for self-help projects in a wide variety of areas such as low-income housing, credit unions, worker cooperatives, legal assistance, and neighborhood and community organizations. Efforts that enable the poor to participate in the ownership and control of economic resources are especially important.

201. Poor people must be empowered to take charge of their own futures and become responsible for their own economic advancement. Personal motivation and initiative, combined with social reform, are necessary elements to assist individuals in escaping poverty. By taking advantage of opportunities for education, employment, and training, and by working together for change, the poor can help themselves to be full participants in our economic, social, and political life.

202. d. *The tax system should be continually evaluated in terms of its impact on the poor.* This evaluation should be guided by three principles. First, the tax system should raise adequate revenues to pay for the public needs of society, especially to meet

the basic needs of the poor. Secondly, the tax system should be structured according to the principle of progressivity, so that those with relatively greater financial resources pay a higher rate of taxation. The inclusion of such a principle in tax policies is an important means of reducing the severe inequalities of income and wealth in the nation. Action should be taken to reduce or offset a disproportionate burden on those with lower incomes. Thirdly, families below the official poverty line should not be required to pay income taxes. Such families are, by definition, without sufficient resources to purchase basic necessities of life. They should not be forced to bear the additional burden of paying income taxes.

203. e. *All of society should make a much stronger commitment to education for the poor.* Any long-term solution to poverty in this country must pay serious attention to education, public and private, in school and out of school. Lack of adequate education, especially in the inner city setting, prevents many poor people from escaping poverty. In addition, illiteracy, a problem that affects tens of millions of Americans, condemns many to joblessness or chronically low wages. Moreover, it excludes them in many ways from sharing in the political and spiritual life of the community. Since poverty is fundamentally a problem of powerlessness and marginalization, the importance of education as a means of overcoming it cannot be overemphasized.

204. Working to improve education in our society is an investment in the future, an investment that should include both the public and private school systems. Our Catholic schools have the well-merited reputation of providing excellent education, especially for the poor. Catholic inner-city schools provide an otherwise unavailable educational alternative for many poor families. They provide one effective vehicle for disadvantaged students to lift themselves out of poverty. We commend the work of all those who make great sacrifices to maintain these inner-city schools. We pledge ourselves to continue the effort to make, Catholic schools models of education for the poor.

205. We also wish to affirm our strong support for the public school system in the United States. There can be no substitute for quality education in public schools, for that is where the large majority of all students, including Catholic students, are educated. In Catholic social teaching, basic education is a fundamental human right. In our society a strong public school system is essential if we are to protect that right and allow everyone to develop to their maximum ability. Therefore, we strongly endorse the recent calls for improvements in and support for public education, including improving the quality of teaching and enhancing the reward for the teaching profession. At all levels of education we need to improve the ability of our institutions to provide the personal and technical skills that are necessary for participation not only in today's labor market but also in contemporary society.

206. f. *Policies and programs at all levels should support the strength and stability of families, especially those adversely affected by the economy.* As a nation, we need to examine all aspects of economic life and assess their effects on families. Employment practices, health insurance policies, income security programs, tax policy, and service programs can either support or undermine the abilities of families to fulfill their roles in nurturing children and caring for infirm and dependent family members.

207. We affirm the principle enunciated by John Paul II that society's institutions and policies should be structured so that mothers of young children are not forced by economic necessity to leave their children for jobs outside the home. The nation's social welfare and tax policies should support parents' decisions to care for their own

children and should recognize the work of parents in the home because of its value for the family and for society.

208. For those children whose parents do work outside the home, there is a serious shortage of affordable, quality day care. Employers, governments, and private agencies need to improve both eh availability and the quality of child care services. Likewise, families could be assisted by the establishment of parental leave policies that would assure job security for new parents.

209. The high rate of divorce and the alarming extent of teenage pregnancies in our nation are distressing signs of the breakdown of traditional family values. These destructive trends are present in all sectors of society: rich and poor; white, black and brown; urban and rural. However, for the poor they tend to be more visible and have more damaging economic consequences. These destructive trends must be countered by a revived sense of personal responsibility and commitment to family values.

210. g. *A thorough reform of the nations' welfare and income- support programs should be undertaken.* For millions of poor Americans the only economic safety net is the public welfare system. The programs that make up this system should serve the needs of the poor in a manner that respects their dignity and provides adequate support. In our judgment the present welfare system does not adequately meet these criteria. We believe that several improvements can and should be made within the framework of existing welfare programs. However, in the long run, more far-reaching reforms that go beyond the present system will be necessary. Among the immediate improvements that could be made are the following:

211. (1) *Public assistance programs should be designed to assist recipients, wherever possible, to become self-sufficient through gainful employment.* Individuals should not be worse off economically when they get jobs than when they rely only on public assistance. Under current rules, people who give up welfare benefits to work in low-paying jobs soon lose their Medicaid benefits. To help recipients become self-sufficient and reduce dependency on welfare, public assistance programs should work in tandem with job creation programs that include provisions for training, counseling, placement, and child care. Jobs for recipients of public assistance should be fairly compensated so that workers receive the full benefits and status associated with gainful employment.

212. (2) *Welfare programs should provide recipients with adequate levels of support.* This support should cover basic needs in food, clothing, shelter, health care, and other essentials. At present only 4 percent of poor families with children receive enough cash welfare benefits to lift them out of poverty. The combined benefits of AFDC and food stamps typically come to less than three-fourths of the official poverty level. Those receiving public assistance should not face the prospect of hunger at the end of the month, homelessness, sending children to school in ragged clothing, or inadequate medical care.

213. (3) *National eligibility standards and a national minimum benefit level for public assistance programs should be established.* Currently welfare eligibility and benefits vary greatly among states. In 1985 a family of three with no earnings had a maximum AFDC benefit of $98 a month in Mississippi and $558 a month in Vermont. To remedy these great disparities, which are far larger than the regional differences in the cost of living, and to assure a floor of benefits for all needy people, our nation should establish and fund national minimum benefit levels and eligibility standards in cash assistance programs. The benefits should also be indexed to reflect changes in the cost of living. These changes reflect standards that our nation has already put in place for

ages and disabled people and veterans. Is it not possible to do the same for the children and their mothers who receive public assistance?

214. (4) *Welfare programs should be available to two-parent as well as single-parent families.* Most states now limit participation in AFDC to families headed by single parents, usually women. The coverage of this program should be extended to two-parent families so that fathers who are unemployed or poorly paid do not have to leave home in order for their children to receive help. Such a change would be significant step toward strengthening two-parent families who are poor.

For Further Reading

The following select list of writings provides a mixture of primary and secondary sources related to the major parts of the anthology, and the full text of the works being excerpted will also provide rich additional reading.

Catholic Social Thought: *The Documentary Heritage.* Edited by David J. O'Brien and Thomas A. Shannon. Maryknoll: Orbis, 1992.

Curran, Charles E. *Catholic Moral Theology in the United States: A History.* Washington, DC: Georgetown University Press, 2008.

Curran, Charles E. *Catholic Social Teaching 1891–Present: A Historical, Theological, and Ethical Analysis.* Washington, DC: Georgetown University Press, 2005.

Gustafson, James M. *Protestant and Roman Catholic Ethics: Prospects for Rapprochement.* Chicago: University of Chicago Press, 1978.

McCann, Dennis, and Patrick D. Miller. *In Search of the Common Good.* New York: T&T Clark, 2005.

National Conference of Catholic Bishops, *Contemporary Catholic Social Teaching.* Washington, DC: United States Catholic Conference, 1991.

Unfinished Journey: The Church Forty Years after Vatican II: Essays for John Wilkins. Edited by Austen Ivereigh. New York: Continuum, 2003.

PART 9

Early- to Mid-Twentieth-Century Voices

THE SOCIAL GOSPEL

30

❧ The social gospel movement is in many respects heir to the ideas of human moral progress found in nineteenth-century liberal theology as represented by Albrecht Ritschl. There are also echoes of the transformational impulses we have seen in Bushnell and Maurice. However, if liberal theology in the late nineteenth century was riding a wave of cultural optimism and belief in human progress, the social gospel movement was responding to conditions that belied that hope. Its context was one of recurrent depressions, social conflict, and problems born of urbanization and the industrial revolution. A fairly complex reaction to the new situation, the social gospel movement had both conservative and radical wings. It opposed the naïve glorification of the profit motive and advocated justice for industrial workers and political reforms designed to ameliorate the unjust conditions that kept people from realizing their true potential. Despite the problems it faced, the movement continued to place hope in the possibility moral progress for the good of society.

Washington Gladden (1836–1918) is often considered the first major voice of this tradition. Walter Rauschenbusch is doubtless its most eloquent and prominent exponent. The viability of the movement with its utopian hopes was ultimately undermined by the Great Depression and the outbreak of World War II. Nonetheless, its concern for social justice as an integral part of the church's witness and its understanding of the Kingdom of God as related to the concerns of human history and society has had a lasting impact on American Protestantism.

Selection 1: Washington Gladden, *Social Redemption*

Washington Gladden, a Congregational minister and prolific author, was one of the early spokespersons of the social gospel movement. Here in our excerpt "Social Redemption" from his book The Church and Modern Life *as in his famed Lyman Beecher Lectures,* Social Salvation, *he exhorts the church to commit to the Christianization of the society toward a realization of the Kingdom of God on earth.*

The New Reformation will be wrought out with weapons that are not carnal. One of the lessons that the church has learned, in the nineteen centuries of its history, is that it must keep itself free from all suspicion of entanglement with physical force.

That statement needs qualification. It is not universally true. The Greek church, as we have seen, is still fatally involved in political complications; the Roman church, while forced to abstain from the use of the temporal power, has maintained its right to use it; and other state churches, as those of England and Germany, retain some hold upon the political arm. But we are speaking of the church in our own country; and of the American church it is true that it has ceased to rely upon the power of the state. The entire divorce which our constitution decrees between the government of the church and the government of the state has become, with us, a settled policy, which we do not wish to disturb. It is doubtful whether intelligent Roman Catholics in the United States would be willing to have this condition changed, and no other Christians would for one moment consent to it.

What the church does in the way of improving social conditions must, therefore, be done by purely moral and spiritual agencies. Society is not to be Christianized by any kind of coercion. The church cannot use force in any way, nor can it enter into any coalition with governments that rest on force. "It is not by might nor by power, but by my Spirit, saith the Lord," that the kingdoms of this world are to become the kingdoms of our Lord and of his Christ. It is as irrational to try to propagate Christianity by coercive measures of any description, as it would be to try to make plants grow by applying to them mechanical pressure.

Nor can the church undertake to dictate or prescribe the forms of industrial society. Its function is not the organization of industry. It would not wisely attempt to decide between different methods of managing business.

It would not, for example, be expedient for the church, at the present time, to take sides in the controversy between collectivism and private enterprise. The Socialists declare that the wage system, based on private capital, tends to injustice and oppression; the advocates of the existing system contend that Socialism would destroy the foundations of thrift and welfare. The church cannot be the umpire in this contest, nor can it take sides with either party. Questions of economic method are beyond its province. Its concern is not with the machinery of society, but with the moral motive power. Or, it might be truer to say that it seeks to invigorate the moral life of men, and trusts that reinforced life to make its own economic forms. Its business is to fill men's minds with the truth as it is in Jesus, and to make them see that that truth applies to every human relation; and it ought to believe that when this truth is thus received and thus applied, it will solve all social problems. When employers and employed are all filled with the spirit of Christ, the wage system will not be a system of exploitation, but a means of social service.

Here is an employer of many hundreds of men, at the head of a very large business, which is rapidly increasing. This is not an imaginary case. This employer is a man of flesh and blood, and he is in the very thick of the competitive mêlée; he is using the machinery of the wage system, but he is governing all his business by the principles of Christianity, and the business is thriving in a marvelous way. This does not mean that the manager is piling up money for himself, for he is not: he is living very frugally, and is adding nothing to his own accumulation; but the business is growing by leaps and bounds. The increasing profits, every year, are distributed in the form of stock among the laborers who do the work, and the customers who purchase the goods. The men who do the work are buying for themselves beautiful homes in the vicinity of the factory; in a few more years they will own a large part of the stock of the concern. This manager is not getting rich; but he has the satisfaction of seeing his business prospering in his hands; he is helping a great many men to find the ways of comfort and independence, and he insists that he has himself found the secret of a happy life. It is evident that if all employers were governed by the same motives, the wage system would be an instrument of philanthropy. Whether this man is a church member or not does not appear, but he is certainly a Christian; he has learned the way of Jesus, and is walking in it. If the church could inspire all its members with this kind of social passion, all social questions would be solved. And this is the church's business—to inspire its members with this kind of social passion. Without this spirit in their hearts, no matter what the social machinery might be, the outcome would be envying and strife and endless unhappiness.

We have had the inside history of some of the many communistic enterprises that have come to grief, and all of them have been wrecked by the selfishness of their members, most of whom were seeking for soft places, and shirking their duties—each trying to get as much as he could out of the commonwealth and to give in return for it as little service as possible. These contrasted cases show that the machinery of the wage system cannot prevent the exercise of brotherliness, and that the machinery of communism will not secure it. No kind of social machinery will produce happiness or welfare when selfish men are running it; and no kind of social machinery will keep brotherly men from behaving brotherly.

We are often told by Socialists that the present régime of individual initiative and private capital tends to make men selfish and unbrotherly, while the tendency of Socialism would be to make men unselfish and fraternal. If the church were sure that this is the truth, she would be inclined to throw her influence on the side of Socialism. But, on the other hand, it is urged that Socialism tends to merge the individual in the mass, to destroy the virtues of self-respect and self-reliance, and to weaken the fibre of manhood. If the church were sure that this is true, she would be constrained to pause before committing herself to the socialistic programme.

She knows, in fact, that there is truth in both these contentions. That the individualistic régime has bred a fearful amount of heartlessness and rapacity is painfully evident; that such socialistic experiments as have been tried have weakened human virtue appears to be true. Under which régime the greater damage would be done is not yet quite clear. Therefore the church cannot commit herself to either of these methods. The best work she can do, at the present time, is to inspire men with a love of justice and a spirit of service. She must rear up a generation of men who hate robbery in all its disguises; who are determined never to prosper at the expense of their neighbors, and who know how to find their highest pleasure in helping their fellow men. If the Christian morality means anything, it means all this. A church which represents Jesus Christ on the earth must set before herself no lower aim than this. And a generation of men whose hearts are on fire with this purpose may be trusted to fill the earth with righteousness and peace, whether they work with the machinery of the wage system or with the machinery of Socialism.

There are many good men, outside the church as well as within it, who believe that the existing social order can never be Christianized; that it must be replaced by a new social system. But most of us are still clinging to the belief that the existing social order can be Christianized, so that justice may be established in it, and good-will find expression through it. That it has been sadly perverted we all confess; we acknowledge with shame that it has become, in large measure, the instrument of injustice and oppression. But we believe that it may be reformed, so that it shall represent, in some fair degree, the kingdom of God.

The redemption of the social order is, then, the problem now before us. Can it be accomplished? President Roosevelt thinks that it can, and those who stand with him and support him assume that the existing competitive régime can be moralized and made to represent the interests of equity and fair dealing. If this can be done, nothing more is needed. If it cannot be done, the existing régime must make way for something better. The conviction that it can be done is finding expression just now in the vigorous efforts that are being made to amend and strengthen the laws which restrain plunderers and oppressors, so that opportunities may be equalized and the paths to success be kept open for men of all ranks and capacities. This is simple justice, and for this the church of God must stand with all the might of her influence.

That she has been derelict in the discharge of this duty must be confessed. If she had kept the charge committed to her, the inequalities and spoliations now burdening society would not be in existence. For although it is not the business of the church to furnish to the world an economic programme, it is her business to see that no economic programme is permitted to exist under which injustice and oppression find shelter. The right to reprove and denounce all social arrangements by which the few prosper at the expense of the many is one of her chartered rights as the institute of prophecy. A church which fails to exercise this function is faithless to her primary obligation.

That the church has incurred heavy blame because of the feebleness of her testimony against such wrongs must now be confessed, and the least she can do to make amends for this infidelity is to speak now and henceforth, with commanding voice, against all the corporate wrongs that infest society. It may be that by her testimony the magistrates will be strengthened so to enforce the laws that aggressors shall be restrained, and freedom and opportunity secured to all; and that thus the existing industrial order may become, so far as law can make it, the servant of justice and good-will.

*   *   *

The more earnestly, therefore, we contend that the business of the church is the Christianization of the social order, the more strenuously we must maintain that she is powerless to do this work except as her life is fed by faith and prayer. The redemption of the social order is the greatest task she has undertaken, and she needs for it a strength that can only come from conscious fellowship with God. If she ever needed inspiration, she needs it now. If there ever was a time when she could dispense with the divine guidance and grace, that time is not now. The churches which desert the places of prayer, and think to substitute the wisdom of men for the power of God, are not going to give much aid in this struggle.

Selection 2: Walter Rauschenbusch, *A Theology for the Social Gospel*

> *Walter Rauschenbusch (1861–1918) was a Baptist clergymen and professor of theology whose name became virtually synonymous with the social gospel movement. For him the "Kingdom of God" and its establishment were central. This selection captures what this meant to him.*

If theology is to offer an adequate doctrinal basis for the social gospel, it must not only make room for the doctrine of the Kingdom of God, but give it a central place and revise all other doctrines so that they will articulate organically with it.

This doctrine is itself the social gospel. Without it, the idea of re deeming the social order will be but an annex to the orthodox conception of the scheme of salvation. It will live like a negro servant family in a detached cabin back of the white man's house in the South. If this doctrine gets the place which has always been its legitimate right, the practical proclamation and application of social morality will have a firm footing.

To those whose minds live in the social gospel, the Kingdom of God is a dear truth, the marrow of the gospel, just as the incarnation was to Athanasius, justification by faith alone to Luther, and the sovereignty of God to Jonathan Edwards. It was just as dear to Jesus. He too lived in it, and from it looked out on the world and the work he had to do.

Jesus always spoke of the Kingdom of God. Only two of his reported sayings contain the word "Church," and both passages are of questionable authenticity. It is safe to say that he never thought of founding the kind of institution which afterward claimed to be acting for him.

Yet immediately after his death, groups of disciples joined and consolidated by inward necessity. Each local group knew that it was part of a divinely founded fellowship mysteriously spreading through humanity, and awaiting the return of the Lord and the establishing of his Kingdom. This universal Church was loved with the same religious faith and reverence with which Jesus had loved the Kingdom of God. It was the partial and earthly realization of he divine Society, and at the Parousia the Church and the Kingdom would merge.

But the Kingdom was merely a hope, the Church a present reality. The chief interest and affection flowed toward the Church. Soon, through a combination of causes, the name and idea of "the Kingdom" began to be displaced by the name and idea of "the Church" in the preaching, literature, and theological thought of the Church. Augustine completed this process in his De Civitate Dei. The Kingdom of God which has, throughout human history, opposed the Kingdom of Sin, is today embodied in the Church. The millennium began when the Church was founded. This practically substituted the actual, not the ideal Church for the Kingdom of God. The beloved ideal of Jesus became a vague phrase which kept intruding from the New Testament. Like Cinderella in the kitchen, it saw the other great dogmas furbished up for the ball, but no prince of theology restored it to its rightful place. The Reformation, too, brought no renascence of the doctrine of the Kingdom; it had only eschatological value, or was defined in blurred phrases borrowed from the Church. The present revival of the Kingdom idea is due to the combined influence of the historical study of the Bible and of the social gospel.

When the doctrine of the Kingdom of God shriveled to an undeveloped and pathetic remnant in Christian thought, this loss was bound to have far-reaching consequences. We are told that the loss of a single tooth from the arch of the mouth in childhood may spoil the symmetrical development of the skull and produce malformations affecting the mind and character. The atrophy of that idea which had occupied the chief place in the mind of Jesus, necessarily affected the conception of Christianity, the life of the Church, the progress of humanity, and the structure of theology. I shall briefly enumerate some of the consequences affecting theology. This list, however, is by no means complete.

1. Theology lost its contact with the synoptic thought of Jesus. Its problems were not at all the same which had occupied his mind. It lost his point of view and became to some extent incapable of understanding him. His ideas had to be rediscovered in our time. Traditional theology and the mind of Jesus Christ became incommensurable quantities. It claimed to regard his revelation and the substance of his thought as divine, and yet did not learn to think like him. The loss of the Kingdom idea is one key to this situation.

2. The distinctive ethical principles of Jesus were the direct outgrowth of his conception of the Kingdom of God. When the latter disappeared from theology, the former disappeared from ethics. Only persons having the substance of the Kingdom ideal in their minds, seem to be able to get relish out of the ethics of Jesus. Only those church bodies which have been in opposition to organized society and have looked for a better city with its foundations in heaven, have taken the Sermon on the Mount seriously.

3. The Church is primarily a fellowship for worship; the Kingdom is a fellowship of righteousness. When the latter was neglected in theology, the ethical force of Christianity was weakened; when the former was emphasized in theology, the importance of worship was exaggerated. The prophets and Jesus had cried down sacrifices and ceremonial performances, and cried up righteousness, mercy, solidarity. Theology now reversed this, and by its theoretical discussions did its best to stimulate sacramental actions and priestly importance. Thus the religious energy and enthusiasm which might have saved mankind from its great sins, were used up in hearing and endowing masses, or in maintaining competitive church organizations, while mankind is still stuck in the mud. There are nations in which the ethical condition of the masses is the reverse of the frequency of the masses in the churches.

4. When the Kingdom ceased to be the dominating religious reality, the Church moved up into the position of the supreme good. To promote the power of the Church and its control over all rival political forces was equivalent to promoting the supreme ends of Christianity. This increased the arrogance of churchmen and took the moral check off their policies. For the Kingdom of God can never be promoted by lies, craft, crime or war, but the wealth and power of the Church have often been promoted by these means. The medieval ideal of the supremacy of the Church over the State was the logical consequence of making the Church the highest good with no superior ethical standard by which to test it. The medieval doctrines concerning the Church and the Papacy were the direct theological outcome of the struggles for Church supremacy, and were meant to be weapons in that struggle.

5. The Kingdom ideal is the test and corrective of the influence of the Church. When the Kingdom ideal disappeared, the conscience of the Church was muffled. It became possible for the missionary expansion of Christianity to halt for centuries without creating any sense of shortcoming. It became possible for the most unjust social conditions to fasten themselves on Christian nations without awakening any consciousness that the purpose of Christ was being defied and beaten back. The practical undertakings of the Church remained within narrow lines, and the theological thought of the Church was necessarily confined in a similar way. The claims of the Church were allowed to stand in theology with no conditions and obligations to test and balance them. If the Kingdom had stood as the purpose for which the Church exists, the Church could not have fallen into such corruption and sloth. Theology bears part of the guilt for the pride, the greed, and the ambition of the Church.

6. The Kingdom ideal contains the revolutionary force of Christianity. When this ideal faded out of the systematic thought of the Church, it became a conservative social influence and increased the weight of the other stationary forces in society. If the Kingdom of God had remained part of the theological and Christian consciousness, the Church could not, down to our times, have been salaried by autocratic class governments to keep the democratic and economic impulses of the people under check.

7. Reversely, the movements for democracy and social justice were left without a religious backing for lack of the Kingdom idea. The Kingdom of God as the fellowship of righteousness, would be advanced by the abolition of industrial slavery and the disappearance of the slums of civilization; the Church would only indirectly gain through such social changes. Even today many Christians cannot see any religious importance in social justice and fraternity because it does not increase the number of conversions nor fill the churches. Thus the practical conception of salvation, which is the effective theology of the common man and minister, has been cut back and crippled for lack of the Kingdom ideal.

8. Secular life is belittled as compared with church life. Services rendered to the Church get a higher religious rating than services rendered to the community.' Thus the religious value is taken out of the activities of the common man and the prophetic services to society. Wherever the Kingdom of God is a living reality in Christian thought, any advance of social righteousness is seen as a part of redemption and arouses inward joy and the triumphant sense of salvation. When the Church absorbs interest, a subtle asceticism creeps back into our theology and the world looks different.

9. When the doctrine of the Kingdom of God is lacking in theology, the salvation of the individual is seen in its relation to the Church and to the future life, but not in its relation to the task of saving the social order. Theology has left this important point in a condition so hazy and muddled that it has taken us almost a generation to see that the salvation of the individual and the redemption of the social order are closely related, and how.

10. Finally, theology has been deprived of the inspiration of great ideas contained in the idea of the Kingdom and in labor for it. The Kingdom of God breeds prophets; the Church breeds priests and theologians. The Church runs to tradition and dogma; the Kingdom of God rejoices in forecasts and boundless horizons. The men who have contributed the most fruitful impulses to Christian thought have been men of prophetic vision, and their theology has proved most effective for future times where it

has been most concerned with past history, with present social problems, and with the future of human society. The Kingdom of God is to theology what outdoor colour and light are to art. It is impossible to estimate what inspirational impulses have been lost to theology and to the Church, because it did not develop the doctrine of the Kingdom of God and see the world and its redemption from that point of view.

These are some of the historical effects which the loss of the doctrine of the Kingdom of God has inflicted on systematic theology. The chief contribution which the social gospel has made and will make to theology is to give new vitality and importance to that doctrine. In doing so it will be a reformatory force of the highest importance in the field of doctrinal theology, for any systematic conception of Christianity must be not only defective but incorrect if the idea of the Kingdom of God does not govern it.

The restoration of the doctrine of the Kingdom has already made progress. Some of the ablest and most voluminous works of the old theology in their thousands of pages gave the Kingdom of God but a scanty mention, usually in connection with eschatology, and saw no connection between it and the Calvinistic doctrines of personal redemption. The newer manuals not only make constant reference to it in connection with various doctrines, but they arrange their entire subject matter so that the Kingdom of God becomes the governing idea.

In the following brief propositions I should like to offer a few suggestions, on behalf of the social gospel, for the theological formulation of the doctrine of the Kingdom. Something like this is needed to give us "a theology for the social gospel."

1. The Kingdom of God is divine in its origin, progress and consummation. It was initiated by Jesus Christ, in whom the prophetic spirit came to its consummation, it is sustained by the Holy Spirit, and it will be brought to its fulfillment by the power of God in his own time. The passive and active resistance of the Kingdom of Evil at every stage of its advance is so great, and the human resources of the Kingdom of God so slender, that no explanation can satisfy a religious mind which does not see the power of God in its movements. The Kingdom of God, therefore, is miraculous all the way, and is the continuous revelation of the power, the righteousness, and the love of God. The establishment of a community of righteousness in mankind is just as much a saving act of God as the salvation of an individual from his natural selfishness and moral inability. The Kingdom of God, therefore, is not merely ethical, but has a rightful place in theology. This doctrine is absolutely necessary to establish that organic union between religion and morality, between theology and ethics, which is one of the characteristics of the Christian religion. When our moral actions are consciously related to the Kingdom of God they gain religious quality. Without this doctrine we shall have expositions of schemes of redemption and we shall have systems of ethics, but we shall not have a true exposition of Christianity. The first step to the reform of the Churches is the restoration of the doctrine of the Kingdom of God.

2. The Kingdom of God contains the teleology of the Christian religion. It translates theology from the static to the dynamic. It sees, not doctrines or rites to be conserved and perpetuated, but resistance to be overcome and great ends to be achieved. Since the Kingdom of God is the supreme purpose of God, we shall understand the Kingdom so far as we understand God, and we shall understand God so far as we understand his Kingdom. As long as organized sin is in the world, the Kingdom of God is characterized by conflict with evil. But if there were no evil, or after evil has been overcome, the Kingdom of God will still be the end to which God is lifting the

race. It is realized not only by redemption, but also by the education of mankind and the revelation of his life within it.

3. Since God is in it, the Kingdom of God is always both present and future. Like God it is in all tenses, eternal in the midst of time. It is the energy of God realizing itself in human life. Its future lies among the mysteries of God. It invites and justifies prophecy, but all prophecy is fallible; it is valuable in so far as it grows out of action for the Kingdom and impels action. No theories about the future of the Kingdom of God are likely to be valuable or true which paralyze or postpone redemptive action on our part. To those who postpone, it is a theory and not a reality. It is for us to see the Kingdom of God as always coming, always pressing in on the present, always big with possibility, and always inviting immediate action. We walk by faith. Every human life is so placed that it can share with God in the creation of the Kingdom, or can resist and retard its progress. The Kingdom is for each of us the supreme task and the supreme gift of God. By accepting it as a task, we experience it as a gift. By labouring for it we enter into the joy and peace of the Kingdom as our divine fatherland and habitation.

4. Even before Christ, men of God saw the Kingdom of God as the great end to which all divine leadings were pointing. Every idealistic interpretation of the world, religious or philosophical, needs some such conception.

Within the Christian religion the idea of the Kingdom gets its distinctive interpretation from Christ. (a) Jesus emancipated the idea of the Kingdom from previous nationalistic limitations and from the debasement of lower religious tendencies, and made it world-wide and spiritual. (b) He made the purpose of salvation essential in it. (c) He imposed his own mind, his personality, his love and holy will on the idea of the Kingdom. (d) He not only foretold it but initiated it by his life and work. As humanity more and more develops a racial consciousness in modern life, idealistic interpretations of the destiny of humanity will become more influential and important. Unless theology has a solidaristic vision higher and fuller than any other, it can not maintain the spiritual leadership of mankind, but will be outdistanced. Its business is to infuse the distinctive qualities of Jesus Christ into its teachings about the Kingdom, and this will be a fresh competitive test of his continued headship of humanity.

5. The Kingdom of God is humanity organized according to the will of God. Interpreting through the consciousness of Jesus we may affirm these convictions about the ethical relations within the Kingdom: (a) Since Christ revealed the divine worth of life and personality, and since his salvation seeks the restoration and fulfillment of even the least, it follows that the Kingdom of God, at every stage of human development, tends toward a social order which will best guarantee to all personalities their freest and highest development. This involves the redemption of social life from the cramping influence of religious bigotry, from the repression of self-assertion in the relation of upper and lower classes, and from all forms of slavery in which human beings are treated as mere means to serve the ends of others. (b) Since love is the supreme law of Christ, the Kingdom of God implies a progressive reign of love in human affairs. We can see its advance wherever the free will of love supersedes the use of force and legal coercion as a regulative of the social order. This involves the redemption of society from political autocracies and economic oligarchies; the substitution of redemptive for vindictive penology; the abolition of constraint through hunger as part of the industrial system; and the abolition

of war as the supreme expression of hate and the completest cessation of freedom. (c) The highest expression of love is the free surrender of what is truly our own, life, property, and rights. A much lower but perhaps more decisive expression of love is the surrender of any opportunity to exploit men. No social group or organization can claim to be clearly within the Kingdom of God which drains others for its own ease, and resists the effort to abate this fundamental evil. This involves the redemption of society from private property in the natural resources of the earth, and from any condition in industry which makes monopoly profits possible. (d) The reign of love tends toward the progressive unity of mankind, but with the maintenance of individual liberty and the opportunity of nations to work out their own national peculiarities and ideals.

6. Since the Kingdom is the supreme end of God, it must be the purpose for which the Church exists. The measure in which it fulfils this purpose is also the measure of its spiritual authority and honour. The institutions of the Church, its activities, its worship, and its theology must in the long run be tested by its effectiveness in creating the Kingdom of God. For the Church to see itself apart from the Kingdom, and to find its aims in itself, is the same sin of selfish detachment as when an individual selfishly separates himself from the common good. The Church has the power to save in so far as the Kingdom of God is present in it. If the Church is not living for the Kingdom, its institutions are part of the "world." In that case it is not the power of redemption but its object. It may even become an anti-Christian power. If any form of church organization which formerly aided the Kingdom now impedes it, the reason for its existence is gone.

7. Since the Kingdom is the supreme end, all problems of personal salvation must be reconsidered from the point of view of the Kingdom. It is not sufficient to set the two aims of Christianity side by side. There must be a synthesis, and theology must explain how the two react on each other. The entire redemptive work of Christ must also be reconsidered under this orientation. Early Greek theology saw salvation chiefly as the redemption from ignorance by the revelation of God and from earthliness by the impartation of immortality. It interpreted the work of Christ accordingly, and laid stress on his incarnation and resurrection. Western theology saw salvation mainly as forgiveness of guilt and freedom from punishment. It interpreted the work of Christ accordingly, and laid stress on the death and atonement. If the Kingdom of God was the guiding idea and chief end of Jesus—as we now know it was—we may be sure that every step in His life, including His death, was related to that aim and its realization, and when the idea of the Kingdom of God takes its due place in theology, the work of Christ will have to be interpreted afresh.

8. The Kingdom of God is not confined within the limits of the Church and its activities. It embraces the whole of human life. It is the Christian transfiguration of the social order. The Church is one social institution alongside of the family, the industrial organization of society, and the State. The Kingdom of God is in all these, and realizes itself through them all. During the Middle Ages all society was ruled and guided by the Church. Few of us would want modern life to return to such a condition. Functions which the Church used to perform, have now far outgrown its capacities. The Church is indispensable to the religious education of humanity and to the conservation of religion, but the greatest future awaits religion in the public life of humanity.

Reinhold Niebuhr 31

❧ *Reinhold Niebuhr (1892–1971) is arguably the most widely influential native-born American theologian of the twentieth century. His unsentimental social analysis in tandem with the insights of his Christian heritage—his "Christian realism"—influenced a generation of socially concerned Americans both inside and outside the churches. Readily associated with the neo-orthodox theologies of his day, Niebuhr believed that the illusions of liberalism regarding human potential for moral progress frustrated any possibility of an effective social ethics. If the reality of sin is ignored, all social teachings are reduced to pious and irrelevant incantations.*

His extensive writings over a long period of time display frequent shifts in his positions but not at the cost of his basic insights. The most complete account of his social ethics is doubtless his two-volume work, The Nature and Destiny of Man. *However, the excerpts that follow from his shorter works convey key ideas of his views in a more compressed form.*

Selection 1: *An Interpretation of Christian Ethics*

The relevance of an impossible ethical ideal shows Niebuhr's basic approach. He stresses the importance of the "law of love as a basis of even the most minimal social standards, yet calls it "an impossible ideal."

Prophetic Christianity faces the difficulty that its penetration into the total and ultimate human situation complicates the problem of dealing with the immediate moral and social situations which all men must face. The common currency of the moral life is constituted of the "nicely calculated less and more" of the relatively good and the relatively evil. Human happiness in ordinary intercourse is determined by the difference between a little more and a little less justice, a little more and little less freedom, between varying degrees of imaginative insight with which the self enters the life and understands the interests of the neighbor. Prophetic Christianity, on the other hand, demands the impossible; and by that very demand emphasizes the impotence and corruption of human nature, wresting from man the cry of distress and contrition, "The good that I would, do I do not: but the evil that I would not, that I do. . . . Woe is me . . . who will deliver me from the body of this death." Measuring the distance between mountain peaks and valleys and arriving at the conclusion that every high mountain has a "timber line" above which life cannot maintain itself, it is always tempted to indifference toward the task of building roads up the mountain-side, and of coercing its wilderness into an sufficient order to sustain human life. The latter task must consequently be assumed by those who are partly blind to the total dimension of life and, being untouched by its majesties and tragedies, can give themselves to the immediate tasks before them.

Thus prophetic religion tends to disintegrate into two contrasting types of religion. The one inclines to deny the relevance of the ideal of love, to the ordinary problems of existence, certain that the tragedy of human life must be resolved by something more than moral achievement. The other tries to prove the relevance of the religious ideal to the problems of everyday existence by reducing it to conformity with the prudential rules of conduct which the common sense of many generations and the experience of the ages have elaborated. Broadly speaking, the conflict between these two worldviews is the conflict between orthodox Christianity and modern secularism. In so far as liberal Christianity is a compound of prophetic religion and secularism it is drawn into the debate in a somewhat equivocal position but, on the whole, on the side of the secularists and naturalists.

Against orthodox Christianity, the prophetic tradition in Christianity must insist on the relevance of the ideal of love to the moral experience of mankind on every conceivable level. It is not an ideal magically superimposed upon life by a revelation which has no relation to total human experience. The whole conception of life revealed in the Cross of Christian faith is not a pure negation of, or irrelevance toward, the moral ideals of "natural man." While the final heights of the love ideal condemn as well as fulfill the moral canons of common sense, the ideal is involved in every moral aspiration and achievement. It is the genius and the task of prophetic religion to insist on the organic relation between historic human existence and that that which is both the ground and the fulfillment of this existence, the transcendent.

Moral life is possible at all only in a meaningful existence. Obligation can be felt only to some system of coherence and some ordering will. Thus moral obligation is always an obligation to promote harmony and to overcome chaos. But every conceivable order in the historical world contains an element of anarchy. Its world rests upon contingency and caprice. The obligation to support and enhance it can therefore only arise and maintain itself upon the basis of a faith that it is the partial fruit of a deeper unity and the promise of a more perfect harmony than is revealed in any immediate situation. If a lesser faith than this prompts moral action, it results in precisely those types of moral fanaticism which impart unqualified worth to qualified values and thereby destroy even their qualified worth. The prophetic faith in a God who is both the ground and the ultimate fulfillment of existence, who is both the creator and the judge of the world, is thus involved in every moral situation. Without it the world is seen either as being meaningless or as revealing unqualifiedly good and simple meanings. In either case the nerve of moral action is ultimately destroyed.

The dominant attitudes of prophetic faith are gratitude and contrition; gratitude for Creation and contrition before Judgment; or, in other words, confidence that life is good in spite of its evil and that it is evil in spite of its good. In such a faith both sentimentality and despair are avoided. The meaningfulness of life does not tempt to premature complacency, and the chaos which always threatens the world of meaning does not destroy the tension of faith and hope in which all moral action is grounded.

The prophetic faith, that the meaningfulness of life and existence implies a source and end beyond itself, produces a morality which implies that every moral value and standard is grounded in and points toward an ultimate perfection of unity and harmony, not realizable in any historic situation. An analysis of the social history of mankind validates this interpretation.

In spite of the relativity of morals every conceivable moral code and every philosophy of morals enjoins concern for the life and welfare of the other and seeks to restrain the unqualified assertion of the interests of the self against the other. There is thus a fairly universal agreement in all moral systems that it is wrong to take the life or the property of the neighbor, though it must be admitted that the specific applications of these general principles vary greatly according to time and place. This minimal standard of moral conduct is grounded in the law of love and points toward it as ultimate fulfillment. The obligation to affirm and protect the life of others can arise at all only if it is assumed that life is related to life in some unity and harmony of existence. In any given instance motives of the most calculating prudence rather than a high sense of obligation may enforce the standard. Men may defend the life of the neighbor merely to preserve those processes of mutuality by which their own life is protected. But that only means that they have discovered the inter-relatedness of life through concern for themselves rather than by an analysis of the total situation. This purely prudential approach will not prompt the most consistent social conduct, but it will nevertheless implicitly affirm what it ostensibly denies—that the law of life is love.

Perhaps the clearest proof, that the law of love is involved as a basis of even the most minimal social standards, is found in the fact that every elaboration of minimal standards into higher standards makes the implicit relation more explicit. Prohibitions of murder and theft are negative. They seek to prevent one life from destroying or taking advantage of another. No society is content with these merely negative prohibitions. Its legal codes do not go much beyond negatives because only minimal standards can be legally enforced. But the moral codes and ideals of every advanced society demand more than mere prohibition of theft and murder. Higher conceptions of justice are developed. It is recognized that the right to live implies the right to secure the goods which sustain life. This right immediately involves more than mere prohibition of theft. Some obligation is felt, however dimly, to organize the common life so that the neighbor will have fair opportunities to maintain his life. The various schemes of justice and equity which grow out of this obligation, consciously or unconsciously imply an ideal of equality beyond themselves. Equality is always the regulative principle of justice; and in the ideal of equality there is an echo of the law of love, "Thou shalt love they neighbor AS THYSELF." If the question is raised to what degree the neighbor has a right to support his life through the privileges and opportunities of the common life, no satisfactory, rational answer can be given to it, short of one implying equalitarian principles: He has just as much right as you yourself.

This does not mean that any society will ever achieve perfect equality. Equality, being a rational, political version of the law of love, shares with it the quality of transcendence. It ought to be, but it never will be fully realized. Social prudence will qualify it. The most equalitarian society will probably not be able to dispense with special rewards as inducements to diligence. Some differentials in privilege will be necessary to make the performance of certain social functions possible. While a rigorous equalitarian society can prevent such privileges from being perpetuated from one generation to another without regard to social function, it cannot eliminate privileges completely. Nor is there any political technique which would be a perfect guarantee against abuses of socially sanctioned privileges. Significant social functions are endowed by their very nature with a certain degree of social power. Those who possess power, however socially restrained, always have the opportunity of deciding that the function which they perform is entitled to more privilege than any ideal scheme of justice would allow. The ideal of equality is thus qualified in any possible society by the necessities of social cohesion and corrupted by the sinfulness of men. It remains, nevertheless, a principle of criticism under which every scheme of justice stands and a symbol of the principle of love involved in all moral judgments.

But the principle of equality does not exhaust the possibilities of the moral ideal involved in even the most minimal standards of justice. Imaginative justice leads beyond equality to a consideration of the special needs of the life of the other. A sensitive parent will not make capricious distinctions in the care given to different children. But the kind of imagination which governs the most ideal family relationships soon transcends this principle of equality and justifies special care for a handicapped child and, possibly, special advantages for a particularly gifted one. The "right" to have others consider one's unique needs and potentialities is recognized legally only in the most minimal terms and is morally recognized only in very highly developed communities. Yet the modern public school, which began with the purpose of providing equal educational opportunities for all children, has extended its services so that both handicapped and highly gifted children receive special privileges from it. Every one of these achievements in the realm of justice is logically related, on the one hand, to the most minimal standards of justice, and on the other to the ideal of perfect love—i.e., to the obligation of affirming the life and interests of the neighbor as much as those of the self. The basic rights to life and property in the early community, the legal minima of rights and obligations of more advanced communities, the moral rights and obligations recognized in these communities beyond those which are legally enforced, the further refinement of standards in the family beyond those recognized in the general community—all these stand in an ascending scale of moral possibilities in which each succeeding step is a closer approximation of the law of love.

The history of corrective justice reveals the same ascending scale of possibilities as that of distributive justice. Society begins by regulating vengeance and soon advances to the stage of substituting public justice for private vengeance. Public justice recognizes the right of an accused person to a more disinterested judgment than that of the injured accuser. Thus the element of vengeance is reduced, but not eliminated, in modern standards of punitive justice. The same logic which forced its reduction presses on toward its elimination. The criminal is recognized to have rights as a human being, even when he has violated his obligations to society. Therefore modern criminology, using psychiatric techniques, seeks to discover the cause of antisocial conduct in order that it may be corrected. The reformatory purpose attempts to displace the purely punitive intent. This development follows a logic which must culminate in the command, "Love your enemies." The more imaginative ideals of the best criminologists are, of course, in the realm of unrealized hopes. They will never be fully realized. An element of vindictive passion will probably corrupt the corrective justice of even the best society. The collective behavior of mankind is not imaginative enough to assure more than minimal approximations of the ideal. Genuine forgiveness of the enemy requires a contrite recognition of the sinfulness of the self and of the mutual responsibility for the sin of the accused. Such spiritual penetration is beyond the capacities of collective man. It is the achievement of only rare individuals. Yet the right to such understanding is involved in the most basic of human rights and follows logically if the basic right to life is rationally elaborated. Thus all standards of corrective justice are organically related to primitive vengeance on the one hand, and the ideal of forgiving love on the other. No absolute limit can be placed upon the degree to which human society may yet approximate the ideal. But it is certain that every achievement will remain in the realm of approximation. The ideal in its perfect form lies beyond the capacities of human nature.

Moral and social ideals are always a part of a series of infinite possibilities not only in terms of their purity, but in terms of their breadth of application. The most tender and imaginative human attitudes are achieved only where consanguinity and contiguity support the unity of life with life, and nature aids spirit in creating harmony. Both law and morality recognize rights and obligations within the family which are not recognized in the community, and within the community which are not accepted beyond the community. Parents are held legally responsible for the neglect of their children but not for the neglect of other people's children. Modern nations assume qualified responsibilities for the support of their unemployed, but not for the unemployed of other nations. Such a sense of responsibility may be too weak to function adequately without the support of political motives, as, for instance, the fear that hungry men may disturb the social peace. But weak as it is, it is yet strong enough to suggest responsibilities beyond itself. No modern people is completely indifferent toward the responsibility for all human life. In terms of such breadth the obligation is too weak to become the basis for action, except on rare occasions. The need of men in other nations must be vividly portrayed and dramatized by some great catastrophe before generosity across national boundaries expresses itself. But it can express itself, even in those rare moments, only because all human life is informed with an inchoate sense of responsibility toward the ultimate law of life—the law of love. The community of mankind has no organs of social cohesion and no instruments for enforcing social standards (and it may never have more than embryonic ones); yet that community exists in a vague sense of responsibility toward all men which underlies *all* moral responsibilities in limited communities.

As has been observed in analyzing the ethic of Jesus, the universalism of prophetic ethics goes beyond the demands of rational universalism. In rational universalism obligation is felt to all life because human life is conceived as the basic value of ethics. Since so much of human life represents only potential value, rational universalism tends to qualify its position. Thus in Aristotelian ethics the slave does not have the same rights as the freeman because his life is regarded as of potentially less value. Even in Stoicism, which begins by asserting the common divinity of all men by reason of their common rationality, the obvious differences in the intelligence of men prompts Stoic doctrine to a certain aristocratic condescension toward the "fools." In prophetic religion the obligation is toward the loving will of God; in other words, toward a more transcendent source of unity than any discoverable in the natural world, where men are always divided by various forces of nature and history. Christian universalism, therefore, represents a more impossible possibility than the universalism of Stoicism. Yet it is able to prompt higher actualities of love, being less dependent upon obvious symbols of human unity and brotherhood. In prophetic ethics the transcendent unity of life is an article of faith. Moral obligation is to this divine unity; and therefore it is more able to defy the anarchies of the world. But this difference between prophetic and rational universalism must not obscure a genuine affinity. In both cases the moral experience on any level of life points toward an unrealizable breadth of obligation of life to life.

If further proof were needed of the relevance of the love commandment to the problems of ordinary morality it could be found by a negative argument: Natural human egoism, which is sin only from the perspective of the law of love, actually results in social consequences which prove this religious perspective to be right. This point must be raised not against Christian orthodoxy, which has never denied this negative relevance of the law of love to all human situations but against a naturalism which regards the law of love as an expression of a morbid perfectionism, and declares "we will not aim so high or fall so low." According to the thesis of modern naturalism, only excessive egoism can be called wrong. The natural self-regarding impulses of human nature are accepted as the data of ethics; and the effort is made to construct them into forces of social harmony and cohesion. Prophetic Christianity, unlike modern liberalism, knows that the force of egoism cannot be broken by moral suasion and that on certain levels qualified harmonies must be achieved by building conflicting egoisms into a balance of power. But, unlike modern naturalism, it is unable to adopt a complacent attitude toward the force of egoism. It knows that it is sin, however natural and inevitable it may be, and its sinfulness is proved by the social consequences. It is natural enough to love one's own family more than other families and no amount of education will ever eliminate the inverse ratio between the potency of love and the breadth and extension in which it is applied. But the inevitability of narrow loyalties and circumscribed sympathy does not destroy the moral and social peril which they create. A narrow family loyalty is a more potent source of injustice than pure individual egoism, which, incidentally, probably never exists. The special loyalty which men give their limited community is natural enough; but it is also the root of international anarchy. Moral idealism in terms of the presuppositions of a particular class is also natural and inevitable; but it is the basis of tyranny and hypocrisy. Nothing is more natural and, in a sense, virtuous, than the desire of parents to protect the future of their children by bequeathing the fruits of their own toil and fortune to them. Yet this desire results in laws of testation by which social privilege is divorced from social function. The social injustice and conflicts of human history spring neither from a pure egoism nor from the type of egoism which could be neatly measured as excessive or extravagant by some rule of reason. They spring from those virtuous attitudes of natural man in which natural sympathy is inevitably compounded with natural egoism. Not only excessive jealousy, but the ordinary jealousy, from which no soul is free, destroys the harmony of life with life. Not only excessive vengeance, but the subtle vindictiveness which insinuates itself into the life of even the most imaginative souls, destroys justice. Wars are the consequence of the moral attitudes not only of unrighteous but of righteous nations (righteous in the sense that they defend their interests no more than is permitted by all the moral codes of history). The judgment that "whosoever seeketh to gain his life will lose it" remains true and relevant to every moral situation even if it is apparent that no human being exists who does not in some sense lose his life by seeking to gain it.

A naturalistic ethics, incapable of comprehending the true dialectic of the spiritual life, either regards the love commandment as possible of fulfillment and thus slips into utopianism, or it is forced to relegate it to the category of an either harmless

or harmful irrelevance. A certain type of Christian liberalism interprets the absolutism of the ethics of the sermon on the mount as Oriental hyperbole, as a harmless extravagance, possessing a certain value in terms of pedagogical emphasis. A
purely secular naturalism, on the other hand, considers the absolutism as a harmful
extravagance. Thus Sigmund Freud writes: "The cultural super-ego . . . does not
trouble enough about the mental constitution of human beings; it enjoins a command
and never asks whether it is possible for them to obey it. It presumes, on the contrary,
that a man's ego is psychologically capable of anything that is required of it, that it
has unlimited power over the id. This is an error; even in normal people the power of
controlling the id cannot be increased beyond certain limits. If one asks more of them
one produces revolt or neurosis in individuals and makes them unhappy.

The command to love the neighbor as ourselves is the strongest defense there is
against human aggressiveness and it is a superlative example of the unpsychological
attitude of the cultural super-ego. The command is impossible to fulfill; such an enormous inflation of the ego can only lower its value and not remedy its evil. This is a
perfectly valid protest against a too moralistic and optimistic love perfectionism. But
it fails to meet the insights of a religion which knows that the law of love is an impossible possibility and knows how to confess, "There is a law in my members which wars
against the law that is in my mind." Freud's admission that the love commandment is
"the strongest defense against human aggressiveness" is, incidentally, the revelation
of a certain equivocation in his thought. The impossible command is admitted to be
a necessity, even though a dangerous one. It would be regarded as less dangerous by
Freud if he knew enough about the true genius of prophetic religion to realize that
it has resources for relaxing moral tension as well as for creating it. If the relevance
of the love commandment must be asserted against both Christian orthodoxy and
against certain types of naturalism, the impossibility of the ideal must be insisted
upon against all those forms of naturalism, liberalism, and radicalism which generate
utopian illusions and regard the love commandment as ultimately realizable because
history knows no limits of its progressive approximations.

Selection 2: *Justice and Love*

> *Niebuhr distinguished but did not separate justice and love. This was an impor-
> tant step away from the sort of dualism that made love simply a matter of Chris-
> tian personal behavior while justice held sway in worldly matters. This kind of
> dichotomous thinking led to a quietistic attitude in the church's relation to the
> world. Love cannot avoid the concerns of justice. At the same time this little essay
> shows Niebuhr's realism in the face of tragic choices that the quest for justice may
> entail and thereby makes clear his sharp difference from the Social Gospel move-
> ment that preceded him.*

"A Christian," declared an eager young participant in a symposium on Christianity
and politics, "always considers the common welfare before his own interest." This
simple statement reveals a few of the weaknesses of moralistic Christianity in dealing
with problems of justice. The statement contains at least two errors, or perhaps one
error and one omission.

The first error consists in defining a Christian in terms which assume that consistent selflessness is possible. No Christian, even the most perfect, is able "always" to consider the common interest before his own. At least he is not able to do it without looking at the common interest with eyes colored by his own ambitions. If complete selflessness were a simple possibility, political justice could be quickly transmuted into perfect love; and all the frictions, tensions, partial cooperations, and overt and covert conflicts could be eliminated. If complete selflessness without an admixture of egoism were possible, many now irrelevant sermons and church resolutions would become relevant. Unfortunately there is no such possibility for individual men; and perfect disinterestedness for groups and nations is even more impossible.

The other error is one of omission. To set self-interest and the general welfare in simple opposition is to ignore nine tenths of the ethical issues that confront the consciences of men. For these are concerned not so much with the problem of the self against the whole as with problems of the self in its relation to various types of "general welfare." "What do you mean by common interest?" retorted a shrewd businessman in the symposium referred to. Does it mean the family or the nation? If I have to choose between "my family" and "my nation," is the Christian choice inevitably weighted in favor of the nation since it is the larger community? And if the choice is between "my" nation and another nation, must the preference always be for the other nation on the ground that concern for my own nation represents collective self-interest? Was the young pacifist idealist right who insisted that if we had less "selfish concern for our own civilization" we could resolve the tension between ourselves and Russia, presumably by giving moral preference to a communist civilization over our own?

Such questions as these reveal why Christian moralism has made such meager contributions to the issues of justice in modern society. Justice requires discriminate judgments between conflicting claims. A Christian justice will be particularly critical of the claims of the self as against the claims of the other, but it will not dismiss them out of hand. Without this criticism all justice becomes corrupted into a refined form of self-seeking. But if the claims of the self (whether individual or collective) are not entertained, there is no justice at all. There is an ecstatic form of agape which defines the ultimate heroic possibilities of human existence (involving, of course, martyrdom) but not the common possibilities of tolerable harmony of life with life.

In so far as justice admits the claims of the self, it is something less than love. Yet it cannot exist without love and remain justice. For without the "grace "of love, justice always degenerates into something less than justice.

But if justice requires that the interests of the self be entertained, it also requires that they be resisted. Every realistic system of justice must assume the continued power of self-interest, particularly of collective self-interest. It must furthermore assume that this power will express itself illegitimately as well as legitimately. It must therefore be prepared to resist illegitimate self-interest, even among the best men and the most just nations. A simple Christian moralism counsels men to be unselfish. A profounder Christian faith must encourage men to create systems of justice which will save society and themselves from their own selfishness.

But justice arbitrates not merely between the self and the other, but between the competing claims upon the self by various "others." Justice seeks to determine what I owe my family as compared with my nation; or what I owe this segment as against that segment of a community. One of the strange moral anomalies of our times is that there are businessmen and men of affairs who have a more precise sense of justice in feeling their way through the endless relativities of human relations than professional teachers of morals. Practical experience has made them sensitive to the complex web of values and interests in which human decisions are reached, while the professional teachers of religion and morals deal with simple counters

of black and white. This certainly is one of the reasons why the pulpit frequently seems so boring and irrelevant to the pew. At his worst the practical man of affairs is morally heedless and considers only his own interest, mistaking collective self-interest for selfless virtue. At his best he has been schooled in justice, while his teacher confuses the issue by moral distinctions which do not fit the complexities of life.

The realm of justice is also a realm of tragic choices, which are seldom envisaged in a type of idealism in which all choices are regarded as simple. Sometimes we must prefer a larger good to a smaller one, without the hope that the smaller one will be preserved in the larger one. Sometimes we must risk a terrible evil (such as an atomic war) in the hope of avoiding an imminent peril (such as subjugation to tyranny) . Subsequent events may prove the risk to have been futile and the choice to have been wrong. If there is enough of a world left after such a wrong choice we will be taxed by the idealists for having made the wrong choice; and they will not know that they escaped an intolerable evil by our choice. Even now we are taxed with the decision to resist naziism, on the ground that the war against naziism has left us in a sad plight. The present peril of communism seems to justify an earlier capitulation to naziism. But since we are men and not God, we could neither anticipate all the evils that would flow from our decision to resist naziism, nor yet could we have capitulated to the immediate evil because another evil was foreshadowed.

The tragic character of our moral choices, the contradiction between various equal values of our devotion, and the incompleteness in all our moral striving, prove that " if in this life only we had hoped in Christ, we are of all men most miserable." No possible historic justice is sufferable without the Christian hope. But any illusion of a world of perfect love without these imperfect harmonies of justice must ultimately turn the dream of love into a nightmare of tyranny and injustice.

Selection 3: *Christian Faith and Natural Law*

As we have seen from previous selections of Roman Catholic social teaching in particular, natural law has been a primary resource. It has also enjoyed prominence in some Protestant thought as well. Here Niebuhr gives his version of this concept as over against classical Roman Catholic and Protestant views.

In his challenging article entitled "Theology Today," the Archbishop of York presents several questions which in his opinion require a fresh answer in the light of contemporary history. One of these questions is: "Is there a natural order which is from God, as Catholic tradition holds, or is there only natural disorder, the fruit of sin, from which Christ delivers us, as Continental Protestantism has held?" I should like to address myself to this question and suggest that the facts of human history are more complex than either the traditional Catholic or Protestant doctrines of natural order and natural law suggest.

According to Thomistic doctrine, the Fall robbed man of a *donum superadditum* but left him with a *pura naturalia*, which includes a capacity for natural justice. What is lost is a capacity for faith, hope, and love—that is, the ability to rise above the natural order and have communion with divine and supernatural order, to know God and, in fellowship with him, to be delivered of the fears, anxieties, and sins which result from this separation from God. The fallen man is thus essentially an incomplete man, who is completed by the infusion of sacramental grace, which restores practically, though not quite, all of the supernatural virtues which were lost in the Fall. The Fall does not seriously impair man's capacity for natural justice. Only this is an incomplete perfection, incapable of itself to rise to the heights of love.

According to Protestant theology, the Fall had much more serious consequences. It left man "totally corrupt" and "utterly leprous and unclean." The very reason which in Catholic thought is regarded as the instrument and basis of natural justice is believed in Protestant thought to be infected by the Fall and incapable of arriving at any true definition of justice. Calvin is slightly more equivocal about the effects of sin upon reason than Luther, and as a consequence Calvinism does not relegate the natural law and the whole problem of justice so completely to the background as does Lutheranism. Nevertheless, the theory of total depravity is only slightly qualified in Calvinism.

I should like to maintain that the real crux of the human situation is missed in both the Catholic and the Protestant version of the effect of sin upon man's capacity for justice. Something more than a brief paper would be required to prove such a thesis; I must content myself therefore with suggesting the argument in general outline.

The Biblical conception of man includes three primary terms: (a) he is made in the image of God, (b) he is a creature, and (c) he is a sinner. His basic sin is pride. If this pride is closely analyzed, it is discovered to be man's unwillingness to acknowledge his creatureliness. He is betrayed by his greatness to hide his weakness. He is tempted by his ability to gain his own security to deny his insecurity, and refuses to admit that he has no final security except in God. He is tempted by his knowledge to deny his ignorance. (This is the source of all "ideological taint" in human knowledge.) It is not that man in his weakness has finite perspectives that makes conflicts between varying perspectives so filled with fanatic fury in all human history; it is that man denies the finiteness of his perspectives that tempts him to such fanatic cruelty against those who hold convictions other than his own. The quintessence of sin is, in short, that man "changes the glory of the incorruptible God into the image of corruptible man." He always usurps God's place and claims to be the final judge of human actions.

The loss of man's original perfection therefore never leaves him with an untarnished though incomplete natural justice. All statements and definitions of justice are corrupted by even the most rational men through the fact that the definition is colored by interest. This is the truth in the Marxist theory of rationalization and in its assertion that all culture is corrupted by an ideological taint. The unfortunate fact about the Marxist theory is that it is used primarily as a weapon in social conflict. The enemy is charged with this dishonesty, but the Marxist himself claims to be free of it. This is, of course, merely to commit the final sin of self-righteousness and to imagine ourselves free of the sin which we discern in the enemy. The fact that we do not discern it in ourselves is a proof of our sin and not of our freedom from sin. Christ's parable of the mote and the beam is a perfect refutation of this illusion.

The fact remains, nevertheless, that reason is not capable of defining any standard of justice that is universally valid or acceptable. Thus Thomistic definitions of justice are filled with specific details which are drawn from the given realities of a feudal social order and may be regarded as "rationalizations" of a feudal aristocracy's dominant position in society. (The much-praised Catholic prohibition of usury could be maintained only as long as the dominant aristocratic class were borrowers rather than lenders of money. When the static wealth of the landowners yielded to the more dynamic wealth of the financiers and industrialists, the prohibition of usury vanished. Catholics hold Protestantism responsible for this development, but it is significant that the Catholic Church makes no effort to impose the prohibition of usury upon its own bourgeois members.)

Bourgeois idealists of the eighteenth century invented new natural law theories and invested them with bourgeois rather than feudal-aristocratic content. The natural law of the eighteenth century was supposed to be descriptive rather than prescriptive. It was, more exactly, a "law of nature" rather than a "law of reason." But its real significance lay in its specific content. The content of this law justified the bourgeois classes in their ideals, just as the older law justified the feudal aristocrats. In short, it is not possible to state a universally valid concept of justice from any particular sociological locus in history. Nor is it possible to avoid either making the effort or making pretenses of universality which human finiteness does not justify. This inevitable pretense is the revelation of "original sin" in history. Human history is consequently more tragic than Catholic theology assumes. It is not an incomplete world yearning for completion, and finding it in the incarnation. It is a tragic world, troubled not by finiteness so much as by "false eternals" and false absolutes, and expressing the pride of these false absolutes even in the highest reaches of its spirituality. It is not the incarnation as such that is the good news of the gospel, but rather the revelation of a just God who is also merciful; this is the true content of the incarnation. That is, it is the atonement that fills the incarnation with meaning.

But Catholic thought not only fails to do justice to the positive character of the sinful element in all human definitions and realizations of natural justice. It also fails to do justice to the relation of love to justice. In its conception, natural justice is good as far as it goes, but it must be completed by the supernatural virtue of love. The true situation is that anything short of love cannot be perfect justice. In fact, every definition of justice actually presupposes sin as a given reality. It is only because life is in conflict with life, because of sinful self-interest, that we are required carefully to define schemes of justice which prevent one life from taking advantage of another. Yet no scheme of justice can do full justice to all the variable factors which the freedom of man introduces into human history. Significantly, both eighteenth-century and medieval conceptions of natural law are ultimately derived from Stoic conceptions. And it is the very nature of Stoic philosophy that it is confused about the relation of nature to reason. This confusion is due to the fact that it does not fully understand the freedom of man. In all Greco-Roman rationalism, whether Platonic, Aristotelian, or Stoic, it is assumed that man's freedom is secured by his rational transcendence over nature. Since reason and freedom are identified, it is assumed that the freedom that man has over nature is held in check and disciplined by his reason. The real situation is that man transcends his own reason, which is to say that he is not bound in his 'actions by reason's coherences and systems. His freedom consists in a capacity for self-transcendence in infinite regression. There is therefore no limit in reason for either his creativity or his sin. There is no possibility of giving a rational definition of a just relation between man and man or nation and nation short of a complete love in which each life affirms the interests of the other. Every effort to give a definition of justice short of this perfect love invariably introduces contingent factors, conditions of time and place, into the definition. Love is the only final structure of freedom. Human personality as a system of infinite potentialities makes it impossible to define absolutely what I owe to my fellow man, since nothing that he now is exhausts what he might be. Human personality as capacity for infinite self-transcendence makes it impossible from my own standpoint to rest content in any ordered relation with my fellow men. There is no such relation that I cannot transcend to imagine a better one in terms of the ideal of love. Provisional definitions of justice short of this perfect love are, of course, necessary. But they are much more provisional than any natural law theory, whether medieval or modern, realizes. The freedom of man is too great to make it possible to define any scheme of justice absolutely in terms of "necessary" standards.

According to Catholic theology, it is this structure of ultimate freedom that is lost in the Fall just as the accompanying virtue of love is lost. The real situation is that "original justice" in the sense of a mythical "perfection before the Fall "is never completely lost. It is not a reality in man but always a potentiality. It is always what he ought to be. It is the only goodness completely compatible with his own and his fellow man's freedom—that is, with their ultimate transcendence over all circumstances of nature. Man is neither as completely bereft of "original justice" nor as completely in possession of "natural justice" as the Catholic theory assumes.

Protestant theory, on the other hand, partly because of Luther's nominalistic errors, has no sense of an abiding structure at all. Luther's theory of total depravity is, in fact, more intimately related to his nominalism than is generally realized. Only in nominalistic terms, in which love is regarded as good by the fiat of God and not because it is actually the structure of freedom, can it be supposed that life could be completely at variance with itself. "Sin," said Saint Augustine quite truly, "cannot tear up nature by the roots." Injustice has meaning only against a background of a sense of justice. What is more, it cannot maintain itself without at least a minimal content of justice. The "ideological taint" in all human truth could have no meaning except against the background of a truth that is not so tainted. Men always jump to the erroneous conclusion that because they can conceive of a truth and a justice that completely transcend their interests, they are therefore also able to realize such truth and such justice. Against this error of the optimists, Protestant pessimism affirms the equally absurd proposition that sin has completely destroyed all truth and justice.

Protestantism has been betrayed into this error partly by its literalism, by which it defines the Fall as a historic event and "perfection before the Fall" as a perfection existing in a historical epoch before the Fall. When Luther essays to define this perfection he indulges in all kinds of fantastic nonsense. The perfection before the Fall is always an ideal possibility before the act. It describes a dimension of human existence rather than a period of history. It is the vision of health whicl even a sick man has. It is the structure of the good without which there could be no evil. The anarchy of Europe is evil only because it operates against an ideal possibility and necessity of order in Europe. The blindness of the eye is evil only because the ideal possibility is sight.

Protestant pessimism has been rightfully accused by Catholic thinkers of leading to obscurantism in culture and to antinomianism in morals; and it would be difficult to estimate to what degree our present anarchy is due to Protestant errors. But Catholics forget that Protestant pessimism is but a corrupted form of a prophetic criticism which Christianity must make even against its own culture, and that the medieval culture was subject to such .a criticism by reason of its inability to recognize to what degree Christianity as a culture and as an institution is involved not only in the finiteness of history but in the sin of history that is, precisely in the effort to hide finiteness and to pretend a transcendent perfection which, cannot be achieved in history.

It may be useful to apply to contemporary history the theory that all human life stands under an ideal possibility purer than the natural law, and that at the same time it is involved in sinful reality much more dubious than the natural justice that Catholic thought declares to be possible. I will choose one specific example, prompted by the Archbishop of York's splendid wireless address in October last in favor of negotiated "rather than an "imposed" peace. The peace of Versailles was an imposed peace. Its territorial provisions were really more just than is sometimes supposed at the present moment. But among its provisions it contained the forced admission of guilt by the vanquished, a piece of psychological cruelty which reveals self-righteousness at its worst. (It is interesting how our worst sins are always derived from self-righteousness, which is what gives Christ's contest with the Pharisees such relevance.) Against such a peace his Grace, and with him many others, are now pleading for a negotiated peace. They rightly believe that only in such a peace can Europe find security.

Yet it must be recognized that there is no definition of natural justice that can give us a really adequate outline of a just peace. Justice cannot be established in the world by pure moral suasion. It is achieved only as some kind of decent equilibrium of power is established. And such an equilibrium is subject to a thousand contingencies of geography and history. We cannot make peace with Hitler now because his power dominates the Continent, and his idea of a just peace is one that leaves him in the security of that dominance. We believe, I think rightly, that a more just peace can be established if that dominance is broken. But in so far as the Hitlerian imperial will must be broken first, the new peace will be an imposed peace. We may hope that a chastened Germany will accept it and make it its own. But even if vindictive passions are checked, as they were not in 1918, the fact that Germany will be defeated will rob her of some ideal possibilities in Europe, which she might have had but for her defeat in the war.

Nor is it possible for us to be sure that our conception of peace in Europe, in even our most impartial moments, could do full justice to certain aspects of the European situation that might be seen from the German but not from our perspective. On the other hand, we must assume that even the most chastened Germany would not be willing, except as she is forced, to accept certain provisions for the freedom of Poland and Czechoslovakia and the freedom of small nations generally. The inclination of the strong to make themselves the sponsors of the weak, and to claim that they are doing this not for their own but for the general good, is not a German vice. The Germans have merely accentuated a common vice of history and one that influences every concrete realization of justice. The concretion of justice in specific historic instances always depends upon a certain equilibrium of forces, which prevents the organizing will of the strong from degenerating into tyranny. Without resistance even the best ruler, oligarchy, or hegemonous nation would be tempted to allow its creative function of organization to degenerate into tyranny. Furthermore, even the most resolute moral resistance against vindictive passion cannot prevent retributive justice from degenerating into vindictiveness, if the foe is so thoroughly defeated as to invite the type of egotism which expresses itself in vindictiveness. It is significant, moreover, that no "rational" standard of retributive justice can be defined. What is worked out in each particular instance is always some *ad hoc* compromise between vindictiveness on the one hand and forgiveness on the other. This is particularly true of international disputes in which there are no genuinely impartial courts of adjudication. (Neutral nations are interested in the particular balance of power that emerges out of each conflict.) The structure of justice that emerges from each overt conflict must therefore be established to a very considerable degree by the disputants in the conflict, more particularly by the victors.

Yet men are not completely blinded by self-interest or lost in this maze of historical relativity. What always remains with them is not some uncorrupted bit of reason, which gives them universally valid standards of justice. What remains with them is something higher—namely, the law of love, which they dimly recognize as the law of their being, as the structure of human freedom, and which, in Christian faith, Christ clarifies and redefines, which is why he is called the "second Adam." It is the weakness of Protestant pessimism that it denies the reality of this potential perfection and its relevance in the affairs of politics.

The effort of the Christian church in Britain at the present moment to stem the tide of vindictiveness, which it rightly anticipates as an inevitable danger after the war, is a truer expression of the Christian spirit than pacifist disavowals of war as such. It is not possible to disavow war absolutely without disavowing the task of establishing justice. For justice rests upon a decent equilibrium of power; and all balances of power involve tension; and tension involves covert conflict; and there will be moments in history when covert conflict becomes overt. But it is possible to transcend a conflict while standing in it. Forgiveness is such a possibility. But forgiveness to the foe is possible only if I know myself to be a sinner—that is, if I do not have some cheap or easy sense of moral transcendence over the sinful reality of claims-and counterclaims which is the very stuff of history.

This does not mean that it would ever' be possible to establish 'a justice based upon perfect forgiveness after a war. The sinfulness of human nature will relativize every ideal possibility. Vindictiveness (which is an egoistic corruption of justice) cannot be completely eliminated. But the quality of justice that can be achieved in a war will depend upon the degree to which a "Kingdom of God" perspective can be brought upon the situation. It is this higher imagination rather than some unspoiled rational definition of retributive justice that pulls justice out of the realm of vindictiveness.

Human nature is, in short, a realm of infinite possibilities of good and evil because of the character of human freedom. The love that is the law of its nature is a boundless self-giving. The sin that corrupts its life is a boundless assertion of the self. Between these two forces all kinds of ad hoc restraints may be elaborated and defined. We may call this natural law. But we had better realize how very tentative it is. Otherwise we shall merely sanction some traditional relation between myself and my fellow man as a "just" relation, and quiet the voice of conscience which speaks to me of higher possibilities. What is more, we may stabilize sin and make it institutional; for it will be discovered invariably that my definition of justice guarantees certain advantages to myself to which I have no absolute right, but with which I have been invested by the accidents of history and the contingencies of nature and which the "old Adam" in me is only too happy to transmute into absolute rights.

PAUL TILLICH 32

❧ *Born in Germany in 1886, Paul Tillich had made a name for himself as a leading philosopher and theologian in that country as well as an active voice for religious socialism. When he came to the United States and Union Theological Seminary in New York in 1933 as a result of the Nazi rise to power, his thought underwent change in the face of a new social political context. However, the basic themes of his thought and his methodology remained consistent with his earliest work.*

Our selection from his mature work in Systematic Theology *introduces us to some of the social ethical ramifications of Tillich's work with the biblical and theological theme of the Kingdom of God, which has become such a potent and formative concept in contemporary Christian social teaching. For Tillich the churches are agents of the Kingdom of God in history as they seek to balance the horizontal line of social transformation with vertical line of salvation in a manner appropriate to the ambiguities of historical existence.*

Selection 1: "The Kingdom of God in History," *Systematic Theology, Volume Three*

The Kingdom of God and the Ambiguities of Historical Self-Integration

We have described the ambiguities of history as consequences of the ambiguities of life processes in general. The self-integration of life under the dimension of history shows the ambiguities implied in the drive toward centeredness: the ambiguities of "empire" and of "control," the first appearing in the drive of expansion toward a universal historical unity, and the second, in the drive toward a centered unity in the particular history-bearing group. In each case the ambiguity of power lies behind the ambiguities of historical integration. So the question arises: What is the relation of the Kingdom of God to the ambiguities of power? The answer to this question is also the answer to the question of the relation of the churches to power.

The basic theological answer must be that, since God as the power of being is the source of all particular powers of being, power is divine in its essential nature. The symbols of power for God or the Christ or the church in biblical literature are abundant. And Spirit is the dynamic unity of power and meaning. The depreciation of power in most pacifist pronouncements is unbiblical as well as unrealistic. Power is the eternal possibility of resisting non-being. God and the Kingdom of God "exercise" this power eternally. But in the divine life—of which the divine kingdom is the creative self-manifestation—the ambiguities of power, empire, and control are conquered by unambiguous life.

Within historical existence this means that every victory of the Kingdom of God in history is a victory over the disintegrating consequences of the ambiguity of power. Since this ambiguity is based on the existential split between subject and object, its conquest involves a fragmentary reunion of subject and object. For the internal power structure of a history-bearing group, this means that the struggle of the Kingdom of God in history is actually victorious in institutions and attitudes and conquers, even if only fragmentarily, that compulsion which usually goes with power and transforms the objects of centered control into mere objects. In so far as democratization of political attitudes and institutions serves to resist the destructive implications of power, it is a manifestation of the Kingdom of God in history. But it would be completely wrong to identify democratic institutions with the Kingdom of God in history. This confusion, in the minds of many people, has elevated the idea of democracy to the place of a direct religious symbol and has simply substituted it for the symbol "Kingdom of God." Those who argue against this confusion are right when they point to the fact that aristocratic hierarchical systems of power have for long periods prevented the total transformation of men into objects by the tyranny of the strongest. And beyond this they also correctly point out that by their community and personality-creating effects aristocratic systems have developed the democratic potential of leaders and masses. However, this consideration does not justify the glorification of authoritarian systems of power as expressions of the will of God. In so far as the centering and liberating elements in a structure of political power are balanced, the Kingdom of God in history has conquered fragmentarily the ambiguities of control. This is, at the same time, the criterion according to which churches must judge political actions and theories. Their judgment against power politics should not be a rejection of power but an affirmation of power and even of its compulsory element in cases where justice is violated ("justice" is used here in the sense of protection of the individual as a potential personality in a community). Therefore, although the fight against "objectivation" of the personal subject is a permanent task of the churches, to be carried out by prophetic witness and priestly initiation, it is not their function to control the political powers and force upon them particular solutions in the name of the Kingdom of God. The way in which the Kingdom of God works in history is not identical with the way the churches want to direct the course of history.

The ambiguity of self-integration of life under the historical dimensions is also effective in the trend toward the reunion of all human groups in an empire. Again it must be stated that the Kingdom of God in history does not imply the denial of power in the encounter of centered political groups, for example, nations. As in every encounter of living beings, including individual men, power of being meets power of being and decisions are made about the higher or lower degree of such power—so it is in the encounter of political power groups. And as it is in the particular group and its structure of control, so it is in the relations of particular groups to each other that decisions are made in every moment in which the significance of the particular group for the unity of the Kingdom of God in history is actualized. In these struggles it might happen that a complete political defeat becomes the condition for the greatest significance a group gets in the manifestation of the Kingdom of God in history—as in Jewish history and, somehow analogously, in Indian and Greek history. But it also may be that a military defeat is the way in which the Kingdom of God, fighting in history, deprives national groups of a falsely claimed ultimate significance—as in the case of Hitler's Germany. Although this was done through the conquerors of naziism, their victory did not give them an unambiguous claim that they themselves were the bearers of the reunion of mankind. If they raised such a claim they would, by this very fact, show their inability to fulfill it. (See, for example, some hate propaganda in the United States and the absolutism of Communist Russia.)

For the Christian churches this means that they must try to find a way between a pacifism which overlooks or denies the necessity of power (including compulsion) in the relation of history-bearing groups and a militarism which believes in the possibility of achieving the unity of mankind through the conquest of the world by a particular historical group. The ambiguity of empire-building is fragmentarily conquered when higher political unities are created which, although they are not without the compulsory element of power, are nonetheless brought about in such a way that community between the united groups can develop and none of them is transformed into a mere object of centered control.

This basic solution of the problem of power in expansion toward larger unities should determine the attitude of the churches to empire-building and war. War is the name for the compulsory element in the creation of higher imperial unities. A "just" war is either a war in which arbitrary resistance against a higher unity has to be broken (for example, the American Civil War) or a war in which the attempt to create or maintain a higher unity by mere suppression is resisted (for example, the American Revolutionary War). There is no way of saying with more than daring faith whether a war was or is a just war in this sense. This incertitude, however, does not justify the cynical type of realism which surrenders all criteria and judgments, nor does it justify utopian idealism which believes in the possibility of removing the compulsory element of power from history. But the churches as representatives of the Kingdom of God can and must condemn a war which has only the appearance of a war but is in reality universal suicide. One never can start an atomic war with the claim that it is a just war, because it cannot serve the unity which belongs to the Kingdom of God. But one must be ready to answer in kind, even with atomic weapons, if the other side uses them first. The threat itself could be a deterrent.

All this implies that the pacifist way is not the way of the Kingdom of God in history. But certainly it is the way of the churches as representatives of the Spiritual Community. They would lose their representative character if they used military or economic weapons as tools for spreading the message of the Christ. The church's valuation of pacifist movements, groups, and individuals follows from this situation. The churches must reject political pacifism but support groups and individuals who try symbolically to represent the "Peace of the Kingdom of God" by refusing to participate in the compulsory element of power struggles and who are willing to bear the unavoidable reactions by the political powers to which they belong and by which they are protected. This refers to such groups as the Quakers and to such individuals as conscientious objectors. They represent within the political group the resignation of power which is essential for the churches but cannot be made by them into a law to be imposed on the body politic.

The Kingdom of God and the Ambiguities of Self-Creativity

While the ambiguities of historical self-integration lead to problems of political power, the ambiguities of historical self-creativity lead to problems of social growth. It is the relation of the new to the old in history which gives rise to conflicts between revolution and tradition. The relations of the generations to each other is the typical example for the unavoidable element of unfairness on both sides in the process of growth. A victory of the Kingdom of God creates a unity of tradition and revolution in which the unfairness of social growth and its destructive consequences, "lies and murder," are overcome.

They are not overcome by rejection of revolution or tradition in the name of the transcendent side of the Kingdom of God. The principal antirevolutionary attitude of many Christian groups is fundamentally wrong, whether unbloody cultural or unbloody and bloody political revolutions are concerned. The chaos which follows any kind of revolution can be a creative chaos. If history-bearing groups are unwilling to take this risk and are successful in avoiding any revolution, even an unbloody one, the dynamics of history will leave them behind. And certainly they cannot claim that their historical obsolescence is a victory of the Kingdom of God. But neither can this be said of the attempt of revolutionary groups to destroy the given structures of the cultural and political life by revolutions which are intended to force the fulfilment of the Kingdom of God and its justice "on earth." It was against such ideas of a Christian revolution to end all revolutions that Paul wrote his words in Romans, chapter 13, about the duty of obedience to the authorities in power. One of the many politico-theological abuses of biblical statements is the understanding of Paul's words as justifying the anti-revolutionary bias of some churches, particularly the Lutheran. But neither these words nor any other New Testament statement deals with the methods of gaining political power. In Romans, Paul is addressing eschatological enthusiasts, not a revolutionary political movement.

The Kingdom of God is victorious over the ambiguities of historical growth only where it can be discerned that revolution is being built into tradition in such a way that, in spite of the tensions in every concrete situation and in relation to every particular problem, a creative solution in the direction of the ultimate aim of history is found.

It is the nature of democratic institutions, in relation to questions of political centeredness and of political growth, that they try to unite the truth of the two conflicting sides. The two sides here are the new and the old, represented by revolution and tradition. The possibility of removing a government by legal means is such an attempted union; and in so far as it succeeds it represents a victory of the Kingdom of God in history, because it overcomes the, split. But this fact does not remove the ambiguities inherent in democratic institutions themselves. There have been other ways of uniting tradition and revolution within a political system, as is seen in federal, pre-absolutistic organizations of society. And we must not forget that democracy can produce a mass conformity which is more dangerous for the dynamic element in history and its revolutionary expression than is an openly working absolutism. The Kingdom of God is as hostile to established conformism as it is to negativistic non-conformism.

If we look at the history of the churches we find that religion, including Christianity, has stood overwhelmingly on the conservative-traditionalistic side. The great moments in the history of religion when the prophetic spirit challenged priestly doctrinal and ritual traditions are exceptions. These moments are comparatively rare (the Jewish prophets,

Jesus and the apostles, the reformers)—according to the general law that the normal growth of life is organic, slow, and without catastrophic interruptions. This law of growth is most effective in realms in which the given is vested with the taboo of sacredness and in which, consequently, every attack on the given is felt as a violation of a taboo. The history of Christianity up to the present is full of examples of this feeling and consequently of the traditionalist solution. But whenever the spiritual power produced a spiritual revolution, one stage of Christianity (and religion in general) was transformed into another. Much tradition-bound accumulation is needed before a prophetic attack on it is meaningful. This accounts for the quantitative predominance of religious tradition over religious revolution. But every revolution in the power of the Spirit creates a new basis for priestly conservation and the growth of lasting traditions. This rhythm of the dynamics of history (which has analogies in the biological and psychological realms) is the way in which the Kingdom of God works in history.

The Kingdom of God and the Ambiguities of Historical Self-Transcendence

The ambiguities of self-transcendence are caused by the tension between the Kingdom of God realized in history and the Kingdom as expected. Demonic consequences result from absolutizing the fragmentary fulfillment of the aim of history within history. On the other hand if the consciousness of realization is completely absent, utopianism alternates with the inescapable disappointments that are the seedbed of cynicism.

Therefore no victory of the Kingdom of God is given if either the consciousness of realized fulfillment or the expectation of fulfillment is denied. As we have seen, the symbol of the "third stage" can be used in both ways. But it also can be used in such a way as to unite the consciousness of the presence and the not-yet-presence of the Kingdom of God in history. This was the problem of the early church, and it remained a problem for all church history, as well as for the secularized forms of the self-transcending character of history. While it is comparatively easy to see the theoretical necessity of the union of the presence and not-yet-presence of the Kingdom of God, it is very difficult to keep the union in a state of living tension without letting it deteriorate into a shallow "middle way" of ecclesiastical or secular satisfaction. In the case of either ecclesiastical or secular satisfaction, it is the influence of those social groups which are interested in the preservation of the status quo that is largely, though not exclusively, responsible for such a situation. And the reaction of the critics of the status quo leads in each case to a restatement of the "principle of hope" (Ernst Bloch) in utopian terms. In such movements of expectation, however unrealistic they may be, the fighting Kingdom of God scores a victory against the power of complacency in its different sociological and psychological forms. But of course, it is a precarious and fragmentary victory because the bearers of it tend to ignore the given, but fragmentary, presence of the Kingdom.

The implication of this for the churches as representatives of the Kingdom of God in history is that it is their task to keep alive the tension between the consciousness of presence and the expectation of the coming. The danger for the receptive (sacramental) churches is that they will emphasize the presence and neglect the expectation; and the danger for the activistic (prophetic) churches is that they will emphasize the expectation and neglect the consciousness of the presence. The most important expression of this difference is the contrast between the emphasis on individual salvation in the one group and on social transformation in the other. Therefore it is a victory of the Kingdom of God in history if a sacramental church takes the principle of social transformation into its aim or if an activistic church pronounces the Spiritual Presence under all social conditions, emphasizing the vertical line of salvation over against the horizontal line of historical activity. And since the vertical line is primarily the line from the individual to the ultimate, the question arises as to how the Kingdom of God, in its fight within history, conquers the ambiguities of the individual in his historical existence.

KARL BARTH

33

Born in Basel, Switzerland, on May 10, 1886, Karl Barth was Professor
of Theology in various German universities until forced out by Hitler. He then
taught for the remainder of his career in Basel. Influenced by religious socialism he showed a deep interest in social and political questions. In the conflict
of the German Protestant Church with the Nazis, he became one of the main
intellectual resources for the opponents of Hitler. Barth is well known for his
authorship of the Barmen Declaration of 1934 stating the Christian opposition of the "confessing church" to the ideology of National Socialism and those
Christian church leaders who were accommodating to the Nazi regime. He is also
considered the leading figure of "neo-orthodoxy" and its critique of the liberalism associated with theologians like Ritschl and Harnack that arose in the late
nineteenth century.

After World War II, Barth took a more positive view of the possibility of
Christian life under Communism. Naziism with its anti-Semitic attack against
Jesus Christ and, therefore, the triune God was a more substantial threat than
the primitive atheism of Communism with its denial of a general revelation of
God, a concept that Barth denied also in his emphasis on divine self-revelation as
the only avenues to the knowledge of God.

The following selection is a portion of an essay that first appeared in German in 1946 and is now included in a collection of three essays in a volume
entitled Community, State, and Church. It provides a good illustration of his
influential social-ethical method.

Selection 1: *The Christian Community and the Civil Community*

By the "Christian community" we mean what is usually called "the Church" and by
the "civil community" what is usually called "the State."

The use of the concept of the "community" to describe both entities may serve at
the very outset to underline the positive relationship and connection between them.
It was probably with some such intention in mind that Augustine spoke of the *civitas
coelestis* and *terrena* and Zwingli of divine and human justice. In addition, however,
the twofold use of the concept "community" is intended to draw attention to the fact
that we are concerned in the "Church" and the "State" not merely and not primarily
with institutions and offices but with human beings gathered together in corporate
bodies in the service of common tasks. To interpret the "Church" as meaning above

all a "community" has rightly become more recognised and normal again in recent years. The Swiss term "civil community"—in Swiss villages the residential, civil, and ecclesiastical communities often confer one after the other in the same inn, and most of the people involved belong to all three groups—the "civil community" as opposed to the "Christian community" may also remind Christians that there are and always have been communities outside their own circle in the form of States, i.e. political communities. The "Christian community" (the Church) is the commonalty of the people in one place, region, or country who are called apart and gathered together as "Christians" by reason of their knowledge of and belief in Jesus Christ. The meaning and purpose of this "assembly" (*ekklesia*) is the common life of these people in one Spirit, the Holy Spirit, that is, in obedience to the Word of God in Jesus Christ, which they have all heard and are all needing and eager to hear again. They have also come together in order to pass on the Word to others. The inward expression of their life as a Christian community is the one faith, love, and hope by which they are all moved and sustained; its outward expression is the Confession by which they all stand, their jointly acknowledged and exercised responsibility for the preaching of the Name of Jesus Christ to all men and the worship and thanksgiving which they offer together. Since this is its concern, every single Christian community is as such an ecumenical (catholic) fellowship, that is, at one with the Christian communities in all other places, regions, and lands.

The "civil community" (the State) is the commonalty of all the people in one place, region, or country in so far as they belong together under a constitutional system of government that is equally valid for and binding on them all, and which is defended and maintained by force. The meaning and purpose of this mutual association (that is, of the polis) is the safeguarding of both the external, relative, and provisional freedom of the individuals and the external and relative peace of their community and to that extent the safeguarding of the external, relative, and provisional humanity of their life both as individuals and as a community. The three essential forms in which this safeguarding takes place are (a) legislation, which has to settle the legal system which is to be binding on all; (b) the government and administration which has to apply the legislation; (c) the administration of justice which has to deal with cases of doubtful or conflicting law and decide on its applicability.

II

When we compare the Christian community with the civil community the first difference that strikes us is that in the civil community Christians are no longer gathered together as such but are associated with non-Christians (or doubtful Christians). The civil community embraces everyone living within its area. Its members share no common awareness of their relationship to God, and such an awareness cannot be an element in the legal system established by the civil community. No appeal can be made to the Word or Spirit of God in the running of its affairs. The civil community as such is spiritually blind and ignorant. It has neither faith nor love nor hope. It has no creed and no gospel. Prayer is not part of its life, and its members are not brothers and sisters. As members of the civil community they can only ask, as Pilate asked: What is truth? Since every answer to the question abolishes the presuppositions of the very existence of the civil community. "Tolerance" is its ultimate wisdom in the "religious" sphere—"religion" being used in this context to describe the purpose of the Christian community. For this reason the civil community can only have external, relative, and provisional tasks and aims, and that is why it is burdened and defaced by something which the Christian community can, characteristically, do without: physical force, the "secular arm" which it can use to enforce its authority. That is why it lacks the ecumenical breadth and freedom that are so essential to Christianity. The polis has walls. Up till now, at least, civil communities have always been more or less clearly marked off from one another as local, regional, national, and therefore competing and colliding units of government. And that is why the State has no safeguard or corrective against the danger of either neglecting or absolutising itself and its particular system and thus in one way or the other destroying and annulling itself. One cannot in fact compare the Church with the State without realising how much weaker, poorer, and more exposed to danger the human community is in the State than in the Church.

III

It would be inadvisable, however, to make too much of the comparison. According to the fifth thesis of the Theological Declaration of Barmen (1934), the Christian community also exists in "the still unredeemed world," and there is not a single problem harassing the State by which the Church is not also affected in some way or other. From a distance it is impossible clearly to distinguish the Christian from the non-Christian, the real Christian from the doubtful Christian even in the Church itself. Did not Judas the traitor participate in the Last Supper? Awareness of God is one thing, Being in Cod quite another. The Word and Spirit of Cod are no more automatically available in the Church than they are in the State. The faith of the Church can become frigid and empty; its love can grow cold; its hope can fall to the ground; its message become timid and even silent; its worship and thanksgiving mere formalities; its fellowship may droop and decay.

Even the Church does not simply "have" faith or love or hope. There are dead churches, and unfortunately one does not have to look far to find them anywhere. And if, normally, the Church renounces the use of physical force and has not shed blood, sometimes the only reason has been lack of opportunity; struggles for power have never been entirely absent in the life of the Church. Again, side by side with other and more far-reaching centrifugal factors, local, regional, and national differences in the Church's way of life have been and still are strong. The centripetal forces which it needs are still weak enough to make even the unity of Christian communities among themselves extremely

The activity of the State is, as the Apostle explicitly stated (Romans 13:4, 6), a form of divine service. As such it can be perverted just as the divine service of the Church itself is not exempt from the possibility of perversion. The State can assume the face and character of Pilate. Even then, however, it still acts in the power which God has given it ("Thou couldest have no power at all against me, except it were given thee from above": John 19:1 1). Even in its perversion it cannot escape from God; and His law is the standard by which it is judged. The Christian community therefore acknowledges "the benefaction of this ordinance of His with thankful, reverent hearts" (Barmen Thesis No. 5). The benefaction which it acknowledges consists in the external, relative, and provisional sanctification of the unhallowed world which is brought about by the existence of political power and order. In what concrete attitudes to particular political patterns and realities this Christian acknowledgement will be expressed can remain a completely open question. It makes one thing quite impossible, however: a Christian decision to be indifferent; a non-political Christianity. The Church can in no case be indifferent or neutral towards this manifestation of an order so clearly related to its own mission. Such indifference would be equivalent to the opposition of which it is said in Romans 13:2 that it is a rebellion against the ordinance of God—and rebels secure their own condemnation.

VII

The Church must remain the Church. It must remain the inner circle of the Kingdom of Christ. The Christian community has a task of which the civil community can never relieve it and which it can never pursue in the forms peculiar to the civil community. It would not redound to the welfare of the civil community if the Christian community were to be absorbed by it (as Rothe has suggested that it should) and were therefore to neglect the special task which it has received a categorical order to undertake. It proclaims the rule of Jesus Christ and the hope of the Kingdom of God. This is not the task of the civil community; it has no message to deliver; it is dependent on a message being delivered to it. It is not in a position to appeal to the authority and grace of God; it is dependent on this happening elsewhere. It does not pray; it depends on others praying for it. It is blind to the whence and whither of human existence; its task is rather to provide for the external and provisional delimitation and protection of human life; it depends on the existence of seeing eyes elsewhere. It cannot call the human hybris into question fundamentally, and it knows of no final defence against the chaos which threatens it from that quarter; in this respect, too, it depends on ultimate words and insights existing elsewhere. The thought and speech of the civil community waver necessarily between a much too childlike optimism and a much too peevish pessimism in regard to man—as a matter of course it expects the best of everybody and suspects the worst! It obviously relies on its own view of man being fundamentally superseded elsewhere. Only an act of supreme disobedience on the part of Christians could bring the special existence of the Christian community to an end. Such a cessation is also impossible because then the voice of what is ultimately the only hope and help which all men need to hear would be silent.

VIII

The Christian community shares in the task of the civil community precisely to the extent that it fulfils its own task. By believing in Jesus Christ and preaching Jesus Christ it believes in and preaches Him who is Lord of the world as He is Lord of the Church. And since they belong to the inner circle, the members of the Church are also automatically members of the wider circle. They cannot halt at the boundary where the inner and outer circles meet, though are entrusted (whether or not they believe it to be a divine revelation) to provide "according to the measure of human insight and human capacity" for temporal law and temporal peace, for an external, relative, and provisional humanisation of man's existence. Accordingly, the various political forms and systems are human inventions which as such do not bear the distinctive mark of revelation and are not witnessed to as such—and can therefore not lay any claim to belief. By making itself jointly responsible for the civil community, the Christian community participates—on the basis of and by belief in the divine revelation—in the human search for the best form, for the most fitting system of political organisation; but it is also aware of the limits of all the political forms and systems which man can discover (even with the co-operation of the Church), and it will beware of playing off one political concept—even the "democratic" concept—as the Christian concept, against all others. Since it proclaims the Kingdom of God it has to maintain its own hopes and questions in the face of all purely political concepts. And this applies even more to all political achievements. Though the Christian will be both more lenient and more stern, more patient and more impatient towards them than the non-Christian, he will not regard any such achievement as perfect or mistake it for the Kingdom of God—for it can only have been brought about by human insight and human ability. In the face of all political achievements, past, present, and future, the Church waits for "the city which hath foundations, whose builder and maker is God" (Hebrews 11:10). It trusts and obeys no political system or reality but the power of the Word, by which God upholds all things (Hebrews 1:3; Barmen Thesis No. 5), including all political things.

X

In this freedom, however, the Church makes itself responsible for the shape and reality of the civil community in a quite definite sense. We have already said that it is quite impossible for the Christian to adopt an attitude of complete indifference to politics. But neither can the Church be indifferent to particular political patterns and realities. The Church "reminds the world of God's Kingdom, God's commandment and righteousness and thereby of the responsibility of governments and governed" (Barmen Thesis No. 5). This means that the Christian community and the individual Christian can understand and accept many things in the political sphere—and if necessary suffer and endure everything. But the fact that it can understand much and endure everything has nothing to do with the "subordination" which is required of it, that is, with the share of responsibility which it is enjoined to take in the political sphere. That responsibility refers rather to the decisions which it must make before God: "must" make, because, unlike Christian understanding and suffering, Christian intentions and decisions are bound to run in a quite definite direction of their own. There will always be room and need for discussion on the details of Christian intentions and decisions, but the general line on which they are based can never be the subject of accommodation and compromise in the Church's relations with the world. The Christian community "subordinates" itself to the civil community by making its knowledge of the Lord who is Lord of all its criterion, and distinguishing between the just and the unjust State, that is, between the better and the worse political form and reality; between order and caprice; between government and tyranny; between freedom and anarchy; between community and collectivism; between personal rights and individualism; between the State as described in Romans 13 and the State as described in Revelation 13. And it will judge all matters concerned with the establishment, preservation, and enforcement of political order in accordance with these necessary distinctions and according to the merits of the particular case and situation to which they refer. On the basis of the judgment which it has formed it will choose and desire whichever seems to be the better political system in any particular situation, and in accordance with this choice and desire it will offer its support here and its resistance there. It is in the making of such distinctions, judgments, and choices from its own centre, and in the practical decisions which necessarily flow from that centre, that the Christian community expresses its "subordination" to the civil community and fulfills its share of political responsibility.

XI

The Christian decisions which have to be made in the political sphere have no idea, system, or programme to refer to but a direction and a line that must be recognised and adhered to in all circumstances. This line cannot be defined by appealing to the so-called "natural law." To base its policy on "natural law" would mean that the Christian community was adopting the ways of the civil community, which does not take its bearings from the Christian centre and is still living or again living in a state of ignorance. The Christian community would be adopting the methods, in other words, of the pagan State. It would not be acting as a Christian community in the State at all; it would no longer be the salt and the light of the wider circle of which Christ is the centre. It would not only be declaring its solidarity with the civil community: it would be putting itself on a par with it and withholding from it the very things it lacks most. It would certainly not be doing it any service in that way. For the thing the civil community lacks (in its neutrality towards the Word and Spirit of God) is a firmer and clearer motivation for political decisions than the so-called natural law can provide. By "natural law" we mean the embodiment of what man is alleged to regard as universally right and wrong, as necessary, permissible, and forbidden "by nature," that is, on any conceivable premise. It has been connected with a natural revelation of God, that is, with a revelation known to man by natural means. And the civil community as such—the civil community which is not yet or is no longer illuminated from its centre—undoubtedly has no other choice but to think, speak, and act on the basis of this allegedly natural, or rather of a particular conception of the court of appeal which is passed off as the natural law. The civil community is reduced to guessing or to accepting some powerful assertion of this or that interpretation of natural law. All it can do is to grope around and experiment with the convictions which it derives from "natural law," never certain whether it may not in the end be an illusion to rely on it as the final authority and therefore always making vigorous use, openly or secretly, of a more or less refined positivism. The results of the politics based on such considerations were and are just what might be expected. And if they were and are not clearly and generally negative, if in the political sphere the better stands alongside the worse, if there were and still are good as well as bad States—no doubt the reality is always a curious mixture of the two!—then the reason is not that the true "natural law" has been discovered, but simply the fact that even the ignorant, neutral, pagan civil community is still in the Kingdom of Christ, and that all political questions and all political efforts as such are founded on the gracious ordinance of God by which man is preserved and

his sin and crime confined. What we glimpse in the better kind of State is the purpose, meaning, and goal of this divine ordinance. It is operative in any case, even
though the citizens of the particular State may lack any certain knowledge of the
trustworthy standards of political decision, and the overwhelming threat of mistaking an error for the truth may be close at hand. The divine ordinance may operate
with the co-operation of the men and women involved, but certainly without their
having deserved it: *Providentia Dei, confusione hominum* ("God's providence, human's
shame"). If the Christian community were to base its political responsibility on
the assumption that it was also interested in the problem of natural law and that it
was attempting to base its decisions on so-called natural law, this would not alter
the power which God has to make good come of evil, as He is in fact always doing
in the political order. But it would mean that the Christian community was sharing human illusions and confusions. It is bad enough that, when it does not risk
going its own way, the Christian community is widely involved in these illusions
and confusions. It should not wantonly attempt to deepen such involvement. And
it would be doing no less if it were to seek the criterion of its political decisions in
some form of the so-called natural law. The tasks and problems which the Christian community is called to share, in fulfillment of its political responsibility, are
"natural," secular, profane tasks and problems. But the norm by which it should be
guided is anything but natural: it is the only norm which it can believe in and accept
as a spiritual norm, and is derived from the clear law of its own faith, not from the
obscure workings of a system outside itself: it is from knowledge of this norm that
it will make its decisions in the political sphere.

XII

It is this reliance on a spiritual norm that makes the Christian community free to
support the cause of the civil community honestly and calmly. In the political sphere
the Church will not be fighting for itself and its own concerns. Its own position,
influence, and power in the State are not the goal which will determine the trend
of its political decisions. "My Kingdom is not of this world. If my Kingdom were of
this world, then would my servants fight that I should not be delivered to the Jews,
but now is my Kingdom not from hence" (John 18:36). The secret contempt which
a Church fighting for its own interests with political weapons usually incurs even
when it achieves a certain amount of success is well deserved. And sooner or later
the struggle generally ends in mortifying defeats of one sort or of the Jesus Christ
who came and is to come again. But it cannot do this by projecting, proposing, and
attempting to enforce a State in the likeness of the Kingdom of God. The State is
quite justified if it refuses to countenance all such Christian demands. It belongs
to the very nature of the State that it is not and cannot become the Kingdom of
God. It is based on an ordinance of God which is intended for the "world not yet
redeemed" in which sin and the danger of chaos have to be taken into account with
the utmost seriousness and in which the rule of Jesus Christ, though in fact already
established, is still hidden. The State would be disavowing its own purpose if it were
to act as thou its task was to become the Kingdom of God. And the Church that
tried to induce it to develop into the Kingdom of God could be rightly reproached
for being much too rashly presumptuous. If its demand were to have any meaning at

all, it would have to believe that its own duty was also to develop into the Kingdom of God. But, like the State, the Church also stands "in the world not yet redeemed." And even at its best the Church is not an image of the Kingdom of God. It would appear that when it makes this demand on the State, the Church has also confused the Kingdom of God with a mere ideal of the natural law. Such a Church needs to be reminded again of the real Kingdom of God, which will follow both State and Church in time. A free Church will not allow itself to be caught on this path.

XIV

The direction of Christian judgments, purposes, and ideals in political affairs is based on the analogical capacities and needs of political organisation. Political organisation can be neither a repetition of the Church nor an anticipation of the Kingdom of God. In relation to the Church it is an independent reality; in relation to the Kingdom of God it is (like the Church itself) a human reality bearing the stamp of this fleeting world. An equating of State and Church on the one hand and State and Kingdom of God on the other is therefore out of the question. On the other hand, however, since the State is based on a particular divine ordinance, since it belongs to the Kingdom of God, it has no autonomy, no independence over against the Church and the Kingdom of God. A simple and absolute heterogeneity between State and Church on the one hand and State and Kingdom of God on the other is therefore just as much out of the question as a simple and absolute equating. The only possibility that remains—and it suggests itself compellingly—is to regard the existence of the State as an allegory, as a correspondence and an analogue to the Kingdom of God which the Church preaches and believes in. Since the State forms the outer circle, within which the Church, with the mystery of its faith and gospel, is the inner circle, since it shares a common centre with the Church, it is inevitable that, although its presuppositions and its tasks are its own and different, it is nevertheless capable of reflecting indirectly the truth and reality which constitute the Christian community. Since, however, the peculiarity and difference of its presuppositions and tasks and its existence as an outer circle must remain as they are, its justice and even its very existence as a reflected image of the Christian truth and reality cannot be given once and for all and as a matter of course but are, on the contrary, exposed to the utmost danger; it will always be questionable whether and how far it will fulfill its just purposes. To be saved from degeneration and decay it needs to be reminded of the righteousness which is a reflection of Christian truth. Again and again it needs a historical setting whose goal and content are the moulding of the State into an allegory of the Kingdom of God and the fulfillment of its righteousness. Human initiative in such situations cannot proceed from the State itself. As a purely civil community, the State is ignorant of the mystery of the Kingdom of God, the mystery of its own centre, and it is indifferent to the faith and gospel of the Christian community. As a civil community it can only draw from the porous wells of the so-called natural law. It cannot remind itself of the true criterion of its own righteousness, it cannot move towards the fulfillment of that righteousness in its own strength. It needs the wholesomely disturbing presence, the activity that revolves directly around the common centre, the participation of the Christian community in the execution of political responsibility. The Church is not the

Kingdom of God, but it has knowledge of it; it hopes for it; it believes in it; it prays in the name of Jesus Christ, and it preaches His Name as the Name above all others. The Church is not neutral on this ground, and it is therefore not powerless. If it achieves only the great and necessary *metabasis eis alto genos* which is the share of political responsibility which it is enjoined to assume, then it will not be able to be neutral and powerless and deny its Lord in the other genos. If the Church takes up its share of political responsibility, it must mean that it is taking that human initiative which the State cannot take: it is giving the State the impulse which it cannot give itself; it is reminding the State of those things of which it is unable to remind itself. The distinctions, judgments, and choices which it makes in the political sphere are always intended to foster the illumination of the State's connexion with the order of divine salvation and grace and to discourage all the attempts to hide this connexion. Among the political possibilities open at any particular moment it will choose those which most suggest a correspondence to, an analogy and a reflection of, the content of its own faith and gospel.

In the decisions of the State, the Church will always support the side which clarifies rather than obscures the Lordship of Jesus Christ over the whole, which includes this political sphere outside the Church. The Church desires that the shape and reality of the State in this fleeting world should point towards the Kingdom of God, not away from it. Its desire is not that human politics should cross the politics of God, but that they should proceed, however distantly, on parallel lines. It desires that the active grace of God, as revealed from heaven, should be reflected in the earthly material of the external, relative, and provisional actions and modes of action of the political community. It therefore makes itself responsible in the first and last place to God—the one God whose grace is revealed in Jesus Christ—by making itself responsible for the cause of the State. And so, with its political judgments and choices, it bears an implicit, indirect, but none the less real witness to the gospel. Even its political activity is therefore a profession of its Christian faith. By its political activity it calls the State from neutrality, ignorance, and paganism into co-responsibility before God, thereby remaining faithful to its own particular mission. It sets in motion the historical process whose aim and content are the moulding of the State into the likeness of the Kingdom of God and hence the fulfillment of the State's own righteous purposes.

XV

The Church is based on the knowledge of the one eternal God, who as such became man and thereby proved Himself a neighbor to man, by treating him with compassion (Luke 10:36f.). The inevitable consequence is that in the political sphere the Church will always and in all circumstances be interested primarily in human beings and not in some abstract cause or other, whether it be anonymous capital or the State as such (the functioning of its departments!) or the honour of the nation or the progress of civilisation or culture or the idea, however conceived, of the historical development of the human race. It will not be interested in this last idea even if "progress" is interpreted as meaning the welfare of future generations, for the attainment of which man, human dignity, human life in the present age are to be trampled underfoot. Right itself becomes wrong (*summum ius summa iniuria*) when it is allowed to rule as an abstract form, instead of serving the limitation and hence the preservation of man. The Church is at all times and in all circumstances the enemy of the idol Juggernaut. Since God Himself became man, man is the measure of all things, and man can and must only be used and, in certain circumstances, sacrificed, for man. Even the most wretched man—not man's egoism, but man's humanity—must be resolutely defended against the autocracy of every mere "cause." Man has not to serve causes; causes have to serve man.

XVI

The Church is witness of the divine justification, that is, of the act in which God in Jesus Christ established and confirmed His original claim to man and hence man's claim against sin and death. The future for which the Church waits is the definitive revelation of this divine justification. This means that the Church will always be found where the order of the State is based on a commonly acknowledged law, from submission to which no one is exempt, and which also provides equal protection for all. The Church will be found where all political activity is in all circumstances regulated by this law. The Church always stands for the constitutional State, for the maximum validity and application of that twofold rule (no exemption from and full protection by the law), and therefore it will always be against any degeneration of the constitutional State into tyranny or anarchy. The Church will never be found on the side of anarchy or tyranny. In its politics it will always be urging the civil community to treat this fundamental purpose of its existence with the utmost seriousness: the limiting and the preserving of man by the quest for and the establishment of law.

XVII

The Church is witness of the fact that the Son of man came to seek and to save the lost. And this implies that—casting all false impartiality aside—the Church must concentrate first on the lower and lowest levels of human society. The poor, the socially and economically weak and threatened, will always be the object of its primary and particular concern and it will always insist on the State's special responsibility for these weaker members of society. That it will bestow its love on them, within the framework of its own task (as part of its service), is one thing and the most important thing; but it must not concentrate on this and neglect the other thing to which it is committed by its political responsibility: the effort to achieve such a fashioning of the law as will make it impossible for "equality before the law" to become a cloak under which strong and weak, independent and dependent, rich and poor, employers and employees, in fact receive different treatment at its hands: the weak being unduly restricted, the strong unduly -protected: The Church must stand for social justice in the political sphere. And in choosing between the various socialistic possibilities (social-liberalism? co-operativism? syndicalism? free trade? moderate or radical Marxism?) it will always choose the movement from which it can expect the greatest measure of social justice (leaving all other considerations on one side).

XVIII

The Church is the fellowship of those who are freely called by the Word of grace and the Spirit and love of God to be the children of God. Translated into political terms, this means that the Church affirms, as the basic right which every citizen must be guaranteed by the State, the freedom to carry out his decisions in the politically lawful sphere, according to his own insight and choice, and therefore independently, and the freedom to live in certain spheres (the family, education, art, science, religion, culture), safeguarded but not regulated by law. The Church will not in all circumstances withdraw from and oppose what may be practically a dictatorship, that is, a partial and temporary limitation of these freedoms, but it will certainly withdraw from and oppose any out-and-out dictatorship such as the totalitarian State. The adult Christian can only wish to be an adult citizen, and he can only want his fellow citizens to live as adult human beings.

XIX

The Church is the fellowship of those who, as members of the one Body of the one Head, are bound and committed to this Lord of theirs and therefore to no other. It follows that the Church will never understand and interpret political freedom and the basic law which the State must guarantee to the individual citizen other than in the sense of the basic duty of responsibility which is required. This was never made particularly clear in the classic proclamations of so-called "human rights" in America and France.) The citizen is responsible in the whole sphere of his freedom, political and non-political alike. And the civil community is naturally responsible in the maintenance of its freedom as a whole. Thus the Christian approach surpasses both individualism and collectivism. The Church knows and recognises the "interest" of the individual and of the "whole," but it resists them both when they want to have the last word. It subordinates them to the being of the citizen, the being of the civil community before the law, over which neither the individuals nor the "whole" are to hold sway, but which they are to seek after, to find, and to serve—always with a view to limiting and preserving the life of man.

XX

As the fellowship of those who live in one faith under one Lord on the basis of a Baptism in one Spirit, the Church must and will stand for the equality of the freedom and responsibility of all adult citizens, in spite of its sober insight into the variety of human needs, abilities, and tasks. It will stand for their equality before the law that unites and binds them all, for their equality in working together to establish and carry out the law, and for their equality in the limitation and preservation of human life that it secures. If, in accordance with a specifically Christian insight, it lies in the very nature of the State that this equality must not be restricted by any differences of religious belief or unbelief, it is all the more important for the Church to urge that the restriction of the political freedom and responsibility not only of certain classes and races but, supremely, of that of women is an arbitrary convention which does not deserve to be preserved any longer. If Christians are to be consistent there can be only one possible decision in this matter.

XXI

Since the Church is aware of the variety of the gifts and tasks of the one Holy Spirit in its own sphere, it will be alert and open in the political sphere to the need to separate the different functions and "powers"—the legislative, executive, and judicial— inasmuch as those who carry out any one of these functions should not carry out the others simultaneously. No human being is a god able to unite in his own person the functions of the legislator and the ruler, the ruler and the judge, without endangering the sovereignty of the law. The "people" is no more such a god than the Church is its own master and in sole possession of its powers. The fact is that within the community of the one people (by the people and for the people) definite and different services are to be performed by different persons, which, if they were united in one human hand, would disrupt rather than promote the unity of the common enterprise. With its awareness of the necessity that must be observed in this matter, the Church will give a lead to the State.

XXII

The Church lives from the disclosure of the true God and His revelation, from Him as the Light that has been lit in Jesus Christ to destroy the works of darkness. It lives in the dawning of the day of the Lord and its task in relation to the world is to rouse it and tell it that this day has dawned. The inevitable political corollary of this is that the Church is the sworn enemy of all secret policies and secret diplomacy. It is just as true of the political sphere as of any other that only evil can want to be kept secret. The distinguishing mark of the good is that it presses forward to the light of day. Where freedom and responsibility in the service of the State are one, whatever is said and done must be said and done before the ears and eyes of all, and the legislator, the ruler, and the judge can and must be ready to answer openly for all their actions— without thereby being necessarily dependent on the public or allowing themselves to be flurried. The statecraft that wraps itself up in darkness is the craft of a State which, because it is anarchic or tyrannical, is forced to hide the bad conscience of its citizens or officials. The Church will not on any account lend its support to that kind of State.

XXIII

The Church sees itself established and nourished by the free Word of God—the Word which proves its freedom in the Holy Scriptures at all times. And in its own sphere the Church believes that the human word is capable of being the free vehicle and mouthpiece of this free Word of God. By a process of analogy, it has to risk attributing a positive and constructive meaning to the free human word in the political sphere. If it trusts the word of man in one sphere it cannot mistrust it on principle in the other. It will believe that human words are not bound to be empty or useless or even dangerous, but that the right words can clarify and control great decisions. At the risk of providing opportunities for empty, useless, and dangerous words to be heard, it will therefore do all it can to see that there is at any rate no lack of opportunity for the right word to be heard. It will do all it can to see that there are opportunities for mutual discussion in the civil community as the basis of common endeavours. And it will try to see that such discussion takes place openly. With all its strength it will be on the side of those who refuse to have anything to do with the regimentation, controlling, and censoring of public opinion. It knows of no pretext which would make that a good thing and no situation in which it could be necessary.

XXIV

As disciples of Christ, the members of His Church do not rule: they serve. In the political community, therefore, the Church can only regard all ruling that is not primarily a form of service as a diseased and never as a normal condition. No State can exist without the sanction of power. But the power of the good State differs from that of the bad State as *potestas* differs from *potentia*. Potestas is the power that follows and serves the law; potentia is the power that precedes the law, that masters and bends and breaks the law—it is the naked power which is directly evil. Bismarck—not to mention Hitler—was (in spite of the Daily Bible Readings on his bedside table) no model statesman because he wanted to establish and develop his work on naked power. The ultimate result of this all-too-consistently pursued aim was inevitable: "all that draw the sword shall perish by the sword." Christian political theory leads us in the very opposite direction.

XXV

Since the Church is ecumenical (catholic) by virtue of its very origin, it resists all abstract local, regional, and national interests in the political sphere. It will always seek to serve the best interests of the particular city or place where it is stationed. But it will never do this without at the same time looking out beyond the city walls. It will be conscious of the superficiality, relativity, and temporariness of the immediate city boundaries, and on principle it will always stand for understanding and cooperation within the wider circle. The Church will be the last to lend its support to mere parochial politics. *Pacta sunt servanda? Pacta sunt concludenda!* All cities of the realm must agree if their common cause is to enjoy stability and not fall to pieces. In the Church we have tasted the air of freedom and must bring others to taste it, too.

DIETRICH BONHOEFFER

34

❧ *Born on February 4, 1906, in Breslau, Germany, Dietrich Bonhoeffer was executed by the Nazis at Flossenberg concentration camp for his alleged connections to the July 20, 1944, plot on Hitler's life. It was a cruel and meaningless act as the Third Reich was collapsing and, tragically, only two weeks later the camp was liberated by the United States Army.*

A young theologian of great promise, he first called attention to the problems of Christian ethics in his book The Cost of Discipleship *(1937) with its famous attack on "cheap grace"—grace without discipleship. A leader in the "confessing church," he was soon involved in the struggle against Naziism. He was imprisoned in April 1943 and remained so until his death.*

His courageous opposition to Hitler and his martyrdom have added luster and gravity to his already profound theological contributions. Because of his long imprisonment and early death, his work, though extensive, is incomplete. Nonetheless, Ethics, *from which we are drawing, is a large collection and, along with his other writings, including* Letters and Papers from Prison, *has been highly influential. Bonhoeffer continues to command the attention of theologians and ethicists to this day.*

Selection 1: "The Concrete Commandment and the Divine Mandates," *Ethics*

One of the questions Bonhoeffer raised was "How does the will of God become concrete?" He tried to avoid "general principles" for Christian ethics and his "mandates" are an attempt to safeguard the concrete commandment in and of Christ as the basis of Christian social action. While not dispensing with the traditional term, "orders" (the church, marriage, culture, and government) the term "mandate" helps to make the point that these structures of life are the creation of God's command revealed in Christ, thus avoiding the suggestion in the logic of the term orders that they have their own intrinsic authority apart from Christ. For some Christians in that day the idea of government as an order of creation tended to militate against opposition to the Third Reich.

The Commandment of God revealed in Jesus Christ embraces in its unity all of human life. Its claim on human beings and the world through the reconciling love of God is all-encompassing. This commandment encounters us concretely in four different forms that find their unity only in the commandment itself, namely, in the church, marriage and family, culture, and government. God's commandment is not to be found anywhere and everywhere, not in theoretical speculation or private enlightenment, not in historical forces or compelling ideals, but only where it gives itself to us. God's commandment can only be spoken with God's own authorization; and only insofar as God authorizes it can the commandment be legitimately declared His. God's commandment is to be found not wherever there are historical forces, strong ideals, or convincing insights, but only where there are divine mandates which are grounded in the revelation of Christ. We are dealing with such mandates in the church, in marriage and family, in culture, and in government.

By "mandate" we understand the concrete divine commission grounded in the revelation of Christ and the testimony of scripture; it is the authorization and legitimization to declare a particular divine commandment, the conferring of divine authority on an earthly institution. A mandate is to be understood simultaneously as the laying claim to, commandeering of, and formation of a certain earthly domain by the divine command. The bearer of the mandate acts as a vicarious representative, as a stand-in for the one who issued the commission. Understood properly, one could also use the term "order" [Ordnung] here, if only the concept did not contain the inherent danger of focusing more strongly on the static element of order rather than on the divine authorizing, legitimizing, and sanctioning, which are its sole foundation. This then leads all too easily to a divine sanctioning of all existing orders per se, and thus to a romantic conservatism that no longer has anything to do with the Christian doctrine of the four mandates. If these misinterpretations could be purged from the concept of order, then it would be very capable of expressing the intended meaning in a strong and convincing way. The concept of "estate," which has proven reliable since the time of the Reformation, also suggests itself here. However, in the course of history it has become so obscured that it simply can no longer be employed in its original purity. The word carries too many overtones of human favoritism and of privileges to allow us still to hear its original humble dignity. Finally, the concept of "office" [Amt] has become so secularized and so closely connected to institutional-bureaucratic thinking that it no longer conveys the solemnity of the divine decree. Lacking a better word we thus stay, for the time being, with the concept of mandate. Nevertheless, our goal, through clarifying the issue itself, is to contribute to renewing and reclaiming the old concepts of order, estate, and office.

The divine mandates depend solely on God's one commandment as it is revealed in Jesus Christ. They are implanted in the world from above as organizing structures—"orders"—of the reality of Christ, that is, of the reality of God's love for the world and for human beings that has been revealed in Jesus Christ. They are thus in no way an outgrowth of history; they are not earthly powers, but divine commissions. Church, marriage and family, culture, and government can only be explained and understood from above, from God. The bearers of the mandate are not commissioned from below, executing and representing particular expressions of the collective will of human beings. Instead, they are in a strict and unalterable sense God's commissioners, vicarious representatives, and stand-ins. This is true regardless of the particular historical genesis of a church, a family, or a government. Within the domain of the mandates, God's authorization has thus designated an irrevocable above and below.

God's commandment therefore always seeks to encounter human beings within an earthly relationship of authority, within an order that 395 is clearly determined by above and below. However, this above and below immediately requires a more precise definition: (1) It is not identical with an earthly power relation. Under no circumstances may the more powerful simply invoke the divine mandate in their dealings with the weaker. It is, on the contrary, part of the nature of the divine mandate to correct and order the earthly power relations in its own way. (2) It must further be emphasized that the divine mandate creates not only the above, but in fact also the below. Above and below belong together in an inseparable and mutually delimiting relationship that must still be more precisely defined at a later point. (3) It is true that above and below refer not to a relation between concepts and things, but between persons. However, it is a relation between the kind of people who submit to God's commission, and to it alone, regardless of whether they find themselves above or below. Even a master has a Master, and this fact alone makes him a master and authorizes and legitimizes him I the servant. Master and servant owe one another the respect that springs from their respective participation in God's mandate. Abuse of being below is equal to and just as frequent as the abuse of being above that inflicts injury on the person below. Apart from personal misconduct, the abuse of being above and being below is inevitable when the grounding of both in God's mandate is no longer recognized. Being above is then understood, grasped, and unscrupulously exploited as an arbitrary favor of fate, just as being below is considered an unjust discrimination, and must correspondingly lead to outrage and rebellion. However, those who are below can become conscious of their inherent powers; they can reach the critical moment in which they feel, through a sudden act of insight and self-liberation, the dark forces of destruction, of negation, of doubt, and of rebellion converging upon themselves; in this moment, through these chaotic forces, they feel superior to anything that exists, to anything above. At that very moment the relationship between above and below has been turned on its head. There is no longer an authentic above and below. Instead, those above derive their authorization and legitimization solely from below, and those below regard those who are above—seen from their perspective—merely as the embodied claim of those who are below to get above. Thus those below become an ongoing and inevitable threat to those who are above. Such people can only maintain their position "above" by fomenting ever-increasing unrest below, while at the same time using terror against the rebellious forces at work below. At this stage of inversion and dissolution the relation between above and below is one of deepest hostility, of mistrust, deception, and envy. In this atmosphere even the purely personal abuse of being above and of being below thrives as never before. Trembling before the forces of rebellion, the fact that an authentic order instituted from above had been possible at all must appear as what it actually is, a miracle. The authentic order of above and below lives out of faith in the commission from "above," in the "Lord" of "lords." Such faith alone banishes the demonic powers, which arise from below. When this faith breaks down, then the entire arrangement that has been implanted in the world from above collapses like a house of cards. Some then say that it was a deception of the people while others claim that it was a miracle. Both groups must nevertheless be astounded by the power of faith.

Only in their being with-one-another [Miteinander], for-one-another [Füreinander], and over-against-one-another [Gegeneinander] do the divine mandates of church, marriage and family, culture, and government communicate the commandment of God as it is revealed in Jesus Christ. None of these mandates exists self-sufficiently, nor can one of them claim to replace all the others. The mandates are *with-one-another* or they are not divine mandates. However, in being with-one-another they are not isolated and separated from one another but oriented toward one another. They are *for-one-another* or they are not God's mandates. But in this being-with-one-another and being-for-one-another, each of them is also limited [begrenzt] by the other, and, in the context of being-for-one-another, this limitation is necessarily experienced as a being-over-against-one-another. Where *being-over-against-one-another* is no longer present, God's mandate no longer exists. Being above [das Obensein] is thus limited in a threefold way, each of which works differently. It is limited by God who issues the commission, by the other mandates, and by the relation to those below [das Untensein]. These limits at the same time also safeguard being above. This safeguard serves to encourage the exercise of the divine mandate, just as the limit is the warning not to transgress it. Safeguard and limit are two sides of the same coin. God safeguards by limiting, and encourages by warning.

The Commandment of God in the Church

*   *   *

On the basis of Holy Scripture the preaching office proclaims Jesus Christ as the Lord and Savior of the world. There is no legitimate proclamation by the church that is not proclamation of Christ. The church does not have a twofold word, the one general, rational, and grounded in natural law and the other Christian—that is, it does not have one word for unbelievers and another for believers. Only a pharisaical arrogance can lead the church to withhold the proclamation of Christ from some but not from others. The word of the church is justified and authorized solely by the commission of Jesus Christ. Therefore any of its words that fail to take this authorization into account must be just empty chatter. For example, let us take the church's encounter with the government, whose mandate is certainly not to confess Christ. Instead, government should be challenged about very specific problems whose remedy is part of its divine mandate. In so doing, however, the church cannot simply cease to be church. Only by fulfilling its own mandate can it legitimately question the government about fulfilling its mandate. The church also does not have a twofold commandment at its disposal, one for the world and one for the Christian congregation. Instead, its commandment is the one commandment of God revealed in Jesus Christ, which it proclaims to the whole world.

The church proclaims this commandment by giving witness to Jesus Christ as the Lord and Savior of Christ's church-community and the world, thus calling everyone into community with Christ.

Jesus Christ, the eternal Son with the Father in eternity—this means that nothing created can be conceived and essentially understood in its nature apart from Christ, the mediator of creation. Everything has been created through Christ and toward Christ, and everything has its existence only in Christ (Col. 1:15ff.). Seeking to understand God's will with creation apart from Christ is futile.

Jesus Christ, the God who became human—this means that God has bodily taken on human nature in its entirety, that from now on divine being can be found nowhere else but in human form, that in Jesus Christ human beings are set free to be truly human before God. Now the "Christian" is not something beyond the human, but it wants to be in the midst of the human. What is "Christian" is not an end in itself, but means that human beings may and should live as human beings before God. In becoming human, God is revealed as the one who seeks to be there not for God's own sake but "for us." To live as a human being before God, in the light of God's becoming human, can only mean to be there not for oneself, but for God and for other human beings.

Jesus Christ, the crucified Reconciler—this means, first, that by its rejection of Jesus Christ the entire world has become godless, and that no effort on its part can lift this curse from it. In the cross of Christ the worldliness of the world has once and for all received its identifying mark. However, Christ's cross is the cross of the world's reconciliation with God. Therefore, precisely the godless world simultaneously stands under the identifying mark of reconciliation as freely instituted by God. The cross of reconciliation sets us free to live before God in the midst of the godless world, sets us free to live in genuine worldliness [*Weltlichkeit*]. The proclamation of the cross of reconciliation frees us to abandon futile attempts to deify the world, because it has overcome the divisions, tensions, and conflicts between the "Christian" and the "worldly," and calls us to single-minded action and life in faith in the already accomplished reconciliation of the world with God. A life of genuine worldliness is possible only through the proclamation of the crucified Christ. Thus I not possible in contradiction to the proclamation, and also not beside it in some kind of autonomy of the worldly; but it is precisely "in, with, and under" the proclamation of Christ that a genuinely worldly life is possible and real. The godlessness and godforsakenness of the world cannot be recognized apart from or in opposition to the proclamation of the cross of Christ, for the worldly will always seek to satisfy its unquenchable desire for its own deification. Where the worldly nevertheless establishes its own law beside the proclamation of Christ, there it falls completely under its own spell, and in the end must set itself in God's place. In both cases the worldly ceases to be worldly. Left to its own devices, the worldly is neither willing nor able to be only worldly, but it desperately and frantically seeks its own deification. Consequently it is precisely this decidedly and exclusively worldly life that becomes trapped in a halfhearted pseudo-worldliness. It lacks the freedom and courage for a genuine and full-blown worldliness, that is, the freedom and courage to let the world be what it really is before God, namely, a world that in its godlessness is reconciled with God. The substantive characteristics of this "genuine worldliness" we will have to discuss later. What is decisive here is only that *there is genuine worldliness only and precisely because of the proclamation of the cross of Jesus Christ.*

Jesus Christ, the risen and exalted Lord—this means that Jesus Christ has overcome sin and death, and is the living Lord to whom has been given all power in heaven and on earth. All worldly powers are subject to and bound to serve Christ, each in its own way. The proclamation of Christ is now addressed to all creatures as the liberating call to come under the lordship of Jesus Christ. This proclamation is not subject to any earthly limitations; it is ecumenical, which means it is not possible in contradiction to the proclamation, and also not beside it in some kind of autonomy of the worldly; but it is precisely "in, with, and under" the proclamation of Christ that a genuinely worldly life is possible and real. The godlessness and godforsakenness of the world cannot be recognized apart from or in opposition to the proclamation of the cross of Christ, for the worldly will always seek to satisfy its unquenchable desire for its own deification. Where the worldly nevertheless establishes its own law beside the proclamation of Christ, there it falls completely under its own spell, and in the end must set itself in God's place. In both cases the worldly ceases to be worldly. Left to its own devices, the worldly is neither willing nor able to be only worldly, but it desperately and frantically seeks its own deification. Consequently it is precisely this decidedly and exclusively worldly life that becomes trapped in a halfhearted pseudo-worldliness. It lacks the freedom and courage for a genuine and full-blown worldli-ness, that is, the freedom and courage to let the world be what it really is before God, namely, a world that in its godlessness is reconciled with God. The substantive char-acteristics of this "genuine worldliness" we will have to discuss later. What is decisive here is only that *there is genuine worldliness only and precisely because of the proclamation of the cross of Jesus Christ.*

Jesus Christ, the risen and exalted Lord—this means that Jesus Christ has overcome sin and death, and is the living Lord to whom has been given all power in heaven and on earth. All worldly powers are subject to and bound to serve Christ, each in its own way. The proclamation of Christ is now addressed to all creatures as the liberating call to come under the lordship of Jesus Christ. This proclamation is not subject to any earthly limitations; it is ecumenical, which means it encompasses the entire globe. The lordship of Jesus Christ is not a foreign rule, but the lordship of the Creator, Reconciler, and Redeemer. It is the lordship of the one through whom and toward whom all created being exists, indeed the one in whom alone all created being finds its origin, essence, and goal. Jesus Christ does not impose a foreign law on created being, but neither does Christ permit created being to have an autonomy [Eigeng-esetzlichkeit] apart from Christ's commandment. The commandment of Jesus Christ, the living Lord, sets created being free to fulfill its own law; that is the law inherent in it from its origin, essence, and goal in Jesus Christ. The commandment of Jesus Christ does not establish the rule of the church over government, nor the rule of gov-ernment over family, nor of culture over government and church, or whatever other relationships of dominance may be conceivable here. To be sure, the commandment of Jesus Christ rules church, family, culture, and government. But it does so by simul-taneously setting each of these mandates free to exercise their respective functions. Jesus Christ's claim to rule as it is proclaimed by the church simultaneously means that family, culture, and government are set free to be what they are in their own nature as grounded in Christ. Only through this liberation, which springs from the proclaimed rule of Christ, can the divine mandates be properly with-one-another, for-one-another, and against-one-another, as we will have to discuss extensively at a later point.

We just said that the rule of Christ's commandment over all created being is not synonymous with the rule of the church. With this assertion we have touched upon a crucial problem of the church's mandate, which we can no longer avoid.

It is the mandate of the church to proclaim God's revelation in Jesus Christ. However, it is the mystery of this name that it denotes not merely an individual human being, but at the same time comprises all of human nature within itself. Jesus Christ can always only be proclaimed and witnessed to as the one in whom God has bodily taken on humanity. Jesus Christ is one in whom there is the new humanity, the community of God [Gemeinde Gottes]. In Jesus Christ the word of God and the community-of-God are inextricably bound together. Through Jesus Christ the word of God and the community-of-God belong inseparably together. Thus, where Jesus Christ is proclaimed according to the divine mandate, there is also always a church-community. To begin with, this simply means that there are human beings who accept, believe, and simply allow themselves to receive the word of Christ, in contrast to others who do not accept but reject it. It means that there are human beings who allow themselves to receive what, from God's perspective, all human beings should actually receive; it means that there are human beings who stand vicariously in the place [stellvertretend dastehen] of all other human beings, of the whole world. To be sure, they are human beings who at the same time lead their worldly lives in family, culture, and government, and do so as those who through Christ's word1 have been set free for life in the world. However, gathering around the divine word, having been chosen by and living in this word, they now also constitute a corporate entity [Gemeinwesen], a body in its own right that is separate from the worldly orders. This "corporate entity" is now our subject, specifically and first of all with regard to its necessary distinction from the divine mandate of proclamation. The word of God, as it is proclaimed by virtue of the divine mandate, rules over and governs all the world. The "corporate entity" that comes into being around this word does not rule over the world, but only serves the fulfilling of the divine mandate. The law within this "corporate entity" can never and may never become the law of the worldly orders lest an alien rule be established. Conversely, the law of a worldly order can never and may never become the law of this corporate entity. The uniqueness of the divine mandate of the church thus consists in the fact that the proclamation of Christ's lordship over all the world needs to remain distinct from the "law" of the church as a corporate entity, while, on the other hand, the church as a corporate entity cannot be separated from the office of proclamation.

The church as a distinct corporate entity serves to fulfill the divine mandate and does so in a twofold way: *first,* in that everything in this corporate entity is oriented toward effectively proclaiming Christ to all the world—which means that the church-community itself is merely an instrument, a means to an end; *second,* in that by this action of the church-community on behalf of the world and in its stead, the goal of the divine mandate of proclamation and the beginning of its fulfillment has already been reached. Thus the church-community, precisely by seeking to be merely an instrument and a means to an end, has in fact become the goal and center of all that God is doing with the world. The concept of vicarious representative action [Stellvertretung] defines this dual relationship most clearly. The Christian community stands in the place in which the whole world should stand. In this respect it serves the world as vicarious representative; it is there for the world's sake. On the other hand, the place where the church-community stands is the place where the world fulfills its own destiny; the church-community is the "new creation," the "new creature," the goal of God's ways on earth. In this dual vicarious representation, the church-community is in complete community with its Lord; it follows in discipleship the one who was the Christ precisely in being there completely for the world and not for himself.

The church as a distinct corporate entity is thus subject to a double divine purpose, to both of which it must do justice, namely, being oriented toward the world, and, in this very act, simultaneously being oriented toward itself as the place where Jesus Christ is present. As a distinct corporate entity, it is characteristic of the church to express the unlimited message of Christ within the delimited domain of its own cultural [geistig] and material resources, and it is precisely the unlimitedness of the message of Christ that calls people back into the delimited domain of the church-community.

Selection 2: *Letters and Papers from Prison*

> *These passages are taken from his letters to his friend Eberhard Bethge written on June 8, 1944, and July 16, 1944. They express ideas about human autonomy in a "world come of age." This phrase and Bonhoeffer's insights briefly stated in these letters were to spark considerable discussion among theologians and ethicists of very different theological orientations, including those who pursued the theme of a "religionless Christianity."*

June 8, 1944

The movement toward human autonomy (by which I mean discovery of the laws by which the world lives and manages its affairs in science, in society and government, in art, ethics, and religion), which began around the thirteenth century (I don't want to get involved in disputing exactly when), has reached a certain completeness in our age. Human beings have learned to manage all important issues by themselves, without recourse to "Working hypothesis: God." In questions of science or art, as well as in ethical questions, this has become a matter of course, so that hardly anyone dares rock the boat anymore. But in the last hundred years or so, this has also become increasingly true of religious questions; it's becoming evident that everything gets along without "God" and does so just as well as before. As in the scientific domain, so in human affairs generally, "God" is being pushed further and further out of our life, losing ground. The historical views of both Catholics and Protestants agree that this development must be seen as the great falling-away from God, from Christ, and the more they lay claim to God and Christ in opposing this, and play them off against it, the more this development considers itself anti-Christian. The world, now that it has become conscious of itself and the laws of its existence, is sure of itself in a way that it is becoming uncanny for us. Failures, things going wrong, can't shake the world's confidence in the necessity of its course and its development; such things are accepted with fortitude and sobriety as part of the bargain, and even an event like this war is no exception. In very different forms the Christian apologetic is now moving against this self-confidence. It is trying to persuade this world that has come of age that it cannot live without "God" as its guardian. Even after we have capitulated on all worldly matters, there still remain the so-called ultimate questions—death, guilt—which only "God" can answer, and for which people need God and the church and the pastor. So in a way we live off these so-called ultimate human questions. But what happens if some day they no longer exist as such, or if they are being answered "without God"? Here is where the secularized offshoots of Christian theology come in, that is, the existential philosophers and the psychotherapists, to prove to secure, contented ,and happy human beings that they are in reality miserable and desperate and just don't want to admit that they are in a perilous situation, unbeknown to themselves, from which only existentialism or psychotherapy can rescue them. Where there is health, strength, security, and simplicity, these experts scent sweet fruit on which they can gnaw or lay their corrupting eggs. They set about to drive people to inner despair, and then they have a game they can win. This is secularized Methodism. And whom does it reach? A small number of intellectuals, of degenerates, those who consider themselves most important in the world and therefore enjoy being preoccupied with themselves. A simple man who spends his daily life with work and family, and certainly also with various stupid affairs, won't be affected. He has neither time nor inclination to be concerned with his existential despair, or to see his perhaps modest share of happiness as having "perilous," "worrisome," or "disastrous" aspects. I consider the attack by Christian apologetics on the world's coming of age as, first of all, pointless, second, ignoble, and, third, unchristian. Pointless—because it appears to me like trying to put a person who has become an adult back into puberty, that is, to make people dependent on a lot of things on which they in fact no longer depend, to shove them into problems that in fact are no longer problems for them. Ignoble—because an attempt is being made here to exploit people's weaknesses for alien purposes to which they have not consented freely. Unchristian—because it confuses Christ with a particular stage of human religiousness, namely, with a human law. More about this later, but first a few more words about the historical situation. The question is Christ and the world that has come of age. The weakness of liberal theology was that it allowed the world the right to assign to Christ his place within it; that it accepted, in the dispute between church and world, the—relatively mild—peace terms dictated by the world. Its strength was that it did not try to turn back the course of history and really took up the battle (Troeltsch!), even though this ended in its defeat. Defeat was followed by capitulation and the attempt at a completely new beginning, based on "regaining awareness" of its own foundations in the Bible and the Reformation. Heim sought, along pietist-methodist lines, to convince individuals that they were confronted with the alternatives "despair or Jesus." He was winning "hearts." Althaus (continuing the modern positivist line in a strongly confessional direction) tried to regain from the world some room for Lutheran doctrine (ministry) and Lutheran ritual, otherwise leaving the world to its own devices. Tillich undertook the religious interpretation of the development of the world itself—against its will—giving it its form through religion. That was very brave, but the world threw him out of the saddle and galloped on by itself. He too thought he understood the world better than it did itself, but the world felt totally misunderstood and rejected such an insinuation. (The world does need to be understood in a better way than it does itself! But not "religiously," the way the religious socialists want to do.) Barth was the first to recognize the error of all these attempts (which were basically all still sailing in the wake of liberal theology, without intending to do so) in that they all aim to save some room for religion in the world or over against the world. He led the God of Jesus Christ forward to battle against religion, *pneuma* against *sarx*. This remains his greatest merit (the second edition of The Epistle to the Romans, despite all the neo-Kantian eggshells t). Through his later Dogmatics he has put the church in a position to carry this distinction in principle all the way through. It was not in his ethics that he eventually failed, as is often said—his ethical observations, so far as they exist, are as important as his dogmatic ones—but in the nonreligious interpretation of theological concepts he gave no concrete guidance, either in dogmatics or ethics. Here he reaches his limit, and that is why his theology of revelation has become positivist, a "positivism of revelation," as

I call it. To a great extent the Confessing Church now has forgotten all about Barth's approach and lapsed from positivism into conservative restoration. Its significance is that it holds fast to the great concepts of Christian theology, but it appears to be exhausting itself gradually in the process. Certainly these concepts contain the elements of genuine prophecy (which include the claim to the truth as well as mercy, as you mentioned) and of genuine ritual, and only to that extent does the message of the Confessing Church get attention, a hearing—and rejection.

Both remain undeveloped, remote, because they lack interpretation. Those who, like, for example, P. Schutz or the Oxford or Berneuchen movements, who long for "movement" and "life," are dangerous reactionaries, backward looking, because they want to go back before the beginnings of revelation theology and seek "religious" renewal. They haven't understood the problem at all, so their talk is completely beside the point. They have no future whatsoever (except possibly the Oxford people, if only they weren't so lacking in biblical substance). As for Bultmann, he seems to have sensed Barth's limitation somehow, but misunderstands it in the sense of liberal theology, and thus falls into typical liberal reductionism (the "mythological" elements in Christianity are taken out, thus reducing Christianity to its "essence"). My view, however, is that the full content, including the "mythological" concepts, must remain— the New Testament is not a mythological dressing up of a universal truth, but this mythology (resurrection and so forth) is the thing itself!—but that these concepts must now be interpreted in a way that does not make religion the condition for faith (cf. the *peritomei* in Paul!). Only then, in my opinion, is liberal theology overcome (which still determines even Barth, if only in a negative way), but at the same time the question it asks is really taken up and answered (which is not the case with the Confessing Church's positivism of revelation!). The fact that the world has come of age is no longer an occasion for polemics and apologetics, but is now actually better understood than it understands itself, namely, from the gospel and from Christ.

Now to your question of whether the church has any "ground" left to stand on, or whether it is losing it altogether, and the other question, whether Jesus himself used the human "predicament" as a point of contact, so that "achine," criticized above, is in the right.

July 16, 1944

Now for a few more thoughts on our topic. I'm just working gradually toward the nonreligious interpretation of biblical concepts. I am more able to see what needs to be done than how I can actually do it. Historically there is just one major development leading to the world's autonomy. In theology it was Lord Herbert of Cherbury who first asserted that reason is sufficient for religious understanding. In moral philosophy Montaigne and Bodin substitute rules for life for the commandments. In political philosophy Macchiavelli separates politics from general morality and founds the doctrine of reason of state. Later H. Grotius, very different from Macchiavelli in content, but following the same trend toward the autonomy of human society, sets up his natural law as an international law, which is valid *etsi deus non daretur*, "as if there were no God." Finally, the philosophical closing line: on one hand, the deism of Descartes: the world is a mechanism that keeps running by itself without God's intervention; on the other hand, Spinoza's pantheism: God is nature. Kant is basically a deist; Fichte and Hegel are pantheists. In every case the autonomy of human beings and the world is the goal of thought. (In the natural sciences this obviously begins with Nicholas of Cusa and Giordano Bruno and their—"heretical"—doctrine of the infinity of the universe [der Welt]. The cosmos of antiquity is finite, as is the created world of medieval thought. An infinite universe—however it is conceived—is self-subsisting, "etsi deus non daretur." However, modern physics now doubts that the universe is infinite, yet without falling back to the earlier notions of its finitude.) As a working hypothesis for morality, politics, and the natural sciences, God has been overcome and done away with, but also as a working hypothesis for philosophy and religion (Feuerbach!). It is a matter of intellectual integrity to drop this working hypothesis, or eliminate it as far as possible. An edifying scientist, physician, and so forth is a hybrid. So where is any room left for God? Ask those who are anxious, and since they don't have an answer, they condemn the entire development that has brought them to this impasse. I have already written to you about the various escape routes out of this space that has become too narrow. What could be added to that is the *salto mortale* back to the Middle Ages. But the medieval principle is heteronomy, in the form of clericalism. The return to that is only a counsel of despair, a sacrifice made only at the cost of intellectual integrity. It's a dream, to the tune of "Oh, if only I knew the road back, the long road to childhood's land!" There is no such way—at least not by willfully throwing away one's inner integrity, but only in the sense of Matt. 18:3, that is, through repentance, through ultimate honesty! And we cannot be honest unless we recognize that we have to live in the world "etsi deus non daretur." And this is precisely what we do recognize—before God! God himself compels us to recognize it. Thus our coming of age leads us to a truer recognition of our situation before God. God would have us know that we must live as those who manage their lives without God. The same God who is with us is the God who forsakes us (Mark 15:34!). The same God who makes us to live in the world without the working hypothesis of God is the God before whom we stand continually. Before God, and with God, we live without God. God consents to be pushed out of the world and onto the cross; God is weak and powerless in the world and in precisely this way, and only so, is at our side and helps us. Matt. 8:17 makes it quite clear that Christ helps us not by virtue of his omnipotence but rather by virtue of his weakness and suffering! This is the crucial distinction between Christianity and all religions. Human religiosity directs people in need to the power of God in the world, God as deus ex machina. The Bible directs people toward the powerlessness and the suffering of God; only the suffering God can help. To this extent, one may say that the previously described development toward the world's coming of age, which has cleared the way by eliminating a false notion of God, frees us to see the God of the Bible, who gains ground and power in the world by being powerless. This will probably be the starting point for our "worldly interpretation."

For Further Reading

The following select list of writings provides a mixture of primary and secondary sources related to the major parts of the anthology, and the full text of the works being excerpted will also provide rich additional reading.

Barth, Karl. *Ethics.* Edited by Dietrich Braun. Translated by Geoffrey Bromily. New York: Seabury, 1981.

Bonhoeffer, Dietrich. *Discipleship.* Translated from the German Edition by Martin Kuske and Ilse Tödt. English Edition edited by Geffrey Ke. Minneapolis: Fortress Press, 2001.

Dorn, Jacob Henry. *Washington Gladden: Prophet of the Social Gospel.* Columbus: Ohio State University Press, 1968.

Lovin, Robin. *Reinhold Niebuhr.* Nashville: Abingdon, 2008.

Minus, Paul M. *Walter Rauschenbusch: American Reformer.* New York: Macmillan; London: Collier Macmillan, 1988.

Niebuhr, Reinhold. *Moral Man and Immoral Society: A Study in Ethics and Politics.* Louisville: Westminster John Knox, 2001.

———. *The Nature and Destiny of Man: A Christian Interpretation.* 2 Volumes. Introduction by Robin W. Lovin. Westminster John Knox, 1996.

Rasmussen, Larry L. *Dietrich Bonhoeffer: Reality and Resistance.* Louisville: Westminster John Knox, 2005.

Rauschenbusch, Walter. *Selected Writings.* Edited by Winthrop S. Hudson. New York: Paulist, 1984.

Tillich, Paul. *Love, Power and Justice: Ontological Analysis and Ethical Applications.* London and New York: Oxford University Press, 1971.

———. *The Protestant Era.* Chicago: University of Chicago Press, 1957.

———. *Theology of Peace.* Edited by Ronald H. Stone. Louisville: Westminster John Knox, 1990.

Webster, J. S. *Barth's Moral Theology: Human Action in Barth's Thought.* Grand Rapids: Eerdmans, 1998.

PART 10

Twentieth-Century Feminist
and Womanist Ethics

❧ *As an expression of Christian social teaching, feminist theology and ethics develops within and alongside the broader social movements that have sought equal rights for women. However, feminist theology and ethics has gone beyond issues of civil rights and equal opportunity and equal treatment in the workplace to concern itself with all forms of patriarchal oppression in social roles and in the institutional practices and biases of the churches. This statement by Lisa Sowle Cahill from our third selection below is an apt definition of feminists ethics as an outgrowth of feminist theology. "The central, most direct, and most obvious way that feminist theology has influenced ethics is in its advocacy for women's concerns and women's perspective, expressed ethically as justice for women. Justice for women means to regard women as the social equals of men and to support their equal participation in the social roles that contribute to the common good, as well as their equal share in those benefits comprised by it." No one working in Christian social ethics today can ignore the contributions of feminist ethicists.*

Selection 1: Rosemary Radford Ruether, *Sexism and God-Talk*

Rosemary Radford Ruether (born 1936) is a distinguished church historian and theologian who is considered one of the most influential pioneers in feminist theology. The term God/ess, which is appears in our excerpt is one she coined to challenge the male dominated language of traditional theology and to make the point that we do not possess a satisfactory way to name God. In this excerpt from Sexism and God-Talk, *one of her most heralded books, we gain a sense of her feminist social critique as it speaks both to church and society.*

Ministry and Community for a People Liberated from Sexism

We have named sexism as a serious expression of human sinfulness, of alienation from authentic existence. Such a recognition of sexism as sin requires a radical redefinition of ministry and church. The grace of conversion from patriarchal domination opens up a new vision of humanity for women and men, one that invites us to recast and re-create all our relationships. Church, as the avant-garde of liberated humanity, should be the support system for this process. Conversion to a new humanity cannot take place in isolation. Psychologically, one cannot affirm a feminist identity against the historical weight of patriarchal oppression by oneself. Theologically, it is essential to understand redemption as a communal, not just an individual, experience. Just as sin implies alienation and broken community, so rebirth to authentic selfhood implies a community that assembles in the collective discovery of this new humanity and that provides the matrix of regeneration.

It is precisely when feminists discover the congruence between the Gospel and liberation from sexism that they also experience their greatest alienation from existing churches. The discovery of alternative possibilities for identity and the increasing conviction that an alternative is a more authentic understanding of the Gospel make all the more painful and insulting the reality of most historical churches. These churches continue to ratify, by their language, institutional structures, and social commitments, the opposite message. The more one becomes a feminist the more difficult it becomes to go to church.

The women's movement does create its own alternative expressions of community. Women bond together in support groups and coalitions for action. They gather in many places, often outside the formal organizations of church and society, to share experiences and analysis. They begin to build their own organizations. Seldom does such feminist networking allow women to name the religious dimension of their struggle or to get in touch with healing spiritual power to support their new options. Religious feminists experience a starvation of sacramental nourishment, a famine of the Word of God/ess. The churches, the great symbol-making institutions of their traditions, operate as a countersign to their hopes.

Is the Christian Church usable as ecclesia for women and men seeking liberation from patriarchy? Will the increasing participation of women in ministry provide alternative options in the foreseeable future? Or has the recent entry of women into ministry in token numbers failed to challenge, for the most part, the patriarchal interpretation of Christianity? We need to recapitulate briefly the theologies that have excluded women from ministry and also those that have included women. This will lead us to ask what kind of ministry women (and men) can exercise in the Church today that is compatible with liberation from patriarchy.

Women and Ministry: Theologies of Exclusion and Inclusion

The patriarchal theology that has prevailed throughout most of Christian history in most Christian traditions has rigidly barred women from ministry. The arguments for this exclusion are identical with the arguments of patriarchal anthropology. Women are denied leadership in the churches for the same reasons they are denied leadership in society. Contrary to some recent apologetics, the Christian tradition never affirmed women's inclusion in social leadership while arguing for women's exclusion from ministry based on the special nature of ministry. The arguments for women's exclusion from ministry are applications of the general theology of male headship and female subordination. This subordination, while attributed to women's physiological role in procreation, extends to an inferiority of mind and soul as well. Women are categorized as less capable than men of moral self-control and reason. They can play only a passive role in the giving and receiving of ministry. They should keep silent.

Priestly traditions also define women's "uncleanness" in religious terms. Female bodiliness is seen as polluting and defiling the sacred. Women must be distanced from the Holy. Holiness becomes a male mystery that annuls the finitude and mortality of birth from the female. Women may be baptized, but they cannot represent this process of rebirth and nourishment in the realm of male holiness. The near hysteria that erupted in recent years in the Episcopal Church when women began visibly to use the priestly sacramental symbols reveals the pathology that underlies the exclusion of women from ministry. The pathology seems to be even more violent when the issue is not just women as preachers but women as priests. This shows the extent to which the rejection of woman as maternal flesh adds another dimension beyond simply negation of woman as teacher. The most extreme repugnance against the idea of women in ministry typically is expressed in the question "Can you imagine a pregnant woman at the altar?"

Recent feminist scholarship has pointed to the existence of an alternative tradition in the Jesus movement and early Christianity. This alternative Christianity could have suggested a very different construction of Christian theology: women as equal with men in the divine mandate of creation, restored to this equality in Christ; the gifts of the Spirit poured out on men and women alike; the Church as the messianic society, not over against creation but over against the systems of domination. We see hints of this vision in the New Testament. But the Deutero-Pauline recasting of Christianity in patriarchal terms made this inclusive theology nonnormative.

Inclusive or "counter-cultural Christianity" did not disappear, but it went underground. It became identified with heretical sects whose traditions are preserved only in fragments or through the polemics of the dominant religion. Moreover, the Gnostic interpretation of this inclusive Christianity in the second and third centuries creates a dualism between the eschatological realm and the world of material creation. Gnosticism thus shares with patriarchal Christianity the as-assumption that women are subordinate in the material or pro-creational order. Only as an ascetic elite do women and men share leadership power in anticipation of the heavenly realm above, in which there is no procreation and no sexual division.

The difference between this Gnostic option and the patriarchal Church lies in the Gnostic assumption that the Church and its ministry follow the eschatological, not the creational, order.' This concept of the Church led by an inclusive celibate elite was rediscovered in Albigensian sects that appeared in the Middle Ages and in the Shakers in the early modern period. But the dominant patriarchal Church marginalized even this idea of women's public ministry as members of the celibate elite.

Prophetic charisms have also been a way of including women in ministry. The Christian churches have never denied that the gifts of the Spirit are poured out on men and women alike. But in the second and third centuries rising episcopal power struggled to suppress the autonomous power of prophets. The historical ministry of bishops, as keepers of the keys and discerners of spirits, claimed the right to judge and control the occasional ministry of prophets and prophetesses. It routinized the power of the Spirit as automatically transmitted through apostolic succession and thus illegitimized any prophecy not under episcopal control.'

Nevertheless, the phenomenon of independent prophets and prophetesses does not disappear from popular Christianity. Medieval Christianity sought either to discipline such persons within religious orders or to suppress them as heretics, as is evident by the contrary fates of Franciscans' and Waldensians. The initial power accorded Joan of Arc testifies to the medieval openness to the prophetess as long as she appeared to be winning. Her execution and subsequent exoneration by the French monarchy she helped restore to power reflects a conflict between contrary alignments of ecclesiastical and political power—the one seeking to illegitimate her victories by defining her as a witch, the other legitimating their own power by vindicating her as a true prophet-emissary from God.

In the left-wing sects of the Reformation is a new appearance of groups who define the free prophetic Spirit as the true author of Christian ministry. For radical Puritan sects in the seventeenth century, the Spirit can raise up preachers of the Word who speak with authority, not from the authorized channels of feudal priest or university cleric but among the humble weavers and spinsters of the lower orders of society." In movements in which the Spirit authorizes ministerial gifts directly, in which the community rather than the institutional authorities validate the authenticity of the gifts, women occasionally are found as preachers. This is the case among Baptists and Quakers in the seventeenth-century English Civil War sects and again in the nineteenth-century American Pentecostal and Holiness movements. The Spirit is no discriminator among persons on the basis of gender but can empower whomever it will. Ministry is proven by its gifts, not by its credentials.

But prophecy is unstable as a means of long-term inclusion of women in ministry. Movements that accepted in the first generation women's right to preach and teach as prophetesses later become institutionalized, and the gifts of the Spirit are routinized in an ordained clergy that excludes the participation of women. Women's ministry based on charismatic gifts is both continually reborn in practice and continually marginalized from power in historical Church institutions.

Nineteenth-century America represents a new stage in the conflict between woman's capacity for holiness and her right to exercise ministerial roles. The disestablishment of the churches and the privatization of religion shift the cultivation of piety to the home. Femininity and piety become increasingly identified. This suggests to many women that they are uniquely capable of evangelizing others. Conservative churchmen seek to control this by segregating women's evangelical role strictly within the home, as uplifter of husband and children, and within the private women's prayer group."

But once empowered, women's evangelizing activities constantly break out of these domestic limits. The prayer group turns into a revival meeting with women as organizers and then as preachers. Benevolent societies turn into women's home and foreign missionary societies with their own budgets, their own leadership in women's hands. From these roles as evangelical preachers and organizers of benevolent societies women begin to demand ordained ministry.

Liberal feminism succeeds in opening up the ordained ministry to women. The liberal tradition reclaims the idea of women's equality in the imago dei, but it secularizes it. Women are declared to be sharers of a common human nature, which is the basis of social rights. Natural rights become the ideological basis for renovating the social order. The arguments for women's ordination in the nineteenth century also draw on prophetic and romantic themes. The text of Acts 2:17-18, in which the gifts of the Spirit are said to be poured out on men and women alike, was constantly evoked to justify women's right to preach. Likewise it is said that women's altruistic and nurturing nature and her natural spirituality especially suit her for ministry. But these arguments carry weight only when combined with the liberal assumption that a just social order should grant equal rights and opportunities to all its members.

These various traditions were brought together in the sermon delivered by Luther Lee, an evangelical preacher who led the ordination service for Antoinette Brown, the first woman ordained to the Congregational ministry, in 1853. Lee took his text from Galatians 3:28: "In Christ there is neither male nor female." And he combined it with Acts 2:17-18. He argued that the preaching office is the same as the prophetic office. Since the gifts of prophecy are given to women as well as men in the New Testament, there has never been any excuse for excluding women from the ordained ministry. The preaching office was given to women by Christ. Lee's argument depended on the identification of prophetic charisms and historic ministry.

Antoinette Brown's ordination was part of the first wave of liberal feminism, which is manifest in the Seneca Falls Women's Rights Convention of 1848. The leaders of this convention base their Declaration of the Rights of Women on the American Declaration of Independence and Bill of Rights. They protest against patriarchal theology, declare the equality of women and men in creation to be the authentic Biblical view, and call for the inclusion of women in theological study, teaching, and ministry. Among the "repeated injuries and usurpations on the part of man toward woman, having the direct object of establishing an absolute tyranny over her," against which they protest in this document are numerous matters having to do with male religious privilege. The document ends with a final resolution, offered by Lucretia Mott, herself a Quaker minister, which reads:

> *Resolved:* that the speedy success of our cause depends upon the zealous and untiring efforts of both men and women for the overthrow of the monopoly of the pulpit, and for the securing to women of equal participation with men in various trades, professions and commerce.

A few Protestant groups begin to ordain women in the nineteenth century, it is not until the mid-1950s to 1970s that most major American Protestant denominations begin to ordain women. Only since 1970 have sufficient numbers of women begun to attend seminary and to become ordained for ministry that the implications for the nature of Church and ministry have begun to be raised. We begin to see that the securing of women's ordination through liberal assumptions contains the seeds of its own contradiction. Women are included in ministry through a concept of justice as equal opportunity. But this perspective neglects any critique of the public order beyond a demand for equal opportunity of all persons in it regardless of gender. The shaping of the form and symbols of ministry by patriarchal culture, to the exclusion of women, is not seen as making the historic form of ministry itself problematic. Women win inclusion in this same ministry, without asking whether ministry itself needs to be redefined.

The patriarchal symbols and the hierarchical relationship of the ministry to the laity are still taken as normative. Women are allowed in token numbers to integrate themselves into this male-defined role. They adopt the same garb, the same titles (Reverend, if not Father), the same clerical modes of functioning in a hierarchically structured church. They too stand in the phallically designed pulpit and bring down the "seminal" word upon the passive body of the laity. Women's ordained status thus remains symbolically and socially anomalous. Even winning the legal right to ordination is not secure. Later, a backlash against it may occur, as in the Swedish Lutheran Church, in which male priests and theologians dragged out all the old arguments linking maleness and priesthood, including pollution taboos, to argue for the illegitimacy of women's ordination." Women play the ministerial role by endlessly proving that they can think, feel, and act like "one of the boys." The "boys," in turn, accept them only in token numbers that do not threaten their monopoly on ecclesiastical power (anything above five percent is perceived as a threat to this monopoly). But they continually subvert women in practice, intimating that they should retain their "femininity" by exercising a different ministry from men, as assistant minister in charge of children, youth, and the aged, not as "the Minister" with full authority. Women in ministry, like all women trying to function in public roles under male rules, find themselves in a double bind. They are allowed success only by being better than men at the games of masculinity, while at the same time they are rebuked for having lost their femininity. In such a system it is not possible for women to be equal, but only to survive in a token and marginal way at tremendous physical and psychological cost.

Ministry and Community for Liberation from Patriarchy

Church as Liberation Community

Feminist liberation theology starts with the understanding of Church as liberation community as the context for under-standing questions of ministry, creed, worship, or mission. Without a community committed to liberation from sexism, all questions such as the forms of ministry or mission are meaningless. Conversion from sexism means both freeing oneself from the ideologies and roles of patriarchy and also struggling to liberate social structures from these patterns. A feminist liberation Church must see itself as engaged in both of these struggles as the center of its identity as Church. Joining the Church means entrance into a community of people who share this commitment and support one another in it.

*   *   *

The New Earth: Socioeconomic Redemption from Sexism

Christianity has, in its New Testament foundations, traditions that would affirm the equality of woman in the image of God and the restoration of her full personhood in Christ. But even the primarily marginalized traditions that have affirmed this view through the centuries have not challenged the socioeconomic and legal subordination of women. Equality in Christ has been understood to apply to a new redeemed order beyond creation, to be realized in Heaven. Even when anticipated on earth, equality in Christ is confined to the monastery or the Church, the eschatological community. Patriarchy as order of nature or creation remains the underlying assumption of mainstream and radical Christianity alike. If woman becomes equal as virgin, prophetess, martyr, mystic, or even preacher, it is because these roles are seen as gifts of the Spirit and harbingers of a transcendent order. Only with the Enlightenment is there a shift to an egalitarian concept of "original nature" that challenges the "naturalness" of hierarchical social structures.

The claim that redemption in Christ has a social dimension has come about in modern Christianity only by an identification of its inherited messianic symbols with their secular interpretation in liberalism and socialism. But this new consciousness is still under continuous challenge by conservative Christians who seek to invalidate any theology, whether from a feminist, class, or racial minority perspective, that would make socioeconomic liberation an intrinsic part of the meaning of redemption. Such Christians would claim that redemption is a purely spiritual matter and has nothing to do with socio-economic changes.

This individualizing and spiritualizing of salvation is the reverse side of the individualizing of sin. Sin is recognized only in individual acts, not structural systems. One is called to examine one's sinfulness in terms of abuses of oneself and personal unkindness to one's neighbor, but not in terms of the vast collective structures of war, racism, poverty, and, least of all, the oppression of women. In more sophisticated circles, Reinhold Niebuhr's division between "moral man" and "immoral society" is used to declare that altruism and love is possible, if at all, only on the interpersonal level. Collective groups, especially large ones, like nation-states, can only pursue an ethic of self-interest.

This "realism" is distorted by neoconservatives into an attack on any effort to create a more just society as fanatical and utopian. Liberation theology is condemned as a "heretical" effort to transcend the limits of historical existence, as though the present Western capitalist society represented the "limits" of historical existence and the "best of all possible worlds."' Such thinking neglects the early Niebuhr for whom such reflections on human limits are also an effort to find a solid basis for building a more just society. Niebuhr's working model of a more just society was democratic socialism. And he did not hesitate to think that even violent revolution might be ethically justified, at times, to break chains of colonial oppression and bring about the basis for such a new possibility.

The working assumption of this feminist theology has been the dynamic unity of creation and redemption. The God/ess who underlies creation and redemption is One. We cannot split a spiritual, antisocial redemption from the human self as a social being, embedded in sociopolitical and ecological systems. We must recognize sin precisely in this splitting and deformation of our true relationships to creation and to our neighbor and find liberation in an authentic harmony with all that is incarnate in our social, historical being. Socioeconomic humanization is indeed the outward manifestation of redemption.

The search for the good self and the good society exists in an unbreakable dialectic. One cannot neglect either side. One cannot assume, with Marxism, that new, just social institutions automatically will produce the "new humanity." But one also cannot suppose that simply building up an aggregate of converted individuals will cause those individuals to act differently, changing society without any attention to its structures. The sensitized consciousness causes individuals to band together to seek a transformed society, and new and more just social relations cause many people to act and become different.

In this chapter I examine different traditions of feminist liberation. . . .

LIBERAL FEMINISM

Liberal feminism has its roots in a feminist appropriation of the liberal traditions of equal rights, rooted in the doctrine of a common human nature of all persons. The liberal feminist agenda has been focused on the historic exclusion of women from access to and equal rights in the traditional male public sphere. It has sought to dismantle the historic structure of patriarchal law that denied women civil rights as autonomous adults. It has sought the full equality of women before the law, as citizens. This has entailed the repeal of discriminatory laws that denied property rights to married women especially, under the common-law rubric that the married woman was "civilly dead" and that her husband was her legal representative.

*   *   *

SOCIALIST FEMINISM

Socialism, like liberalism, operates under an unstated androcentric bias. It assumes that the male work role is the normative human activity. Women are to be liberated by being incorporated into the male realm. Liberalism would extend to women the legal right to do so, while socialism would provide women with the economic capacity to the advantage of such rights. Both assume that women are liberated insofar as they are able to function like men in the public realm.

*   *   *

RADICAL FEMINISM

For radical feminism the core issue is women's control over their own persons, their own bodies as vehicles of autonomous sexual expression, and their own reproduction. Patriarchy means above all, the subordination of women's bodies, sexuality, and reproduction to male ownership and control. Rape, wide beating, sexual harassment, pornography, the ideologies, culture, and fashions that socialize women to becoming objects of male sexual control, the denial of birth control and abortion, and, ultimately, the denial of female initiation and control over sexual relations—all are ramifications of the fundamental nature of patriarchy, the expropriation of woman as body by man. Any theory of women's liberation that stops short of liberating women from male control over their bodies has not reached the root of patriarchy.

*   *   *

IS THERE AN INTEGRATIVE FEMINIST VISION OF SOCIETY?

The search for an integrative vision starts with the assumption that feminism must include the liberal, socialist, and radical traditions. Each of these traditions shows its limitations precisely at the point where it tries to become final and to encapsulate itself within its own system. It remains insightful and authentic to the extent that it also remains open-ended. We have seen how the insufficiencies of each perspective suggest the need for the others. Liberal feminism opens into the questions of the economic hierarchies of work explored by socialist feminism. Radical feminism moves into an increasingly isolated, separatist utopianism that largely fails to address the real possibilities of most women and men, and so calls for its reintegration back into questions of social reorganization of mainstream society. Each of these perspectives can provide a part of a larger whole to the extent that we refuse the temptation to set up any one in a mutually exclusive relationship to the others.

What is the society we seek? We seek a society that affirms the values of democratic participation, of the equal value of all persons as the basis for their civil equality and their equal access to the educational and work opportunities of the society. But more, we seek a democratic socialist society that dismantles sexist and class hierarchies, that restores ownership and management of work to the base communities of workers themselves, who then create networks of economic and political relationships. Still more, we seek a society built on organic community, in which the processes of childraising, of education, of work, of culture have been integrated to allow both men and women to share child nurturing and homemaking and also creative activity and decision making in the larger society. Still more, we seek an ecological society in which human and nonhuman ecological systems have been integrated into harmonious and mutually supportive, rather than antagonistic, relations.

There are two ways to imagine going about building this new society. One is to build an alternative, communitarian system by a small voluntary group with a high intentionality and consciousness. Such a group would seek to put together all aspects of this feminist, socialist, communitarian, and ecological vision in a small experiment conducted on a separate social and economic base from the larger society. Such communal experiments have been carried out within history. They can be reasonably successful in fusing all aspects of the vision. Their limitation lies precisely in their inability to move beyond the small voluntary group and create a base for the larger society. A second method is to work on pieces of the vision separately: a communal child-care unit within an educational institution or workplace; an alternative energy system for an apartment building; solar greenhouses for a neighborhood; a women's collective that produces alternative culture for the society. We might develop within a self-managed institution less hierarchical forms of organization, more equal remuneration for all workers, men and women, regardless of their jobs. We might plan communities that allow more humanized relationships between the various aspects of people's lives. We might encourage a plurality of household patterns, homosexual as well as heterosexual, voluntary as well as blood- and marriage-related, where groups can share income and homemaking. We can think of these separate pieces of a mosaic that we are putting in place, gradually replacing the present picture with a new vision.

But the alternative nonsexist, nonclassist and nonexploitative world eludes us as a global system. This is not so much because of our inability to imagine it correctly as because of the insufficient collective power of those already converted to an alternative vision. The powers and principalities are still very much in control of most of the world. The nucleus of the alternative world remains, like the Church (theologically, as the Church), harbingers and experimenters with new human possibilities within the womb of the old.

Selection 2: Lisa Sowle Cahill, "Feminism and Christian Ethics," *Freeing Theology: The Essentials of Theology in Feminist Perspective*

Lisa Sowle Cahill is the J. Donald Monan, S.J., Professor at Boston College where she has taught since 1976. She is a major figure in Catholic social ethics in the United States and has been a prolific writer in the areas of sexuality and gender, bioethics, and matters of social justice and global concerns. Her article from which this segment is taken provides a helpful introduction to key aspects of feminist ethics in general and its engagement with traditional natural law thinking in Catholic ethics in particular.

The central, most direct, and most obvious way that feminist theology has influenced ethics is in its advocacy for women's concerns and women's perspective, expressed ethically as justice for women. Justice for women means to regard women as the moral and social equals of men and to support their equal participation in the social roles that contribute to the common good, as well as their equal share in those benefits comprised by it. For instance, the U.S. Catholic bishops in their recent pastoral letter on the economy' were explicitly concerned with the situation of women. The social and economic marginalization of many women and its attendant ill effects on women, their children, and their families were directly addressed in that document as they had not been in earlier Catholic social teaching. Previous documents, by contrast, had tended to speak generically of the rights and duties of "man?" Women's perspectives are also more important in traditional areas of so-called personal ethics. While abortion, for instance, was once simply treated as a simple matter of an unborn child's right to life versus the mother's interests, such as her own life or other lesser values, which could be objectively assessed, the woman's situation is now more frequently seen as lending a distinctive texture to the complexity of the abortion situation. Pope John Paul II writes sympathetically of the unwed mother, abandoned by the father of her child, who is pressured into an abortion. More importantly, women themselves are seen as indispensable contributors to the moral analysis of abortion.

In addition, feminism has influenced moral theology at a more fundamental level by shaping its questions and methods. At this level, feminism's influence is distinctive, though not unique. In other words, the characteristic contributions of feminist thinking are reflected in other, related approaches to ethics, especially that of liberation theology, of which feminist theology is usually understood to be a part.

These more fundamental contributions of feminism to theological ethics can be placed in three interdependent categories: (1) a revision of natural law as the basis of ethics; (2) an emphasis on the social and historical contexts of ethics, including a cross-cultural perspective; and (3) a renewal of Scripture as a source for ethics.

Feminism's special contribution of advocacy for women's liberation and these three fundamental but shared contributions to ethical method will be developed in turn. Then I will explore the contributions of feminism to Christian ethics at the practical level through discussing two areas of applied ethics: sex and gender, and war and peace.

Christian Feminism and Fundamental Ethics

Anne E. Patrick has defined feminism as endorsing "(1) a solid conviction of the equality of women and men, and (2) a commitment to reform society, including religious society, so that the full equality of women is respected, which requires also reforming the thought systems that legitimate the present unjust social order.'" Feminist theology is never merely theoretical but is also always practical. The integral relation of theory and practice (or, to use the Marxist term, praxis) is a premise of all political and liberation theologies. These theologies arise out of an experienced situation of oppression and have as a primary aim the deconstruction of unjust social structures and institutions. Thus, by definition, liberation theology is at the same time ethics.

Feminist theology emerges from women's experience of exclusion from social opportunity and power; it also aims at social change. The distinctive characteristic of liberation theology in its feminist variety is that it identifies with women as an oppressed group (as well as with men as also constrained by narrow gender-derived definitions of human identity) and that it seeks to introduce into the social agenda the importance of women's cause. Feminist theology begins with women's concrete reality, which it uses to critically address received traditions viewing women primarily in the service of institutionalized male dominance (patriarchy). As Margaret Farley asserts, "Feminist ethics traces its origins to women's growing awareness of the disparity between received traditional interpretations of their identity and function and their own experience of themselves and their lives." As such, it also claims a special "vantage point in a focus on women's experience precisely as disadvantaged." The moral test, from a feminist point of view, is the effect of an ethical position, moral decision, or policy on the actual lives of women. The feminist moral ideal is to transform persons and societies toward more mutual and cooperative relationships between women and men, reflecting their equality as human persons.

Natural Law as a Basis for Ethics: The Feminist Revision
Feminists often appeal to the full human stature of women as their moral criterion and call for its recognition. Farley insists that the "most fundamental" principle of feminism is that "women are fully human and are to be valued as such." This claim is also foundational to Rosemary Ruether's ethics. "The critical principle of feminist theology is the promotion of the full humanity of women. Whatever denies, diminishes, or distorts the full humanity of women is, therefore, appraised as not redemptive." This criterion, especially as proposed by these two prominent Catholic theologians, serves as an important point of contact with the natural law tradition and also suggests resources for its renewal.

The most distinctive characteristic of the Roman Catholic tradition of ethics is its foundation in the natural law morality of Thomas Aquinas. In the thirteenth century, Aquinas combined the theology of Augustine, with Aristotelian philosophy to locate morality within creation and redemption, and he also gave great importance to reason and human experience in discerning specific moral values and actions. The natural law he defined as humans' innate inclination toward what promotes human fulfillment; it has been instilled in the creature by God and is knowable by reason. By reflecting on experience itself, the human person can understand what sort of personal and political life will be most fulfilling for, humans and, with a somewhat lesser degree of certitude, what specific actions best fulfill in the concrete the universal moral values that can be, generalized from human behavior. For instance, all human beings seek to preserve their own lives, procreate and educate their young, live in society with others, and know the truth about God. By considering these general principles in relation to the specific requirements of life in society, we may arrive at moral rules about issues such as self-defense, war, capital punishment, or monogamous marriage, contraception, and abortion. Even though the exact formulation of such rules and their application may vary among cultures or situations, Aquinas's natural law morality provides a base on which to build a community of moral discourse that transcends cultures and unites individuals and societies. In this sense, the natural law morality is a reasonable and objective morality.

It is important to realize that while Aquinas himself took an inductive and flexible approach to natural law, exhibiting caution about the absoluteness of specific conclusions from the general principles, some of his neoscholastic heirs (under the influence of Cartesian and Kantian philosophy, with their ideals of clear concepts and absolute norms) turned the morality of nature into a rigid, ahistorical system, which functioned to control and sanction experience rather than to reflect-it. Treatments of sexual morality and bioethics illustrate this point. Ethical reflection tended to stake its authority on absolute principles, such as the primacy of procreation or the inviolability of all innocent human life, and then to derive from them specific conclusions (the immorality of all contraception and abortion), upon which were conferred the same absoluteness. What ethicists overlooked was the fact that this process of derivation, as well as the formulation of the starting principles, always takes place within a historical setting in which the perspectives of some will be privileged over those of others and in which the perceived need to address social and moral problems can result in distortions of ostensibly universal values. Yet both Aquinas and his more recent interpreters allow that objectivity is attained historically and inductively and therefore always partially. The natural law approach is of lasting value for today in that it grounds an experiential morality while holding to an ideal of shared human truth, and manifests a confidence that God's will for persons is revealed in creation as an ongoing process of discovering God in human life.

Feminists who speak of "full humanity" as an ethical norm or test share the confidence of the natural law tradition in several areas: in seeing ethics as an objective enterprise; in building an understanding of basic and shared human characteristics through reflection on human life itself; and in viewing the fulfillment of human characteristics as imbued with moral value.

Feminists also claim that women and men share one human nature and that, whatever their functional biological differences and the exaggerated gender roles that have separated them historically, the commonality of that nature warrants similar moral treatment. Men's and women's virtues and vices are like enough so that their fundamental social contributions, duties, and claims may also be equal. Most feminists reject "two natures" theories that result in separate spheres dividing men and women and securing the dominance of one sex by the submission of the other. On the contrary, they believe it is possible to build on agreement about human purposes, goals, and values in order to challenge and begin to change sinful social structures perpetuating inequality.

While the concerns of many Roman Catholic feminists coincide with the natural law approach, they also introduce some new emphases. According to feminists, the patriarchal model of virtue that dominated neoscholastic ethics emphasized rationality, control, and certitude over effectively, rationality, and dialogue. It also focused on the individual to the detriment of interdependence and community. Although few feminists today would want to argue that women are intrinsically more prone to affective relationships and men to individualist rationality, they would recognize that historically different qualities have been socially encouraged in men and women and that the perspectives of women can introduce into ethics a more complete view of human moral capacity. For Christian feminists, virtue consists not only in the integrity and rectitude of the rational Self. It also requires a relational concern for building communities in which all can contribute to mutual fulfillment, communities secured on a base of justice and ascending toward the completion and transformation of love.

Just as feminists avoid a two-natures theory of women's and men's emotional, cognitive, and moral characteristics, so they reject the idea that justice and love mean something essentially different for women than for Men. Ruether has written of a "cult of true womanhood" that followed nineteenth-century industrialization in Western countries, an ideology that both idealized women and confined them to the home and domesticity. Women were seen as more religious, spiritual, and moral than men, and it was their destiny to sacrifice themselves for husband and children." This separation of women's and men's spheres and the subordination of women's talents to the family were reinforced by a particular Christian ideal of love as self-sacrifice—an ideal that was applied unevenly to women and men. In a landmark essay, Valerie Saiving pointed out that the prevalent Christian definition of sin as self-assertion and virtue as, self-sacrifice was addressed more to the male situation in history than to the female and that women may face different temptations, against which they need to cultivate different virtues. Ideally, all Christians should experience a sacrificial and self-transcending love. At the same time, the cult of maternal and wifely sacrifice encourages in women the sin of self-negation rather than that of will-to-power. As she puts it, "A woman can give too much of herself, so that nothing remains of her own uniqueness; she can become merely an emptiness, almost a zero, without value to herself, to her fellow men, or, perhaps, even to God."

Christian ethicists today seek ways of defining love that, retain its aspect of self-offering while giving new emphasis to a mutuality or reciprocity that makes possible and completes the genuinely interpersonal and relational dimensions of love. The reconceptualization of love has had far-reaching effects in moral theology. For instance, John Paul II, even in defending the traditional ban on contraception, does not claim that women's proper role is at the heart of the family but instead appeals to the "total reciprocal self-giving of husband and wife." Although the fact that he also alludes to women's "true femininity," which should not be diluted by roles outside the home, introduces a note of ambiguity into his endorsement of mutuality in marital love, the pope still exemplifies a notable shift in the premises of moral theology regarding one of its central virtues. This shift is carried through by authors like

Christine Gudorf, who uses her own experience as a parent as a point of departure for arguing that Christian love is not disinterested but involved. All love requires sacrifice but also aims at mutuality, at the extension and sharing of the love relationship.

Christian ethics today is considering anew whether shared and even universal human values are able to provide any sort of a reasonable and objective-base for morality. This question is all the more urgent given heightened awareness of cultural and historical pluralism, as we shall see clearly in the next section. Feminist thought helps to clarify that all claims about what is natural to persons arise out of limited, partisan, and provisional experiences. The particularity of experience and of moral insight does not invalidate them as sources for an objective ethics; however, it does require that any proposal about a universally human or Christian morality be subjected to critical scrutiny and revision in light of the testimony of persons and groups of which natural law theorists may not have taken full account. For example, feminists have reexamined moral theology's tradition of assigning special virtues to women, especially self-sacrifice as wives and mothers, which in fact worked to exclude women from full humanity. Natural law ethics is not dead, but it is certainly more inductive, dialectical, and cautious in its method, thanks to feminism and other critical social movements that have unmasked the partiality of false universalisms whose proponents presented their own experiences and interests as absolute. A revised natural law method in Christian ethics bases morality on goods for persons, such as freedom, mutual love, justice, and association in the common good. However, it will constantly reexamine the status quo in light of the concrete requirements of these goods and, in particular, will enter into dialogue with diverse interpretations of the fundamental human goods.

The Social Context and Content of Ethics

All ethics is social ethics. Our discussion of natural law has already made evident that all ethics is socially situated; moreover, even so-called personal moral decisions and relations have a social dimension. In the feminist motto, "the personal is political." Attention to the moral agent or moral subject must be accompanied by recognition of the subject's social context. From the middle of the twentieth century, Catholic theology has been characterized by the "turn to the subject" influenced by the philosopher Immanuel Kant and demonstrated in the work of Karl Rahner. In Rahner's thought, the person as free subject in relation to God is the reference point of a theological anthropology that portrays morality, especially love of neighbor, as the response of the individual to the ever-present summons of the divine love. But in recent ethics, this stress on the free, acting subject has been complemented by a revived interest in the social nature of the person. Social structures and expectations impinge on all persons and all their ethical decisions, whether in the areas of economics or sex, just war or the termination of medical treatment.

Feminism highlights the social side of all morality by critically evaluating sexual and family practices in the light of patriarchy and showing their economic and political ramifications. Thus it furthers this general movement in Christian ethics to integrate personal decision making with the social location of the agent and the social reverberations of action. The common good, interdependence, and sociality have all been used to counteract strains of liberal individualism in Christian ethics. In Catholic feminist writing, this emphasis on the communal and social dovetails with the Thomistic tradition of posing social issues in terms of the common good rather than in terms of individual rights. Human persons are "essentially relational as well as autonomous and free."

In an essay on method in Christian ethics, June O'Connor draws together themes of sociality with those of a revised natural law epistemology. The fact that ethics is consciously experiential means that it must recognize both that there are sources of insight in addition to reason and also that experience and moral insight are communal. O'Connor notes that contemporary religious ethics attends to noncognitive capacities for moral insight, such as the affections and emotions. Contemporary ethics also acknowledges that many of our visions of reality operate pre-reflectively and hence their social sources and implications must be critically examined. "Feminist critiques of society detail ways in which attitudes about women shape personal behaviors and social policies." Feminist thought also exemplifies an increasing trend to acknowledge that "communities of shared faith" (whether religious or not) shape values and visions of life and to commend "a cross-cultural consciousness" to the ethical enterprise.

When the social dimension of all morality is adequately recognized, it also becomes possible to view moral norms in relation to their social conditions and effects rather than as abstract absolutes. In Catholic social teaching and social ethics, it has long been recognized that general moral principles may demand an application that is nuanced to particular sociopolitical settings. In writings about political organization, the economy, or war and peace, normative ethics has offered a general framework rather than systems of specific absolutes. For instance, workers may be said to have a right to a living wage, without specifying the precise amount of a minimum salary or whether it is up to employers or the government to guarantee it or how to accommodate the fact that some households will include more than one wage earner. Similarly, just war theory stipulates several criteria of legitimacy for armed conflict (for example, defense of the common good, last resort, right intention, proportionality, immunity of civilians) without trying to specify exactly which concrete policies, actions, or decisions meet or do not meet these criteria. But in areas of so-called personal, especially sexual, morality, Catholic ethics has operated on the basis of absolute norms about specific physical acts. This inconsistency of approach has been widely noted by moral theologians, and a sexual morality that is more nuanced to situations has been proposed.

Another angle on the same problem is provided by the revival of "virtue" ethics, replacing the manualist focus on individual moral acts. The manuals of moral theology that were the staples of seminary education in the first half of this century tended to isolate decisions from the full texture of the moral life. An ethics of virtue stresses the continuity of one's moral character, as expressed in decisions and actions. A feminist vision supports the cultivation of virtue understood in relational terms, not only as the righteousness of the agent as such. Moral acts find their meaning in the character of an integral moral life, realized in community with others, and consisting in the cultivation of personal, social, and religious values.

In summary, Catholic ethics today incorporates the importance of the social on at least two levels. First, it acknowledges that moral thinking always occurs within a sociohistorical context. This context shapes one's moral point of view, insights, and conclusions. Moral principles, norms, and decisions have a special relevance to this context, developing in response to its needs and standing to be enlarged or redefined when the relevance of other contexts of experience and thought become clear. Second,

Catholic ethics now recognizes that there is no such thing as purely individual or even interpersonal morality. All morality is social, not only because it arises from the social context, but also because individual choices and relationships always affect and are affected by social practices, institutions, and the common good. The old dualism of personal and social morality was a false one. Still needed in Catholic ethics is a coherent moral methodology that would recognize in both personal and social life the need for norms, as well as the need to nuance their application sensitively to situation and context, and to place specific applications within an integrally virtuous life.

Scripture and Feminist Ethics

A revisionist, iconoclastic, and subversive approach to images and roles of women in the Bible has been a mainstay of Christian feminism. Feminist biblical interpretation, like feminist theology, is inherently political in its inspiration and aims, and hence it is also ethical. Feminist ethics reflects the renewed interest in Scripture that has made gradual headway in Catholic moral theology since Vatican II.

Since Catholic ethics has been primarily an ethics of the natural law, the inclusion of biblical resources has presented to it two special challenges. The first is to confront the fact that Jesus' teachings about discipleship may be at odds with the most "obvious" conclusions of rational, objective ethical thinking. No doubt the clearest examples are Jesus' commands to love one's neighbor and even enemy and his example of nonviolence (see the Sermon on the Mount, Mt. 5–7). In general, Jesus summons his hearers to a new way of life in the kingdom of God, even if the result for those who follow him is rejection or persecution. The ethical implications of the New Testament call into question any morality based on individual rights, self-defense, or even justice in the usual senses of equal regard or equal treatment.

A second and related challenge lies in the fact that the Bible takes sides. Jesus establishes a radically inclusive community in which the sinner, the poor, the outcast, and the marginal (including women) have a new place and are even preferred in God's eyes. Once more, the Bible calls into question the objective and universal ethics of the natural law tradition. Instead, the Bible seems to function ethically in providing models of how the early Christian communities undermined the reigning power relations of their day by establishing inclusive communities of reciprocity, forgiveness, and even love. This is not to say that the early Christians embodied the kingdom of God perfectly in their lives. However, many scholars use sociology and social history to illumine the settings of biblical texts and to read through the text the relation of the early churches to their surrounding cultures. As a result, they can claim that the nonviolence and sharing of goods practiced by early Christian communities may have offered critical alternatives to societies structured by the dominance of the wealthy over the poor and torn by revolutionary movements, hatred among religious and racial groups, and blood vendettas for redressing wrongs.

The appropriation of these challenges in Catholic ethics is an ongoing process, as yet incomplete. Catholic moral theologians tend to want to preserve both the community of moral discourse guaranteed by natural law and the special inspiration of Jesus' teaching. Hence they maintain that, while religious commitment provides a unique motivation for fulfilling the moral law, "human" and "Christian" morality are substantively the same. The Christian will not behave differently in the concrete than the morally sincere and prudent atheist, though he or she may locate moral agency against the transcendent horizon of God's redeeming love.

Liberation theology, as a movement within Catholicism, has, however, intro-duced into the mainstream a somewhat different response to the biblical challenges by means of the theme of a "preferential option for the poor.' This preemptive special concern for those who are least well off is certainly reinforced by feminist theology. The preferential option has appeared particularly in economic ethics (for instance, in the U.S. bishops' pastoral letter, "Economic Justice for All"), and is often applied first of all to women and children, who, among the poor, suffer most. Moreover, as the U.S. bishops noted, since there are a greater number of women and children than men in poverty, Jesus' preference for the excluded must be directed in a special way to them.

In summary, the Bible has been important in the renewal of post–Vatican II Catholic ethics. A biblical ethics places more emphasis on conversion, on the tran-scendent meaning and aim of all moral activity, and on the importance of responding compassionately to those in need rather than on adherence to abstract moral rules. The New Testament also seems to challenge some of the central principles of the natural law and to propose radical gospel-based communities of mercy and love. An unresolved problem in Catholicism is how to combine a genuine attentiveness to the biblical kingdom witness with the traditional natural law commitment to moral uni-versality and objectivity.

Christian Feminism and Applied Ethics

We have seen that feminist ethics adopts an advocacy stance for women; it builds on the experiential base of natural law ethics; it highlights the social nature of personal relationships; and it turns to Scripture to heighten compassion and solidarity as moral values. Now we will explore the ways in which these contributions are influencing Roman Catholic approaches to the ethics of sex and gender and to the problem of war.

Sex and Gender

The area of sex and gender is without a doubt the one in which the ethical influence of feminist thought has been most conspicuous. Very important here is the "turn to experience," especially the experience of women. Up until the 1960s, Catholic ethics continued to define the primary purpose of sexuality as procreation and to under-stand women's role primarily in relation to motherhood. The basis of this teaching was the "nature" of sex, understood in terms of its physical function of procreation, to which the potentials of sex to give pleasure and to enhance companionship and love were subordinated. The isolation of the procreative meaning of sex as its moral key occurred under the influence of a variety of historical factors, among the most impor-tant of which were the need for Christianity to defend sex and procreation from attack by ancient and medieval dualist philosophies and religions, which denied the good-ness of the body and discouraged sexual relations and childbearing. Also, theologians worked within a cultural framework that valued marriage, childbearing, and women in relation to patriarchal kinship and inheritance patterns. These contingent factors were obscured when the resulting sexual ethic was expressed in abstract definitions of the "nature" of sex that absolutized one particular aspect of human sexual experience.

During the Second Vatican Council and subsequently, Catholic sexual teaching responded to the modern possibility that marriage could be a partnership, not only of economic and domestic cooperation and parenthood but also of love. It was the incipient recognition in Western culture of women as equal in dignity to men that made it possible to view men and women as entering into authentic friendship in marriage, which sexual union can augment. Both the Council's Pastoral Constitution on the Church in the Modern World and the "birth control encyclical," *Humanae vitae*, presented sex and marriage as having two equal purposes, love and procreation. Even though the magisterium continues to defend specific sexual norms based originally on the old procreative focus (like the ban on artificial contraception), so fundamental a change has occurred in the understanding of sexuality that its concrete effects have no doubt not yet been fully realized.

Another major development in the Christian attitude to sex is that it is not now understood so much in terms of sex acts as in terms of sexuality and of sexual relationships, of which genital expression is only one part. This development reflects the general ethical shift away from a morality of acts governed by stringent norms and toward a personal and social morality guided by the integration of a virtuous Christian life. Philosophers and theologians such as Paul Ricoeur and Andre Guindon have characterized sex as a "language," and even official teaching has incorporated the new formulation. Sex, in papal writings, is "the 'language of the body' [which has] an important interpersonal meaning, especially in reciprocal relationships between man and woman."

Women's writing about sexuality clearly reflects an interest in placing sexual expression within the totality of an ongoing relationship or friendship. Christian feminists tend to see sexuality as above all a relational capacity undergirding intimacy and commitment, not just as consolidating economic, kinship, and procreative relationships. "At the heart of sexual intimacy . . . is the desire to wholly express and nurture the mutuality of committed relationship. Commitment . . . requires the same kind of vulnerability, openness, risk-taking, and trust at the level of genital sexuality as it does within every other dimension of the partnership."

The displacement of the procreative purpose of sex by its affective and communicative ones also has signaled increased openness toward lesbian and gay relationships, although moralists vary in the interpretation given to them. However, even ethicists who regard the significance of shared parenthood to be a cross-cultural human meaning of sex, entailing a privileged status for heterosexual marriage, may regard the committed sexual relationships of homosexual couples as morally acceptable. Neither condemnation of gay persons nor the demand that they remain celibate is easy to reconcile with the fact that sexual orientation is a deep component of personal identity and the realization that gay persons are as capable as heterosexual ones of manifesting a range of human and Christian virtues in their lives."

The relationship between sex and gender is one area in which the ability to know a moral "law of nature" has been called radically into question. The contemporary perception that definitions of nature are perspectival and hence must be held broadly accountable to experience is crucial here. As we have seen, the twentieth century has witnessed a remarkable change in Christian (and philosophical) understandings of the meaning of sex, since the potential of sex to express affection, friendship, and commitment has moved into the foreground. The old biologist standard of procreative sex, contained within a marital union seen as a vehicle for the education of children, has widely been judged inadequate to the full human experience of sexuality.

But an unfinished agenda for a contemporary Christian sexual ethics is to relocate parenthood positively in relation to sexuality. Parenthood, despite inevitable distortions in reality, is a fulfilling human relationship that unites a sexual couple and binds the generations. Yet many personalist interpretations of sex, in displacing procreation as the normative meaning of sex, lose sight of it altogether. If procreation is not to be seen as the absolute norm for sex, then what legitimate moral role should it in fact play?

The first step toward reintegrating parenthood with sexual morality is to take conception and childbearing out of the old "act" morality and to place them in a new relational one. Bearing and nurturing children are not reducible to biogenetic procreation but involve parenthood as an enduring and demanding relationship. Although the fundamental human paradigm for the parental endeavor may be children conceived sexually and raised by two parents committed to one another, many analogous forms of parenthood are morally commendable, especially adoption. One issue for the new sexual morality is how to define which forms of parenthood are morally desirable and which, however well intentioned, come into conflict with other important values, such as the integrity of the marital bond. This issue is relevant in light of new reproductive technologies and infertility therapies, especially those that use "surrogate mothers" or "donors" of eggs, sperm, or embryos.

Feminist thinking has been important in the evolution of a sexual-parental morality. Feminists have especially inspected, criticized, and reinterpreted the human meaning of motherhood, revealing how women's experience of parenthood has been institutionalized in patriarchal cultures. Feminists not only question whether parenthood is a natural role for women more than for men, but also unveil how constricting social interpretations of it have narrowed women's contributions in other areas. Many feminists seek ways to offer positive construals of the actual experience of being a mother, while breaking the bonds of a "biology is destiny" ideology.

A philosopher offering a creative reconsideration of motherhood is Sara Ruddick, whose work has been noted by many Christian ethicists. She advances what she calls a "practicalist" conception of knowledge akin to Catholic moral theology's inductive reformulations of a morality of nature. Ruddick examines the practice of motherhood, drawing on her own experience, in order to illuminate its salient qualities, especially the virtues that it requires. "Maternal practice begins with a double vision—seeing the fact of' biological vulnerability as socially significant and as demanding care." Although women's appreciation of this "demand" may be heightened by pregnancy and labor, Ruddick seems to see "maternal work" as the calling of all parents. The mother's special works are preservative love, nurturance, and training, the distinguishing virtue of which is the "attentive love" of "maternal thinking." Attentive love can degenerate into self-loss and can be contradicted by motherhood's peculiar vices—"anxious or inquisitorial scrutiny, domination, intrusiveness, caprice, and self-protective cheeriness." But at its zenith, attentive love is (in the words of Simone Weil) an "intense, pure, disinterested, gratuitous, generous attention." The virtues cultivated through the parental relationship are a valuable moral education for other spheres of life.

Noting the oppressive situations of women cross-culturally, Christine Gudorf laments that conditions are far from adequate for a positive ethic of motherhood worldwide, since in many cultures women lack the opportunity to reflect on their most essential experience of motherhood and to shape their parental and social roles accordingly. Too often it is still the case that women "are given and taken in marriage, seized for rape and battery, mutilated and sterilized as matters of policy, and assigned more work than men." Necessary conditions for the development of an acceptable practice of motherhood include respect for women's bodies, sexuality, and decisions about them; the opening of alternative female roles in addition to motherhood; equal responsibility of men in the care of children and the home; social support like maternity leave and day care, which would allow all parents to undertake both domestic and public roles successfully; social initiatives to alleviate the poverty that affects women and children most of all.

In summary, the ethics of sex and gender demonstrates the commitment of contemporary Catholic ethics to reexamining natural law categories on the basis of experience and to incorporating the testimony of those engaged practically in the relevant areas, especially when their voices have been in the past neglected or excluded. Current understandings of sexuality also emphasize its relational over its procreative capacity, although the weaving into the sexual relation of a morally attractive notion of parenthood for women and for men is an ongoing task. This project has been furthered by feminist readings of motherhood, as an important human

Selection 3: Beverly Wildung Harrison, *Making the Connections: Essays in Feminist Social Ethics*

> *Beverly Wildung Harrison is Carolyn Williams Beaird Professor Emeritus at Union Theological Seminary, New York City. She is a noted feminist social ethicist whose work has been referenced extensively by other feminist scholars.*

The Effect of Industrialization on Women's Political Consciousness

Many nineteenth-century English feminists looked to the United States as a place where the heavy hand of tradition and social myth vis-à-vis women might be broken. There were solid grounds for these hopes, at least as they applied to women of European extraction. During the colonial period, European visitors often commented that under conditions of settlement in the wilderness, women in the new nation were called on to exhibit strength, endurance, and a wide range of skills that middle-strata women in Europe had ceased to express. After the United States gained independence from Great Britain, distinguished English feminists such as Harriet Martineau came to the United States to see first-hand the prospects for a "new woman" in a nation where sex role rigidities had weakened. Martineau's perceptions as an observer of life in the United States have led modern feminists to classify her as one of the first sociologists. Her observations here confirmed others' accounts of the extraordinary diversity of social roles played by women in the young nation. However, she also signaled concern that two forces threatened positive change. She worried that both the low ratio of women to men and pressures on the rural frontier increased the trend toward a drastically lower marriage age for both men and women. Martineau recognized that this pattern of early marriage, with the resultant high rate of early childbirth, would offset the relative gains women in the United States had made in escaping the developed European bourgeois traditions of genteel womanhood.

In the United States, the social base of feminism varied from state to state and region to region The seeds of the ideology that women are born to be homemakers and nurturers of children had been planted early in colonies founded by dissenting Protestant groups, but neither Puritans nor dissenters originally endorsed that distinctive and, later, urban-industrial cult of genteel womanhood and its sharply differentiated sex role divisions. This ideology did not subvert the more egalitarian roles of the rural frontier until capital accumulation created an extensive, new monied class. The factory system, accelerated by the Civil War, permeated where capital was concentrated, especially in the Northeast. As in England, the new myth of women's nature took hold precisely in the region where women were the first to work in the factories, illustrating again that this myth flourishes best where it is least apt.

The early factory system in the United States was even more dependent on the wage labor of women than was the English factory system because until immigration form Europe accelerated, labor was in short supply. Textiles and clothing were the core of early industry in New England, and women had the necessary skills for this work. Women, often lacking other modes of economic survival, also were willing to work for low wages. Resentment of women as laborers was a major factor in the slow development of an organized labor movement in the United States. Male industrial workers experienced women's lower wages as a menace to their demands for adequate salaries and better working conditions. Often male workers refused to organize with women or support the early strikes women initiated for better wages and working conditions. Masses of indigent European immigrants began to arrive in the newly industrialized United States. Those who did not find their way to cheap or free land on the frontier began to swell the industrial labor force, and women and children competed with men for extremely low-paying factory positions. The competition between men, women, and children for jobs was intense. Labor laws restricting children from factory work and limiting hours or setting special working conditions for them or for women were often supported by working men chiefly as a means of restricting competition for industrial jobs.

Even in the face of the grim reality of most women's lives, the capitalist centers of Boston and New York became the places where the bourgeois cult of true womanhood flourished. The locus of early American feminism took root elsewhere, in the Middle Atlantic region, where left-wing Protestant religion and the egalitarian conditions of small-town life had produced a feminism religious in its motivation and anti-elitist in its social orientation. In that milieu, women had actively scoffed at the thesis that they were, by nature, especially gentle and virtuous.

Slowly but surely this egalitarian feminism gave way to the accelerating pressures of the rising affluent ideal. By the time the women's suffrage movement became a widespread force at the end of the nineteenth century, many feminists themselves used the arguments of women's "special nature" as a reason why women should have political suffrage. Needless to say, by that time a few affluent women even hinted that genteel women would join their male counterparts in upholding "civilization" against the encroachments of the immigrant masses and black former slaves.

In the southern United States, the social base of feminism was all but nonexistent. The dominant plantation system evolved, dependent on slavery for free labor. Since the legitimation of the slave system was a basic ideological requirement, interesting permutations in the prevailing ideology of "women's special nature" were required to sustain it. In the southern slave-holding states, a virulent pedestalism came to characterize the social myth of "women's nature," though of course "women" referred only to white women. The gap between the actual experience of even the plantation master's wife and this ideology was dramatic, however, as many historians have observed. Increasingly, white women were portrayed as asexual and chaste, in contrast to black women stereotyped to legitimate the frequent sexual liaisons forced on them by their white masters. Since the black woman was fantasized as earthy, erotic, and promiscuous, the white woman was imaged as the opposite. Hence, the classic split in western male consciousness that projects women as either virgin or whore grounded the social mythologies that variously entrapped white and black women in the slave-holding states. The vast number of poor white women who were neither masters' wives nor slaves were all but invisible. They lived not only as rural poor women always have had to do, at the margins of survival, but they also labored under strong ideological constraints to identify with the master's wife, if only to avoid the fate of falling as low as the female slave.

The ideology of "effete womanhood" in the industrially affluent northeastern United States and the schizophrenic ideology of "pure white womanhood" required by the southern slave system converged. It is little wonder that the efforts of newly conscious women, grounded in demands for religious, social, and political equality, fared badly in the wake of the rising tide of industrial affluence. Early "radical feminism" of the U.S. frontier, which espoused full personhood for women and which, if not revolutionary, was at least radically reformist and egalitarian in its social vision, gradually gave way to a more moderate, middle-strata congenial reformist women's perspective. Great freedom in dress, movement, and personal expression ensued, but these changes only masked the subtle erosion of the social and economic base of women's social power.

In the United States, as elsewhere, war has been a major force accelerating centralization and monopoly of the industrial system and of technological innovation. During wartime, women were needed in industrial production, but the postwar periods saw strong consolidation of the ideology of "women's place." Home and family life became ever more critical to those in a war-weary population, who now could afford to revert to private concerns. Note, however, that the line between the private and the public world clearly divided the family and the economy. The thesis some have advanced that the 1960s women's movement in the United States was the result of middle-class women being underchallenged in their spotless, mechanized kitchens fails totally to explain the broad-based structural reasons for women's dissatisfactions.

In the United States, as the gross national product skyrocketed, access to middle-strata existence appeared to be a panacea available to all who worked hard enough. Here, as in Britain, aspiration to middle-class status reinforced the hold of ideologies about what women should be. As always when the role of women is at issue, the reality of women's lives lay elsewhere. In the post-World War II period, women's role as housewives and mothers was everywhere celebrated. Some jobs briefly accessible to women during the early feminist period were largely closed after the war. In reality, increasing numbers of women were moving into the wage labor force out of economic necessity. Increasingly, women found employment only in castelike labor sectors that constitute "women's work"—clerical and stenographic positions, retail sales, and work that parallels domestic labor. The new, postwar technological professions required and expertise and psychological orientation that "privatized woman" had not acquired.

Those women who remained in the home began to experience the frustration attendant on their new economic role—that of being expert consumers. Those who worked, whether out of economic necessity or to escape the boredom engendered by the social powerlessness of the middle-strata home, found little respite from the powerlessness in the world of "feminine" work. These were the dynamics that engendered the feminist renaissance of the late 1960s and 1970s. Black women and other minority women, who have always carried either the double or triple jeopardy of racism, sexism, and class, moved to develop an analysis of gender equality more adequate to their lives than white feminists' interpretations. In spite of the ways that power and ideology separate and isolate women across boundaries of race and class, the social base for the rising consciousness of women is broad in the United States today.

Advanced capitalist industrial development needs the social myth of women's "special nature and place" to keep women out of productive work or, failing that, out of the labor movement, precisely as earlier political and economic systems needed women to stay in place as reproducers. To provide justice for women under advanced capitalist economies would require fundamental political and economic change. So far, postcapitalist systems of production, industrially centralized as capitalist systems have been, also have not redressed the injustices of women's dual role. In postcapitalist economies, men and women may have more equal access to wage labor, but women usually tend to home and children alone. Women's political and economic powerlessness in all industrialized societies, then, is and will remain a deep source of social instability. Whether we are pressured to stay in the domestic sphere, as in capitalist modes of production, or encouraged to do both wage and domestic labor, as in some post-capitalist societies, advanced industrialized and centralized production double-binds us all. Under these conditions women must either internalize a self-image of female impotence or bear the double load of social and domestic labor. In either case, the myths of female identity that are foisted on us are so remote from the reality of our lives as to force us to risk madness or begin to demystify the power relations under which we live. The evidence is growing that more and more women have begun the demystification process, which is why feminism is likely to remain a potent force no matter what resistance it meets.

The Specific Feminist Theological Agenda within Christianity

The critique we feminists make of Christianity involves a long agenda for theological change. It requires an extended and profound rethinking of all the language, images, and metaphors central to Christian theology, a re-visioning that will surely not be exhausted soon. The unrealistic expectations of our opponents are often aimed at discrediting our work. Those who complain because we have not already or instantly produced liturgies, rituals, and theological imagery that are exemplary theological alternatives to long-established Christian practice are making an unjust demand. To expect a decade of feminist work to produce a fully mature, nonsexist Christian theology that rivals the presumed grandeur of Elizabethan English, or even the greatest literary productions created by a huge male theological caste working over centuries, is silly. Developing a feminist literary tradition, including a liturgy and a significant corpus of theological reflection, is a task for numerous and culturally diverse women, over many lifetimes and many generations. And much of our early work must aim at critical de-construction of existing imagery, the "digging" necessary to remember the ignored or forgotten work of our foresisters.

Even so, there are, I believe, three matters of particular urgency on the Christian feminist theological agenda, if we are to heal the special oppressiveness of masculinist Christian practice that daily shatters women's lives. Priority must be given not only to the language of Christian theology but to the images that Christian theology relies on in describing our God-relation. The frequent dismissal by male theologians of this matter is itself one of the great scandals of contemporary Christianity. Christian male theologians have celebrated God's speaking, as logos, as "the Word," throughout Christian history. No metaphors for God are more overworked in Christian theological imagination than the speech metaphors. The Christian theological community that claims that God's speaking to us is itself the primary metaphor of divine disclosure can hardly also insist, with any integrity, that the issue of sexist theological language and image ins a minor problem. The spiritual schizophrenia expressed here never ceases to amaze me. Surely one of the reasons that sexism in theological language can be so readily, if erroneously, dismissed is that many Christian theologians have lost the capacity to recognize the fundamental, imagistic character of the language in which they confess the faith of the Christian community. It I am right on this point, then feminist theology, precisely because of women's insistence on the foundational character of image and metaphor, will contribute to a desperately needed refurbishment of Christian theological imagination.

As I have acknowledged here, it was my early feminist consciousness that made me aware of how glibly some white male Christian theological colleagues invoked God as "wholly other," as "transcendent" to all human time, space, and experience. With this awareness cam a persistent puzzlement at their apparent inability to notice the complete loss of religious substance and meaning that followed from this kind of negative, abstract imagery about God. Slowly I began to realize that one of the dynamics I had previously overlooked was the way in which male gender primacy masks the effect of the abstractions of these primal God metaphors used by male theologians. They often operate with a split consciousness because they employ vague and impersonal concepts and language about God on the one hand and simultaneously draw on the concrete male imagery of Christian tradition on the other. Even when these theologians spoke of God as totally transcendent, they nevertheless did not lose entirely a continuing analogy between God and their own experience. The positive analogy between their lives and God was sustained by the male biblical imagery that their abstract concepts denied. Many men, I now believe, do not really experience the complete spiritual emptiness of God's "radical transcendence" because their ongoing recital of the stories of scripture and liturgical tradition continually reiterates images for God that invoke analogies to male identity and men's experience. This "wholly other" God is, for them, still Father, Lord, King, all concrete terms of male agency. He remains, always, whatever else they aver of God, a male image. Men can insist on the complete disconnectedness of God and "man" yet not have to cope with what it means theologically to create a total gulf between human experience and God. No wonder male theologians often seem to me not to be hearing what they are saying!

For many of us women, by contrast, this abstract "otherness" language, taken together with imagery derived so exclusively from concrete historical male experience, combines to obliterate all divine-human connection. Is it any wonder that we protest and insist that this is not our experience of faith? No positive analogy for divine-human relationship is present for us. The image and language of "wholly other" and "father" combine to render us totally invisible, empty of any connecton to God, and reinforce a double disidentification of ourselves with God. Women are not being ornery or irreverent, then, in protesting male theological practice. Only if we pay attention as much to the sources or our images as to explicit gender references in the structure of language do we see the depth of the problem imposed on a feminist theology.

A second urgent matter for a contemporary Christian feminist theological agenda, touched on in my earlier historical discussion, is the split endemic in dominant Christian tradition, especially the split between spiritualistic mind and body. The sources of this split in dominant theological tradition are many, and I have addressed some of them elsewhere. Here I need only to underscore how much the purported "differences" between male and female, and the social inequality of women, have legitimated and grounded this split. "Male" has been a pervasive symbol for mind, power, intellect, that which is truly "spirit"; female has been symbol for nature, "irrational" feeling, "mere body," earth, the less than fully human. Women are body and men (actually, only dominant, power-identified males) are mind or reason. In some streams of classic Hellenic and late Hellenistic traditions, women were held to be, literally, deficient in the capacity for reason, and we are still living with that judgment and internalizing it. But even in the more holistic Hebraic tradition, men were most often portrayed as bearing nepesh, spirit, more readily able to be the spokespersons for Yahweh's breath and power.

I have already insisted that over the centuries this body/mind split has rendered dominant Christian traditions inept, idealized, incapable of addressing very fundamental issues of life, existence, and intellectuality. Not only has the dualism led to an ascetic, antisexual, antiphysical theology, encouraging dominant Christianity's constant and perpetual spiritualizing of life, but it has conditioned Christian inability to recognize that material well-being and bodily health are fundamental to spiritual blessedness and to authentic "redemption." This split is also clearly implicated in the way in which Christianity, in the modern period, has become not merely complacent toward but actively collusive with capitalist ideology. The inability of Christians to affirm, appreciate, and celebrate pleasure as a gift of God given for our enjoyment is also rooted in this dualism. Christian masochism is the perfect psychological foil to support a workaholic culture that nevertheless finds little or no joy or pleasure in work.

Finally, feminist theology must address the very deep nature/history split in the Christian past, especially in the western tradition. Since women are held to be "mere" nature, men are therefore understood as the real historical agents. The sharp dichotomy between history and nature runs through much of our theology, our ethics, and our reflection, and it conditions our actions and worldviews in ways too numerous to elaborate here. Those who have analyzed the cultural roots of the ecological crisis point to the complicity of Christian tradition in encouraging unrestrained "domination" of nature. Even if these charges are overdrawn, we still have to acknowledge that the "stewardship" of our avowedly Christian culture in relation to nature has been appalling. Can anyone really deny that there is no connection between Christianity and a Christian-dominant culture's belief that it is acceptable to consume resources rapaciously, to plunder and destroy the land, to control nature in any way we choose? As Christians, we have learned to think of ourselves as "above" nature, as its superior.

It is not only feminist theology that makes this protest. Feminists press the issue in a foundational way, the more so because women have been imaged as a nature and bearers of nature, and we have learned the value of not repudiating this connection In our identification with nature, we feminists do need to avoid nature romanticism, which can lead to abdication of historical responsibility by construing human life as merely cyclical and evolutionist. We do possess the power of historical agency or creative capacity to affect and change the world. Still, modern Christian theology has overemphasized the nature/history distinction by interpreting humanity (males) primarily as the makers of history rather than as subjects of natural/historical relationship. Technical, not personal-relational images have been primary in our conception of nature. What a feminist theological critique demands, by contrast, is not a complete rejection of human historical agency but a profound recovery of a sense that we are, ourselves, species-dependent, in nature, culture, and history. As natural, historical, and cultural creators, we are profoundly dependent on each other and the rest of the natural/historical/cultural order. There is in fact a clear dialectic between our responsibility to nature and our capacity to become fresh, creative, and humane historical-cultural agents. If we do not recover a new respect for our deep interdependence as natural/historical and cultural beings, understanding our reciprocity with each other and nature as a dimension and condition of our freedom, all of us are doomed.

Womanist Voices

36

Womanist theology and ethics developed as a voice that was not being heard in either the feminist movements or the black liberation theology of the second half of the twentieth century. Womanist theology embraces the concerns of gender discrimination associated with feminist thinkers but distinguishes itself from them by virtue of its concern with the issues of racial discrimination that compound the plight of African American women and that present its own particular agenda of socio economic issues. In many respects the "Ain't I a Woman" speech of Sojourner Truth (see above) anticipates the womanist cause as will be particularly evident in the selection from Jacquelyn Grant.

Selection 1: Katie Geneva Cannon, *Katie's Canon: Womanism and the Soul of the Black Community*

Katie Geneva Cannon (b. 1949) is the Anne Scales Rogers Professor of Christian Ethics at Union Presbyterian Seminary. She is the first African American woman to be ordained in the United Presbyterian Church (U.S.A.). Her book, Katie's Canon, *from which we have taken this selection, is one of her best-known works. The impact of her womanist perspective on Christian ethics has been powerful. Her contention that womanist ethics will profit greatly by engaging the writings of African American women as a principle resource for understanding how Black women have dealt with their lives under oppressive circumstances is an important contribution to its methodology.*

Black Womanist Consciousness

From the period of urbanization of World War II to the present, Black women find that their situation is still a situation of struggle, a struggle to survive collectively and individually against the continuing harsh historical realities and pervasive adversities in today's world. The Korean and Vietnam wars, federal government programs, civil rights movements, and voter education programs have all had a positive impact on the Black woman's situation, but they have not been able to offset the negative effects of inherent inequities that are inextricably tied to the history and ideological hegemony of racism, sexism, and class privilege.

The Black woman and her family continue to be enslaved to hunger, disease, and the highest rate of unemployment since the Depression of the 1930s. Advances in education, housing, health care, and other necessities that came about during the mid- and late 1960s are deteriorating faster now than ever before. Both in informal day-to-day life and in the formal organizations and institutions in society. Black women are still the victims of the aggravated inequities of the tridimensional phenomenon of race/class/gender oppression. This is the backdrop of the historical context for the emergence of the Black feminist consciousness.

In essence, the Bible is the highest source of authority for most Black women. In its pages, Black women have learned how to refute the stereotypes that depict Black people as minstrels or vindictive militants, mere ciphers who react only to omnipresent racial oppression. Knowing the Jesus stories of the New Testament helps Black women be aware of the bad housing, overworked mothers, underworked fathers, functional illiteracy, and malnutrition that continue to prevail in the Black community. However, as God-fearing women they maintain that Black life is more than defensive reactions to oppressive circumstances of anguish and desperation. Black life is the rich, colorful creativity that emerged and reemerges in the Black quest for human dignity. Jesus provides the necessary soul for liberation.

Understanding the prophetic tradition of the Bible empowers Black women to fashion a set of values on their own terms, as well as mastering, radicalizing, and sometimes destroying the pervasive negative orientations imposed by the larger society. Also, they articulate possibilities for decisions and action that address forthrightly the circumstances that inescapably color and shape Black life. Black women serve as contemporary prophets, calling other women forth so that they can break away from the oppressive ideologies and belief systems that presume to define their reality.

Black feminist consciousness may be more accurately identified as Black womanist consciousness, to use Alice Walker's concept and definition. As an interpretive principle, the Black womanist tradition provides the incentive to chip away at oppressive structures, bit by bit. It identifies those texts that help Black womanists to celebrate and rename the innumerable incidents of unpredictability in empowering ways. The Black womanist identifies with those biblical characters who hold on to life in the face of formidable oppression. Often compelled to act or to refrain from acting in accordance with the powers and principalities of the external world, Black womanists search the Scriptures to learn how to dispel the threat of death in order to seize the present life.

Womanist Perspectival Discourse and Canon Formation

My fascination with words has no conscious beginning. I cannot recall the year, the month, the week, or the day when I first realized the magic that lay in the mix of alphabets, words, and stories. However, I do remember as a preschooler spending recess romping through the graveyard at the Mt. Calvary Lutheran Church. The words inscribed on the tombstones mesmerized me. I loved tracing the outline of the granite-carved letters, reading the epitaphs aloud, and spellbinding my classmates with creative stories about the deceased. Even as a small child I was participating in a ritual of honor for my ancestors whose lives and words belong not merely to the past but live on—in, with, and beyond their descendants.

As a womanist theological ethicist my research continues to look directly at ancestral cultural material as well as relatively fixed literary forms. Womanist ethics examines the expressive products of oral culture that deal with our perennial quest for liberation, as well as written literature that invites African Americans to recognize "the distinction between nature in its inevitability and culture in its changeability." When understood in its essentials, my work as a womanist ethicist focuses on the four following areas.

1. The creation of womanist pedagogical styles. African American women in the academy design new modes of rigorous inquiry for teaching critical consciousness in our various disciplines. We invite women and men of contemporary faith communities to a more serious encounter with the contributions Black women and Black men have made and continue to make to theological and religious studies.

2. The emergence of distinctive investigative methodologies. Black women scholars engage in constructing cognitive maps of the "logic" that sets the perimeters for the intelligibility and legitimacy of race, sex, and class oppression, so that we may discern the hierarchical, mechanistic patterns of exploitation that must be altered in order for justice to occur.

3. Reconsideration of the established theories, doctrines, and debates of Eurocentric, male-normative ethics. By juxtaposing traditional principles of character and the regulative standards of action with the judgment and criticism of ourselves in relation to others, we define, elaborate, exemplify, and justify the integration of being and doing.

4. The adjudicative function of womanist scholars. We formulate fresh ethical controversies relevant to our particular existential realities as they are recorded in the writings of African American women. I maintain that Black women writers stay intimately attuned to the social, cultural, and political environment in which Black life is lived and that their writings enlarge our theopolitical consciousness and our concept of ethics altogether. This aspect of womanist scholarship is built on the assumption that the African American women's literary tradition is a many-splendored art form and that our task as ethicists is not to read theoethical meaning into texts but to resonate with what is there. By respecting the autonomy of the novel and short story as literary art, I do not explain African American women's literature away by referencing it to Christian symbolic function nor do I dwell on thematic elements that are traditionally related to religious beliefs and moral conduct (i.e., immanence, transcendence, sin, salvation, grace, and forgiveness). Instead, what seems most reasonable for my purpose in this aspect of womanist research are the organizing intertextuality questions: What books are important in the writing of womanist ethics? Whose texts are we conscious of when we write? In this essay, therefore, I will identify some of the generative themes in the texts of African American women writers that womanist ethicists need to address.

My personal title for this essay is "Katie's Canon," wherein I identify the critical contestable issues at the center of Black life—issues inscribed on the bodies of Black people.' As a womanist liberation ethicist I have a solemn responsibility to investigate the African American women's literary tradition by asking hard questions and pressing insistently about the responsibility of this canon of books to the truthful, consistent, and coherent representation of Black existence in contemporary society. I am arguing that there is a certain distinguishable body of writings by African American women characterized by fidelity in communicating the baffling complexities and the irreducible contradictions of the Black experience in America. When seen through critical, theoethical lenses, Black women writers skillfully and successfully supply the patterns of conduct, feeling, and contestable issues that exist in the real-lived context that lies behind this literature.

Black Woman Ethicist as Noncanonical Other

The dilemma of the Black woman ethicist as the noncanonical other is defined as working in opposition to the academic establishment, yet building upon it. The liberation ethicist works both within and outside the guild. The Black womanist scholar receives the preestablished disciplinary structures of intellectual inquiry in the field of ethics and tries to balance the paradigms and assumptions of this intellectual tradition with a new set of questions arising from the context of Black women's lives. The tension is found in the balancing act of simultaneously trying to raise the questions appropriate to the discipline while also trying to understand what emphasis ought properly to be placed on the various determinants influencing the situation of Black women. In order to work toward an inclusive ethic, the womanist struggles to restructure the categories so that the presuppositions more readily include the ethical realities of Black women.

The womanist scholar identifies the pervasive White and male biases deeply embedded in the field of study. As a liberationist, she challenges and reshapes the traditional inquiry and raises candid questions between the two locales of whiteness and maleness. She insists that new questions guide the research so that Black women's moral wisdom can provide the answers. In essence, she seeks to determine why and how Black women actively negotiate their lives in a web of oppression."

The Black woman's ethical analysis distinguishes between "possibilities in principle" and "possibilities in fact." She extends Black women's existential reality above the threshold of that frustrating and illusory social mobility that forms the core of the American dream. That is, she strips away false, objectified conceptualities and images that undergird the apparatuses of systemic oppression.

The intersection of race, sex, and class gives womanist scholars a different ethical orientation with a different ideological perspective. The experience of being both the participant from within and the interpreter from without results in an inescapable duality to the character of womanist ethics. Beginning with her own historical, socio-ethical situation, the Black woman scholar cuts off what is untrue and adds what is most urgent. In other words, she refutes what is inimical and coopts the positive. This task is difficult since Black women in general are dealing with vague, amorphous social ideals, on the one hand, and with the long-standing effects of American racism, sexism, and class elitism on the other.

For example, Black female ethicists endure with a certain grace the social restrictions that limit their own mobility, and at the same time they demand that the relationships between their own condition and the condition of those who have a wide range of freedom be recognized. They bring into clear focus the direct correlation of economic, political, and racial alienation. As participant-interpreters, they have direct contact with the high and the lowly, the known and the unrecognized, the comic and the tragic that makes them conscious of the myriad value systems that are antithetical to Black survival. To demystify large and obscure ideological relations, social theories, and, indeed, the heinous sociopolitical reality of tridimensional oppression is a moral act. To do ethics inside out and back again is the womanist norm.

In other words, as the noncanonical other, these women rightly recognize how family life, cultural expression, political organization, and social and economic roles shape the Black community. Furthermore, they identify the way Black women as moral agents persistently attempt to strip away the shrouding of massive dislocation and violence exacerbated in recent years by the nation's fiscal crisis. Under extremely harsh conditions, Black women buttress themselves against the dominant coercive apparatuses of society. Using a series of resistance modes, they weave together many disparate strands of survival skills, styles, and traditions in order to create a new synthesis that, in turn, serves as a catalyst for deepening the wisdom-source that is genuinely their own."

Black women ethicists use this framework of wisdom to compare and contrast Black female moral agency with the agency of those in society who have the freedom to maximize choice and personal autonomy. The womanist scholar focuses on describing, documenting, and analyzing the ideologies, theologies, and systems of values that perpetuate the subjugation of Black women. At the same time, she emphasizes how Black women are shaping their own destinies within restricted possibilities, resisting and overthrowing those restrictions, and sometimes, in the interest of survival, acting in complicity with the forces that keep them oppressed.

To make this point clearer: Black women ethicists constantly question why Black women are considered merely ancillary, no more than throwaway superfluous appendages in a society that claims "life, liberty, and the pursuit of happiness" as "inalienable rights." What theological systems relegate Black women to the margins of the decision-making mainstream of American religious, political, and economic life? And what qualitative judgments and social properties establish a chasm between the proposition that Black women, first and foremost, are human beings and the machinations that allow glaring inequities and unfulfilled promises to proceed morally unchecked?

The womanist scholar stresses the role of emotional, intuitive knowledge in the collective life of the people. Such intuition enables moral agents in situations of oppression to follow the rule within, and not be dictated to from without. Untrammeled by external authority, Black female moral agents' intuitive faculties lead them toward a dynamic sense of moral reasoning. They designate the processes, the manners, and subtleties of their own experiences with the least amount of distortion from the outside. They go below the level of racial, sexual structuring and into those areas where Black people are simply human beings struggling to reduce to consciousness all of their complex experiences. Communion with one's own truths makes one better able to seize and delineate with unerring discrimination the subtle connections among people, institutions, and systems that serve as silent accessories to the perpetuation of flagrant forms of injustice.

Intrigued by the largely unexamined questions that have fallen through the cracks between feminist ethics and Black male theology, the womanist scholar insists on studying the distinctive consciousness of Black women within Black women's institutions, clubs, organizations, magazines, and literature." Appropriating the human condition in their own contexts, Black women collectively engage in revealing the hidden power relations inherent in the present social structures. A central conviction is that theoethical structures are not universal, color-blind, apolitical, or otherwise neutral. Thus, the womanist ethicist tries to comprehend how Black women create their own lives, influence others, and understand themselves as a force in their own right. The womanist voice is one of deliverance from the deafening discursive silence that the society at large has used to deny the basis of shared humanity.

Conclusion

In order to move toward a Black liberation ethic, attention must be paid to an ethical vision that includes Black women. The substantial omission of Black women from theological discourse flows quite naturally from male theologians using analytical concepts and frameworks that take the male experience as the norm. An inclusive liberation ethic must focus—on the particular questions of women in order to reveal the subtle and deep effects of male bias on recording religious history. As scholars, we must demonstrate the hidden assumptions and premises that lie behind our ethical speculations and inferences. Our task is to change the imbalance caused by an andro-centric view, wherein it is presumed that only men's activities have theological value. If we are willing to unmask the male assumptions that dominate religious thought, we will discover whole new areas of ethical inquiry.

Second, in moving toward a Black liberation ethic we must examine Black women's contributions in all the major fields of theological studies—Bible, history, ethics, mission, worship, theology, preaching, and pastoral care. The Black male biases operate not so much to omit Black women totally as to relegate Black church women to the position of direct object instead of active subject. Too often Black women are presented in a curiously impersonal dehumanizing way as the fused backbone in the body of the church.

A womanist liberation ethic requires us to gather information and to assess accurately the factual evidence regarding Black women's contribution to the Black church community. Black women organized voluntary missionary societies, superintended church schools, led prayer meetings, took an active part in visiting and ministering to the sick and needy, and raised large amounts of money to defray the expenses of the Black church. Black women are conscious actors who have altered the theological picture in significant ways. Furthermore, this second area of research does more than increase our understanding of Black women in the church community; it also elicits reinterpretation of old conclusions about the church universal.

Finally, the development of an inclusive ethic requires us to recognize and condemn the extent to which sex differences prevail in the institutional church, in our theological writings, and in the Black church's practices. A womanist liberation ethic directs critical attention not only to scholarship in the fields of study but also to its concrete effects on women in the pews. The work has to be done both from the basis of church practices and from the basis of continuing academic investigation. For instance, we need to do an analysis of sexist content of sermons in terms of reference to patriarchal values and practices. Particular attention needs to be given to the objectification, degradation, and subjection of the female in Black preaching. At the same time, we need to analyze the social organization of the Black church—curricula, music, leadership expectation, pastor-member interactions—as well as outright sex discrimination. Far too often, the organization of the church mirrors male dominance in the society and normalizes it in the eyes of both female and male parishioners.

Whether the discipline of ethics has almost completely neglected Black women (as in White male scholarship) or treated them as incidental to central issues (as in Black male scholarship) or considered gender as the important factor for research (as in White feminist scholarship), the cumulative effect of womanist scholarship is that it moves us toward a fundamental reconceptualization of all ethics with the experience of Black women at center stage.

Selection 2: Jacquelyn Grant, *White Women's Jesus and Black Woman's Christ: Feminist Christology and Womanist Response*

Jacquelyn Grant (b. 1948) is professor and director and founder of the Center for Black Women in Church and Society at the Interdenominational Theological Center in Atlanta. She ranks as one of the foundational thinkers of womanist theology and ethics. This selection from her Christology provides further insight into the agenda that womanist ethics must engage. The fact that it is a Christology laden with important commentary on the task of Christian social teaching reminds the church that the two finally cannot be separated.

The Starting Point for Womanist Theology

Because it is important to distinguish Black and White women's experiences, it is also important to note these differences in theological and Christological reflection. To accent the difference between Black and White women's perspective in theology, I maintain that Black women scholars should follow Alice Walker by describing our theological activity as "womanist theology." The term "womanist" refers to Black women's experiences. It accents, as Walker says, our being responsible, in charge, outrageous, courageous and audacious enough to demand the right to think theologically and to do it independently of both White and Black men and White women.

Black women must do theology out of their tridimensional experience of racism/sexism/classism. To ignore any aspect of this experience is to deny the holistic and integrated reality of Black womanhood. When Black women, say that God is on the side of the oppressed, we mean that God is in solidarity with the struggles of those on the underside of humanity.

In a chapter entitled "Black Women: Shaping Feminist Theory," Hooks elaborates the interrelationship of the threefold oppressive reality of Black women and shows some of the weaknesses of White feminist theory. Challenging the racist and classist assumption of White feminism, Hooks writes:

> Racism abounds in the writings of white feminists, reinforcing white supremacy and negating the possibility that women will bond politically across ethnic and racial boundaries. Past feminist refusal to draw attention to and attack racial hierarchy suppressed the link between race and class. Yet

class structure in American society has been shaped by the racial politics of white supremacy.

This means that Black women, because of oppression' determined by race and their subjugation as women, make up a disproportionately high percentage of the poor and working classes. However, the fact that Black women are a subjugated group even within the Black community and the White women's community does not mean that they are alone in their oppression within those communities. In the women's community poor White women are marginalized, and in the Black community, poor Black men are also discriminated against. This suggests that classism, as well as racism and sexism, has a life of its own. Consequently, simply addressing racism and sexism is inadequate to bring about total liberation.49 Even though there are dimensions of class which are not directly related to race or sex, classism impacts Black women in a peculiar way which results in the fact that they are most often on the bottom of the social and economic ladder. For Black women doing theology, to ignore classism would mean that their theology is no different from any other bourgeois theology. It would be meaningless to the majority of Black women, who are themselves poor. This means that addressing only issues relevant to middle class women or Blacks will simply not do: the daily struggles of poor Black women must serve as the gauge for the verification of the claims of womanist theology.

The Use of the Bible in the Womanist Tradition

Theological investigation into the experiences of Christian Black women reveals that Black women considered the Bible to be a major source for religious validation in their lives. Though Black women's relationship with God preceded their introduction to the Bible, this Bible gave some content to their God-consciousness? The source for Black women's understanding of God has been twofold: first, God's revelation directly to them, and secondly, God's revelation as witnessed in the Bible and as read and heard in the context of their experience. The understanding of God as creator, sustainer, comforter, and liberator took on life as they agonized over their pain, and celebrated the hope that as God delivered the Israelites, they would be delivered as well. The God of the Old and New Testament became real in the consciousness of oppressed Black women. Though they were politically impotent, they were able to appropriate certain themes of the Bible which spoke to their reality. For example, Jarena Lee, a nineteenth century Black woman preacher in the African Methodist Episcopal Church constantly emphasized the theme "Life and Liberty" in her sermons which were always biblically based. This interplay of scripture and experience was exercised by many other Black women. An ex-slave woman revealed that when her experience negated certain oppressive interpretations of the Bible given by White preachers, she, through engaging the biblical message for herself rejected them. Consequently, she also dismissed White preachers who distorted the message in order to maintain slavery. Her grandson, Howard Thurman, speaks of her use of the Bible in this way:

> "During the days of slavery," she said, "the master's minister would occasionally hold services for the slaves. Always the white minister used as his text something from Paul. 'Slaves be obedient to them that are your masters . . .,

as unto Christ.' Then he would go on to show how, if we were good and happy slaves, God would bless us. I promised my Maker that if I ever learned to read and if freedom ever came, I would not read that part of the Bible.

What we see here is perhaps more than a mere rejection of a White preacher's interpretation of the Bible, but an exercise in internal critique of the Bible. The Bible must be read and interpreted in the light of Black women's own experience of oppression and God's revelation within that context. Womanists must, like Sojourner, "compare the teachings of the Bible with the witness" in them.

To do Womanist Theology, then, we must read and hear the Bible and engage it within the context of our own experience. This is the only way that it can make sense to people who are oppressed. Black women of the past did not hesitate in doing this and we must do no less.

The Role of Jesus in the Womanist Tradition

In the experiences of Black people, Jesus was "all things." Chief among these however, was the belief in Jesus as the divine co-sufferer, who empowers them in situations of oppression. For Christian Black women in the past, Jesus was their central frame of reference. They identified with Jesus because they believed that Jesus identified with them. As Jesus was persecuted and made to suffer undeservedly, so were they. His suffering culminated in the crucifixion. Their crucifixion included rape, and babies being sold. But Jesus' suffering was not the suffering of a mere human, for Jesus was understood to be God incarnate. As Harold Carter observed of Black prayers in general, there was no difference made between the persons of the trinity, Jesus, God, or the Holy Spirit. "All of these proper names for God were used interchangeably in prayer language. Thus, Jesus was the one who speaks the world into creation. He was the power behind the Church . . .

Black women's affirmation of Jesus as God meant that White people were not God. One old slave woman clearly demonstrated this as she prayed:

> "Dear Massa Jesus, we all uns beg Ooner [you] come make us a call dis yore day. We is nutting but poor Etiopian women and people ain't tink much 'bout we. We ain't trust any of dem great high people for come to we church, but do' you is de one great Massa, great too much dan Massa Linkum, you ain't shame to care for we African people."

This slave woman did not hesitate to identify her struggles and pain with those of Jesus. In fact, the common struggle made her know that Jesus would respond to her beck and call.

> "Come to we, dear Massa Jesus. De sun, he hot too much, de road am dat long and boggy (sandy) and we ain't got no buggy for send and fetch Ooner. But Massa, you 'member how you walked dat hard walk up Calvary and ain't weary but tink about we all dat way. We know you ain't weary for to come to we. We pick out de torns, de prickles, de brier, de backslidin' and de quarrel and de sin out of you path so dey shan't hurt Ooner pierce feet no more."

As she is truly among the people at the bottom of humanity, she can make things comfortable for Jesus even though she may have nothing to give him-no water, no food-but she can give tears and love. She continues:

"Come to we, dear Massa Jesus. We all uns ain't got no good cool water for give you when you thirsty. You know, Massa, de drought so long, and the well so low, ain't nutting but mud to drink.But we gwine to take de 'munion cup and fill it wid de tear of repentance, and love clean out of we heart. Dat all we hab to gib you, good Massa."

For Black women, the role of Jesus unraveled as they encountered him in their experience as one who empowers the weak. In this vein, Jesus was such a central part of Sojourner Truth's life that all of her sermons made him the starting point. When asked by a preacher if the source of her preaching was the Bible, she responded "No honey, can't preach from de Bible-can't read a letter." Then she explained; "When I preaches, I has jest one text to preach from, an' I always preaches from this one. My text is, 'When I found Jesus!'" In this sermon Sojourner Truth recounts the events and struggles of her life from the time her parents were brought from Africa and sold "up an' down, an' hither an' yon . . ." to the time that she met Jesus within the context of her struggles for dignity of Black people and women. Her encounter with Jesus brought such joy that she became overwhelmed with love and praise:

Praise, praise, praise to the Lord! An' I begun to feel such a love in my soul as I never felt before-love to all creatures. An' then, all of a sudden, it stopped, an' I said, Dar's de white folks that have abused you, an' beat you, an' abused your people-think o' them! But then there came another rush of love through my soul, an' I cried out loud-'Lord, I can love even de white folks!

This love was not a sentimental, passive love. It was a tough, active love that empowered her to fight more fiercely for the freedom of her people. For the rest of her life she continued speaking at abolition and women's rights gatherings, condemning the horrors of oppression.

The Significance of Jesus in the Womanist Tradition

More than anyone, Black theologians have captured the essence of the significance of Jesus in the lives of Black people which to an extent includes Black women. They all hold that the Jesus of history is important for understanding who he was and his significance for us today. By and large they have affirmed that this Jesus is the Christ, that is, God incarnate. They have argued that in the light of our experience, Jesus meant freedom. They have maintained that Jesus means freedom from the sociopsychological, psychocultural, economic and political oppression of Black people. In other words, Jesus is a political messiah "To free (humans) from bondage was Jesus' own definition of his ministry." This meant that as Jesus identified with the lowly of his day, he now identifies with the lowly of this day, who in the American context are Black people. The identification is so real that Jesus Christ in fact becomes Black. It is important to note that Jesus' blackness is not a result of ideological distortion of a few Black thinkers, but a result of careful Christological investigation. Cone examines the sources of Christology and concludes that Jesus is Black because "Jesus was a Jew." He explains:

> It is on the basis of the soteriological meaning of the particularity of his Jewishness that theology must affirm the christological significance of Jesus' present blackness. He is black because he was a Jew. The affirmation of the Black Christ can be understood when the significance of his past Jewishness is related dialectically to the significance of his present blackness. On the one hand, the Jewishness of Jesus located him in the context of the Exodus, thereby connecting his appearance in Palestine with God's liberation of oppressed Israelites from Egypt. Unless Jesus were truly from Jewish ancestry, it would make little theological sense to say that he is the fulfillment of God's covenant with Israel. But on the other hand, the blackness of Jesus brings out the soteriological meaning of his Jewishness for our contemporary situation when Jesus' person is understood in the context of the cross and resurrection are Yahweh's fulfillment of his original intention for Israel.

The condition of Black people today reflects the cross of Jesus. Yet the resurrection brings the hope that liberation from oppression is immanent. The resurrected Black Christ signifies this hope.

Cone further argues that this christological title, "The Black Christ" is not validated by its universality, but, in fact, by its particularity. Its significance lies in whether or not the christological title "points to God's universal will to liberate particular oppressed people from inhumanity." These particular oppressed peoples to which Cone refers are characterized in Jesus' parable on the Last Judgment as "the least." "The least in America are literally and symbolically present in Black people." This notion of "the least" is attractive because it descriptively locates the condition of Black women. "The least" are those people who have no water to give, but offer what they have, as the old slave woman cited above says in her prayer. Black women's experience in general is such a reality. Their tri-dimensional reality renders their particular situation a complex one. One could say that not only are they the oppressed of the oppressed, but their situation represents "the particular within the particular."

But is this just another situation that takes us deeper into the abyss of theological relativity? I would argue that it is not, because it is in the context of Black women's experience where the particular connects up with the universal. By this I mean that in each of the three dynamics of oppression, Black women share in the reality of a broader community. They share race suffering with Black men; with White women and other Third World women, they are victims of sexism; and with poor Blacks and Whites, and other Third World peoples, especially women, they are disproportionately poor. To speak of Black women's tridimensional reality, therefore, is not to speak of Black women exclusively, for there is an implied universality that connects them with others.

Likewise, with Jesus Christ, there was an implied universality that made him identify with others—the poor, the woman, the stranger. To affirm Jesus' solidarity with the "least of the people" is not an exercise in romanticized contentment with one's oppressed status in life. For as the Resurrection signified that there is more to life than the cross for Jesus Christ, for Black women it signifies that their tri-dimensional oppressive existence is not the end, but it merely represents the context in which a particular people struggle to experience hope and liberation. Jesus Christ thus represents a three-fold significance: first he identifies with the "little people," Black women, where they are;

secondly, he affirms the basic humanity of these, "the least"; and thirdly, he inspires active hope in the struggle for resurrected, liberated existence.

To locate the Christ in Black people is a radical and necessary step, but an understanding of Black women's reality challenges us to go further. Christ among the least must also mean Christ in the community of Black women. William Eichelberger was able to recognize this as he further particularized the significance of the Blackness of Jesus by locating Christ in Black women's community. He was able to see Christ not only as Black male but also Black female.

> God, in revealing Himself and His attributes from time to time in His creaturely existence, has exercised His freedom to formalize His appearance in a variety of ways. . . . God revealed Himself at a point in the past as Jesus the Christ a Black male. My reasons for affirming the Blackness of Jesus of Nazareth are much different from that of the white apologist. . . . God wanted to identify with that segment of mankind which had suffered most, and is still suffering. . . . I am constrained to believe that God in our times has updated His form of revelation to western society. It is my feeling that God is now manifesting Himself, and has been for over 450 years, in the form of the Black American Woman as mother, as wife, as nourisher, sustainer and preserver of life, the Suffering Servant who is despised and rejected by men, a personality of sorrow who is acquainted with grief. The Black Woman has borne our griefs and carried our sorrows. She has been wounded because of American white society's transgressions and bruised by white iniquities. It appears that she may be the instrumentality through whom God will make us whole.

Granted, Eichelberger's categories for God and woman are very traditional. Nevertheless, the significance of his thought is that he was able to conceive of the Divine reality as other than a Black male messianic figure.

Challenges for Womanist Christology

Although I have argued that the White feminist analysis of theology and Christology is inadequate for salvific efficacy with respect to Black women, I do contend that it is not totally irrelevant to Black women's needs. I believe that Black women should take seriously the feminist analysis, but they should not allow themselves to be coopted on behalf of the agendas of White women, for as I have argued, they are often racist unintentionally or by intention.

The first challenge therefore, is to Black women. Feminists have identified some problems associated with language and symbolism of the church, theology, and Christology. They have been able to show that exclusive masculine language and imagery are contributing factors undergirding the oppression of women.

In addressing the present day, womanists must investigate the relationship between the oppression of women and theological symbolism. Even though Black women have been able to transcend some of the oppressive tendencies of White male (and Black male) articulated theologies, careful study reveals that some traditional symbols are inadequate for us today. The Christ understood as the stranger, the outcast, the hungry, the weak, the poor, makes the traditional male Christ (Black and White) less significant. Even our sisters, the womanist of the past though they exemplified no problems with the symbols themselves, they had some suspicions about the effects of a male image of the divine, for they did challenge the oppressive and distorted use of it in the church's theology. In so doing, they were able to move from a traditional oppressive Christology, with respect to women, to an egalitarian Christology. This kind of equalitarian Christology was operative in Jarena Lee's argument for the right of women to preach. She argued ". . . the Saviour died for the woman as well as for the man." The crucifixion was for universal salvation, not just for male salvation or, as we may extend the argument to include, not just for White salvation. Because of this Christ came and died, no less for the woman as for the man, no less for Blacks as for Whites.

> If the man may preach, because the Saviour died for him, why not the woman? Seeing he died for her also. Is he not a whole Saviour, instead of half one? as those who hold it wrong for a woman to preach, would seem to make it appear.

Lee correctly perceives that there is an ontological issue at stake. If Jesus Christ were a Savior of men then it is true the maleness of Christ would be paramount. But if Christ is a Saviour of all, then it is the humanity—the wholeness—of Christ that is significant. Sojourner was aware of the same tendency of some scholars and church leaders to link the maleness of Jesus and the sin of Eve with the status of women and she challenged this notion in her famed speech "Ain't I A Woman?"

> Then that little man in black there, he says women can't have as much rights as men, 'cause Christ wasn't a woman! Where did your Christ come from? Where did your Christ come from? From God and a woman. Man had nothing to do with Him.

> If the first woman God ever made was strong enough to turn the world upside down all alone, these women together ought to be able to turn it back, and get it right side up again! And now they is asking to do it, the men better let them.

I would argue, as suggested by both Lee and Sojourner, that the significance of Christ is not his maleness, but his humanity. The most significant events of Jesus Christ were the life and ministry, the crucifixion, and the resurrection. The significance of these events, in one sense, is that in them the absolute becomes concrete. God becomes concrete not only in the man Jesus, for he was crucified, but in the lives of those who will accept the challenges of the risen Saviour the Christ.

For Lee, this meant that women could preach; for Sojourner, it meant that women could possibly save the world; for me, it means today, this Christ, found in the experiences of Black women, is a Black woman. The commitment that to struggle not only with symptoms (church structures, structures of society), as Black women have done, but with causes (those beliefs which produce and reinforce structures) yield deeper theological and christological questions having to do with images and symbolism. Christ challenges us to ask new questions demanded by the context in which we find ourselves.

The second challenge for Black women is that we must explore more deeply the question of what Christ means in a society in which class distinctions are increasing.

If Christ is among "the least" then who are they? Because our foreparents were essentially poor by virtue of their race, there was no real need for them to address classism as a separate reality. Today, in light of the emerging Black middle class we must ask what is the impact of class upon our lives and the lives of other poor Black and Third World women and men.

Another way of addressing the class issue in the church is to recognize the fact that although our race/sex analyses may force us to realize that Blacks and women should share in the leadership of the church, the style of leadership and basic structures of the church virtually insure the continuation of a privileged class.

Contemporary Black women in taking seriously the Christ mandate to be among the least must insist that we address all three aspects of Black women's reality in our analyses. The challenge here for contemporary Black women is to begin to construct a serious analysis which addresses the structural nature of poverty. Black women must recognize that racism, sexism and classism each have lives of their own, and that no one form of oppression is eliminated with the destruction of any other. Though they are interrelated, they must all be addressed.

The third and final challenge for Black women is to do constructive Christology. This Christology must be a liberating one, for both the Black women's community and the larger Black community. A Christology that negates Black male humanity is still destructive to the Black community. We must, therefore, take seriously only the usable aspects of the past.

To be sure, as Black women receive these challenges, their very embodiment represents a challenge to White women. This embodiment (of racism, sexism and classism) says to White women that a wholistic analysis is a minimal requirement for wholistic theology. The task of Black women then, is constructive.

As we organize in this constructive task, we are also challenged to adopt the critical stance of Sojourner with respect to the feminist analysis as reflected in her comment:

> I know that it feel a kind o' hissin' and ticklin' like to see a colored woman get up and tell you about things, and woman's rights. We have all been thrown down so low that nobody thought we' ever get up again, but we have been long enough trodden now; we will come up again, and now I am here. . . .

> . . . I wanted to tell you a mite about Woman's Rights, and so I came out and said so. I am sittin' among you to watch; and every once in a while I will come out and tell you what time of night it is.

Selection 3: Delores S. Williams, "*Womanist* Theology: Black Women's Voice"

Delores Williams is Paul Tillich Professor Emerita of Theology and Culture at Union Theological Seminary in New York City. She is one of womanist theology's original thinkers who articulated the particular issues facing black women as distinguished from feminism and male centered black theology.

DAUGHTER: Mama, why are we brown, pink, and yellow, and our cousins are white, beige, and black?

MOTHER: Well, you know the colored race is just like a flower garden, with every color flower represented.

DAUGHTER: Mama, I'm walking to Canada and I'm taking you and a bunch of slaves with me.

MOTHER: It wouldn't be the first time.

In these two conversational exchanges, Pulitzer Prize-winning novelist Alice Walker begins to show us what she means by the concept "womanist." The concept is presented in Walker's *In Search of Our Mother's Gardens*, and many women in church and society have appropriated it as a way of affirming themselves as black while simultaneously owning their connection with feminism and with the Afro-American community, male and female. The concept of womanist allows women to claim their roots in black history, religion and culture.

What then is a womanist? Her origins are in the black folk expression "You acting womanish," meaning, according to Walker, "wanting to know more and in greater depth than is good for one—outrageous audacious, courageous and willful behavior." A womanist is also "responsible, in charge, serious." She can walk to Canada and take others with her. She loves, she is committed, she is a universalist by temperament.

Her universality includes loving men and woman, sexually or nonsexually. She loves music, dance, the spirit, food and roundness, struggle, and she loves herself. "Regardless."

Walker insists that a womanist is also "committed to survival and wholeness of entire people, male and female." She is no separatist, "except for health." A womanist is a black feminist or feminist of color. Or as Walker says, "Womanist is to feminist as purple to lavender."

Womanist theology, a vision in its infancy, is emerging among Afro-American Christian women. Ultimately many sources—biblical, theological, ecclesiastical, social, anthropological, economic, and material from other religious traditions will inform the development of this theology. As a contribution to this process, I will demonstrate how Walker's concept of womanist provides some significant clues for the work of womanist theologians. I will then focus on method and God-content in womanist theology. This contribution belongs to the work of prolegomena—prefatory remarks, introductory observations intended to be suggestive and not conclusive.

Codes and Contents

In her definition, Walker provides significant clues for the development of womanist theology. Her concept contains what black feminist scholar Bell Hooks in From Margin to Center identifies as cultural codes. These are words, beliefs, and behavioral patterns of a people that must he deciphered before meaningful communication can happen cross-culturally. Walker's codes are female-centered and they point beyond themselves to conditions, events, meanings. and values that have crystallized in the Afro-American community around women's activity and formed traditions.

A paramount example is mother-daughter advice: Black mothers have passed on wisdom for survival—in the white world, in the black community, and with men—for as long as anyone can remember. Female slave narratives, folk tales, and some contemporary black poetry and prose reflect this tradition. Some of it is collected in "Old Sister's Advice to Her Daughters," in *The Book of Negro Folklore*, edited by Langston Hughes and Ama Bontemps (Dodd Mead 1958).

Walker's allusion to skin color points to a historic tradition of tension between black women over the matter of some black men's preference for light-skinned women. Her reference to black women's love of food and roundness points to customs of female care in the black community (including the church) associated with hospitality and nurture.

These cultural codes and their corresponding traditions are valuable resources for indicating and validating the kind of data upon which womanist theologians can reflect as they bring black women's social, religious, and cultural experience into the discourse of theology, ethics, biblical and religious studies. Female slave narratives, imaginative literature by black women, autobiographies, the work by black women in academic disciplines, and the testimonies of black church women will be authoritative sources for womanist theologians.

Walker situates her understanding of a womanist in the context of nonbourgeois black folk culture. The literature of this culture has traditionally reflected more egalitarian relations between men and women, much less rigidity in male-female roles, and more respect for female intelligence and ingenuity than is found in bourgeois culture.

The black folk are poor less individualistic than those who are better off, they have, for generations, practiced various forms of economic sharing. For example, immediately after Emancipation mutual aid societies pooled the resources of black folk to help pay for funerals and other daily expenses. *The Book of Negro Folklore* describes the practice of rent parties that flourished during the Depression. The black folk stressed togetherness and a closer connection with nature. They respect knowledge gained through lived experience monitored by elders who differ profoundly in social class and worldview from the teachers and education encountered in American academic institutions. Walker's choice of context suggests that womanist theology can establish its lines of continuity in the black community with nonbourgeois traditions less sexist than the black power and black nationalist traditions.

In this folk context, some of the black female-centered cultural codes in Walker's definition (e.g., "Mama, I'm walking to Canada and I'm taking you and a bunch of slaves with me") point to folk heroines like Harriet Tubman, whose liberation activity earned her the name "Moses" of her people. This allusion to Tubman directs womanist memory to a liberation tradition in black history in which women took the lead, acting as catalysts for the community's revolutionary action and for social change. Retrieving this often hidden or diminished female tradition of catalytic action is an important task for womanist theologians and ethicists. Their research may well reveal that female models of authority have been absolutely essential for every struggle in the black community and for building and maintaining the community's institutions.

Freedom Fighters

The womanist theologian must search for the voices, actions, opinions, experience, and faith of women whose names sometimes slip into the male-centered rendering of black history, hut whose actual stories remain remote. This search can lead to such little-known freedom fighters as Milla Granson and her courageous work on a Mississippi plantation. Her liberation method broadens our knowledge of the variety of strategies black people have used to obtain freedom. According to scholar Sylvia Dannett, in Profiles in Negro Womanhood:

Milla Granson, a slave, conducted a midnight school for several years. She had been taught to read and write by her former master in Kentucky, and in her little school hundreds of slaves benefited from her learning. After laboring all day for their master, the slaves would creep stealthily to Milla's "schoolroom" (a little cabin in a hack alley). The doors and windows had to be kept tightly sealed to avoid discovery. Each class was composed of twelve pupils and when Milla had brought them up to the extent of her ability, she "graduated" them and took in a dozen more. Through this means she graduated hundreds of slaves. Many of whom she taught to write a legible hand forged their own passes and set out for Canada,

Women like Tubman and Granson used subtle and silent strategies to liberate themselves and large numbers of black people. By uncovering as much as possible about such female liberation, the womanist begins to understand the relation of black history to the contemporary folk expression: "If Rosa Parks had not sat down, Martin King would not have stood up."

While she celebrates and emphasizes black women's culture and way of being in the world, Walker simultaneously affirms black women's historic connection with men through love and through a shared struggle for survival and for a productive quality of life (e.g., "wholeness"). This suggests that two of the principal concerns of womanist theology should he survival and community building and maintenance. The goal of this community building is, of course, to establish a positive quality of life—economic, spiritual, educational—for black women, men, and children. Walker's understanding of a womanist as "not a separatist" ("except for health"), however, reminds the Christian womanist theologian that her concern for community building and maintenance must ultimately extend to the entire Christian community and beyond that to the larger human community.

Yet womanist consciousness is also informed by women's determination to love themselves. "regardless." This translates into an admonition to black women to avoid the self-destruction of hearing a disproportionately large burden in the work of community building and maintenance. Walker suggests that women can avoid this trap by connecting with women's communities concerned about women's rights and well-being. Her identification of a womanist as also a feminist joins black women with their feminist heritage extending back into the nineteenth century in the work of black feminists like Sojourner Truth, Frances W. Harper, and Mary Church Terrell.

In making the feminist-womanist connection, however, Walker proceeds with great caution. While affirming an organic relationship between womanists and feminists, she also declares a deep shade of difference between them ("Womanist is to feminist as purple to lavender.") This gives womanist scholars the freedom to explore the particularities of black women's history and culture without being guided by what white feminists have already identified as women's issues.

But womanist consciousness directs black women away from the negative divisions prohibiting community building among women. The womanist loves other women sexually and nonsexually. Therefore, respect for sexual preferences is one of the marks of womanist community. According to Walker, homophobia has no place. Nor does "Colorism" (i.e., "yella" and half-white black people valued more in the black world than black-skinned people), which often separates black women from each other. Rather, Walker's womanist claim is that color variety is the substance of universality. Color, like birth and death, is common to all people. Like the navel, it is a badge of humanity connecting people with people. Two other distinctions are prohibited in Walker's womanist thinking. Class hierarchy does not dwell among women who ". . . love struggle, love the Folks . . . are committed to the survival and wholeness of an entire people." Nor do women compete for male attention when they ". . . appreciate and prefer female culture . . . value . . . women's emotional flexibility . . . and women's strength."

The intimations about community provided by Walker's definition suggest no genuine community building is possible when men are excluded (except when women's health is at stake). Neither can it occur when black women's self-love, culture, and love for each other are not affirmed and are not considered vital for the community's self-understanding. And it is thwarted if black women are expected to bear "the lion's share" of the work and to sacrifice their well-being for the good of the group.

Yet, for the womanist, mothering and nurturing are vitally important. Walker's womanist reality begins with mothers relating to their children and is characterized by black women (not necessarily bearers of children) nurturing great numbers of black people in the liberation struggle (e.g., Harriet Tubman). Womanist emphasis upon the value of mothering and nurturing is consistent with the testimony of many black women. The poet Carolyn Rogers speaks of her mother as the great black bridge that brought her over. Walker dedicated her novel The Third Life of Grange Copeland to her mother ". . . who made a way out of no way." As a child in the black church, I heard women (and men) give thanks to God for their mothers . . . who stayed behind and pulled the wagon over the long haul."

It seems, then, that the clues about community from Walker's definition of a womanist suggest that the mothering and nurturing dimension of Afro-American history can provide resources for shaping criteria to measure the quality of justice in the community. These criteria could be used to assure female-male equity in the presentation of the community's models of authority. They could also gauge the community's division of labor with regard to the survival tasks necessary for building and maintaining community.

Womanist Theology and Method

Womanist theology is already beginning to define the categories and methods needed to develop along lines consistent with the sources of that theology. Christian womanist theological methodology needs to be informed by at least four elements: (1) a multidialogical intent, (2) a liturgical intent, (3) a didactic intent, and (4) a commitment both to reason and to the validity of female imagery and metaphorical language in the construction of theological statements.

A multidialogical intent will allow Christian womanist theologians to advocate and participate in dialogue and action with many diverse social, political, and religious communities concerned about human survival and productive quality of life for the oppressed. The genocide of cultures and peoples (which has often been instigated and accomplished by Western white Christian groups or governments) and the nuclear threat of omnicide mandates womanist participation in such dialogue/ action. But in this dialogue/action the womanist also should keep her speech and action focused upon the slow genocide of poor black women, children, and men by exploitative systems denying them productive jobs, education, health care, and living space. Multidialogical activity may, like a jazz symphony, communicate some of its most important messages in what the harmony-driven conventional ear hears as discord, as disruption of the harmony in both the black American and white American social, political, and religious status quo.

If womanist theological method is informed by a liturgical intent, then womanist theology will he relevant to (and will reflect) the thought, worship, and action of the black church. But a liturgical intent will also allow womanist theology to challenge the thought/worship/action of the black church with the discordant and prophetic messages emerging from womanist participation in multidialogics. This means that womanist theology will consciously impact critically upon the foundations of liturgy, challenging the church to use justice principles to select the sources that will shape the content of liturgy. The question must be asked: "How does this source portray blackness/ darkness, women and economic justice for nonruling-class people?" A negative portrayal will demand omission of the source or its radical reformation by the black church. The Bible, a major source in black church liturgy, must also be subjected to the scrutiny of justice principles.

A didactic intent in womanist theological method assigns a teaching function to theology. Womanist theology should teach Christians new insights about moral life based on ethics supporting justice for women, survival, and a productive quality of life for poor women, children, and men. This means that the womanist theologian must give authoritative status to black folk wisdom (e.g., Brer Rabbit literature) and to black women's moral wisdom (expressed in their literature) when she responds to the question, "How ought the Christian to live in the world?" Certainly tensions may exist between the moral teachings derived from these sources and the moral teachings about obedience, love, and humility that have usually buttressed presuppositions about living the Christian life. Nevertheless, womanist theology, in its didactic intent, must teach the church the different ways God reveals prophetic word and action for Christian living.

These intents, informing theological method, can yield a theological language whose foundation depends as much upon its imagistic content as upon reason. The language can be rich in female imagery, metaphor, and story. For the black church, this kind of theological language may be quite useful, since the language of the black religious experience abounds in images and metaphors. Clifton Johnson's collection of black conversion experiences, God Struck Me Dead, illustrates this point.

The appropriateness of womanist theological language will ultimately reside in its ability to bring black women's history, culture, and religious experience into the interpretive circle of Christian theology and into the liturgical life of the church. Womanist theological language must, in this sense, he an instrument for social and theological change in church and society.

Who Do You Say God Is?

Regardless of one's hopes about intentionality and womanist theological method, questions must be raised about the God-content of the theology. Walker's mention of the black womanist's love of the spirit is a true reflection of the great respect Afro-American women have always shown for the presence and work of the spirit. In the black church, women (and men) often judge the effectiveness of the worship service not on the scholarly content of the sermon nor on the ritual nor on orderly process. Rather, worship has been effective if "the spirit was high," i.e., if the spirit was actively and obviously present in a balanced blend of prayer, of cadenced word (the sermon), and of syncopated music ministering to the pain of the people.

The importance of this emphasis upon the spirit is that it allows Christian womanist theologians, in their use of the Bible, to identify and reflect upon those biblical stories in which poor oppressed women had a special encounter with divine emissaries of God, like the spirit. In the Hebrew Testament, Hagar's story is most illustrative and relevant to Afro-American women's experience of bondage, of African heritage, of encounter with God/emissary in the midst of fierce survival struggles. Katie Cannon among a number of black female preachers and ethicists urges black Christian women to regard themselves as Hagar's sisters.

In relation to the Christian or New Testament, the Christian womanist theologian can refocus the salvation story so that it emphasizes the beginning of revelation with the spirit mounting Mary, a woman of the poor: ". . . the Holy Spirit shall come upon thee, and the power of the Highest shall overshadow thee (Luke 1:35). Such an interpretation of revelation has roots in nineteenth-century black abolitionist and feminist Sojourner Truth. Posing an important question and response, she refuted a white preacher's claim that women could not have rights equal to men's because Christ was not a woman. Truth asked, "Whar did your Christ come from? From God and a woman! Man had nothin' to do wid Him!" This suggests that womanist theology could eventually speak of God in a well-developed theology of the spirit. The sources for this theology are many. Harriet Tubman often "went into the spirit" before her liberation missions and claimed her strength for liberation activity came from this way of meeting God. Womanist theology has grounds for shaping a theology of the spirit informed by black women's political action.

Christian womanist responses to the question "who do you say God is?" will be influenced by these many sources. Walker's way of connecting womanists with the spirit is on/v one clue. The integrity of black church women's faith, their love of Jesus, their commitment to life, love, family, and politics will also yield vital clues. And other theological voices (black liberation, feminist, Islamic, Asian, Hispanic, African, Jewish, and Western white male traditional) will provide insights relevant for the construction of the God-content of womanist theology.

Each womanist theologian will add her own special accent to the understandings of God emerging from womanist theology. But if one needs a final image to describe women coming together to shape the enterprise, Bess B. Johnson in God's Fierce Whimsy offers an appropriate one. Describing the difference between the play of male and female children in the black community where she developed, Johnson says: the boys in the neighborhood had this game with rope . . . tug-o'-war.. till finally some side would jerk the rope away from the others, who'd fall down. . . . Girls. . . weren't allowed to play with them in this tug-o'-war; so we figured out how to make our own rope—out of . . . little dandelions. You just keep adding them, one to another, and you can go on and on. . . . Anybody, even the boys, could join us. . . . The whole purpose of our game was to create this dandelion chain—that was it. And we'd keep going, creating till our mamas called us home.

Like Johnson's dandelion chain, womanist theological vision will grow as black women come together and connect piece with piece. Between the process of creating and the sense of calling, womanist theology will one day present itself in full array, reflecting the divine spirit that connects us all.

For Further Reading

The following select list of writings provides a mixture of primary and secondary sources related to the major parts of the anthology, and the full text of the works being excerpted will also provide rich additional reading.

Brubaker, Pamela. *Women Don't Count: the Challenge of Women's Poverty for Christian Ethics.* Atlanta: Scholars, 1994.

Coleman, Monica A. *Making a Way Out of No Way: A Womanist Theology.* Minneapolis: Fortress Press, 2008.

Fiorenza, Elisabeth Schüssler. *In Memory of Her: A Feminist Theological Reconstruction of Christian Origins.* New York: Crossroad, 1983.

———. *The Power of the Word: Scripture and the Rhetoric of Empire.* Minneapolis: Fortress Press, 2007.

Floyd-Thomas, Stacey. *Mining the Mother Lode: Methods in Womanist Ethics.* Cleveland: Pilgrim, 2006.

Harrison, Beverly Wildung. *Justice in the Making: Feminist Social Ethics.* Edited by Elizabeth M. Bounds. Louisville: Westminster John Knox, 2004.

A Just and True Love: Feminism at the Frontiers of Theological Ethics. Essays in Honor of Margaret Farley. Edited by Maura A. Ryan and Brian F. Li. Notre Dame: Notre Dame University Press, 2007.

Kirk-Duggan, Cheryl. *Exorcizing Evil: A Womanist Perspective on the Spirituals.* Maryknoll: Orbis, 1997.

Ross, Rosetta. *Witnessing and Testifying: Black Women, Religion, and Civil Rights.* Minneapolis: Fortress Press, 2003.

Ruether, Rosemary Radford. *Women and Redemption: A Theological History*, 2nd edition. Minneapolis: Fortress Press, 2012.

Russell, Letty. *Human Liberation in a Feminist Perspective.* Philadelphia: Westminster, 1974.

Townes, Emilie. *In a Blaze of Glory: Womanist Spirituality as Social Witness.* Nashville: Abingdon, 1995.

Trible, Phyllis. *Texts of Terror: Literary-Feminist Readings of Biblical Narratives.* Philadelphia: Fortress Press, 1984.

West, Traci. *Disruptive Christian Ethics: When Racism and Women's Lives Matter.* Louisville: Westminster John Knox, 2006.

Womanist Theological Ethics: A Reader. Edited by Katie Geneva Cannon, Emilie M. Townes, and Angela D. Sims. Louisville: Westminster John Knox, 2011.

PART 11

Contemporary Issues:
The Mid-Twentieth Century to the Present

In addition to the themes of liberation evident in feminist and womanist theology and ethics, the latter half of the twentieth century has seen a powerful upsurge in the literature of liberation theology and its concern for social justice. The examples below feature two of the foremost representatives of Latin American liberation theology and in the person of James Cone a dominant figure in Black Theology of liberation. Martin Luther King Jr. was not in the strictest sense a liberation theologian, but his call for freedom from oppression and the witness of his life and work place him at the head of this chapter.

Selection 1: Martin Luther King Jr., Letter from a Birmingham Jail

Martin Luther King Jr.'s open letter to fellow clergy was written while in jail for his leadership in the civil rights campaign in Birmingham. In it he chides the leaders of the church for their failure to take up the cause of justice with the urgency it deserves. He lays out and defends his philosophy of nonviolence.

16 April 1963

My Dear Fellow Clergymen:

While confined here in the Birmingham city jail, I came across your recent statement calling my present activities "unwise and untimely." Seldom do I pause to answer criticism of my work and ideas. If I sought to answer all the criticisms that cross my desk, my secretaries would have little time for anything other than such correspondence in the course of the day, and I would have no time for constructive work. But since I feel that you are men of genuine good will and that your criticisms are sincerely set forth, I want to try to answer your statement in what I hope will be patient and reasonable terms.

I think I should indicate why I am here in Birmingham, since you have been influenced by the view that argues against "outsiders coming in." I have the honor of serving as president of the Southern Christian Leadership Conference, an organization operating in every southern state, with headquarters in Atlanta, Georgia. We have some eighty-five affiliated organizations across the South, and one of them is the Alabama Christian Movement for Human Rights. Frequently we share staff, educational and financial resources with our affiliates. Several months ago the affiliate here in Birmingham asked us to be on call to engage in a nonviolent direct action program if such were deemed necessary. We readily consented, and when the hour came we lived up to our promise. So I, along with several members of my staff, am here because I was invited here. I am here because I have organizational ties here.

But more basically, I am in Birmingham because injustice is here. Just as the prophets of the eighth century B.C. left their villages and carried their "thus saith the Lord" far beyond the boundaries of their home towns, and just as the Apostle Paul left his village of Tarsus and carried the gospel of Jesus Christ to the far corners of the Greco Roman world, so am I compelled to carry the gospel of freedom beyond my own home town. Like Paul, I must constantly respond to the Macedonian call for aid.

Moreover, I am cognizant of the interrelatedness of all communities and states. I cannot sit idly by in Atlanta and not be concerned about what happens in Birmingham. Injustice anywhere is a threat to justice everywhere. We are caught in an inescapable network of mutuality, tied in a single garment of destiny. Whatever affects one directly, affects all indirectly. Never again can we afford to live with the narrow, provincial "outside agitator" idea. Anyone who lives inside the United States can never be considered an outsider anywhere within its bounds.

You deplore the demonstrations taking place in Birmingham. But your statement, I am sorry to say, fails to express a similar concern for the conditions that brought about the demonstrations. I am sure that none of you would want to rest content with the superficial kind of social analysis that deals merely with effects and does not grapple with underlying causes. It is unfortunate that demonstrations are taking place in Birmingham, but it is even more unfortunate that the city's white power structure left the Negro community with no alternative.

In any nonviolent campaign there are four basic steps: collection of the facts to determine whether injustices exist; negotiation; self-purification; and direct action. We have gone through all these steps in Birmingham. There can be no gainsaying the fact that racial injustice engulfs this community. Birmingham is probably the most thoroughly segregated city in the United States. Its ugly record of brutality is widely known. Negroes have experienced grossly unjust treatment in the courts. There have been more unsolved bombings of Negro homes and churches in Birmingham than in any other city in the nation. These are the hard, brutal facts of the case. On the basis of these conditions, Negro leaders sought to negotiate with the city fathers. But the latter consistently refused to engage in good faith negotiation.

Then, last September, came the opportunity to talk with leaders of Birmingham's economic community. In the course of the negotiations, certain promises were made by the merchants—for example, to remove the stores' humiliating racial signs. On the basis of these promises, the Reverend Fred Shuttlesworth and the leaders of the Alabama Christian Movement for Human Rights agreed to a moratorium on all demonstrations. As the weeks and months went by, we realized that we were the victims of a broken promise. A few signs, briefly removed, returned; the others remained. As in so many past experiences, our hopes had been blasted, and the shadow of deep disappointment settled upon us. We had no alternative except to prepare for direct action, whereby we would present our very bodies as a means of laying our case before the conscience of the local and the national community. Mindful of the difficulties involved, we decided to undertake a process of self-purification. We began a series of workshops on nonviolence, and we repeatedly asked ourselves: "Are you able to accept blows without retaliating?" "Are you able to endure the ordeal of jail?" We decided to schedule our direct action program for the Easter season, realizing that except for Christmas, this is the main shopping period of the year. Knowing that a strong economic-withdrawal program would be the byproduct of direct action, we felt that this would be the best time to bring pressure to bear on the merchants for the needed change.

Then it occurred to us that Birmingham's mayoral election was coming up in March, and we speedily decided to postpone action until after election day. When we discovered that the Commissioner of Public Safety, Eugene "Bull" Connor, had piled up enough votes to be in the run off, we decided again to postpone action until the day after the run off so that the demonstrations could not be used to cloud the issues. Like many others, we waited to see Mr. Connor defeated, and to this end we endured postponement after postponement. Having aided in this community need, we felt that our direct action program could be delayed no longer.

You may well ask: "Why direct action? Why sit ins, marches, and so forth? Isn't negotiation a better path?" You are quite right in calling for negotiation. Indeed, this is the very purpose of direct action. Nonviolent direct action seeks to create such a crisis and foster such a tension that a community which has constantly refused to negotiate is forced to confront the issue. It seeks so to dramatize the issue that it can no longer be ignored. My citing the creation of tension as part of the work of the nonviolent resister may sound rather shocking. But I must confess that I am not afraid of the word "tension." I have earnestly opposed violent tension, but there is a type of constructive, nonviolent tension which is necessary for growth. Just as Socrates felt that it was necessary to create a tension in the mind so that individuals could rise from the bondage of myths and half-truths to the unfettered realm of creative analysis and objective appraisal, so must we see the need for nonviolent gadflies to create the kind of tension in society that will help men rise from the dark depths of prejudice and racism to the majestic heights of understanding and brotherhood. The purpose of our direct action program is to create a situation so crisis packed that it will inevitably open the door to negotiation. I therefore concur with you in your call for negotiation. Too long has our beloved Southland been bogged down in a tragic effort to live in monologue rather than dialogue.

One of the basic points in your statement is that the action that I and my associates have taken in Birmingham is untimely. Some have asked: "Why didn't you give the new city administration time to act?" The only answer that I can give to this query is that the new Birmingham administration must be prodded about as much as the outgoing one, before it will act. We are sadly mistaken if we feel that the election of Albert Boutwell as mayor will bring the millennium to Birmingham. While Mr. Boutwell is a much more gentle person than Mr. Connor, they are both segregationists, dedicated to maintenance of the status quo. I have hope that Mr. Boutwell will be reasonable enough to see the futility of massive resistance to desegregation. But he will not see this without pressure from devotees of civil rights. My friends, I must say to you that we have not made a single gain in civil rights without determined legal and nonviolent pressure. Lamentably, it is an historical fact that privileged groups seldom give up their privileges voluntarily. Individuals may see the moral light and voluntarily give up their unjust posture; but, as Reinhold Niebuhr has reminded us, groups tend to be more immoral than individuals.

We know through painful experience that freedom is never voluntarily given by the oppressor; it must be demanded by the oppressed. Frankly, I have yet to engage in a direct action campaign that was "well timed" in the view of those who have not suffered unduly from the disease of segregation. For years now I have heard the word "Wait!" It rings in the ear of every Negro with piercing familiarity. This "Wait" has almost always meant "Never." We must come to see, with one of our distinguished jurists, that "justice too long delayed is justice denied."

We have waited for more than 340 years for our constitutional and God given rights. The nations of Asia and Africa are moving with jetlike speed toward gaining political independence, but we still creep at horse and buggy pace toward gaining a cup of coffee at a lunch counter. Perhaps it is easy for those who have never felt the stinging darts of segregation to say, "Wait." But when you have seen vicious mobs lynch your mothers and fathers at will and drown your sisters and brothers at whim; when you have seen hate filled policemen curse, kick and even kill your black brothers and sisters; when you see the vast majority of your twenty million Negro brothers smothering in an airtight cage of poverty in the midst of an affluent society; when you suddenly find your tongue twisted and your speech stammering as you seek to explain to your six year old daughter why she can't go to the public amusement park that has just been advertised on television, and see tears welling up in her eyes when she is told that Funtown is closed to colored children, and see ominous clouds of inferiority beginning to form in her little mental sky, and see her beginning to distort her personality by developing an unconscious bitterness toward white people; when you have to concoct an answer for a five year old son who is asking: "Daddy, why do white people treat colored people so mean?"; when you take a cross county drive and find it necessary to sleep night after night in the uncomfortable corners of your automobile because no motel will accept you; when you are humiliated day in and day out by nagging signs reading "white" and "colored"; when your first name becomes "nigger," your middle name becomes "boy" (however old you are) and your last name becomes "John," and your wife and mother are never given the respected title "Mrs."; when you are harried by day and haunted by night by the fact that you are a Negro, living constantly at tiptoe stance, never quite knowing what to expect next, and are plagued with inner fears and outer resentments; when you are forever fighting a degenerating sense of "nobodiness"—then you will understand why we find it difficult to wait. There comes a time when the cup of endurance runs over, and men are no longer willing to be plunged into the abyss of despair. I hope, sirs, you can understand our legitimate and unavoidable impatience. You express a great deal of anxiety over our willingness to break laws. This is certainly a legitimate concern. Since we so diligently urge people to obey the Supreme Court's decision of 1954 outlawing segregation in the public schools, at first glance it may seem rather paradoxical for us consciously to break laws. One may well ask: "How can you advocate breaking some laws and obeying others?" The answer lies in the fact that there are two types of laws: just and unjust. I would be the first to advocate obeying just laws. One has not only a legal but a moral responsibility to obey just laws. Conversely, one has a moral responsibility to disobey unjust laws. I would agree with St. Augustine that "an unjust law is no law at all."

Now, what is the difference between the two? How does one determine whether a law is just or unjust? A just law is a man-made code that squares with the moral law or the law of God. An unjust law is a code that is out of harmony with the moral law.

To put it in the terms of St. Thomas Aquinas: An unjust law is a human law that is not rooted in eternal law and natural law. Any law that uplifts human personality is just. Any law that degrades human personality is unjust. All segregation statutes are unjust because segregation distorts the soul and damages the personality. It gives the segregator a false sense of superiority and the segregated a false sense of inferiority. Segregation, to use the terminology of the Jewish philosopher Martin Buber, substitutes an "I it" relationship for an "I thou" relationship and ends up relegating persons to the status of things. Hence segregation is not only politically, economically and sociologically unsound, it is morally wrong and sinful. Paul Tillich has said that sin is separation. Is not segregation an existential expression of man's tragic separation, his awful estrangement, his terrible sinfulness? Thus it is that I can urge men to obey the 1954 decision of the Supreme Court, for it is morally right; and I can urge them to disobey segregation ordinances, for they are morally wrong.

Let us consider a more concrete example of just and unjust laws. An unjust law is a code that a numerical or power majority group compels a minority group to obey but does not make binding on itself. This is difference made legal. By the same token, a just law is a code that a majority compels a minority to follow and that it is willing to follow itself. This is sameness made legal. Let me give another explanation. A law is unjust if it is inflicted on a minority that, as a result of being denied the right to vote, had no part in enacting or devising the law. Who can say that the legislature of Alabama which set up that state's segregation laws was democratically elected? Throughout Alabama all sorts of devious methods are used to prevent Negroes from becoming registered voters, and there are some counties in which, even though Negroes constitute a majority of the population, not a single Negro is registered. Can any law enacted under such circumstances be considered democratically structured?

Sometimes a law is just on its face and unjust in its application. For instance, I have been arrested on a charge of parading without a permit. Now, there is nothing wrong in having an ordinance which requires a permit for a parade. But such an ordinance becomes unjust when it is used to maintain segregation and to deny citizens the First-Amendment privilege of peaceful assembly and protest.

I hope you are able to see the distinction I am trying to point out. In no sense do I advocate evading or defying the law, as would the rabid segregationist. That would lead to anarchy. One who breaks an unjust law must do so openly, lovingly, and with a willingness to accept the penalty. I submit that an individual who breaks a law that conscience tells him is unjust, and who willingly accepts the penalty of imprisonment in order to arouse the conscience of the community over its injustice, is in reality expressing the highest respect for law.

Of course, there is nothing new about this kind of civil disobedience. It was evidenced sublimely in the refusal of Shadrach, Meshach and Abednego to obey the laws of Nebuchadnezzar, on the ground that a higher moral law was at stake. It was practiced superbly by the early Christians, who were willing to face hungry lions and the excruciating pain of chopping blocks rather than submit to certain unjust laws of the Roman Empire. To a degree, academic freedom is a reality today because Socrates practiced civil disobedience. In our own nation, the Boston Tea Party represented a massive act of civil disobedience.

We should never forget that everything Adolf Hitler did in Germany was "legal" and everything the Hungarian freedom fighters did in Hungary was "illegal." It was "illegal" to aid and comfort a Jew in Hitler's Germany. Even so, I am sure that, had

I lived in Germany at the time, I would have aided and comforted my Jewish brothers. If today I lived in a Communist country where certain principles dear to the Christian faith are suppressed, I would openly advocate disobeying that country's antireligious laws.

I must make two honest confessions to you, my Christian and Jewish brothers. First, I must confess that over the past few years I have been gravely disappointed with the white moderate. I have almost reached the regrettable conclusion that the Negro's great stumbling block in his stride toward freedom is not the White Citizen's Counciler or the Ku Klux Klanner, but the white moderate, who is more devoted to "order" than to justice; who prefers a negative peace which is the absence of tension to a positive peace which is the presence of justice; who constantly says: "I agree with you in the goal you seek, but I cannot agree with your methods of direct action"; who paternalistically believes he can set the timetable for another man's freedom; who lives by a mythical concept of time and who constantly advises the Negro to wait for a "more convenient season." Shallow understanding from people of good will is more frustrating than absolute misunderstanding from people of ill will. Lukewarm acceptance is much more bewildering than outright rejection.

I had hoped that the white moderate would understand that law and order exist for the purpose of establishing justice and that when they fail in this purpose they become the dangerously structured dams that block the flow of social progress. I had hoped that the white moderate would understand that the present tension in the South is a necessary phase of the transition from an obnoxious negative peace, in which the Negro passively accepted his unjust plight, to a substantive and positive peace, in which all men will respect the dignity and worth of human personality. Actually, we who engage in nonviolent direct action are not the creators of tension. We merely bring to the surface the hidden tension that is already alive. We bring it out in the open, where it can be seen and dealt with. Like a boil that can never be cured so long as it is covered up but must be opened with all its ugliness to the natural medicines of air and light, injustice must be exposed, with all the tension its exposure creates, to the light of human conscience and the air of national opinion before it can be cured.

In your statement you assert that our actions, even though peaceful, must be condemned because they precipitate violence. But is this a logical assertion? Isn't this like condemning a robbed man because his possession of money precipitated the evil act of robbery? Isn't this like condemning Socrates because his unswerving commitment to truth and his philosophical inquiries precipitated the act by the misguided populace in which they made him drink hemlock? Isn't this like condemning Jesus because his unique God consciousness and never ceasing devotion to God's will precipitated the evil act of crucifixion? We must come to see that, as the federal courts have consistently affirmed, it is wrong to urge an individual to cease his efforts to gain his basic constitutional rights because the quest may precipitate violence. Society must protect the robbed and punish the robber. I had also hoped that the white moderate would reject the myth concerning time in relation to the struggle for freedom. I have just received a letter from a white brother in Texas. He writes: "All Christians know that the colored people will receive equal rights eventually, but it is possible that you are in too great a religious hurry. It has taken Christianity almost two thousand years to accomplish what it has. The teachings of Christ take time to come to earth." Such an attitude stems from a tragic misconception of time, from the strangely irrational notion that there is something in the very flow of time that will inevitably cure all ills. Actually, time itself is neutral; it can be used either destructively or constructively. More and more I feel that the people of ill will have used time much more effectively than have the people of good will. We will have to repent in this generation not merely for the hateful words and actions of the bad people but for the appalling silence of the good people. Human progress never rolls in on wheels of inevitability; it comes through the tireless efforts of men willing to be coworkers with God, and without this hard work, time itself becomes an ally of the forces of social stagnation. We must use time creatively, in the knowledge that the time is always ripe to do right. Now is the time to make real the promise of democracy and transform our pending national elegy into a creative psalm of brotherhood. Now is the time to lift our national policy from the quicksand of racial injustice to the solid rock of human dignity.

You speak of our activity in Birmingham as extreme. At first I was rather disappointed that fellow clergymen would see my nonviolent efforts as those of an extremist. I began thinking about the fact that I stand in the middle of two opposing forces in the Negro community. One is a force of complacency, made up in part of Negroes who, as a result of long years of oppression, are so drained of self-respect and a sense of "somebodiness" that they have adjusted to segregation; and in part of a few middle-class Negroes who, because of a degree of academic and economic security and because in some ways they profit by segregation, have become insensitive to the problems of the masses. The other force is one of bitterness and hatred, and it comes perilously close to advocating violence. It is expressed in the various black nationalist groups that are springing up across the nation, the largest and best known being Elijah Muhammad's Muslim movement. Nourished by the Negro's frustration over the continued existence of racial discrimination, this movement is made up of people who have lost faith in America, who have absolutely repudiated Christianity, and who have concluded that the white man is an incorrigible "devil."

I have tried to stand between these two forces, saying that we need emulate neither the "do nothingism" of the complacent nor the hatred and despair of the black nationalist. For there is the more excellent way of love and nonviolent protest. I am grateful to God that, through the influence of the Negro church, the way of nonviolence became an integral part of our struggle. If this philosophy had not emerged, by now many streets of the South would, I am convinced, be flowing with blood. And I am further convinced that if our white brothers dismiss as "rabble rousers" and "outside agitators" those of us who employ nonviolent direct action, and if they refuse to support our nonviolent efforts, millions of Negroes will, out of frustration and despair, seek solace and security in black nationalist ideologies—a development that would inevitably lead to a frightening racial nightmare.

Oppressed people cannot remain oppressed forever. The yearning for freedom eventually manifests itself, and that is what has happened to the American Negro. Something within has reminded him of his birthright of freedom, and something without has reminded him that it can be gained. Consciously or unconsciously, he has been caught up by the Zeitgeist, and with his black brothers of Africa and his brown and yellow brothers of Asia, South America and the Caribbean, the United States Negro is moving with a sense of great urgency toward the promised land of racial justice. If one recognizes this vital urge that has engulfed the Negro community, one should readily understand why public demonstrations are taking place. The Negro has many pent up resentments and latent frustrations, and he must release them. So let him march; let him make prayer pilgrimages to the city hall; let him go on freedom rides—and try to understand why he must do so. If his repressed emotions are not released in nonviolent ways, they will seek expression through violence; this is not a threat but a fact of history. So I have not said to my people: "Get rid of your discontent." Rather, I have tried to say that this normal and healthy discontent can be channeled into the creative outlet of nonviolent direct action. And now this approach is being termed extremist. But though I was initially disappointed at being categorized as an extremist, as I continued to think about the matter I gradually gained a measure of satisfaction from the label. Was not Jesus an extremist for love: "Love your enemies, bless them that curse you, do good to them that hate you, and pray for them which despitefully use you, and persecute you." Was not Amos an extremist for justice: "Let justice roll down like waters and righteousness like an ever flowing stream." Was not Paul an extremist for the Christian gospel: "I bear in my body the marks of the Lord Jesus." Was not Martin Luther an extremist: "Here I stand; I cannot do otherwise, so help me God." And John Bunyan: "I will stay in jail to the end of my days before I make a butchery of my conscience." And Abraham Lincoln: "This nation cannot survive half slave and half free." And Thomas Jefferson: "We hold these truths to be self evident, that all men are created equal . . ." So the question is not whether we will be extremists, but what kind of extremists we will be. Will we be extremists for hate or for love? Will we be extremists for the preservation of injustice or for the extension of justice? In that dramatic scene on Calvary's hill three men were crucified. We must never forget that all three were crucified for the same crime--the crime of extremism. Two were extremists for immorality, and thus fell below their environment. The other, Jesus Christ, was an extremist for love, truth and goodness, and thereby rose above his environment. Perhaps the South, the nation and the world are in dire need of creative extremists.

I had hoped that the white moderate would see this need. Perhaps I was too optimistic; perhaps I expected too much. I suppose I should have realized that few members of the oppressor race can understand the deep groans and passionate yearnings of the oppressed race, and still fewer have the vision to see that injustice must be rooted out by strong, persistent and determined action. I am thankful, however, that some of our white brothers in the South have grasped the meaning of this social revolution and committed themselves to it. They are still all too few in quantity, but they are big in quality. Some—such as Ralph McGill, Lillian Smith, Harry Golden, James McBride Dabbs, Ann Braden and Sarah Patton Boyle—have written about our struggle in eloquent and prophetic terms. Others have marched with us down nameless streets of the South. They have languished in filthy, roach infested jails, suffering the abuse and brutality of policemen who view them as "dirty nigger-lovers." Unlike so many of their moderate brothers and sisters, they have recognized the urgency of the moment and sensed the need for powerful "action" antidotes to combat the disease of segregation. Let me take note of my other major disappointment. I have been so greatly disappointed with the white church and its leadership. Of course, there are some notable exceptions. I am not unmindful of the fact that each of you has taken some significant stands on this issue. I commend you, Reverend Stallings, for your Christian stand on this past Sunday, in welcoming Negroes to your worship service on a nonsegregated basis. I commend the Catholic leaders of this state for integrating Spring Hill College several years ago.

But despite these notable exceptions, I must honestly reiterate that I have been disappointed with the church. I do not say this as one of those negative critics who can always find something wrong with the church. I say this as a minister of the gospel, who loves the church; who was nurtured in its bosom; who has been sustained by its spiritual blessings and who will remain true to it as long as the cord of life shall lengthen.

When I was suddenly catapulted into the leadership of the bus protest in Montgomery, Alabama, a few years ago, I felt we would be supported by the white church. I felt that the white ministers, priests and rabbis of the South would be among our strongest allies. Instead, some have been outright opponents, refusing to understand the freedom movement and misrepresenting its leaders; all too many others have been more cautious than courageous and have remained silent behind the anesthetizing security of stained glass windows.

In spite of my shattered dreams, I came to Birmingham with the hope that the white religious leadership of this community would see the justice of our cause and, with deep moral concern, would serve as the channel through which our just grievances could reach the power structure. I had hoped that each of you would understand. But again I have been disappointed.

I have heard numerous southern religious leaders admonish their worshipers to comply with a desegregation decision because it is the law, but I have longed to hear white ministers declare: "Follow this decree because integration is morally right and because the Negro is your brother." In the midst of blatant injustices inflicted upon the Negro, I have watched white churchmen stand on the sideline and mouth pious irrelevancies and sanctimonious trivialities. In the midst of a mighty struggle to rid our nation of racial and economic injustice, I have heard many ministers say: "Those are social issues, with which the gospel has no real concern." And I have watched many churches commit themselves to a completely other worldly religion which makes a strange, un-Biblical distinction between body and soul, between the sacred and the secular.

I have traveled the length and breadth of Alabama, Mississippi and all the other southern states. On sweltering summer days and crisp autumn mornings I have looked at the South's beautiful churches with their lofty spires pointing heavenward. I have beheld the impressive outlines of her massive religious education buildings. Over and over I have found myself asking: "What kind of people worship here? Who is their God? Where were their voices when the lips of Governor Barnett dripped with words of interposition and nullification? Where were they when Governor Wallace gave a clarion call for defiance and hatred? Where were their voices of support when bruised and weary Negro men and women decided to rise from the dark dungeons of complacency to the bright hills of creative protest?"

Yes, these questions are still in my mind. In deep disappointment I have wept over the laxity of the church. But be assured that my tears have been tears of love. There can be no deep disappointment where there is not deep love. Yes, I love the church. How could I do otherwise? I am in the rather unique position of being the son, the grandson and the great grandson of preachers. Yes, I see the church as the body of Christ. But, oh! How we have blemished and scarred that body through social neglect and through fear of being nonconformists.

There was a time when the church was very powerful—in the time when the early Christians rejoiced at being deemed worthy to suffer for what they believed. In those days the church was not merely a thermometer that recorded the ideas and principles of popular opinion; it was a thermostat that transformed the mores of society. Whenever the early Christians entered a town, the people in power became disturbed and immediately sought to convict the Christians for being "disturbers of the peace" and "outside agitators.'" But the Christians pressed on, in the conviction that they were "a colony of heaven," called to obey God rather than man. Small in number, they were big in commitment. They were too God-intoxicated to be "astronomically intimidated." By their effort and example they brought an end to such ancient evils as infanticide and gladiatorial contests. Things are different now. So often the contemporary church is a weak, ineffectual voice with an uncertain sound. So often it is an archdefender of the status quo. Far from being disturbed by the presence of the church, the power structure of the average community is consoled by the church's silent—and often even vocal—sanction of things as they are.

But the judgment of God is upon the church as never before. If today's church does not recapture the sacrificial spirit of the early church, it will lose its authenticity, forfeit the loyalty of millions, and be dismissed as an irrelevant social club with no meaning for the twentieth century. Every day I meet young people whose disappointment with the church has turned into outright disgust.

Perhaps I have once again been too optimistic. Is organized religion too inextricably bound to the status quo to save our nation and the world? Perhaps I must turn my faith to the inner spiritual church, the church within the church, as the true ekklesia and the hope of the world. But again I am thankful to God that some noble souls from the ranks of organized religion have broken loose from the paralyzing chains of conformity and joined us as active partners in the struggle for freedom. They have left their secure congregations and walked the streets of Albany, Georgia, with us. They have gone down the highways of the South on tortuous rides for freedom. Yes, they have gone to jail with us. Some have been dismissed from their churches, have lost the support of their bishops and fellow ministers. But they have acted in the faith that right defeated is stronger than evil triumphant. Their witness has been the spiritual salt that has preserved the true meaning of the gospel in these troubled times. They have carved a tunnel of hope through the dark mountain of disappointment. I hope the church as a whole will meet the challenge of this decisive hour. But even if the church does not come to the aid of justice, I have no despair about the future. I have no fear about the outcome of our struggle in Birmingham, even if our motives are at present misunderstood. We will reach the goal of freedom in Birmingham and all over the nation, because the goal of America is freedom. Abused and scorned though we may be, our destiny is tied up with America's destiny. Before the pilgrims landed at Plymouth, we were here. Before the pen of Jefferson etched the majestic words of the Declaration of Independence across the pages of history, we were here. For more than two centuries our forebears labored in this country without wages; they made cotton king; they built the homes of their masters while suffering gross injustice and shameful humiliation—and yet out of a bottomless vitality they continued to thrive and develop. If the inexpressible cruelties of slavery could not stop us, the opposition we now face will surely fail. We will win our freedom because the sacred heritage of our nation and the eternal will of God are embodied in our echoing demands. Before closing I feel impelled to mention one other point in your statement that has troubled me profoundly. You warmly commended the Birmingham police force for keeping "order" and "preventing violence." I doubt that you would have so warmly commended the police force if you had seen its dogs sinking their teeth into unarmed, nonviolent Negroes. I doubt that you would so quickly commend the policemen if you were to observe their ugly and inhumane treatment of Negroes here in the city jail; if you were to watch them push and curse old Negro women and young Negro girls; if you were to see them slap and kick old Negro men and young boys; if you were to observe them, as they did on two occasions, refuse to give us food because we wanted to sing our grace together. I cannot join you in your praise of the Birmingham police department.

It is true that the police have exercised a degree of discipline in handling the demonstrators. In this sense they have conducted themselves rather "nonviolently" in public. But for what purpose? To preserve the evil system of segregation. Over the past few years I have consistently preached that nonviolence demands that the means we use must be as pure as the ends we seek. I have tried to make clear that it is wrong to use immoral means to attain moral ends. But now I must affirm that it is just as wrong, or perhaps even more so, to use moral means to preserve immoral ends. Perhaps Mr. Connor and his policemen have been rather nonviolent in public, as was Chief Pritchett in Albany, Georgia, but they have used the moral means of nonviolence to maintain the immoral end of racial injustice. As T. S. Eliot has said: "The last temptation is the greatest treason: To do the right deed for the wrong reason."

I wish you had commended the Negro sit inners and demonstrators of Birmingham for their sublime courage, their willingness to suffer and their amazing discipline in the midst of great provocation. One day the South will recognize its real heroes. They will be the James Merediths, with the noble sense of purpose that enables them to face jeering and hostile mobs, and with the agonizing loneliness that characterizes the life of the pioneer. They will be old, oppressed, battered Negro women, symbolized in a seventy two year old woman in Montgomery, Alabama, who rose up with a sense of dignity and with her people decided not to ride segregated buses, and who responded with ungrammatical profundity to one who inquired about her weariness: "My feets is tired, but my soul is at rest." They will be the young high school and college students, the young ministers of the gospel and a host of their elders, courageously and nonviolently sitting in at lunch counters and willingly going to jail for conscience' sake. One day the South will know that when these disinherited children of God sat down at lunch counters, they were in reality standing up for what is best in the American dream and for the most sacred values in our Judaeo Christian heritage, thereby bringing our nation back to those great wells of democracy which were dug deep by the founding fathers in their formulation of the Constitution and the Declaration of Independence.

Never before have I written so long a letter. I'm afraid it is much too long to take your precious time. I can assure you that it would have been much shorter if I had been writing from a comfortable desk, but what else can one do when he is alone in a narrow jail cell, other than write long letters, think long thoughts and pray long prayers?

If I have said anything in this letter that overstates the truth and indicates an unreasonable impatience, I beg you to forgive me. If I have said anything that understates the truth and indicates my having a patience that allows me to settle for anything less than brotherhood, I beg God to forgive me.

I hope this letter finds you strong in the faith. I also hope that circumstances will soon make it possible for me to meet each of you, not as an integrationist or a civil-rights leader but as a fellow clergyman and a Christian brother. Let us all hope that the dark clouds of racial prejudice will soon pass away and the deep fog of misunderstanding will be lifted from our fear drenched communities, and in some not too distant tomorrow the radiant stars of love and brotherhood will shine over our great nation with all their scintillating beauty.

> Yours for the cause of Peace and Brotherhood,
> Martin Luther King Jr.

Selection 2: James H. Cone, *A Black Theology of Liberation*

James Cone (b. 1938) is the Charles A. Briggs Distinguished Professor of Systematic Theology at Union Theological Seminary in New York. Cone was the first theologian to bring the philosophy of Black power to theological expression in his 1969 book, Black Theology and Black Power, *followed in 1970 by* A Black Theology of Liberation, *from which the following excerpt is taken. In challenging and for some disturbing rhetoric, Cone identifies "blackness" with God in God's concern for the victims of racist oppression. The call to be God's person in the quest for justice is a call to become black.*

The reader is entitled to know what to expect in this book. It is my contention that Christianity is essentially a religion of liberation. The function of theology is that of analyzing the meaning of that liberation for the oppressed community so they can know that their struggle for political, social, and economic justice is consistent with the gospel of Jesus Christ. Any message that is not related to the liberation of the poor in the society is not Christ's message. Any theology that is indifferent to the theme of liberation is not Christian theology.

In a society where men are oppressed because they are black, Christian theology must become Black Theology, a theology that is unreservedly identified with the goals of the oppressed community and seeking to interpret the divine character of their struggle for liberation. "Black Theology" is a phrase that is particularly appropriate for contemporary America because of its symbolic power to convey both what whites mean by oppression and what blacks mean by liberation. However, I am convinced that the patterns of meaning centered in the idea of Black Theology are by no means restricted to the American scene, since blackness symbolizes oppression and liberation in any society.

It will be evident, therefore, that this book is written primarily for the black community and not for white people. Whites may read it and to some degree render an intellectual analysis of it, but an authentic understanding is dependent on the blackness of their existence in the world. There will be no peace in America until white people begin to hate their whiteness, asking from the depths of their being: "How can we become black?" It is hoped that enough people will begin to ask that question that this country will no longer be divided on the basis of color. But until then, it is the task of the Christian theologian to do theology in the light of the concreteness of human oppression as expressed in color, and to interpret for the oppressed the meaning of God's liberation in their community.

*   *   *

Unfortunately, American white theology has not been involved in the struggle for black liberation. It has been basically a theology of the white oppressor, giving religious sanction to the genocide of Indians and the enslavement of black people. From the very beginning to the present day, American white theological thought has been "patriotic," either by defining the theological task independently of black suffering (the liberal northern approach) or by defining Christianity as compatible with white racism (the conservative southern approach). In both cases theology becomes a servant of the state, and that can only mean death to black people. It is little wonder that an increasing number of black religionists are finding it difficult to be black and also to be identified with traditional theological thought forms.

The appearance of Black Theology on the American scene then is due exclusively to the failure of white religionists to relate the gospel of Jesus to the pain of being black in a white racist society/It arises from the need of black people to liberate themselves from white oppressors. Black Theology is a theology of liberation because it is a theology which arises from an identification with the oppressed blacks of America, seeking to interpret the gospel of Christ in the light of the black condition. It believes that the liberation of black people is God's liberation.

The task of Black Theology then is to analyze the "nature of the gospel of Jesus Christ in the light of oppressed black people so they will see the gospel as inseparable from their humiliated condition, bestowing on them the necessary power to break the chains of oppression. This means that it is a theology of and for the black community, seeking to interpret the religious dimensions of the forces of liberation in that community.

There are two reasons why Black Theology is Christian theology and possibly the only expression of Christian theology in America. First, there can be no theology of the gospel which does not arise from an oppressed community. This is so because God in Christ has revealed himself as a God whose righteousness is inseparable from the weak and helpless.

The goal of Black Theology is to interpret God's activity as he is related to the oppressed black community.

Second, Black Theology is Christian theology because it centers on Jesus Christ. There can be no Christian theology which does not have Jesus Christ as its point of departure. Though Black Theology affirms the black condition as the primary datum of reality which must be reckoned with, this does not mean that it denies the absolute revelation of God in Jesus Christ. Rather it affirms it. Unlike white theology which tends it to make the Christ-event an abstract, intellectual idea, Black Theology believes that the black community itself is precisely where Christ is at work. The Christ-event in twentieth-century America is a black-event, an event of liberation taking place in the black community in which black people recognize that it is incumbent upon them to throw off the chains of white oppression by whatever means they regard as suitable. This is what God's revelation means to black and white America, and why Black Theology may be the only possible theology in our time.

It is to be expected that some persons will ask, "Why Black Theology? Is it not true that God is color blind? Is it not true that there are others who suffer as much as, if not more in some cases than, black people?" These questions reveal a basic lack of understanding regarding Black Theology, and also a superficial view of the world at large. There are at least three points to be made here.

First, in a revolutionary situation there can never be just theology. It is always theology identified with a particular community. It is either identified with those who inflict oppression or with those who are its victims. A theology of the latter is authentic Christian theology, and a theology of the former is a theology of the Antichrist. Insofar as Black Theology is a theology arising from an identification with the oppressed black community and seeks to interpret the gospel of Jesus Christ in the light of the liberation of that community, it is Christian theology. American white theology is a theology of the Antichrist, insofar as it arises from an identification with the white community, thereby placing God's approval on white oppression of black existence.

Second, in a racist society, God is never color blind. To say God is color blind is analogous to saying that God is blind to justice and injustice, to right and wrong, to good and evil. Certainly this is not the picture of God revealed in the Old and New Testaments. Yahweh takes sides. On the one hand, he sides with Israel against the Canaanites as she makes her settlement in Palestine. On the other hand, he sides with the poor within the community of Israel against the rich and other political oppressors. In the New Testament, Jesus is not for all, but for the oppressed, the poor and unwanted of society, and against oppressors. The God of the biblical tradition is not uninvolved or neutral regarding human affairs; rather he is quite involved. He is active in human history, taking sides with the oppressed of the land. If God is not involved in human history, then all theology is useless, and Christianity itself is a mockery, a hollow, meaningless diversion.

The meaning of this message for our contemporary situation is clear. God, because he is a God of the oppressed, takes sides with black people. He is not color blind in the black-white struggle, but has made an unqualified identification with black people. This means that the movement for black liberation is the work of God himself, effecting his will among men.

Thirdly, there are, to be sure, many people who suffer, and they are not all black. Many white liberals receive a certain joy in reminding black militants that two thirds of the poor in America are white people. Of course one could observe that this means that the proportion of poor blacks is five times as great as that of poor whites, when we consider the total population of each group. But it is not our intention to debate white liberals on this issue, since it is not the purpose of Black Theology to minimize the suffering of others, including white people. Black Theology merely tries to discern the activity of the Holy One as he effects his purpose in the liberation of man from the forces of oppression. We must make decisions about where God is at work so we can join him in his fight against evil.

*   *   *

Black Theology's emphasis also rejects any identification with the recent "death of God" theology. The death-of-God question is a white issue which arises out of the white experience. Questions like "How do we find meaning and purpose in a world in which God is absent?" are questions of an affluent society. Whites may wonder how to find purpose in their lives, but our purpose is forced upon us. We do not want to know how we can get along without God, but how we can survive in a world permeated with white racism.

God Is Black

Because black people have come to know themselves as black, and because that blackness is the cause of their own love of themselves and hatred of whiteness, God himself must be known only as he reveals himself in his blackness. The blackness of God, and everything implied by it in a racist society, is the heart of Black Theology's doctrine of God. There is no place in Black Theology for a colorless God in a society when people suffer precisely because of their color. The black theologian must reject any conception of God which stifles black self-determination by picturing God as a God of all peoples. Either God is identified with the oppressed to the point that their experience becomes his or he is a God of racism. Authentic identification, as Camus pointed out, is not "a question of psychological identification—a mere subterfuge by which the individual imagines that it is he himself who is being offended." It is "identification of one's destiny with that of others and a choice of sides." Because God has made the goal of black people his own goal, Black Theology believes that it is not only appropriate but necessary to begin the doctrine of God with an insistence on his blackness.

The blackness of God means that God has made the oppressed condition his own condition. This is the essence of the biblical revelation. By electing Israelite slaves as his people and by becoming the Oppressed One in Jesus Christ, God discloses to men that he is known where men experience humiliation and suffering. It is not that he feels sorry and takes pity on them (the condescending attitude of those racists who need their guilt assuaged for getting fat on the starvation of others); quite the contrary, his election of Israel and incarnation in Christ reveal that the liberation of the oppressed is a part of the innermost nature of God himself. This means that liberation is not an afterthought, but the essence of divine activity.

The blackness of God then means that the essence of the nature of God is to be found in the concept of liberation. Taking seriously the Trinitarian view of the Godhead, Black Theology says that as Father, God identified with oppressed Israel participating in the bringing into being of this people; as Son, he became the Oppressed One in order that all may be free from oppression; as Holy Spirit, he continues his work of liberation. The Holy Spirit is the Spirit of the Father and the Son at work in the forces of human liberation in our society today. In America, the Holy Spirit is black people making decisions about their togetherness, which means making preparation for an encounter with white people.

It is Black Theology's emphasis on the blackness of God that distinguishes it sharply from contemporary white views of God. White religionists are not capable of perceiving the blackness of God because their satanic whiteness is a denial of the very essence of divinity. That is why whites are finding and will continue to find the black experience a disturbing reality. White theologians would prefer to do theology without reference to color, but this only reveals how deeply racism is embedded in the thought forms of this culture. To be sure, they would probably concede that the concept of liberation is essential to the biblical view of God. But it is still impossible for them to translate the biblical emphasis on liberation to the black-white struggle today. Invariably they quibble on this issue, moving from side to side, always pointing out the dangers of extremism on both sides. (In the black community, we call this shuffling.) They really cannot make a decision, because it has been made already for them. The way in which scholars would analyze God and black people was decided when black slaves were brought to this land, while churchmen sang "Jesus, Lover of My Soul." Their attitude today is no different from that of the Bishop of London who assured the slaveholders that Christianity, and the embracing of the Gospel, does not make the least Alteration in Civil property, or in any Duties which belong to Civil Relations; but in all these Respects, it continues Persons just in the same State as it found them. The Freedom which Christianity gives, is a Freedom from the Bondage of Sin and Satan, and from the dominion of Man's Lust and Passions and inordinate Desires; but as to their outward Condition, whatever that was before, whether bond or free, their being baptized and becoming Christians, makes no matter of change in it. Of course white theologians today have a "better" way of putting it, but what difference does that make? It means the same thing to black people. "Sure," as the so-called radicals would say, "God is concerned about black people." And then they go on to talk about God and secularization or some other white problem unrelated to emancipation of black people. This style is a contemporary white way of saying that "Christianity . . . does not make the least alteration in civil property."

In contrast to this racist view of God, Black Theology proclaims his blackness. People who want to know who God is and what he is doing must know who black people are and what they are doing. This does not mean lending a helping hand to the poor and unfortunate blacks of the society. It does not mean joining the war on poverty! Such acts are sin offerings that represent a white way of assuring themselves that they are basically a "good" people. Knowing God means being on the side of the oppressed, becoming one with them and participating in the goal of liberation. We must become black with God.

It is to be expected that white people will have some difficulty with the idea of "becoming black with God." The experience is not only alien to their existence as they know it to be, it appears to be an impossibility. "How can white people become black?" they ask. This question always amuses me because they do not really want to lose their precious white identity, as if it is worth saving. They know, as everyone in this country knows, a black man is anyone who says he is black, despite his skin color. In the literal sense a black man is anyone who has "even one drop of black blood in his veins."

But "becoming black with God" means more than just saying "I am black," if it involves that at all. The question "How can white people become black?" is analogous to the Philippian jailer's question to Paul and Silas, "What must I do to be saved?" The implication is that if we work hard enough at it, we can reach the goal. But the misunderstanding here is the failure

to see that blackness or salvation (the two are synonymous) is the work of God and not man. It is not something we accomplish; it is a gift. That is why they said, "Believe in the Lord Jesus and you will be saved." To believe is to receive the gift and utterly to reorient one's existence on the basis of the gift. The gift is so unlike what humans expect that when it is offered and accepted, we become completely new creatures. This is what the Wholly Otherness of God means. God comes to us in his blackness which is wholly unlike whiteness, and to receive his revelation is to become black with him by joining him in his work of liberation.

Even some black people will find this view of God hard to handle. Having been enslaved by the God of white racism so long, they will have difficulty believing that God is identified with their struggle for freedom. Becoming one of his disciples means rejecting whiteness and accepting themselves as they are in all their physical blackness. This is what the Christian view of God means for black people.

Selection 3: Gustavo Gutiérrez, *A Theology of Liberation: History, Politics, and Salvation*

Gustavo Gutiérrez (b. 1928), a Peruvian theologian and Dominican priest, is the John Cardinal O'Hara Professor of Theology at the University of Note Dame. He is one of the founders of Latin American liberation theology, which developed in response to the needs of the poor as embodied in the liberationist principle of the "preferential option for the poor." This concern is evident in this excerpt. Also featured here is his description of the key methodological conviction of Latin American liberation theology: theology as critical reflection on practice (praxis). A companion to this precept is the notion of "orthopraxy" as an antidote to the church's overemphasis on orthodoxy at the expense of concern for justice in history.

Theology as Critical Reflection on Praxis

The function of theology as critical reflection on praxis has gradually become more clearly defined in recent years, but it has its roots in the first centuries of the Church's life. The Augustinian theology of history which we find in The City of God, for example, is based on a true analysis of the signs of the times and the demands with which they challenge the Christian community.

Historical Praxis

For various reasons the existential and active aspects of the Christian life have recently been stressed in a different way than in the immediate past.

In the first place, charity has been fruitfully rediscovered as the center of the Christian life. This has led to a more Biblical view of the faith as an act of trust, a going out of one's self, a commitment to God and neighbor, a relationship with others.' It is in this sense that St. Paul tells us that faith works through charity: love is the nourishment and the fullness of faith, the gift of one's self to the Other, and invariably to others. This is the foundation of the praxis of Christians, of their active presence in history. According to the Bible, faith is the total human response to God, who saves through love.' In this light, the understanding of the faith appears as the understanding not of the simple affirmation—almost memorization—of truths, but of a commitment, an overall attitude, a particular posture toward life.

In a parallel development, Christian spirituality has seen a significant evolution. In the early centuries of the Church there emerged the primacy, almost exclusiveness, of a certain kind of contemplative life, hermitical, monastic, characterized by withdrawal from the world, and presented as the model way to sanctity. About the twelfth century the possibility of sharing contemplation by means of preaching and other forms of apostolic activity began to be considered. This point of view was exemplified in the mixed life (contemplative and active) of the mendicant orders and was expressed in the formula: *contemplata aliis tradere* ("to transmit to others the fruits of contemplation"). Viewed historically this stage can be considered as a transition to Ignatian spirituality, which sought a difficult but fruitful synthesis between contemplation and action: in *actione contemplativus* ("contemplative in action"). This process, strengthened in recent years by the search for a spirituality of the laity, culminates today in the studies on the religious value of the profane and in the spirituality of the activity of the Christian in the world."

Moreover, today there is a greater sensitivity to the anthropological aspects of revelation. The Word about God is at the same time a promise to the world. In revealing God to us, the Gospel message reveals us to ourselves in our situation before the Lord and with other humans. The God of Christian revelation is a God incarnate, hence the famous comment of Karl Barth regarding Christian anthropocentrism, "Man is the measure of all things, since God became man." All this has caused the revaluation of human presence and activity in the world, especially in relation to other human beings. On this subject Congar writes: "Seen as a whole, the direction of theological thinking has been characterized by a transference away from attention to the being per se of supernatural realities, and toward attention to their relationship with man, with the world, and with the problems and the affirmations of all those who for us represent the Others." There is no horizontalism in this approach. It is simply a question of the rediscovery of the indissoluble unity of humankind and God.

On the other hand, the very life of the Church appears ever more clearly as a *locus theologicus*. Regarding the participation of Christians in the important social movements of their time, Chenu wrote insightfully more than thirty years ago: "They are active *loci theologici* for the doctrines of grace, the Incarnation, and the redemption, as expressly promulgated and described in detail by the papal encyclicals. They are poor theologians who, wrapped up in their manuscripts and scholastic disputations, are not open to these amazing events, not only in the pious fervor of their hearts but formally in their science; there is a theological datum and an extremely fruitful one, in the presence of the Spirit." The so-called new theology attempted to adopt this posture some decades ago. The fact that the life of the Church is a source for all theological analysis has been recalled to mind often since then. The Word of God gathers and is incarnated in the community of faith, which gives itself to the service of all.

Vatican Council II has strongly reaffirmed the idea of a Church of service and not of power. This is a Church which is not centered upon itself and which does not "find itself" except when it "loses itself," when it lives "the joys and the hopes, the griefs and the anxieties of persons of this age" (*Gaudium et spes*, no. 1). All of these trends provide a new focus for seeing the presence and activity of the Church in the world as a starting point for theological reflection.

What since John XXIII and Vatican Council II began to be called a theology of the signs of the times can be characterized along the same lines, although this takes a step beyond narrow ecclesial limits. It must not be forgotten that the signs of the times are not only a call to intellectual analysis. They are above all a call to pastoral activity, to commitment, and to service. Studying the signs of the times includes both dimensions. Therefore, *Gaudium et spes*, no. 44, points out that discerning the signs of the times is the responsibility of every Christian, especially pastors and theologians, to hear, distinguish, and interpret the many voices of our age, and to judge them in the light of the divine Word. In this way, revealed truths can always be more deeply penetrated, better understood, and set forth to greater advantage. Attributing this role to every member of the People of God and singling out the pastors—charged with guiding the activity of the Church—highlights the call to commitment which the signs of the times imply. Necessarily connected with this consideration, the function of theologians will be to afford greater clarity regarding this commitment by means of intellectual analysis. (It is interesting to note that the inclusion of theologians in the above-mentioned text met opposition during the conciliar debates.)

Another factor, this time of a philosophical nature, reinforces the importance of human action as the point of departure for all reflection. The philosophical issues of our times are characterized by new relationships of humankind with nature, born of advances in science and technology. These new bonds affect the awareness that persons have of themselves and of their active relationships with others.

Maurice Blondel, moving away from an empty and fruitless spirituality and attempting to make philosophical speculation more concrete and alive, presented it as a critical reflection on action. This reflection attempts to understand the internal logic of an action through which persons seek fulfillment by constantly transcending themselves. Blondel thus contributed to the elaboration of a new apologetics and became one of the most important thinkers of contemporary theology, including the most recent trends.

To these factors can be added the influence of Marxist thought, focusing on praxis and geared to the transformation of the world. The Marxist influence began to be felt in the middle of the nineteenth century, but in recent times its cultural impact has become greater. Many agree with Sartre that "Marxism, as the formal framework of all contemporary philosophical thought, cannot be superseded." Be that as it may, contemporary theology does in fact find itself in direct and fruitful confrontation with Marxism, and it is to a large extent due to Marxism's influence that theological thought, searching for its own sources, has begun to reflect on the meaning of the transformation of this world and human action in history. Further, this confrontation helps theology to perceive what its efforts at understanding the faith receive from the historical praxis of humankind in history as well as what its own reflection might mean for the transformation of the world.

Finally, the rediscovery of the eschatological dimension in theology has also led us to consider the central role of historical praxis. Indeed, if human history is above all else an opening to the future, then it is a task, a political occupation, through which we orient and open ourselves to the gift which gives history its transcendent meaning: the full and definitive encounter with the Lord and with other humans. "To do the truth," as the Gospel says, thus acquires a precise and concrete meaning in terms of the importance of action in Christian life. Faith in a God who loves us and calls us to the gift of full communion with God and fellowship with others not only is not foreign to the transformation of the world; it leads necessarily to the building up of that fellowship and communion in history. Moreover, only by doing this truth will our faith be "verified," in the etymological sense of the word. From this notion has recently been derived the term orthopraxis, which still disturbs the sensitivities of some. The intention, however, is not to deny the meaning of orthodoxy, understood as a proclamation of and reflection on statements considered to be true. Rather, the goal is to balance and even to reject the primacy and almost exclusiveness which doctrine has enjoyed in Christian life and above all to modify the emphasis, often obsessive, upon the attainment of an orthodoxy which is often nothing more than fidelity to an obsolete tradition or a debatable interpretation. In a more positive vein, the intention is to recognize the work and importance of concrete behavior, of deeds, of action, of praxis in the Christian life. "And this, it seems to me, has been the greatest transformation which has taken place in the Christian conception of existence," said Edward Schillebeeckx in an interview. "It is evident that thought is also necessary for action. But the Church has for centuries devoted its attention to formulating truths and meanwhile did almost nothing to better the world. In other words, the Church focused on orthodoxy and left orthopraxis in the hands of nonmembers and nonbelievers."

*   *   *

Theology as a critical reflection on Christian praxis in the light of the Word does not replace the other functions of theology, such as wisdom and rational knowledge; rather it presupposes and needs them. But this is not all. We are not concerned here with a mere juxtaposition. The critical function of theology necessarily leads to redefinition of these other two tasks. Henceforth, wisdom and rational knowledge will more explicitly have ecclesial praxis as their point of departure and their context. It is in reference to this praxis that an understanding of spiritual growth based on Scripture should be developed, and it is through this same praxis that faith encounters the problems posed by human reason. Given the theme of the present work, we will be especially aware of this critical function of theology with the ramifications suggested above. This approach will lead us to pay special attention to the life of the Church and to commitments which Christians, impelled by the Spirit and in communion with others, undertake in history. We will give special consideration to participation in the process of liberation, an outstanding phenomenon of our times, which takes on special meaning in the so-called Third World countries.

This kind of theology, arising from concern with a particular set of issues, will perhaps give us the solid and permanent albeit modest foundation for the theology in a Latin American perspective which is both desired and needed. This Latin American focus would not be due to a frivolous desire for originality, but rather to a fundamental sense of historical efficacy and also—why hide it?—to the desire to contribute to the life and reflection of the universal Christian community. But in order to make our contribution, this desire for universality—as well as input from the Christian community as a whole—must be present from the beginning. To concretize this desire would be to overcome particularistic tendencies—provincial and chauvinistic—and produce something unique, both particular and universal, and therefore fruitful.

"The only future that theology has, one might say, is to become the theology of the future," Harvey Cox has said. But this theology of the future must necessarily be a critical appraisal of historical praxis, of the historical task in the sense we have attempted to sketch. Moltmann says that theological concepts "do not limp after reality. . . . They illuminate reality by displaying its future." In our approach, to reflect critically on the praxis of liberation is not to "limp after" reality. The present in the praxis of liberation, in its deepest dimension, is pregnant with the future; hope must be an inherent part of our present commitment in history. Theology does not initiate this future which exists in the present. It does not create the vital attitude of hope out of nothing. Its role is more modest. It interprets and explains these as the true underpinnings of history. To reflect upon a forward-directed action is not to dwell on the past. It does not mean being the caboose of the present. Rather it is to penetrate the present reality, the movement of history, that which is driving history toward the future. To reflect on the basis of the historical praxis of liberation is to reflect in the light of the future which is believed in and hoped for. It is to reflect with a view to action which transforms the present. But it does not mean doing this from an armchair; rather it means sinking roots where the pulse of history is beating at this moment and illuminating history with the Word of the Lord of history, who irreversibly committed himself to the present moment of humankind to carry it to its fulfillment.

It is for all these reasons that the theology of liberation offers us not so much a new theme for reflection as a new way to do theology. Theology as critical reflection on historical praxis is a liberating theology, a theology of the liberating transformation of the history of humankind and also therefore that part of humankind—gathered into ecclesia—which openly confesses Christ. This is a theology which does not stop with reflecting on the world, but rather tries to be part of the process through which the world is transformed. It is a theology which is open—in the protest against trampled human dignity, in the struggle against the plunder of the vast majority of humankind, in liberating love, and in the building of a new, just, and comradely society—to the gift of the Kingdom of God.

*   *   *

Perspectives

"The lottery vendor who hawks tickets 'for the big one,' "wrote Vallejo in another poem, "somehow deep down represents God." But every person is a lottery vendor who offers us "the big one": our encounter with that God who is deep down in the heart of each person" Nevertheless, the neighbor is not an occasion, an instrument, for becoming closer to God: We are dealing with a real love of persons for their own sake and not "for the love of God," as the well-intended but ambiguous and ill-used cliché would have it—ambiguous and ill-used because many seem to interpret it in a sense which forgets that the love for God is expressed in a true love for persons themselves. This is the only way to have a true encounter with God. That my action towards another is at the same time an action towards God does not detract from its truth and concreteness, but rather gives it even greater meaning and import.

It is also necessary to avoid the pitfalls of an individualistic charity. As it has been insisted in recent years, the neighbor is not only a person viewed individually. The term refers also to a person considered in the fabric of social relationships, to a person situated in economic, social, cultural, and racial coordinates. It likewise refers to the exploited social class, the dominated people, the marginated. The masses are also our neighbor, as Chenu asserts. This point of view leads us far beyond the individualistic language of the I-Thou relationship. Charity is today a "political charity," according to the phrase of Pius XII. Indeed, to offer food or drink in our day is a political action; it means the transformation of a society structured to benefit a few who appropriate to themselves the value of the work of others. This transformation ought to be directed toward a radical change in the foundation of society, that is, the private ownership of the means of production.

Our encounter with the Lord occurs in our encounter with others, especially in the encounter with those whose human features have been disfigured by oppression, despoliation, and alienation and who have "no beauty, no majesty" but are the things "from which men turn away their eyes" (Isa. 53:2-3). These are the marginal groups, who have fashioned a true culture for themselves and whose values one must understand if one wishes to reach them." The salvation of humanity passes through them; they are the bearers of the meaning of history and "inherit the Kingdom" (James 2:5). Our attitude towards them, or rather our commitment to them, will indicate whether or not we are directing our existence in conformity with the will of the Father. This is what Christ reveals to us by identifying himself with the poor in the text of Matthew. "A theology of the neighbor, which has yet to be worked out, would have to be structured on this basis."

A Spirituality of Liberation

To place oneself in the perspective of the Kingdom means to participate in the struggle for the liberation of those oppressed by others. This is what many Christians who have committed themselves to the Latin American revolutionary process have begun to experience. If this option seems to separate them from the Christian community, it is because many Christians, intent on domesticating the Good News, see them as wayward and perhaps even dangerous. If they are not always able to express in appropriate terms the profound reasons for their commitment, it is because the theology in which they were formed—and which they share with other Christians—has not produced the categories necessary to express this option, which seeks to respond creatively to the new demands of the Gospel and of the oppressed and exploited peoples of this continent. But in their commitments, and even in their attempts to explain them, there is a greater understanding of the faith, greater faith, greater fidelity to the Lord than in the "orthodox" doctrine (some prefer to call it by this name) of reputable Christian circles. This doctrine is supported by authority and much publicized because of access to social communications media, but it is so static and devitalized that it is not even strong enough to abandon the Gospel. It is the Gospel which is disowning it.

But theological categories are not enough. We need a vital attitude, all-embracing and synthesizing, informing the totality as well as every detail of our lives; we need a "spirituality." Spirituality, in the strict and profound sense of the word is the dominion of the Spirit. If "the truth will set you free" (John 8:32), the Spirit "will guide you into all the truth" (John 16:13) and will lead us to complete freedom, the freedom from everything that hinders us from fulfilling ourselves as human beings and offspring of God and the freedom to love and to enter into communion with God and with others. It will lead us along the path of liberation because "where the Spirit of the Lord is, there is liberty" (2 Cor. 3:17).

A spirituality is a concrete manner, inspired by the Spirit, of living the Gospel; it is a definite way of living "before the Lord," in solidarity with all human beings, "with the Lord," and before human beings. It arises from an intense spiritual experience, which is later explicated and witnessed to. Some Christians are beginning to live this experience as a result of their commitment to the process of liberation. The experiences of previous generations are there to support it, but above all, to remind them that they must discover their own way. Not only is there a contemporary history and a contemporary Gospel; there is also a contemporary spiritual experience which cannot be overlooked. A spirituality means a reordering of the great axes of the Christian life in terms of this contemporary experience. What is new is the synthesis that this reordering brings about, in stimulating a deepened understanding of various ideas, in bringing to the surface unknown or forgotten aspects of the Christian life, and above all, in the way in which these things are converted into life, prayer, commitment, and action.

The truth is that a Christianity lived in commitment to the process of liberation presents its own problems which cannot be ignored and meets obstacles which must be overcome. For many, the encounter with the Lord under these conditions can disappear by giving way to what he himself brings forth and nourishes: love for humankind. This love, however, does not know the fullness of its potential. This is a real difficulty, but the solution must come from the heart of the problem itself. Otherwise, it would be just one more patchwork remedy, a new impasse. This is the challenge confronting a spirituality of liberation. Where oppression and human liberation seem to make God irrelevant—a God filtered by our longtime indifference to these problems—there must blossom faith and hope in him who came to root out injustice and to offer, in an unforeseen way, total liberation. This is a spirituality which dares to sink roots in the soil of oppression-liberation.

A spirituality of liberation will center on a conversion to the neighbor, the oppressed person, the exploited social class, the despised ethnic group, the dominated country. Our conversion to the Lord implies this conversion to the neighbor. Evangelical conversion is indeed the touchstone of all spirituality. Conversion means a radical transformation of ourselves; it means thinking, feeling, and living as Christ—present in exploited and alienated persons. To be converted is to commit oneself to the process of the liberation of the poor and oppressed, to commit oneself lucidly, realistically, and concretely. It means to commit oneself not only generously, but also with an analysis of the situation and a strategy of action. To be converted is to know and experience the fact that, contrary to the laws of physics, we can stand straight, according to the Gospel, only when our center of gravity is outside ourselves.

Conversion is a permanent process in which very often the obstacles we meet make us lose all we had gained and start anew. The fruitfulness of our conversion depends on our openness to doing this, our spiritual childhood. All conversion implies a break. To wish to accomplish it without conflict is to deceive oneself and others: "No one is worthy of me who cares more for father or mother than for me." But it is not a question of a withdrawn and pious attitude. Our conversion process is affected by the socio-economic, political, cultural, and human environment in which it occurs. Without a change in these structures, there is no authentic conversion. We have to break with our mental categories, with the way we relate to others, with our way of identifying with the Lord, with our cultural milieu, with our social class, in other words, with all that can stand in the way of a real, profound solidarity with those who suffer, in the first place, from misery and injustice. Only thus, and not through purely interior and spiritual attitudes, will the "new person" arise from the ashes of the "old."

Christians have not done enough in this area of conversion to the neighbor, to social justice, to history. They have not perceived clearly enough yet that to know God is to do justice. They still do not live in one sole action with both God and all humans. They still do not situate themselves in Christ without attempting to avoid concrete human history. They have yet to tread the path which will lead them to seek effectively the peace of the Lord in the heart of social struggle.

A spirituality of liberation must be filled with a living sense of gratuitousness. Communion with the Lord and with all humans is more than anything else a gift. Hence the universality and the radicalness of the liberation which it affords. This gift, far from being a call to passivity, demands a vigilant attitude. This is one of the most constant Biblical themes: the encounter with the Lord presupposes attention, active disposition, work, fidelity to God's will, the good use of talents received. But the knowledge that at the root of our personal and community existence lies the gift of the self-communication of God, the grace of God's friendship, fills our life with gratitude. It allows us to see our encounters with others, our loves, everything that happens in our life as a gift. There is a real love only when there is free giving—without conditions or coercion. Only gratuitous love goes to our very roots and elicits true love.

Prayer is an experience of gratuitousness. This "leisure" action, this "wasted" time, reminds us that the Lord is beyond the categories of useful and useless." God is not of this world. The gratuitousness of God's gift, creating profound needs, frees us from all religious alienation and, in the last instance, from all alienation. The Christian committed to the Latin American revolutionary process has to find the way to real prayer, not evasion. It cannot be denied that a crisis exists in this area and that we can easily slide into dead ends." There are many who—nostalgically and in "exile," recalling earlier years of their life—can say with the psalmist: "As I pour out my soul in distress, I call to mind how I marched in the ranks of the great to the house of God, among exultant shouts of praise, the clamor of the pilgrims" (Ps. 42:4). But the point is not to backtrack; new experiences, new demands have made heretofore familiar and comfortable paths impassable and have made us undertake new itineraries on which we hope it might be possible to say with Job to the Lord, "I knew of thee then only by report, but now I see thee with my own eyes" (42:5). Bonhoeffer was right when he said that the only credible God is the God of the mystics. But this is not a God unrelated to human history. On the contrary, if it is true, as we recalled above, that one must go through humankind to reach God, it is equally certain that the "passing through" to that gratuitous God strips me, leaves me naked, universalizes my love for others, and makes it gratuitous. Both movements need each other dialectically and move toward a synthesis. This synthesis is found in Christ; in the God-Man we encounter God and humankind. In Christ humankind gives God a human countenance and God gives it a divine countenance." Only in this perspective will we be able to understand that the "union with the Lord," which all spirituality proclaims, is not a separation from others; to attain this union, I must go through others, and the union, in turn, enables me to encounter others more fully. Our purpose here is not to "balance" what has been said before, but rather to deepen it and see it in all its meaning.

The conversion to one's neighbors, and in them to the Lord, the gratuitousness which allows me to encounter others fully, the unique encounter which is the foundation of communion of persons among themselves and of human beings, with God, these are the source of Christian joy. This joy is born of the gift already received yet still awaited and is expressed in the present despite the difficulties and tensions of the struggle for the construction of a just society. Every prophetic proclamation of total liberation is accompanied by an invitation to participate in eschatological joy: "I will take delight in Jerusalem and rejoice in my people" (Isa. 65:19). This joy ought to fill our entire existence, making us attentive both to the gift of integral human liberation and history as well as to the detail of our life and the lives of others. This joy ought not to lessen our commitment to those who live in an unjust world, nor should it lead us to a facile, low-cost conciliation. On the contrary, our joy is paschal, guaranteed by the Spirit (Gal. 5:22; 1 Tim. 1:6; Rom. 14:17); it passes through the conflict with the great ones of this world and through the cross in order to enter into life. This is why we celebrate our joy in the present by recalling the passover of the Lord. To recall Christ is to believe in him. And this celebration is a feast (Apoc. 19:7), a feast of the Christian community, those who explicitly confess Christ to be the Lord of history, the liberator of the oppressed. This community has been referred to as the small temple in contradistinction to the large temple of human history." Without community support neither the emergence nor the continued existence of a new spirituality is possible.

The Magnificat expresses well this spirituality of liberation. A song of thanksgiving for the gifts of the Lord, it expresses humbly the joy of being loved by him: "Rejoice, my spirit, in God my Savior; so tenderly has he looked upon his servant, humble as she is. . . . So wonderfully has he dealt with me, the Lord, the Mighty One" (Luke 1:47-49). But at the same time it is one of the New Testament texts which contains great implications both as regards liberation and the political sphere. This thanksgiving and joy are closely linked to the action of God who liberates the oppressed and humbles the powerful. "The hungry he has satisfied with good things, the rich sent empty away" (vv. 52-53). The future of history belongs to the poor and exploited. True liberation will be the work of the oppressed themselves; in them, the Lord saves history. The spirituality of liberation will have as its basis the spirituality of the anawim. Living witnesses rather than theological speculation will point out, are already pointing out, the direction of a spirituality of liberation." This is the task which has been undertaken in Latin America by those referred to above as a "first Christian generation."

Selection 4: Jon Sobrino, *The Principle of Mercy: Taking the Crucified People from the Cross*

Jon Sobrino, S.J. (b. 1938) has been a prominent voice in Latin American liberation theology. In 1989 he narrowly escaped death when a unit of the Salvadorian military broke into the rectory at the University of Central America in

San Salvador and murdered six of Sobrino's fellow Jesuits. Sobrino had founded
this university and taught there until being admonished by the Vatican and the
Congregation for the Doctrine of the Faith for certain of his teachings in 2007
and then prohibited from teaching by his archbishop. The Vatican's concerns are
not clearly reflected in this selection, however. Here Sobrino deftly relates the
liberation of the forgiveness of sins to commitment to the liberation of the poor.

Forgiveness as Liberation

What we have said so far shows not only that forgiveness is central to the New Testament but that, in its quality as acceptance and not mere absolution, forgiveness is formally liberating.

The forgiveness of acceptance bestowed by Jesus in the gospel accounts is something not merely beneficial, but liberating. An important expression of liberation appears in those accounts. The context is the contempt and social ostracism (at times deserved, one could think, but often hypocritical) to which sinners are subjected. The fact that Jesus addresses sinners, receives them into his company, and takes his meals with them is a forthright expression of victory over social segregation. But especially, Jesus restores sinners their lost dignity. Here is how Joachim Jeremias describes what must have happened to Zacchaeus. "That Jesus should wish to be a guest in his home—in the home of this despised person shunned by all—is inconceivable to him. Jesus restores to him his lost honor by entering his house as a guest and breaking bread with him." The forgiveness that is acceptance opens up a new, positive future to sinners. It opens social space to them in the sight of others, and inner space to them in their own sight. Truly Jesus can tell them, "Go in peace."

There is another element in the liberation bestowed by the forgiveness that is acceptance, one that has been observed by exegetes with raised eyebrows. In a number of the incidents of healing, and in one of the scenes of forgiveness, Jesus pronounces these surprising final words: "Your faith has healed you" or "has been your salvation." Jesus is saying that acceptance of the sinner has sparked an authentic interior renewal in the person. He is saying that forgiveness is more than something merely good but external to the person. In the declaration "Your faith has been your salvation" appears the salvific power of the God who wishes to effect, and is able to effect, a person's real, interior transformation. And there appears what we may call God's consummate delicacy, which says "You can." Doubtless that delicacy implies that God has forgiven the sinner; but in accepting sinners, what is of interest to God is not winning some kind of triumph but encouraging sinners to change and convincing them that they can change—that their potential is greater than they had thought.

Conversion, then, is not a Pelagian affair, but an enabled one. More than anything else, however, it is real. It is really the human being who is now changed, justified, and liberated.

The conversion that is acceptance delivers human beings from their sin, surely. But more than that, it delivers them from themselves—from what they regard as being their truth. As we have said, it is no easy thing to come to the recognition of one's own sin. It is not easy because sin has the innate tendency to hide from itself and even to try to pass for the contrary. Thus, in John, the sinner is a "liar." And it is not easy because a forthright acknowledgment of one's own sin—without the possibility of forgiveness—would logically lead a human being to paralysis, anguish, and despair. However to know oneself a sinner in the art of learning to be forgiven facilitates the acknowledgment of one's own sin, since now the latter is perceived no longer only in its dark, enslaving side, but under the light of forgiveness, as well. This is what can shatter human hubris, which had rather retain its own than retract itself, rather cling to the negative than enfeeble the keenness with which persons cleave to themselves (the hubris overcome by Christ in the transcendent declaration of Phil. 2:6). Forgiveness, then, is liberation from the lie about oneself, with which human beings seek to oppress their own truth.

Finally, forgiveness liberates the human being to recognize God as God actually is—to recognize God in the essential divine dimension of gratuity and partiality. Standing in correlation to our tendency to wish to appear just before God is the view of God shown in justice. But to accept forgiveness is also the way in which one asserts God's authentic reality as gratuitous and partial. What theology emphasizes with respect to the relationship between God and the poor must also be emphasized with respect to the relationship between God and the sinner. Both relationships introduce us to the authentic reality of God.

Not to accept efficaciously the possibility of God's forgiving acceptance—to ignore it or regard it as of lesser importance—would mean failing to recognize God. Not to accept, as something central in God, the ultimate joy of God's acceptance of the sinner, would be tantamount to not believing in God. Conversely, allowing oneself to be accepted forgivingly by God is believing in God and making it plain in what God one believes.

The forgiveness that is acceptance, therefore, is something good, and also something formally liberative. Forgiveness is a benefit because it is liberation from the lie with which we seek to conceal forgiveness from ourselves and exclude it from our view of God.

Liberation from Personal Sin and Eradication of Historical Sin

All that we have said is a central truth in God's revelation and, furthermore, in a surprising way. The difficult recognition of one's own sin, and the difficult actualization of conversion proceed, in the last analysis, from forgiveness in its quality as light shed upon one's own truth and strength for one's own conversion. Since forgiveness is truth, it cannot be opaque to itself, nor can it establish itself through a logic proceeding from any source beyond the fact itself. Simply, God is thus.

Theologically, however, we are responsible for reflecting on the manner in which this central truth is integrated into theological reflection and, in the present instance, into the reflection of the theology of liberation. More concretely, what does this truth say to a theology that takes as its specific finality the eradication of structural historical sin? What relationship obtains between allowing oneself to be personally forgiven by God and the practice of the Reign conducted for the purpose of uprooting the anti-Reign? Let us state from the outset that there is no question here of manipulating either truth in favor of another. Our concern is to assert both truths as central, in terms of the premise—a faith premise, to be sure, but a premise maintained on the basis of reflection, as well—that both truths converge in the truth of total liberation, that of the interior human being and that of human history, to comprise what is called integral liberation.

If we ask ourselves how personal liberation from sin supports historical liberation, a number of critical questions may arise. It can be alleged that what we have been saying, while true enough, is too utopian (not even Jesus, we shall hear, enjoyed a great deal of success in this area) and excessively individualistic; historically, it can actually foster an escapist attitude. And we basically agree. We grant that our proposition entails its danger. We admit that no truth, however central or "key," must be elevated to the status of sole truth. This would be just another manifestation of human greed. But we also believe that the plural truths in which the single truth of God is manifested, converge. We hold, a priori, that a positive, mutually complementary relation must obtain between personal forgiveness and the eradication of concrete, historical sin. A posteriori, this relationship will be observable in the light of concrete, historical reality.

A priori, we must assert that the logic of revelation forbids us to make anything of our "own" as central and sole, even something as important as our own forgiveness and salvation. Not even God makes anything of "God's own" the central thing. The divine self-revelation is that of a God-for-others, and more specifically, a God-for-the-weak. Hence the logic—the logic of reality, rather than the logic of sheer concept—that one forgiven, a person who has allowed herself to be accepted by God, would not make that acceptance the core thing, the ultimate fact. Rather, a person accepted by God would become accepting of others: The forgiven person would become a forgiving one.

This is the logic of the first letter of John: Being loved by God issues in love for one's siblings. It is the logic of the theology of liberation, as Gustavo Gutiérrez has enunciated it: "Loved in order to love," and "liberated in order to liberate."

Let us now formulate this in terms of concrete history. We must inquire not only into the what, but also into the for what of our own forgiveness, our own liberation. Were there to be no for what that transcends the forgiven individual as such, personal forgiveness would remain shut up in that forgiven individual, and this would run counter to the ultimate logic of God's revelation. If the forgiven person were to focus exclusively on this personal forgiveness, he would be transformed once more into the selfish human being. He would become—in Christian logic—the ingrate, and we should even have to doubt whether this person had actually permitted his forgiving acceptance by God.

That from which forgiveness delivers the forgiven one has now been sent forth. For what it delivers him or her is next in order of analysis. Forgiveness frees a person, in the first place—in virtue of the concrete, historical nature of forgiveness—to accept and forgive others. But more generally, it sets a person free to engage in a positive effectuation of God's love with regard to the world, of which this created person has had a personal experience. One of the essential elements of the divine love is that it sees the world as it really is, in its truth and not in its lie, and that it effectuates, in the truth of that world, the divine will. Liberation from personal sin, experienced as letting oneself be accepted by God's love, thereupon leads one to render present in the world the love of God that has now been experienced. The only essential further specification is that, on the level of the concrete, historical world, to forgive the sin of the world is to uproot it.

Concretely, one must ask precisely what personal forgiveness contributes to the eradication of historical sin. Substantially, it contributes the possibility of an enhanced liberation praxis, one superior in its direction, its intensity, and its values—all of which can have an influence on persons and groups committed to liberation.

As we have seen, the forgiven one is delivered from her own lie. But according to John himself, while "lying" is the formal anthropological assertion with regard to the sinner's sin, its material content is "murderous." The words are harsh (and must be understood analogically). But this must not detract from the importance of the basic intuition, which is the following. The sinful human being simultaneously wreaks a double vitiation: of the verum, and of the bonum—a twin subjugation of truth through the lie and goodness through murder—a double rejection of his creatureliness, so as to be (falsely) more than what this being is before God (Adam's original sin), and so as to be (wickedly) more than his sibling (Cain's original sin). It will be open to theological discussion which of these two poles enjoys anthropological priority, but in any case we must accept their dialectic, the reciprocation that prevails between the "lying" and the "murderous," between defending oneself from God and offending one's sister or brother.

In other words, sin is "lie," but it has a content: "to kill." In forgiveness, human beings become knowers of their lie and of the content of their lie. They become aware of the gravity of the one as of the other. And while this may appear minimal, it is not, for now one's eyes are opened to know what one is and what one does—the supreme wickedness of one's hubris and its historical product. And as these "knowledges" are offered in forgiveness, it becomes possible to attain to them and to maintain them in all their raw realism, and thus to live in truth. We live in a world that murders, and in this is the most radical truth of that world.

Traditional theology and piety have always maintained that, in order to know what sin is, one must gaze on Christ crucified. Christ is the forgiving one, but he is also the offended one, and in a precise way: It is he who has been put to death. Today, as well, those who forgive open their eyes and know just what it is that is being forgiven: responsibility in the continued crucifixion of entire peoples.

To be able to see with new eyes the genuine reality of the world, to be able to stare it in the face despite its tragedy, to be able to perceive what it is to which God says a radical "no," is (logically) the first fruit of allowing oneself really to be pardoned by God.

The freely forgiven one is the grateful one. And it is the gratitude of knowing oneself to be accepted that moves a person to a de-centering from self, to generous action, to a life of eager striving that the love of God that has been experienced may be a historical reality in this world. The logic of the forgiven and grateful one—with all due caution when it comes to the enthusiasm of new converts—is what opens the heart to a limitless salvific, historical practice. The prototype here is Paul, who feels so loved by Christ that he makes of his life a total, absorbing apostolate in behalf of others, to the very point of neglecting his own salvation in order to concentrate on the salvation of his brothers and sisters. The phenomenon recurs in Ignatius Loyola, who is so overcome with gratitude for being accepted and forgiven that he can only ask himself, as he stands before Christ crucified, "What am I doing for Christ?" and "What ought I to do for Christ?" These questions are the most complete, the most adequate, concrete historical expression of gratitude. Here is not only a grateful responding, but a generous corresponding to the reality of the one who has accepted me and forgiven me.

Hence it is that the experience of the love of God moves a person to render that same love real in the world, and to do so with limitless generosity: in the language of Ignatius, to act for the greater glory of God.

These experiences of Paul and Ignatius have their historical translation today. Forgiven persons, who have had their eyes opened to the death that reigns in today's world and to their own shared responsibility in the same (analogously, depending on the case), are impelled to produce their gratitude, and this they do. Like Ignatius before Jesus crucified, they ask themselves before a crucified people, "What have I done to crucify them? What am I doing to take them down from their cross? What ought I to do that a crucified people may rise again?"

Forgiveness, then, does not remain shut up within the forgiven one but overflows in gratitude in the historical practice of mercy (with all conjunctural and structural mediations of objective transformation, of accompaniment in suffering and hope, and so on).

The contribution to liberation made by the forgiven is the memory of their own sinfulness, the real, and still possible, sinfulness of those who steer their lives in the direction of a liberation practice. This recollection, once more, is not t masochistic. It is a salvific recollection, just as is the "perilous memory Jesus." Demanding though it be, it pulls us back to the truth, back to honesty with the real. The recall of one's own sin engenders a fruitful humility. It makes it easier to recognize (and remedy) the limitations to which liberation processes are subject, however necessary, good, and just these processes may be. It makes it easier to perceive (and remedy) the dogmatisms, chauvinisms, and reductionisms that constitute the inevitable by-product of these processes.8 In a word, the memory of one's own sin—a memory that, being honest and not neurotic, has only been made possible by forgiveness—helps minimize the hubris that comes into the practice of liberation. To "wage a revolution as one forgiven," as Gonzalez Faus puts it so well is a boon for the practice of liberation. It renders that practice more humane and more humanizing; it tends to preserve it from the dangers that lurk along its path; and it even makes it, in the long run, more effective.

The Poor and Oppressed: Historical Mediation of a Forgiveness That Is Acceptance

An emphasis on the fact that sin is rediscovered precisely in the light of a forgiveness that is acceptance obviously calls for a reflection on the concrete, historical mediation of that forgiveness. Otherwise, everything we have said up until now will have been said in vain. From the standpoint of liberation, it calls for a reflection on whether any role in that forgiveness falls to the poor and oppressed, and what that role would be. That is, we must reflect on whether, as the offended, they are "forgivers," and whether, as forgivers, they reveal the magnitude of the offense that afflicts them.

What we wish to state here is that, throughout the history of the church and theology, many historical mediations of pardon, of the forgiveness that is absolution, have been developed, but the question of the mediation of the forgiveness that is acceptance remains open, especially in the case of those sins (as also structural sin in itself) that oppress and deal death on all sides. And our thesis (obvious in its formulation, but by no means obvious in its corresponding practice) is that those who offer the forgiveness that is acceptance today—structurally, and in concrete expressions— are the poor and oppressed of this world.

The elevation of the poor of this world to the status of mediators of the forgiveness that is acceptance has nothing of the rhetorical about it; nor, in principle, ought it to cause any astonishment. In the reflection maintained by biblical theology, and in current systematic theology, the presentation of the poor—including their collective presentation—is a constant in crucial aspects of revelation: God's self-manifestation, immediate and with partiality, to an oppressed people; a salvation emerging from this same people, as it takes on the sin of the world; the basic ethical requirement of serving the poor; the right of the poor to demand conversion; and, in the beautiful, unprecedented words of Puebla, their evangelizing capacity. To these familiar core affirmations, John Paul II has added another very important one: On the day of judgment, the peoples of the Third World will judge the peoples of the First World. To put this in theological language: The Son of Man, still present today in the poor, will preside at the last judgment through the poor.

HUMAN SEXUALITY

🔖 *Once thought to be matters of personal ethics, issues of human sexuality have in recent decades become a topic of widespread public debate inside and outside the churches. Traditional norms of sexual morality have been challenged and for many have been superseded by new models of sexual ethics as new understandings of sexuality have emerged. Those in the churches who are deeply involved in this emotionally charged debate over changing sexual mores are often concerned about how disagreements over sexual ethics will affect scriptural authority. However, they are also convinced that the stance taken by the churches is critical to Christian social witness since sexuality and sexual conduct are so much a part of the fabric of our humanity and relationships at the heart of society.*

Selection 1: Charles Curran, "Catholic Social and Sexual Teaching: A Methodological Comparison"

Charles Curran (b. 1934) is the Elizabeth Scurlock University Professor of Human Values at Southern Methodist University in Dallas, Texas. He is a distinguished, widely published, and influential contemporary Catholic ethicist. A loyal priest of the Roman Catholic Church, Curran has nonetheless been critical of its approach to sexual ethics. In the excerpt from his article comparing the church's methodology in social teaching with that of its methodology in sexual ethics, his positive appraisal of the former stands in contrast to his view of the latter. Our selection picks up with the discussion of sexual ethics.

The focus now shifts to official Catholic teaching in the area of sexual morality. Three recent documents will be examined: "Declaration of Sexual Ethics," issued by the Congregation for the Doctrine of the Faith on December 29, 1975, "Letter to the Bishops of the Catholic Church on the Pastoral Care of Homosexual Persons," promulgated by the Congregation for the Doctrine of the Faith on October 1, 1986, and "Instruction on Respect for Human Life in its Origin and on the Dignity of Procreation," issued by the Congregation for the Doctrine of the Faith on February 22, 1987.

The present discussion centers on methodological issues, but something must be said briefly about the authoritative nature of these documents. There is a hierarchy of official Catholic Church documents. These three documents are not from the pope himself but from one of the Roman congregations. By their very nature, such documents are not expected to break new ground. However, it is interesting that the documents have received wide public discussion. Catholics owe a religious respect to the teaching of these documents, but they are of less authoritative weight than the documents issued by the pope himself.

For our present purposes, the focus is on the methodological approaches taken in these documents. Study will show that these methodological approaches differ sharply from the three methodological approaches found in the contemporary documents on Catholic social teaching.

(1) Classicist rather than historically conscious. The "Declaration of Sexual Ethics" of 1975 shows very little historical consciousness. In the very beginning of the document, the emphasis on the eternal and the immutable is very clear:

> Therefore there can be no true promotion of human dignity unless the essential order of human nature is respected. Of course, in the history of civilization many of the concrete conditions and need of human life have changed and will continue to change. But all evolution of morals and every type of life must be kept within the limits imposed by the immutable principles based upon every human person's constitutive elements and essential relations—elements and relations which transcend historical contingencies.

> These fundamental principles which can be grasped by reason are contained in "the divine law—eternal, objective, and universal—whereby God orders, directs, and governs the entire universe and all the ways of the human community by a plan conceived in wisdom and love. Human beings have been made by God to participate in this law with the result that under the gentle disposition of divine providence they can come to perceive ever increasingly the unchanging truth." This divine law is accessible to our mind (n. 3).

The "Letter to the Bishops of the Catholic Church on the Pastoral Care of Homosexual Persons" in 1986 bases its teaching on "the divine plan" and "the theology of creation," which tell us of "the creator's sexual design" (nn. 1-7). The "theocratic law" (n. 6) found in Scripture also attests to the church's teaching. Emphasis is frequently put on the will of God, which is known in the above mentioned ways and is what the church teaches.

This letter points out that many call for a change in the church's teaching on homosexuality because the earlier condemnations were culture-bound (n. 4). The letter acknowledges that the Bible was composed in many different epochs with great cultural and historical diversity and that the church today addresses the gospel to a world which differs in many ways from ancient days (n. 5). In the light of this recognition of historical consciousness, one is not prepared for the opening sentence of the next paragraph: "What should be noticed is that, in the presence of such remarkable diversity, there is nevertheless a clear consistency within the Scriptures themselves on the moral issue of homosexual behavior" (n. 5). Historical consciousness is mentioned only to deny it in practice.

The "Instruction of Respect for Human Life in its Origin and on the Dignity of Procreation," promulgated in 1987, appeals to the unchangeable and immutable laws of human nature. The laws are described as "inscribed in the very being of man and of woman" (II, B, n. 4). These laws are "inscribed in their persons and in their union" (Introduction, n. 5).

This instruction describes its own methodology as deductive: "The moral criteria for medical intervention in procreation are deduced from the dignity of human persons, of their sexuality, and of their origins" (II, B, n. 7). "A first consequence can be deduced from these principles" of the natural law (Introduction, n. 3). In summary, these documents show little or no historical consciousness in their approach to questions of sexuality.

(2) The emphasis is on nature and faculties rather than on the person. In the official hierarchical teaching on sexuality, the methodology gives much more significance to nature and faculties than it does to the person. This has been a constant complaint against the older Catholic methodology in sexual ethics that has led to its teaching on masturbation, artificial contraception, sterilization, artificial insemination, homosexual acts, etc. The manuals of moral theology based their sexual ethics on the innate purpose, God-given structure, and finality of the sexual faculty. The sexual faculty has a twofold purpose—procreation and love union. Every sexual actuation must respect that twofold finality and nothing should interfere with this God-given purpose. The sexual act itself must be open to procreation and expressive of love. Such an understanding forms the basis of the Catholic teaching that masturbation, contraception, and artificial insemination, even with the husband's seed, are always wrong. In the popular mentality, it was often thought that Catholic opposition to artificial contraception was based on a strong pronatalist position, but such is not the case. Catholic teaching has also condemned artificial insemination with the husband's seed that is done precisely in order to have a child. In my judgment, this condemnation points up the problematic aspect in the methodology of Catholic sexual teaching: the sexual faculty can never be interfered with and the sexual act must always be open to procreation and expressive of love. This natural act must always be present. With many other Catholic revisionist theologians, I maintain that for the good of the person or the good of the marriage one can and should interfere with the sexual faculty and the sexual act. I have claimed that the official teaching is guilty of a physicalism that insists the human person cannot interfere with the physical, biological structure of the sexual faculty or the sexual act. There is no doubt that the official documents under discussion here continue to accept and propose this basic understanding.

The "Declaration on Sexual Ethics" points out that the sexual teaching of the Catholic Church is based "on the finality of the sexual act and on the principal criterion of its morality: it is respect for its finality that ensures the moral goodness of this act" (n. 5). Sexual sins are described often in this document as "abuses of the sexual faculty" (n. 6, also nn. 8, 9). The nature of the sexual faculty and the sexual act—not the person—form the ultimate moral criterion in matters of sexual morality.

The letter on homosexuality cites the earlier "Declaration of Sexual Ethics" to point out that homosexual acts are deprived of their essential and indispensable finality and are intrinsically disordered (n. 3). This letter points out that only within marriage can the use of the sexual faculty be morally good (n. 7). However, there does seem to be a development in this letter in terms of a greater appeal to personalism. The teaching claims to be based on the reality of the human person in one's spiritual and physical dimensions (n. 2). There are more references to the human person throughout this document than in the earlier declaration, but the change is only verbal. The methodology is ultimately still based on the nature of the faculty and of the act, which are then assumed to be the same thing as the person.

The instruction on some aspects of bioethics is very similar to the letter on homosexuality in this regard. There are references to the "intimate structure" of the conjugal act and to the conjugal act as expressing the self gift of the spouses and their openness to the gift of life. The document also appeals to the meaning and values that are expressed in the language of the body and in the union of human persons (II, B, n. 4). Thus, the terms (the finality of the faculty, and of the act and the abuse of the faculty) are not used, but the basic teaching remains the same. There are many more references to the person and to the rights of persons than in the earlier documents, but the change remains verbal and does not affect the substance of the teaching.

(3) Ethical model. There can be no doubt that the documents in official Catholic teaching on sexuality employ the law model as primary. The "Declaration of Sexual Ethics" in its discussion of ethical methodology insists on the importance of the divine law—eternal, objective, and universal—whereby God orders, directs, and governs the entire universe (n. 3). This document bases its teaching on the "existence of immutable laws inscribed in the constitutive elements of human nature and which are revealed to be identical in all beings endowed with reason" (n. 4). Throughout the introductory comments, there is no doubt whatsoever that this declaration follows a legal model.

> Since sexual ethics concern certain fundamental values of human and Christian life, this general teaching equally applies to sexual ethics. In this domain, there exist principles and norms which the church has always unhesitatingly transmitted as part of her teaching, however much the opinions and morals of the world may have been opposed to them. These principles and norms in no way owe their origin to a certain type of culture, but rather to knowledge of the divine law and of human nature. They therefore cannot be considered as having become out of date or doubtful under the pretext that a new cultural situation has risen (n. 5).

The "Letter to the Bishops of the Catholic Church on the Pastoral Care of Homosexual Persons" is by its very nature more concerned with pastoral care than with an explanation of the moral teaching and the ethical model employed in such teaching (n. 2). However, the occasional references found in this pastoral letter indicate the deontological model at work. There are frequent references to the will of God, the plan of God, and the theology of creation. Traditional Catholic natural law is the basis for this teaching. The teaching of Scripture on this matter is called "theocratic law" (n. 6). The recent instruction on bioethics definitely employs a deontological model:

> Thus, the Church once more puts forward the divine law in order to accomplish the work of truth and liberation. For it is out of goodness—in order to indicate the path of life—that God gives human beings his commandments and the grace to observe them (Introduction, n. 1).

The natural moral law expresses and lays down the purposes, rights, and duties which are based upon the bodily and spiritual nature of the human person. Therefore, this law cannot be thought of as simply a set of norms on the biological level; rather, it must be defined as the rational order whereby the human being is called by the Creator to direct and regulate one's life and action and in particular to make use of one's own body (Introduction, n. 3).

This document also cites the following quotation from Mater et Magistra: "The transmission of human life is entrusted by nature to a personal and conscious act and as such is subject to the all-holy laws of God: immutable and inviolable laws, which must be recognized and observed" (Introduction, n. 4). Biomedical science and technology have grown immensely in the last few years, but "science and technology require, for their own intrinsic meaning, an unconditional respect for the fundamental criteria of the moral law" (Introduction, n. 2).

A very significant practical difference between a law model and a relationality-responsibility model is illustrated by the teaching proposed in these documents. In a legal model, the primary question is the existence of law. If something is against the law, it is wrong; if there is no law against it, it is acceptable and good. Within such a perspective, there is very little gray area. Something is either forbidden or permitted. Within a relationality-responsibility model, there are more gray areas. Here one recognizes that in the midst of complexity and specificity one cannot always claim a certitude for one's moral positions.

III

The contemporary official Catholic teaching on social issues with its relationality-responsibility model recognizes significant gray areas. Octogesima Adveniens acknowledges the pluralism of options available and the need for discernment. The two recent pastoral letters of the United States Roman Catholic bishops on peace and the economy well illustrate such an approach. The documents make some very particular judgments, but they recognize that other Catholics might in good conscience disagree with such judgments. The bishops' letters call for unity and agreement on the level of principles, but they recognize that practical judgments on specific issues cannot claim with absolute certitude to be the only possible solution. The pastoral letter on peace, for example, proposes that the first use of nuclear weapons is always wrong but recognizes that other Catholics in good conscience might disagree with such a judgment.

In the contemporary official Catholic teaching on sexual issues, there is little or no mention of such gray areas. Something is either forbidden or permitted. Even in the complex question of bioethics, the same approach is used. Certain technologies and interventions are always wrong; others are permitted. Thus, the very way in which topics are treated, namely, either forbidden or permitted, indicates again that a legal model is at work in the hierarchical sexual teaching.

The thesis and the conclusions of this paper are somewhat modest, but still very significant. There can be no doubt that there are three important methodological differences between hierarchical Roman Catholic teaching on social morality and the official hierarchical teaching on sexual morality. Whereas the official social teaching has evolved so that it now employs historical consciousness, personalism, and a relationality-responsibilty ethical model, the sexual teaching still emphasizes classicism, human nature and faculties, and a law model of ethics. The ramifications of these conclusions are most significant and must be thoroughly explored.

Selection 2: Christine Gudorf, "Life without Anchors: Sex, Exchange, and Human Rights in a Postmodern World"

Along with Margaret Farley (see below) and others, Christine Gudorf, Professor of Theology at Florida International University has been one of the influential women in Christian ethics writing on the subject of sexuality. Her comments on the end of sexual dimorphism illustrate the impact of contemporary research on our thinking about sexuality and the implications of its claims for public policy matters such as gay marriage and for the teachings of the churches in matters of sexual orientation.

The End of Sexual Dimorphism

Recently we have seen a contemporary attack on sexual dimorphism by both citizen groups, on the one hand, and academics and medical professionals, on the other hand. In the First World, we now have associations of persons who call themselves transgendered or third sexed, as well as a multitude of social scientists reporting on societies in which sexuality does not present itself dimorphically. As elaborated by Karen Lebacqz at the 1997 annual meeting of the Society of Christian Ethics, the Intersex Society of North America opposes sexual (re)assignment and surgical/medical intervention in the case of children born with ambiguous genitalia; it argues instead for social acceptance of diverse forms of sexuality. Many medical researchers point out that sexual dimorphism no longer explains large numbers of cases in which persons lack agreement between their chromosomal sex, hormonal sex, sex of the brain, gonadal sex, sex of the internal reproductive organs, and sex of the external genitalia. Sexual orientation is under similar attack, not only rom bisexuals who have long argued that bisexuality was more than simple indeterminacy between poles of homo- and heterosexuality, but also from anthropologists who have studied human cultures in which there is no evidence of any fixed sexual orientation.

A great deal of the literature in the multidisciplinary attack on sexual dimorphism point to present and past cultures with third-sex roles, as in the more than a hundred Native American tribes with two-spirit or man-woman roles, or the Hawaiian *aikane* and the Tahitian *mahu*, not to mention historical third-sex roles, such as Middle-Eastern eunuchs or Christian *castrati*.

Rejection of sexual dimorphism challenges the most basic categories in which we think. Feminism defines itself in terms of support for the equality of women with men, but what if humanity is more varied? What if there are more than two sexual divisions, and the borders of maleness and femaleness are not where they had been assumed to be? The feminist claim would have to be adapted to such sociohistorical changes in the central terms of feminist arguments. At the least, "sex" and "gender" would no longer signify different concepts. Sex—maleness and femaleness—would no longer be construed as a biological category, but rather as a culturally assigned one, like gender. For if the objections to sexual dimorphism are correct, to use external genitalia as the criterion by which to assign sex reveals a cultural, not a scientific, decision to elevate external genitalia (or the other front-runner among the biological determinants, chromosomal sex) over all the other biological definitions or determinants of sex.

The implications of polymorphism for human rights would be similarly profound and obvious. As a dimension of self-determination, would individuals have a right to decide their own sex, as the Intersex Society asserts that those who are born with ambiguous genitalia do? If individuals were to have the right to decide their own sex, would there be any limiting criteria to be imposed on their choice? What responsibilities would fall to society with regard to respecting and protecting this individual right to choose one's sex?

From the perspective of the Christian churches, the end of sexual dimorphism has radical implications for the notion of sexual sin. Once the traditional categories of male and female become ambiguous, prohibition of homosexuality and the reservation of marriage to heterosexuals become impossible to enforce. Conservative notions linking Christian virtue to traditional sex roles (for example, 1 Timothy: "Yet woman will be saved by childbearing, if she continues in faith and love and holiness, with modesty") also become more ambiguous. Perhaps the most contentious issue in the churches would be the most basic: whether sexual dimorphism, because assumed and applied in the Bible, is therefore divinely revealed and beyond question.

Other than the environmental challenge, I can think of no more profound challenge to human societies than this scientifically grounded challenge to human sexual dimorphism. If it really is the paradigm shift that it appears to be, it may well be more revolutionary than any of the previous scientific shifts of the modern period. Like the theories of Copernicus, Galileo, William Harvey, and even Werner Heisenberg and Albert Einstein, it would affect matters of scientific theory and belief, but unlike those earlier discoveries, the abandonment of sexual dimorphism would also affect the everyday customs, self-understandings, and patterns of relationship of all human beings in all human societies.

The basic options are taking shape in terms of the familiar dichotomy of reformist and radical, and, as usual, there are troubling aspects in both. The more modernist position attempts to save the established theory by reforming it: human sexuality is broadened from its dimorphic division to include a third sex/gender. This is undoubtedly the most popular option, because it seems closest to the already familiar. Trimorphism allows the majority who understand themselves as "normal" to nearly dispose of all the "abnormals" in a category that offers them quasi-normalcy. Ultimately the problem is that such a reform is not conceptually clear. Persons born without internal reproductive organs, persons sexually attracted to the same sex, persons who like to dress and act like the "other" sex, persons who want the body of the "other" sex, persons whose birth sex is ambiguous—anybody who does not fully correspond to the heterosexual male or female role in his or her society would be assigned to the third sex/gender. One troubling sign that already suggests the instability of this category is that in large cities across the United States there are already separate organizations of transsexuals, of transgendered persons, of intersex persons, in addition to gay, lesbian, and bisexual groups.

The other alternative to sexual dimorphism is erasing all sex/gender distinctions whatsoever, or at least attempting to move in that direction. What we have understood as the constituents of human sexuality (external genitalia, gonadal sex, hormonal sex, and so forth) would all come to be understood as variable individual characteristics like shoe size, characteristics of no social, and little interpersonal, significance. A move in this direction has the potential to tremendously increase individual human freedom for self-creation. It would seem to offer relief to the many who have felt oppressed by the failure of their bodies, their desires, or their character traits to fit the sex/gender expectations of society. Erasing sexual categories by extensive multiplication would seem to undermine any dualist hierarchy in sexuality, thus satisfying feminist, gay and lesbian, and other sexual rights claims.

Some feminists and human rights advocates may ask whether social blindness to sexuality is the appropriate solution to unjustified sexual discrimination. Perhaps some discrimination based on sex, they may say, is a precondition for justice for "women." Remember the institution of chromosome testing to protect women's sports from male transsexual dominance? The end of sexual categories need not, of course, mean the end of categories. Justice for "women" in sports could come through categories based on height or weight or muscle-mass, rather than sex. We may find that sexually undifferentiated restrooms are no more dangerous than racially undifferentiated drinking fountains. We can still give social support to those who bear and raise children, whether we call them women or parent or whatever.

My most severe reservations, however, concern the impact of such erasure of sex/gender distinctions on human socialization of the young and the process of individuation. The complexity of late modern/postmodern society—compounded by increasing human specialization, population density, and technology—already exerts enormous pressure on our young, especially adolescents, as they maneuver through the individuation process. Youth, through rock music and videos, were the first cohort to recognize the challenge to sexual dimorphism, and they have been playing with it for a decade or more. It is, however, a very different thing for a few performers to experiment with cross dressing and bisexuality, than for society to totally erase sexual distinctions. The first may be exciting; the second has tremendous potential for complicating and confusing the process of adolescence, not to mention adulthood. We know that suicides among teens are at an all-time high, and that the highest rates are among teens loosely identified as gay and lesbian. While I agree that one important way to decrease such suicides is to put these teens in touch with gay and lesbian organizations, I am not so sure that the fundamental problem is a repressive heterosexist society; the fundamental problem may be, instead, socially structured sexual confusion. Our society is heterosexist, and it is still often sexually repressive. But most young teens are sexually confused because human sexual individuation is complicated and because socialization in this area is largely indirect and confusing— and those who do not find many clues to their own feelings and desires in the models around them are at higher risk and are more likely to despair. The suicide rate among confused but presumed heterosexual teens is also high. Should we raise the level of confusion and insecurity for all of them?

In the last few centuries, we have progressively destroyed, in the name of individual freedom, most of the taken-for-granted, socially assigned aspects of personhood. Today we demand of our children that they make personal decisions as to their adult occupation, their geographical location, their religion, their spouse, their political ideology, their hobbies, and their civic affiliations. In areas of migration (I speak from Miami), youngsters are often also given choices about migration and nationality. Many indigenous and racial culture groups ask youngsters to decide between separatist and assimilationist practices and movements, and even to decide how they want to define themselves. My adopted youngest son has been variously classified by his school board over twelve years as black (by color), white (by race of legal mother), racially mixed, and a person of color. Each of these invokes in him a different social ideology to which he must adapt his understanding of himself.

One of the only assurances we give our babies about who they will be is that they are girls (or boys) and will grow up to be women (or men). That message used to be more extended —we used to tell the girls that they would marry men, be homemakers, and have babies, but we now recognize that these are only some of the possibilities open to them. Is it or is it not a big step to go from telling a child he or she can decide whether to have long or short hair, to prefer baths or showers, to teach kindergarten or drive a semi, to bake pies of fix a transmission, to telling a child to choose whether to be male or female? As before, the primary thing the child cannot decide is whether to be a sperm or ovum contributor in reproduction. All that changes at the level of individual options is that the labels "male" and "female" are no longer attached to the type of gamete contribution.

On the other hand, imagine dating in a sexually undifferentiated society, where sexual interest in, even desire for, another person would frequently precede information as to the type of genitalia and preferred sexual practices of that person. Would the churches still teach us to refrain from sex until marriage in such a society? The potential for expanding our sexual preferences in such a society, I am told, would be awesome. I am persuaded, however, that the potential for disappointment and suffering would also be awesome—and already is for partners of growing numbers of persons whose sexual identity is unconventional, in transition, or otherwise unpredictable.

Humans have a yen for freedom, but we also need—psychologically as well as physically —structure and stability in the world out of which we must construct our identities. Real human freedom cannot be solely focused on the deconstruction of society; it must also involve reconstruction, because the humanity of all of us depends in some critical ways upon the health and consistency of the societies that socialize us. If, as seems the be the case, we are moving inexorably toward greater pluralism and freedom in sexual identities, are there any ways to minimize the confusion and suffering?

Selection 3: The Lambeth Conference 1998, *Resolution I.10 Human Sexuality*

While voices for change in the churches' attitudes on sexuality have become louder and more numerous, there remains significant opposition on behalf of upholding traditional teachings. Church bodies with an international constituency and organization experience something of a division between the sometimes more open churches of Europe and North America and their partners in the churches of the southern hemisphere. The Lambeth Conference of the Anglican

Communion is illustrative. The resolutions reported from the Appendix, though defeated, nonetheless express the strong sentiments of those churches.

This Conference:

a.   commends to the Church the subsection report on human sexuality [1];

b.   in view of the teaching of Scripture, upholds faithfulness in marriage between a man and a woman in lifelong union, and believes that abstinence is right for those who are not called to marriage;

c.   recognises that there are among us persons who experience themselves as having a homosexual orientation. Many of these are members of the Church and are seeking the pastoral care, moral direction of the Church, and God's transforming power for the living of their lives and the ordering of relationships. We commit ourselves to listen to the experience of homosexual persons and we wish to assure them that they are loved by God and that all baptised, believing and faithful persons, regardless of sexual orientation, are full members of the Body of Christ;

d.   while rejecting homosexual practice as incompatible with Scripture, calls on all our people to minister pastorally and sensitively to all irrespective of sexual orientation and to condemn irrational fear of homosexuals, violence within marriage and any trivialisation and commercialisation of sex;

e.   cannot advise the legitimising or blessing of same sex unions nor ordaining those involved in same gender unions;

f.   requests the Primates and the ACC to establish a means of monitoring the work done on the subject of human sexuality in the Communion and to share statements and resources among us;

g.   notes the significance of the Kuala Lumpur Statement on Human Sexuality and the concerns expressed in resolutions IV.26, V.1, V.10, V.23 and V.35 on the authority of Scripture in matters of marriage and sexuality and asks the Primates and the ACC to include them in their monitoring process.

1. Called to Full Humanity—Section 1 Report

Subsection 3—Human Sexuality

Human sexuality is the gift of a loving God. It is to be honoured and cherished by all people. As a means for the expression of the deepest human love and intimacy, sexuality has great power.

The Holy Scriptures and Christian tradition teach that human sexuality is intended by God to find its rightful and full expression between a man and a woman in the covenant of marriage, established by God in creation, and affirmed by our Lord Jesus Christ. Holy Matrimony is, by intention and divine purpose, to be a life-long, monogamous and unconditional commitment between a woman and a man. The Lambeth Conference 1978 and 1998 both affirmed 'marriage to be sacred, instituted by God and blessed by our Lord Jesus Christ'.

The New Testament and Christian history identify singleness and dedicated celibacy as Christ-like ways of living. The Church needs to recognise the demands and pressures upon both single and married people. Human beings define themselves by relationships with God and other persons. Churches need to find effective ways of encouraging Christ-like living, as well as providing opportunities for the flourishing of friendship, and the building of supportive community life.

We also recognise that there are among us persons who experience themselves as having a homosexual orientation. Many of these are members of the Church and are seeking the pastoral care, moral direction of the Church, and God's transforming power for the living of their lives and the ordering of relationships. We wish to assure them that they are loved by God, and that all baptised, believing and faithful persons, regardless of sexual orientation, are full members of the Body of Christ. We call upon the Church and all its members to work to end any discrimination on the basis of sexual orientation, and to oppose homophobia.

Clearly some expressions of sexuality are inherently contrary to the Christian way and are sinful. Such unacceptable expression of sexuality include promiscuity, prostitution, incest, pornography, paedophilia, predatory sexual behaviour, and sado-masochism (all of which may be heterosexual and homosexual), adultery, violence against wives, and female circumcision. From a Christian perspective these forms of sexual expression remain sinful in any context. We are particularly concerned about the pressures on young people to engage in sexual activity at an early age, and we urge our Churches to teach the virtue of abstinence.

All human relationships need the transforming power of Christ which is available to all, and particularly when we fall short of biblical norms.We must confess that we are not of one mind about homosexuality. Our variety of understanding encompasses:

- those who believe that homosexuality is a disorder, but that through the grace of Christ people can be changed, although not without pain and struggle.
- those who believe that relationships between people of the same gender should not include genital expression, that this is the clear teaching of the Bible and of the Church universal, and that such activity (if unrepented of) is a barrier to the Kingdom of God.
- those who believe that committed homosexual relationships fall short of the biblical norm, but are to be preferred to relationships that are anonymous and transient.
- those who believe that the Church should accept and support or bless monogamous covenant relationships between homosexual people and that they may be ordained.

It appears that the opinion of the majority of bishops is not prepared to bless same sex unions or to ordain active homosexuals. Furthermore many believe that there should be a moratorium on such practices.

We have prayed, studied and discussed these issues, and we are unable to reach a common mind on the scriptural, theological, historical, and scientific questions which are raised. There is much that we do not yet understand. We request the Primates and the Anglican Consultative Council to establish a means of monitoring work done in the Communion on these issues and to share statements and resources among us.

The challenge to our Church is to maintain its unity while we seek, under the guidance of the Holy Spirit, to discern the way of Christ for the world today with respect to human sexuality. To do so will require sacrifice, trust and charity towards one another, remembering that ultimately the identity of each person is defined by Christ.

There can be no description of human reality, in general or in particular, outside the reality of Christ. We must be on guard, therefore, against constructing any other ground for our identities than the redeemed humanity given to use in him. Those who understand themselves as homosexuals, no more and no less than those who do not, are liable to false understandings based on personal or family histories, emotional dispositions, social settings and solidarities formed by common experiences or ambitions. Our sexual affections can no more define who we are than our class race or nationality. At the deepest ontological level, therefore, there is no such thing as "a" homosexual or "a" hetrosexual; therefore there are human beings, male and female, called to redeemed humainty in Christ, endowed with a complex variety of emotional potentialities and threatened by a complex variety of forms of alienation.

12. An examination of the theological Principles Affecting the Homosexual Debate, St Andrew's Day Statement 1995.

Appendix

Resolutions of Sections and Regions referred to in Subsection (f) of Resolution I.10 (Human Sexuality)
Resolution V.1 from Central and East Africa Region

This Conference:

a. believes in the primary authority of the Scriptures, according to their own testimony; as supported by our own historic tradition. The Scriptural revelation of Jesus the Christ must continue to illuminate, challenge and transform cultures, structures, systems and ways of thinking; especially those secular views that predominate our society to day;

b. consequently, reaffirms the traditional teaching upholding faithfulness between a husband and wife in marriage, and celibacy for those who are single;

c. noting that the Holy Scriptures are clear in teaching that all sexual promiscuity is a sin, is convinced that this includes homosexual practices, between persons of the same sex, as well as heterosexual relationships outside marriage;

d. believes that in this regard, as in others, all our ordained Ministers must set a wholesome and credible example. Those persons who practise homosexuality and live in promiscuity, as well as those Bishops who knowingly ordain them or encourage these practices, act contrary to the Scriptures and the teaching of the Church. We call upon them to repent;

e. respects as persons and seeks to strengthen compassion, pastoral care, healing, correction and restoration for all who suffer or err through homosexual or other kind of sexual brokenness.

f.   affirms that it is therefore the responsibility of the Church to lead to repentance all those who deviate from the orthodox teaching of the Scriptures and to assure them of God's forgiveness, hope and dignity.

Note: This Resolution was put to the Conference in the form of an amendment to Resolution I.10 and was defeated.

Resolution V.10 from the Latin American Region
This Conference recognises the importance of strengthening Christian family values, and thereby reaffirms traditional Anglican sexual ethics.
Note: This Resolution was put to the Conference in the form of an amendment to Resolution I.10 and was withdrawn by the mover.

Resolution V. 23 from the South East Asia Region
This Conference receives the Kuala Lumpur Statement on Human Sexuality with gratitude as an authentic expression of Anglican moral norms.
Note: This Resolution was not voted upon, as the Conference agreed to pass to next business.

Resolution V.35 from the West Africa Region

This Conference:

a.   (noting that—
   (i)   the Word of God has established the fact that God created man and woman and blessed their marriage;
   (ii)   many parts of the Bible condemn homosexuality as a sin;
   (iii) homosexuality is one of the many sins that Scripture has condemned;
   (iv)   some African Christians in Uganda were martyred in the 19th century for refusing to have homosexual relations with the king because of their faith in the Lord Jesus and their commitment to stand by the Word of God as expressed in the Bible on the subject;
b.   stands on the Biblical authority and accepts that homosexuality is a sin which could only be adopted by the church if it wanted to commit evangelical suicide.

Note: This Resolution was put to the Conference in the form of an amendment to Resolution I.10 and was defeated.

Selection 4: World Council of Churches' contributions to the discussions on human sexuality: From Harare to Porto Alegre, *Background Document*, Geneva 2006

> *Unlike other selections that have presented a point of view, this report from the World Council of Churches provides an overview of the issues of human sexuality that the WCC has been working on. One can see from the report that this is a multifaceted endeavor with considerable differences to be faced among the participating churches. The decision to move beyond the question of homosexual orientation to the broader consideration of human sexuality is further testimony to the fact that the discourse on human sexuality has become more extensive in scope.*

Historical Background: From New Delhi to Canberra

It was over forty years ago when, at the request of its member churches, the World Council of Churches (WCC) began to address the issues of human sexuality. The foci and nature of the work done have been influenced by the aspects the churches felt challenged to address at a given time. The survey carried out by Birgitta Larsson best explains how the Council dealt with issues of human sexuality in the period between the New Delhi Assembly (1961) and the Canberra Assembly (1991). The major findings were published in "A Quest for Clarity" (Birgitta Larsson, *The Ecumenical Review*, Vol. 50/1, WCC Publications, Geneva. 1998).

Several General Assemblies made reference to new questions facing the church. The New Delhi Assembly, for instance, stated:

> The churches have to discover what positions and actions to take in regard to sex relations before and after marriage; illegitimacy; in some cultures polygamy or concubinage as a social system sanctioned by law and customs; in some Western cultures short-term marriages, or liaisons, easy divorce; in all parts of the world mixed marriages (inter-faith, inter-confessional and inter-racial) with the diminishing of caste and class systems and of racial prejudice. . . . All this, and much else, forces the churches to re-examine their teaching, preaching and pastoral care and their witness and service to society.

The Uppsala Assembly in 1968 took the entry point of the debate on "birth control", but continued to state:

> Family patterns change in different social settings, and Christian marriage can find its expression in a variety of ways. *We should like materials elaborating the problems of polygamy, marriage and celibacy, birth control, divorce, abortion and also of homosexuality to be made available for responsible study and action.*

Inspired by the reflections on "alternative life-styles" by the ecumenical consultation on Sexism in the 1970s (June 1974, Berlin), the Nairobi Assembly (1975) called for "a theological study of sexuality, taking into account the culture of the member churches":

Whereas we recognize the urgent need to examine ways in which women and men can grow into partnership of mutual interdependence, it is recommended that the WCC urge the member churches to

1. affirm the personhood and mutual interdependence of individuals in families;
2. affirm the personhood and worth of people living in different life situations.

The Christian Church is in a key position to foster and support the partners to marriage in their search for mutuality. The church is in the same unique position in respect to persons living in different life situations (e.g. single people living in isolation, single parents), extended families and persons living in communal patterns. There is evidence that these people are not fully accepted by many societies and are often ignored by the church.

The assemblies in Vancouver (1983) and Canberra (1991) came up with similar statements, including additional concerns related to biotechnology. Responding to recommendations by the Vancouver Assembly, the Central Committee called for a thorough re-examination of values in sexuality, with special emphasis on how churches develop educational and pastoral care systems in this area, and initiated a study on female sexuality. Because of the rich diversity of the findings, a second study was commissioned on Sexuality and Human Relations. The 1989 Moscow Central Committee asked to circulate this study for comment in the regions. The result of this process was the very comprehensive and very carefully edited publication on *Living in Covenant with God and One Another: A Guide to the Study of Sexuality and Human Relations* . . . (Geneva: WCC, 1990), which still is a very good resource for study encounters and group discussion at different levels.

Whilst churches expected the WCC to contribute to more clarity and perhaps even a common position, it proved to be difficult for the Council to respond to such requests. The member churches through the WCC were obviously more successful in identifying a range of key issues that need to be addressed in different contexts and in creating opportunities for careful considerations of the various aspects and perspectives involved.

Birgitta Larsson's survey suggests that:

- very different and changing family patterns and life-styles challenge the churches to address a wider range of issues of human sexuality; frequently noted are issues of pre-marital sex, short term marriages or extra-marital sex, polygamy, marriage and celibacy, homosexuality, etc.;
- the WCC addressed issues of human sexuality through different studies in response to requests coming from the member churches, which were taken up by the decision making bodies;

- studies were successful in so far as they did not pretend to lead to a WCC position taken by the Central Committee, but rather provided information and considerations for careful discussions by the member churches together and in their different cultural contexts.

The WCC has functioned well as a space for facilitating and enabling the dialogue on issues related to human sexuality.

From Canberra to Harare

In the period since the Canberra Assembly, the issue of homosexuality progressively has taken center stage. Gay and Lesbian Caucus met during the Canberra Assembly and drafted a letter to the new moderator of Central Committee asking that work on sexual orientation be transferred from Family Life Education to Justice Unit. The decisive turning point was, however, the 1994 Central Committee meeting in Johannesburg. The Unit III Committee report was hotly debated in the plenary in response to references to violence against women, particularly lesbians. The announcement of Harare as the venue for the Eighth Assembly prompted a Dutch journalist at a press conference to raise the question about reports of police in Zimbabwe randomly arresting gays in the streets of Harare. As the preparations for the Harare Assembly got underway, the WCC was increasingly confronted with strong reactions from gay groups and gay-friendly churches, condemning the fact that the Zimbabwe government continued to attack homosexuals in the country as a severe violation of human rights.

A first staff workshop, facilitated by former WCC staff member Alan Brash, was organized in July 1995. Alan Brash also produced a statement on the issues at stake that was later published in the Risk Series under the title *Facing Our Differences*.

In December 1996 the Orthodox-Protestant dialogue in Antelias spent much time on the sexual orientation issue and agreed on the human rights aspects of the issue. This was, however, later challenged by Orthodox as well as by some Protestant voices in the WCC, prompting a WCC human rights consultation in 1998 to reject any reference to sexual orientation in a document for Harare. On the other hand, the WCC received correspondence from some member churches emphasizing the human rights aspect, particularly the United Church of Christ in USA and the Evangelical Lutheran Church in the Kingdom of The Netherlands; the latter church subsequently withdrew from participation in the Harare Assembly.

A small consultation in 1997 in Geneva underlined that issues of human sexuality were already on the agenda of many of the member churches and that the different approaches and positions taken posed serious new challenges to the quest for the visible unity of the church. Contributions to this consultation were published by *The Ecumenical Review* in 1998. This constructive ecumenical approach to the issue was strengthened by the idea to prepare Padare1 sessions on sexual orientation that would allow for mutual encounter and discussion in a safe environment.

The workshops in Harare, on sexual orientation were experienced by most of the participants as a helpful contribution by the WCC to create a space for dialogue. This became even more important after the very difficult experience of the Lambeth Conference of the Anglican communion, which rather deepened the differences and divisions within the Anglican Communion on sexual orientation. As in other churches, the focus on a decision by a decision-making body or an authoritative statement on the issues at stake proved to be mostly counterproductive. The approach of creating an enabling ecumenical space for mutual encounter, analysis and dialogue seems to be more promising.

Based on the Padare sessions at Harare the Programme Guidelines recommended to the assembly a shift of focus from sexual orientation to human sexuality. The Programme Guidelines Committee report emphasized the need for the WCC to address issues of personal and interpersonal ethics. It noted:

As we stand at the dawn of a new millennium, one of the most significant tasks for the churches will be to address the contemporary ethical issues growing out of the enormous advances in fields such as genetic engineering and electronic communication. Issues of personal and interpersonal ethics must also be addressed. The WCC should offer space and direction for conversation and consultation enabling member churches to discuss these difficult issues—including human sexuality—which cause division within and among its member churches. This conversation must build on the shared theological and hermeneutical reflection that has informed earlier ecumenical ethical discussions on issues such as racism.

With the ecumenical map changing rapidly, the WCC must continue to encourage and support bilateral and multilateral discussion on local and regional levels, offering space for reflection, conversation and evaluation of progress and process for those actively on the road to unity." (Excerpts from the programme guidelines report, Harare Assembly)

The assembly further urged the WCC "to engage in a study of human sexuality, in all of its diversity, to be made available for member churches."

Post-Harare Developments and Achievements

Further reflections on the recommendations by the Programme Committee convinced the Council that the process should move beyond stating the issue as merely a difficult one to be avoided because of potential conflict or divisions, to a situation in which spaces are opened up for discussion, debate, analysis and action. It is apparent that, because of the openness that has developed in some churches, there is less denial of the importance of the issues and their impact on members of the community and churches. There is more clarity on methods of how to talk about human sexuality. Many member churches are involved in discussions of different aspects of human sexuality although it has to be noted that few have yet moved to specific programme or educational work.

At the Harare Assembly it was clear that the churches did not feel it appropriate to establish a specific programme on human sexuality. The mandate of the Assembly was not to start a programme but to "provide space" through which the member churches are enabled to discuss the difficult issues related to human sexuality. For this reason the general secretary, with the support of the WCC Officers, decided to approach the issue in the following way.

A. Reference Group on Human Sexuality

The General Secretary invited a number of representatives from member churches to form a WCC Reference Group on Human Sexuality. The terms of reference of the group are:

- To advise the general secretary on the development and content of the WCC work related to human sexuality, taking into account the link with all other areas of WCC work that have bearing on the implementation of the governing bodies' recommendations.
- To advise and accompany the WCC's Human Sexuality Staff Group in carrying out the recommendations of the WCC governing bodies, helping to evaluate its work and offering advice on further development of the work.
- To ensure the participation of representatives from WCC member churches in their confessional, cultural and religious diversity.

The group met on several occasions - November 2000, July 2001 and April 2003 in Geneva. The work done includes:

- Followed up on WCC programmatic work linked to the issue of human sexuality
- Set up a list server (e-mail group) for sharing ideas and information within the Reference and Staff Groups
- Developed a timeline of work up to the 2006 Ninth General Assembly
- Provided a detailed analysis of the church statements received and preparation of the Bossey Seminar 2001 following the WCC General Secretary's invitation to all WCC member churches to submit their official statements on all aspects of human sexuality. (see below for further details).
- Reviewed a congregational study guide prepared by the Anglican Diocese of Johannesburg, South Africa.
- Gathered substantive theological, pastoral and ethical reflections for publication in a Study Guide to be completed by June 2004.
- Gathered stories from the regions for a Risk Book to be published in 2006
- Regional seminars were organised (2003–2004) on biblical texts, similar to the third Bossey seminar, in Asia (Bangalore, India), Lebanon, Fiji, Nairobi, Latin America and the Caribbean, North America, and Europe in preparation for the plenary presentation to the WCC CC in August 2005. One member of the reference group organized the meeting and another one from outside the region participated.

B. Staff group on human sexuality

The General Secretary appointed a Human Sexuality Staff Group within WCC. The terms of reference for the group requires that it "develop a process that responds to the mandate from the Assembly (which shall be facilitated) in ways which will enable the member churches to engage in dialogue with one another as well as with congregations."

Both groups have been engaged in exploring questions of human sexuality so as to offer advice to him on these issues. The staff group has worked on

- Publishing two articles in the July 2002 issue (Volume 54, Number 3) of *The Ecumenical Review*:

  "Reclaiming the Sacredness and the Beauty of the Body: The Sexual Abuse of Women and children from a church Leader's Perspective" by David Coles

  "The Body as Hermeneutical Category: Guidelines for a Feminist Hermeneutics of Liberation" by Nancy Cardoso Pereira

- Publishing of a theme issue on "Human Sexuality": *The Ecumenical Review* October 2004 (Volume 56, Number 4)
- Compilation of a bibliography on human sexuality issues.
- Linking the issue of human sexuality to WCC programmatic work (see following section).
- Review of a study guide on Human Sexuality, prepared by the Anglican Diocese of Johannesburg.
- Preparation of an informal hearing session on Human Sexuality at the August 2002 Central Committee and for a Plenary Hearing at the Central Committee of 2005.
- Preparing and acting as an advisory body for planning the Bossey Seminars on human sexuality (see section on Bossey below).
- Facilitated archiving of materials - in Spring 2002 materials and correspondence relating to these issues, especially leading up to the General Assembly in Harare, were properly archived and lodged in the WCC library. This represents nearly nine years of exploring appropriate and effective ways and methods of discussing and addressing the issues involved.

C. Review of Church Statements on Human Sexuality:
Recognising that several churches around the world were wrestling with different dimensions of the issues surrounding human sexuality, the Reference Group decided to analyse what the churches have said on the issue.

Therefore in 2001, the General Secretary of the WCC sent a letter to the churches calling on them to share with the WCC their statements and actions on the issue. Over 60 documents were received and range from reports to resolutions to recommendations. These were collated and summarized by the Reference Group members. It was acknowledged that there are serious gaps in the information received from the churches—there are very few received from churches in Asia, Africa, Middle East, the Pacific or Latin America, or from the family of the Orthodox churches.

What is significant is that almost every document that was received from the churches is meant for study and further reflection and dialogue within the church and therefore does not claim to possess the status of official church positions. While the reviewed documents clearly reflect a plurality of approaches vis a vis their theological, ethical and heremeutical methodology—they do share certain features. "For instance, almost all statements acknowledge the existence of some real discontinuity between "traditional" church positions on human sexuality and the actual reality "out there". Most statements consider the Bible as the main foundation for ethical decision- making, albeit in different ways and with various emphases. Except for a few statements, the vast majority of the church documents tend to adopt a humble approach by recognizing the need for further study and reflection on this highly sensitive issue of human sexuality. Yet the most glaring aspect of these documents is their diversity." (Fr. George Mathew Nalunakkal from the Reference Group who helped review the statements.)

The documents received from the churches can be found in the WCC Library in the archives.

D. The Bossey Seminars

By providing a laboratory for testing and further developing the approach chosen by the Programme Guidelines Committee and the Reference Group, the three Bossey Seminars became the most comprehensive contribution to the process in the period between the WCC Assemblies in Harare and Porto Alegre. All three seminars were introduced by a meditation on the theme of **pilgrimage**. In terms of methodology, the seminars were also facilitated by a professional from outside WCC who tested the consensus of the group all the way through each meeting in order to allow for development to take place. At the beginning all the participants were invited to make a contract of confidentiality, attentiveness to the process and honoring of the others' convictions.

The **first seminar** (July 2001) invited a broad range of participants from various regions to share their cultural, local and global perspectives on human sexuality. The participants expressed that the best kind of theology emerges from real life experience in relation to sacred traditional theology. The degree to which the individual participants were able to reach openness and vulnerability determined the quality of shared reflection and theologizing. Many participants experienced the pressure of their local culture very strongly. The interaction of culture with practice, faith and scripture was an enduring concern. Human sexuality is not just about matters of same-sex sexuality as it has often arisen in ecumenical discussions. Rather, human sexuality is very basic to all human beings and affects them often at points of extreme vulnerability.

Personal stories of pain, guilt, celebration were shared within a confidential sharing space in the Bossey seminar where people spoke voluntarily of their lives of engagement with infidelity, failures of sex lives in marriages and relationships, identity questions, and a panoply of other experiences. These experiences could not be categorized along the lines of gender, orientation, and culture. instead, they were marked by openness and became encounters with sacred humanness. Traditional sexual ethics are inadequate because a) they themselves are flawed, and b) they are inadequate to deal with the new world that the people of God find themselves in. A new practice and theology of sexuality need to be forged. This theology needs to reclaim the theology of the body and to practice pastoral care and approaches that are more appropriate for the varied human sexual experiences.

Regional experiences were shared. In Sub-Saharan Africa, widespread concern was expressed concerning patriarchal gender differentiation and human rights violation of women particularly on cultural/ritual control of women's sexualities and violence against women. For many African women, "the marriage certificate is a death certificate." Sexual networking, polygamy, and other sexual practices spread HIV/AIDS like wildfire in the continent. The use of condom continues to be a church issue that is hotly debated. In Asia, colonization brought massive repression of traditional expressions of sacred sexualities. Globalization promotes commodification of the body, particularly of women and children and gives rise to issues of injustice. In North America and Western Europe, post-modernity has a huge impact on sexual practices. Debates on homosexuality are dominant in church discussions. There is a deep sense of the pain of family rejection. Violence against women, abuse of children and rising divorce rates are still major problems. In all regions, churches are in a position of silence and shame about sexuality, and sexuality exclusive to marriage is fundamentally challenged.

The **second Bossey seminar** (April 2002) dealt with the summary and analysis of church statements collated by the international Reference Group. The statements identified the issues and approaches the churches were struggling with. The participants discovered the gaps between church statements and lived realities and that most of the responses are from the north. Two inputs on confessional perspectives were given by the Finnish Orthodox Church and United Methodist Church, USA. While various forms of life in communities were celebrated, the dimensions of challenges in human sexuality varied in different communities—monastic communities, mixed marriages, marriages within the traditional faith communities, gay and lesbian communities. There were painful moments created by hardening of church positions on human sexuality. Other issues and responses presented during the seminar were HIV/AIDS pandemic in Africa and responses of non-governmental organizations, and sexual abuse among clergy or church leaders and a church response from Aotearoa-New Zealand.

The **third Bossey seminar** (April 2003) focused on Bible studies. Three approaches were used in the study of the Bible—body of Christ, pilgrimage and Trinity. The study of the Bible and the sharing from confessional perspectives provided a lively entry point in identifying issues on human sexuality that had not been explored in the past. These situations have arisen from the realization that family structures or patterns are changing. There is an increasing number of mother-headed families where the male role has become irrelevant, causing fathers to be thrown out of the homes; more people would like to remain single or get married but not raise children. In Africa, because of AIDS, families are beginning to be left to the care of grandmothers and even children as parents die of AIDS. In Europe and North America gay and lesbian communities would like to raise their own children through adoptions or through children they brought from previous relationships, or through in-vitro fertilization. Other issues identified were disabilities and sexuality, polygamy, fidelity, extra marital and pre-marital sex, homosexuality, abortion and contraception. The participants affirmed the sharing of stories and challenged the prescriptive and normative model of engaging in the issues of human sexuality. The participants affirmed an enabling and facilitating approach to theology, ethics, and Bible studies in dealing with the varied dimensions of human sexuality. They affirmed the nature of theology that is provisional, that shows signposts along the life journey, that is not prescriptive. There is a need to explore eschatological reversal and counter-culture as another lens in reading the Bible.

E. Work on HIV/AIDS

Churches engaged early with HIV/AIDS, and many have excellent care, education and counseling programs. But the challenge to the churches is felt at a deeper level than this. As the pandemic has unfolded, it has exposed fault lines that reach to the heart of our theology, our ethics, our liturgy and our practice of ministry. Today, churches are being obliged to acknowledge that they have—however unwittingly—contributed both actively and passively to the spread of the virus. The difficulty in addressing issues of sex and sexuality has often made it painful to engage, in any honest and realistic way, with issues of sex education and HIV prevention. The tendency to exclude others and certain interpretations of the scriptures have combined to promote the stigmatization, exclusion and suffering of people with HIV or AIDS. This has undermined the effectiveness of care, education and prevention efforts and inflicted additional suffering on those already affected by the HIV. Given the extreme urgency of the situation, and the conviction that the churches do have a distinctive role to play in the response to the epidemic, what is needed is a rethinking of the mission, and the transformation of structures and ways of working.

The work on curricula for theological education that has begun has identified the need for more positive affirmation of the human body and of sexual relationships. The issue of Human Sexuality has been substantively incorporated into the Ecumenical HIV & AIDS training programmes for Theological Institutions and also the programmes of Theological Education by extension, especially in Africa. More resources material have been prepared and more training opportunities have been made available through the various regional HIV & AIDS Initiatives- in the different regions of the world. HIV/AIDS provides an opportunity for the churches to engage more openly and in a pastoral way with issues of human sexuality.

F. Violence against Women

The issue of violence against women has been on the agenda of the WCC for over a decade now. In their analysis of this violence, women today increasingly make a link with issues related to human sexuality and violence. Whenever there is war or conflict, there is reference to rape and other acts of sexual violence against women. What makes this even more difficult to bear is the evidences of sexual violence against women and children even in refugees centers in the hands of humanitarian aid workers. But sexual violence against women is a reality in times of peace, too.

Regrettably, sexual violence takes place even in the so-called safe environment of the church. Recent revelations of sexual abuse by clergy show it to be a closely guarded secret that happens in many churches in all parts of the world. Women in the WCC constituency also point to the violence that lesbian women experience in most societies. All this has made women identify more clearly the link between the violence they experience and their sexuality. The WCC is committed to working with women in challenging the churches to speak out more clearly on these issues and to offer solidarity and pastoral support to women who experience violence.

G. Other important contributions

Links continue to be made between the Reference Group and current WCC programmes through the work of the staff group on

- theological anthropology
- ETE (Ecumenical Theological Education) curricula
- EDAN (Ecumenical Disabilities Advocacy Network)
- Biotechnology

In the process of this work WCC has established contact with church related organizations addressing issues of human sexuality in their own contexts (e.g., the European Forum of Lesbian and Gay Christian Groups Assembly in Spring 2003). One way of linking such organizations within and between regions is to facilitate participation of individuals from other contexts. Reports and experiences of the participants at these events will contribute to the data that the WCC is collecting and will be shared with the churches and others who express interest.

The Programme Committee report to the 1999 meeting of the Central Committee stated that "new attention is needed to the spiritual dimensions of caring for life, particularly as they relate to ethical questions arising from bio-technology, birth control, abortion and human sexuality."

The Reference Group hopes that from the work done, the churches will be helped to realize that the issues of human sexuality that members are wrestling with are not only about homosexuality. There are diversities in human sexual experience that should be celebrated and addressed through open spaces for discussion.

H. Central Committee, February 2005

The Reference Group on Human Sexuality reported to the Central Committee (Feb. 2005) on the steps that have been taken in response to the Eighth Assembly mandate to create the climate for a discussion on human sexuality. It affirmed both the complexity of the discussions and the variety of church positions and discussions.

"The reference group has reflected on a broad spectrum of issues on human sexuality and brings it now to the attention of the Central Committee. The issues raised are questions of justice in human relationship and call for a redemptive approach of healing and reconciliation." (Dr. Erlinda Senturias, Moderator, Reference Group.)

It was acknowledged that the two important contributions made by the WCC in this process are:

i.) The review of Church Statements which affirm the diversity of positions among the churches and the series of three seminars held at the Ecumenical Institute in Bossey described earlier which provided a methodology of respect for diversity, sensitivity and an atmosphere of dialogue.

ii.) The Bossey seminars offered a safe space and encouraged the sharing of experiences. "The interaction of culture with practice, faith and scripture was an enduring concern. The Church, among other institutions, is faced with sensitive issues such as HIV and AIDS, marriage instability, sexual abuse and questions concerning sexual orientation. In all regions, churches seem to struggle with a position of silence and shame about sexuality and with the fact that sexuality exclusive to marriage is fundamentally challenged. The degree to which the individual participants were able to open themselves up to the others in accepting their own vulnerability and respecting the vulnerability of the others determined the quality of shared reflection and theologizing. The participants underlined that the best kind of theology emerges from real life experience in relation to sacred traditional theology." (Valburga Striek)

The Central Committee called for pastoral wisdom in dealing with the difficult and even divisive ethical questions posed to the churches by issues of human sexuality.

In table discussions CC members shared some of the challenges faced in their own church contexts. This hearing plenary of the Central Committee, within a mode of consensus, paved the way for a continuing discussion among the churches.

Some Conclusions

There have been many contacts and inquiries from member churches and groups in churches asking for more information on human sexuality to enrich their own discussions. Some of these discussions have been provoked partly through discussions on HIV/AIDS, partly through educational curricula and, not least, because it is one of the human rights issues currently on the agenda in many communities and churches.

Three insights seem to be central throughout the journey of the WCC's response to issues of human sexuality:

- to concentrate on the mainstreaming of positions and the production of authoritative statements is obviously counterproductive and deepens the rifts within and among churches; there is a need for ecumenical spaces for encounter, analysis, dialogue and education following an enabling and pastoral approach to the issues at stake;
- to neglect the diversity of contexts and the different issues that are of concern for the churches in different regions is not helpful; the recommendation of the Harare Programme Guidelines Committee to move from sexual orientation to human sexuality in its rich diversity provided useful guidance;
- the entry point should always be the celebration of the gift of life and human bodies instead of a narrow focus on normative and prescriptive guidelines.

As a global fellowship of churches the WCC is in a unique situation to engage member churches holding different views and positions on human sexuality. By not being part of the local and national church scene the WCC is privileged to offer a space for fruitful encounter rather than being directly involved in the immediate debates. The churches' response to the request of the WCC general secretary has made the Council a trusted custodian of the diverse church perspectives on the issue. This challenges the WCC to develop the capacity for listening and hearing different church voices telling different but authentic stories and experiences.

One of the fruits of this capacity to listen and discern is the Council's growing ability to challenge and help the churches to overcome the syndrome of denial—at least as is evidenced by the outcome of the three Bossey seminars that were organized to follow up the recommendations by the Programme Guideline Committee. This may be a huge step forward towards a better understanding and higher level of mutual acceptability.

The WCC also plays an important role in communicating to the wider fellowship what the churches are saying and doing about the issue of human sexuality. In this way the Council brings churches into living contacts with each other on this otherwise potentially dividing issue and offers the global ecumenical platform to deal with it responsibly.

Through involvement in this issue the WCC is becoming a fellowship of churches in a deeper sense—it is being seen as a brother and sister ("fellow") to those who are otherwise feeling alienated and excluded from their fellowship and ecclesial community.

The Ninth Assembly in Porto Alegre in February 2006, will have an ecumenical conversation on the issue and workshops in the mutirão so that the dialogue can continue.

Selection 5: Margaret Farley, *Just Love: A Framework for Christian Sexual Ethics*

Margaret Farley, Order of the Sisters of Mercy, is the Gilbert L. Stark Professor of Christian Ethics emerita at the Yale Divinity School. A feminist ethicist, she has written on a variety of subjects including notable work in medical ethics. Her 2006 book Just Love *has received wide acclaim and wide use in churches and schools. Notwithstanding the challenges to traditional sexual morality in the present day—which Farley discusses thoroughly in her book—there is still a need for norms that can (arguably) keep faith with a Christian perspective on sexual relationships. Farley's use of norms of justice speaks to both the human community in general and the ethos of Christian love in particular.*

Norms for Just Sex

Some preliminary clarifications are important for understanding the specific norms for a sexual ethic. First, the norms that I have in mind are not merely ideals; they are bottom-line requirements. Second, and as a qualification of the first, all of these norms admit of degrees. This means that there is a sense in which they are stringent requirements, but they are also ideals. In both senses, they are all part of justice. That is, they can be understood in different contexts as norms of what I shall call "minimal" or "maximal" justice. While minimal justice is always required, maximal justice can go beyond this to what is "fitting." Maximal justice may, in fact, point to an ideal that exceeds the exacting requirement of minimal justice. Third, the specific norms are not mutually exclusive. Although each of them emphasizes something the others do not, they nonetheless overlap enough that, as we shall see, some sexual behaviors and relationships are governed by more than one norm. Fourth, since humans are embodied spirits, inspirited bodies, theirs is an embodied autonomy and an embodied relationality. The norms that I will lay out, therefore, are to be understood as requiring respect for an embodied as well as inspirited reality. I turn now to the specific norms that I propose for a contemporary human and Christian sexual ethic.

1. Do No Unjust Harm

The first general ethical norm we may identify is the obligation not to harm persons unjustly. This is grounded in both of the obligating features of personhood, for it is because persons are persons that we experience awe of one another and the obligation of respect. "Do no harm" echoes through the experience of "do not kill" the other. To harm persons may be to violate who they are as ends in themselves. But there are many forms that harm can take—physical, psychological, spiritual, relational. It can also take the form of failure to support, to assist, to care for, to honor, in ways that are required by reason of context and relationship. I include all of these forms in this norm.

In the sexual sphere, "do no unjust harm" takes on particular significance. Here each person is vulnerable in ways that go deep within. As Karen Lebacqz has said, "Sexuality has to do with vulnerability. Eros, the desire for another, the passion that accompanies the wish for sexual expression, makes one vulnerable . . . capable of being wounded. And how may we be wounded or harmed? We know the myriad ways. Precisely because sexuality is so intimate to persons, vulnerability exists in our embodiment and in the depths of our spirits. Desires for pleasure and for power can become bludgeons in sexual relations. As inspirited bodies we are vulnerable to sexual exploitation, battering, rape, enslavement, and negligence regarding what we know we must do for sex to be "safe sex." As embodied spirits we are vulnerable to deceit, betrayal, disparity in committed loves, debilitating "bonds" of desire, seduction, the pain of unfulfillment. We have seen in previous chapters the role sex can play in conflict, the ways in which it is connected with shame, the potential it has for instrumentalization and objectification. We have also seen human vulnerability in the context of gender exclusionary practices and gender judgments: "Terrible things are done to those who deviate."

Actions and social arrangements that are typically thought to be harmful in the sexual sphere include all forms of violence, as well as pornography, prostitution, sexual harassment, pedophilia, sadomasochism. Most of these are controversial today, so that they cannot be rejected out of hand, judged without assessment of their injustice or justice. Many of these are governed by other principles for a sexual ethic that we have yet to explore. I will therefore return to them again, though all too briefly, placing them in the whole of the framework for sexual ethics that I am proposing.

"Do no unjust harm" goes a long way toward specifying a sexual ethic, but not far enough. It is necessary to identify additional principles for a sexual ethic that aims to take account of the complex concrete realities of persons. I said above that autonomy and relationality, two equally primordial features of human persons, provide the ground and the content for sexual ethics. They provide a ground or basis, as we have seen, for the principle that forbids unjustifiable harm. Together they yield six more specific and positive norms: a requirement of free choice, based on the requirement to respect persons' autonomy, and five further norms that derive from the requirement of respect for persons' relationality. Hence, we move from our first norm, "do no unjust harm" to a second norm for a sexual ethic: freedom of choice.

2. Free Consent

We have already seen the importance of freedom of freedom (autonomy, or a capacity for self-determination) as a ground for a general obligation to respect persons as ends in themselves. This capacity for self-determination, however, also undergirds a more specific norm. The requirement articulated in this norm is all the more grave because it directly safeguards the autonomy of persons as embodied and inspirited, as transcendent and free. I refer here to the particular obligation to respect the right of human persons to determine their own actions and their relationships in the sexual sphere of their lives. This right or this obligation to respect individual autonomy sets a minimum but absolute requirement for the free consent of sexual partners. This means, of course, that rap, violence, or any harmful use of power against unwilling victims is never justified. Moreover, seduction and manipulation of persons who have limited capacity for choice because of immaturity, special dependency, or loss of ordinary power, are ruled out. The requirement of free consent, then, opposes sexual harassment, pedophilia, and other instances of disrespect for persons' capacity for, and right to, freedom of choice.

Derivative from the obligation to respect free consent on the part of sexual partners are also other ethical norms such as a requirement for truth-telling, promise-keeping, and respect for privacy. Privacy, despite contentions over its legal meanings, requires respect for what today is named "bodily integrity." "Do not touch, invade, or use" is the requirement unless an individual freely consents. What this recognizes is that respect for embodied freedom is necessary if there is to be respect for the intimacy of the sexual self.

Whatever other rationales can be given for principles of truth-telling and promise-keeping, their violation limits and hence hinders the freedom of choice of the other person: deception and betrayal are ultimately coercive. If I lie to you, or dissemble when it comes to communicating my intentions and desires, and you act on the basis of what I have told you, I have limited your options and hence in an important sense coerced you. Similarly, if I make a promise to you with no intention of keeping the promise, and you make decisions on the basis of this promise, I have deceived, coerced, and betrayed you. Along with the requirement of free consent, then, these other obligations belong to a sexual ethic as well.

Relationality, I have argued, is equiprimordial with autonomy as an essential feature of human personhood, and along with autonomy grounds the obligation to respect persons as ends in themselves. Like autonomy, relationality does more than ground obligations to respect persons as persons, it specifies the content of this obligation. To treat persons as ends and not as mere means includes respecting their capacities and needs for relationship. Sexual activity and sexual pleasure are instruments and modes of relation; they can enhance relationships or hinder them, contribute to them and express them. Sexual activity and pleasure are optional goods for human persons in the sense that they are not absolute, peremptory goods which could never be subordinated to other goods, or for the sake of other goods be let go, but they are, or certainly can be, very great goods, mediating relationality and the general well-being of persons.

Hence, insofar as one person is sexually active in relation to another, sex must not violate relationality, but serve it. Another way of saying this is that it is not sufficient to respect the free choice of sexual partners. In addition to "do no harm" and the requirement of free consent, relationality as a characteristic of human persons yields five specific norms for sexual activity and sexual relationships: mutuality, equality, commitment, fruitfulness, and what I will designate in general terms, "social justice." For an adequate contemporary sexual ethic, we need to explore the meaning and implications of each of these norms.

3. Mutuality

Respect for persons together in sexual activity requires mutuality of participation. It is easy for us today to sing the songs of mutuality in celebration of sexual love. We are in disbelief when we learn that it has not always been so. Yet traditional interpretations of heterosexual sex are steeped in images of the male as active and the female passive, the woman as receptacle and the man as fulfiller, the woman as ground and the man as seed. No other interpretation of the polarity between the sexes has had so long and deep-seated an influence on men's and women's self-understandings. Today we think such descriptions quaint or appalling, and we recognize the danger in them. For despite the seeming contradiction between the active/passive model of sexual relations and the sometime interpretations of women's sexuality as insatiable, the model formed imaginations, actions and roles which in turn determined that he who embodied the active principle was greater than she who simply waited—for sex, for gestation, for birthing which was not of her doing and not under her control.

Today we believe we have a completely different view. We have learned that male and female reproductive organs do not signal activity only for one and passivity for the other, nor do universalizable male and female character traits signal this. We can even appreciate all the ways in which, even at the physical level, men's bodies receive, encircle, embrace, and all the ways women's bodies are active, giving, penetrating. Today we also know that the possibilities of mutuality exist for many forms of relationship—whether heterosexual or gay, whether with genital sex or the multiple other ways of embodying our desires and our loves. The key for us has become not activity/passivity but active receptivity and receptive activity—each partner active, each one receptive. Activity and receptivity partake of one another, so that activity can be a response to something received (like loveliness), and receptivity can be a kind of activity, as in "receiving" a guest.

Underlying the norm of mutuality is a view of sexual desire that does not see it as a search only for the pleasure to be found in the relief of libidinal tension, although it may include this. Human sexuality, rather, because it is fundamentally relational, seeks ultimately what contemporary philosophers have called a "double reciprocal incarnation," or mutuality of desire and embodied union. No one can deny that sex may, in fact, serve many functions and be motivated by many kinds of desire. Nonetheless, central to its meaning, necessary for its fulfillment, and normative for its morality when it is within an interpersonal relation is some form and degree of mutuality.

Yet we have learned to be cautious before too high a rhetoric of mutuality, too many songs in praise of it. Like active/passive relations, mutuality, too, has its dangers. Insofar as, for example, we assume it requires total and utter self-disclosure, we know that harm lurks unless sexual relations have matured into justifiable and mutual trust. Insofar as we think that sex is just and good only if mutuality is perfected, we know that personal incapacities large and small can undercut it. We know that patience, as well as trust, and perhaps unconditional love are all needed for mutuality to become what we dream it can be. But what is asked of us, demanded of us, for the mutuality of a one night stand, or of a short-term affair, or of a lifetime of committed love, differs in kind and degree.

Indeed, the mutuality that makes sexual love and activity just (and, one must add, that makes for "good sex" in the colloquial sense of the term) can be expressed in many ways, and it does admit of degrees. No matter what, however, it entails some degree of mutuality in the attitudes and actions of both partners. It entails some form of activity and receptivity, giving and receiving—two sides of one shared reality on the part of and within both persons. It requires, to some degree, mutuality of desire, action, and response. Two liberties meet, two bodies meet, two hearts come together—metaphorical and real descriptions of sexual mutuality. Part of each person's ethical task, or the shared task in each relationship, is to determine the threshold at which this norm must be respected, and below which it is violated.

4. Equality

Our considerations of mutuality lead to yet another norm that is based on respect for relationality. Free choice and mutuality are not sufficient to respect persons in sexual relations. A condition for real freedom and a necessary qualification of mutuality is equality. The equality that is at stake here is equality of power. Major inequalities in social and economic status, age and maturity, professional identity, interpretations of gender roles, and so forth, can render sexual relations inappropriate and unethical primarily because they entail power inequalities—and hence, unequal vulnerability, dependence, and limitation of options. The requirement of equality, like the requirement of free consent, rules out treating a partner as property, a commodity, or an element in market exchange. Jean-Paul Sartre describes, for example, a supposedly free and mutual exchange between persons, but an exchange marked by unacknowledged domination and subordination: "It is just that one of them pretends . . . not to notice that the Other is forced by the constraint of needs to sell himself as a material object."

Of course here, too, equality need not be, may seldom be, perfect equality. Nonetheless, it has to be close enough, balanced enough, for each to appreciate the uniqueness and difference of the other, and for each to respect one another as ends in themselves. If the power differential is too great, dependency will limit freedom, and mutuality will go awry. This norm, like the others, can illuminate the injury or evil that characterizes situations of sexual harassment, psychological and physical abuse, at least some forms of prostitution, and loss of self in a process that might have led to genuine love.

5. Commitment

Strong arguments can be made for a fifth norm in sexual ethics, also derivative of a responsibility for relationality. At the heart of the Christian community's understanding of the place of sexuality in human and Christian life has been the notion that some form of commitment, some form of covenant or at last contract, must characterize relations that include a sexual dimension. In the past, this commitment, of course, was largely identified with heterosexual marriage. It was tied to the need for a procreative order and a discipline of unruly sexual desire. It was valued more for the sake of family arrangements than for the sake of the individuals themselves. Even when it was valued in itself as a realization of the life of the church in relation to Jesus Christ, it carried what today are unwanted connotations of inequality in relations between men and women. It is possible, nonetheless, that when all meanings of commitment in sexual relations are sifted, we are left with powerful reasons to retain it as an ethical norm.

As we have already noted, contemporary understandings of sexuality point to different possibilities for sex than were seen in the past—possibilities of growth in the human person, personal garnering of creative power with sexuality as a dimension not an obstacle, and the mediation of human relationship. On the other hand, no one argues that sex necessarily leads to creative power in the individual or depth of union between persons. Sexual desire left to itself does not seem able even to sustain its own ardor. In the past, persons feared that sexual desire would be too great; in the present, the rise of impotency and sexual boredom makes persons more likely to fear that sexual desire will be too little. There is growing evidence that sex is neither the indomitable drive that early Christians (and others) thought it was nor the primordial impulse of early psychoanalytic theory. When it was culturally repressed, it seemed an inexhaustible power, underlying other motivations, always struggling to express itself in one way or another. Now that it is less repressed, more and more free and in the open, it is easier to see other complex motivations behind it, and to recognize its inability in and of itself to satisfy the affective yearning of persons. More and more readily comes the conclusion drawn by many that sexual desire without interpersonal love leads to disappointment and a growing disillusionment. The other side of this conclusion is that sexuality is an expression of something beyond itself. Its power is a power for union, and its desire is a desire for intimacy.

One of the central insights from contemporary ethical reflection on sexuality is that norms of justice cannot have as their whole goal to set limits to the power and expression of human sexuality. Sexuality is of such importance in human life that it needs to be nurtured, sustained, as well as disciplined, channeled, controlled. There appear to be at least two ways which persons have found to keep alive the power of sexual desire within them. One is through novelty of persons with whom they are in sexual relation. Moving from one partner to another prevents boredom, sustains sexual interest and the possibility of pleasure. A second way is through relationship extended sufficiently through time to allow the incorporation of sexuality into a shared life and an enduring love. The second way seems possible only through commitment.

Both sobering evidence of the inability of persons to blend their lives together, and weariness with the high rhetoric that has traditionally surrounded human covenants, yield a contemporary reluctance to evaluate the two ways of sustaining sexual desire and living sexual union. At the very least it may be said, however, that although brief encounters open a lover to relation, they cannot mediate the kind of union—of knowing and being known, loving and being loved—for which human relationality offers the potential. Moreover, the pursuit of multiple relations precisely for the sake of sustaining sexual desire risks violating the norms of free consent and mutuality, risks measuring others as apt means to our own ends, and risks inner disconnection from any kind of life-process of our own or in relation with others. Discrete moments of union are not valueless (though they may be so, and may even be disvalues), but they can serve to isolate us from others and from ourselves.

On the other hand, there is reason to believe that sexuality can be the object of commitment, that sexual desire can be incorporated into a covenanted love without distortion or loss, but rather, with gain, with enhancement. Given all the caution learned from contemporary experience, we may still hope that our freedom is sufficiently powerful to gather up our love and give it a future; that thereby our sexual desire can be nurtured into a tenderness that has not forgotten passion. We may still believe that to try to use our freedom in this way is to be faithful to the love that arises in us or even the yearning that rises from us. Rhetoric should be limited regarding commitment, however, for particular forms of commitment are themselves only means, not ends. As Robin Morgan notes regarding the possibility of process only with an enduring relation, "Commitment gives you the leverage to bring about change—and the time in which to do it."

A Christian sexual ethic, then, may well identify commitment as a norm for sexual relations and activity. Even if commitment is only required in the form of a commitment not to harm one's partner, and a commitment to free consent, mutuality, and equality (as I have described these above), it is reasonable and necessary. More than this, however, is necessary if our concerns are for the wholeness of the human person—for a way of living that is conducive to the integration of all of life's important aspects, and for the fulfillment of sexual desire in the highest forms of friendship. Given these concerns, the norm must be a committed love.

6. Fruitfulness

A sixth norm derivative from the obligating feature of relationality is what I call "fruitfulness." Although the traditional procreative norm of sexual relations and activity no longer holds absolute sway in Christian sexual ethics in either Protestant or Roman Catholic traditions, there remains a special concern for responsible reproduction of the human species. Traditional arguments that if there is sex it must be procreative have changed to arguments that if sex is procreative it must be within a context that assures responsible care of offspring. The connection between sex and reproduction is a powerful one, for it allows individuals to reproduce and to build families, it allows a sharing of life full enough to issue in new lives, and it allows the human species to perpetuate itself. Relationality in the form of sexual reproduction, moreover, does not end with the birth of children; it stretches to include the rearing of children, the initiation of new generations into a culture and civilization, and the ongoing building of the human community.

At first glance, it appears that "procreation" belongs only to, is only possible for, some persons; and even for them, it has come to seem quite optional. How, then, can it constitute a norm for sexual activity and relations? Even if it were recognized as a norm for fertile heterosexual couples, what would this mean for infertile heterosexual couples or for heterosexual couples who choose not to have children, for gays and lesbians, for single persons, for ambiguously gendered persons? For these other individuals and partners, would it signal, as it has in the past, a lesser form of sex and lesser forms of sexual relationships? Or is it possible that a norm of fruitfulness can and ought to characterize all sexual relationships?

It is certainly true that all persons can participate in the rearing of new generations; and some of those who cannot reproduce in traditional ways do even have their own biological children by means of the growing array of reproductive technologies—from infertility treatments to artificial insemination to in vitro fertilization to surrogate mothering. All of this is not only true but significant. Yet an ethically normative claim on sexual partners to reproduce in any of these ways seems unwarranted.

Something more is at stake. Beyond the kind of fruitfulness that brings forth biological children, there is a kind of fruitfulness that is a measure, perhaps, of all interpersonal love. Love between persons violates relationality if it closes in upon itself and refuses to open to a wider community of persons. Without fruitfulness of some kind, any significant interpersonal love (not only sexual love) becomes an égoisme à deux. If it is completely sterile in every way, it threatens the love and the relationship itself. But love brings new life to those who love. The new life within the relationship of those who share it may move beyond itself in countless ways; nourishing other relationships; providing goods, services, and beauty for others; informing the fruitful work lives of the partners in relations; helping to raise other people's children; and on and on. All of these ways and more may constitute the fruit of a love for which persons in relations are responsible. A just love requires the recognition of this as the potentiality of lovers; and it affirms it, each for the other, both together in the fecundity of their love. Interpersonal love, then, and perhaps in a special way, sexual love insofar as it is just, must be fruitful.

The articulation of this norm, however, moves us to another perspective in the development of a sexual ethic. There are obligations in justice that the wider community owes to those who choose sexual relationships. Hence, our final norm is of a different kind.

7. Social Justice

This norm derives from our obligation to respect relationality, but not only from this. It derives more generally from the obligation to respect all persons as ends in themselves, to respect their autonomy and relationality, and this not to harm them but to support them. A social justice norm in the context of sexual ethics relates not specifically to the justice between sexual partners. It points to the kind of justice that everyone in a community or society is obligated to affirm for its members as sexual beings. Whether persons are single or married, gay or straight, bisexual or ambiguously gendered, old or young, abled or challenged in the ordinary forms of sexual expression, they have claims to respect from the Christian community as well as the wider society. These are claims to freedom from unjust harm, equal protection under the law, an equitable share in the goods and services available to others, and freedom of choice in their sexual lives—within the limits of not harming or infringing on the just claims of the concrete realities of others. Whatever the sexual status of persons, their needs for incorporation into the community, for psychic security and basic well-being, make the same claims for social cooperation among us as do those of us all. This is why I call the final norm "social justice." If our loves for one another are to be just, then this norm obligates us all.

There is one way in which, of course, this norm qualifies sexual relationships themselves, obligating sexual partners as well as the community around them. That is, sexual partners have always to be concerned about not harming "third parties." As Annette Baier observes, "in love there are always third parties, future lovers, children who may be born to one of the lovers, their lovers and their children." At the very least, a form of 'social justice" requires of sexual partners that they take responsibility for the consequences of their love and their sexual activity—whether the consequences are pregnancy and children, violation of the claims that others may have on each of them, public health concerns, and so forth. No love, or at least no great love, is just for "the two of us," so that even failure to share in some way beyond the two of us the fruits of love may be a failure in justice.

My focus in articulating this norm, however, is primarily on the larger social world in which sexual relationships are formed and sustained. It includes, therefore, the sorts of concerns I identified above, but larger concerns as well. A case in point is the struggle for gender equality and (in particular) women's rights in our own society and around the world. This is relevant to the sexual ethic I am proposing because it has a great deal to do with respect for gender and sexuality as it is lived in concrete contexts of sexual and gender injustice.

Here we could identify numerous other issues of utmost importance. Sexual and domestic violence might head the list, both at home and abroad. But it would include also racial violence that is perpetrated on men and women and that all too often has to do with false sexual stereotypes. Development, globalization, and gender bias would be high on the list of the issues I have in mind. The myths and doctrines of religious and cultural traditions that reinforce gender bias and unjust constriction of gender roles become important here as well. Included, too, must be the disproportionate burden that women bear in the world-wide AIDS pandemic.

We have already seen in the previous chapter the kinds of injustices inflicted on persons whose gender and sexuality do not fall into the usual categories. We should add issues surrounding the explosion of reproductive technologies—many of which have proven to offer a great benefit for individuals, but many of which remain questionable, such as technologies for sex-selection. Other issues also require moral assessment, such as the availability (or not) of contraceptives, and the repercussions for some women of the marketing of male remedies for impotence. It is neither possible nor necessary to detail all of these issues here. My point is only that they, too, fall within the concerns of an adequate human and Christian sexual ethic. They signal social and communal obligations not to harm one another unjustly and to support one another in what is necessary for basic well-being and a reasonable level of human flourishing for all. These obligations stretch to a common good—one that encompasses the sexual sphere along with the other significant spheres of human life.

In summary, what I have tried to offer here is a framework for sexual ethics based on norms of justice—those norms which govern all human relationships and those which are particular to the intimacy of sexual relations. Most generally, the norms derive from the concrete reality of persons and are focused on respect for their autonomy and relationality. This is to respect persons as ends in themselves. It yields an injunction to do no unjust harm to persons. It also yields specifications both of what it means to respect autonomy and relationality and what it means to do no harm. Autonomy is to be respected through a requirement of free consent from sexual partners, with related requirements for truthtelling, promise-keeping, and respect for privacy. Relationality is to be respected through requirements of mutuality, equality, commitment, fruitfulness, and social justice.

Even more specifically, we may in terms of this framework say things like: sex should not be used in ways that exploit, objectify, or dominate; rape, violence, and harmful uses of power in sexual relationships are ruled out; freedom, wholeness, intimacy, pleasure are values to be affirmed in relationships marked by mutuality, equality, and some form of commitment; sexual relations like other profound interpersonal relations can and ought to be fruitful both within and beyond the relationship; the affections of desire and love that bring about and sustain sexual relationships are all in all genuinely to affirm both lover and beloved.

I recognize full well that it is not an easy task to introduce considerations of justice into every sexual relation and the evaluation of every sexual activity. Critical questions remain unanswered, and serious disagreements are all too frequent, regarding the concrete reality of persons and the meanings of sexuality. What can be normative and what exceptional—that is, what is governed by the norms I have identified and what can be exceptions to these norms—is sometimes a matter of all too delicate judgment. But if sexuality is to be creative and not destructive in personal and social relationships, then there is no substitute for discerning ever more carefully the norms whereby it will be just.

ENVIRONMENTAL ETHICS   39

❧ *Since the mid-twentieth century up to the present, the fate of the environment has become an international concern for scientists, philosophers, public policy makers, non-governmental organizations, and no less theologians and ethicists who have given expression to this urgent issue for Christian social teaching.*

Selection 1: Joseph Sittler, "Called to Unity" (1962)

Contributions to Christian social teaching in the area of environmental ethics would not be complete without recognition of the pioneering work of Joseph Sittler (1904–1987). This brief excerpt from his famous speech to the 1962 New Delhi assembly of the World Council of Churches grounds the care of creation in Christology, thereby drawing the environmental obligations of the Christian churches into the center of the faith; the unity of church and the unity of all things are centered in the cosmic Christ.

He is the image of the invisible God, the firstborn of all creation; for him all things were created, in heaven and on earth, visible and invisible, whether thrones or dominions or principalities or authorities—all things were created through him and for him. He is before all things, and in him all things hold together. He is the head of the body, the church; he is the beginning, the firstborn from the dead, that in everything he might be preeminent. For in him all the fullness of God was pleased to dwell, and through him to reconcile to himself all things, whether on earth or in heaven, making peace by the blood of his cross. Colossians 1:15-20

There are two reasons for placing these five verses from the Colossian letter at the beginning of what I wish to say about the unity of Christ's Church. (1) These verses say clearly *that* we are called to unity, and (2) they suggest *how* the gift of that unity may be waiting for our obedience.

These verses say that we are called to unity, that the One who calls us is God, that this relentless calling persists over and through all discouragements, false starts, and sometimes apparently fruitless efforts; it is these verses that have engendered the ecumenical movement among the churches and steadily sustain them in it.

These verses sing out their triumphant and alluring music between two huge and steady poles—"Christ," and "all Things." Even the Ephesian letter, rich and large as it is in its vision of the church moves not within so massive an orbit as this astounding statement of the purpose of God. For it is here declared that the sweep of God's restorative action in Christ is no smaller than the six-times repeated *ta pant*. Redemption is the name for this will, this action, and this concrete man who is God with us and God for us—and all things are permeable to his cosmic redemption because all things subsist in him. He comes to all things, not as a stranger, for he is the firstborn of all creation, and in him all things were created. He is not only the matrix and *prius* of things; he is the intention, the fullness, and the integrity of all things: For all things were created through him and for him. Nor are all things a rumbled multitude of facts in an unrelated mass, for in him all things hold together.

Why does St. Paul, in this letter, as in the letter to the Ephesians, expand his vocabulary so radically far beyond his usual terms? Why do the terms guilt, sin, the law, and the entire Judaic catalogue of demonic powers here suddenly become transposed into another vocabulary, general in its character, cosmic in its scope, so vastly referential as to fill with Christic energy and substance the farthest outreach of metaphysical speculation?

The apostle does that out of the same practical pastoral ardor as caused him, when he wrote to his Philippian community, to enclose a deceptive petty problem of human recalcitrance within the overwhelming therapy of grace. Just as selfishness and conceit in Philippi are drowned in the sea of the divine charity "found in human form . . . humbled himself and became obedient unto death, even the death of the cross,"—so here. The Colossian error was to assume that there were "thrones, dominions, principalities and authorities" which have a life and power apart from Christ, that the real world was a dualism, one part of which (and that part ensconcing the power of evil) was not subject to the Lordship of the Creator in his Christ.

Against that error which, had it persisted, would have trapped Christ within terms of purely moral and spiritual power and hope, Paul sets off a kind of chain reaction for the central atom, and the staccato ring of *ta panta* is the sounding of its reverberations into the farthest reaches of human fact, event, and thought. All is claimed for God, and all is Christic. The fugue-like voices of the separate claims—of him, in him, through him, for him—are gathered up the quiet coda—"For in him all the fullness of God was pleased to dwell."

We must not fail to see the nature and the size of the issue that Paul confronts and encloses in this vast Christology. In propositional form it is simply this: A doctrine of redemption is meaningful only when it swings with the larger orbit of a doctrine of creation. For God's creation of earth cannot be redeemed in any intelligible sense of the word apart from a doctrine of the cosmos which is his home, his definite place, the theater of his selfhood under God, in cooperation with his neighbor, and in caring relationship with nature, his sister.

> Unless one is prepared to accept a dualism which condemns the whole physical order as being not of God and interprets redemption simply as release from the physical order, then one is forced to raise the question of cosmic redemption, not in contrast with but as an implication of personal redemption. Physical nature cannot be treated as an indifferent factor—as the mere

stage and setting of the drama of personal redemption. It must either be condemned as it itself evil, or else it must be brought within the scope of God's redemptive act.

Unless the reference and the power of the redemptive act includes the whole of man's experience and environment, straight out to its farthest horizon, then the redemption is incomplete. There is and will always remain something of evil to be overcome. And more. The actual man in his existence will be tempted to reduce the redemption of man, to what purgation, transformation, forgiveness, and blessedness is available by an "angelic" escape from the cosmos of natural and historical fact—and in the option accept some sort of dualism which is as offensive to biblical theology as it is beloved of all Gnosticism, then as now.

*   *   *

The Split between Grace and Nature in Western Thought

The doctrinal cleavage, particularly fateful in western Christendom, has been an element in the inability of the church to relate the powers of grace to the vitalities and processes of nature. At the very time, and in that very part of the world where men's minds were being deepeningly determined by their understanding and widened control of the powers of nature they were so identifying the realm of history and the moral as the sole realm of grace as to shrink to no effect the biblical Christology of nature. In the midst of vast changes in man's relation to nature the sovereignty and scope of grace was, indeed, attested and liberated by the Reformers. But post-Reformation consolidations of their teaching permitted their Christic recovery of all of nature as a realm of grace to slip back into a minor theme.

In the Enlightenment the process was completed. Rationalism, on the one hand, restricted redemption by grace to the moral soul, and Pietism, on the other hand, turned down the blaze of the Colossian vision so radically that its ta panta was effective only as a moral or mystical incandescence. Enlightenment man could move in on the realm of nature and virtually take it over because grace had either ignored or repudiated it. A bit of God died with each new natural conquest; the realm of grace retreated as more of the structure and process of nature was claimed by not autonomous man. The rood-screen in the Church, apart from its original meaning, has become a symbol of man's devout but frightened thought permitting to fall asunder what God joined together.

*   *   *

Claiming Nature for Christ

Is it possible to fashion a theology catholic enough to affirm redemption's force enfolding nature, as we have affirmed redemption's force enfolding history? That we should make that effort is, in my understanding, the commanding task of this moment in our common history. And by common history I refer to that which is common to all of the blessed obediences of the household of faith: Antioch and Aldersgate, Constantinople and Canterbury, Geneva and Augsburg, Westminster and Plymouth.

For the problem which first drove the Church, as our text reminds us, to utter a Christology of such amplitude is a problem that has persisted and presses upon us today with absolute urgency. We are being driven to claim the world of nature for God's Christ just as in the time of Augustine that Church was driven to claim the world of history as the city of God, for his Lordship and purpose. For fifteen centuries the Church has declared the power of grace to conquer egocentricity, to expose idolatry, to inform the drama of history with holy meaning. But in our time we have beheld the vision and promises of the Enlightenment come to strange and awesome maturity. The cleavage between grace and nature is complete. Man's identity had been shrunken to the dimensions of privatude within social determinism. The doctrine of the creation has been made a devout datum of past time. The mathematization of meaning in technology and its reduction to operational terms in philosophy has left no mental space wherein to declare that nature, as well as history, is the theater of grace and the scope of redemption.

When millions of the world's people, inside the church and outside of it, know that damnation now threatens nature as absolutely as it has always threatened men and societies in history, it is not likely that witness to a light that does not enfold and illumine the world-as-nature will be even comprehensible. For the root-pathos of our time is the struggle by the peoples of the world dominions, principalities" which restrict and ravage human life.

If, to this longing of all men everywhere we are to propose "Him of whom, and through whom, and in whom are all thing," then that proposal must be made in redemptive terms that are forged in the furnace of man's crucial engagement with nature as both potential to blessedness and potential to hell.

The matter might be put another way: The address of Christian thought is most weak precisely where man's ache is most strong. We have had, and have, a Christology of the moral soul, a Christology of history, and, if not a Christology of the ontic, affirmations so huge as to fill the space marked out by ontological questions. But we do not have, at least not in such effective force as to have engaged the thought of the common life, a daring, penetrating, life-affirming Christology of nature. The theological magnificence of cosmic Christology lies, for the most part, still tightly folded in the Church's innermost heart and memory. Its power is nascent among us all in our several styles of preaching, teaching, worship its waiting potency in available for release in kerygmatic theology, in moral theology, in liturgical theology, in sacramental theology. And the fact that our separate traditions inclines us to one another of these as central does not diminish either the fact, or our responsibility. For it is true of us all that the imperial vision of Christ as coherent in ta panta had not broken open the powers of grace to diagnose, judge, and heal the ways of men as they blasphemously strut about this hurt and threatened world as if they owned it. Our vocabulary of praise has become personal, pastoral, too purely spiritual, static. We have not affirmed as inherent in Christ—God's proper man for man's proper selfhood and society—the world political, the world economical, the world aesthetic, and all other commanded orderings of actuality which flow from the ancient summons to tend this garden of the Lord. When atoms are disposable to the ultimate hurt then the very atoms must be reclaimed for God and his will.

*   *   *

It is the thesis of this address that our moment in history is heavy with the imperative that faith proposes for the madly malleable and grandly possible potencies of nature—that holiest, vastest, confession: That by him, for him, and through him all things subsist in God, and therefore are to be used in joy and sanity for his human family.

The Church is both thrust and lured towards unity. The thrust is from behind and within: It is grounded in God's will and promise. The lure is God's same will and promise operating upon the Church from the needs of history within which she lives her life. The thrust of the will and the promise is a steady force in the Church's memory: The lure is and the promise is a steady force in the Church's memory: The lure is clamant in the convulsions that twist our times in the Church's present. The way forward is from Christology expanded to its cosmic dimensions, made passionate by the pathos of this threatened earth, and made ethical by the love and wrath of God. For as it was said in the beginning that God beheld all things and declared them good, so it was uttered by an angel in the apocalypse of St. John, ". . . ascending from the east, having the seal of the living God: and he cried with a loud voice to the four angels, to whom it was given to hurt the earth and the sea, saying, Hurt not the earth neither the sea, nor the trees . . ." (Revelation 7:2-3, KJV). The care of the earth, the realm of nature as a theater of grace, the ordering of the thick, material procedures that make available to or deprive men of bread and peace—these are Christological obediences before they are practical necessities.

Selection 2: Larry L. Rasmussen, "Is Eco-Justice Central to Christian Faith?" *Earth Community, Earth Ethics*

> *Larry L. Rasmussen is the Reinhold Niebuhr Professor of Social Ethics Emeritus at Union Theological Seminary in New York. His book* Earth Community, Earth Ethics *won the coveted Grawenmeyer Award in Religion in 1997. His theme in that book, which links human community and care of the earth as essential to environmental wholeness, is echoed in this more recent article. Here Rasmussen raises the crucial question for Christian faith and ethics regarding the centrality of eco-justice in faith and practice. The challenge is reminiscent of Sittler's claim that care for creation is a Christic obligation (see above).*

The mission of the churches beyond 2000 is to help create community among structured enemies in a shared but humanly dominated biosphere. The task is reconciling and reconciled socioenvironmental community. And the obstacle is not diversity, bio- or otherwise. It is injustice, moral privilege, and moral exclusion, just as it is also a cosmology that fails to understand community comprehensively—the sociocommunal, biophysical, and geoplanetary together.

Such reconciling and reconciled local "Earth" community is in fact the only community that genuinely saves, whether the dividing lines of hostility be racial-ethnic, gendered, sexual, class-borne, species-borne, national, or cultural. Such community is the only truly redeemed community, the only expression of genuinely "new creation." Community is not reformed or redeemed, if, to recall Jesus's words, we only love redundantly, if we love only those who like us and who are like us. But such community is a work of art far more difficult than present language lets on. Exuberant declarations "celebrating" differences and "embracing" community cover harsher realities. Ask Carl Lee Haley. Or, if you could, ask those species now extinct at human hands.

"Eco-justice" is one way to name the moral norm and goal. "The Community of Life" is another way to name it, "Earth Community" yet another. Until we register this moral universe and this notion of community in our explication of incarnation, creation, and redemption, eco-justice will not be central to Christian faith.

*   *   *

More specifically, what would community spiritual-moral formation for such comprehensive community mean for churches working together with other institutions and movements? It would mean a different "social" Christianity as well as a different "ecological" one. Most simply put, it would require shedding the remnants of complex domination systems that have oppressed both peoples and land and sea. There are assumptions necessary to this task. While not all of them can be elaborated here, at least the following must be included.

- Until matters of "eco-justice" are seen to rest somewhere near the heart of Christian faith, "the environment" will be relegated to the long list of important "issues" clamoring for people's attention. The proper subject of justice is not only society. Nor is it "the environment." It is "creation" as Earth—the more-than-human and human, together, Carl Lee Haley and Jake Bregenz and their daughters and all those creatures and eco-systems in the Museum of Natural History.
- Differently said, all creation has standing before God and is the object of redemption. Creation's well-being rests at the center, not the edge, of Christian moral responsibility and practices, liturgical and contemplative practices included. The theological line of thought should not run "God—Church—World" but "God—Cosmos—Earth—Church."
- A significant work for Christian communities for the foreseeable future is adapting their major teachings and practices—the "deep traditions" of Christianity, together with its reading of Scripture—to the task of revaluing nature/culture together so as to prevent their destruction and contribute to their sustainability.
- There are no pristine Christian traditions for this task. This means that conversions to Earth on the part of Christianity are crucial to Christianity's

part in the interreligious, pan-human vocation of Earthkeeping. "Conversion" here means what it has commonly meant in religious experience, namely, both a break with the past and yet a preservation of essential trajectories; both a rupture and new direction, yet a sense that the new place is also "home" or truly "home"; both a rejection of elements of tradition yet the making of new tradition in fulfillment of the old; both difference from what has gone before and solidarity with it. Substantively, "conversion to Earth" means measuring all Christian impulses by one stringent criterion: their contribution to Earth's well-being.

- A valorizing of Christina pluralism is necessary and desirable. It is necessary for the sake of the integrity of diverse Christian traditions themselves. They are many, they are wildly different from one another, even in the same family, and they ought to be treated in ways that even in the same family, and they ought to be treated in ways that honor their genealogy and merit the respect and recognition of their devotees. "Catholicity" is the name for the nature of the church as the community of churches, present and past, that manifest the ecumenical range of historically incarnate faiths lived across two millennia on most of Earth's continents. Such catholicity is inherently plural; it can only exist as internally diverse. A faithful remembering of the Christian past thus means respecting and retrieving this variety. This is not—to point up the contrast—"faithfulness" in the manner of imperial Christianities large and small, which consists in the selective forgetting or repression of this variety, usually in the name of theological heresy, moral or cultural deviance.

- Valorizing Christian pluralism is desirable for another reason. The "eco-crisis" is comprehensive of nature and culture together. No one tradition, religious or secular, can satisfactorily address the full range of matters that require planetary attention. It is therefore necessary to think ecologically about ecumenism and ecumenically about ecological well-being.

The effort to offer a different Christian cosmology and moral universe from the assumptions and vignettes just enumerated, one in accord with "eco-justice," has been made in recent years by World Council of Churches work on justice, peace, and creation. There the metaphor of the whole household of God—Earth as *oikos*—has been developed so as to integrate these plural concerns within the same cosmological-theological-moral frame of reference. Ernst Conradie's summary is a succinct way of reporting this effort and gathering the interlocking elements of the single creational household. World Council emphases have been these: "1) the integrity of the biophysical foundations of this house (the earth's biosphere); 2) the economic management of the household's affairs; 3) the need for peace and reconciliation amidst ethnic, religious and domestic violence within this single household; 4) a concern for issues of health and education; 5) the place of women and children within this household; 6) a 'theology of life' and recovery of indigenous peoples' voices and wisdom; and 7) an ecumenical sense of the unity not only of the church, but also of the human community as a whole and of all of God's creation, the whole inhabited world (*oikoumene*)."

With all this in place, we can say more about the kind of moral theory and moral formation necessary if eco-justice is to be central to Christian faith.

*   *   *

Part of this conversion is a reconstruction of the working moral notions that guide our sense of what is valued, how it is valued, and the actions deemed appropriate in light of ascribed value Mary Midgely takes up the tradition initially most prominent in the Anglo-Saxon world but now a part of the sweep of globalization; namely, the notion of life by implicit and explicit contract, a tradition identified with a list of influential thinkers from John Locke to John Rawls. But before her discussion I interject a note from living influences often associated with Kant and Descartes. What these share that continues to be reflected in the way we live our daily lives is the Enlightenment turn to the human subject as the sole subject of morality and religion, a turn that, I add, builds upon medieval Catholicism's and the Protestant Reformation's obsession with the standing of the naked human subject in guilt before God, and which then built upon the Protestant Reformation's distinction, in its doctrine of justification by grace through faith, between the person and the person's works, a distinction that asserted individual dignity as given by God in Christ. As noted earlier from Barbour's summary, salvation and redemption are intensely personal here; but they are not communal and cosmic. This helps prepare for an Enlightenment narrative that understands humanity as a species apart, just as it fails to block a rendering of the rest of nature in Cartesian and Kantian terms. Kant himself was utterly clear about the radical turn to the human subject and its solitary status: "Animals are not self-conscious and are there merely as a means to an end. That end is man." As we noted, Kant might have gone another direction. In awe of "the moral law within and the starry heavens without," he chose only "within." Interestingly, and fatefully, Descartes, too, could have gone another direction and did not. In his famous *Discourse on Method and Meditations*, Descartes says there are two possible sources of a practical philosophy based in certain knowledge. It will be knowledge "I . . . find within myself, or perhaps the great book of nature." He then forgets the latter and, like Kant and the fabled turn to the human subject of Western Enlightenment thought, gives centrality to the nature and resources of the autonomous, rational, individual self, with reliable knowledge rooted in human subjectivity. He also regarded other creatures as automatons, organic machines of a sort, without consciousness and feeling, not to say reason. Thus it came to be that even the venerable traditions of "natural law" and "natural rights" do not include the laws and rights of nature, but the laws and rights of humans alone. Nature, when it is there, is an array of raw material serving active, purposive human subjects. This is, as many have pointed out, a notion that beautifully serves the narrative of the new economy, capitalism, where nature is rendered as resources available for human transformation through labor. This is where and how value itself comes to nature, namely, by way of its service to humankind and its transformation by humankind.

Yet, it is not truly even "humankind," of course, nor genuine "homocentricity" in ethics. Women and children, indigenous peoples and peoples of color, Jews, Muslims, and slaves did not share equal rights even when Enlightenment rights and law language was "universal" in voice. Still, the point is that even when the scope of rights and the domain of moral law comes to claim a wider range of human subjects as deepseated gentlemanly prejudices against slaves, women, and non-Western peoples and religions are combated in the name of a more genuine and hard-won universalism, that scope stops short of other members in the Community of Life. Thus even such a treasure as the Universal Declaration of Human Rights assumes a universe of morally self-sufficient human beings ranged over against passive nature. Dignity is ascribed to humans, and properly so, but to naught else. That Christians did not clamor in protest, "but ALL creation has standing in, with, and before God" is, in retrospect, one of our gravest sins of the modern era. We, too, performed the magic of the incredible shrinking cosmos and left no one standing, morally speaking, other than God and these curious "birds without feathers," as one ancient wag described us.

But if the way of Kantian duty and the genuine achievement of human rights discourse does not set us on the path of righteousness for the great work, what about that strongest tradition of all, social contract theory? We got off on the wrong path with "physics envy" as Locke and capitalism modeled social contract theory on seventeenth-century Newtonian science. Human society and its ways of spelling out obligation—duty, right, justice, law, morality—were the product of free contract between rational individual agents as though these agents were separate, distinct, independent atoms who relate not by nature but by choice. Our animal and biophysical nature is split off in a way that parallels Descartes' reduction of trustworthy reality to the conscious human mind, and—this is key—we have no duties to non-contractors. The Yahwist's insistence that we, as all else, are creatures of the soil, Adam from Adama, is simply gone in the Christian versions of this, as is the theocentric universe of medieval cosmology, with all nature alive as an ocean of symbols linking earth to heaven and a fecund expression of living, divine emanation.

Mary Midgley, in "Duties Concerning Island," has performed the useful service of listing those who are left out of this moral universe of rational contracting agents but to whom, she argues, we have non-contractual obligation. It turns out that social contract morality omits a great deal that keeps much of the world humming in this era of globalization. Here is the list: our ancestors are omitted, as are posterity, children, the senile, the temporarily insane, the permanently insane, so-called "defectives," ranging down to "human vegetables, embryos, sentient animals, nonsentient animals, plants of all kinds, artifacts, including works of art, inanimate but structured objects—rivers, rock, crystals, etc., unchosen groups of all kinds, including families and species, ecosystems, landscapes, villages, warrens, cities, etc., countries, the biosphere, oneself and God. "As far as the numbers go," Midgley says in her understated way, "this is no minority of the beings with whom we have to deal." In short, our most commonly utilized moral apparatus simply leaves out the greater part of our actual communities and obligations. The sharp antithesis Kant and Descartes drew between living persons and all else, or Locke between the contracts of rational agents with one another and all else, simply fails as a guide for the morality that must of needs "arise out of our membership in complex biological and ecological communities that are to a great extent invisible to us" but of which we are part, upon which our lives and other lives depend utterly, and which we impact fatefully. As David Toolan nicely puts it, "we are literally parented by these ecosystems," but we render them no due. "Eco-justice" is the name of the moral universe that renders them their due.

*   *   *

The four interactive norms of eco-justice that flow from our discussion but that are formulated by Hessel are: (a) solidarity with other people and creatures in Earth community; (b) ecological sustainability, i.e., environmentally-fitting habits that enable life to flourish; (c) sufficiency as a standard of organized sharing; (d) socially just participation in decisions about how to obtain sustenance and manage the common good. These are genuinely public norms, whose appeal is to all persons of good will. Yet the point here is that they belong to Christian faith as an Earth-honoring faith whose boundaries and substance encompass, on both core confessional and utterly practical grounds, the whole Community of Life. They are thus central to that faith.

Selection 3: Sallie McFague, *The Body of God: An Ecological Theology*

Sallie McFague (b. 1933) is E. Rhodes and Leona B. Carpenter Professor of Theology Emerita at Vanderbilt University and Distinguished Theologian in Residence at Vancouver School of Theology. The first paragraph of our excerpt captures the thrust of the book's title and perspective. An additional theme contributing to the discourse of eco-justice is the powerful notion of the environment as among the "poor" with whom Christians are called to unite in solidarity.

The Shape of the Body: The Christic Paradigm

In this and the following sections on the shape and scope of the body, we will be suggesting two interrelated moves in regard to Christology: the first is to relativize the incarnation in relation to Jesus of Nazareth and the second is to maximize it in relation to the cosmos. In other words, the proposal is to consider Jesus as paradigmatic of what we find everywhere: everything that is is the sacrament of God (the universe as God's body), but here and there we find that presence erupting in special ways. Jesus is one such place for Christians, but there are other paradigmatic persons and events—and the natural world, in a way different from the self-conscious openness to God that persons display, is also a marvelous sacrament in its diversity and richness.

But if knowing and doing are embodied, are concrete and particular, as we have assumed throughout this essay, then we must begin with the story of Jesus, not with everything that is. We stand within particular historical, cultural communities and see the world through those perspectives. We gain our hints and clues, our metaphors of reality, through formative traditions that we also are called upon to re-form. Our first step, then, is to read the central story of Christian faith from the perspective of the organic model. The Christic paradigm must precede the cosmic Christ; the hints and clues for an embodied theology should arise from the particular, concrete insights and continuities of the tradition's basic story This in no way privileges Scripture as the first or last word, but only as the touchstone text that Christians return to as a resource (not the source) for helping them to construct for their own time the distinctiveness of their way of being in the world.

Christianity's Distinctive Embodiment: Inclusion of the Neglected Oppressed

The point at issue is distinctive embodiment; that is, what does, could, Christian faith have to say that is special, important, different, illuminating about embodiment—in relation to God, to ourselves, and to the natural world? Religious traditions will say many and different things about embodiment, and, as scholars have reminded us, Eastern, Goddess, and Native traditions, to mention a few, may say more and better things than does the Christian tradition. The question, however, for those of us who choose to remain Christian is, What does, can, the Christian faith contribute to an embodied theology, to an ecological sensibility?

*　　*　　*

What does Christian faith, and especially the story of Jesus, have to offer in terms of a distinctive perspective on embodiment? What is the shape that it suggests for God's body, the universe, enlivened by the breath of God's spirit? Christianity is par excellence the religion of the incarnation and, in one sense, is about nothing but embodiment, as is evident in its major doctrines. In another sense, as we noted earlier, Christianity has denied, subjugated, and at times despised the body, especially female human bodies and bodies in the natural world. This is not the place for a treatise on the sorry history of Christianity's treatment of bodies or even on the rich complexities of various incarnational theologies such as those of Paul, John, Irenaeus, certain medieval mystics, and so on. I want to make a more simple, direct proposal: *The story of Jesus suggests that the shape of God's body includes all, especially the needy and outcast.* While there are many distinctive features of the Christian notion of embodiment, in an ecological age when the development of our sensibility concerning the vulnerability and destruction of nonhuman creatures and the natural environment is critical, we ought to focus on one: the inclusion of the neglected oppressed—the planet itself and its many different creatures, including outcast human ones. The distinctive characteristic of Christian embodiment is its focus on oppressed, vulnerable, suffering *bodies*, those who are in pain due to the indifference or greed of the more powerful. In an ecological age, this ought to include oppressed nonhuman animals and the earth itself.

We need to pause and consider this suggestion, for it is shocking by conventional human standards. Until recently, most people found the notion that the earth is vulnerable, that its many species as well as the ecosystems supporting life are victims, are oppressed, absurd. And many still do. Many will even deny that the destabilizing love that we see in Jesus' parables, which overturns the conventional dualisms of rich and poor, righteous and sinner, Jew and Gentile, should include the dualism of humans over nature. And yet a cosmological or ecological perspective demands this radicalization of divine love: God's love is unlimited and oriented especially toward the oppressed—whoever the oppressed turn out to be at a particular time. The definition of who falls into this group has changed over the centuries, most recently focusing not on the spiritually poor, but the physically poor, those oppressed through the deprivation of bodily needs or through discrimination because of skin color or gender. Thus, the liberation theologies based on oppression due to poverty, race, or gender (and their interconnections) have arisen to claim that the gospel of Jesus of Naza-reth has a preferential option for the poor, the poor in body, those whose bodies and bodily needs are not included in the conventional hierarchy of value. These are bodies that are devalued, discarded, and destroyed; these are bodies that can claim no intrin-sic value in themselves but are of worth only because they are useful to others. In the organic model, bodies are basic, we have suggested, and how they are treated—how they are fed and housed, valued in their differences, honored in their integrity—is the primary issue. One of the most fundamental aspects of the story of Jesus, the love that overturns conventional dualistic hierarchies to reach out to the outcast and the victim, ought, we suggest, be extended to another dualistic hierarchy, that of human-ity over nature. Nature is the "new poor," and in an embodiment, organic perspective, this means bodily poverty.

It is important to be clear about this suggestion of nature as the new poor. It does not mean that the "old poor" —poor human beings—are being replaced, or that every microorganism is included in God's love in the same way as human beings are. It does, however, suggest that nature is the "also" poor, and that even microorganisms have their place in creation, a place that is not merely their usefulness (or threat) to human beings. There are two interrelated issues in the notion of nature as the new poor. The first is nature's value as such and to God; the second is its relation to human beings as well as what human beings are presently doing to nature. A statement from the World Council of Churches on the meaning of the phrase "the integrity of creation" is helpful here: "The value of all creatures in and for themselves, for one another, and for God, and their interconnectedness in a diverse whole that has unique value for God, together constitute the integrity of creation." This definition underscores the intrinsic value that each living being has in and for itself as a creature loved by God as well as the instrumental value that living beings have for one another and for God as parts of an evolutionary, weblike creation.

Intrinsic versus instrumental value is the critical issue. It means, quite simply, that other creatures as well as our planet as a whole were not created for our benefit, as we have already learned from the common creation story. Therefore, when we consider some part of it solely in terms of usefulness to ourselves as, for instance, in the metaphors of "silo" (food), "laboratory" (experimental material), "gymnasium" (recreation), or "cathedral" (spiritual uplift), we transgress "the integrity of creation." Nature as the new poor does not mean that we should sentimentalize nature or slip into such absurdities as speaking of "oppressed" mosquitoes or rocks. Rather, nature as the new poor means that we have made nature poor. It is a comment not about the workings of natural selection but of human sin. It is a hard, cold look at what one part of nature, we human beings, have done to the rest of it: we have broken the integrity of creation by the excesses of our population and life-style, by our utilitarian attitude toward other creatures as well as toward our own vulnerable sisters and brothers, by our refusal to acknowledge the value of each and every aspect of creation to itself and to God. Nature is not necessarily and as such poor; it is so only because of *one* species, our own, which threatens the vitality and viability of the rest of nature. To say that the inclusive love of Jesus' destabilizing parables ought to be extended to nature does not, then, imply a sentimental divine love for each and every cell or bacterium. Rather, it brings to mind the righteous judgment of the Creator whose body, composed of many valuable, diverse forms, is being diminished on our planet by one greedy, thoughtless, albeit self-conscious and hence responsible, part of that body—ourselves. It means that nature needs to be liberated and healed because we have enslaved it and made it sick. This perspective claims that in the twentieth century on our planet, human beings have caused nature to be the new poor in the same way that a small elite of the human population has created and continues to create the old poor—through a gross imbalance of the haves and have-nots. Those "other" people (the old poor) and nature (the new poor) are, in both cases, there "for our use."

Of course, all aspects of creation—including human beings—have instrumental as well as intrinsic value (we all live on top of, in between, and inside each other), but this cannot mean within the Hebrew and Christian traditions that *any* aspect of creation is nothing but fuel or fodder for others. The recognition of intrinsic value means, at the very least, that when we use other creatures for our benefit, we do so with humility, respect, and thanksgiving for these other lives. Moreover, to add nature as the new poor to God's inclusive love does not mean that each and every cell, elephant, or Douglas fir will thrive and prosper any more than it means that each and every poor human being does. In our complex world of natural selection, fortune and misfortune, human freedom as well as sin, nothing could be further from reality. It might mean, however, that we would look at nature with new eyes, not as something to be misused or even just used, but as our kin, that of which we are a part, with each creature seen as valuable in itself and to God. Indeed, we might see nature in our time as the new poor of Jesus' parables.

A cosmological and theocentric perspective—valuing the natural bodies around us because they are intrinsically worthwhile in themselves and to God, rather than for our purposes—is conventionally alien to us, but so is the overturning of the other hierarchies in the message of Jesus. The central claim of the gospel is, then, not only that the Word became flesh, but the particular shape that flesh took—one that presented a shock to our natural way of considering things in terms of value to ourselves. And for us to admit that nature is the "new poor" is also a direct affront to our anthropocentric sensibility. Our first response, in fact, might well be that such a radical perspective, a theocentric-cosmological one, is useless in light of the ecological crisis we face, where increasing numbers of poor, needy people *must* use the natural environment to provide for their own basic needs. We so not need to add yet another category of the oppressed, especially that of nature. But the shape of the body of God from a Christian perspective suggests otherwise. That shape, we have suggested, is given its basic outlines from one of the central features of Jesus' ministry—his destabilizing parables that side with the outcast. Extended to the natural world, to our planet and its many nonhuman creatures, the parabolic ministry of Jesus names a new poor, which is by definition poor in body, for those creatures and dimensions of our planet are primarily body. An incarnational religion, a bodily tradition, such as Christianity, should not have to strain to include the natural world and its creatures, for they epitomize the physical. They are, as it were, the *representative* bodies.

If we press this issue still further in light of other motifs in the ministry of Jesus—his healings and eating practices—we can develop our theme more deeply. Jesus' healing ministry has often been an embarrassment to the church, especially in light of the church's spiritualization of salvation; moreover, the healings appear to fall into the category of miracles and thus suggest a breaking of natural laws. But they are unmistakably central in all versions of Jesus' ministry, as central as the parables. As a symbol of focused concern, of what counts, the healing stories are crucial. We have suggested that in the organic model the body is the main attraction, and the healing stories seem to agree. Whatever else one wants to say about them, they focus attention on bodily pain and bodily relief. Since Christians understand Jesus of Nazareth as at least paradigmatic of God, that his ministry is a place to gain hints and clues about divine concern, then the centrality of the healing stories stands full square against any minimizing of the body. Bodies count, claims the healing ministry of Jesus, in the eyes of God. This perspective, of course, fits very well indeed with an ecological sensibility. It suggests that redemption should be enlarged to salvation: redemption means to "buy back" or "repay" through, for instance, a sacrifice, whereas salvation means healing of preserving from destruction. The first applies only to human beings who have offended (sinned) and hence need to be rescued through a substitutionary act of reconciliation, while the second can include the natural order, which, along with human beings, needs to be healed and preserved.

The healing metaphor for salvation is a modest claim. It does not suggest ecstatic fulfillment of all desires but rather preservation from destruction or, at most, the restoration to adequate bodily functioning. If the parables are the deconstructive phase of Jesus' ministry, overturning the oppressive, dualistic hierarchies, then the healing stories are the middle or reconstructive phase, not promising the kingdom but only what in ecological terms is called "sustainability," the ability to function in terms of bodily needs. The healings are a modest statement in light of the radical character of the parables. And yet, in another sense, at least in a cosmological or ecological context, they deepen the radicality of the parables, for they imply that bodily health and well-being is a priority of the gospel—and given the inclusiveness of the parabolic message and its bias toward the needy, this must mean not just human bodies but other vulnerable ones as well.

A third characteristic aspect of Jesus' ministry, his practice of eating with sinners, might be called the *prospective* phase, in contrast to the *deconstructive* (parables) and *reconstructive* (healing) dimensions. This practice was as much a scandal to Jesus' contemporaries as were the destabilizing parables and the miraculous healings. It is also, although for different reasons, scandalous to an ecological era. It suggests that all are invited to the banquet of life. In the stories of Jesus feeding the multitudes as well as in his unconventional invitations to the outcasts to share his table, two motifs emerge. First, whatever food there is, be it only a few loaves, should be shared and, second, is the hope of abundance, of a feast that satisfies the deepest hungers of all creatures, of all creation. One could say there is a minimal and a maximal vision: the exhortation that the basic needs of all creatures, including the most needy, be met from available resources, and the faith that the deepest needs will also be met in the future. By focusing on food, which, along with breath, is the most immediate and necessary component of bodily health, the motif of God's love for all, especially the outcast and the vulnerable, is deepened and radicalized. Moreover, the food imagery includes, without any additional explanation or rationalization, the nonhuman creatures and the plants of our planet. Food is basic to all life and is, increasingly, a symbol of the planet's crisis: the exponential growth of the human population and the life-style of some in that population at the expense of all other living things. So, this one metaphor of food includes not only what is most basic but also what is deepest. The eating practices and feeding stories of Jesus not only suggest a survival strategy for the diversity of life-forms, but also project a vision when all shall gather at one table—the lion, the lamb, and human beings—and eat their fill. It is a vision of salvation as wholeness, characterized not by the overcoming of differences, but by their acceptance and inclusion. Such visions have a prophetic edge, for they serve both as a critique of current practices as well as a goal toward which to strive. They are not, then, so much about the future as about the present; they propose an alternative to the present, not necessarily realizable but at least as giving a direction toward which to aim.

Jesus' eating stories and practices suggest that physical needs are basic and must be met—food is not a metaphor here but should be taken literally. All creatures deserve what is basic to bodily health. But food also serves as a metaphor of fulfillment at the deepest level of our longings and desires. The church picked up and developed the second, metaphorical emphasis, making eating imagery the ground of its vision of spiritual fulfillment, especially in the eucharist. But just as the tradition focused on the second birth (redemption), often neglecting the first birth (creation), so also it spiritualized hunger as the longing of the soul for God, conveniently forgetting the source of the metaphor in basic bodily needs. But the aspects of Jesus' ministry on which we have focused—the parables, healings, and eating stories—do not forget this dimension; in fact, Jesus' activities and message, according to this interpretation, are embarrassingly bodily. The parables focus on oppression that people feel due to their concrete, cultural setting, as servants rather than masters, poor rather than rich, Gentile rather than Jew; the healing stories are concerned with the bodily pain that some endure; the eating stories have to do with physical hunger and the humiliation of exclusion. None of these is primarily spiritual, though each assumes the psychosomatic unity of human nature and can serve as a symbol of eschatological fulfillment—the overcoming of all hierarchies, the health and harmony of the cosmos and al its creatures, the satiety of the deepest groanings and longings of creation.

Our focus, however, has been on the bodily basics, because the major established traditions within Christianity (except for sectarian, monastic, and now liberations theologies) have neglected them, and because it allows us to include human as well as planetary well-being. The shape, then, of God's body from some central motifs in the ministry of Jesus is one that includes the rich diversity of created forms, especially in regard to their basic needs for physical well-being. *The body of God must be fed.*

But even this exhortation, let alone the fulfillment of creation's deepest longings, is difficult, perhaps impossible, to bring about. We have suggested that the distinctive feature of a Christian view of embodiment is inclusion of the outcast and the oppressed. This is a scandal by conventional human standards and (here the issue deepens and darkens) in light of the process of natural selection in evolutionary biology. In neither framework do the vulnerable get the basics, let alone any glory.

Evolution and Solidarity with the Oppressed

We have looked at this scandal in terms of conventional human standards, but what of natural selection? What consonance can there possibly be between Christianity's inclusion of the outcasts of society, as well as our extension to include our vulnerable planet and its many creatures, and biological evolution, in which millions are wasted, individuals are sacrificed for the species, and even whole species are wiped out in the blinking of an eye? Does not the Christian overturning of hierarchies, the healing of bodies, and the concern with basics of life for all seem like an absurdity—or, at least, hopelessly naïve? Is there any fit between the distinctive embodiment perspective of

Jesus' ministry and the common creation story? The answer is both yes and no; there is both consonance and dissonance.

Jesus voiced the yes in the stories we have of his life and death: human beings can choose to side with the vulnerable and the outcast Evolution is not only or solely biological; it is also historical and cultural. Once evolutionary history reaches the human, self-conscious stage, natural selection is not the only operative principle, for natural selection can be countered with the principle of solidarity. The notion of siding with the vulnerable is not the sole insight of Christianity by any means. All human beings, despite the historically dismal record of slavery, oppression of women and homosexuals, and genocide, just to name a few of our more heinous crimes against the vulnerable, have, nonetheless, the option of deciding differently—and sometimes do. That is, once evolutionary history reaches the self-conscious level, other principles can function as to which individuals and species live and thrive. Cultural evolution can expand ethical regard to include more and more others besides the dominant males of a culture: women, people of all races and classes, the physically challenged, gays and lesbians—and even animals and the earth. This is a democratizing tendency that counters the fang and claw of genetic evolution as well as its two basic movers, chance and law. Human choice, the expansion of who survives and prospers, can and has enlarged the pool, so that, for instance, the physically challenged are not necessarily cast aside as they would be if only genetic selection were operative. Enlarging the pool, however, is often a minimal step, for we all know that equality for all does not follow. Ethical regard is practiced differently for African-Americans than for whites and for gays and lesbians than for heterosexuals.

Nonetheless, once the scales have fallen from our eyes and we recognize that human beings have reached a plateau where both choice and power are involved in who lives and how well they live, we see that cultural evolution is as (if not more) important than natural selection—at least on the planet at this time. We now know that natural selection is not the only principle: something else is possible. We know that the recognition of the intrinsic value of other life-forms is an alternative. Some form of this insight is evident in the practice of most cultures and religions, though which life-forms count varies enormously. The point is that some do; that is, all life-forms are not simply grist for the biological mill, as natural selection holds. The issue becomes, then, where one draws the line in terms of intrinsic value. The model of the universe as God's body, composed of billions of different bodies, implies that all are valuable. The theocentric-cosmocentric view implicit in the organic model is radically inclusive: God loves the entire creation and finds it valuable. The Christic paradigm suggests a further shaping of the body, with particular attention to those parts of the body that hitherto have been excluded by human sin. In this reading, Christianity intensifies a cultural process we find in many different forms and place in human history: a radicalization of intrinsic value that is counter to the principle of natural selection (and this occurred, of course, centuries before those principles were known).

Solidarity with the oppressed, then, becomes the Christian form of both consonance with and defiance of the evolutionary principle. It is consonant with it because it claims that there is a next stage of evolution on our planet, one that is not primarily genetic but cultural: the necessity, for survival and well-being, for all life-forms to share the basic goods of the planet. It is defiant of it because it suggests that the principle needed for this to occur is not natural selection or the survival of the fittest, but the solidarity of each with all. We have reached the point where war, ecological destruction, sexual and racial discrimination, poverty and homelessness, are counter-productive to planetary well-being. We have also reached the point where we realize that the interrelationships and interconnections among all forms of life are so deep, permanent, and mysterious that the various species of plants and animals need one another. But solidarity of each with all should perhaps remain at this utilitarian level: we need each other to survive. The scandal of Christianity goes further: it insists on solidarity with the outsider the outcast, the vulnerable. Does not this make Christian faith a surd, if not absurd, in view of postmodern science, rather than merely counter to it? Would not the planet be better off without these "outcast" types?

At this point, I believe we have no choice but to admit that the radical inclusiveness that is at the heart of Christian faith, especially inclusion of the oppressed, is not compatible with evolution, even cultural evolution. For as we have seen, its view of sinful human nature deepens the notion of the ecological sinner: the bloated self-refusing to share. Hence, even the best of cultural evolution, from a Christian perspective, is lacking, for we "naturally" construct our worlds to benefit ourselves, including only those who are useful to us. Christian solidarity with the oppressed, therefore, will have some special, peculiar characteristics that are both counterrevolutionary and countercultural. One form will entail resistance to evil or the liberation of the oppressed, and another will involve suffering with those who, nonetheless, suffer. The first form is the primary one, what we have discussed under the rubric of the embodiment ministry of Jesus—his parables, healings, and eating practices that attempt in deconstructive, reconstructive, and prospective ways to free suffering bodies and fulfill their needs. The second form, the suffering of God—and ourselves—with those who, nonetheless, suffer, recognizes that irremediable, unconscionable, unremitting, horrific suffering *does* occur both to individuals and to whole species, suffering that is beyond our best efforts to address and seemingly beyond God's as well.

In both forms of Christian solidarity with the oppressed, the active and the passive, liberation and suffering, the cross and resurrection of the Christic paradigm are central to an embodiment theology. The death of our natural, sinful preference for hierarchical dualisms that favor the wealthy, healthy, well-fed bodies is a necessary prerequisite in the embodiment ministry of Jesus. His parables, healing stories, and eating practices demand our deaths—just as the practice of his embodiment ministry also brought about his own death. Neither biological nor cultural evolution includes this radical next step of identification with the vulnerable and needy through the death of the self. What is clear in the New Testament stories of the Christic paradigm is that for those who respond to its call, the way of solidarity with the oppressed with demand the cross (in some form or another). What is less clear, but hinted at, is that *bodies*, all suffering bodies, will live again to see a new day. Regardless of the difficulty of imagining what resurrection might mean, then or now, what is clear is the focus on the body, the physical basis of life. Faith in the resurrection of the body is the belief that the spirit that empowers the universe and all its living forms is working with us, in life and in death, to bring about the well-being and fulfillment of all the bodies in creation. Resurrection of the body puts the emphasis where it should be in an ecological theology: on the physical basis of life. As often as Christianity has forgotten sand repudiated that basis, its most ancient and treasured belief in the resurrection of the body reminds it of its denial of the physical.

*   *   *

The Scope of the Body: The Cosmic Christ

The suffering of creation—undoubtedly the greater reality for most creatures, human as well as nonhuman—is addressed by the scope of the body of the cosmic Christ. Whatever happens, says our model, happens to God also and not just to us. The body of God, shaped by the Christic paradigm, is also the cosmic Christ –the loving, compassionate God on the side of those who suffer, especially the vulnerable and excluded. All are included, not only in their liberation and healing, but also in their defeat and despair. Even as the life-giving breath extends to all bodies in the universe, so also does the liberating, healing, and suffering love of God. The resurrected Christ is the cosmic Christ, the Christ freed from the body of Jesus of Nazareth, to be present in and to all bodies. The New Testament appearance stories attest to the continuing empowerment of the Christic paradigm in the world: the liberating, inclusive love of God for all is alive in and through the entire cosmos. We are not alone as we attempt to practice the ministry of inclusion, for the power of God is incarnate throughout the world, erupting now and then where the vulnerable are liberated and healed, as well as where they are not. The quiescent effect on human effort of the motif of sacrificial suffering in the central atonement theory of Christianity has made some repudiate any notion of divine suffering, focusing entirely on the active, liberating phase of God's relation to the world. But there is a great difference between a sacrificial substitutionary atonement in which the Son suffers for the sins of the world and the model of the God as the body within which our bodies live and who suffers with us, feeling our pain and despair. When we have, as disciples of Jesus' paradigmatic ministry, actively fought for the inclusion of excluded bodies, but nonetheless are defeated, we are not alone, even here. And the excluded and the outcast bodies for which we fought belong in and are comforted by the cosmic Christ, the body of God in the Christic paradigm.

The Direction of Creation and the Place of Salvation

The immediate and concrete sense of the cosmic Christ—God with us in liberation and in defeat—is the first level of the scope or range of God's body. But there are two additional dimensions implied in the metaphor that need focused and detailed attention. One is the relationship between creation and salvation in which salvation is the direction of creation and creation is the place of salvation. The metaphor of the cosmic Christ suggests that the cosmos is moving toward salvation and that this salvation is taking place in creation. The other dimension is that God's presence in the form or shape of Jesus' paradigmatic ministry is available not just in the years 1–30 ce and not just in the church as his mystical body, but everywhere, in the cosmic body of the Christ. Both of these dimensions of the metaphor of the cosmic Christ are concerned with *place* and *space*, with where God's body is present in its Christic shape. Christian theology has not traditionally been concerned with or interested in spatial matters, as we have already noted, priding itself on being a historical religion, often deriding such traditions as Goddess, Native, and "primitive" for focusing on place, on sacred spaces, on the natural world. But it is precisely place and space, as the common creation story reminds us, that must now enter our consciousness. An ecological sensibility demands that we broaden the circle of salvation to include the natural world, and the practical issues that face us will, increasingly, be on a finite limited planet, arable land with water will become not only the symbol of privilege but, increasingly, the basis of survival. Geography, not history, is the ecological issue. Those in the Christian tradition who have become accustomed to thinking or reality in a temporal model—the beginning in creation; the middle in the incarnation, ministry, and death of Jesus Christ; and the end at the eschaton when God shall bring about the fulfillment of all things - need to modify their thinking in a spatial direction. We need to ask where is this salvation occurring here and now, and what is the scope of this salvation?

In regard to the first dimension of the cosmic Christ, what does it mean to say that salvation is the *direction* of creation and creation is the *place* of salvation? To say that salvation is the direction of creation is a deceptively simple statement on a complex, weighty matter. It is a statement of faith in the face of massive evidence to the contrary, evidence that we have suggested when we spoke of the absurdity of such a claim in light of both conventional standards and natural selection. Some natural theologies, theologies that begin with creation, try to make the claim that evolutionary history contains a teleological direction, an optimistic arrow, but our claim is quite different. It is a retrospective, not a prospective claim; it begins with salvation, with experiences of liberation and healing that one wagers are from God, and reads back into creation the hope that the whole creation is included within the divine liberating, healing powers. It is a statement of faith, not of fact; it takes as its standpoint a concrete place where salvation has been experienced—in the case of Christians, the paradigmatic ministry of Jesus and similar ministries of his disciples in different, particular places—and projects the shape of these ministries onto the whole. What is critical, then, in this point of view about the common creation story is not that this story tells us anything about God or salvation but, rather, that it gives us a new, contemporary picture with which to remythologize Christian faith. The entire fifteen-billion-year history of the universe and the billions of galaxies are, from a Christian perspective, from this concrete, partial, particular setting, seen to be the cosmic Christ, the body of God in the Christic paradigm. Thus, the direction or hope of creation, all of it, is nothing less than what I understand that paradigm to be for myself and for other human beings: the liberating, healing, inclusive love of God.

To say that creation is the place of salvation puts the emphasis on the here-and-now aspect of spatiality. While the direction motif takes the long view, speaking of the difficult issue of an evolutionary history that appears to have no purpose, the place motif underscores the concrete, nitty-gritty, daily, here-and-now aspect of salvation. In contrast to all theologies that claim or even imply that salvation is an otherworldly affair, the place motif insists that salvation occurs in creation, in the body of God. The cosmic Christ is the physical, available, and needy outcast in creation, in the space where we live. In Christian thought creation is often seen as merely the backdrop of salvation, of lesser importance than redemption, the latter being God's main activity. We see this perspective in such comments as "creation is the prologue to history" or "creation provides the background and setting for the vocation of God's people," and in Calvin's claim that nature is the stage for salvation history. In this way of viewing the relation between creation and redemption, creation plays no critical role: it is only the stage on which the action takes place, the background for the real action. But in our model of the body of God as shaped by the Christic paradigm, creation is of central importance, for creation—meaning our everyday world of people and cities, farms and mountains, birds and oceans, sun and sky—is the place where it all happens and to whom it happens. Creation as the place of salvation means that the health and well-being of all creatures and parts of creation is what salvation is all about—it is God's place and our place, the one and only place. Creation is not one thing and salvation something else; rather, they are related as scope and shape, as space and form, as place and pattern. Salvation is for all of creation. The liberating, healing, inclusive ministry of Christ takes pace *in* and *for* creation.

These two related motifs of the direction of creation and the place of salvation both underscore expanding God's liberating, healing, inclusive love to all of the natural world. This expansion does not eclipse the importance of needy, vulnerable human beings, but it suggests that the cosmic Christ, the body of Christ, is not limited to the church or even to human beings but, as coextensive with God's body, is also the direction of the natural world and the place where salvation occurs.

Selection 4: James Nash, *Loving Nature: Ecological Integrity and Christian Responsibility*

> *James Nash (1938–2008) served as executive director of the Massachusetts Council of Churches and subsequently as executive director of the Church's Center for Theology and Public Policy in Washington, DC. Nash ranks as one of the most important environmental ethicists of our time. His book* Loving Nature *is one of the most thoroughly theological in its account of a Christian approach to ecological ethics. In this excerpt he examines in what sense the Christian love ethic can be the basis of ecological ethics.*

Once we root Christian ecological ethics in a theology and ethic of love, however, we immediately encounter mental quagmires in defining Christian love and determining its implications for responsible relations in ecological contexts. Vigorous debates abound in Christian ethics about the definitions, types, characteristics, possibilities, demands, and dilemmas of love. Nearly all these earnest and complicated controversies have focused exclusively on divine-human and interhuman relationships. Perplexity and complexity are compounded, however, in ecological situations where damaging and killing are biological necessities for existence (rather than strategic responses to moral evil, as in war), and where human relations with other creatures are between *un*equals.

The ethical debates commence with the definition of Christian love. Christians have no consensus on the meaning of love—and apparently neither does the New Testament. Garth Hallett, for instance, argues that six rival rules of preference of types of love—from self-preference to self-denial—have been represented in Christian history and are within Christian bounds. All are altruistic norms; all can require considerable sacrifice; all can be compatible with the sacrifice of Calvary. But the behavioral differences can sometimes be significant. The most strongly supported, but not the only, norm in the New Testament, claims Hallett, is self-subordination, seeking one's own benefit only on condition that benefits to others are first assured. The problem is obviously complex—and Hallett never deals with the additional moral complications of ecological relations! Love, of course, is an ambiguous work in common parlance. It has multiple meanings, most of which connote amorous sentimentality or drooling passions. The internal Christian problem of definition is not so wide or vague, but it is sufficiently confounding in its own right, especially when love is the basic norm of Christian ethics. It is fair to say that Christian ethics has a nebulous norm.

The problem, moreover, only begins with definition; it branches out to cover a broad spectrum of ethical issues. A sampling of the key and overlapping questions indicates the character of the debate and the dilemmas of interpreting Christian love in any context, let alone in an ecological one. What is the nature of agape (the prime Greek word for love in the New Testament) and what are its characteristics? What is the relationship, if any, between agape and eros? Are they antitheses, as Anders Nygren contends? Or can they be synthesized in some way; are eros and other "human loves" incorporated into agape, as D. D. Williams argues? To what degree is love self-sacrificing in relation to goals of self-realization? Is love "equal regard," "other regard," self-disregard, or some other normative relationship between the self and others? To what degree should Christians be suspicious of egoism, or even of claims to altruism? What role, if any, does mutuality—sharing, reciprocal giving and receiving in a caring community - play in Christian love? What kinds and expressions of love are psychologically and sociologically possible for human beings? What is the relationship between love as disposition and deeds, or attitude and acts? What is the relation of justice to love? What are the "most love-embodying rules and/or acts" in the midst of the tragic choices often associated with conflicting values and claims?

In these complex debates, the starting assumptions about the nature of Christian love obviously will affect the specific applications. Moreover, the meaning of Christian love has been manipulated in a multitude of ways to correspond with self-interest, to reduce the costs to the self of obligations to others. This problem is particularly acute in ecological relationships where humans have exercised a distortion of dominion by denying moral obligations to nonhuman creatures. Excessive self-love is really the root sin of lovelessness, the imperialistic preference for the self and, therefore, the absence or perversion of love for others. It is persistent and imaginative, and constantly corrupts Christian love in practice and dilutes it in theory. The problem is inevitable (even if unnecessary). But an awareness of our human inclinations to whittle away at love may minimize some of its worst effects, like self-deception and self-aggrandizement.

Despite this dissensus in Christian thought, it is still essential and possible to specify some basic implications of Christian love in an ecological context. In what follows, I intentionally have avoided a "radical" definition and opted for a more moderate interpretation of this unfathomable phenomenon we call love. One reason is to enable a wider palatability. Another is the desire to minimize the risks of overstating the case—particularly important in the light of our feeble and vague understandings of love. In effect, I am acknowledging that Christian love may demand more of Christians ecologically, but it certainly demands no less. Even when offered in modest proportions, however, Christian love has an unnervingly demanding quality. Sacrifice of personal interests is an inherent part of love.

By definition, Christian love, as disposition and/or deed, is always at least caring and careful service, self-giving and other-regarding outreach, in response to the needs of others (human and otherkind), out of respect for their God-endowed intrinsic value and in loyal response to the God who is love and who loves all. It seeks the other's good or well-being and, therefore, is always other-regarding (only the degree is up for debate). This love is expressed through kindness, mercy, generosity, compassion, justice, and a variety of other commendable qualities. Love is a relational concept and initiative; it seeks to establish connections and build caring relationships. Its ideal forms are expressed in such terms as *reconciliation, communion, community, harmony,* and *shalom.* These features characterize love in every situation, social and ecological.

Love and Predation

In reality, love is always compromised, sometimes severely. The human situation is that we are confronted with a host of conflicting, often irreconcilable moral claims that make it impossible to "do no harm," but only to minimize the harm we inevitably do. Moral purity and perfection are illusions; moral ambiguity and selectivity are the normal conditions of ethical decision-making. We must choose the "greater good" or the "lesser evil"—the "best possible"—among sometimes lousy options. War and abortion are two extreme examples of the standard moral dilemma of struggling to love under the conditions of "necessary evil." In ecological relations, the complexities are compounded, because the "necessary evil" is natural and not only moral. The evil is built into the ecosphere (thus, natural or nonmoral evil); it is an inherent tragedy, entailing no human moral blame or sin except insofar as humans normally exacerbate the tragedy by going beyond environmental use to abuse, by exceeding the limits of human abilities and nature's capacities.

To be human is to be initially a *natural predator,* along with all other creatures, in relation to the rest of the biophysical world. I am using the term *predator* broadly to cover not only biological predation per se, but all forms of human destruction and consumption of other life forms and their habitats—both as herbivore and carnivore, both as deliberate and unavoidable acts. Whether in a broad or narrow sense, however, predation is a primary condition of human existence. We are not a special creation, a species segregated from nature. That is bad biology which leads to bad theology and ethics. Humans are totally immersed in and totally dependent on the biophysical world for our being. We cannot talk about humans and nature, but only humans *in* nature. We have evolved with all other creatures through adaptive interactions from shared ancestors. We are biologically (and theologically) relatives—albeit remote—of caterpillars, strawberries, the dinosaurs, the oaks, the protozoa, and all other forms of being.

Nevertheless, it is morally imperative that we not romanticize these biological connections, as some "nature lovers' are prone to do. The biophysical creation in which we humans are participants is not a world of "natural harmony" or "biological community" or "familial cooperation." These commonly used terms have ethical implications as eschatological concepts, as I will argue later in this chapter. In natural history, however, these terms romanticize and distort reality, hindering our understanding of the moral dilemmas in human relationships with the rest of the biophysical world. That world is a morally ambiguous reality. It is a symbiotic system of predators and prey, edible flora and consuming fauna, parasites and hosts, scavengers and decomposers. The so-called "dynamic equilibrium" of the whole depends upon such primary interactions as lethal competition and amoral mutualism, in which the blood and guts—literally—of deceased creatures provide the nutrients for the generation of new life. In this practically endless recycling of life and death, every member of a species struggles against, uses, and/or feed on members of other species in order to survive. Euphemisms such as harmony, cooperation, community, or family are hardly fit descriptions of a reality in which species eat and otherwise destroy one another.

Thus, humans are naturally predators—including consumers and self-defenders—in this order. Killing is a biological necessity for existence. We *must* kill and use other life forms and destroy their habitats in order to satisfy human needs (for food, fuel, shelter, etc.), to protect our lives and health from other predators and pathogenic parasites (for which our very bodies are environmental habitats), and to build and maintain the structures of culture. Whatever else human beings may be, we cannot avoid being initially natural predators.

How is it possible, then, to express Christian love in such morally constricted circumstances? Since humans are predators by necessity, is it possible to act as *altruistic predators*—as beings who seek to minimize the ecological harm that we inevitably cause and who consume caringly and frugally to retain and restore the integrity of the ecosphere? Or is altruistic predation a contradiction in terms? The answers to these questions are important, because the development of a Christian ecological ethic depends on the possibility of humans expressing love in an ecological context, on the possibility of humans becoming altruistic predators. Though the answers are by no means easy, they do not appear in principle to be relevantly different from the responses that Christian ethicists generally give to other types of moral dilemmas. Whether the issue is moral evil or natural evil, the ethical problem remains essentially the same: making discriminate judgments to discern the best possible balance, the most love-embodying acts and/or principles under the circumscribed conditions of necessary evil. If the just war theory can provide much of Christian ethics with a means of expressing love in warfare by restricting the conditions and conduct of war, then surely love is relevant in an ecological context—where, unlike human interactions, killing is indisputably necessary—as a means of preventing and restricting environmental despoliation.

Qualifications of Ecological Love

Christian love in an ecological context is not an exact replica of love in an interpersonal or social context. Relevant differences exist between these contexts, and warrant relevant adjustments in the applications of love.

First, even if interpersonal love can rightly be defined as "equal regard," (which I doubt, since this concept seems insufficiently flexible to cover the spectrum of possible forms, from self-sacrifice to self-affirmation, which love ought to take in different situations), this concept seems totally inappropriate as a definition of ecological love. "Equal regard" for others assumes ontological equality of worth between the lover and the loved. That quality, however, is not evident in a comparison of humans with other species. Morally relevant differences exist that justify disparate and preferential treatment for humans.

Humans are more than one among the multitude of natural predators. We are also the *creative predator*—unique, unlike any other creature. This claim does not deny or ignore the fact that nonhuman creatures, probably all in one respect or another, have powers that are superior to those of humans—the speed of the cheetah, the strength of the elephant and the proportionate strength of the ant, the flight of birds and insects, the echolocation of bats, the web-weaving of spiders, the eyesight of raptors, the hearing of owls and deer, and the chemical production of plants, to name only a few. Some species—especially but not exclusively among mammals—display rational and quasi-moral qualities, including courage, compassion, deception, sympathy, grief, joy, fear, mutual aid, and learning abilities. Human superiority over other creatures is restricted and not rigidly demarcated.

Nevertheless, our rational and moral powers, and therefore, our creative capacities—no matter how weak they may appear in relation to our norms—so radically exceed the powers of any other species that major differences in quantity or degree are legitimately regarded as differences in quality or kind. We can never transcend nature, contrary to that mainstream theological tradition which contrasted nature and spirit. Human psychic-spiritual capacities are not additives to nature, but derivatives from nature. In history, we are inextricably immersed in nature. We can, however, transcend some instinctive necessities and realize some of the rational, moral, and spiritual *potentialities* in nature, far beyond the capacities of any other creature. That apparently is what Paul Tillich meant in describing the human, with slight exaggeration, as "finite freedom" in comparison with the "finite necessity" of other life forms. We are the only creatures with moral agency, that is, relative freedom and rationality to transcend instinct sufficiently in order to define and choose good or evil, right or wrong. We, therefore, are the only creatures who now can be *altruistic predators*—or *profligate predators*.

We are the only creatures capable of intentionally creating and regulating our own environments—and, in fact, destroying every other creature's environment while recognizing the demonic effects of our actions. We are the only species that can create cultures, whether primary or complex, and a multitude of cultural artifacts, from artistic expressions to computer systems, from religious rituals to architectural structures, from moral designs to political orders. Only humans, according to traditional Christian doctrine, have the potential to serve as the image of God and to exercise dominion in creation. Despite historical misinterpretations and abuse, these concepts recognize a basic biological fact: humans alone have evolved peculiar rational, moral, and therefore, creative capacities that enable us alone to serve as responsible representatives of God's interests and values, to function as protectors of the ecosphere and deliberately constrained consumers of the world's goods. We alone are the creative predators. In the light of that fact, it seems unreasonable to put humans on a moral par with other creatures.

Biotic egalitarianism strikes me as a moral absurdity and, in some cases, as an antihuman ideology. The claim of Schweitzer and some "deep ecologists" that the choice of one life form over another, including humans, is "arbitrary and subjective" or "an irrational and arbitrary bias," cannot be sustained in the light of the unique capacities of humans, to experience and create moral, spiritual, intellectual, and aesthetic goods. The value-creating and value-experiencing capacities of humans are morally relevant differences between us and all other species, and justify differential and preferential treatment in conflict situations. I shall have more to say on this problem in the next chapter. In the meantime, it is important to note that while my viewpoint affirms the primacy of human values, it also denies the exclusivity of human values. Other creatures also have intrinsic value—for themselves and for God—which warrants respect from human beings. However, their value is not equal to that of humans. If moral preference for human needs and rights is "speciesism," I plead guilty, but I think with just cause. Thus, in my view, *Christian love* in an ecological context is not equal regard, but it must remain at a high level of other regard.

Second, the definition of *Christian love* cannot be restricted to self-sacrifice, especially not in an ecological context of inequality. Reinhold Niebuhr's idea that the essence or highest form of love is self-sacrifice, as symbolized by the cross of Christ, makes sacrificial love into an end in itself, rather than a means to an end. But love is relational. Its ultimate intention is to create and enhance caring and sharing relationships, to unite giving and receiving. It is best described in such relational concepts as reconciliation, harmony, and communion. Sacrificial love, ranging in forms from simple acts of generosity to death on a cross, is a means of advancing the goal of reconciled relationship; it is not the end in itself. In Christian symbols, the instrument of Crucifixion cannot be isolated from its objectives, the reconciling events of the Resurrection, communion, and consummation. The cross is not an end in itself; it is a means to restore broken communion.

Nevertheless, there is an element of self-sacrifice that is an inherent part of every form and context of love. Niebuhr was clearly right on this point: the sacrificial love of the cross stands in judgment on our truncated models of mutuality, and prevents self-regarding motives from pretending to be the ultimate fulfillment of love. Love entails giving up at least some of our own interests and benefits for the sake of the well-being of others in communal relationships. This mandate applies in both human and ecological communities. The agonizing but unavoidable question, then, that Christian love continually poses for us is: what human interests and benefits must be sacrificed in this age of ecological crisis in order to serve the needs of other creatures and to enhance the health of the biotic community of which we and they are interdependent parts?

Third, some dimensions of Christian love appear to be inapplicable in an ecological context. Forgiveness, for example, is a fundamental facet of love in Christian understandings of human relationships with God and with one another. Forgiveness of sins, for example, is the core of Luther's doctrine of justification by faith. But forgiveness is relevant only in interactions between moral agents, parties with moral capacities—to judge right and wrong, to do good or evil, to repent and pardon, to retaliate or return good for evil. Nonhuman creatures, so far as is known in their present evolutionary state, lack moral agency. Forgiveness is irrelevant in direct relationships with creatures that act instinctively or submorally and are incapable of sin or remorse. In fact, an argument for the relevance of forgiveness in this context might be a dangerous anthropomorphism, since it could legitimate a counter-argument for revenge or retribution against nonhuman creatures "guilty" of some "offense" against humans—like biting or attacking. It is best to keep forgiveness and its opposite out of these relationships. Nevertheless, appeals for divine forgiveness for our sins against the ecosphere and its all-pervasive life forms are essential for a vital Christian piety. Repentance and petitions for pardon for our profligate predation need to be part of ritualized prayer in Christian churches. Karl Barth uncharacteristically said very little about ecological responsibilities, and much of the little he did say seems confused. Yet one point is potent. Barth notes that the killing of animals, which is morally legitimate only under the "pressure of necessity" and only when accompanied by a protest against it, is theologically possible only as "a deeply reverential act of repentance, gratitude and praise on the part of the forgiven sinner in face of the One who is the Creator and Lord of man and beast." That perspective is valid for all dimensions of human ecological consumption.

These three qualifications mean that Christian love in an ecological context will be less rigorous than in human social relations. Relevant differences in the situations justify different levels of moral expectation, just as we hold different standards for family life and international affairs. This fact, however, certainly does not imply that Christian love makes no serious ethical demands upon human beings in ecological interactions. It does! Christian love has many dimensions, and most of them are relevant and relatively rigorous in an ecological context.

Ecological Dimensions of Love

A popular and sentimental song from the fifties was called "Love Is a Many-Splendored Thing." Neither the title nor the lyrics deserve any poetic acclaim; still, the title suggests more wisdom than a horde of homilies. The meaning of Christian love cannot be encapsulated in simple definitions or a single dimension. Christian love is multidimensional. No single dimension exhausts its meaning; its full brilliance depends upon seeing the multiple facets of love together. My intention, therefore, is to outline several interpenetrating dimensions of Christian love as they apply to ecological relationships.

These dimensions are love as *beneficence, other-esteem, receptivity, humility, understanding, communion,* and *justice.* I shall reserve a discussion of love as justice for the next chapter, because this topic deserves special and extensive treatment.

1. Beneficence

Love as beneficence is looking not only to one's "own interests, but to the interests of others" (Phil. 2:4). It is being "servants to one another" (Gal. 5:13, RSV) by seeking "to do good to one another and to all" (1 Thess. 5:15). It is serving Christ by ministering to the hungry, naked, lonely, and incarcerated (Matt. 25:31-46; cf. Isa. 58)— and following the principle of the reasonable extension of love to its uncontainable inclusivity, this mandate for ministry applies to all God's creatures in their natural habitats.

Beneficence means *doing* good, or, realistically, the maximum possible good in the circumstances, rather than merely wanting or willing good. It includes nonmaleficence, doing as little harm or wrong to others (Rom. 13:10) as feasible, and refusing to inflict needless suffering or destruction. It goes beyond that negative duty to a positive quest of the neighbor's good, within the limits imposed by nature. Beneficence is caring and careful service on behalf of the well-being of others, human and otherkind, simply because a need exists, without regard for the earned or instrumental merit of the recipients and without the expectations of *quid pro quos.* Other life forms may have no direct utility for human needs, and most cannot respond to love in kind, but these considerations are irrelevant from the perspective of beneficence or other dimensions of Christian love. Christian love cannot be reduced to beneficence, but it is decrepit without beneficence.

Love as beneficence may be simple acts of kindness to wild creatures, like letting a dead tree stand in the yard as a food source and nesting site for woodpeckers or refraining from too-frequent visits to a fox den. Moreover, love as beneficence can be manifested in every way that Christians and other citizens function as protectors of the biosphere—by preventing, for example, the toxication of the air, water, soil, and stratosphere or by saving the stability and diversity of species in their essential habitats. Lobbying for a clean air act or a pesticide control bill may be an act of beneficence. Similarly, preventing radical reductions and extinctions of species by struggling against deforestation and habitat fragmentation has the character of beneficence. Even human population control is implied by beneficence, since it is necessary, among other reasons, to insure that all species have sufficient living space. Love expressed in the compassionate caring of beneficence is an indispensable element of a Christian ecological ethic.

Distinguishing love as beneficence from love as justice is not always easy, and often it isn't especially useful, except to academic purists. But one thing is clear: beneficence should never be a substitute for justice, as some suggest. In my view, beneficence exceeds the expectations of justice; it begins only when the demands of justice have been satisfied. It is the mercy that tempers justice, the "extra mile" that adds kindness to the calculations of "less and more." In a simple example, ecological justice might allow us to let the mourning dove with the raw, defeathered underwing freeze in the sub-zero temperatures of a New England winter. After all, those are the breaks in the natural struggle for survival. However, beneficence cannot resist feeding and sheltering the bird in the study until the wing heals. In many interpretations, moreover, beneficence has an optional quality, whereas justice is morally mandatory. Again, while beneficence generally connotes doing good, justice deals with the proper distribution of that good. Consequently, it seems important to insist that beneficence should be regarded as a supplement of justice, probably even the primary motivation for justice, but not as a substitute for justce.

2. Other-Esteem

Love as other-esteem "does not insist on its own way" (1 Cor. 13:5). It appreciates and celebrates the existence of the other to the empathic point that "if one member suffers, all suffer together with it; if one member is honored, all rejoice together with it" (1 Cor. 12:26). Other-esteem values, honors, and respects the integrity of the other, as a precious gift of God.

*　　*　　*

Other-esteem is an expression of eros in the classical sense, since it is evoked by the love-worthy qualities or meritorious features in the beloved. But this fact does not disqualify other-esteem for consideration as a form of agape. On the contrary, other-esteem is incorporated into agape, because it values the otherness of distinctiveness of the beloved as a good in itself, and treats the beloved accordingly.

Love as other-esteem speaks forcefully against a variety of forms of ecologically debilitating anthropocentrism. It renounces that anthropocentrism which views the natural world as created for humans, and which values that world only for its contributions to human wants—measuring even ancient forests of sequoias in board feet, evaluating verdant plains and valleys as "worthless" land until "improved" by development, and describing huntable animals as "game" or "trophies" to be "harvested." It rejects that anthropocentrism which treats other creatures kindly only to the extent that they conform to human standards of "beauty" and "civility," and which, therefore, offers bounties on "moral offenders," the "bad" "varmints" like cougars and coyotes. It disdains that anthropocentrism which yearns to transform nature's wild, chaotic order into a Disneyland tameness, with gardens of manicured shrubs, pesticided grass, concrete esplanades, and tender beasts for petting. That anthropocentrism is blind even to the beauty of an untended lawn recuperating from domesticity and overflowing with dandelions.

Other-esteem, in contrast, does not wish to be the manager, gardener, or zoo keeper of the biosphere. It rejects these despotic metaphors for responsible relationships of humans with otherkind. Other-esteem respects the integrity of wild nature— its diversity, relationality, complexity, ambiguity, and even prodigality. It is quite content to let the natural world work out its own adaptations and interactions without "benefit" of human interventions, except insofar as necessary to remedy human harm to nature's integrity and to satisfy vital human interests. Other-esteem groans with the travail of creation, but it also accepts the fact that natural habitats and their inhabitants are generally served best by the absence of human schemes for improvement, beautification, or domestication.

3. Receptivity
Love as receptivity is "not envious or boastful or arrogant or rude" (1 Cor. 13:4-5), because it recognizes its dependency. Receptivity is a step beyond love as other-esteem. It too values otherness, but, additionally, it is an acute consciousness that the human community is incomplete, weakened, and even homicidal apart from others. We need the others, the biotic and abiotic components of the ecosphere. Consequently, receptivity is a yearning for relationship, not only to give to but to receive from the treasured others. Like other-esteem, it also is eros. It desires; it longs for the presence and pleasures of the beloved. But it is a self-giving love in the very process of being self-getting, because receptivity gives honor to the gifts of the others by recognizing our deficiencies and our dependencies on the others' gifts.

Receptivity stands in sharp contrast to the self-sufficiency so characteristic of human interactions with the ecosphere. We humans tend to celebrate our uniqueness and completeness in a virtual orgy of anthropocentrism, reminiscent of the competitive rallying boast of "We're Number One"! In our depletion of the ozone layer, our indiscriminate use of pesticides, our destruction of temperate and tropical rain forests, and our indifference to extinctions, we act as if we have no dependence on other parts of the body of earth. Receptivity, however, is a recognition of the intricately interdependent connections between humankind and the rest of the earth and an acknowledgment of our kinship with all earth's elements. It acts caringly to nurture and sustain the vitality, stability, and productivity of the relationship. Receptivity reminds us that love in an ecological context is not a "one night stand"!

Moreover, a full-fledged receptivity desires the raw, unadorned world with a virtually erotic passion. Despite the dangers to life and limb that generate justifiable fears, receptive lovers of nature yearn to be in the presence of the beloved and share in the intimate and omnipresent pleasures. They marvel at the miracles around them. They are filled with awe and humility and mystery. They feel "biophilia." For Christians, receptivity is a celebration of the sacramental presence of the Spirit, discussed in chapter 4. Reflecting my own prejudices, I suspect that many serious ornithologists have experienced these feelings, and probably (though I confess to mystification) so have many herpetologists. Love as receptivity reminds us that the natural world must be protected and nurtured not only for humanity's physical existence, but also for our spiritual well-being. This receptive attitude has aptly been described as "descendentalism," the spiritual appreciation of the earthy, and it has been, as John Muir exemplified, a powerful force in initiating and sustaining the environmental movement. We therefore need to nurture receptivity not only for is inherent value, but also for its dynamic power to promote changes, in environmental policy.

4. Humility

Love as humility is not thinking of ourselves more highly (or more lowly) than we ought to think (Rom. 12:3. Cf. Matt. 23:11-12; Luke 14:11; 18:9-14). It is a realistic virtue rejecting both self-deprecation and self-aggrandizement. In response to arrogance, however, humility is other-regarding to the extent that it is self-deflating. It knows the weaknesses in human knowledge and character, and thus, recognizes that we are neither wise enough nor good enough to control the powers we can create or to comprehend the mysterious power that created us. Humility is the counter to hubris, the arrogant denial of creaturely limits on human ingenuity and technology. It is the antidote for triumphalism, the forgetting of our finitude and folly in the midst of celebrating human creativity. It is also a remedy for profligate predation—the excessive production and consumption that strain the limits of nature's capacities and disrespect the intrinsic value of our kin in creation. Humility, therefore, expresses itself as simplicity and frugality—that temperance which undoes self-indulgence.

Humility sits with the lowliest human as an equal (James 2:1-9), and even with unequals in an ecological context, in the manner of the self-emptying God who also sat with ontological unequals by entering and identifying with the human condition (Phil. 2:1-11). It seeks to puncture, therefore, any exaggerations about human powers and any undervaluations of other creatures. It is untroubled by human kinship with all other species. It accepts its relations. Humility recognizes that to be human is to be from the humus and to return to the humus. It regards all creatures as worthy of moral consideration.

Humility is cautious love or careful caring. It thrives in the manifestation of modesty, or choosing restrained, rather than ambitious, means and ends as ways of minimizing the risks of disaster in the light of the virtual inevitability of human error and evil. Undue risks represent the antithesis of humility, since, as that semi-cynical adage notes, if anything can go wrong, it will! Historian Herbert Butterfield spoke forcefully against the arrogance of immodesty:

> The hardest strokes of heaven fall in history upon those who imagine that they can control things in a sovereign manner, as though they were kings of the earth, playing Providence not only for themselves but for the far

future—reaching out into the future with the wrong kind of farsightedness, and gambling on a lot of risky calculations in which there must never be a single mistake.

To counteract this arrogance, no virtue will be in greater demand than humility as modesty if we are to avoid ecological catastrophes in the years ahead. The 1989 sludging of Prince William Sound with eleven million gallons of Alaskan crude from the wrecked supertanker Exxon Valdez is only one of countless examples of environmental destruction resulting from the sin of immodesty—that exaggerated confidence in human and technical reliability, and the failure to make due allowance for error and evil, the unpredictable and the unknown. Technology, as the contemporary clichés remind us, is both "promise and peril." Technological innovations can provide us with indispensable knowledge and assistance in alleviating some ecological problems. For instance, we would not even know about ozone depletion or be able to reduce toxic emissions without sophisticated technology. Yet, technology also has caused serious ecological damage, and it probably offers no answers to some ecological problems—certainly not to extinctions—to which it has contributed. Moreover, even the most reliable technologies are always subject to breakdowns, technical misuse, and power abuse. Humility as modesty, therefore, cautions us not to be confident, let alone overconfident, in "technological fixes." It warns us that no human plans or techniques are fail-safe, so long as humans are relatively free and definitely finite. It urges us to remember the Achilles' heel of human creativity: the powers to shape the earth contain the powers to destroy it.

The meek or humble may not inherit the earth, but they will dramatically increase the odds that a healthy earth will be there to inherit.

5. Understanding

Love as understanding is loving God with our whole mind (Luke 10:27) and therefore loving the created beings that God loves with our whole mind. Not only faith seeks understanding; so does love. Love wants to know everything about the beloved—likes and dislikes, aspirations and anxieties, but above all, the other's needs. In fact, the only way to nurture and serve others adequately is to know their needs. Love requires understanding, or cognitive and emotional comprehension—and that is no less true in an ecological context than in a personal context. In fact, the amount of essential knowledge is far greater ecologically, because of the multitude of creatures in intricate interactions in complex ecosystems.

Knowledge about ecological dynamics is essential for ecological love. A large portion of environmental damage, in both personal and corporate settings, is a consequence not of malice but of ignorance—indeed, seemingly invincible ignorance. Too few are aware of even the seemingly obvious ecological effects of their actions. I once talked with a woman who was complaining about the decline of nesting birds in her backyard, and then in the next breath, she indicated that she had tripled the use of pesticides to combat gypsy moths. She did not recognize the linkage, despite Rachel Carson's work and despite widespread publicity about the destructive effects of pesticides like DDT on bald eagles, peregrine falcons, and other wildlife. The problem is magnified many-fold when we are dealing with major corporations dumping massive amounts of diverse pollutants into the air, soil, and water. The ecological effects of industrial and technological wastes on ozone depletion, global warming, acid rain, and species' reductions are difficult to trace. Discovery depends on extensive and expensive technical research. Ecological studies in a number of specialties and sub-specialties have expanded dramatically in recent years, but we remain a long way from an adequate understanding of the intricate interdependencies in nature.

Despite the impressive knowledge explosion in the twentieth century, the more impressive fact about the human condition is how little we know. Much of human knowledge about ecology is fragmentary and disconnected. Scientific specialists know only a small percentage of the pieces of the ecological puzzle, and far less about how the pieces fit together in the intricate complexity of ecosystems, not to mention the ecosphere. Not even the number of species is known, and dramatically less is known about how these species depend on one another in the interactions of countless food chains.

One danger in this context is that some human act of negligence combined with ignorance, such as the use of a particular pesticide, could destroy an unrecognized "keystone" species, on which many species in an ecosystem depend directly and indi-rectly for their survival. The whole ecosystem would then crumble. Such acts of igno-rance are commonplace in history, ancient and modern. The great North American ecological disaster of the 1930s, the Dust Bowl, was largely a consequence of agricul-tural malpractice confronting drought. Ecosystems in the United States have suffered heavy damage from the introduction of exotic aliens, without regard for the absence of natural control mechanisms—from kudzu in the Southeast and feral burros in the Southwest to starlings and house sparrows everywhere! Benjamin Franklin cites an ironic example of ecological ignorance from the eighteenth century, along with a wise warning:

> Whenever we attempt to amend the scheme of Providence, and to interfere with the government of the world, we had need to be very circumspect, lest we do more harm than good. In New England they once thought black-birds useless, and mischievous to the corn. They made efforts to destroy them. The consequence was, the blackbirds were diminished; but a kind of worm, which devoured heir grass, and which the blackbirds used to feed on, increased prodigiously; then finding their loss in grass greater than their saving in the corn, they wished again for their blackbirds.

Ecological ignorance, then, is hardly bliss; it is a prime ingredient for ecological catastrophes (which may be a single calamity, like an oil spill or, more frequently, an accumulation of abuses that create a composite calamity, like ozone depletion).

In this context, environmental research and education are important expres-sions of love. The advancement of ecological understanding is a key responsibility of our educational and ecclesiastical institutions. Knowledge is not virtue, contrary to Socrates, but knowledge is a necessary condition of objectively virtuous behavior in personal and corporate contexts. Knowledge certainly is power. It is power not only to control and manipulate, but also to care and mend. Ecological understanding is essential for acting lovingly.

6. Communion

Love as communion "binds everything together in perfect harmony" (Col. 3:14). It is "the unity of the Spirit in the bond of peace" (Eph. 4:3; cf. 4:15-16), for Christ has broken down all the partitions of alienation (Eph. 2:14). It is the pursuit of "what makes for peace and for mutual upbuilding" in community (Rom. 14:19). Love as communion is the consummation of love; it is the completion of the "drive toward the reunion of the separated." It is the solvent of separation, the adhesive for wholeness and fullness in relations, the final sign of the bonding power of love. Communion is the full extension of love as receptivity and other-esteem. It means that the goal of Christian love is inherently and concretely relational. Communion is not satisfied with the other dimensions of love; it knows that love is incomplete without solidarity, without friendship and partnership in fully interdependent and shared relationships, without the interpenetration of giving *and* receiving. Communion not only wants the loved ones to be in their distinctiveness; it wants them to be *our* loved ones in fully reconciled relationships. Love as communion, then, is reconciliation, harmony, koinonia, shalom. Ultimately, it is salvation, for the Reign of God is the consummation of communion or reconciliation.

Such a love, however, is only partially and provisionally known in history. We experience at best precious fragments of this love, which prompt our urges for more. This is especially true in natural history where systemic alienation and predation prevail. The Isaianic vision (Isa. 11:6-9; 65:25) of a lion resting with a lamb, of a child leading a harmonious band of carnivores and herbivores, of a serpent eating only dust, is "unnatural" in history. Indeed, it is a utopian illusion to believe that such possibilities exist in history (except for the ambiguous distortions in domestication). The "peaceable kingdom" is an ultimate ideal or eschatological hope.

Yet, this vision of love as communion is by no means irrelevant to history, human and natural. It functions not only as a judgment on human deficiencies in expressing the demands of love, but also as a goad pressing us to reach out to the limits of love in history. Though we cannot now experience the full harmony of the New Creation, we can approximate it to the fullest extent that the moral ambiguity of this creation makes possible.

Biomedical Ethics 40

❧ *The advances of medical science during the latter half of the twentieth century have spawned a burgeoning field of biomedical ethics. These new developments have posed serious issues for the churches' witness on behalf of the sanctity of life.*

Selection 1: Paul Ramsey, *Fabricated Man*

Paul Ramsey (1913–1988), a professor of religion at Princeton University for forty years, was one of the most influential Protestant ethicists of the twentieth century. He wrote on a wide variety of topics. He brought a compassionate and conservative voice to the emerging field of biomedical ethics. His cautionary reflections on the possibilities for the management of human genesis and human "self-modification" represent not only Ramsey's perspective but also the continuing task of biomedical ethics.

Chapter 3: Parenthood and the Future of Man by Artificial Donor Insemination, Etcetera, Etcetera

Aldous Huxley's fertilizing and decanting rooms in the Central London Hatchery (Brave New World) will become a possibility within the next fifteen to fifty years. I have no doubt they will become actualities—at least as a minority practice in our society. One reason this will come to pass is that philosophers, theologians and moralists, churches and synagogues, do not have the persuasive power to prevent the widespread social acceptance of morally objectionable technological "achievements" if they occur. Philosophers whose business it is to transmit wisdom which begins in wonder and theologians whose business it is to transmit wisdom which begins in fear of the Lord, 1 while criticizing, reshaping, and enlivening these wisdoms, have collectively abandoned understanding, and their voices. This may seem a harsh and despairing charge. Perhaps the dehumanizing tendencies of technology in all advanced societies should simply be described as irresistible. But, if so, a first evidence of that irresistibility is the way in which leading intelligences, including theologians and churchmen, rush to offer the sacrament of confirmation or to celebrate a Bar Mitzvah before the event whenever they hear of any new means by which man will become a "self-modifying system"—his own creator, the unlimited lord of the future.

The Fascinating Prospect of Man's Limitless Self-Modification

There are profound anthropological and ethical issues raised by the possible future technical biological control and change of the human species (just as there are profound anthropological and ethical issues raised by the challenge to individual human self-awareness by the prospect of keeping alive a wholly "spare-parts" or an "artificial" man). To follow out either of these directions and long-range consequences of present research and development (which originates, to be sure, in a legitimate concern for the treatment of present human ills) would be to take a larger overview than in either previous chapter.

Physicians generally are content to stick close to present and near-future patient care—waiting until the longer day's dawning to consider whether some of the notorious things now proposed and only remotely possible should ever be done. Biochemists and molecular biologists, however, are keenly aware that research and development in the self-modification of the human species cuts all questions loose from the moorings of an ethics of medical practice and from the ethics upon which our civilization has so far been founded.

The fascinating prospect of man's limitless self-modification is almost daily placed before the public in magazine and news articles. With these prospects we must deal, and at least make the attempt to articulate the elements of a possible line of moral reasoning concerning them.

I intend, therefore, to draw together some of the themes introduced by the preceding two chapters and to set them in the perspective of additional possibilities ahead. Thus we shall see what may happen to medical ethics, or to ethics in general, when the future of the species is taken to be a patient who is to be reworked by biological technology and through new forms of human "reproduction."

One journal article, by David M. Rorvik, in the April 1969 issue of *Esquire*, was accompanied by appropriate pictures of specially bred astronauts, legless for efficiency on long space-voyages; a completely germ-free human being for colonizing outer space; short-legged stocky dwarfs for planets with high gravitational pressure; four-legged human types for Jupiter; men with prehensile feet and tails to hang on to planets with low gravitational pull; clones of Barbra Streisands, Mahalia Jacksons, Joe Namaths, and Adolph Hitlers to entertain us here on earth; chimeras and cybogs to do janitors' work. This, of course, was sensational journalism. The wonder is that there is no outcry.

At the same time, the *Esquire* article printed the Rand Corporation's table of human expectations: artificial in-ovulation in humans by 1972; genetic surgery by 1995; routine animal cloning by 2005; widespread human cloning by 2020; routine breeding of hybrids and specialized human mutants by 2025 A.D., that is! And there was good, if sparse, scientific information contained in the article. This included accounts of: the work of the French scientist, Jean Rostand, in parthenogenesis by jolting frogs' eggs; H. J. Muller's campaign for germinal choice from banks; the experiments of Dr. J. K. Sherman of the University of Arkansas in successfully impregnating women with sperm from stocks frozen for prolonged periods at 385° below zero; Dr. Sophia

Kleegman's practice of artificial insemination from anonymous donors (AID) at $25 per masturbation; the transportation of an entire "herd of prize sheep" by air from Europe in the form of tiny embryos kept alive in the uterus of a single rabbit and then implanted in ewes—showing what can soon be done by inovulating humans; the way in which human motherhood could be made obsolete by ectogenesis—a combination of test-tube babies and the artificial placenta; the work of Dr. O. S. Heynes of South Africa in putting women during the last stage of pregnancy in a special decompression chamber to increase the flow of oxygen to the fetus so as to produce more intelligent children; how to avoid the limitations of the human female pelvis so the human brain can grow bigger; the laser beam that will make genetic manipulation possible; and, finally, the major "evolutionary perturbation" of clonal reproduction which men can seize for their profitable self-modification as a species.

Artificial Insemination with Donor (AID) is only the first breach of what has until recently been understood to be human parenthood as a basic form of humanity. Then there is artificial inovulation. And after artificial inovulation comes "germinal selection" from ovum and semen banks for the management and self-modification of the future of our species. Then, electro-tickle parthenogenesis, whose result would be only women, men no longer being needed. Then, women hiring mercenaries to bear their children, as now they secure the cooperation of semen donors. "Sooner or later," writes Dr. Roderic Gorney of the UCLA School of Medicine, "a patient will request and get artificial gestation for her baby just because she is tired of the restrictions of pregnancy and wants to take a round-the-world tour or go skiing." Or there will be a woman offering to give gestation to the child of a dying sister who wants before passing away to leave her husband a child? There will be: babies produced by reworking male and female germinal material in hatcheries, which unfortunately would at first still require somebody's womb to bring the fetus to term; the making of "carbon-copies" of people by clonal reproduction (using nuclear transplantation); clonal farming, offering everyone who can afford it a supply of "identical twin" organs whenever he needs a transplant; the manufacture of short-legged astronauts or of a race of serfs by combining human with animal chromosomal material; the predetermination of the sex of our children, involving the zygotic, embryonic or fetal destruction of the unwanted sort. Compulsory, or at least the socially sanctioned, injection of young women with long-time contraceptives to enable them to maneuver through their early years without pregnancy (this might be a condition for admission to college).

The latest article to appear on these apparently fascinating prospects is "The Second Genesis" by the distinguished science writer, Albert Rosenfeld, published in Life magazine in the June 13, 1969 issue. Beneath a sense of man's boundless freedom Rosenfeld's writing is suffused by a sense of man's boundless determinism: man the self-creator seems also the slave of the actions that biology now makes possible. The control of life is "coming," according to the book's subtitle. The miracle worker is bound to do these actions, because he can, or someone will; and the doer of miracles is destined to be indefinitely reshaped by performances to which he seems drawn out of dizziness before the prospects.

Rosenfeld covers the ground we have already traversed—"solitary generation" (Rostand's phrase); artificial androgenesis (producing all males, as parthenogenesis would produce all females); banks of ova and sperm; propagation by cuttings; sex selection by diaphragms to separate androsperm from gynosperm; in vitro babies ("too great to resist"); hybridization with animals; offspring not of particular couples even in culture but of the entire species or entirely fabricated according to specification; the peddling of Celebrity Seed; women competing with women not for marriage partners but for sex partners while more and more men cop out because of the celebrated female orgasmic powers; wholesale automanipulation; and Dr. E. S. E. Hafez's projects for combining AID with the production of centuplets by induced superovulation in women, to secure a supermarket of embryos for use on earth and to miniaturize the people to be sent aloft to colonize the planets.

It is evident that women who are to be freed by "labor saving devices" are also to be limitlessly used. This is only a special case of the "limitless freedom/limitless submission" (Dostoevski) which will result with the destruction of parenthood as a basic form of humanity, and its recombination in various ways for extrinsic purposes.

In the end, Rosenfeld remarks:

> In our current circumstances, the absence of a loved one saddens us, and death brings terrible grief. Think how easily the tears could be wiped away if there were no single "loved one" to miss that much—or if that loved one were readily replaceable by any of several others. And yet—if you (the hypothetical in vitro man) did not miss anyone very much, neither would anyone miss very much. Your absence would cause little sadness, your death little grief. You too would be readily replaceable.

The aloneness many of us feel on this earth is assuaged, more or less effectively, by the relationships we have with other human beings. . . . These relationships are not always as deep or as abiding as we would like them to be, and communication is often distressingly difficult. Yet . . . there is always the hope that each man and woman who has not found such relationships will eventually find them. But in the in vitro world, or in the tissue-culture world, even the hope of deep, abiding relationships might be hard to sustain. Could society devise adequate substitutes? If each of us is "forever a stranger and alone" here and now, how much more strange, how much more alone, would one feel in a world where we belong to no one, and no one belongs to us. Could the trans-humans of post-civilization survive without love as we have known it in the institutions of marriage and family?

The American public, when questioned about their approval or disapproval of these ways of "improving" human reproduction, manifest a surprising degree of approval of them. A Harris Poll published in Life magazine, on June 13, 1969, showed that two people disapproved for every one who approved of AID, artificial inovulation and in vitro babies. But the fact that one out of three approved was the remarkable thing. It is notable, however, that people's approval is based on interpreting these proposals as treatments. They do not have in mind the primary purpose and effects that are often in view in the case of some scientists. While fifty- six percent disapproved and nineteen percent approved of AID upon a simple description of the procedure, thirty-five percent approved when this was explained as the only way by which a couple could have a child or a normal child. By contrast, a larger number, thirty-six percent of both men and women, surprisingly approved of artificial inovulation if the husband fertilized the egg. The explanation was that both the men and the women believed that men feel emasculated by AID. In vitro babies won the approval of twenty-five percent of both men and women, while thirty percent of the men and thirty-five percent of the women approved if the wife might die or be crippled from childbirth. The hazards to babies in learning how to achieve this were not brought into consideration by the pollsters. Purposely making genetic changes in order to "give a child to an otherwise childless marriage" won sixty-two percent approval; to avoid retarded babies won fifty-eight percent approval; while producing superior people through genetics was roundly rejected by fifty-seven percent to twenty-one percent. Again, the hazards to the unborn child were not reported to have been brought into question.

The conclusion to be drawn from the Harris Poll is that approval of such novel proposals is related to the treatment of infertility in marriage, the prevention of birth defects, and the preservation of man's sense of wholeness. The remarkable thing was not the degree of acceptance but that the acceptance was based on care of the persons involved in the family or of one another. The poll also disclosed a great amount of pro-natalist sentiment and the belief that people must have children.

Little comfort should be drawn from these observations, however, if the future development of people's acceptance and future behavior patterns in our society show that treatments offered in primary patients, people's present care of one another, and even their pronatalism by any means may be readily misused and molded into self-modifications of the transmission of life as a means to other goals. This could be the inexorable result of our present fascination with biological techniques applied to the origins of life.

How Far Are These Procedures Legitimate Treatments?

I am aware that many of the researchers and practitioners who are developing these exquisite "remedies" are motivated primarily by therapeutic goals. Several examples of such good uses of the relevant scientific know-how can be given.

Artificial insemination was first developed to enable a husband and wife to have children. Making it possible for a woman to have a child is the purpose even when nonhusband donors are used. The practice need not be directed to the improvement of that celebrated non-patient, the human species.

Artificial inovulation also has a therapeutic purpose and effect. If a woman's ovum for some reason cannot reach the place of impregnation or be impregnated by her husband, it is possible for the physician to extract it, fertilize it with semen from her husband, and then implant it in her uterus. This assists fertility in the marriage. Such an excellent treatment, however, becomes at once a possible way of circumventing the normal parameters of parenthood, and a possible way of treating future multitudes.

Similarly, caesarian sections constitute descriptively and ethically one sort of procedure when it is indicated that normal birth would be unsafe for both mother and child. But the use of caesarian sections routinely on all women who have babies in hospitals in order to overcome the restrictions of the human pelvis and let the human brain grow larger and larger over generations to come' (suggested by Joshua Lederberg)—that, morally, would be altogether a different procedure. It would introduce unknown evolutionary perturbations and use today's women for the purpose of doctoring the species in a later time.

Again, the improvement of present incubator methods—an artificial placenta, no less—might have great value in saving the lives of the prematurely born. This cannot be regarded, however, as a procedure to be chosen in place of the fetus' being nine months in the womb of its mother, when one remembers the disadvantages of prematurity—ranging from greater mortality to serious mental and physical impairments in development.

Let us imagine that there can be developed an artificial placenta as good for the child as the womb—or better, because it abolishes the limits imposed by the human pelvis upon brain development, and makes the child accessible to "the management's" improvement. Even so, such a technical development skips over the crucial ethical question. Prescinding from the "good" ends in view, the decisive moral verdict must be that we cannot rightfully get to know how to do this without conducting unethical experiments upon the unborn who must be the "mishaps" (the dead and the retarded ones) through whom we learn how. It is amazing that, in discussions of man's self-modification of the future of his species by prenatal refabrication, this simple, decisive ethical objection is so seldom mentioned. This can only mean that our ethos is well prepared to make human waste for the sake of these self-elected goals.

Intrauterine monitoring for the purpose of detecting in the unborn genetic or developmental defects which may be corrected by fetal surgery or other procedure is an obvious accomplishment in extending treatment at a time when it might be beneficial—treatment to which physicians formerly did not have access. (Whether by these extraordinary means unborn lives should always be saved is another question.) But at least some forms of "screening" (in contrast to monitoring and treatment) focus upon patients other than the unborn, and propose the elimination of some genetic defect from the species by eliminating these primary patients after they are here among us as lives yet unborn—including those who are only carriers and would themselves be quite healthy. The public is dimly aware of the fact that abortion as a means of population control is only a form of increasing the death rate (where, as in our age, the control of death has helped to create the population problem). But still fewer people are aware that abortion—even abortion on the so-called "fetal indications" of a probability of grave mental or physical defect in the child—can readily cease to be even a form of alleged therapy for that child. "The abortion dilemma," it has recently been pointed out, "is only the currently visible small fraction of the very large iceberg dealing with the control of the quality of human life," which is the generalized "patient" to be dealt with by these abortions and other procedures. Abortion will soon become a way of doctoring that non-patient: the species.

Amniocentesis to detect congenital defects (and if the defects are sex-related, the sex of the child) has therapeutic value where there is some present or future method of extending care to the patient. The proposed use of this procedure, however, or the use of artificial inovulation, to predetermine the sex of the child (in the latter case, by not implanting the undesired sort) departs from the parameters of human parenthood so far as to raise the gravest social and ethical questions.

In our present society, for example, this would likely lead to a serious imbalance between the sexes of the children chosen to be born. In spite of what we say about the equality of the sexes, and about liking girl-children as much as boys, our operative decisions would be to the contrary. Statistics plainly show that parents seek to have an additional child when they already have one, two, three, or four girl-children far more frequently than they do when—in each of these classifications—they already have one, two, three, or four boys. Generally, people often try again for a boy, less often for a girl. Professor Amitai Etzioni, sociologist at Columbia University, has pointed out the widespread social, moral and political repercussions—including a return to the frontier atmosphere in this country—that would follow any attempt to predetermine the sex of our children.

Finally, genetic surgery by means of laser beams or some chemical to reverse mutations might be a wholly acceptable procedure for treating the primary patient—to correct some serious genetic defect with which a child is otherwise going to be born. In this case, any mishap resulting from the process of trying to knock out a nucleotide or change the child's genetic makeup would be a great tragedy; but it would be a consequence of decisions and actions taken in behalf of the child's health. This must be classed among the normal hazards of proper medical care. If there is some miscarriage, it is not a miscarriage of justice—as would be the case if the mishap resulted from experimenting on the child in a program of positive eugenics for the supposed sake of the species.

Since the foregoing point repeats the judgment I have made elsewhere concerning the treatment-value of genetic surgery—perhaps the most exquisite of all the procedures we have under review—let us look more closely at the question of whether this is a choice-worthy treatment and at the ethically relevant circumstances that could morally deny us this option.

Soon laboratories will be submitting requests for federal research funds to finance the search for viruses to manipulate defective genes. The alteration of genes by viruses will, of course, be done first in animals. If promising viruses are discovered, application must then be made to the Food and Drug Administration to license the material for testing in humans. This brings us to the crucial point of whether our knowledge at that stage will be such that any mishap can correctly be classed among tragedies in the practice of medicine—this time, upon a hypothetical human being, the unconceived child—or whether the hazards will be such that it would be immoral to proceed further with the attempt to learn how to use viruses to change genes.

As I understand it, one gene must be replaced by another; to manipulate out a bad gene entails the introduction of another genetic determiner. It may be possible to find a virus that would carry only the desired gene, or at least one that would be known to carry no deleterious genes. In that case the moral objection about to be raised would not pertain. However, the biophysicist, Leroy G. Augenstein, of Michigan State University, describes the situation we might face in deciding whether to begin testing genetic surgery on human beings. "Suppose we were to find a virus which carried the necessary DNA for correcting diabetes and made all the boys very tall (good basketball teams) and raised their IQ's by fifteen points (no flunking out of school)." Then if anything went wrong, it would be tragic, not an immoral act we had. done. Suppose, however, Augenstein continues, "we were unlucky and the virus contained not only a certain amount of DNA enabling people to make their own insulin, but additional DNA so that the group tested either went on to have defective children or developed schizophrenia. We would have a whole generation with extensive genetic changes before we even knew they were in trouble."

Obviously, if we knew beforehand that these would be the results, the introduction of a virus to correct the insulin production of an as yet unconceived child would be no proper treatment. It would rather be a wicked thing to do. But suppose we do not know that these terrible consequences of tampering with the gene for insulin will be forthcoming? What then? Is it only tragedy as a hazard of proper medical care if and when these things result? I should say not. Given the intricate and wonderful structure of the genes and the lottery that produces the genotype which is or becomes a human being, we ought morally to require a far higher degree of knowledge that there are no hazards of such gravity. It is not enough not to know, one must rather know that there are not these hazards, before this homing-in on the gene for insulin could possibly be a choice-worthy treatment of a hypothetical human being, as yet unconceived, who seems likely to become diabetic.

This is not only because insulin injections are better treatments. Suppose it were judged that diabetes is serious enough for the individual and that the increasing number of diabetics arising from the gene pool is so serious that something must be done about it. Still, we ought not to choose genetic surgery at the risk of producing individuals who may, in increased numbers, become schizophrenic in the first generation and who may be the mothers and fathers of children who are defective in the second generation, even if their defects are deemed to be no greater than diabetes. The reason for this conclusion is that there is a third alternative for treating the unborn. We are not forced to choose between doing nothing about diabetes as an inherited disease and correcting it by genetic manipulation under these supposed conditions. The indicated treatment for preventing the transmission of diabetes would be having no children or fewer children. The treatment would be continence or not getting married or using three contraceptives at the same time or voluntary sterilization. Only someone who is more of a pro-natalist than the Roman Catholic Church ever was, or who strictly believes that every human being has an absolute right to have children, can avoid the conclusion that these are more choice-worthy options than visiting upon hypothetical children the risks that we are supposing are associated with the removal of diabetes, or that we must suppose have not been removed from the realm of possibility. The treatment of choice would be to do everything possible to correct the consequences of "achievements" of the past, when from an unlimited and unexamined pro-natalism we learned how to enable diabetic women to have children.

Let us make the case a harder one, to see if these ethical conclusions do or do not still hold true for the meaning of genetic responsibility. Suppose the bad gene believed to be manipulable by a virus is far, far more serious than diabetes, e.g., a recessive trait like cystic fibrosis or PKU; or a dominant trait like achondroplasia (dwarfism) or Huntington's chorea where the defect will be passed on with a fifty-fifty probability (like brown hair or brown eyes). What, we now ask, ought rightfully to be done in behalf of, first, the child prenatally and, secondly, the hypothetical child preconceptually?

If amniocentesis, intrauterine monitoring, etc., disclose the fact that an unborn child has two doses of the recessive genes for a serious illness or has proved unlucky on the fifty-fifty chances that he will be a victim of one of these serious dominant defects, without question his parents can rightfully consent to drastic prenatal treatments—since these treatments may, it is reasonable to believe, be beneficial to him. Then if the worst befall, it would be the tragic result of rightful actions. We could go further and say that even if the unborn child is not certainly afflicted with one of these diseases, he may be one of a limited population at grave risk. (Amniocentesis, etc., backed up by a reading of the unborn child's maternal and paternal genetic history can indicate this risk.) We could say that parents can validly consent in behalf of such an unborn child medically, permitting the physician to use possibly beneficial trial treatments that, however drastic, do not place the child at greater risk than now surrounds him as one of a specially endangered population.

It is obvious, however, that canons of loyalty involved in the treatment of an as yet unconceived life—canons of loyalty similar in any way to those that are standard for our treatment of an actual child prenatally or postnatally—will require far more certainty of possible overall benefit to the hypothetical child before genetic surgery could be the treatment of choice. There would have to be far more than a fifty-fifty probability that a hypothetical child relieved of dwarfism would not be afflicted with schizophrenia (or would not produce children with other defects in the second generation), or that the child would not suffer worse mishap if relieved of the statistical likelihood that he will suffer Huntington's chorea or cystic fibrosis.

This way of expressing the option is, in fact, quite false, since we are not forced to choose between genetic surgery and doing nothing at all to prevent the conception and birth of these children. A hypothetical child is nothing—or at least nothing until we begin working on him preconceptually upon the fixed assumption that he will be engendered. Therefore, there would have to be at least no discernible risks before genetic surgery would be for him the treatment of choice. Before a child is at all actual he has no title to be born. Men and women have no unqualified right to have children. The treatments for the prevention of cystic fibrosis, Huntington's chorea, achondroplasia, some forms of muscular dystrophy, PKU, amaurotic idiocy, and other chromosomal abnormalities (if and when our Early Genetic Warning System can be perfected to detect them before conception) are continence, not getting married to a particular person, not having any children, using three contraceptives at once, or sterilization.

In discussing the ethics of the crucial step that begins the trial of genetic surgery upon humans, we should demand to know why these alternatives are not genetically more responsible. Finally, we must observe with some amazement that we live in an age that can calmly contemplate these two contradictory procedures: (1) abortion when there is likelihood that the child will be seriously impaired mentally or physically, and (2) learning how to do genetic surgery on humans although this may lead to the conception of children who may be seriously impaired mentally or physically (the mishaps).

It may be unfair to attribute to geneticists, who write as if they are not to be deterred by a proper ethics of treating hypothetical children, the pro-natalist attitudes of past traditional societies. If not, the explanation of their easy assumption that genetic surgery is a procedure which, when it becomes feasible, should be put into actual use may be that for them "genetic manipulation is only the currently visible small fraction of the very large iceberg dealing with the control of quality of human life" generally, having in view man's improving self-modification. A subtle but significant shift has taken place from doctoring primary patients to doctoring that nonpatient, the human race. For this reason, patients now alive or in the first and second generation may be passed over lightly, hypothetical children can be thought of as actualities to be improved at risk, and one can even contemplate permitting harm to come to them (with abortion as an escape prepared for the injured) for the sake of knowledge and learning the techniques ordered to the good to come.

While in the foregoing I have unavoidably stepped upon the terrain of ethical reasoning, my chief intention has been to show that actions whose objective is treatment and actions whose objective is the control of the future of our species are different sorts of actions, even when descriptively they may look alike; and that these two different sorts of actions may be subject to opposed ethical limits or evaluations.

The Ethical Questions

"If a scientist fixated upon the technical difficulties of the feat produces a clonal offspring cultivated from some medical student's intestinal cells, no judge can then decide, when someone comes tardily to court, that the baby should be uncreated." The same can be said of the other feats we have reviewed. If a mishap from trying genetic surgery upon humans comes tardily to court, the judge cannot say that baby should be uncreated. If an embryo created and nurtured to development in vitro comes tardily to the court of public opinion, we cannot say that baby should be uncreated. It will be too late to say it ought not to have been created. Discussion of the moral questions raised by the new biology must begin now. In this discussion the public should be engaged, and from it no helpful perspective should be excluded. The humanity of man is at stake. In ensuring that man shall remain man when and after he does any of these projected procedures for the increase of knowledge and for his own improvement, consequences are an important consideration. In fact there is nothing more important in the whole of ethics than the consequences for good or ill of man's actions and abstentions—except right relations among men, justice, and fidelity one with another. The moral quality of our actions and abstentions are determined both by the consequences for all men and by keeping covenant man with man.

We need to raise the ethical questions with a serious and not a frivolous conscience. A man of frivolous conscience announces that there are ethical quandaries ahead that we must urgently consider before the future catches up with us. By this he often means that we need to devise a new ethics that will provide the rationalization for doing in the future what men are bound to do because of new actions and interventions science will have made possible.1 9 In contrast, a man of serious conscience means to say in raising urgent ethical questions that there may be some things that men should never do. The good things that men do can be made complete only by the things they refuse to do.

Unavoidably, in outlining and analyzing the prospects before us, we already have introduced ethical considerations. I propose in the following sections of this chapter to raise four questions that seem to me crucial in making a proper response to the issues raised by the new biology (only the first of which has strictly to do with the consequences for good or ill of the adoption of one or another of these proposals for doctoring the species): (1) the question of whether or not man has or can reasonably be expected to have the wisdom to become his own creator, the unlimited lord of the future; (2) the anthropological and basic ethical question concerning the nature and meaning of human parenthood, and of actions that would be destructive of parenthood as a basic form of humanity; (3) the questionableness of actions and interventions that are consciously set within the context of aspirations to godhood; and (4) the question of human species-suicide. Some of these topics will be discussed more fully than others, and it is quite impossible (as we shall see from the very beginning) to keep them separate from one another. Questions of ethics are from the beginning questions of philosophy, of total worldview, of metaphysical or ultimately religious outlooks and "on-looks." It may be helpful to bring these things to the surface, in an age when many men imagine there can be ethics without ultimates.

A Question of Wisdom

First, then, the question of whether man is or will ever be wise enough to make himself a successful self-modifying system or wise enough to begin doctoring the species. When concern for the species replaces care for the primary patient, and means are adopted that are deep invasions of the parameters of human parenthood as it came to us from the Creator, will we not be launched on a sea of uncertainty where lack of wisdom may introduce mistakes that are uncontrollable and irreversible?

To this it is no answer to say that changes are already taking place in human kind, or that men are constantly modifying themselves by changes now consciously or unconsciously introduced, for example, in the environment. It is no answer to say simply that in the future proposed to us by the revolutionary biologists the changes we are now undergoing will only be accelerated in rate or that the self-modifications then going on will simply be deliberate in major ways. It is true that man adapts to his environment and that his environmental changes change him. The point now being made, however, may be cinched by saying that, from man's rape of the earth and his folly in exercising stewardship over his environment by divine commission, there can be derived no reason to believe that he ought now to reach for dominion over the modifications of his own species as well. It is almost a complete answer to these revolutionary proposals simply to say that "to navigate by a landmark tied to your own ship's head is ultimately impossible." Many or most of the proposals we are examining are exercises in "What To Do When You Don't Know The Names Of The Variables," not even the variables which our beginning to act upon the proposals, or our making of the proposals, may bring to pass in human society generally. The proposals are speculative speculations, not programs. They could not be otherwise. We do not even know how to learn to predict the consequences of presently projected lordships over the future in remote future human situations whose values and milieu we have no means of controlling. The following proposition is, therefore, as good as any other. Man cannot endure if there is no creation beneath him, assumed in his being, on which he ought not to lay his indefinitely tampering hands.

Selection 2: Joseph Fletcher, *Morals and Medicine*

Joseph Fletcher (1905–1991) taught Christian ethics at both the Episcopal Divinity School at Cambridge, Massachusetts, and Harvard Divinity School. Many know him best for his book Situation Ethics: The New Morality, *in which he advocated setting aside the rigid rules of traditional morality in favor of discerning what love should do given the situation. Fletcher was also an early contributor among Christian ethicists in the field of bioethics and brought his situationist perspective to bear upon these issues. In this selection he tackles the often vexing of problem of how to have a "good death" in the face of modern medicine's ability to keep us alive under extreme conditions. This issue remains a serious concern to this day.*

Euthanasia and Anti-Dysthanasia

The patient's right to die on his way to the hospital, a minister stops at a house near his church to say a word of personal sympathy to a couple sitting on the porch with their family doctor. Upstairs the man's mother is in bed, the victim of a series of small cerebral hemorrhages over the last eleven years. Her voice went two years ago and there is now no sign that she hears anything. Communication has ended. Says the son, with a complex question-asking glance at his wife, "My mother is already dead."

Listening to those telltale words the doctor shakes his head sympathetically and helplessly. To the minister, that involuntary gesture seems almost a ritual. Earlier that day another doctor did exactly the same thing when the minister told him about his talk with a family whose twenty-year-old son has been lying in the "living death" of complete coma for four years. An auto crash hopelessly shattered his cerebral cortex. Since then only the brain stem has sustained life. All thought and feeling have been erased, and he hasn't moved a single muscle of his body since the accident. But he is in "excellent health," although he feels no stimulus of any kind, from within or without. Once an angular blond youth of sixteen, he is now a baby-faced brunette, seemingly ten years old. He is fed through an indwelling nasal tube. He suffers no pain, only reacts by reflex to a needle jab. His mother says, "My son is dead."

Later, at the hospital, the minister visits a woman in her early seventies. He had last seen her at her fiftieth wedding anniversary party two months earlier. She has now been in the hospital for a week with what was tentatively thought to be "degenerative arthritis." But the diagnosis is bone cancer. Both legs were already fractured when she arrived at the hospital and little bits of her bones are splintering all the time; she has agonizing shaking attacks that break them off. She turns away from her clerical caller and looks at her husband. "I ought to die. Why can't I die?" It is the living that fear death, not the dying.

The minister leaves, somehow feeling guilty, and goes upstairs to Surgical. An intern and a young resident in surgery grab his arms and say, "Come on, join our council of war." They go into an empty room where two staff physicians and the chaplain are waiting. In the next room, a man is dying, slowly, in spite of their ingenious attempt to save him from pneumonic suffocation by means of a "tracheotomy," a hole cut in his throat through which an artificial respirator is used. The question is: should they take away the oxygen tank, let the patient go? The chaplain is pulled two ways. One of the doctors is against it, the other joins the resident in favor. The intern says he doesn't "like" it. The visiting clergyman says, "I would." They do. The oxygen is removed, the light turned off, the door closed behind them. Then they send the chaplain to comfort the widow out in the alcove at the end of the hall, saying, "We are doing everything we can."

This heartbreaking struggle over mercy death has become a standard drama in hospital novels—most recently in Richard Frede's *The Interns.* Physicians and clergymen struggle constantly in the most vital, intimate, and highly personal centers of human existence. The "primary events" of birth, procreation, and death are their daily fare. Ultimate as well as immediate concerns tax their capacity for creative and loving decisions. Squarely and continually confronting them is death, the prospect of nonbeing which lurks out of sight though never wholly out of mind for most of us. Because most people cannot look it in the eye, they cling to irrational, phobic, and sentimental attitudes about voluntary death and the medical control of dying.

They cannot see death as experienced doctors and ministers do—in perspective, a familiar adversary. This is the case even among psychologists. For example, many aspects were discussed in a recent symposium, The Meaning of Death, at a convention of the American Psychological Association. But nothing whatever was said about the growing problem of dying in dignity. Bad words such as "euthanasia" were unmentioned.

We are, however, becoming somewhat less irrational than our forebears on this subject. At the level of sheer logic, one of the most curious features of the "theological era" of the past is that most people feared and sought to avoid death at any and every cost, except sometimes for honor's sake. Even though they professed to have faith in personal survival after death, it was their worst enemy. Nowadays, when faith is waning not only in the prospect of hell but even of heaven, there is a trend toward accepting death as a part of reality, just as "natural" as life. Churchmen, even clergymen, are dropping the traditional faith in personal survival after death, just as many unbelievers do. Curiously, it is the skeptics about immortality who appear to face death more calmly. They seem somehow less inclined to hang on desperately to life at the cost of indescribable and uncreative suffering for themselves and others.

But a painful conflict persists. For instance, not long ago a man came to me deeply depressed about his role, or lack of one, in his mother's death. She had been an invalid for years, requiring his constant care and attention. At last her illness reached a "terminal" stage and she had to be taken to the hospital. One Saturday after work when he arrived in her semi-private room, the other patient greeted him by crying out, "I think your mother has just passed away. See. Quick!" His immediate reaction was relief that her suffering, and his, were now ended; so he hesitated to act on the other patient's plea to breathe into his mother's mouth in an effort to resuscitate her. Ever since, he had been troubled by a profound sense of guilt. His "conscience" accused him. This conflict is a "lay" version of what many doctors, if not most, feel when they forgo some device that might sustain a patient's life a little longer. Some are comforted when their action, or inaction, is interpreted to them as a refusal to prolong the patient's death.

Vegetable or Human?

In truth, the whole problem of letting people "go" in a merciful release is a relatively new one. It is largely the result of our fabulous success in medical science and technology. Not long ago, when the point of death was reached, there was usually nothing that could be done about it. Now, due to the marvels of medicine, all kinds of things can keep people "alive" long after what used to be the final crisis. For example, there is the cardiac "pacemaker," a machine that can restart a heart that has stopped beating. Turn off the machine, the heart stops. Is the patient alive? Is he murdered if it is taken away? Does he commit suicide if he throws it out the window? Artificial respirators and kidneys, vital organ transplants, antibiotics, intravenous feeding— these and many other devices have the double effect of prolonging life and prolonging dying. The right to die in dignity is a problem raised more often by medicine's successes than by its failures. Consequently, there is a new dimension in the debate about "euthanasia." The old-fashioned question was simply this: "May we morally do anything to put people mercifully out of hopeless misery?" But the issue now takes a more troubling twist: "May we morally omit to do any of the ingenious things we could do to prolong people's suffering?"

For doctors, this dilemma challenges the Hippocratic oath which commits them to increasingly incompatible duties—to preserve life and to relieve suffering. This conflict of conscience is steadily magnified by the swelling numbers of elderly people. Medical genius and sanitation have resulted in greater longevity for most of our population. In consequence, the predominant forms of illness are now degenerative—the maladies of age and physical failure—not the infectious diseases. Disorders in the metabolic group, renal problems, malignancy, cardiovascular ills, are chronic rather than acute. Adults in middle life and beyond fill the beds of our hospitals, and the sixty-five-and-over class grows fastest of all. Under these circumstances, many people fear the prospect of senility far more than they fear death.

Unless we face up to the facts with moral sturdiness, our hospitals and homes will become mausoleums where the inmates exist in a living death. In this day of "existential" outlook, in its religious and nonreligious versions, we might think twice on Nietzsche's observation, "In certain cases it is indecent to go on living." Perhaps it is a supreme lack of faith and self-respect to continue, as he put it, "to vegetate in a state of cowardly dependence upon doctors and special treatments, once the meaning of life, the right to life, has been lost."

Consider an actual case, in a topflight hospital. After a history of rheumatic heart disease, a man was admitted with both mitral and aortic stenosis—a blockage of the heart valves by something like a calcium deposit. The arts and mechanics of medicine at once went into play. First, open-heart surgery opened the mitral valve. Then—the patient's heart still sluggish—the operation was repeated. But the failure of blood pressure brought on kidney failure. While the doctors weighed a choice between a kidney transplant and an artificial kidney machine, staphylococcal pneumonia set in. Next, antibiotics were tried and failed to bring relief, driving them to try a tracheotomy. Meanwhile, the heart action flagged so much that breathing failed even through the surgical throat opening. The doctors then tried oxygen through nasal tubes, and failed; next, they hooked him into an artificial respirator. For a long time, technically speaking, the machine did his breathing. Then, in spite of all their brilliant efforts, he died.

Should they have "let him go" sooner into the Christian heaven or Lucretius' "long good night"? If so, at what point? Would it have been "playing God" to stop before the second operation? Before the tracheotomy? Before the respirator? Only the ignorant imagine that these are easy decisions. In practice, they are complex, even for those who favor merciful deaths in principle. Doctors as responsible ministers of medicine carry an awesome responsibility. Indeed, by their very use of surgical, chemical, and mechanical devices they are, in a fashion, playing God. In this case from the beginning some of the doctors had little hope, but they felt obliged to do what they could. A few insisted that they had to do everything possible even if they felt sure they would fail. Where can we draw the line between prolonging a patient's life and prolonging his dying?

The ugly truth is that sometimes patients in extremis try to outwit the doctors and escape from medicine's ministrations. They swallow kleenex to suffocate themselves, or jerk tubes out of their noses or veins, in a cat-and-mouse game of life and death which is neither merciful nor meaningful. Medical innovation makes it ever easier to drag people back to "life" in merely physiological terms. Yet when these patients succeed in outwitting their medical ministrants, can we say that they have committed suicide in any real sense of the word? Who is actually alive in these contrivances and contraptions? In such a puppet-like state most patients are, of course, too weakened and drugged to take any truly human initiative.

The classical deathbed scene, with its loving partings and solemn last words, is practically a thing of the past. In its stead is a sedated, comatose, betubed object, manipulated and subconscious, if not subhuman. This is why, for example, one desperate woman is trying to guarantee herself a fatal heart attack to avoid anything like her mother's imbecile last years. It is an unnerving experience to any sensitive person to hear an intern on the terminal ward of a hospital say with defensive gallows humor that he has to "go water the vegetables" in their beds.

Families—and their emotional and economic resources —deserve some reckoning too. And finally, all of us are potential patients. Surely we need to give these questions a fresh look, even though the obligation lies heaviest on leaders in medicine and allied fields.

Medical Morals and Civil Law

It is an oversimplification to think of the issue any longer as "euthanasia" and decide for or against it. Euthanasia, meaning a merciful or good death, may be achieved by direct or indirect methods. If it is direct, a deliberate action or "mercy-killing" to shorten or end life, it is definitely murder as the law now stands. But indirect euthanasia is another matter, the more complicated and by far the more frequent form of the problem. There are three forms it can take: (1) administering a death-dealing painkiller, (2) ceasing treatments that prolong the patient's life—or death, if you prefer, and (3) withholding treatment altogether.

An example of the first form is the administration of morphine in doses which are pyramided to toxic, fatal proportions. The doctor has been forced to choose between doing nothing further to alleviate suffering, or giving a merciful dose which kills both the pain and the patient. Usually he chooses the latter course. An example of the second form is the hospital scene described earlier when two doctors, a resident, an intern, a chaplain, and a visiting minister agreed to "pull the plug" and disconnect the bubbling life-prolonging oxygen tank.

To illustrate the third form of indirect euthanasia, we might look at this practical problem. A poliomyelitis patient—a young woman—is struck down by an extensive paralysis of the respiratory muscles. Lacking oxygen, her brain suffers irreparable damage from suffocation. She could be kept "alive" for months—maybe longer—by artificial respiration through a tracheostomy. However, is there anything in moral law, either the law of nature, the law of Scripture, or the law of love, that obliges us to use such extraordinary means, such gimmicks? If we forgo their use, and let the patient die of natural asphyxiation, we have "euthanised" in the third indirect form. Both Protestant and Catholic teachers have favored such a course. Or, to take another case, if a patient with incurable cancer gets pneumonia, may we morally withhold antibiotics that would cure the pneumonia and let the patient "go," thus escaping a protracted and pain-ridden death? Roman Catholics are not so sure about this one, but most others are agreed that the best and most loving course would be to withhold the antibiotics.

Some of those who have tried to face these issues—the Euthanasia Societies in America and England, for example —have wanted to restrict both direct and indirect euthanasia to voluntary situations where the patient has consented. Such a concept is applicable to people—of whom there are many—who have private understandings with doctor friends and with their families in anticipation of the end. But what of the patient who has never stated his wishes and is past making a mentally competent choice? Under this code, mercy would have to be denied no matter how hideous and hopeless his suffering. Yet in modern medical practice most terminal patients are in precisely this submoral condition. Therefore, many moralists are prepared to approve even involuntary forms of indirect euthanasia. Pope Pius XII, for example, said that in deciding whether to use reanimation techniques, if life is ebbing hopelessly, doctors may cease and desist, "to permit the patient, already virtually dead, to pass on in peace." This decision could be made by the family and the doctor for the patient. In the same vein, an Archbishop of Canterbury (Cosmo, Lord Lang) agreed that "cases arise in which some means of shortening life may be justified." Both of these church leaders of the recent past preferred to leave the decision as to when in the physician's hands.

This is probably the wisest policy, provided the doctors do not take a rigid or idolatrous view of their role as "life" savers. Medicine's achievements have created some tragic and tricky questions. Margaret Mead, the anthropologist, in a recent lecture on medical ethics at Harvard Medical School, called for an end to the present policy of pushing the responsibility off on physicians. It is certainly unfair to saddle the doctors with all the initiative and responsibility, to create such a "role image" for them, when pastors and relatives might take it. There is some wisdom, nevertheless, in the Pope's injunction to the family of the dying to be guided by the doctors' advice as to when "vital functions" have ceased and only minimal organic functioning continues.

The direct ending of a life, with or without the patient's consent, is euthanasia in its simple, unsophisticated, and ethically candid form. This is opposed by many teachers, Roman Catholics, and others. They claim to see a moral difference between deciding to end a life by deliberately doing something and deciding to end a life by deliberately not doing something. To many others this seems a very cloudy distinction. What, morally, is the difference between doing nothing to keep the patient alive and giving a fatal dose of a pain-killing or other lethal drug? The intention is the same, either way. A decision not to keep a patient alive is as morally deliberate as a decision to end a life. As Kant said, if we will the end, we will the means. Although differences persist in its application, the principle of mercy death is today definitely accepted, even in religious circles where the pressures of death-fear have been strongest. Disagreements concern only the "operational" or practical question—who does what under which circumstances?

Doctors and laymen have asked lawmakers to legalize direct euthanasia, thus far unsuccessfully. While this writer's decision is in favor of the direct method, it may be necessary to settle temporarily for an intermediate step in the law. One distinguished jurist, Glanville Williams, has suggested that since there is little immediate hope of having the direct method proposal adopted, it might be more practical to try for a law to safeguard the doctors in the indirect forms of mercy death which they are now practicing anyway, and which leading moralists of all persuasions could endorse. Such a measure would provide that a medical practitioner is not guilty of

any offense if he has sought to speed or ease the death of a patient suffering a painful and fatal disease. Doctors would then have protection under the law, freedom
to follow their consciences. To bring this matter into the open practice of medicine
would harmonize the civil law with medical morals, which must be concerned with
the quality of life, not merely its quantity.

The Vitalist Fallacy

The biggest obstacle to a compassionate and honest understanding of this problem
is a superstitious concept of "nature" inherited from an earlier, prescientific culture.
People often feel that death should be "natural"—that is, humanly uncontrolled and
uncontrived. Sometimes they say that God works through nature and therefore any
"interference" with nature by controlling what happens to people in the way of illness and death—interferes with God's activity. This argument has a specious aura of
religious force. For example, one doctor with an eighty-threeyear-old patient, para-
lyzed by a stroke and a half dozen other ailments, tells the compassionate family that
he will do nothing, "leave it to God." But God does not cooperate; their mother goes
on gasping. Maybe the doctor needs a better and more creative theology.

For the fact is that medicine itself is an interference with nature. It freely
cooperates with or counteracts and foils nature to fulfill humanly chosen ends.
As Thomas Sydenham said three hundred years ago, medicine is "the support of
enfeebled and the coercion of outrageous nature." Blind, brute nature imposing an
agonizing and prolonged death is outrageous to the limit, and to bow to it, to "leave
things in God's hands" is the last word in determinism and fatalism. It is the very
opposite of a morality that prizes human freedom and loving kindness.

The right of spiritual beings to use intelligent control over physical nature,
rather than submit beastlike to its blind workings, is the heart of many crucial
questions. Birth control, artificial insemination, sterilization, and abortion are all
medically discovered ways of fulfilling and protecting human values and hopes in
spite of nature's failures or foolishnesses. Death control, like birth control, is a
matter of human dignity. Without it persons become puppets. To perceive this is
to grasp the error lurking in the notion—widespread in medical circles—that life
as such is the highest good. This kind of vitalism seduces its victims into being
more loyal to the physical spark of mere biological life than to the personality
values of self-possession and human integrity. The beauty and spiritual depths of
human stature are what should be preserved and conserved in our value system,
with the flesh as the means rather than the end. The vitalist fallacy is to view life at
any old level as the highest good. This betrays us into keeping "vegetables" going
and dragging the dying back to brute "life" just because we have the medical know-
how to do it.

Medicine, however, has a duty to relieve suffering equal to preserving life. Furthermore, it needs to reexamine its understanding of "life" as a moral and spiritual
good—not merely physical. The morality of vitalism is being challenged by the
morality of human freedom and dignity. Natural or physical determinism must give
way to the morality of love. Doctors who will not respirate monsters at birth—the
start of life—will not much longer have any part in turning people into monsters at
the end of life.

Selection 3: Richard A. McCormick, *How Brave a New World: Dilemmas in Bioethics*

Richard A. McCormick, S.J. (1922–2000) was one of the foremost interpreters and teachers of Catholic social teaching. He brought fresh insight and serious dialogue with the social and cultural context of his day. In this excerpt he offers a carefully nuanced discussion of the ethical issues involved in in vitro fertilization raising related questions regarding the status of nascent life at the earliest stage, questions that touch on the Roman Catholic church's strong opposition to abortion and anticipating the debate over embryonic stem cell research that we will meet up with in Selection 4.

"In vitro" Fertilization

R. G. Edwards notes that there are three areas of medicine that could benefit greatly from the studies surrounding in vitro fertilization: (1) Some forms of infertility (blockage of the oviduct) could possibly be cured. (2) Knowledge useful for contraceptive technology could be gained. (3) Knowledge and methods could be obtained leading to the alleviation of genetic disorders and even other deformities.

The simplest instance of in vitro fertilization is extraction of the wife's oocytes by laparoscopy, fertilization with husband's sperm followed by laboratory culture to the blastocyst stage, then embryo transfer (implantation) into the wife's uterus. The procedure would be aimed at overcoming sterility due to obstruction of the fallopian tubes. This is the "simplest" instance because it does not raise the further issues of donor sperm, host wombs, and totally artificial gestation.

The ethical issues involved in such a procedure are multiple, even if only this simplest form is in question. They involve considerations of justice, the beginning of human life, and the value of life, in addition to the questions of parenthood and sex. First, there is the question of embryo wastage. Only one or two of the eggs taken from the mother would be transferred back into her. The remaining embryos would be discarded although such discarding is not essential to the procedure. Those who are convinced that human personhood begins with fertilization would reject in vitro fertilization on that ground alone, for apparently it would involve the deliberate destruction of human life to achieve a pregnancy.

However, other ethicists argue that there is a genuine doubt about whether we are dealing with a human person at this stage of development. The existence of such a doubt leads to a variety of conclusions. Some say that the very probability of human personhood constitutes "an absolute veto against this kind of experimentation." Others, while remaining basically negative, argue that given such a positive doubt, "the reasons in favor of experimenting might carry more weight, considered rationally, than the uncertain rights of a human being whose very existence is in doubt." Finally, there are some who would undoubtedly agree with Joseph Fletcher that the product of in vitro fertilization is but human tissue, "fallopian and uterine material."

Edwards' response to these serious ethical concerns seems unconvincing. He notes that in discarding embryos experimenters are doing nothing more than women who use intrauterine contraceptive devices. However, rather than an argument supporting embryo wastage, this could be viewed as an objection against intrauterine devices—to the extent that they achieve contraceptive effectiveness by expelling embryos. The same response could be made to his assertion that "in a society which sanctions the abortion of a fully formed fetus, the discarding of such a minute, undifferentiated embryo should be acceptable to most people." Such an argument says nothing of the moral rightness or wrongness of abortion, but only of a particular society's toleration or sanctioning of it. As a form of ethical argument, it is equivalent to saying that a society that tolerates obliteration bombing of cities should not object to a little selective torture of enemy prisoners. While that may be true in terms of ethical consistency, it says nothing about the moral rightness or wrongness of either procedure.

The second serious ethical problem with in vitro fertilization is its experimental character. It has been argued that, given the unknown hazards associated with laboratory culture and embryonic transfer, and the inability to overcome such unknown hazards, in vitro fertilization with subsequent implantation constitute potentially hazardous experimentation with a human subject without his consent—that is, risks are chosen for the future human being without his consent. More concisely, the experimental phase of this technology can be shown to be risk-free only by exposing a certain number of subjects to unethical experiments. Therefore we can never get to know how to perform such procedures in an ethical way. The argument does not rest on ascription of personal status to the embryo who is eventually discarded during development of the technology (though, as noted above, some ethicists would see a serious problem here too). Rather, it points to the possible harm to be inflicted on living children who come to be born after in vitro fertilization and laboratory culture. There is at present no way of finding out whether the viable progeny of these procedures will be deprived or retarded. Nor would a willingness to practice abortion on the deformed solve the problem, since many such deformities cannot and will not be identifiable by amniocentesis.

Others contend that this argument is not altogether persuasive, for procreation by natural processes produces a certain percentage of deformed, crippled, or retarded children. Thus the natural process of sexual intercourse also imposes serious hazards on future children without their consent and is no less "experimental" in this sense than laboratory fertilization with embryo transfer. Thus the problem is to bring the dangers associated with in vitro fertilization procedures to an acceptable level. No one has insisted that "natural" procreation be completely safe for the fetus before it is undertaken. Even in the most severe cases (women with phenylketonuria, whose offspring are virtually certain of receiving damage during gestation), it is argued that we do not constrain such couples from procreating except by moral suasion. "If we accept the morality of couples making this childbearing decision, can we deny the needs of a couple childless because of the woman's blocked oviducts?"

A possible double response could be made to this argument. First, we have no way of knowing the comparative risk ratios of the two methods of reproduction, since discovering the percentage of risk of in vitro procedures would expose a certain, perhaps very large, number of human subjects to serious risk without their consent. Second, when it is known that husband and wife are carriers of the same severe recessive, genetic disease, the course of moral responsibility demands that they not run the hazards of procreation. Therefore, when faced with the possible deformities from in vitro technology, the proper response is not to point to similar deformities in natural processes as justification for creating them by technology, but to use that technology to diminish them in the natural processes.

At some point, then, this discussion opens on the morality of risk-taking even within so-called natural procreative processes. What is the responsible course for couples who are carriers for the same deleterious recessive disease (for example, phenylketonuria) when there is a one-in-four chance that the child will be afflicted? Many, if not all, philosophers and theologians who have discussed the problem hold that running such a risk is morally irresponsible, and indeed that partners with such recessive defects ought not as a general rule to marry. As Medawar puts it: "If anyone thinks or has ever thought that religion, wealth, or color are matters that may properly be taken into account when deciding whether or not a certain marriage is a suitable one, then let him not dare to suggest that the genetic welfare of human beings should not be given equal weight." The problem remains, however, of where to draw the line where risk-taking is involved. Some would argue that a one-in-four chance of a seriously afflicted child is a tolerable risk. Others would disagree.

Here, however, several points must be made to structure the ethical discussion. First, even though abstention from childbearing may be the only responsible decision in these cases, it is another matter altogether whether this abstention should be compelled by law. Second, there is a line to be drawn where inherited defects are involved. Some diseases are relatively minor and manageable; others are enormously crippling and catastrophic for the child. Finally, in a highly technological and comfort-oriented society, the fear of having a defective child can easily become pathological. That is particularly possible in a society unwilling (unable?) to adjust itself to the needs of its most disadvantaged citizens.

The third set of arguments against in vitro fertilization concerns what it is likely to lead to, especially through the mentality it could easily foster. For instance, if in vitro fertilization is successfully (with safety and normality) introduced to treat sterility within a marriage, will there not be extensions beyond the marriage if either husband's sperm or wife's ovum is defective? And this raises all the ethical and theological problems associated with AID. Furthermore, the standard use of in vitro fertilization for infertility involves viewing infertility as a disease. But the accuracy of that description has been challenged not only because sterility is not a disease in the ordinary sense (since it is the incapacity or dysfunction of a couple, not of an individual), but above all because viewing it as a disease tends to undermine, in thought and practice, the bond between childbearing and the marriage covenant. Those who have no problem with AID would see little force in this type of argument, or would see it overridden by the value of providing the couple with their own child. But that is where the issue is.

If these arguments are overcome, there remain other issues of ethical relevance. For instance, would children conceived by in vitro fertilization suffer any identity or status problems? Would they experience a possibly harmful pressure to research their mental, physical, and emotional development? If the technology were widely used, would that distort the priorities of the health-care system in a way that would do harm by neglect in other, more urgent areas?

In vitro fertilization can also be undertaken with donor sperm, to be followed by embryonic transfer to the wife of the sterile husband, or to a host womb. Or it could occur with the sperm of the husband and an egg of another woman to be implanted in the wife (adopted embryo). Where donor sperm or ovum is used, not only is there the issue of unknown hazards imposed without consent, but once again the relation of procreation to marriage becomes the focus of concern. The issue is intensified when a host or surrogate womb (not the wife's) is used for the pregnancy, for not only does one of the agents of fertilization come from outside the marriage, but also the entire period of pregnancy and delivery is outside the marriage.

Such a rather exotic arrangement raises further formidable problems. What if the surrogate "mother" were to become disenchanted with the pregnancy and desire an abortion? What if the genetic parents desired such an abortion and tried to force the surrogate mother to undergo one? What if the genetic husband and wife are determined to have a healthy child and refuse to accept the deformed or retarded child that is born of the surrogate mother? There are additional ethical problems with the social identity of the child. Who is truly the child's mother? Who has rights and responsibilities with regard to such a child? A society, it can be argued, that already has enormous problems with marital stability would be unwise in the extreme to add freely to those problems.

My own view is that at the level of the individual couple's decision, there seems to be no argument that shows with clarity and certainty that husband-wife in vitro procedures using their own sperm and ovum are necessarily and inherently wrong, if abortion of a possibly deformed child is excluded and the risks are acceptably low. This is not to say that in vitro procedures are without problems and dangers. They are not. But such dangers issue only in a prudential caution, not necessarily a moral judgment that each instance is morally wrong. Let me take each of the major arguments once again in systematic form to make this clear.

1. Technologizing marriage.
There are two forms this argument takes. The first is associated with Pius XII and his statements on artificial insemination by husband. The Pope excluded this, and especially on the grounds that it separated the "biological activity from the personal relation of the married couple." Rather, "in its natural structure, the conjugal act is a personal act. . . ." In summary, Pius XII viewed the conjugal act as having a natural and God-given design that joins the love-giving dimension with the life-giving dimension. On this basis he excluded both contraception and artificial insemination—and a fortiori in vitro fertilization with embryo transfer. It is safe to say that this structured the negative responses of some theologians and bishops when they spoke of the "unnatural."

I believe that this is substantially the approach of Donald McCarthy." He refers to the "integrity of the procreative process" and argues that artificial fertilization is among those "actions that violate human dignity or the dignity of human procreation." Such actions are inhuman in themselves.

The second form of this argument is a softer form. It is a general concern that too much technology introduced into a highly personal context (parenting, family) can mechanize and depersonalize the context. The argument issues in a prudential caution, not necessarily a moral judgment that each instance is morally wrong on this account alone—as noted earlier. This argument is also justifiably concerned with objectifying the child into a consumer item ("what sex?" "what color eyes?" etc.).

What might be said of these arguments? I shall comment on only the first, since the second is a dictate of common sense, and leaves the question fairly well open. It is clear that at least very many theologians have not been able to accept "the natural . . . design of the conjugal act" as this was interpreted by Pius XII-that is, they have not viewed it as an inviolable value. Thus they can allow for contraception at times.

Similarly, and in some consistency, they have not been able to see that artificial insemination by the husband is necessarily a violation of nature. Gindel states it well when he says that the child must be the expression and embodiment of love, but that sexual intercourse is not the only or necessary source for this expression and embodiment. Many would respond in a similar fashion to Donald McCarthy's assertion that artificial fertilization always attacks the integrity of the procreative process. How can one establish that plausibly? We can intuit it, but intuitions notoriously differ. And in this case, such dehumanization has not been perceived by at least very many commentators (most recently Bernard Haring, George Lobo, Roger Troisfontaines, Karl Rahner et al.).

That is not to say that the separation of procreation from sexual love-making is a neutral thing. To say that would be to minimize the physical aspects of our being in a dualistic way. Rather the artificial route to pregnancy is a disvalue and one that needs justification. John R. Connery, S.J., has caught this well (though by saying this I do not imply that he should necessarily be associated with the analysis as one approving it). Whether it can find such justification is the burden of some of the other arguments—especially that of the "slippery slope" involving possible undesirable future developments.

In summary, it seems very difficult to reject in vitro fertilization with embryo transfer on the sole ground of artificiality or the separation of the unitive and the procreative in that sense—unless one accepts this physical inseparability as an inviolable value.

2. Abortion and discarded zygotes.

It is admitted that at present in the process of in vitro fertilization with embryo transfer more than one ovum is fertilized. Those not used will perish. As I noted there are those who view zygotes as persons with rights and therefore condemn the procedure outright as abortion. Others see them as simply "human tissue" and find no problem in their creation and loss, the more so because so many fertilized ova are lost in in vivo attempts at pregnancy. Still a third group would assess the zygote as somewhere in between these alternatives—not yet a person, but a living human being deserving of respect and indeed protection. How much protection is the key question.

With no claim of saying the last word, I would suggest the following for consideration. First, the discussion ought not to center around the personhood of the fertilized ovum. It is difficult to establish this, and there are reputable theologians and philosophers in large numbers who deny such an evaluation at this stage. Moreover, it is unnecessary; for many of those who deny personhood insist that the zygote is not just a thing, but also deserves our respect and awe.

Second, it is one thing to fertilize in vitro in order to experiment and study the product of conception. It is quite another to do so in order to achieve a pregnancy. It seems to me that the respect due nascent life, even if not yet personal life, rubs out the first alternative at least as a general rule. Some research is necessary, of course, prior to implementation of transfer technology. I do not see this, given our strong doubts about zygote status, as incompatible with respect. This is, however, the gray and most difficult and controversial area. Kass has stated that the "presumption of ignorance ought to err in the direction of not underestimating the basis for respect." That seems correct, and it is the same as the traditional principle that states that in factual doubts life generally deserves the preference.

Third, the term "abortion" must be carefully used when there is question of discarded zygotes. We know that a very high percentage of naturally fertilized ova never implant, are lost. This means that there is a tacit acceptance on the part of the couple that their normal sexual relations will lead to this as the price of having a child.

The response often given to this explanation is that we may not reproduce by artifice everything that happens in nature. Thus, though people inevitably die, we do not kill them. Though there are life-taking earthquakes in nature, we ought not manufacture life-taking earthquakes. Perhaps a distinction is called for here between replicating nature's disasters and replicating nature's achievements. Is there anything particularly wrong about achieving artificially— f cute de mieux— what occurs otherwise naturally? We are not exactly replicating disasters, but rather achievements even with unavoidable disvalues. If it is by no means clear that couples engaging in normal sexual relations are "causing abortions" because foreseeably many fertilized ova do not implant, it is not clear that the discards from artificial procedures must be called "abortions," especially if the ratio of occurrence is roughly similar.

Put this in the language of rights to life on the supposition that the zygote is a person. It is not a violation of the right to life of the zygote if it is spontaneously lost in normal sexual relations. Why is it any more so when this loss occurs as the result of an attempt to achieve pregnancy artificially? The matter of discards is serious, indeed crucial for those of us who believe that human life must be protected and respected from its very beginning. These reflections are meant only as probes into a difficult area.

3. Harm to the possible child.
The argument here is that the very procedure that gives life is inseparable from risks, physical and psychological. These may be small risks, but even so it is morally wrong to induce for a nonconsenting child even a small risk of great harm. This seems to be Ramsey's key argument.

On the other hand, the counterstatement (by Kass and others) is that the risk of harm need not be positively excluded. It is sufficient if it is equivalent to or less than the risks to the child from normal procreation.

The response to this assertion, as I noted, is that we could never get to know that without exposing a certain number of children to unknown risk to get the statistic. This seems to some to be an insuperable argument for ever starting the in vitro procedures. However, once this statistic is had, is the objection any longer telling? In other words, even though Steptoe and Edwards may have acted wrongfully (in ignorance of the risks), after it is clear that the risks are equivalent to normal conception, are those who follow necessarily acting wrongfully?

4. The extension beyond marriage.
This reasoning takes two forms. First, once in vitro fertilization is used successfully in marriage, it will go beyond marriage to third-party donors (semen, ovum), host wombs, etc. This extension is seen as a radical attack on marriage, the family, human sexuality, personal identity, and lineage of the child. The argument is one

of inevitability, given the cultural acceptance by many of AID (donor insemination) already. As Kass says: "There will almost certainly be other uses involving third parties." However, possible abuses need not morally indict legitimate uses. With discretion and judgment human beings are, I believe, capable of drawing lines. Abuses, therefore, are not inevitable, though it would be naïve to think that some will not occur.

The second form of the argument, an extension of the first, is that the wedge argument is primarily a matter of the logic of justification—that is, the principles now used to justify husband-wife in vitro fertilization already justify in advance other procedures. The strict validity of this second argument, it seems to me, depends on the "principles now used to justify." If the principle is that an infertile couple, using their own gametes, may licitly use artificial means, that is one thing. If, on the other hand, it is less precise (for example, couples may licitly overcome their sterility with in vitro procedures), then all the problems involved in the second form of the argument strike home.

In summary, then, at the level of the individual couple's decision, there seems to be no argument that shows with clarity and certainty that in vitro procedures using their own sperm and ovum are necessarily and inherently wrong, if abortion of a possibly deformed child is excluded and the risks are acceptably low." This is not to say that such procedures are without problems and dangers. They are not.

I would conclude, therefore, that in vitro fertilization with embryo transfer is ethically acceptable under a fourfold condition: (1) the gametes are those of husband and wife; (2) embryo wastage is not significantly higher in the artificial process than it is in vivo; (3) the likelihood of fetal abnormality is no greater than it is in normal procreation; (4) there is no intention to abort if abnormality does occur.

Another, and an extremely interesting, moral problem is the question of government funding of in vitro research. In my own—at this time very tentative—judgment, public policy should not support in vitro fertilization where research alone (not embryo transfer) is the purpose. Respect for germinating life calls for at least this. Granted, there is potentially a good deal to be learned from study of fertilized ova (genetic disease, contraception, fertility). But I do not see how this can be done without stripping nascent life of the minimal respect we owe it. Some research is necessary, of course, prior to implementation of transfer technology. I do not see this, given our doubts about zygote status, as incompatible with respect.

As for in vitro fertilization with embryo transfer at the research stage (I mean clinical trials—for I think it quite clear that government should not support clinical practice), this should not be supported with government funds in the present circumstances (compare below) though it should not be prohibited by law or policy. Why "not be supported"? Because of the cumulative impact of many arguments: The dangers of going beyond marriage are almost certainly unavoidable in our present atmosphere; the distorted priorities of medicine this introduces (for example, prenatal care for children already in utero is unavailable to very many); the almost unavoidable dangers of proceeding to independent zygote research and the manipulation of the implanted fetus (compare our abortion culture) with the assault on nascent life that this involves; the readiness to abort that this procedure presently entails; the trauma this would visit on an already deeply divided nation (on abortion) by asking that tax money be used for purposes against the consciences of many and not necessary to the public good; the disproportion of benefits (to a relatively few) with costs; the growing neglect of more radically therapeutic (oviduct reconstruction) and preventive (of gonorrhea) interventions; government reinforcement of the dubious, perhaps noxious, notion that women's lives are unfulfilled if they cannot have their "own children."

It should be remembered that funding implies fostering. Whether it is appropriate to foster depends on what is being fostered. And that depends to some extent on the circumstances. Thus if we cannot fund in vitro fertilization between husband and wife without in our circumstances funding (and fostering) practices beyond that, we should not do so. I believe this to be the case. In other circumstances we could draw a different conclusion.

Cloning

The reproductive technology known as cloning represents the most intense intervention of all. At the present, cloning in the human species still pertains to the area of science fiction. Were it to occur at some future date it would involve removing insemination and fertilization from the marriage relationship, and it would also remove one of the partners from the entire process. Its purported advantages are eugenic in character (removal of deleterious genetic material from the gene pool, and programming the genotype in such a way as to maximize certain desirable traits—for example, intelligence, creativity, artistic ability).

There are those who judge such procedures as desirable and moral in terms of their consequences and advantages. If such manipulative reproduction would heighten the intelligence (or artistic, or creativity) quotient of the race, or provide solutions to some particularly difficult and intractable human problems, it is good. To the objection or at least suspicion that there might be something inhuman in laboratory reproduction of human beings, it is asserted that "man is a maker and a selector and a designer, and the more rationally contrived and deliberate anything is, the more human it is." On this basis it is concluded that "laboratory reproduction is radically human compared to conception by ordinary heterosexual intercourse. It is willed, chosen, purposed, and controlled, and surely these are among the traits that distinguish Homo sapiens from others in the animal genus."

Whether such value judgments are the only ones capable of supporting the ethical character of cloning may be debatable. However, they do suggest that there comes a point in the moral discourse surrounding reproductive interventions when one must step aside from the casuistry of individual interventions and view the future possibilities and directions in aggregate and in the light of over-all convictions about what the "human" is. When that is done, some of the following questions arise. Will such reproductive interventions, even if they provide certain short-term remedies or advantages, actually improve the over-all quality of human life? If so, how is the improvement to be specified? What is the notion of the human that functions in the description of an "improvement"? And who decides this? If the development and application of such technology are likely to be humanly destructive, why will they be such? And if the more advanced forms of reproductive technology threaten some profoundly cherished human values and institutions (parenthood, marriage, the family), and are therefore something to be avoided, or at least stringently controlled, how are these values threatened, and where was the first wrong step or threatening one taken? Those are the questions that will be asked for decades as technology becomes increasingly sophisticated.

If the questions surrounding basic values are not asked, not asked seriously, not asked publicly, not asked continually, and in advance of the use of reproductive technologies, the danger is that we will identify the humanly and morally good with the technologically possible. That is why so much is at stake in reproductive interventions—not only in the conclusions that are drawn, but also in the criteria and form of moral reasoning involved.

Selection 4: James Gustafson, *The Contributions of Theology to Medical Ethics*

> *James Gustafson (b. 1925) is a prominent Christian ethicist out of the United Church of Christ tradition who has taught at Yale, The University of Chicago, and Emory University. His two-volume work,* Ethics from a Theocentric Perspective, *is a work of singular importance in the foundational work of Christian ethics. In our brief excerpt he reflects on the contribution of theology and theological ethics to the discourse of biomedical ethics.*

From my perspective, ethics, like theology, is reflection on human experience. It is reflection on human experience in its moral dimensions. The salient aspect of human experience in which moral dimensions occur is action. Ethics is an intellectual activity like theology. Its principal subject matter is human action. It is not all human action, however, but human action that is prescribed, governed, and judged by moral values and by moral principles. The task of a moral philosopher is two-fold: to analyze the necessary conditions for moral activity (including moral judgments, and choices, and actions) to occur, and to indicate normatively what moral principles and values ought to govern human action. Ethics, like theology, is the work of finite and fallible human agents.

The religious qualification of moral experience and more particularly of moral action, takes place through the awareness that action is not only in response to other persons, events, and things, but also in response to the ultimate power that sustains and stands over against creation. Moral experience in the context of religious life is qualified affectively and intellectually by the experience of the reality of God. The theological qualification of ethics takes place through the articulation of the significance of the ultimate power both as a necessary condition for moral action, and as a necessary justification for moral values and principles that judge, prescribe, and govern action. The theologian who concentrates on ethics has the same two tasks as the moral philosopher: to analyze the necessary conditions for moral activity to occur, and to indicate normatively what moral principles and values ought to govern action. His difference from the moral philosopher is not in the form of thought, nor is the substance of this thought unique. His thought is qualified by his experience of and belief in the reality of God. Thus, his analysis of the necessary conditions for moral activity to occur will move to the theological margins of moral experience, and to the theological grounds of all experience. His indication of normative moral principles and values will be, in some manner, justified by his theology.

Medicine, I take it, merely specifies an arena of human action of which morality is a dimension. Thus medical ethics addresses this arena.

The Contribution of Theology to Medical Ethics

The contribution that theology can make to medical ethics depends upon what claims are made and defended about God, the ultimate power, and about human beings as moral agents in relation to God. Particularly it depends upon whether the symbols or concepts of God provide a basis for drawing moral inferences with reference to human activity. Moral inferences from theological claims have been made in many ways in the history of the Christian tradition. God has been claimed to be the giver of the moral law through persons such as Moses and through the moral order of creation via his gracious creative act. God has been claimed to be the commander who speaks to people in a direct and immediate way in particular circumstances. Stories and symbols of God and his activities have been used to interpret the religious and moral significance of events and circumstances in such a way that a particular course of human moral action "follows" from such interpretation. "If a religious utterance is not a moral utterance no moral inferences can be derived from it. . . ." In the Western religious traditions many "utterances" about God have moral terms.

The claims made about God that are bases for drawing moral inferences, it must be noted, are not always straightforward predicates, like "God is love," nor are they always general indicative statements, like "God intends the well-being of the creation." Often they have been made in other forms of discourse, God is like a King, or a Father, or a Shepherd; analogies to social roles imply certain relations, which in turn are sources for delineating certain moral purposes or duties. God chastizes his people for their religious and moral wrongs through the activity of their political and military enemies; culpability is punished and thus the laws given to guide his people are reinforced. God's rule is like a Kingdom which will come; from some perceptions of that Kingdom inferences are drawn about the moral order that anticipates it. It is not possible here to develop the variety of religious language about God, and to show how choices of significant symbols that refer to him and to his activity richly affect the ways in which the contributions of theology to medical ethics can be made. God's purposes, and his relations to creation about which Psalmists spoke poetically, and prophets vividly, must be indicated in briefer and more prosaic terms.

To develop the contributions of theology to medical ethics briefly, I have selected three theological themes to be used illustratively. Inevitably this selection skews the presentation, and invites possible misinterpretations; yet in order to indicate both in substance and in form what the contribution of theology can be, it must be made. Two of these themes are primarily about God, one is primarily about humans.

First, God intends the well-being of the creation. This statement about God's intention clearly contains a value term, well-being. It is a declaration about God's purpose, or about what God values.

Second, God is both the ordering power that preserves and sustains the well-being of the creation and the power that creates new possibilities for well-being in events of nature and history. This theme is about the characteristic activities of the ultimate power. It also contains the value term, well-being. To use language more appropriate to humans, the first statement refers to the intention of God's "intellect" and the second to the intention of his "will" or "activity."

These statements about God, I believe, are plausible as inferences drawn from the religious dimensions of experience as that has been reflected upon by the Jewish and Christian communities, and expressed both in vivid symbols and in doctrinal statements. The experiences which make these symbolic and doctrinal affirmations plausible have been the occasions for the poetic and prayerful celebrations of the goodness of life in the tradition. The experiences which render them dubious have been the occasions for the most profound human quarrels with God, such as those of Job and Jeremiah, and for the elements of eschatological hope that are present in the tradition such as the expectation of a messiah, a return of the Lord, or the coming of God's Kingdom. "Philosophical" theologians have also on occasion found bases for making similar affirmations. I cannot here develop the grounds for plausibility of these statements; persons who find them plausible can follow the remainder of the argument with some conviction; persons who do not might follow it as a thought-experiment."

The human race has developed in such a way that it has unique capacities among the whole of creation, namely those which enable its members to act intentionally to affect the course of the creation for its well-being. The human race has a role of "deputyship" or "stewardship" within creation. Humans are part of creation; they are finite. They are limited in information, understanding, and power, though in all three respects their capacities are beyond that of other creatures. In addition, distinctive human capacities are the conditions for a basic anxiety; human perceptions of life with its threats to individual and collective human well-being lead to inordinate efforts to secure and defend a time and space of stability to the cost of other persons and communities and other aspects of creation. Thus, relative to the ultimate power, God, humans are finite; relative to God's purpose and activity for the well-being of the whole of creation, humans are inordinately curved in upon their narrow self-interests in efforts to find security. Our third statement sums this up. Humans are finite and "sinful" agents whose actions have a large measure of power to determine whether the well-being of the creation is sustained and fulfilled.

Whether the well-being of the creation will be preserved and sustained, and whether it will develop in response to events in history and nature that create new possibilities, depends to a large measure upon human action. Therein is built the principal bridge between theological beliefs and human morality. To reiterate, to determine whether wellbeing occurs, or whether something less than or opposite to it occurs, is in a large measure within the capacities of human agents. Medical research and practice is an arena in which finite and sinful humans have capacities to intervene in the biological processes of life in such a way that God's intention for the wellbeing of the creation is furthered or frustrated, in such a way that God's power to sustain and preserve that well-being is actualized or not, in such a way that the new possibilities that the creative power of God brings into being are fulfilled, partially realized, or turned to the devastation of the creation. The more precise arenas are many: clinical situations in which life can be prolonged, fetal life aborted, and disturbed patients committed to institutions; public health issues in which diseases can be controlled by pesticides, and resistance to illness developed by improvement in nutrition; medical research in which pharmacological means are developed to increase the stature of dwarfed humans or to control aggressive behavior, and genetic research in which inherited physical defects are isolated for potential therapy.

The issues that the argument must address can now be made more precise. What do these belief statements contribute to human moral action in the arena of medical practice and research? What do they contribute to an interpretation of the necessary conditions for moral action? What do they contribute to the establishment of moral principles and values which ought to be used to judge and guide action? How are these contributions made? . . .

1. These beliefs contribute to medical ethics by providing a moral point of view, that is, a fundamental moral perspective on medical care and research. 2. These beliefs contribute to medical ethics by grounding and informing certain attitudes toward life which are significant for medical ethics. These beliefs contribute to medical ethics by grounding and informing a basic ethical intentionality that gives direction to intervention in the biological processes of life.

Selection 5: Paul T. Jersild, "Theological and Moral Reflections on Stem Cell Research"

Paul T. Jersild is Professor Emeritus of Theology and Ethics at Lutheran Theological Southern Seminary in Columbia, South Carolina, and former Visiting Research Professor at the University of South Carolina Bioethics Center. This article provides a good introduction to the ethical issues currently under debate in matters of stem cell research. The conversation is continuing and new discoveries stimulate further thought in the field of ethics.

Rather than discussing the scientific aspects of embryonic stem cell (ESC) research, I will turn immediately to the central issue of the stem cell debate for people of faith: the theological and moral status of the embryo. Christians historically have been concerned to respect life at every stage of its development, but what I call a gradualist or developmental understanding of human life recognizes the need of making distinctions in the way we understand our obligation toward that life as it emerges. A gradualist understanding has found significant support among Christian theologians from the beginning, and it appeals to me today as an eminently sensible and responsible point of view with obvious implications both for abortion and stem cell research.

I believe the gradualist view expresses the implications of a Lutheran anthropology. Our understanding of human nature is relational, which means we understand who we are in terms of the relations that literally make our human identity possible. At the embryonic level we are potentially but not actually human subjects because we are not yet relational beings. Thus we become who we are as human beings in relation to God and to our fellow human beings. As the embryo in the womb becomes a fetus and progresses to term, the reality of living in relationship—the reality of one's humanity—is more intensely anticipated from the side of the mother and family, reflecting the growing moral status of prenatal life. This view runs counter to the Roman Catholic position that takes a substantialist view, which means that because the elements of human life are present in the embryo, its moral worth must be equal to that of persons living in relationship.

Those who maintain the substantialist view might argue that the relational view fails in its subjectivity. Our humanity is due to the fact that it is God who stands in relation to us, bestowing our humanity from our microscopic beginnings. The fact that our subjectivity, the capacity to relate, and other marks of human identity are absent is thus irrelevant. The developmentalist response is that relationships are the prerequisite to moral obligation. The remoteness of life in its beginning stages inevitably means that our sense of obligation to it does not carry the moral weight that life in relationship confers. The moral argument on behalf of life in its beginning stages betrays a theoretical character compared to the obligations we experience toward actual human beings. Furthermore, the developmentalist would note that the very process of reproduction refutes the substantialist claim. Some 40 to 60 percent of fertilized eggs never complete their journey to implantation and eventual birth. It staggers one's credulity to attribute a divinely bestowed humanity, conferring the rights of citizenship, upon millions of embryos destined to destruction.

Churchly deliberations concerning the human soul also have a bearing on the ESC debate. The Catholic position going back to Thomas Aquinas is called creationism, meaning that each soul is created by an act of God. Since the mid-nineteenth century, and contrary to the thinking of Thomas and many other theologians, the Catholic Church has placed ensoulment at the point of conception. In the current discussion this means that from that moment a fully human being is present who is worthy of the full protection of the law. The theology of Lutheranism (and the Eastern Orthodox Church) has taken a different route, espousing the traducianist view that regards both soul and body as a parental inheritance; they develop together in the womb until reaching their completion at birth. Current developments in Christian thinking about the soul render these older distinctions less than helpful or germane; nevertheless, the gradualist position in the ESC debate obviously relates better to the traducianist than to the creationist position.

It goes without saying that human life demands respect whatever the circumstance or condition being addressed, but the gradualist position calls for distinctions to be made concerning the nature of that respect during the course of embryonic and fetal development. Thus, contrary to the way it is commonly framed, the issue is not when human life begins; the question, rather, is what the nature of our obligation to human life is as it develops from its beginning stages. From common experience we recognize that the sense of moral obligation toward prenatal life increases as the development of that life proceeds from its microscopic, non-sentient state to a recognizable member of the human family. This point is validated in the way we respond to miscarriage, for example, as well as to abortion, which causes far greater moral anguish if it occurs at a late stage in the pregnancy.

There is another significant aspect to this argument. The setting for ESC research is the laboratory rather than the womb. Through in vitro fertilization (IVF) an embryo is produced in a Petri dish, which lacks the nurture that guarantees a future with eventual birth. Thus the dismantling and destruction of an embryo that takes place in stem cell research ought not be labeled an abortion. Jewish law acknowledges this point by not attributing legal status to genetic materials outside the uterus, even if embryos are involved; such materials lack potential humanity until they are implanted in a woman's womb. But the question can still be raised, "Are we acting irresponsibly before God and the human family when we work with genetic materials in the laboratory?" My answer to this question is twofold: Given the fact that human life in its beginning stages has long been the object of laboratory manipulation, and because of its non-sentient, microscopic character in this setting, it does allow for experimentation under carefully maintained guidelines. However, this is a responsible position only if the reasons for such experimentation are morally acceptable: where it is motivated by the promise of regenerative medicine and the desire to alleviate the tragedy and anguish of genetic diseases. Within that context, it is indeed responsible for scientists to pursue ESC research.

An argument often raised and which until recently had been persuasive in my own thinking is whether there may not be serious, detrimental moral consequences for society—a general cheapening of human life—if we are systematically engaged in the continuing destruction of embryos. Here I believe the argument of Francis S. Collins, Director of the Human Genome Project and confessing Christian, is pertinent. He notes that an important goal of ESC research is to arrive at the point where stem cell nuclear transfer (SCNT), commonly called cloning, can be successfully achieved. It is a procedure that overcomes the immunity problem because it involves taking the patient's own genetic material and inserting it in the diseased tissue. SCNT does not involve the fusion of sperm and egg as in IVF, which creates an embryo; it involves taking a single cell from a person's skin (we shed millions of them daily), which provides the DNA instructions, and uniting it with an enucleated egg. It is an artificial procedure performed in the laboratory that does not occur in nature "and is not part of God's plan to create a human individual." I share Collins' conviction that this procedure does not constitute a meaningful assault on our moral sensibilities, and seriously doubt that there could be any long-term detrimental consequences as a result of it.

Successful utilization of SCNT still eludes us, however, and current practice involves the destruction of embryonic life. While I reject the notion that this research destroys the lives of human subjects, or "actual" human life, it is obviously preferable to avoid taking life in any form if alternative procedures are available. Pursuing such alternatives is an expression of our respect for embryonic life. One option is to limit the use of embryos to those that are left over from IVF procedures in fertility clinics, destined to destruction rather than implantation and eventual birth. Unfortunately, the policy of the current administration prevents scientists from pursuing this option since it doesn't allow for a sufficient number of embryos to establish the stem cell lines, or lineage, that are needed. Another often recommended alternative is the use of adult stem cells (ASCs), which at this point have actually provided the most success in stem cell therapy (largely hematopoietic stem cells in combating diseases of the blood). But ASCs appear to lack the plasticity and potency of ESCs, which limits their promise. Scientists point out that research with both ASCs and ESCs is required because of their complementarity; what we learn from research with one contributes to the promise of the other. It is conceivable that ESC research may turn out to be the prerequisite to learning how best to reprogram ASCs to make them as effective therapeutically as ESCs. In other words, ESC research today may well make it unnecessary tomorrow.

Opponents of ESC research argue both deontologically and consequentially in making their case. The former argument maintains that not only is human life present from conception, it bears the same moral value as the lives of human beings living in society. The implications of such a view would require that embryonic life receive the same legal protections enjoyed by a U.S. citizen, which, if pursued (it has been advocated in suits brought before California courts), would lead to a legal nightmare. Among other absurdities, all the embryos in cold storage at fertility clinics—now estimated at over 400,000—would have the right to be born; any denial of such right could constitute an act of homicide.

Among consequential arguments, there is concern over the enormous profits that will likely come from ESC research, causing intense pressure to utilize this research beyond the context of alleviating disease. Are we not naïve in thinking we can harness this research for this purpose alone? This is a legitimate concern; we need a national policy on embryo research that applies to both publicly and privately funded research, carrying significant penalties for those who fail to comply. Among other things, such a policy could prohibit the patenting of information obtained from ESC research to insure that its primary focus remains its healing potential and the common good of society rather than the pursuit of profits. Another common argument cites the deception and hype involved in stem cell research and the raising of false expectations among the public, a situation also related to the pursuit of profits. This is certainly an important point and needs to be addressed by the scientific community. While these consequences (and other "slippery slope" arguments) are important in raising red flags and inspiring an appropriate caution, I do not believe that they should determine national policy on this matter. The potential good of ESC research bears sufficient moral weight to overrule these concerns.

I believe the decisive issue in this debate concerns the moral and theological validity of a gradualist/developmental position that makes a critical moral distinction between microscopic life and personal, human existence. One can certainly argue that human life is all of one fabric, but its beginning as a single thread is far removed from the completed garment—sufficiently removed to require a different set of ethical judgments. The moral impact of destroying embryos in the laboratory by doing research driven by beneficent purposes does not begin to compare with the impact of destroying the lives of individual persons, for whatever reason. Our language about the embryo reveals this fact: it is not injured but damaged; in miscarriage it is not killed but lost; its destruction in the laboratory is an act of disassembling or disaggregating, not killing or murder; we use the impersonal "it" in referring to the embryo because it lacks personal identity. Those who insist on using such terms as killing or murder in this context are straining too hard; they risk credibility in their effort to make a moral point that most of us fail to see.

My conclusion is that when one sees ESC research within the context of potential healing of diseased and suffering people, the moral weight clearly lies on the side of healing people. There is no moral revulsion over the destruction of life at the embryonic level that begins to compare with the anguish and grief caused by the premature demise of people afflicted with a genetic disease, or who are severely disabled by injury. I can appreciate the argument that there are boundaries to what we can achieve in alleviating the pain and burden of human existence, but I'm not convinced that we should draw that boundary in a way that removes the promise of healing in ESC research. To insist that microscopic, non-sentient life must receive the very same respect as living people is to make an intellectual distinction that lacks moral force; it does not compel a strong sense of obligation.

Ian Barbour makes an astute observation that is pertinent to this discussion: "With a new technology, it may be easier to forbid everything or to forbid nothing than to make and enforce careful judgments about potential uses." A more nuanced position is always more demanding in the discernment it requires; it also places a heavier responsibility on those who espouse it because of the risks involved. I would avoid the two opposite poles in the ESC research: the embryo is not a human being with the same moral weight and status as human subjects living in society, but neither is it a mere collection of cells without any moral claim on society. The one viable alternative to these positions is the gradualist/developmental position, driven by the possibilities of healing and adamantly committed to protecting the procedure from every form of self-serving misuse. The end result should be, and I believe can be, the serving of the common good of society.

PACIFISM, JUST WAR, AND TERRORISM

41

❧ *We have already encountered discussions of just war thinking in selections above from Augustine and Aquinas particularly. Previous selections from Origen, the Anabaptists, and the Society of Friends have touched upon Christian pacifism. While just war thinking has prevailed as the dominant position over the long history of Christian discourse about war, pacifism has endured and peacemaking has been the common commitment of Christian social teaching in general. In today's world pacifism continues to have its vigorous defenders, and coping with terrorism has tested the just war theory.*

Selection 1: David A. Hoekema, "A Practical Christian Pacifism"

David A. Hoekema is Professor of Philosophy at Calvin College in Grand Rapids, Michigan. He previously served as Executive Director of the American Philosophical Association at the University of Delaware. This article, which appeared in The Christian Century *in 1986, provides a contemporary defense of pacifism that engages the just war tradition.*

Few moral and theological positions are as deeply cherished by their adherents, yet so quickly dismissed by their opponents, as pacifism. The moral legitimacy of using violence is among the most urgent issues of our time, and yet its discussion slips quickly into an exchange of stereotypes. Pacifists are to be commended, even admired—runs the familiar observation in mainline Protestant, Catholic and evangelical circles—but we who know what the world is really like cannot share their naive optimism. The pacifist's reply has become equally familiar: the principles of just war, noble as they may sound, in practice merely pronounce a blessing upon ruling nations and ideologies.

I have grown increasingly dissatisfied with the gulf separating pacifists from defenders of just war. The church in which I was raised, the Christian Reformed Church, is what one draft board, in refusing a friend's request to be recognized as a conscientious objector during the Vietnam war, aptly termed a "war church." Calvinist theology has long been hostile to pacifism, and most Reformed churches' reflections on war begin by distinguishing justified from unjustified wars. Yet the

Reformed perspectives on the nature of the person and of society can actually support a realistic form of pacifism—a version that has received too little attention in either the "peace churches" or the "war churches."

Pacifism need not be politically naive, nor need it place undue faith in human goodness. These may be telling objections to some pacifists, but a careful articulation of the pacifist vision can meet them. By the same token, pacifists ought not deride just-war theory as merely Realpolitik in vestments, for the just-war tradition, when taken seriously, is just as stringent in its demands as is pacifism.

The case for Christian pacifism has been made frequently and fervently by many writers. The Gospel writers record that Jesus called his followers to a way of life in which violence and division are overcome by sacrificial love. We must not return evil for evil, Jesus taught, but must return good for evil; we must not hate those who wrong us but must love our enemies and give freely to those who hate us. These themes in Jesus' ministry were deeply rooted in the Hebrew prophetic tradition, and Jesus' ministry an his sacrificial death were a continuation and a fulfillment of that tradition. Followers of Jesus, Christian pacifists say, must follow both his example and his teachings: they must show love for all in their actions and seek healing and reconciliation in every situation.

The early Christian community understood Jesus' commands to prohibit the bearing of arms. Christians refused to join the military, even though the Roman army of the period was as much a police force as a conquering army. Those who converted to Christianity while in military service were instructed to refrain from killing, to pray for forgiveness for past acts of violence, and to seek release from their military obligations. A striking example of the pervasiveness of pacifism in the early church is the fact that Tertullian and Origen—church fathers who stood at opposite poles regarding the relation of faith to philosophical reasoning—each wrote a tract supporting Christians' refusal to join the military.

A profound change in the Christian attitude toward war occurred at the time of the emperor Constantine, whose conversion to Christianity helped bring the Christian community from the fringes to the center of Western society. From the time of Constantine to the present, pacifism has been a minority view in the Christian church. The just-war tradition, rooted in the ethical theories of Plato and Cicero and formulated within the Christian tradition by Augustine, Aquinas and the Protestant Reformers, defends military force as a last resort against grave injustice. According to this view, when the innocent are threatened by an unjust aggressor and all other remedies have failed, Jesus' demand for sacrificial love may require us to use lethal force.

Pacifism and just-war theory reach different conclusions only in a narrow range of cases: both positions insist that Christians must strive always for healing and reconciliation and must act out of love for all, and both traditions unequivocally condemn the reasons—whether nationalism, territorial or economic gain, revenge or glory—for which nearly all wars have been fought. Yet the differences that exist are both theologically and politically significant. Just-war defenders argue that if all means short of violence have failed and organized violence promises to be a limited and effective means of reestablishing justice, Christians may participate in war. Pacifists insist that to resort to warfare, even for a moral end, is to adopt a means inconsistent with the Christian's calling.

Why is the pacifist vision of a healing and reconciling ministry of nonviolence not universally embraced in the churches? I would single out five prominent arguments to which pacifists, if they are to make their own position cogent and realistic, must respond.

Pacifism is surrender. "The pacifist viewpoint is appealing in principle, but in practice it means surrendering to the aggressor," is a charge heard often. "Capitulation to the forces of evil cannot be moral."

The problem with this objection is that it equates pacifism with passive nonresistance. Pacifism is not synonymous with "passivism": the pacifist rejection of war is compatible with a great many measures for defense against aggression. In fact, pacifist theorists have urged the development of a civilian-based non-military defense, which would encompass organized but nonviolent resistance, refusal to cooperate with occupying forces, and efforts to undermine enemy morale.

The tendency to equate pacifism with "passivism" and capitulation reflects how little we know of the remarkable historical successes nonviolent tactics have achieved, even in the face of brutal repression. From the courageous Swedish and Danish resistance to Naziism to the transformation of Polish society by the Solidarity labor movement, and from the struggle for Indian self-rule led by Gandhi to the struggle for racial equality in the United States led by Martin Luther King Jr., and others, nonviolence has been a creative and effective force. Whether nonviolent resistance can always overcome aggression and whether its cost in suffering and death will in every case be less than that of war is difficult to say, but at least it cannot be said that pacifism is merely a policy of capitulation.

Pacifism extolls purity. "The main problem with pacifism" runs a second objection, "is that the pacifist places a higher value on his or her own purity of conscience than on saving others' lives. If we are going to fulfill our obligations, we have to be willing to get our hands dirty and not hold ourselves on some higher moral plateau than everyone else. Pacifists enjoy the freedom that others ensure by their willingness to resort to arms.

This objection rests on two confusions. In the first place, pacifism is an objection to war per se, not merely an objection to personal participation in war. Pacifists do not ask for a special exemption because of their high moral views or delicate sensibilities; they refuse to participate in war because it is immoral. Their exemption from military service is simply the compromise position that has developed in a society in which moral objection to war is not unanimously shared.

A second confusion in this argument is the notion that taking part in war shall be regarded as a lesser evil, rendered necessary by extreme circumstances. Such a claim has no part in traditional just-war theory—or, indeed, in any coherent moral theory. The just-war proponent believes that war is sometimes required by justice, in which case it is not the lesser of two evils but is itself a good. The issue is whether intentional killing in war is ever a good thing, not whether one ought to grit one's teeth and bravely commit one wrong rather than another.

Pacifism is based on optimistic humanism. "Pacifism links a noble ideal—the avoidance of violence—to naive and implausible assumptions about the inherent goodness of human nature. If I thought that I could trust people and nations to resolve their differences peaceably and fairly, I would be a pacifist too. But history teaches us differently."

This objection brings us near the heart of the theological argument against pacifism. Indeed, it is a telling argument against some forms of pacifism. Gandhi, for example, was sustained by a deep faith in the goodness of human nature, a goodness he thought nonviolent action could call forth. "If love or non-violence be not the law of our being," he wrote, "the whole of my argument falls to pieces" (in *Gandhi on Non-Violence*, edited by Thomas Merton [New Directions, 1964], p. 25). Similar optimism about human nature seems to have motivated some Quaker writers and much of the pacifism of American church leaders following the First World War. Such optimism requires a selective and unrealistic assessment of human behavior and human capacities. If pacifism rests on a trust that people have a natural capacity and an irrepressible tendency to resolve their differences justly and harmoniously, then pacifism is a delusion, and a dangerous one.

Such trust is not, however, essential to pacifism. There can be a realistic pacifism, a pacifism that gives due weight to the sinfulness and perversity of human nature.

Pacifists and defenders of just war can agree that every life is tainted with sin, and that evil will inevitably arise, but still disagree about how we ought to respond when it does arise. An essential companion to the doctrine of sin is the doctrine of grace. Though human nature is corrupted by sin, it is also illuminated by God's presence and guidance; God's grace shows itself in countless ways in the lives of Christians and non-Christians alike. In light of this fact, evil demands a response that overcomes rather than compounds evil. Such a pacifist stance differs significantly from a Gandhian or humanistic faith in the capacity of the human heart for goodness, while retaining the conviction that there are other remedies for sin besides war.

It should be noted, further, that realism about human nature cuts two ways: if it undermines a pacifism based on optimism, it also undermines the assumption that weapons of destruction and violence intended to restrain evil will be used only for that purpose. The reality of human sinfulness means that the instruments we intend to use for good are certain to be turned to evil purposes as well. There is therefore a strong presumption for using those means of justice that are least likely to be abused and least likely to cause irrevocable harm when they are abused. An army trained and equipped for national defense can quickly become an army of conquest or a tool of repression in the hands of an unprincipled leader. But a nonviolent national defense force, or a peacekeeping force bringing together citizens of a dozen nations, is of little use except for its intended purpose.

Pacifism confuses moral categories. "The basic confusion of pacifists is their assumption that the principles of Christian morality which we ought to follow in our individual lives can be applied to governments. Only individuals can truly be moral; governments are by their very nature 'immoral,' if we judge them as we would judge individuals. Killing is wrong for individuals, but for states an entirely different standard must be applied."

The notion that morality applies to individuals and not to governments is completely contrary to a central doctrine of Reformed theology which is endorsed, in varying forms, by other Christian traditions as well: that Jesus Christ is the Lord not just of the church, nor of a special sphere of religious activity, but of all of the natural and human world. We are not called to serve God in our religious activities and to carry on as usual in the other areas of life—far from it. We are called to live as followers of Jesus Christ in every human activity. Thus, we must obey God's demands for justice and reconciliation not only as families and churches but as societies. There is no room in Christian social thought for excluding governments from the realm of morality. If Christian ethics permits killing in certain circumstances, then violence is legitimate as a last resort, both for individuals and for governments. But if, on the other hand, Jesus did in fact demand that the members of the new Kingdom he inaugurated renounce all killing, then we must restructure both our personal and our institutional lives to fulfill that demand.

Pacifism is too patient. "To suffer wrong rather than harm another, to return nonviolent resistance for violent oppression, might have been appropriate at an earlier stage in our struggle. But the violence inflicted on us for so long leaves us no choice but to use force in return. We can endure no more; only arms can bring justice now."

This argument, the cry raised in Soweto and San Salvador, is painfully familiar, and it is impossible to hear it without feeling the deep pain of those who make it. I am not sure whether this argument can be answered. Those of us who regard it at a comfortable distance may not know the possibilities that remain to those whose lives have been stunted by violence.

Are there wrongs so grave that only violent means can set them right? I do not believe there are, but I do believe that the historical point at which one faces this question is significant. Naziism would surely have been destroyed by sustained nonviolent resistance had Christians and others not averted their gaze from its evil for so long. But whether Naziism could have been destroyed by nonviolent means in 1939 is a far more difficult question. Similarly, the Christian churches of South Africa, both black and white, could once have ended the policy of apartheid through nonviolent reforms, but today, as the black-death toll mounts into the thousands, it is difficult to imagine that the system will fall unless commensurate force is brought to bear against it.

Situations of extreme oppression do not invalidate the pacifist vision of nonviolent change. Active but nonlethal resistance is both theologically and practically defensible even in seemingly hopeless circumstances—as the courageous work of André Trocmé in Vichy France and of several church leaders in South Africa today makes evident. Yet many in such situations turn to violence as their last hope in the struggle for justice. We may dispute their conclusion, but our response should be more one of solidarity than of condemnation.

I have argued that the major objections to pacifism can be met by a pacifism grounded in Christian commitment and realism about human nature. To answer these objections is not to show that pacifism is the only responsible stance that a Christian may adopt. The issue of the justifiability of violence needs to be faced squarely and debated vigorously in the churches, and pacifists and non-pacifists can learn much from each other in this debate. Nevertheless, I believe that the practical pacifism I have described deserves more serious consideration than it has received in Christian circles, especially since the major alternative to pacifism in Christian ethics, the just-war tradition, has significant deficiencies. Important as the just-war tradition has been in the development of Christian thinking about war and peace, it gives insufficient weight to the central Christian calling to be agents of healing and reconciliation.

Furthermore, the radical changes that the nuclear age has brought to the phenomenon of war make it impossible to weigh means against ends in the way required by just-war theory. War is justified, according to just-war criteria, when its good result—the restoration of justice—outweighs the harm it will cause. But when the possible consequences of war include the destruction of humankind and the permanent defacement of the entire natural and human world, we do not know how to balance benefits against such costs. The just-war tradition cannot guide us in thinking about such a prospect.

What are the practical implications of such a pacifist stance? Several first steps can be clearly identified. The cessation of nuclear testing and of the development of new weapons systems, and the subsequent reduction of existing stockpiles of weapons would stabilize the international balance of terror. If at the same time means of international cooperation were created and international authorities strengthened, the threat of war would begin to hang less heavily over us. To go beyond these preliminary steps to abolish war would require far more drastic attacks on the political and economic roots of war.

No one can consistently call for peaceful alternatives to war without reflecting on the ways in which one personally participates in and benefits from social institutions that cause violence. Some people may refuse to take up arms, others may withhold taxes designated for military ends; and others may renounce jobs or possessions that implicate them in injustice. Here there is an urgent need for more open and honest discussion in the churches, for we are too quick to condemn those who bear witness in a way to which we do not feel called. We ought not to demand the same actions from everyone. Out of more open and honest discussion may come new and still untried ways of putting flesh on a shared vision of peace.

Practical Christian pacifism is grounded in faithfulness and hope, but also in realism. It provides not only a moral basis for dealing with conflicts but a framework within which to carry on the vital task of building structures that can eventually eliminate war and its causes.

Selection 2: Address of Pope John Paul II to the Diplomatic Corps, January 13, 2003

In a manner consistent with Catholic social teaching, Pope John Paul II places the reality of war and the threat of terrorism in the larger of context of respect for the sanctity of life in all human activities. While the just war principle of "last resort" is voiced, the emphasis is on the things that make for peace.

Mr. Ambassador, you have also pointed to the legitimate expectations of modern men and women, all too often frustrated by political crises, by armed violence, by social conflicts, by poverty or by natural catastrophes. Never as at the beginning of this millennium has humanity felt how precarious is the world which it has shaped.

2. I have been personally struck by *the feeling of fear which often dwells in the hearts of our contemporaries.* An insidious terrorism capable of striking at any time

and anywhere; the unresolved problem of the Middle East, with the Holy Land and Iraq; the turmoil disrupting South America, particularly Argentina, Colombia and Venezuela; the conflicts preventing numerous African countries from focusing on their development; the diseases spreading contagion and death; the grave problem of famine, especially in Africa; the irresponsible behaviour contributing to the depletion of the planet's resources: all these are so many plagues threatening the survival of humanity, the peace of individuals and the security of societies.

3. *Yet everything can change.* It depends on each of us. Everyone can develop within himself his potential for faith, for honesty, for respect of others and for commitment to the service of others.

It also depends, quite obviously, on political leaders, who are called to serve the common good. You will not be surprised if before an assembly of diplomats I state in this regard *certain requirements* which I believe must be met if entire peoples, perhaps even humanity itself, are not to sink into the abyss.

First, a "YES TO LIFE"! Respect life itself and individual lives: everything starts here, for the most fundamental of human rights is certainly the right to life. Abortion, euthanasia, human cloning, for example, risk reducing the human person to a mere object: life and death to order, as it were! When all moral criteria are removed, scientific research involving the sources of life becomes a denial of the being and the dignity of the person. War itself is an attack on human life since it brings in its wake suffering and death. The battle for peace is always a battle for life!

Next, RESPECT FOR LAW. Life within society—particularly international life—presupposes common and inviolable principles whose goal is to guarantee the security and the freedom of individual citizens and of nations. These rules of conduct are the foundation of national and international stability. Today political leaders have at hand highly relevant texts and institutions. It is enough simply to put them into practice. The world would be totally different if people began to apply in a straightforward manner the agreements already signed!

Finally, the DUTY OF SOLIDARITY. In a world with a superabundance of information, but which paradoxically finds it so difficult to communicate and where living conditions are scandalously unequal, it is important to spare no effort to ensure that everyone feels responsible for the growth and happiness of all. Our future is at stake. An unemployed young person, a handicapped person who is marginalized, elderly people who are uncared for, countries which are captives of hunger and poverty: these situations all too often make people despair and fall prey to the temptation either of closing in on themselves or of resorting to violence.

4. This is why *choices need to be made so that humanity can still have a future.* Therefore, the peoples of the earth and their leaders must sometimes have the courage to say "No".

"NO TO DEATH"! That is to say, no to all that attacks the incomparable dignity of every human being, beginning with that of unborn children. If life is truly a treasure, we need to be able to preserve it and to make it bear fruit without distorting it. "No" to all that weakens the family, the basic cell of society. "No" to all that destroys in children the sense of striving, their respect for themselves and others, the sense of service.

"NO TO SELFISHNESS"! In other words, to all that impels man to protect himself inside the cocoon of a privileged social class or a cultural comfort which excludes others. The life-style of the prosperous, their patterns of consumption, must

be reviewed in the light of their repercussions on other countries. Let us mention for example the problem of water resources, which the United Nations Organization has asked us all to consider during this year 2003. Selfishness is also the indifference of prosperous nations towards nations left out in the cold. All peoples are entitled to receive a fair share of the goods of this world and of the know-how of the more advanced countries. How can we fail to think here, for example, of the access of everyone to generic medicines, needed to continue the fight against current pandemics, an access—alas—often thwarted by short-term economic considerations?

"NO TO WAR"! War is not always inevitable. It is always a defeat for humanity. International law, honest dialogue, solidarity between States, the noble exercise of diplomacy: these are methods worthy of individuals and nations in resolving their differences. I say this as I think of those who still place their trust in nuclear weapons and of the all-too-numerous conflicts which continue to hold hostage our brothers and sisters in humanity. At Christmas, Bethlehem reminded us of the unresolved crisis in the Middle East, where two peoples, Israeli and Palestinian, are called to live side-by-side, equally free and sovereign, in mutual respect. Without needing to repeat what I said to you last year on this occasion, I will simply add today, faced with the constant degeneration of the crisis in the Middle East, that the solution will never be imposed by recourse to terrorism or armed conflict, as if military victories could be the solution. And what are we to say of the threat of a war which could strike the people of Iraq, the land of the Prophets, a people already sorely tried by more than twelve years of embargo? War is never just another means that one can choose to employ for settling differences between nations. As the Charter of the United Nations Organization and international law itself remind us, war cannot be decided upon, even when it is a matter of ensuring the common good, except as the very last option and in accordance with very strict conditions, without ignoring the consequences for the civilian population both during and after the military operations.

5. *It is therefore possible to change the course of events*, once good will, trust in others, fidelity to commitments and cooperation between responsible partners are allowed to prevail. *I shall give two examples.*

Today's Europe, which is at once united and enlarged. Europe has succeeded in tearing down the walls which disfigured her. She has committed herself to planning and creating a new reality capable of combining unity and diversity, national sovereignty and joint activity, economic progress and social justice. This new Europe is the bearer of the values which have borne fruit for two thousand years in an "art" of thinking and living from which the whole world has benefitted. Among these values Christianity holds a privileged position, inasmuch as it gave birth to a humanism which has permeated Europe's history and institutions. In recalling this patrimony, the Holy See and all the Christian Churches have urged those drawing up the future Constitutional Treaty of the European Union to include a reference to Churches and religious institutions. We believe it desirable that, in full respect of the secular state, three complementary elements should be recognized: religious freedom not only in its individual and ritual aspects, but also in its social and corporative dimensions; the appropriateness of structures for dialogue and consultation between the Governing Bodies and communities of believers; respect for the juridical status already enjoyed by Churches and religious institutions in the Member States of the Union. A Europe which disavowed its past, which denied the fact of religion, and which had no spiritual dimension would be extremely impoverished in the face of the ambitious project which calls upon all its energies: constructing a Europe for *all*!

Africa too gives us today an occasion to rejoice: Angola has begun its rebuilding; Burundi has taken the path which could lead to peace and expects from the international community understanding and financial aid; the Democratic Republic of Congo is seriously engaged in a national dialogue which should lead to democracy. The Sudan has likewise shown good will, even if the path to peace remains long and arduous. We should of course be grateful for these signs of progress and we should encourage political leaders to spare no effort in ensuring that, little by little, the peoples of Africa experience the beginnings of pacification and thus of prosperity, safe from ethnic struggles, caprice and corruption. For this reason we can only deplore the grave incidents which have rocked Côte-d'Ivoire and the Central African Republic, while inviting the people of those countries to lay down their arms, to respect their respective constitutions and to lay the foundations for national dialogue. It will then be easy to involve all the elements of the national community in planning a society in which everyone finds a place. Furthermore, we do well to note that Africans are increasingly trying to find the solutions best suited to their problems, thanks to the activity of the African Union and effective forms of regional mediation.

6. Your Excellencies, Ladies and Gentlemen, it is vital to note that *the independence of States can no longer be understood apart from the concept of interdependence*. All States are interconnected both for better and for worse. For this reason, and rightly so, we must be able to distinguish good from evil and call them by their proper names. As history has taught us time and time again, it is when doubt or confusion about what is right and wrong prevails that the greatest evils are to be feared.

If we are to avoid descending into chaos, it seems to me that *two conditions* must be met. First, we must *rediscover* within States and between States *the paramount value of the natural law*, which was the source of inspiration for the rights of nations and for the first formulations of international law. Even if today some people question its validity, I am convinced that its general and universal principles can still help us to understand more clearly the unity of the human race and to foster the development of the consciences both of those who govern and of those who are governed. Second, we need *the persevering work of Statesmen who are honest and selfless*. In effect, the indispensable professional competence of political leaders can find no legitimation unless it is connected to strong moral convictions. How can one claim to deal with world affairs without reference to this set of principles which is the basis of the "universal common good" spoken of so eloquently by Pope John XXIII in his Encyclical *Pacem in Terris*? It will always be possible for a leader who acts in accordance with his convictions to reject situations of injustice or of institutional corruption, or to put an end to them. It is precisely in this, I believe, that we rediscover what is today commonly called "good governance". The material and spiritual well-being of humanity, the protection of the freedom and rights of the human person, selfless public service, closeness to concrete conditions: all of these take precedence over every political project and constitute a moral necessity which in itself is the best guarantee of peace within nations and peace between States.

7. It is clear that, *for a believer*, these motivations are enriched by *faith in a God who is the Creator and Father of all*, who has entrusted man with stewardship of the earth and with the duty of brotherly love. This shows how it is in a State's own interest to ensure that religious freedom—which is a natural right, that is, at one and the same

time both an individual and social right—is effectively guaranteed for all. As I have had occasion to remark in the past, believers who feel that their faith is respected and whose communities enjoy juridical recognition will work with ever greater conviction in the common project of building up the civil society to which they belong. You will understand then why I speak out on behalf of all Christians who, from Asia to Europe, continue to be victims of violence and intolerance, such as happened recently during the celebration of Christmas. Ecumenical dialogue between Christians and respectful contact with other religions, in particular with Islam, are the best remedy for sectarian rifts, fanaticism or religious terrorism. As far as the Catholic Church is concerned, I will mention but one situation which is a cause of great suffering for me: the plight of Catholic communities in the Russian Federation, which for months now have seen some of their Pastors prevented from returning to them for administrative reasons. The Holy See expects from the Government authorities concrete decisions which will put an end to this crisis, and which are in keeping with the international agreements subscribed to by the modern and democratic Russia. Russian Catholics wish to live as their brethren do in the rest of the world, enjoying the same freedom and the same dignity.

8. Your Excellencies, Ladies and Gentlemen, may all of us who have gathered in this place, which is a symbol of spirituality, dialogue and peace, contribute by our daily actions to the advancement of all the peoples of the earth, in justice and harmony, to their progress towards conditions of greater happiness and greater justice, far from poverty, violence and threats of war!º

Selection 3: Jean Bethke Elshtain, *Just War against Terror*

> *Jean Bethke Elshtain (b. 1941) is Laura Spellman Rockefeller Professor of Social and Political Ethics at the University of Chicago. Her book argues for the moral validity of just war thinking in the war against terror she believes it is our obligation to pursue in the world after the September 9, 2011, attacks. Her position is a direct counterpoint to those of her academic peers who have adopted a more pacifist position.*

How well does the post–September 11 war effort fare when assessed according to the just war framework?

The resort to force—or jus ad bellum—stipulates certain criteria for evaluation, as outlined in chapter 3. Let's begin with the triggering event. Surely there can be little doubt in anyone's mind that the attacks of September 11 constituted an act of aggression aimed specifically at killing civilians.1 Indeed, when a wound as grievous as that of September 11 has been inflicted on a body politic, it would be the height of irresponsibility and a dereliction of duty for public officials to fail to respond. A political ethic is an ethic of responsibility. The just war tradition is a way to exercise that responsibility with justice in mind. Such an act of terrorism aims to disrupt fundamental civic peace and tranquility. Good is forced into hiding as we retreat behind closed doors. Preventing further harm and restoring the preconditions for civic tranquility is a justifiable casus belli.

But the argument need not end there. One could go on to make the case that love of our neighbor—in this case, the Afghan people—is implicated as well. Or, less theologically, one could speak of equal regard for others based on human dignity and our common humanity. In Afghanistan under the Taliban, one of every four children died before the age of five; life expectancy was about forty-three years; only 12 percent of the population had access to safe drinking water; and barely 30 percent of the men and only 15 percent of the women could read or write. To be sure, the Taliban took over a country already weakened by war. But rather than restoring services and helping to rebuild the social framework, they devastated it further, becoming violent depredators of their own people. The five years of Taliban rule produced nearly one million refugees, and an estimated six million Afghans, fully one-quarter of the population, were unable to find sufficient food to eat.

"In each of the last few years," writes *New York Times* columnist Nicholas D. Kristof, ". . . 225,000 children died in Afghanistan before the age of 5, along with 15,000 women who died during pregnancy or childbirth. There was no way to save those lives under the Taliban; indeed, international organizations were retreating from Afghanistan even before 9/11 because of the arrests of Christian aid workers." Since the fall of the Taliban, he continues, "aid is pouring in and lives are being saved on an enormous scale. UNICEF, for example, has vaccinated 734,000 children against measles over the last two months, in a country where virtually no one had been vaccinated against disease in the previous 10 years. Because measles often led to death in Afghanistan, the vaccination campaign will save at least 35,000 children's lives each year." Kristof also calculated that 115,000 fewer children under the age of five will die in Afghanistan each year, and that there will be 9,600 fewer maternal deaths. Kristof's point is that military intervention that stops violence saves more civilian lives than are harmed or lost in the conflict itself. Vital human goods, such as healthy children and mothers, cannot be achieved without a minimal level of civic peace.

American forces operating in Afghanistan not only recognize this precondition but are authorized to act on it: As soon as an area is free from pervasive and random violence, troops working as civil affairs teams are paired with local officials. Their task is to reconstruct schools, rebuild hospitals, repair roads, and restore water systems. An article in the *New York Times* describes the reopening of a school that had been closed and gutted by the Taliban. An American civil affairs team paid local workers to ready the school for classes of four thousand girls, grades first through twelfth. I am not arguing that enabling Afghan girls to return to school is a sufficient reason in and of itself to deploy force. But it is clear that the restoration of a fundamental human right to education is a direct outgrowth of the U.S. response to the attacks of September 11. As a result, Afghanistan will be a more just place than if no military action had been taken.

Examining the evidence, we can see that the U.S. military response in Afghanistan clearly meets the just cause criterion of being a war fought with the right intention—to punish wrongdoers and to prevent them from murdering civilians in the future. The right authority criterion was met when both houses of the U.S. Congress authorized statutes and appropriated monies for the war effort. To this we can add the right authority enshrined in Article 51 of the United Nations Charter on self-defense. The Bush administration honored the charter's requirements by giving advance notice to the UN Security Council of its intention to used armed force to punish aggression—for the first time in anyone's living memory, as this notification requirement had become a dead letter. The Security Council, for its part, acknowledged the threat posed by Al Qaeda to the international community.

What of the criterion of last resort? Properly understood, last resort is a resort to armed force taken after deliberation rather than as an immediate reaction. The criterion of last resort does not compel a government to try everything else in actual fact but rather to explore other options before concluding that none seems appropriate or viable in light of the nature of the threat. What is one to do with the likes of bin Laden and Al Qaeda? They present no accountable, organized entity to engage—no sovereign state. They are not parties to any structure of diplomacy and thus cannot be negotiated with; in any event, because what they seek is our destruction, there is nothing to negotiate about. As Michael Quinlan, a British commentator, writes:

> *As we saw amid the wreck of Yugoslavia, to place military action at the very end of the line may mean invoking it only when matters have reached a desperate pass, and when its scale (with the inevitable damage) is larger than its robust use earlier might have entailed. The passage of time is moreover not neutral—if Saddam Hussein had been given longer in Kuwait, or Milosevic in Kosovo, while their mouthpieces filibustered, the delay would have furthered their malign aims.*

What about the prospect of success? This prudential consideration is always tricky, and in this instance I cannot pronounce with any degree of certainty that this criterion is met. Afghanistan has been successfully liberated, even though enormous difficulties lie ahead, including the continuing jostling between rival ethnic and tribal groups and the tension, as a result of military errors, between local authorities, the Afghan government, and American and coalition forces. It is important for the time being that the United States remain engaged there, as the Afghan government is urging us, so that Afghanistan does not fall back into the dismal company of failed states.

Interdicting terrorism of global reach is a tough war aim indeed, even though, and undeniably, the entire world—especially the Muslim world—will be better off if the effort is successful. It is faithful Muslims, more than any other group, who are threatened and tormented when radical Islamists and their terrorist arm hold sway.

*   *   *

Just and Unjust Means

The two key in Bello requirements are proportionality and discrimination, Proportionality refers to the need to use the level of force commensurate with the nature of the threat. If a nation faces a threat from a small. renegade band carrying out indiscriminate assassinations, it does not call in a tactical nuclear strike; rather, it puts a mobile unit in the field to track down this band and stop them. Discrimination refers to the need to differentiate between combatants and noncombatants. Noncombatants historically have been women, children, the aged and infirm, all unarmed persons going about their daily lives, and prisoners of war who have been disarmed by definition.

Knowingly and intentionally placing noncombatants in jeopardy and putting in place strategies that bring the greatest suffering and harm to noncombatants rather than to combatants is unacceptable on just war grounds. According to just war thinking, it is better to risk the lives of one's own combatants than those of enemy noncombatants. In the case of U.S. military strikes in Afghanistan, of course, the noncombatant were not foes because they too had been victims of Al Qaeda and the Taliban. Even as U.S. forces attempted to strike only legitimate war targets, however, the campaign in Afghanistan renewed an old debate about what constitutes a legitimate war target.

Legitimate war targets may vary from conflict to conflict depending on what is deemed essential to the war effort of one's opponents. It is always suspect to destroy the infrastructure of civilian life. People should not be deprived of drinking water, for example. In the early formulations of the principle of proportionality, it was stipulated that wells from which persons and animals drink are never to be poisoned.

Although civilian casualties should be avoided if at all possible, they occur in every war. Inevitably, civilians fall in harm's way because a shell or bomb goes astray and misses its primary target or because war fighters are given faulty intelligence about where combatants are hidden, whether intentionally or unintentionally. The question of "collateral damage" should never be taken lightly. That the United States takes this matter very seriously indeed was noted in chapter 1. Every incident in which civilian lives are lost is investigated and invokes a reevaluation of tactics in an attempt to prevent such incidents in the future. The First Geneva Protocol of 1977, additional to the Geneva Conventions of August 12, 1949, relating to the Protection of Victims of International Armed Conflicts, codified basic just war norms on civilian and nonmilitary targeting, building these into the interstices of international norms on warmaking.

The demands of proportionality and discrimination are strenuous and cannot be alternately satisfied or ignored, depending on whether they serve one's war aims. The norms require that a war-fighting country ask itself critical questions about each criterion. The United States knows that it must try to answer these questions about its war on terrorism, even with all the difficulties attendant upon separating combatants from noncombatants when fighting a shadowy entity that is not a state actor and has neither de jure nor de facto accountability to any wider international community.

During and after a conflict, those animated by the just war tradition assess the conduct of a war-fighting nation by how its warriors conducted themselves. Did they rape and pillage? Were they operating under careful rules of engagement? Did they make every attempt to limit civilian casualties, knowing that, in time of war, civilians are invariably going to fall in harm's way? It is unworthy of the solemn nature of these questions to respond cynically or naively.

Since the Vietnam War and the restructuring of the U.S. military, those who train U.S. soldiers have taken pains to underscore the codes of ethics that derive from the just war tradition. No institution in America pays more attention to ethical restraint on the use of force than does the U.S. military. Thus, we do not threaten to kill and target explicitly three thousand civilians because that number of our own civilians were intentionally slaughtered. The soldier, by contrast to the terrorist, searches out and punishes those responsible for planning, aiding and abetting, and perpetrating the attacks, the act of aggression that served as the trigger for going to war. Preventing future attacks is a critical motivation. Just punishment, which observes restraints, is different from revenge, which knows no limits.

Have in bello criteria been met in the U.S. war on terrorism? On the rule of discrimination, it is clear that every effort is being made to separate combatants from noncombatants, and that targeting civilians has been ruled out as an explicit war-fighting strategy. As the author and war historian Caleb Carr puts it: "Warfare against civilians must never get answered in kind. For as failed a tactic as such warfare has been, reprisals similarly directed at civilians have been even more so—particularly when they have exceeded the original assault in scope. . . . Terror must never be answered with terror; but war can only be answered with war, and it is incumbent on us to devise a style of war more imaginative, more decisive, and yet more humane than anything terrorists can contrive." What the terrorists are planning, if they can acquire effective biological, chemical, and nuclear weapons, are attacks on civilians. What we are planning is to interdict their plans: to stop them without resorting to their methods.

The improved accuracy of the U.S. air war, conducted with weaponry that is more precise and does less damage to the surround than was possible only a few years ago, serves the ends of discrimination. A senior navy officer, quoted by the *New York Times*, observed that: "With precision-guided weapons, you don't have to use as many bombs to achieve the desired effects, and using fewer weapons reduces the risk of collateral damage." It is difficult to assess civilian casualties in a war theater, particularly in the patchwork that is Afghanistan, where different areas are under at least partial control of contesting tribal leaders (some of whom may have called in U.S. strikes against the Taliban when they were in fact trying to kill their own ethnic or tribal rivals, and this on more than one occasion). But attempts to come up with an accurate estimate of civilian deaths in Afghanistan have been made by human rights groups, the U.S. military, and the *Los Angeles Times*. As of July 3, 2002, the consensus was that Afghan civilian casualties numbered between 1,000 and 2,000. The *Los Angeles Times* reviewed more than 2,000 news stories covering 194 incidents. Their count was between 1,067 and 1,201. Relief officials of the Afghan government gave the same figures.

The *Los Angeles Times* concluded that the numbers suggest a very low casualty rate compared with earlier Afghan conflicts. In the early battles between competing Afghan warlords, an estimated 50,000 civilians were killed, according to the International Committee of the Red Cross. Soviet air raids in March 1979 killed 20,000 civilians in a few days in the western city of Herat—just a fraction of the estimated 670,000 civilians who died during the ten-year Soviet occupation. In the current conflict, Afghans themselves report that the big problem is not the accuracy of U.S. weaponry but flawed intelligence.

For example, before it fell, the Taliban put out false information about U.S. warplanes hitting a hospital in central Kabul. "Lies—all lies," said Ghulam Hussain, an emergency room nurse who said he was on duty that night. "Not a single person in this hospital was hurt. No rockets, no bombs, no missiles. Not even a window was broken. "15 The president of the Afghan Red Crescent (the Islamic equivalent of the Red Cross), a foe of the Taliban, is quoted as saying: "The Taliban propaganda created a huge distortion in the outside world, especially early in the war. . . . Civilians were killed, of course, but not nearly as many as the Taliban said, or in the way they said. . . . The Americans were careful and their bombs were very accurate. They checked to see for sure that they were targeting Taliban or al-Qaida bases or convoys. The people who died—it was accidental, not deliberate."

To signal the serious nature of mistaken bombings in which civilians are harmed, Deputy Defense Secretary Paul D. Wolfowitz visited Afghanistan in July 2002 to explore recent incidents and to insist that these incidents be fully investigated. The *New York Times* reported the results of an investigation in which on-site reviews were conducted of eleven locations where airstrikes had killed an estimated four hundred civilians. These reviews "suggest that American commanders have sometimes relied on mistaken information from local Afghans." Another factor was an understandable preference to use airstrikes with precision, high-tech weaponry rather than to put more soldiers in harm's way. American military commanders reiterated that "they take pains to ensure that civilians are spared, often verifying their targets with several sources of information. In many of the cases . . . they insist that they struck valid military targets." The investigation concluded that too many men in the field had been given cell phones to call in intelligence; not all of them shared the interest of the coalition fighting terrorism in trying to uproot the last of the Al Qaeda–Taliban nexus.

The *New York Times* report also suggested that there might be a pattern in the U.S. military of overreliance on air power. During the Kosovo war, I criticized the Clinton administration for its stated zero-casualty policy. In that conflict, we aimed to sacrifice Serbian civilians rather than risk the life of a single American soldier. Such a policy is not acceptable on just war grounds. To his credit, President Bush warned from the beginning that American lives would be at risk and some would be lost. That commitment must always be carried through on the battlefield in order to protect civilians as thoroughly as possible in a theater of modern war.

The United States must do everything it can to minimize civilian deaths—and it is doing so. The United States must express remorse for every civilian death in a way that is not simply rote—and it is doing so. The United States must investigate every incident in which civilians are killed—and it is doing so. The United States must make some sort of recompense for unintended civilian casualties, and it may be making plans to do so—an unusual, even unheard of, act in wartime.

Finally, what about proportionality? Proportionality is a daunting challenge in the fight against terrorism. As the British analyst Clifford Longley writes: "Proportionality is a central concept of conventional just war theory. Under the principle of double effect, for instance, it may be justified to shell or bomb an enemy position even though there may be civilian casualties as a result. But shooting off rounds of ammunition that unintentionally kill civilians would not be justified simply to demonstrate . . . that the gunners are keen and up to scratch." Terrorism aims to kill as many civilians as possible. Terrorists do not assess casualties against traditional war aims: The war aim is the death of civilians and the terrorizing of living civilians. How do we develop a proportional response to a disproportionate intended threat?

We begin by being clear about what we cannot do. We cannot use biochemical, biological, or counter-population nuclear weapons against civilians just because our enemies are setting about doing it. We cannot knowingly target any number of civilians because our opponents are doing it. We can attempt to interdict, disarm, and demolish training camps, weapons stashes, and active combatants, and we can deploy the weapons appropriate to that purpose.

It is fair to say that in Afghanistan the U.S. military is doing its best to respond proportionately. If it were not, the infrastructure of civilian life in that country would have been devastated completely, and it is not. Instead, schools are opening, women are returning to work, movie theaters are filled to capacity, and people can once again listen to music and dance at weddings. This observation is not intended to minimize the suffering and grief that has occurred in too many places, some of it the result of American mistakes in the war effort. But the restoration of a basic structure of civilian rule and a functioning state is a great benefit. We must stay engaged to this peaceful end.

The just war tradition of moral argument affords criteria for determining whether a resort to force is justified. Just war thinking provides guidance as to how a war should be fought and offers a framework of deliberation, evaluation, criticism, and moral challenge. Particularly useful is the tough-minded moral and political realism of just war thinking—not a Machiavellian "anything goes" realism, but an Augustinian realism that resists sentimentalism and insists on ethical restraint. Estrangement, conflict, and tragedy are constant features of the human condition, and just war thinking laced with Augustinian realism offers no assurances that we can ever make the world entirely safe. Augustinianism is skeptical about the exercise of power even as it recognizes the inescapability of power. Augustinian realists are not crusaders, but they do insist that we are called upon to act in a mode of realistic hope with a hardheaded recognition of the limits to action. You do not yourself have to be an Augustinian to recognize the abiding truths and strengths of this position.

Why, and how, have so many in our intellectual and religious life abandoned any such tradition or framework?

THE CHURCH IN THE WORLD
AND THE ETHICS OF VIRTUE 42

❧ *The selections in this chapter are different but connected. John Howard Yoder's theological perspective on the church in the world deeply influenced Stanley Hauerwas in that regard and became foundational for his emphasis on the ethics of virtue and the church as a community of character. Jean Porter as a leading scholar of scholastic thought represents that tradition of virtue ethics in dialogue with Hauerwas.*

Selection 1: John Howard Yoder, *The Priestly Kingdom: Social Ethics as Gospel*

John Howard Yoder (1927–1997) is widely thought of as the premier Mennonite theologian of the past century. His book, Politics of Jesus, has endured as one of the "must read" books on the church in the world. Yoder was a staunch defender of pacifism. He believed that Jesus's call to the Christian community is a radical call to be the church in Christ like discipleship, letting the integrity of this witness be its social witness rather than activistic political engagement in projects of social transformation. This nuanced view of Christianity's relation to democracy is illustrative.

The Christian Case for Democracy

The kind of review of the case of democracy which I suggest could be undertaken from numerous perspectives, traditional and revisionist, within the various disciplines involved. I here suggest only that we add, as one specifically ethical perspective, a theological accounting for the context in which Christians in particular ask whether and why democracy is the preferred form of government. The two pointers from which, I suggest, we might have something to learn are:

(1) A New Testament realism about the nature of governmental power, as exemplified in the political choices of Jesus and the apostles; (2) a free-church realism about the ambivalence of "Christendom," as this doubt has been exemplified in debates

within the Protestant Reformation from Peter of Chelcic to Roger Williams, rebounding in contemporary bicentennial discussion about "civil religion."

It is not a simple matter, going back to our biblical roots to find a clear vision of how the world political order ought to be. We need to correct for our built-in habits of thought, to recognize that prescriptive visions for how things ought to be, in the world beyond the community of faith, did not come naturally to early Christians, or to early Israelites. Israelite nationalists did have a vision for the civil order of their own people. It was theocratic rather than democratic and in historical experience not viable after the first successes of the Maccabees and Zealots.

Obviously the Maccabees knew what they wanted to see happen to imperial pagan government, as did the Zealots. They wanted it to go away. The Maccabean vision included an affirmative design for government according to the will of God, but projected that hope only for the people of God, not for a better empire. There was a prescription for righteous kingship tying together the priest and the prophet in the unity of God's people, but not a vision for a better Rome. Joseph, Daniel, and Mordecai contributed creatively to making more livable the existing pagan imperial system. Frustration with or opposition to a system, or even the desire of the apocalyptic or the Zealot that it should go away, did not yet constitute an alternative affirmative description of what would be the best form of government.

Perhaps an exception to my generalization would be the vision of Micah 4 and Isaiah 2, with all the nations coming to Jerusalem to learn the law and then going home to live in peace. This is in one sense a vision for an alternative way of having God run the world. Yet it is formally marked by not fitting in the frame I am talking about. The event which will attract the nations who come to Jerusalem is not successful empire building, nor effective prophetic critique, nor progressive involvement in political vocations, but the End-time intervention of Yahweh, who will elevate the hill of Zion above all the surrounding mountains and attract the nations to come uncoerced to learn the law. One might speak of this as an alternative vision of a world empire, but it is just as much a vision of the end of world empire.

It obviously did not occur to the early Christians to ask whether empire was or was not the best form of government. Nor is the call for democracy self-evident in most of the rest of the world. The tribesmen or slum dwellers today do not ask the question. Nor do Soviet Baptists or Christians in China. To ask, "What is the best form of government?" is itself a Constantinian question. It is representative of an already "established" social posture. It assumes that the paradigmatic person, the model ethical agent, is in a position of such power (and of such leisure—but that would be a further question) that it falls to him to evaluate alternative worlds and to prefer the one in which he himself (for the model ethical agent assumes himself to be a part of "the people") shares the rule. This paradigmatic ethical agent is assumed to be free, adult, healthy, male (as even our generic pronouns testify), an owner of property, and able to earn.

The Constantinian moral paradigm makes a number of interlocking assumptions about the nature of ethical discourse, each of them self-evident within the system and each of them questionable from a biblical or radical reformation perspective. It is easiest to demonstrate the bearing of these questions by looking at specific applications like the ethics of violence and war, or (in the sixteenth century) like truth-telling and the oath. But as the axioms behind moral logic they reach clear across the board:

1. There is the axiom of generalizability in terms of the social whole as agent. By virtue of the numerical dominance of Christians in society, when you ask what is right for Christians to do, you are asking what the whole society should do.

2. There is the assumption of generalizability through putting myself in the place of the ruler. The meaning of an ethical statement is tested by asking how the society would go if Caesar (or Carter or Reagan) were to administer his society accordingly, not only in his face-to-face relationships but through the legislative and coercive powers of his office.

3. There is the further generalizability of putting myself in the place of "Every-man." I test a moral statement about myself by whether I can wish that it would be a law for all.

Once the question is identified, it is most evident that none of these assumptions about convincing moral discourse would have made sense to the earliest Christians. They do not really make sense today to a dissident Baptist Christian in the Soviet Union, or to Christians in extreme minority situations anywhere else in the world.

Once these assumptions are made, and especially once they are made so sweepingly and so self-evidently as not to be critically conscious, they open the door for a whole new view of the ethics of power. From this point on, there is obvious reason to declare irrelevant many of the biblical models. Therefore one must replace them with something else.

Once these assumptions have been made, then there is no difficulty in elaborating within them why we now see democracy as the best form of government. Each of the above parties claiming paternity (Augustinian, Enlightenment, free churches) can give their reasons, and probably all are right.

Gospel Realism

The simplest expression of a non-Christendom alternative stance that I can offer in this paper will be the conscious anachronism and oversimplification of reaching back to the New Testament to state an alternative. I offer this example not as a proof text nor as prescription, but as a provocative paradigm.

We may see the alternative social analysis simply stated in a text which Luke places most dramatically (Mark and Matthew have its near equivalent earlier in the story) within the conversations in the upper room, just after the "institution of the Eucharist" and between two predictions by Jesus of how his disciples were going to fail him.

"The rulers of the nations lord it over them." Jesus does not suggest that this phenomenon of "lording it" or exercising dominion is one which will go away or for which he has an immediate alternative. He is not an anarchist either in tactics or in theory. He admits the fact of dominion among the nations.

But Jesus does not glorify or ratify this fact. He does not affirm that it is a work of Providence or divine institution. He does not affirm the divine right of rulers, as a majority of Christians since Constantine have done, including the transfer of such

moral ratification to democratic regimes since 1776. Jesus neither says that dominion is good nor that it is bad. There is in his words no ethical evaluation of "dominion" as a good or bad system for the nations. He is, one might say anachronistically,
a positivist. He just says that it is that way.

"Those who exercise authority let themselves be called benefactors."Again the
text is a description and not a moral judgment. Jesus does not say that the rulers of
the nations are benefactors. He reports that they make that moral claim. "They let
themselves be called" is the specific thrust of the middle voice. It is the case that
even the pettiest Caribbean dictator, like the most powerful in Peking or Moscow,
makes claims to be benefactor. But Jesus is not a cynic. He does not say that the
claims are false. He does not, like a modern Marxist, brush them aside as ideological window dressing.

"But it shall not be so among you; you shall be servants because I am a servant."
After having described realistically both the fact of rule and the fact of value claims
being made for that rule, Jesus locates himself and his disciples in a different ethical game. They are not to take over that game of "rulers-making-a-case-for-their-
benevolence" nor are they to attempt to interfere with it. They are called simply to
do something else. The meaning of that "something else" is the alternative answer
to the question of government which is represented by the servant Messiah.

In the immediate context of the narrative of the passion, Jesus was explaining to his disciples why they should see through and reject the Zealot option
which, the text makes very clear, was still their picture of his coming Kingdom.
The pericope began with their argument about their places in the coming government: "Liberation fighters-making-a-case-for-their-beneficence" was their picture
of Jesus and of themselves. He set it aside in favor of the cross-and-servanthood
alternative.

By the time Luke wrote his Gospel, and placed this story in the midst of the
passion narrative, the Zealot ethic was no longer a possibility. We must read Luke
as telling us that this text takes on a wider relevance. Now it is a capsule of a general
view of government as such. This view is wide enough to include both the relative acceptance of the "powers that be" expressed in Romans 13 and the realistic
denunciation of those same powers when their claim to be benefactors is unveiled
as idolatry in Revelation 13.

This statement in Luke deals separately with three levels which we have been
taught to merge. One level is the fact of dominion. It is simply there, independent of
and prior to any process of evaluation. Secondly there is the level of moral rhetoric
used by the bearers of power to legitimize themselves. This legitimation language
comes after the fact of dominion. And then there is the third reality, the ethic of
Jesus and his followers, who take their signals from somewhere else.

Since Constantine we have fused those three levels: the facticity of dominion,
the language of legitimation, and the differentness of the disciples. Thereby we
have confused rather than clarified the proper diversity of language. This mixes the
descriptive and the prescriptive, interweaving the language which justifies coercion
with that which guides voluntary discipleship. Since Constantine, when talking
about government, we have assumed (as Jesus could not have) that we are talking
about government of Christians and by Christians. We have thus lost the distance
which Jesus maintained between his realism about power and his messianic liberty
in servanthood. We have not distinguished between an ethic which can claim the

authority of incarnation for the content of messianic servanthood and that other discourse which talks with the rulers about their claim to be benefactors.

Although in other respects the age of Enlightenment meant the beginning of modernity, in this realm it did not. Bearing fruit (differently) in the American and French Revolutions, Enlightenment thought claimed to reverse the sequence, deriving the fact of dominion from a process of legitimation. Naturally that had to be done, not in favor of the regnant regime, but in favor of and by means of a revolution. Before that was worked out in a secularized form by the philosophes in the name of the dignity of "the people" as bearer of reason, it had been done by the monarchomaques of second-generation Calvinism (Huguenot, Dutch, Scottish, Roundhead) in the name of the Protestant people as bearers of divine justice. Since our revelation succeeded, what we have now must be "government by the people" (as Eusebius had said, "God gave Constantine the victory, so this must be the millennium"). Thus the three-way fusion initiated by the empire's success in hoc signo is replicated in an uncritical, undefined fusion with "democracy."

The benefits to be gained for Christian moral thought from disentangling these three levels again would be multiple.

Instead of dreaming about either past or future situations in which Christians did or would constitute the powerful majority in society, we could accept as normal the diaspora situation in which Christians find themselves in most of the world today and in which voluntarily committed Christians will increasingly be conscious of standing also in the "post-Christian" North Atlantic world. We should be more relaxed and less compulsive about running the world if we made our peace with our minority situation, seeing this neither as a dirty trick of destiny nor as some great new progress but simply as the unmasking of the myth of Christendom, which wasn't true even when it was believed.

Having accepted our minority place within society we shall be freer than before to make fruitful use of the self-justification language of the rulers, whoever they be, as the instrument of our critical and constructive communication with them. If the ruler claims to be my benefactor, and he always does, then that claim provides me as his subject with the language I can use to call him to be more humane in his ways of governing me and my neighbors. The language of his moral claims is not the language of my discipleship, nor are the standards of his decency usually to be identified with those of my servanthood. Yet I am quite free to use his language to reach him. This is potentially as possible for the benefactor claims of a Soviet premier as for those of an elected American president.

When I have the good fortune to find myself in a situation where part of the rulers' language of justification is the claim to have the consent of the governed, then I can use the machinery of democracy and am glad to do so. But I do not therefore believe that I am governing myself or that "we" as "the people" are governing ourselves. We are still governed by an elite, most of whose decisions are not submitted to the people for approval. Of all the forms of oligarchy, democracy is the least oppressive, since it provides the strongest language of justification and therefore of critique which the subjects may use to mitigate its oppressiveness. But it does not make of democracy, and especially it does not make of most regimes which today claim to be democracies, a fundamentally new kind of sociological structure.

The word of Jesus also makes a difference between the facticity of the "lording it" and the justification claimed for it by the rulers themselves. This is the point at which democracies are as much in need of demythologizing as are all the other oligar-chies. The consent of the governed, the built-in controls of constitutionality, checks and balances, and the bill of rights do not constitute the fact of government; they only mitigate it. This is not the case because our government is capitalistic, so that a change in property regimes would make it go away. Nor is it the case because our government has already undergone creeping socialism, so that a return to libertarian anarchy would set us straight. It remains the nature of the civil order itself that its coercive control is prior to any justifications or qualifications thereof.

This biblical realism about the priority of the facticity of the swords over any theories about legitimacy does not mean setting aside the imagery of the "social con-tract," the "state of nature," or any other kind of myth which may be found useful as fulcrum for constructive criticism. But the state of nature and social contract lan-guage lead us seriously astray when they give the impression or support the argument that if Christians don't take over the government we shall fall into anarchy. We are more likely to fall into international anarchy (i.e., war) or into domestic war when people do take over the government with too strong a sense of divine calling to set things right, with the national order as instrument.

It would go beyond our depth in the space available to attempt to unfold, as a complete theory of the church within the civil order, the implications of the separa-tion of the three levels: the brute existence of dominion, the language of benefi-cence whereby the rulers justify themselves and whereby they can thereby be called to greater decency, and the distinctive ethic of the Messiah who chose to serve. Suffice it to say it would throw new light on many of our conversations, dominated as they are by the transfer from royalty to democracy of the claim to be the one righteous social order which glorifies God by its very existence and thus will also be used for God's global purposes.

*　　*　　*

In Favor of Holy Experiments

The negative case for democracy is the one that needed to be made first, for it is the most basic. It applies to the moral claims of any government anywhere. It has concrete textual rootage in the New Testament, not merely superficially in a proof text, but in a crucial christological context. It deals with the reality of government as it is.

It has been important first to clarify that particular call for democracy which is relevant to the more pessimistic view of our situation, to the more Niebuhrian view of the nature of institutions, and to the minority social setting in which Christians have lived in most of the world except for the West between Constantine and modernity. This does not exclude or in any way contradict the more hopeful case for democracy which properly arises in those places where their numbers, or their virtues, or their friends, or their good luck should give to Christians a chance for positive model build-ing. In such favored contexts, there is another "Christian case for democracy" which must also be affirmed. It is the one which once almost succeeded, namely in the age of Milton and Cromwell. This is the vision of the Christian cultic commonwealth as a model for the civil commonwealth. In Christian community, where the Word of God is proclaimed, all should be free to speak and all should listen critically (1 Cor. 14). If that is the way divine truth is to be articulated in the words of our world, then those who have learned those skills of listening critically and speaking prophetically should be able as well to apply them to debates about human justice. The point is not that the Bible is to speak to every question of human justice; that would be the wrong half of the Puritan vision. It is that the people of God should know how to process other issues, once they have learned how dialogically and respectfully to process sacred truths. There is widely recognized evidence for a historic link between the Christian congregation (as the prototype) and the town meeting, between the Christian herme-neutic of dialogue in the Holy Spirit and free speech and parliament, or even between the Quaker vision of "that of God in every man" and nonviolent conflict resolution. It may work very creatively, but it can do so only if it goes all the way, to found its optimism on the logic of servanthood rather than mixing coercive beneficence with claimed theological modesty.

The Cromwellian adventure was sure to fail. It fused two claims: a moral man-date founded on the consensus of the people of God under the Word, and the con-crete sanction of successfully lording it over one's neighbors. The incompatibility of the two modes became clear when the Levellers proposed not only to dismantle ancient privileges through Parliament but to replace the military chain of command with internal democracy in the New Model Army. Cromwell had to go back to taking power as Lord Protector.

The contradiction between consensus and rule was more credible at first in the newly founded Commonwealth of Massachusetts, since it had the privilege of begin-ning without strong adversaries to the left (like the Levellers) or to the right (like the Cavaliers). Yet as Massachusetts matured, it became more visible in its treatment of Friends, Baptists, and Indians that it again had to deny to others the freedom of faith which the founders had sought for themselves. Thus the several strands of the Puri-tan experiment confirmed that the only way to apply, as a paradigm for government, the open conversation of the church under the Word, is first to assure to any and all churches their own freedom by denying to any and all churches any civil privilege.

We keep using the word "democracy" as a code word for a better civil arrange-ment. Yet what is most at stake is not for the demos to be able to rule but rather for other entities, first of all faith communities, and then by implication other voluntary associations and household structures, to pursue their own ends without any more central management, by the demos or anyone else, than the peace of the total com-munity demands. So the irreducible bulwark of social freedom is the dignity of dis-sent; the ability of the outsider, the other, the critic to speak and be heard. This is not majority rule; it is minority leverage. When it goes to seed it can cause anarchy. But without it democracy becomes demagoguery or mindless majoritarian conformity. The crucial need is not to believe that "we, the people" are ruling ourselves. It is to commit ourselves to defending their right to be heard. We will not do that out of the goodness of our hearts. We will only be pushed to do that if their dignity is theo-logically founded along the trajectory from 1 Corinthians 14 to Fox's "that of God in every man."

This is the element of truth in the by now widespread thesis of A. D. Lindsay. The origin of democracy in Puritan and Quaker meetings was not the product of a high view of human wisdom, nor were these people original at the point of their low view of human power. What was new was that peculiar commitment to the dignity of the adversary or the interlocutor which alone makes dialogue an obligation, and which can be rooted only in some transcendent claim.¹⁰ So democracy, when thus defined, does not simply mean that most people get to talk or that everybody gets counted. It means a theologically mandatory vesting of the right of dissent.

This positive correlation between the free church under friendly skies and the viability of a generally dialogical democracy needs repetition, for it is too easily forgotten under the cheaper Enlightenment rhetoric of autonomous human dignity. Yet it hardly needs to be proven once again, or to be advocated. What we need is some way to be ready to revert back to unfriendly skies, without thinking that our only grounds for denouncing tyranny and counting on dialogue would have to be a too sanguine hope for the skies always to be sunny.

In sum: we can contribute to democratization either by using the 'tyrants' legitimation language against them, or by the ripple effect from faith community forms.

Neither of these approaches is the Enlightenment affirmation that "the people" can have the same voice as God, that the majority is right, or that the structures of oppression can be used for good if taken over by the other side. Those views hold that there is some such thing out there as a demos, which is capable of ruling, and that if the demos were to rule we would be well governed. There is no such animal. The demos is a mental construct, a useful cipher to stand for the claim of an insightful minority to express some pertinent criticism of the injustice of the present ruling minority and some credible projects for the alleviation of that injustice.

Each of these ways of approach has the merit of beginning from within what the community of faith knows internally about her own calling, rather than becoming tributary to whatever secular consensus seems strong at the time. From this base, elements of the Enlightenment critique of authoritarianism can be recovered, accountably, because they can be authenticated as transpositions of original Christian testimony. Elements of the optimism of bourgeois or Marxist humanism can be recognized as fragmentary translations of messianic hope, yet without their Promethean autonomy claims.

Selection 2: Stanley Hauerwas, *A Community of Character: Toward a Constructive Christian Social Ethic*

Stanley Hauerwas (b. 1940) is Gilbert T. Rowe Professor of Theological Ethics at Duke Divinity School. Hauerwas is credited with bringing the ethics of character and virtue into prominence among ethicists of the Protestant tradition. Like Yoder, Hauerwas believes the church needs to distinguish itself from the world—not withdraw from the world—and concentrate its witness on its call to be a community of Christian character. This excerpt illustrates his ongoing concern that the church not compromise its integrity by involvement in the social justice projects of political liberalism.

The Church and Liberal Democracy: The Moral Limits of a Secular Polity

1. Christian Social Ethics in a Secular Polity

It has become commonplace that we live in a secular world and society. But attempts to describe and assess the significance of being "secular" are notoriously controversial.' I have no intention of adding further fuel to that particular debate. Rather I want to concentrate on a more limited, but I think no less important, set of challenges a secular polity, such as liberal democracy, presents for Christian social ethics.

By calling attention to the secular nature of our polity I am not trying to provide or defend a theory about what it means to live in the "modern world" or to be a "modern woman or man." All I mean by secular is that our polity and politics gives no special status to any recognizable religious group. Correlatively such a policy requires that public policies be justified on grounds that are not explicitly religious.

American religious groups have been particularly supportive of this understanding of the secular nature of our polity, in that it seems to allow for the free expression of religious convictions without limiting any one group. Of course particular religious groups have in fact been discriminated against socially and politically, but such discrimination, we feel, is not endemic to how our polity should work. Moreover some interpret the secular nature of our polity, that is, our government's acknowledgment of its noncompetency in religion, as a profound confession of the limits of the state appropriate to a recognition of God's sovereignty or as a realistic understanding of human sinfulness."

This positive evaluation presents a decisive challenge to Christian social ethics that we have seldom understood. Even as Christians recover the profound social significance of the Gospel, they find that the terms of expression and justification of those convictions must be secular. Many Christians assume this presents no problem, as the inherent justice of our secular and democratic polity provides the appropriate means for the expression of Christian social concerns. Most recent Christian social ethics in America has thus derived from the largely unexamined axiom that Christians should engage in politics to secure a more nearly just society. Following the lead of the social gospel, social ethics presumes that the task of Christians is to transforms our basic social and economic structures in order to aid individuals in need. Thus political involvement is seen to be the best mechanism to deal with, and perhaps even transform, structures of injustice.

While Christians have sometimes naively overestimated the extent of such transformations, they have also developed extremely sophisticated and influential portrayals of the moral possibilities and limits of our polity. Reinhold Niebuhr took the enthusiasm of the social gospel and made it all the more powerful by suggesting the limits of what love could accomplish through the politics characteristic of our society. Niebuhr saw clearly that love without power is ineffective, but that power must at the same time limit the possibilities of the realization of love. Yet those limits do not lessen the Christian duty to use power to secure the forms of justice possible in our social and political system. To do anything less is to be unfaithful to the Christian's understanding of history and our involvement in it.

Moreover, from this perspective attempts by Christians to avoid political involvement because of the "dirty" nature of politics are rightly condemned as irresponsible, if not unfaithful. Rather it is the task of Christians to be politically involved exactly because we recognize that our politics inherently involves compromise and accommodation. To withdraw from the political in order to remain pure is an irresponsible act of despair. Even more, such withdrawal is self-deceptive as it creates the condition by which the political realm may claim unwarranted significance.

It is my contention, however, that Christian enthusiasm for the political involvement offered by our secular polity has made us forget the church's more profound political task. In the interest of securing more equitable forms of justice possible in our society, Christians have failed to challenge the moral presuppositions of our polity and society. Nowhere is the effect of this seen more powerfully than in the Christian acquiescence to the liberal assumption that a just polity is possible without the people being just.' We simply accepted the assumption that politics is about the distribution of desires, irrespective of the content of those desires, and any consideration of the development of virtuous people as a political issue seems an inexcusable intrusion into our personal liberty.

The more destructive result is that the church has increasingly imitated in its own social life the politics of liberalism. We have almost forgotten that the church is also a polity that at one time had the confidence to encourage in its members virtues sufficient to sustain their role as citizens in a society whose purpose was to counter the unwarranted claims made by other societies and states. Indeed, only if such people exist is it possible for the state to be "secular. " Because the church rarely now engenders such a people and community, it has failed our particular secular polity: Christians have lacked the power that would enable themselves and others to perceive and interpret the kind of society in which we live. Christians have rightly thought that they have a proper investment in making this, and other societies, more nearly just, but have forgotten that genuine justice depends on more profound moral convictions than our secular polity can politically acknowledge.

Christians must again understand that their first task is not to make the world better or more just, but to recognize what the world is and why it is that it understands the political task as it does. The first social task of the church is to provide the space and time necessary for developing skills of interpretation and discrimination sufficient to help us recognize the possibilities and limits of our society. In developing such skills, the church and Christians must be uninvolved in the politics of our society and involved in the polity that is the church. Theologically, the challenge of Christian social ethics in our secular polity is no different than in any time or place—it is always the Christian social task to form a society that is built on truth rather than fear. For the Christian, therefore, the church is always the primary polity through which we gain the experience to negotiate and make positive contributions to whatever society in which we may find ourselves.

⋆ ⋆ ⋆

The Moral Assumptions of Political Liberalism

The American political system has been the testing ground for the viability of liberal theory. To be sure, "liberalism" is a many-faced and historically ambiguous phenomenon, and historically and culturally there were many factors in American life that served to qualify its impact. But it is still the case that America, more than any nation before or after, has been the product of a theory of government. Our assumption has been that, unlike other societies, we are not creatures of history, but that we have the possibility of a new beginning. We are thus able to form our government on the basis of principle rather than the arbitrary elements of a tradition.

Our assumptions in this respect profoundly distort our history, but their power is hard to deny. Liberalism is successful exactly because it supplies us with a myth that seems to make sense of our social origins. For there is some truth to the fact that we originally existed as a people without any shared history, but came with many different kinds of histories. In the absence of any shared history we seemed to lack anything in common that could serve as a basis for societal cooperation. Fortunately, liberalism provided a philosophical account of society designed to deal with exactly that problem: A people do not need a shared history; all they need is a system of rules that will constitute procedures for resolving disputes as they pursue their various interests. Thus liberalism is a political philosophy committed to the proposition that a social order and corresponding mode of government can be formed on self-interest and consent.

From this perspective the achievement of the Constitution is not its fear of tyranny, or even its attempt to limit the totalitarian impulses of the majority. Rather the wisdom and achievement of the Constitution comes from the guiding "assumption that only by institutionalizing the self-interest of the leaders, on the one hand, and of the individual citizen, on the other, could tyranny be averted. " The ethical and political theory necessary to such a form of society was that the individual is the sole source of authority. Thus Hobbes and Locke, to be sure in very different ways, viewed the political problem as how to get individuals, who are necessarily in conflict with one another, to enter into a cooperative arrangement for their mutual self-interest.

Likewise, Madison assumed that "the causes of faction are sown into the nature of man," and since such causes cannot be eliminated without destroying "freedom," the primary task of government is to control the effects of conflict. He argues in the tenth Federalist essay that the chief advantage of an extended republic is that aggregates of self-interested individuals will find it difficult to interfere with the rights of others to pursue their self-interest. Thus, William Hixson argues, Madison justified his understanding of our political character on two suppositions, that the only possible source of public authority is the private need of the independently situated political actors, each of whom is vested with a right to act according to self-defined standards of conscience and interest, and second, that the only legitimate function of "the sovereign" is the preservation of order through the management of conflict between such individuals.

The irony is that our founders thought that the system of competing factions would work only if you could continue to assume that people were virtuous. John Adams in his first year as vice-president under the new constitution said: "We have no government armed with power capable of contending with human passions unbridled by morality and religion. Our constitution was made only for a moral and a religious people. It is wholly inadequate for the government of any other. "Yet the very theory that has formed our public rhetoric and institutions gives no sufficient public basis for the development of such people. It was assumed that in making "morality" a matter of the "private sphere "—that is, what we do with our freedom—it could still be sustained and have an indirect public impact. But we know this has not been the case; our "private" morality has increasingly followed the form of our public life. People feel their only public duty is to follow their own interests as far as possible, limited only by the rule that we do not unfairly limit others' freedom. As a result we have found it increasingly necessary to substitute procedures and competition for the absence of public virtues. The bureaucracies in our lives are not simply the result of the complexities of an industrialized society, but a requirement of a social order individualistically organized.

Many of our current political problems and the way we understand and try to solve them are a direct outgrowth of our liberal presuppositions. For example, the American government is often condemned for its inability to develop an economic or energy policy, but such policies must necessarily be public policies. Just as it has been the genius of the American political system to turn every issue of principle into an issue of interest, so it has been the intention of our polity to make impossible the very idea of public policy or public interest. Public policy cannot exist because society is nothing more than an aggregate of self-interested individuals. The policy that is formulated therefore must be the result of a coalescence of self-interests that is then justified in the name of the greatest good for the greatest number (but too often turns out to be the greatest good for the most powerful). Liberalism thus becomes a self-fulfilling prophecy; a social order that is designed to work on the presumption that people are self-interested tends to produce that kind of people.

It is often pointed out that there is a deep puzzle about the American people, for in spite of being the best off people in the world, their almost frantic pursuit of abundance seems to mask a deep despair and loss of purpose. I suspect that our despair is the result of living in a social order that asks

* * *

The Church as a School for Virtue

If this analysis of our society's polity is even close to being correct, then it is by no means clear what the church's stance ought to be. The temptation is to assume that the task of the church is to find a political alternative or ways to qualify some of the excesses of liberalism. But such a strategy is both theologically and ethically problematic, for it fails to recognize that our society offers no ready alternatives to liberalism. We are all liberals. In fact for us in America, liberalism, a position dedicated to ending our captivity to nature, custom, and coercion, ironically has become our fate. The great self-deception is in thinking that the tradition of liberalism gives us the means to recognize that it is indeed a tradition. Instead it continues to promise us new tomorrows of infinite creation. And the more we are convinced we are free, the more determined we become.

For the church to adopt social strategies in the name of securing justice in such a social order is only to compound the problem. Rather the church must recognize that her first social task in any society is to be herself. At the very least that means that the church's first political task is to be the kind of community that recognizes the necessity that all societies, church and political alike, require authority. But for Christians our authority is neither in society itself nor in the individual; it is in God. As a result the church must stand as a reminder to the pretensions of liberalism that in spite of its claims to legitimate authority, some necessarily rule over others as if they had the right to command obedience.

The church also has a constitution that requires consent, but its constitution takes the form of the story of a savior who taught us to deal with power by recognizing how God limits all earthly claims to power. Because we have been so called and formed, Christians should be free from the fear that fuels the power of coercion for liberal and illiberal states alike. The moral adventure represented by liberalism has been to diffuse the coercive nature of the state and society by developing a culture and government that left the individual to his or her own desires. As a result the coercive aspects of our social order are hidden, since they take the appearance of being self-imposed. Yet the distrust of the other inherent in liberal social and political theory cannot help but create powers that claim our loyalties and destructively run our lives.

Ironically, the most coercive aspect of the liberal account of the world is that we are free to make up our own story. The story that liberalism teaches us is that we have no story, and as a result we fail to notice how deeply that story determines our lives. Accordingly, we fail to recognize the coercive form of the liberal state, as it, like all states, finally claims our loyalty under the self-deceptive slogan that in a democracy the people rule themselves because they have "consented" to be so ruled. But a people who have learned the strenuous lesson of God's lordship through Jesus' cross should recognize that "the people" are no less tyrannical than kings or dictators.

In the absence of anyone knowing the truth, it has been the liberal assumption that "the people, " particularly as they balance one another's desires, limit the power of falsehood. The church accepted such a strategy because it seemed to express a humility about the status of the state that, if not founded on the confession of God's lordship, at least was appropriate to our conviction that God limits all earthly power. Moreover, such a strategy seemed to offer the church freedom to preach the Gospel in a manner few societies had ever been willing to allow. While reveling in such "freedom" we failed to notice that the church had again been coopted into accepting the assumption that the destiny of a particular state and social order was intrinsic to God's Kingdom.

The challenge of the political today is no different than it has always been, though it appears in a new form. The challenge is always for the church to be a "contrast model" for all polities that know not God. Unlike them, we know that the story of God is the truthful account of our existence, and thus we can be a community formed on trust rather than distrust. The hallmark of such a community, unlike the power of the nation-states, is its refusal to resort to violence to secure its own existence or to insure internal obedience. For as a community convinced of the truth, we refuse to trust any other power to compel than the truth itself.

It is in that connection that the church is in a certain sense "democratic," for it believes that through the story of Christ it best charts its future. We rejoice in the difference and diversity of gifts among those in the church, as that very diversity is the necessary condition for our faithfulness. Discussion becomes the hallmark of such a society, since recognition and listening to the other is the way our community finds the way of obedience.40 But the church is radically not democratic if by democratic we mean that no one knows the truth and therefore everyone's opinion counts equally. Christians do not believe that there is no truth; rather truth can only be known through struggle. That is exactly why authority in the church is vested in those we have learned to call saints in recognition of their more complete appropriation of that truth.

Put starkly, the way the church must always respond to the challenge of our polity is to be herself. This does not involve a rejection of the world, or a withdrawal from the world; rather it is a reminder that the church must serve the world on her own terms. We must be faithful in our own way, even if the world understands such faithfulness as disloyalty. But the first task of the church is not to supply theories of governmental legitimacy or even to suggest strategies for social betterment. The first task of the church is to exhibit in our common life the kind of community possible when trust, and not fear, rules our lives.

Such a view of the political task of the church should not sound strange to Christians, whose very existence was secured by people who were willing to die rather than conform to the pretentious claims of government. And we must remember that the demand that religion be freed from state control was not simply an attempt to gain toleration, but to make clear that the church represented a polity truer and more just than the state can ever embody. Simply because we live in a society that has institutionalized "freedom of religion" does not mean the church's political task has thereby been accomplished.

This kind of challenge is all the more needed in a society like ours that is living under the illusion that justice can be based on the assumption that man rather than God controls the world. As John Howard Yoder has suggested, "it is more important to know with what kind of language we criticize the structures of oppression than to suggest that we have the capacity to provide an alternative which would not also be a structure of oppression." As Christians we have a language to describe the problems of liberalism, but we have become hesitant and embarrassed to use it. We must take courage from Solzhenitsyn's example and clearly say that the problem with our society and politics is its sinful presumption that man is born to be happy, when he clearly has to die. A truthful politics is one that teaches us to die for the right thing, and only the church can be trusted with that task.

Moreover, by taking seriously its task to be an alternative polity, the church might well help us to experience what a politics of trust can be like. Such communities should be the source for imaginative alternatives for social policies that not only require us to trust one another, but chart forms of life for the development of virtue and character as public concerns. The problem in liberal societies is that there seems to be no way to encourage the development of public virtue without accepting a totalitarian strategy from the left or an elitist strategy from the right. By standing as an alternative to each, the church may well help free our social imagination from those destructive choices. For finally social and political theory depends on people having the experience of trust rather than the idea of trust.

But we must admit the church has not been a society of trust and virtue. At most, people identify the church as a place where the young learn "morals," but the "morals" often prove to be little more than conventional pieties coupled with a few unintelligible "don'ts." Therefore any radical critique of our secular polity requires an equally radical critique of the church.

And it is a radical critique, for I am not calling for a return to some conservative stance of the church. My call is for Christians to exhibit confidence in the lordship of

Yahweh as the truth of our existence and in particular of our community. If we are so confident, we cannot help but serve our polity, for such confidence creates a society capable of engendering persons of virtue and trust. A people so formed are particularly important for the continued existence of a society like ours, as they can provide the experience and skills necessary for me to recognize the difference of my neighbor not as a threat but as essential for my very life.

Selection 3: Jean Porter, *The Recovery of Virtue: The Relevance of Aquinas for Christian Ethics*

Jean Porter is the John A. O'Brien Professor of Theology at the University of Notre Dame. She has made extensive and highly regarded contributions to Christian ethics and moral theology with particular reference to the resources of the scholastic tradition. With regard to the ethics of virtue, she presents insights from an enduring tradition.

The Concept of Virtue and Concepts of the Virtues

As we saw in the first chapter, the general topic of the virtues has become an important subject for Christian ethics, due in large part to Hauerwas's work. It will be apparent by now that Aquinas' own theory of the virtues is very different from Hauerwas's theory, if only because Aquinas, unlike Hauerwas, grounds his theory of the virtues in a general theory of goodness and the human good. For this reason, it would be misleading to assume that the dichotomies between virtue theory and other sorts of moral theories that Hauerwas emphasizes are also present in Aquinas' work.

A case in point is provided by the sharp distinction that Hauerwas draws between a theory that sees morality as primarily a matter of virtues, and a theory that emphasizes moral rules instead. On Hauerwas' view, moral rules are precisely defined, rigid, and apply mostly to quandaries, whereas virtues are not precisely defined, are flexible, and apply to the whole of life. For this reason, he proposes a theory of virtues as an alternative to rule-oriented accounts of the moral life, although he admits that moral rules do have a subordinate place to play in the moral life.

Whatever the merits of this sort of appeal to a theory of the virtues as an alternative to a theory of moral rules, it would be a mistake to turn to Aquinas for an early example of a moral theorist who offers a theory of virtues rather than a theory of rules. If one means by a morality of rules a theory of morality according to which certain concrete kinds of actions are identified as praiseworthy or blameworthy, then Aquinas certainly espouses a morality of rules as well as a morality of virtues. Indeed, his analysis of the moral value of actions and his analysis of the virtues fit together as two parts of one comprehensive theory of morality. Morally good kinds of actions are conceptually linked to the virtues, in that certain determinate kinds of actions are characteristic of particular virtues and tend to promote them in the individual (although any determinate kind of good action can also be done by one who has no trace of the corresponding virtue). For this reason, we cannot form concepts of particular virtues without some idea of the kinds of actions that correspond to those virtues, even though it is also true that a virtue cannot adequately be understood only as the tendency or capacity to perform a certain kind of action.

The connection between concepts of virtues and concepts of particular kinds of actions is obscured in many contemporary discussions by the relative lack of attention given there to the question of how we arrive at our notions of particular kinds of virtues. Hence, this link may be more evident if we work through the notion of a particular virtue, asking what it is that we know when we know what it is to be virtuous in this particular way.

*   *   *

Justice

When we turn to Aquinas' account of justice, we quickly realize that this virtue cannot be understood in such a way as to put it on a par with temperance and fortitude. As we saw in the last chapter, these virtues are exhibited by actions that are evaluated primarily in terms of their congruity to the well-being of the agent herself. The virtue of justice, on the other hand, is exhibited primarily in external actions which embody right relations among individuals, or between the individual and the community. Hence, we read that "it is proper to justice, among the other virtues, to direct the human person in those things which pertain to another. For it introduces a certain equality . . . ; equality, however, is toward another" (II-II.57.1; cf. I-II.60.2). That is, justice, unlike temperance and fortitude, is oriented directly toward the good of others, and of the community as a whole, and not toward the good of the individual.

For these reasons, the virtue of justice must be located in the will rather than the passions. The will is the immediate source of the external actions that are the proper object of justice (I-II.60.3). Aquinas adds that because the will, unlike the passions, is naturally directed toward the overall good of the individual (as that individual understands it), it needs no additional orientation to direct it toward the pursuit of the agent's own good, but it does need the additional orientation of special virtues (justice and charity) to direct it toward the pursuit of the good of others (I-II.56.6). At the same time, it is precisely because justice orients the will, and thereby the whole person, to the wider goods of other persons and the shared life of the community, that it serves to set the norms by which true temperance and fortitude can be distinguished from incomplete or counterfeit forms of these virtues (II-II.58.5, 6). It takes its ultimate norms from prudence and charity, but since the former is, strictly speaking, an intellectual virtue, and the latter is a theological virtue, Aquinas says that justice is the greatest of the moral virtues properly so called (II-II.58.1, 2).

Our examination of Aquinas' account of justice will raise a number of issues that are central to his moral theory. At the outset, it raises a question that is as urgent for us as it was for him: What is the proper relationship between the good of the individual and the common good? As we shall see, Aquinas insists that the common good takes precedence over individual goods, so much so that he seems to be saying that in moral matters, the well-being of the individual is important only insofar as it fosters the good of the community. Must we conclude, then, that the ideal of individual flourishing that informs temperance and fortitude just gives way to the common good when we come to justice? No; for Aquinas, individual and communal good stand in a reciprocal relationship such that the good of the individual is intrinsic to the common good. But in order to see this, it will be necessary to examine the way in which Aquinas spells out his notions of harm, equality, and the just community. This examination will prove to have further implications for our understanding of Aquinas' moral theory and its relation to present-day concerns.

Common Good and Individual Good

As we saw in the first chapter, normative individualism, once so clearly the supreme moral norm for Christian and secular thinkers alike, has recently come under attack from more than one quarter. The Protestant thinkers analyzed by Outka and, more obliquely, the Catholic moral theologians discussed in the first chapter, may be taken as examples of those who still hold that Christian ethics is grounded in a sense of the irreducible worth of the individual. On the other hand, Gustafson and Hauerwas both insist, albeit on very different grounds, that the good of the community must be given more emphasis, or even complete priority over the good of the individual.' And at first glance, it would seem that Aquinas' moral theory lends unqualified support to the latter view. After all, Aquinas insists, as strongly as any Marxist, that the common good takes precedence over the good of the individual, just as the good of the universe as a whole is a greater good than the good of any one creature, however exalted (II-II.47.10; II-II.58.12; II-II.64.2). And yet, Aquinas is not in fact the one-sided communalist that these remarks, taken alone, would suggest, for, as we saw in chapter 2, he affirms the duty of self-love and the irreducible worth of the individual just as strongly. But for that very reason, if we are to understand Aquinas' theory of justice, we must see how he understands the proper relationship between the common good and the good of the individual. In order to do so, we must see why he gives the common good so much prominence in his theory of morality.

The central importance of the common good in Aquinas' moral thought flows naturally from his anthropology. For him, as for Aristotle, we are intrinsically social beings who can exist and flourish only within the context of a community (I.96.4; II-II.47.10). And we can readily see why he follows Aristotle on this point. In the first place, the community is necessary for our material support. Human children need the care of their parents for several years, and the exigencies of pregnancy and nursing make it extremely difficult, at least, for a woman alone to care for herself and her children. Moreover, the family unit, even the extended household, is not really sufficient for maintaining the necessities of life. Food, shelter, and safety can more readily and securely be provided by an extended group of adults, who can take advantage of the benefits of strength of numbers and some division of labor. Hence, a social life is necessary to secure the material necessities of life to each individual and to bring the next generation expeditiously onto the scene.

And although Aquinas does not say so explicitly, it is clear that his theories of knowledge and language imply that some sort of social life is necessary to the exercise of the rational capacities that are distinctive to the human creature (cf. I.84-88). Because we come to knowledge through a process of discursive reasoning (unlike the angels [I.79.1]), our mental processes presuppose a language and a shared body of knowledge, both of which are cultural artifacts. Moreover, the whole superstructure of human thought and action—language, culture, shared traditions and their informing histories—constitutes a good in itself that transcends the good of any individual who participates in and contributes to it.

These considerations make it easy to see why Aquinas says that the common good transcends the good of the individual. And yet, we have seen other indications in the *ST* that Aquinas is not the one-sided communalist that our observations so far might suggest him to be. In the first place, such an interpretation of Aquinas is difficult to square with his insistence that the proximate norm of temperance and fortitude is the good of the individual. As we have already noted, justice transforms and completes temperance and fortitude by orienting them toward a good that transcends the good of the individual. But if that wider good were not somehow congruent with the good of the individual, it would be hard to see how Aquinas could maintain his thesis of the unity of the virtues, or render even plausible his ideal of the virtuous person as one who lives an ordered and therefore unified life. We have also observed that Aquinas holds that each individual necessarily seeks his own perfection as an individual (as do all creatures), and correlatively, no one can deliberately will what is harmful as such (I-II.29.4). Indeed, Aquinas is so far from condemning this self-love that he insists that each person is under a serious obligation to seek his own good correctly, that is, by pursuing the fundamental inclinations of human life in a way that respects their intrinsic ordering (II-II.26.4). Finally, Aquinas' theological commitments to the importance of the individual are hard to reconcile with an assertion of the absolute priority of the common good. Each individual human being is a potential intimate friend of God, and as such, each individual merits our active love (II-II.25.1, 6).

It begins to appear that if we are to make sense of the full range of what Aquinas has to say concerning individual and communal good, we must take these remarks as implying that correctly understood, the well-being of individual and community are interrelated in such a way that what promotes one promotes the other, and what harms one harms the other as well. And that is indeed the clear implication of his theory of justice. This way of proceeding could easily lead to a sophisticated strategy for throwing a verbal blanket over all sorts of abuses of the individual by the community. It does not do so in Aquinas, because he employs this strategy in the other direction as well. That is, he also defines the good of the community in such a way that it is a necessary condition for the human good that individuals be protected in certain ways, and correlatively, he holds that when these protections are absent, the community may cease to have a claim on the allegiance of its members.

TRINITARIAN THEOLOGY AND SOCIAL ETHICS

Ever since the work of Catholic theologians Karl Rahner and Karl Barth gave special attention to a renewed consideration of trinitarian theology, there has been something of a renaissance in the theology of the Trinity. The emphasis on the relationality of the persons as constituting the unity of the divine life in the communion of love has led to the development of commensurate visions of social justice.

Selection 1: Jürgen Moltmann, *The Trinity and the Kingdom*

Jürgen Moltmann (b. 1926) is acknowledged to be among the most influential theologians of our time. He spent most of his career at the University of Tübingen. His eschatological theology stands, along with Wolfhart Pannenberg, as the paramount expressions of the theology of hope. His books Theology of Hope *and* The Crucified God, *among other of his works, embody within them a strong political theology that influenced liberation theologies. Moltmann is also regarded as one of the major thinkers in contemporary Trinitarian theology. The implications of his approach for a vision of political ethics are clear here.*

1. Political Monotheism

What is the relationship between the religious ideas of any given era and the political constitution of its societies? That is the question asked by political theology.

The originally Stoic concept of political theology presupposes the unity of politics and religion because it was the polis itself that exercised the public practice of religion. Political theology dealt with the sacred rites and sacrifices that the polis had to offer to the gods. To reverence the gods counted as the highest function of the state, for it was the gods who secured the peace and welfare of the whole community. The correspondence between the community's religious ideas and its political constitution counted as being one of life's self-evident premises.

When the churches took on an independent function in the practice of religion, and as differentiations increased in the sphere of both religion and politics, it became increasingly difficult to sum up the relation between religion and politics in any given situation by means of a single definition. The two modern theories about this relationship also prove inadequate in the face of the complex realities of the modern world. The *reflection theory*, according to which economic interests and political relationships are merely reproduced in the superstructure of religion is only applicable to a limited degree; while it is only in a very few cases that the contrary *theory of the secularization of religious ideas* can clearly demonstrate that religion has actually determined politics and economics. Causal reductions and deductions are only very rarely realistic. Reciprocal influence and conditioning is much more frequent. Generally alliances between religious ideas and political options can be discovered, alliances evoked by particular situations and the interests of those involved. Within these alliances one can then discover affinities, correspondences, interdependencies and, occasionally, contradictions as well. Today's political theology, therefore, which enquires into the relationship between religious and political ideas, must note and define the situation and the constellations of interests in which these correspondences and contradictions appear and make themselves felt. This applies to historical situations, and to the present even more.

It was the Christian apologists of the ancient world who developed one of the first forms of political monotheism. Since it meant discipleship of the Jesus who had been crucified by the power of the Roman state, early Christianity was felt to be hostile to the state and godless, and it was because of this that it was persecuted. Consequently it was all-important for the Christian apologists to present their faith as the truly reasonable religion, and hence as the divine worship which really sustained the estate. Following Josephus, they linked biblical tradition about the one rule of the one God with philosophical monotheism. Philosophical monotheism was already associated with the cosmological doctrine of the single, hierarchical world order. The universe itself has a monarchical structure: one deity—one Logos—one cosmos. The fusing of biblical and cosmological monarchism gave rise to the notion of the single, universal pyramid: the one God is Creator, Lord and possessor of his world. His will is its law. In him the world has its unity and its peace. By distinguishing between Creator and creature, the biblical doctrine of creation (compared with Aristotelian and Stoic cosmology) accentuated the idea of God's power of disposal and the dependency of everything on his will. Stoic pantheism was heightened into Christian theism. The universal monarchy was understood in absolutist terms: the world is not the visible 'body' of the invisible deity (Seneca's view); it is the 'work' of God the Creator. The ready convertibility of political into cosmological ideas can already be perceived in Aristotle. His *Metaphysics*, Book 12, expounds the view that the deity is one, indivisible, immovable, impassible and hence perfect. The universe is ruled by the deity through *entelechy* and *eros*. All finite beings are directed towards, and are dependent upon, the infinite divine being. That is why the world has a monarchical constitution. This constitution can be perceived in the hierarchical gradations of inorganic, organic, unconscious, conscious and animate beings. Aristotle closes his remarks on cosmology with the famous statement: 'Being refuses to be badly administered. The rule of the many is not healthy; *let there be only one ruler*. The world must be understood as the ordering lordship of the one, perfect Being over the multiplicity of imperfect and finite things. But this statement is a quotation. It comes from the *Iliad*. And there it was meant politically. Agamemnon unites the divided and mutually hostile Greek cities against the Trojans with this cry: 'Let there be only one ruler!' The question whether Aristotle understood his hierarchical cosmology as a background legitimating the universal empire of Alexander the Great may be left on one side here. But if political rule was legitimated in the ancient world by an appeal to its correspondence with the gods, then polytheism corresponds to the multiplicity of cities and states, whereas cosmological monotheism calls for analogy in a universal imperium that unites the cities and states. This is the only way in which the notion of the correspondence of political and religious ideas can be maintained and used as a legitimation of rule.

The idea of theocracy was very much alive among the martyrs, during the Christian persecutions, and among the theological apologists of Christianity in the first three centuries. Consequently, from a very early period there was a Christian preference for the Roman empire. Remembrance of the Emperor Augustus's peaceful empire outshone even the remembrance of the Christ crucified by Pontius Pilate. The justification of this political choice in favour of the Roman empire ran as follows: The polytheism of the heathen is idolatry. The multiplicity of the nations (which is bound up with polytheism, because polytheism is its justification) is the reason for the continuing unrest in the world. Christian monotheism is in a position to overcome heathen polytheism. Belief in the one God brings peace, so to speak, in the diverse and competitive world of the gods. Consequently Christendom is the one universal religion of peace. In place of the many cults it puts belief in the one God. What political order corresponds to this faith in the one God and the organization of his worship by the one church? It is the Emperor Augustus's kingdom of peace, seen as Rome's enduring obligation and commitment, and as the common hope of the nations.

This political theology was widespread from Origen right down to Eusebius of Caesarea. True, it was not the common stock of the churches. Nor did it convince the Roman Caesars. But it makes it easy to understand why Constantine the Great tried to make out of Christianity a permitted and then a state religion, instead of a persecuted one. The doctrine of sovereignty suggested by Christian monotheism is, as we have seen, more absolutist than the theories based on Aristotle or the Stoics: the one almighty emperor is to a pre-eminent degree *the visible image* of the invisible God. His 'glory' reflects God's glory. His rule represents God's rule. Hence the one God is venerated in him. He is not merely the regent; he is the actual lord and possessor of the imperium. The law which applies to all does not bind him; his will is law, makes laws and changes them. He is ultimately in duty bound to extend the imperium to all peoples, in order to allow everyone to enjoy the peace uniting them: 'The one God, the one heavenly king and the one sovereign nomos and logos corresponds to the one king on earth.' The idea of unity in God therefore provokes both the idea of the universal, unified church, and the idea of the universal, unified state: one God—one emperor—one church—one empire. . . .

It is only when the doctrine of the Trinity vanquishes the monotheistic notion of the great universal monarch in heaven, and his divine patriarchs in the world, that earthly rulers, dictators and tyrants cease to find any justifying religious archetypes any more.

How must a doctrine of the Trinity be formulated if it is to have this intention?

a. The Christian doctrine of the Trinity unites God, the almighty Father, with Jesus the Son, whom he delivered up and whom the Romans crucified, and with the life-giving Spirit, who creates the new heaven and the new earth. It is impossible to form the figure of the omnipotent, universal monarch, who is reflected in earthly rulers, out of the unity of this Father, this Son and this Spirit.

b. If we see the Almighty in trinitarian terms, he is not the archetype of the mighty ones of this world. He is the Father of the Christ who was crucified and raised for us. As the Father of Jesus Christ, he is almighty because he exposes himself to the experience of suffering, pain, helplessness and death. But what he *is* is not almighty power; what he *is* is love. It is his passionate, passible love that is almighty, nothing else.

c. The glory of the triune God is reflected, not in the crowns of kings and the triumphs of victors, but in the face of the crucified Jesus, and in the faces of the oppressed whose brother he became. He is the one visible image of the invisible God. The glory of the triune Go is also reflected in the community of Christ: in the fellowship of believers and of the poor.

d. Seen in trinitarian terms, the life-giving Spirit, who confers on us the future and hope, does not proceed from any accumulation of power, or from the absolutist practice of lordship; he proceeds from the Father of Jesus Christ and from the resurrection of the Son. The resurrection through the life-quickening energy of the Holy Spirit is experienced, not at the spearheads of progress but in the shadow of death.

A political theology which is consciously Christian, and is therefore bound to criticize political monotheism, will ask what is in accord with God—what his correspondences on earth are—which means among other things: in the political constitution of a community? Attempts to restore the unity of religion and politics are mistaken. The result would be the engulfing of the church by the state. But we must ask which political options are in accord with the convictions of the Christian faith, and do not contradict them. We have said that it is not the monarchy of a ruler that corresponds to the triune God; it is the community of men and women, without privileges and without subjugation. The three divine Persons have everything in common, except for their personal characteristics. So the Trinity corresponds to a community in which people are defined through their relations with one another and in their significance for one another, not in opposition to one another, in terms of power and possession.

The monotheistic God is 'the Lord of the world'. He is defined simply through his power of disposal over his property, not through personality and personal relationships. He really has no name—merely legal titles. But the triune God represents an inexhaustible life, a life that the three Persons have in common, in which they are present with one another, for one another and in one another. What the doctrine of the Trinity calls *perichoresis* was also understood by patristic theologians as *the sociality* of the three divine Persons. Two different categories of analogy have always been used for the eternal life of the Trinity: the category of the individual person, and the category of community. Ever since Augustine's development of the psychological doctrine of the Trinity, the first has taken precedence in the West; whereas the Cappadocian Fathers and Orthodox theologians, down to the present day, employ the second category. They incline towards an emphatically social doctrine of the Trinity and criticize the modalistic tendencies in the 'personal' trinitarian doctrine of the Western church. The image of the family is a favourite one for the unity of the Triunity: three Persons—one family. This analogy is not just arbitrary. What it means is that people are made in the image of God. But the divine image is not the individual; it is person with person: Adam and Eve—or, as Gregory of Nazianzus declared, Adam and Eve and Seth—are, dissimilar though they are, an earthly image and parable of the Trinity, since they are consubstantial persons. Whatever we may think about the first human family as Trinitarian analogy, it does point to the fact that the image of God must not merely be sought for in human individuality; we must look for it with equal earnestness in human sociality.

The Christian doctrine of the Trinity provides the intellectual means whereby to harmonize personality and sociality in the community of men and women, without sacrificing the one to the other. In the Western church's doctrine of the Trinity the concept of Person was developed with particular emphasis. This had a strongly formative effect on Western anthropology. If today we understand person as the unmistakable and untransferable individual existence, we owe this to the Christian doctrine of the Trinity. But why was the concept of the perichoresis—the unity and fellowship of the Persons—not developed with equal emphasis? The disappearance of the social doctrine of the Trinity has made room for the development of individualism, and especially 'possessive individualism', in the Western world: everyone is supposed to fulfill 'himself' but who fulfills the community? It is a typically Western bias to suppose that social relationships and society are less 'primal' than the person.

If we take our bearings from the Christian doctrine of the Trinity, personalism and socialism cease to be antitheses and are seen to be derived from a common foundation. The Christian doctrine of the Trinity compels us to develop social personalism or personal socialism For, right down to the present day, the Western cult of the person has allied itself with monotheism, whereas the basis of the socialism of the Eastern countries, if we look at it from a religious viewpoint, is not so much atheistic as pantheistic. That is why Western personalism and Eastern socialism have not hitherto been reconcilable. The human rights of the individual and the rights of society fall apart. Today it is vitally necessary for the two to converge in the direction of a truly 'humane' society; and here the Christian doctrine of the Trinity can play a substantial role. In this respect the new ecumenical conversations about questions of Trinitarian doctrine in the Western and Eastern churches had a trend-setting importance for the future.

Selection 2: Catherine Mowry LaCugna, *God for Us: The Trinity and Christian Life*

Catherine Mowry LaCugna (1952–1997) was a Catholic feminist theologian who held the Nancy Reeves Dreux Chair of Theology at the University of Notre Dame. She developed Karl Rahner's emphasis upon the Trinity as revealed in the economy of salvation; the Trinity as truly God with us and, in turn, we with God and each other. The implications for Christian social teaching flow from there.

The Form of Life of God's Economy: The Reign of God

The historical reconstruction of part I exposed the liabilities of the conceptual separation of *theologia* and *oikonomia*. In brief, the doctrine of the Trinity was cut off from the experience of salvation, from sacramental and liturgical life, from other doctrines. Hence the situation today in which this doctrine has next to no bearing on either theology or on Christian life and practice. The methodological and metaphysical reconstruction in part II showed that the essential unity of *theologia* and *oikonomia* is a *sine qua non* for an adequate Christian theology of God, one that will naturally open out onto the concerns of theological anthropology, sacramental theology, ethics, and ecclesiology.

What might appear, then, as a purely theoretical perspective—the unity of *theologia* and *oikonomia*—and a convenient way to recount the history of doctrinal development, in fact has a direct practical import: *Entering into the life of God means entering in the deepest way possible into the economy, into the life of Jesus Christ, into the life of the Spirit, into the life of others.* Baptism means incorporation into the very life of God, which is indistinguishable from God's life with every creature throughout time, past, present, and future. God's very life, lived out by persons who love and exist together in communion, is what we experience in the economy of creation and salvation. God conceives every creature *ex amore*, God suffuses us with grace and faithful presence, God is assiduously with us and for us, desiring nothing other than to become fully one with each of us, to eradication sin and death, and to live with us for all eternity. Living according to God's economy means adhering to the providential ordering of all things which originate in God, are sustained in existence by God, and are destined for eternal life with God. *Entering into divine life therefore is impossible unless we also enter into a life of love and communion with others.*

The doctrine of the Trinity revolutionizes how we think about God and about ourselves, and also how we think about the form of life, the politics, of God's economy. Just as *orthodoxy* means the conformity of theology and faith to the reality of God's glory, *orthopraxis* mans right practice, right acts, in response to God's life with us. Orthopraxis means doing what is true. The truth about both God and ourselves is that we were meant to exist as persons in communion in a common household, living as persons from and for others, not persons in isolation or withdrawal or self-centeredness. Indeed, the ultimate theological error, the ultimate nonorthodoxy or heresy or untruth about God, would be to think of God as living in an altogether separate household, living entirely for Godself, by Godself, within Godself. This is what the church tried to overcome in Arianism and Eunomianism, but to some degree this "heresy" is incipient even in Trinitarian theologies that make divine self-sufficiency absolute.

Christian orthopraxis must correspond to what we believe to be true about God: that God is personal, that God is ecstatic and fecund love, that God's very nature is to exist toward and for another. The mystery of existence is the mystery of the commingling of persons, divine and human, in a common life, within a common household. We were created from God, *ek theos*, and also for God, *pros ton theon* (John 1:1). God, too, lives from and for another: God the Gather gives birth to the Son, breathes forth the Spirit, elects the creature from before all time. Living from others and for others is the path of glory in which we and God exist together. The light of God's grace and life can indeed be dimmed or possibly even extinguished by sin, which is the absence of praise and the annihilation of communion. The cardinal sin, the sin that lies at the root of all sin (including but not reducible to pride) is whatever binds us to prepersonal or impersonal or antipersonal existence: the denial that we are persons from and for God, from and for others.

Orthopraxis requires that we exercise the modes of relationship that serve the truth of God's economy: words, actions, and attitudes that serve *the reign of God*. The reign of God preached by Jesus is *where God's life rules*. This rule is the opposite of tyranny and arbitrariness. God's rule is accomplished by saving and healing love, by conversion of the heart, through the forgiveness of sins. God's household is administered (economized) by the power of God's Holy Spirit, who rules through justice, peace, charity, love, joy, moderation, kindness, generosity, freedom, compassion, reconciliation, holiness, humility, wisdom, truthfulness, and the gifts of prophecy, healing, discernment of spirits, speaking in tongues, interpretation of tongues. The Spirit of God, Spirit of Christ leads the sinner to atone and rejoice, moves the hardened and selfish heart to compassion for the enemy, enlightens the heart and mind to see the glory of God in the "little ones" of this world, welcomes and accommodates all into its bounty, and even changes our idea of who belongs as a family member in God's household. The reign of God is governance for the sake of communion. It entails a radical reordering of existence: our attachments, our familial relationships, our worship, our fears and anxieties, our way of relating to others.

Jesus Christ is the culmination of God's reign. He not only announces God's rule, he himself lives it, embodies it, and therefore is the criterion for the conclusions we draw about the rule of God's life. Jesus Christ lived in relationship to God, to others, and to himself without sin. All of his words and actions glorified God. To his followers Jesus Christ became more than a model to follow; he is *the means of salvation* by which all of us are reconfigured from death into life, saved from impersonal individualism, now able to live together with others in the one household of God. Jesus Christ is truly the *mediator* of our redemption. Our relationship to others, which is indistinguishable from our relationship to Jesus Christ, determines whether we are or are not finally incorporated into God's household. The reign of God, prepared from the foundation of the world, is present when we feed the hungry, give drink to the thirsty, welcome the stranger, clothe the naked, attend to the sick, or visit the prisoner, for in doing this to another, we do it to Jesus himself.

Jesus inaugurated God's rule by forgiving sins, casting out demons, healing all illnesses and afflictions. He ate with sinners, tax collectors, and lepers. The social conventions of his day made it unusual for him to do so, but he conversed with women, revealed himself to women, counted women among his disciples, appeared to women as the risen Christ. He publicly touched women and was comforted and anointed by women. Jesus offended and scandalized many by these actions.

Jesus amended the conditions under which we may worship: only if we are reconciled with each other, and only if we are not trying to impress others with our piety. He overturned many of the religious conventions of the day, for example, the restriction against healing on the Sabbath. He redrafted the boundaries of family, neighbor, and household: "Whoever does the will of God is my brother and sister and mother." In this new household we live no longer as slaves or wives or children of the *pater familias*, the male head of the patriarchal household, but now are sons and daughters of God. In his adult life Jesus himself had no home; during his ministry he did not belong to someone else's household, and he was not the propertied patriarchal head of a household with wives, slaves, and children.

Jesus strictly interpreted marriage and the law against divorce. He also redefined what are our true daily needs: bread, and God's word. What makes us impure is not the foods we eat or what we drink; what we speak or do against another defiles us. Our lives have meaning only insofar as they serve the gospel. Wealth is an obstacle to perceiving and living according to God's reign; we are likely to acquire treasures that rot and rust and mold, instead of the true treasure that is in heaven. The bounty of God's reign is there for all to partake in, but it is not the bounty of earthy treasures. These are distractions and can give us false reasons for valuing some persons over others.

Those who asked Jesus for a special place in the kingdom were denied; this is God's alone to give and it belongs to those who are last in the world. In the reign of God the first shall be last, the servant shall be the highest. Jesus himself "came not to be served but to serve, and to give his life [as] a ransom for many." Service to others, especially on the part of masters and leaders, is required in God's household. "Truly I tell you, the tax collectors and the prostitutes are going into the kingdom of God ahead of you [chief priests and elders]. For John came to you in the way of righteousness and you did not believe him, but the tax collectors and the prostitutes believed him; and even after you saw it, you did not change your minds and believe him." Yet in the end not even one person is to be excluded from God's household; the shepherd rejoices when he finds the one sheep that has gone astray.

Those who belong to God's reign are to give generously of themselves, like the poor widow who gave two small copper coins, the amount of her subsistence. In God's household there is always more than enough to go around, as the story of the loaves and fishes illustrates. We are to forgive much in order to be forgiven much. Jesus preached in the Sermon on the Mount that the Law does not go far enough. It is not enough not to murder, we also must not be angry with our sister or brother. It is not enough not to commit adultery, we must not desire another in an impersonal way. It is not enough not to swear an oath, all our words must be true and reliable. We must resist revenge and turn the other cheek, give whatever is asked of us, love our enemies and pray for those who persecute us. There is a heavy price for entering the kingdom; those who follow Jesus will be beaten, put on trial, persecuted, betrayed, reviled, lied about, and hated. And we are to rejoice in all this!

Jesus instructed his followers how to pray for the coming of God's reign.

Our Father in heaven, hallowed by your name.
Your kingdom come.
Your will be done, on earth as it is in heaven.
Give us this day our daily bread.
And forgive us our debts, as we also have forgiven our debtors.
And do not bring us to the time of trial, but rescue us from the evil one.

This simple prayer contains the essential elements of life in God's household: the praise of God, constant prayer that God's rule may be established, the granting of what we need to survive, forgiveness of our sins, the grace to forgive others, hope in the future victory of God over sin.

Jesus also specified the commandments or "house rules" that make God's household work:

One of the scribes came near and heard them disputing with one another, and seeing that (Jesus) answered them well, he asked him, "Which commandment is the first of all?" Jesus answered, "The first is, 'Hear, O Israel, the Lord our God, the Lord is one; you shall love the Lord your God with all your heart, and with all your soul, and with all your mind, and with all your strength.' The second is this, 'You shall love your neighbor as yourself'. There is no other commandment greater than these."

False prophets, ravenous wolves disguised as sheep, will emerge and make claims about where to find the true reign of God. Many will proclaim themselves the Messiah, the Savior. Only by their fruits can we distinguish false from true prophets The temptations away from the true reign of God are those that Jesus himself endured and triumphed over: the temptation to live for bread and not for the word of God; the temptation to test God and require that God perform according to our wishes; the temptation to acquire power instead of true worship. The kingdom can come at any time; no one but God knows the day and hour. We must stay in a state of alert and readiness. In the meanwhile we are sent forth to proclaim the good news of the gospel. Whoever welcomes you welcomes me, and whoever welcomes me welcomes the one who sent me."

The power and glory of God's reign are not vested in those who already have social, sexual, political, or religious power, nor riches and entitlements, but in the faith of the hemorrhaging woman and of the man born blind. The early disciples of Jesus gradually 'caught on' to some of the revolutionary implications of his life, teaching, words, deeds, and death. According to the Book of Acts Peter went around preaching about Jesus, preaching the gospel of repentance, and many were converted and baptized. The Spirit of Jesus was alive in the 'church' among the new followers of Jesus who devoted themselves to the apostles' teaching and to communion (*koinonia*) to the breaking of bread, to prayer. They were in awe because of the wonders and signs performed by the apostles in Jesus' name. The daily life of the previously stratified households changed: All believers had their possessions in common (*koina*), they sold their possessions and goods and distributed the proceeds to all, to any who had need. They spent day and night in the temple, broke bread at home, ate food with glad hearts, praising God. Many more were saved. The apostles were filled with the healing power of Jesus: The word of God and Jesus' name healed the sick and cast out demons, converted Saul, and raised the dead.

Through a revelation in a dream Peter came to see that all foods are clean because God has made them. This emboldened him to visit the household of Gentiles who were considered unclean; he ate with the ritually impure and the uncircumcised. The boundaries of God's household changed: Peter was inspired to preach that God shows no partiality, that all who fear God and do what is right are acceptable to God. At this the Gentiles were converted, the Holy Spirit came upon them, and they were baptized.

There was controversy over what one needed to be admitted into God's household: circumcision or baptism. Peter spoke in the assembly: "God, who knows the human heart, testified to [the Gentiles] by giving them the Holy Spirit, just as he did to us: and in cleansing their hearts by faith he has made no distinction between them and us. Now therefore why are you putting God to the test by placing on the neck of the disciples a yoke that neither our ancestors nor we have been able to bear? On the contrary, we believe that we will be saved through the grace of the Lord Jesus, just as they will." This was perhaps the most socially radical development in early Christianity; in God's new household not only uncircumcised males and otherwise ritually unclean Gentiles but also women and slaves were included and were converted and baptized. This new household of God's reign was a drastic departure from cultic and patriarchal religion and household conventions. The reign of God, not the reign as we might be inclined to design it, is the stuff of Christian life. Like the laborers in the vineyard, or the prodigal son the reign of God's making may offend our common-sense notions of how much should be given to whom, what is fair labor practice, who should come first. The parables of the kingdom shake us out of our self-deception that the reign of God is our reign. At the same time, when we are the laborer come late, or the wasteful son, these stories are the good news of our salvation.

Those who come first in God's reign do so not because of their own merit, but because of God. To fulfill the providential plan of God fore-ordained from before all ages, God must overturn and conquer the social, political, economic, racial, sexual stratifications that we ourselves have invented as means of control over others. In Jesus Christ, God heals divisions, reconciles the alienated, gives hope to those who have none, offers forgiveness to the sinner, includes the outcast. In the end God's love and mercy are altogether inclusive, accepting the repentant master as well as the repentant slave. If anyone were to be ultimately excluded from the reign of God it would be because he or she had set up himself or herself as the final criterion of who should be included in God's reign. Still, the exclusion of even a single person is contrary to God's providential plan. In the end only the barriers to eternal and universal communion are excluded from God's reign: sin, death, and despair.

The God whom Jesus loves, relies on, by whose power he heals and forgives sin, is not a political monarch, a tyrant, an aloof authority figure, a castled king or queen whose subjects cannot visit, an isolated figure who cannot suffer because he does not love. The God whose reign Jesus announces rejects the societal and religious conventions of race, sex, standing. The God who calls forth our worship is God for us: sovereign, to be sure, but hardly autonomous or detached from our lives and histories. The *archē*, the origin and ruling principle of Gods life with us is a person, a person who loves another, who suffers with another, a person who unites himself or herself with another in the communion of love. The God of Jesus Christ is, as Bonaventure put it, the *fontalis plenitudo*, the fountain overflowing with mercy and justice, and also the *telos*, the end and fulfillment of every creature. The reign of God cannot definitively be established until every creature is incorporated into the new order of things, the new heaven, the new earth.

The Trinitarian *archē* of God emerges as the basis for mutuality among persons: rater than the sexist theology of complementarity, or the racist theology of superiority, or the clerical theology of privilege, or the political theology of exploitation, or the patriarchal theology of male dominance and control, the reign of God promises the life of true communion among all human beings and all creatures. Mutuality rooted in communion among persons is a non-negotiable truth about our existence, the highest value and ideal of the Christian life, because for God mutual love among persons is supreme. God, the Unoriginate Origin, is personal, not an impersonal or pre-personal substance. God's Covenant with Israel, the ministry and life of Jesus Christ, the new bonds of community created by the Spirit, are icons of God's personal nature.

In sum, the reconception of God's monarchy from a trinitarian perspective was potentially the most far-reaching and radical theological and political fruit of the doctrine of the Trinity It guaranteed that the Christian doctrine of God would be intrinsically connected to politics, ethics, spirituality, and ecclesiology. But as soon as the doctrine of the Trinity became a formal statement about God's 'inner life' instead of a statement about the reign of God and the rule of God's household, monarchy became the most dangerous theological notion of all, ripe for distortion and ideology, and easily confused with the promotion of a form of life contrary to God's life. To this day a properly trinitarian idea of God's *archē* remains notoriously difficult to preserve. It is continually eroded by prevailing patriarchal, racist, and sexist social structures and mythologies, often helped along by rationales thought up by Christian theologians, just as the egalitarian vision of God's reign preached by Jesus Christ was soon eroded within early Christianity by its accommodation to Greco-Roman culture.

The *archē* of God, understood from within a properly trinitarian theology, excludes every kind of subordination among persons, every kind of predetermined role, every kind of reduction of persons to uniformity. The basis for this claim is weakened by the appeal to a metaphysics of intradivine life, even if it is a metaphysics of equality. It there is to be a Christian metaphysics, it must be a metaphysics of the economy of salvation: God, Christ, and Holy Spirit are equally God because of how they accomplish our salvation. To return to the argument of Athanasius and others, to think of Jesus Christ as ontologically subordinate to God vitiates the reality of our salvation through him. Likewise with the Holy Spirit. The great irony and tragedy of so-called orthodox trinitarian theology is that its proponents worked so hard to remove all subordinationism 'within' the Godhead, but then reproduced that same subordinationism in their vision of social and personal relations. This rendered their metaphysical claims empty because untruthful and unorthodox, which is not to say that they were without abidingly deleterious consequences. A reconceived doctrine of the Trinity affirms what Jesus Christ reveals: that love and communion among persons is the truth of existence, the meaning of our salvation, the overcoming of sin, and the means by which God is praised. *Therefore any theological justification for a hierarchy among persons also vitiates the truth of our salvation through Christ.*

For Further Reading

The following select list of writings provides a mixture of primary and secondary sources related to the major parts of the anthology, and the full text of the works being excerpted will also provide rich additional reading.

Justice and Liberation

Bonhoeffer and King: Their Legacies and Import for Christian Social Thought. Edited by Willis Jenkins and Jennifer M. McBride. Minneapolis: Fortress Press, 2010.

Bonino, José Miguez. *Toward a Christian Political Ethic.* Philadelphia: Fortress Press, 1983.

Cone, James H. *God of the Oppressed.* Maryknoll: Orbis, 1997.

De La Torre, Miguel. *Doing Christian Ethics from the Margins.* Maryknoll: Orbis, 2004.
Hall, Douglas John. *The Cross in Our Context: Jesus and the Suffering World.* Minneapolis: Fortress Press, 2003.
Hopkins, Dwight. *Introducing Black Theology of Liberation.* Maryknoll: Orbis, 1999.
Lischer, Richard. *The Preacher King: Martin Luther King Jr. and the Word That Moved America.* New York: Oxford University Press, 1995.
West, Cornel. *Prophesy Deliverance: An Afro-American Revolutionary Christianity.* Philadelphia: Westminster, 1982.

Human Sexuality

Browning, Don S., M. Christian Green, and John Witte Jr., eds. *Sex, Marriage, and Family in World Religions.* New York: Columbia University Press, 2006.
Coakley, Sarah. *The New Asceticism: Sexuality, Gender and the Quest for God.* London and New York: Continuum, 2012.
Gudorf. Christine. *Body, Sex, and Pleasure: Reconstructing Christian Social Ethics.* Cleveland: Pilgrim, 1994.
Hays, Richard B. *Awaiting the Redemption of Our Bodies: The Witness of Scripture Concerning Homosexuality.* Louisville: Westminster John Knox, 1994.
Homosexuality and Christian Community. Edited by Choon-Leong Seow. Louisville: Westminster John Knox, 1996.
Johnson, William Stacey. *A Time to Embrace: Same-Gender Relationships in Religion, Law, and Politics.* Grand Rapids: Eerdmans, 2006.
Jung, Patricia Beattie, Anna Marie Vigen, and John Anderson, eds. *God, Science, Sex, and Gender: An Interdisciplinary Approach to Christian Ethics..* Urbana: University of Illinois Press, 2010.
Nelson, James. *Embodiment: An Approach to Sexuality and Christian Theology.* Minneapolis: Augsburg, 1978.
Salzman, Todd A., and Michael G. Lawler. *The Sexual Person: Toward a Renewed Catholic Anthropology.* Washington, DC: Georgetown University Press, 2008.
Via, Dan O., and Robert A. J. Gagnon, *Homosexuality and the Bible: Two Views.* Minneapolis: Fortress Press, 2003.

Environmental Ethics

Earth Habitat: Eco-Justice and the Church's Response. Edited by Dieter Hessel and Larry Rasmussen. Minneapolis: Fortress Press, 2001.
McFague, Sallie. *A New Climate for Theology: God, the World, and Global Warming.* Minneapolis: Fortress Press, 2008.
Martin-Schramm, James B. *Climate Justice: Ethics, Energy, and Public Policy.* Minneapolis: Fortress Press, 2010.
Rasmussen, Larry L. *Earth Community Earth Ethics.* Maryknoll: Orbis, 1996.
Rolston, Holmes III. *A New Environmental Ethics: The Next Millennium for Life on Earth.* New York and London: Routledge, 2012.

Santmire, H. Paul. *Nature Reborn: The Ecological and Cosmic Promise of Christian Theology*. Minneapolis: Fortress Press. 2000.

Biomedical Ethics

Beauchamp, Tom L. and Childress, James F. *Principles of Biomedical Ethics*. Sixth Edition. Oxford and New York: Oxford University Press, 2009.
Cahill, Lisa Sowle. *Bioethics and the Common Good*. Milwaukee: Marquette University Press, 2004.
Evans, Abigail Rian. *Is God Still at the Bedside? The Medical, Ethical and Pastoral Issues of Death and Dying*. Grand Rapids: Eerdmans, 2011.
Maguire, Daniel C. *Death by Choice*. Second Edition. Garden City: Image, 1984.
Mitchell, C. Ben, Edmund Pellegrino, Jean Bethke Elshtain, John F. Kilmer, and Scott B. Rae. *Biotechnology and the Human Good*. Washington, DC: Georgetown University Press, 2007.
Meilaender, Gilbert. *Bioethics: A Primer for Christians*. Grand Rapids: Eerdmans, 1996.
Peters, Ted, Karen Lebacqz, and Gaymon Bennett. *Why Christians Should Support Stem Cell Research*. Lanham: Rowan and Littlefield, 2008.
Shannon, Thomas A. and Nicholas J. Kockler. *An Introduction to Bioethics*. New York: Paulist, 2009.

Pacifism, Just War, and Terrorism
Holmes, Arthur, Editor. *War and Christian Ethics. Classic and Contemporary Readings on the Morality of War*. Grand Rapids: Baker Academic, 2005.
Long, Edward Leroy, Jr. *Facing Terrorism: Responding as Christians*. Louisville: Westminster John Knox, 2004.
Maguire, Daniel C. *The Horrors We Bless: Rethinking the Just-War Legacy*. Minneapolis: Fortress Press, 2007.
Ramsey, Paul. *War and the Christian Conscience: How Shall Modern War Be Conducted?* Durham: Duke University Press, 1961.
Simpson, Gary M. *War, Peace, and God: Rethinking the Just-War Tradition*. Minneapolis: Fortress Press, 2007.
Stassen, Glen, Editor. *Just Peacemaking: The New Paradigm for the Ethics of Peace and War*. Cleveland: Pilgrim, 2008.
Yoder, John Howard, *The Politics of Jesus*. Grand Rapids: Eerdmans, 1994.
———. *When War Is Unjust: Being Honest in Just-War Thinking*. Maryknoll: Orbis, 1997.

The Church in the World and the Ethics of Virtue

Harrington, Daniel and James F. Keenan. *Jesus and Virtue Ethics: Building Bridges between New Testament Studies and Moral Theology*. Lanham: Rowan and Littlefield, 2002.
———. *Paul and Virtue Ethics: Building Bridges between New Testament Studies and Moral Theology*. Lanham: Rowan and Littlefield, 2010.

Hauerwas, Stanley, Charles Pinches. *Christians among the Virtues: Theological Conversations with Ancient and Modern Ethics.* Notre Dame: Notre Dame University Press, 1997.

Hauerwas, Stanley. *The Peaceable Kingdom: A primer in Christian Ethics.* Notre Dame: University of Notre Dame Press, 1983.

Paris, Peter. *Virtues and Values: The African and African American Experience.* Minneapolis: Fortress Press, 2004.

Pellegrino, Edmund D. and David C. Thomasma. *Christian Virtues in Medical Practice.* Washington, DC: Georgetown University Press, 1993.

Trinitarian Theology and Social Ethics

Boff, Leonardo. *Trinity and Society.* Translated by Paul Burns. Maryknoll: Orbis, 1988.

Grenz, Stanley. *The Social God and the Relational Self: A Trinitarian Theology of the Imago Dei.* Louisville: Westminster John Knox, 2001.

―――. *Rediscovering the Triune God: the Trinity in Contemporary Theology.* Minneapolis: Fortress Press, 2004.

Volf, Miroslav and Michael Welker, Editors. *God's Life in Trinity.* Minneapolis: Fortress Press, 2006.

BIBLIOGRAPHY
OF ORIGINAL SOURCES

Chapter 3

Selection 1: *The Epistle of Barnabas XVII-XXI.* The Apostolic Fathers in English, 3rd edition. Translated and edited by Michael W. Holmes. Grand Rapids: Baker Academic, 2006.

Selection 2: *Justin Martyr The First and Second Apologies. Ancient Christian Writers, 56.* Translated with Introduction by Leslie William Barnard. New York/Mahwah, N.J.: Paulist Press, 1997, 30–35; 41–43.

Selection 3: Irenaeus. *Against Heresies,* Book V, Chapter 24 in The Ante-Nicene Fathers. American Edition, Vol. 1. Grand Rapids: William B. Eerdmans, 1950, 552–553.

Chapter 4

Selection 1: Tertullian. *Apologetical Works and Minucius Felix Octavius. Fathers of the Church, A New Translation series, Volume 10.* Translated by Rudolph Arbesmann, et. al. New York: Fathers of the Church Inc., 1950, 98–110.

Selection 2: Tertullian. *Spectacles* in *Disciplinary, Moral and Ascetical Works.* Translated by Rudolph Arbesmann. Vol. 40, New York: Fathers of the Church, Inc., 1959, 69–76.

Chapter 5

Selection 1: Clement of Alexandria. *The Instructor Book I,* Chapter XIII, *Writings of Clement,* Vol. 1 *Ante-Nicene Christian Library Vol. IV* (Edinburgh Edition). Edinburgh: T&T Clark, 1884, 184–185.

Selection 2: Clement of Alexandria. *The Rich Man's Salvation.* Loeb Classical Library. London: W. Heineman, 1913–1914, 271, 275, 281, 283, 291, 295, 297, 299.

Selection 3: Origen. *Against Celsus,* Book VIII, *Ante-Nicene Christian Library,* Vol. XXIII. Edinburgh: T&T Clark, 1894, 73–75.

Chapter 6

Selection 1: Chrysostem. *Concerning the Statutes, Homily XII*, 9ff, *Nicene and Post-Nicene Fathers*, Vol. IX. Edited by Philip Schaff. New York: Charles Scribner's Sons, 1889, 421–424.

Selection 2: Chrysostem. *Homilies on Matthew* XIX, Ibid, Vol.X, 134–135.

Chapter 7

Selection 1: Augustine. *Enchiridion*, Chap. 9–11, 23–26, *The Works of Saint Augustine: A Translation for the 21st Century*, I, 8. Translated by Bruce Habet. Hyde Park, NY: New City Press, 2005, 277–79; 288–290.

Selection 2: Augustine. *City of God Against the Pagans XIV, 28; XIX, 17, XV, 4, XIX.* Edited and translated by R.W. Dyson. New York: Cambridge University Press, 1998.

Selection 3: Augustine. *Of the Morals of the Catholic Church*, Chapter XV, XXIV, 434, XXVI, and XXVII, *Nicene and Post Nicene Fathers*, Vol. IV. New York: Scribner's, 1889. 48, 54–56.

Selection 4: Augustine. *A Good Marriage*, Fathers *of the Church: A New Translation*. Vol. 27, Chapters 3, 6, 7, 10. New York: Fathers of the Church, Inc., 1955.

Chapter 8

Selection 1: *The Rule of St. Benedict*. New York and London: Penguin Books, 2008.

Selection 2: *The Rule of Saint Francis, Documents of the Christian Church*. Edited by Henry Bettenson. London: Oxford, 1963, 179–184.

Selection 3: Francis of Assisi. *Canticle of the Sun*.

Chapter 9

Selection 1: Bernard of Clairvaux. *On Love of God*, chapters 6, 8–10. Christian Classics Ethereal Library. http://www.ccel.org/ccel/bernard/loving_god.toc.html

Selection 2: Meister Eckhart. *The Talks of Instruction*, nos. 2, 4, 5, 7, 18. Translated by Raymond B. Blankney. New York: Harper Torchbook, 1957, 4, 6–7, 10–11, 25–26.

Selection 3: Catherine of Siena. *The Dialogue or A Treatise of Divine Providence*. Christian Classics Ethereal Library. http://www.ccel.org/ccel/catherine/dialog.iv.ii.vii.html

Chapter 10

Thomas Aquinas. *Summa Theologica*, II/1, Question 90, Article 2; II, 1, Question 91, Articles 1–4; II/1, Question 94, Article 2; II/2, Question 58, Articles 1, 11, 12; II/2, Question 60, Articles 5–6; II/2, Question 64, Articles 2–3 and Question 40, Article 1;

II/2, Question 66, Articles 1–2. Christian Classics Ethereal Library: http://www.ccel.org/ccel/a/aquinas/summa

Chapter 11

Selection 1: Gregory VII. Reg. III, No. 10 a, Translated in Ernest F. Henderson, *Select Historical Documents of the Middle Ages*, (London: George Bell and Sons, 1910), 376–377.

Boniface VIII: Unam Sanctam, Nov. 18, 1302. A New Translation with Notes by Ronald L. Conte, Jr., www.catholicplanet.com

Chapter 12

Selection 1: Martin Luther. *Treatise on Christian Liberty or the Freedom of a Christian. Luther's Works*, Volume 31. Edited by Harold J. Grimm. Translated by W.A. Lambert. Philadelphia: Muhlenberg, 1957, 343–347, 352–355, 358, 361, 366, 369, 371.

Selection 2: ———. *Temporal Authority: To What Extent It Should Be Obeyed. Luther's Works*, Volume 45. Edited by Walther I. Brandt. Translated by J.J. Schindel. Philadelphia: Muhlenberg, 1962, 85–96, 104–105, 109–110, 118–120, 123–125.

Selection 3: ———. *Against the Robbing and Murdering Horde of Peasants. Luther's Works*, Volume 46. Edited by Robert Schultz. Translated by Charles M. Jacobs. Philadelphia: Fortress Press, 1967. 49–55.

Chapter 13

John Calvin. *Institutes of the Christian Religion*. Library of Christian Classics, Volume XX and XXI. Edited by John T. McNeill. Translated and Indexed by Ford Lewis Battles. Philadelphia: Westminster, 1960, 255–56, 271–273, 404, 405, 406, 408–411, 931–932, 1485–1489, 1511–1512, 1518–1521.

Chapter 14

Selection 1: *The Schleitheim Confession of Faith*, Global Anabaptist Mennonite Encyclopedia: www.GAMEO.org.

Selection 2: Thomas Müntzer. "Sermon to the Princes," *Revelation and Revolution: Basic Writings of Thomas Müntzer*. Edited and translated by Michael G. Baylor. Bethlehem: Lehigh University Press, London; Cranbury, NJ: Associated University Presses, 1993, 98–114.

Selection 3: Menno Simons. *Reply to False Accusations, The Complete Writings of Menno Simons*. Translated by Leonard Verduin. Edited by John Christian Wenger. Scottsdale: Herald, 1956, 549–552.

Chapter 15

Selection 1: Francisco Suarez. *A Treatise on Laws and God the Lawgiver, Chap. II. Selections from Three Works of Francisco Suarez, S.J.* Prepared by Gwladys L. Williams, Ammi Brown and John Waldron. Oxford: Clarendon Press, 1944, 372–375.

Selection 2: ———. *A Work in the Three Theological Virtues: Faith, Hope, and Charity; Disputation XIII: On Charity*, Ibid., 800–805.

Chapter 16

Selection 1: *An Agreement of the People.* Gardiner: Constitutional Documents of the Puritan Reformation, www.constution.org/eng/conpur074,htm

Selection 2: Gerard Winstanley. *The Law of Freedom in an Platform* or *True Magistracy Restored* (1652) *The Works of Gerard Winstanley.* Edited by George H. Sabine. Ithaca: Cornell University Press, 1941, 580–582, 599–600.

Chapter 17

Roger Williams. *The Bloody Tenent of Persecution (July 15, 1644)*, Reformed Reader. http://www.reformedreader.org/rbb/williams/btp.htm

Chapter 18

The Rules of Discipline: Advices. Rules of Discipline of the Religious Society of Friends. London: Darton and Harvey, 1834, 1–2, 287–289, 244–246.

Chapter 19

Selection 1: John Locke. *The Reasonableness of Christianity, The Works of John Locke*, Vol. 6, 83–87. The Online Library of Liberty, http://oll.libertyfund.org

Selection 2: Joseph Butler. *Upon the Love of Our Neighbor, Sermon XII.* Fifteen *Sermons Preached at the Rolls Chapel*, Cambridge: Published by Hilliard and Brown; Boston: Hilliard, Gray, Little, and Wilkins, 1827. Transcribed by LeRoy Dagg, 2002 Reproduced with permission of the Bishop Payne Library, Virginia Theological Seminary, 2005 for Project Canterbury: http://anglicanhistory.org/butler/rolls/12.html

Chapter 20

Selection 1: Philip Jacob Spener. *Pia Desideria.* Translated by T.G. Tappert. Philadelphia: Fortress Press, 1964, 87–97.

Selection 2: August Hermann Francke. *Scriptural Rules, Das Zeitalter des Pietismus.* Selection translated by George W. Forell. Bremen: Schünemann, 1965. 82–89.

Chapter 21

Selection 1: John Wesley. *The Use of Money, The Complete Works of John Wesley: Commentary, Sermons, and Other Writings*, Edited by John Emory. New York and Cincinnati: The Methodist Book Concern, c. 1895, Vol. I, 440–448. Also available at http://www.godrules.net/library/wesley/wesley/htm

Selection 2: John Wesley. *Thoughts upon Slavery*. Ibid., Vol. VI, 286–288, 290–293. Also available at http://.gbgm-umc.org/umw/wesley/thoughtsuponslavcry.stm

Selection 3: John Wesley. *Thoughts on the Present Scarcity of Provisions*. Ibid., 274–278.

Chapter 22

Friedrich Schleiermacher. *The Christian Faith*, excerpted in *Friedrich Schleiermacher: Pioneer of Modern Theology*. Edited by Keith W. Clements. Minneapolis: Fortress Press, 1991, 249–253.

Chapter 23

Horace Bushnell. *Politics under the Law of God*. Hartford: Edwin Hunt, 1844, 10–19.

Chapter 24

Frederick Denison Maurice, *The Kingdom of Christ or Hints to a Quaker Respecting the Principles, Constitution and Ordinances of the Catholic Church, Vol. 1*. Edited by Alec R.Vidler. New Edition based on the Second Edition of 1842. London: SCM, 1958, 252–257.

Chapter 25

Selection 1: Sojourner Truth. *Ain't I A Woman?* www.feminist.com/resources/artspeech/genwom/sojour.htm.

Selection 2: Frederick Douglas. "The Meaning of July Fourth for the Negro," *The Life and Writings of Frederick Douglass*. Volume II, Pre-Civil War Decade 1850–1860. New York: Philip S. Foner International, 1950.

Chapter 26

Albrecht Ritschl. *The Christian Doctrine of Justification and Reconciliation*. Edited by H.R. Mackintosh and A.B. MacCaulay. Edinburgh: T&T Clark, 1902, 11–13.

Chapter 27

Selection 1: Leo III. *Rerum Novarum*, May 15, 1891, 1, 22, 23, 24, 36, 37. http://www.vatican.va/holy_father/leo_xiii/douments/hf_enc_l-xiii_15051891_rerum-novarum

Selection 2: Pope Pius XI. *Quadragesimo anno* 1931, 42, 43, 56, 57, 58, 59, 60, 61, 62, 71, 74. http://www.vatican.va/holy_father/plus_xi/encyclicals/documents/hf_p-xi_enc_19310515_quadragesimo

Chapter 28

Selection 1: John XXIII. *Pacem in terris* (1963), 3–7, 11–30. http://www.vatican.va/holy_father/john_xxiii/encyclicals/documents/hf_i-xxiii_enc_11041963_pacem-en.html

Selection 2: Vatican Council II. *Gaudium et spes* (1965), Part I, II, 27–29; Part II, II, 58, 59, III, 71, 72, V, 80, 85, 86 http://www.vatican.va/archive/hist_councils/ii_vatican_council/documents/vat-ii_cons_19651207_gaudium-et-spes_en.html

Chapter 29

Selection 1: U.S. Catholic Bishops. *The Challenge of Peace: God's Promise and Our Response*. Washington, D.C.: United States Conference of Catholic Bishops, 1983, 235–244.

Selection 2: U.S. Catholic Bishops. *Economic Justice for All*. Washington, D.C.: United States Conference of Catholic Bishops, 1986, 136, 137, 151–154, 200c, 201–214.

Chapter 30

Selection 1: Washington Gladden. "Social Redemption," *The Church and Modern Life*, 1908, 41–43, 46. eBook #12290. www.gutenberg.net

Selection 2: Walter Rauschenbusch. *A Theology for the Social Gospel*. New York: Macmillan, 1919, Chapter XIII, 131–145.

Chapter 31

Selection 1: Reinhold Niebuhr. *An Interpretation of Christian Ethics*. New York: Harper and Brothers, 1955, 103–117.

Selection 2: Reinhold Niebuhr. "Justice and Love" in *Love and Justice: Selections from the Shorter Writings of Reinhold Niebuhr*. Edited by D.B. Robertson. Philadelphia: Westminster, 1957, pp. 27–29.

Selection 3: Reinhold Niebuhr. "Christian Faith and Natural Law," Ibid pp. 46–54.

Chapter 32

Paul Tillich. *Systematic Theology*, Volume 3. Chicago: University of Chicago Press, 1963, 385–391.

Chapter 33

Karl Barth. *Community, State and Church*. National Student Christian Federation, 1960, 149–152, 157–158, 161–165, 168–178.

Chapter 34

Selection 1: Dietrich Bonhoeffer. *Ethics*. Edited by Clifford Green. Minneapolis: Fortress Press, 388–394; 399–405.

Selection 2: Dietrich Bonhoffer. *Letters and Papers from Prison*. Edited by John W. de Gruchy. Minneapolis: Fortress Press, 2010, 423–431; 475–480.

Chapter 35

Selection 1: Rosemary Radford Ruether. *Sexism and God-Talk: Toward a Feminist Theology*. Boston: Beacon, 1983, 193–201, 214–216, 232–234.

Selection 2: Lisa Sowle Cahill. "Feminism and Christian Ethics," *Freeing Theology: the Essentials of Theology in Feminist Perspective*. Edited by Catherine Mowry LaCugna. New York: Harper Collins, 1993, 212–220.

Selection 3: Beverly Wildung Harrison. *Making the Connections: Essays in Feminist Social Ethics*. Boston: Beacon, 1985, 48–53, 227–230.

Chapter 36

Selection 1: Katie Geneva Cannon. *Katie's Canon: Womanism and the Soul of the Black Community*. New York: Continuum, 1995. 55–56, 69–70, 124, 128.

Selection 2: Jacquelyn Grant. *White Woman's Christ and Black Woman's Jesus: Feminist Christology and Womanist Respons.*, Atlanta: Scholars, 1989, 209–222.

Selection 3: Delores S. Williams. *"Womanist* Theology: Black Women's Voice" *Christianity and Crisis*, March 2, 1987, 66–70.

Chapter 37

Selection 1: Martin Luther King Jr. "Letter from a Birmingham Jail," African Studies Center—University of Pennsylvania. www.africa.upenn.edu/Articles_Gen/Letter_Birmingham.html.

Selection 2: James H. Cone. *A Black Theology of Liberation.* Maryknoll: Orbis, 1990, 11–12, 22–26, 120–125.

Selection 3: Gutiérrez Gustavo. *A Theology of Liberation: History, Politics, and Salvation.* Translated and edited by Sister Caridad India and John Eagleson. Maryknoll: Orbis, 1988, c 1973, 5–8, 11–12, 116–120.

Selection 4: Jon Sobrino. *The Principle of Mercy: Taking the Crucified People from the Cross.* Maryknoll, N.Y.: Orbis Books, c 1994, 92–97.

Chapter 38

Selection 1: Charles E. Curran. "Catholic Social and Sexual Teaching: A Methodological Comparison," *Theology Today.* Volume 44, January 1988, 425–440.

Selection 2: Christine E. Gudorf. "Life without Anchors: Sex, Exchange, and human Rights in a Postmodern World," *Journal of Religious Ethics*, Volume 26, No.2, 1998, 295–300.

Selection 3: The Lambeth Conference 1998 – *Human Sexuality.* http://www.lambeth conference.org/resolutions/1998/1998-1-10.cfm.

Selection 4: World Council of Churches. From Harare to Porto Alegre, *Background Document*, Geneva, 2006: http://www.oikoumene.org/en/resources/assembly/porto-alegre-2006/3-preparatory-and-background

Selection 5: Margaret A. Farley. *Just Love: A Framework for Christian Sexual Ethics.* NewYork: Continuum: 2006, 215–232.

Chapter 39

Selection 1: Joseph Sittler. "Called to Unity," *The Ecumenical Review.* Volume 14, January, 1962. 177–87.

Selection 2: Larry L Rasmussen. "Is Eco-Justice Central to Christian Faith?" *Union Seminary Quarterly Review*, Volume 54, No, 3–4, 2000, 115, 116–118, 120–124.

Selection 3: Sallie McFague. *The Body of God: An Ecological Theology.* Minneapolis: Fortress Press, 1993, 162–174, 179–182.

Selection 4: James A. Nash. *Loving Nature: Ecological Integrity and Christian Responsibility.* Nashville: Abingdon, 1991, 143–160.

Chapter 40

Selection 1: Paul Ramsey. *Fabricated Man: The Ethics of Genetic Control.* New Haven and London: Yale University Press, 1970, 104–125.

Selection 2: Joseph Fletcher. *Moral Responsibility: Situation Ethics at Work.* Philadelphia: Westminster, 1967, 141–152.

Selection 3: Richard McCormick. A. *How Brave A New World: Dilemmas in Bioethics.* Garden City: Doubleday, 1981, 321–325.

Selection 4: James Gustafson. *The Contributions of Theology to Medical Ethics.* The 1975 Pere Marquette Theology Lecture. Marquette University Theology Department, April 6, 1975, 3–25.

Selection 5: Paul T. Jersild. "Theological and Moral Reflections on Stem Cell Research," *Journal of Lutheran Ethics (JLE)*, Volume 7, Issue 3, March 2007.

Chapter 41

Selection 1: David A. Hoekema. "A Practical Christian Pacifism," *Christian Century*, October 22, 1986, 917–919.

Selection 2: "Address of Pope John Paul II to the Diplomatic Corps," *Osservatore Romano. Weekly Edition in English.* Number 3. January 13, 2003, 3–4.

Selection 3: Jean Bethke Elshtain. *Just War against Terror: The Burden of American Power in a Violent World.* New York: Basic, 2003, 59–62, 65–70.

Chapter 42

Selection 1: John Howard Yoder. *The Priestly Kingdom: Social Ethics as Gospel.* Notre Dame: University of Notre Dame Press, 1984, 153–159, 166–168.

Selection 2: Stanley Hauerwas. *A Community of Character: Toward a Constructive Christian Social Ethic.* Notre Dame and London: University of Notre Dame Press, 1981, pp. 72–74, 77–79, 83–86.

Selection 3: Jean Porter. *The Recovery of Virtue: The Relevance of Aquinas for Christian Ethics.* Louisville: Westminster John Knox, 1990, 104–105, 124–127.

Chapter 43

Selection 1: Jürgen Moltmann. *The Trinity and the Kingdom* Minneapolis: Fortress Press, 1993, 192–195, 197–200.
Selection 2: Catherine Mowry LaCugna. *God for Us: The Trinity and Christian Life.* San Francisco: Harper San Francisco, 1973, 382–388.

INDEX